TACTICS FOR THE TOEFL iBT® TEST

A strategic new approach
to achieving TOEFL success

Christien Lee

OXFORD
UNIVERSITY PRESS

OXFORD
UNIVERSITY PRESS

Oxford University Press is a department of the University of Oxford.
It furthers the University's objective of excellence in research, scholarship,
and education by publishing worldwide. Oxford is a registered trade mark
of Oxford University Press in the UK and in certain other countries.

Published in Canada by
Oxford University Press
8 Sampson Mews, Suite 204,
Don Mills, Ontario M3C 0H5 Canada

www.oupcanada.com

Library and Archives Canada Cataloguing in Publication
Lee, Christien, 1970–, author
Tactics for the TOEFL iBT test / Christien Lee.

ISBN 978-0-19-902017-1 (student book).—ISBN 978-0-19-902018-8 (test pack)

1. Test of English as a Foreign Language—Study guides. 2. English
language—Study and teaching as a second language. 3. English language—
Examinations—Study guides. I. Title.

PE1128.L43 2015   428.0076   C2014-907050-0

Oxford University Press is committed to our environment.
Wherever possible, our books are printed on paper which
comes from responsible sources.

Printed and bound in Canada

1 2 3 4 — 18 17 16 15

Introduction

Achieving a successful score in the TOEFL test can be a challenge, but it's one that millions of students every year must undertake. *Tactics for the TOEFL iBT® Test* is intended as a new kind of coursebook for TOEFL test takers. Each unit in the book focuses on one type of reading, listening, speaking, or writing question that students will see in the TOEFL test. Through a unique combination of detailed explanations, strategic practice, step-by-step guidance, focused vocabulary coverage, and practical test preparation advice and tips, each unit explains what students need to do to achieve success in the TOEFL test and why they need to do it. This approach is based on teaching methods that the author has developed during his 20 years of classroom experience as a TOEFL instructor.

Acknowledgements

Every book involves a team effort; this one more than most.

My grateful thanks to everyone at Oxford University Press who has worked on the book: I truly appreciate your hard work, dedication, encouragement, advice, patience, and passion. Thanks especially to Antoinette and Jennifer for shaping the early manuscript, and to Jason, Nadine, and everyone else at OUP Canada for believing in the book and for turning it into a finished product.

My grateful thanks also to the thousands of students who have trusted me to help them raise their TOEFL scores and whose questions and ideas have helped me develop and hone the strategies and tactics in this book.

Finally, thanks to my family for their support and good advice. Above all, my thanks to Miki for putting up with all of the changed plans, lost weekends, and to Kenzo for the snuggles and for understanding that sometimes Papa was too busy to play trains. I love you both.

—Christien Lee

Oxford University Press would like to acknowledge the advice of teachers from all over the world who participated in online reviews, focus groups, and editorial reviews. We relied heavily on teacher input throughout the extensive development process of the *Tactics for the TOEFL iBT® Test*, and many of the features in the book came directly from feedback we gathered from teachers in the classroom. We are grateful to all who helped. The following reviewers shared their valuable insights with the author and the editorial department:

Patricia Blackstone-Evans, EC Brighton, UK; **Caron Broadbent**, EC Brighton, UK; **Sam Buchan**, EC London, UK; **Beatrice Calixo**, Rennert New York, US; **Judy Chao**, LSI New York, US; **Ray Ming Chao**, Cheng Kung University, Taiwan; **Lori Chinitz**, University of Pennsylvania, US; **Joanna Chung**, CYJ English Academy, Korea; **Cameron Dean**, EC London, UK; **Vern Eaton**, St. Giles International, Canada; **Melody Elliott**, Tokai University, Japan; **Sonia Fantauzzi**, ILSC, Canada; **Dan Genereaux**, Korea University, Korea; **Susan Gilfert**, Kwansei Gakuin University, Japan; **Ted Gray**, Hongik University, Korea; **Sven Greve**, Hansa Language Centre, Canada; **Steve Herder**, Doshisha Women's College, Japan; **Frits Holst**, EC London, UK; **Tsuyoshi Iida**, Doshisha Women's College, Japan; **Greg Jeong**, Live Lecture, Korea; **Yu-Jung Kang**, Ewha University, Korea; **Sotiria Koui**, Harcum College, US; **Shawn Krause**, ILSC, Canada; **Noga Laor**, Rennert New York, US; **Kerry Linder**, LSI New York, US; **Joanna Lockspeiser**, Rennert, US; **Mark Lucas**, Kansai University, Japan; **David McCoy**, Gakushuin University, Japan; **Brian McManus**, University of Pennsylvania, US; **Jesse Miller**, English School of Canada, Canada; **Jo Osborne**, EC Brighton, UK; **Joo-Young Park**, Sungshin Women's University, Korea; **Ben Parkin,** EC Brighton, UK; **Briana Raissi**, GEOS New York, US; **Rosie Roumiana Luczay**, ILSC Toronto, Canada; **Daniel Schulstad**, Embassy CES, US; **Karen Stanley**, Central Piedmont Community College, US; **Claudio Sung**, High Five, Taiwan; **Christos Theodoropulos**, University of Pennsylvania, US; **Ksenia Torutanova-Ducey**, Embassy English, US; **Yvonne Tseng**, Chang Jung University, Taiwan; **Gerald Williams**, Kansai University, Japan; **James Winward-Stuart**, GABA, Japan

About the Author

Christien Lee has been involved in English language teaching and training since 1992. He has specialized in English proficiency tests like TOEFL, IELTS, TOEIC, MELAB, and CELPIP—as an instructor, teacher trainer, and writer. He founded a specialist test preparation academy in Toronto, Canada, in 2004 and ran the school for nine years. During that time, he developed a unique, strategic teaching system that helped thousands of students achieve test success in TOEFL, IELTS, and TOEIC. He regularly speaks about effective ways to teach test preparation classes at conferences for English language teaching professionals. He has also worked with ETS Canada to facilitate teacher training workshops for TOEFL instructors. In addition to writing *Tactics for the TOEFL iBT® Test*, he has written TOEFL practice tests (available at www.oxfordenglishtesting.com) and is a question writer for the Oxford Online Placement Test. He can be contacted via his personal website: www.christienlee.com.

Contents

Writing Tactics   226

Credits   286

Vocabulary Index   287

Practice Test A   291

Practice Test B   315

Tactics for the TOEFL iBT® Test offers a new approach to achieving success in the TOEFL test. It offers a unique combination of innovative tasks that build key skills, authentic test practice, focused test preparation strategies, and high-frequency academic language related to the subjects and topics that most commonly appear in the test.

Reference Sections Provide Detailed Information about Key Aspects of the TOEFL Test

A **general Reference Section** gives students essential information about TOEFL, including how to register, what to expect on the day of the test, and when they will receive their test score.

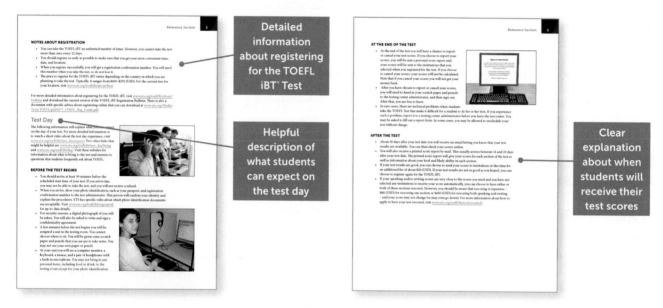

Detailed information about registering for the TOEFL iBT® Test

Helpful description of what students can expect on the test day

Clear explanation about when students will receive their test scores

Individual reference sections for reading, listening, speaking, and writing give students an in-depth understanding of those sections. Students will receive clear instructions for how to answer the different types of questions in each section and detailed information about scoring. They will also see computer screenshots that simulate what they will see in the actual test.

Descriptions of each question type and how students should answer them

Simulated screenshots to show what test takers will see and experience

Detailed information about how the test is scored and how to interpret scores

Diagnostic and Review Tests Provide Authentic Test Practice to Help Students Recognize Areas of Need and Assess Improvement

Each section of *Tactics for the TOEFL iBT® Test* includes both a **diagnostic test** and a **review test** that can be completed in less than one hour. Students can choose how and when to take these tests, but the recommended approach is to take the diagnostic test before starting on a section and the review test after going through the units.

The diagnostic and review tests have a realistic balance of question types that are at the same level as the actual TOEFL test. A score conversion chart at the end of each test lets students get an accurate sense of their likely score on the real TOEFL test.

Realistic balance of question types at the same level as the actual test

Useful score conversion chart that help students judge their likely test score

Two Complete Tests Help Students Practice and Assess Readiness

Tactics for the TOEFL iBT® Test also includes **two full practice tests at the back of the book** that accurately reflect the balance and difficulty of questions in the real TOEFL test. For added authenticity and convenience, **students can take these tests online** using a sophisticated digital testing platform developed by Oxford University Press.

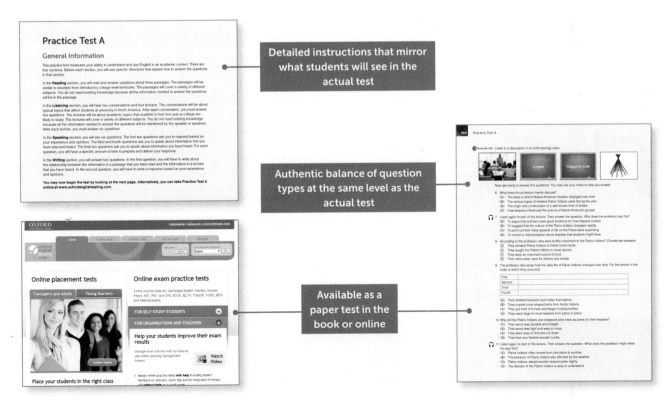

Detailed instructions that mirror what students will see in the actual test

Authentic balance of question types at the same level as the actual test

Available as a paper test in the book or online

Content Units Focus on Individual Question Types in TOEFL plus Useful Vocabulary

Tactics for the TOEFL iBT® Test includes 26 content units that **cover every TOEFL question type** from the reading, listening, speaking, and writing sections of the TOEFL test. In addition, each unit focuses on **one academic subject that often appears in the TOEFL test** as well as **key vocabulary** for achieving test success, including words related to specific academic disciplines and student life at university in North America.

Each content unit begins with a **Warm-up section** designed to get students to think about the focus of that unit, and activate and share their existing knowledge of that subject. Many Warm-up tasks practice key skills for the test like listening, speaking, or writing. Each unit also has one or two **Vocabulary sections that introduce essential words for the TOEFL test** related to the academic subject of the unit.

Each unit contains one or two sections that **analyze and describe a question type from the TOEFL test** in detail. The analysis includes examples of the question type, strategies for how to answer that question and how to recognize and avoid mistakes, plus a realistic practice activity.

> In-depth focus on one or two of the official question types that appear in the TOEFL test

> Each unit focuses on one academic subject; these subjects were chosen based on analysis of TOEFL questions published by ETS

> Detailed analysis of specific question types to help students build knowledge and confidence

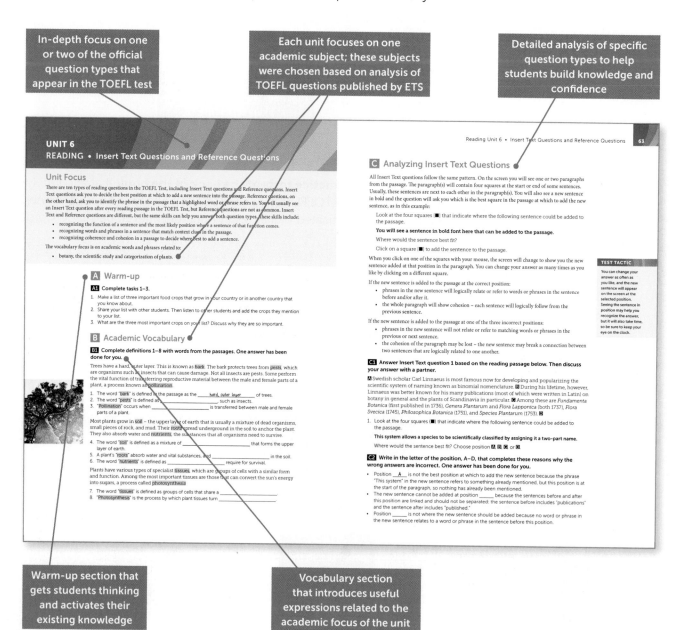

> Warm-up section that gets students thinking and activates their existing knowledge

> Vocabulary section that introduces useful expressions related to the academic focus of the unit

Content Units Introduce and Practice Key Skills and Strategies for TOEFL

Every content unit includes several sections that include multiple tasks designed to help students master **key skills for answering specific question types** accurately and effectively. These sections have a range of activity types.

Some **activities help students build key skills** that will help them answer specific question types. Other activities help students think in the right way or give step-by-step instructions or explanations to achieve improved results. Additional activities provide realistic test questions so that students can practice the key skills and ways of thinking that they have learned.

Tactics for the TOEFL iBT® Test also includes **more than 120 test tactics** that give practical and proven suggestions to raise students' test scores. Some tactics offer a solution to a common problem students have when taking the TOEFL test. Others describe a useful way of thinking or a helpful action that students can take.

Multiple sections that break down key skills into manageable chunks and guide students towards mastery

Each unit has test tactics with practical, proven suggestions and strategies

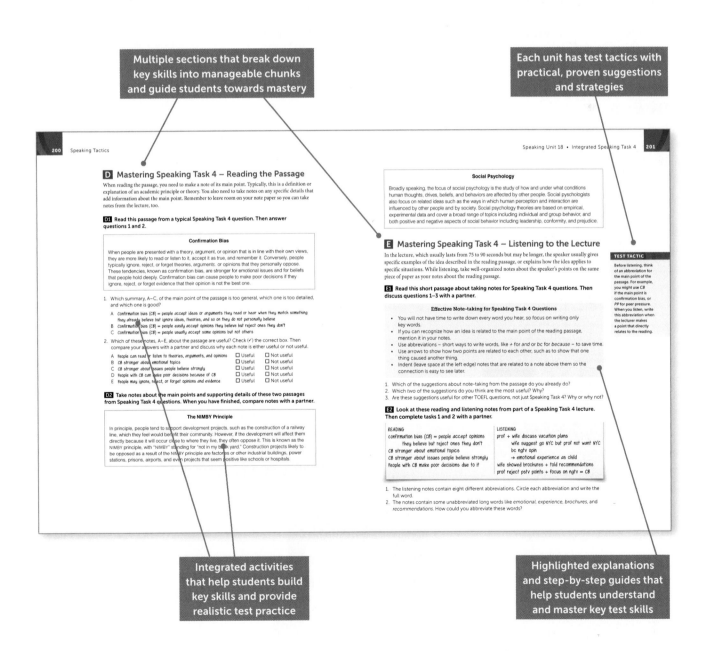

Integrated activities that help students build key skills and provide realistic test practice

Highlighted explanations and step-by-step guides that help students understand and master key test skills

Content Units Provide Authentic Test Practice and Practical Suggestions for Further Study

Every content unit ends with a **Test Challenge** section that provides **realistic test practice** so that students can practice the skills and strategies they have learned. The reading and listening sources in the Test Challenge section were carefully written to include many of the words and phrases that students learned earlier in the unit. They also use many expressions from the **academic word list**.

After the Test Challenge, students will see a **Next Steps** section that offers practical and effective step-by-step activities students can do on their own. These ideas help students build key skills to become better at answering specific question types. The ideas are also designed to help students continue to improve their knowledge of an important academic subject as well as useful vocabulary related to that subject.

Test Challenge section that provides realistic test practice for the question types covered in each unit

Broad coverage of authentic topics and natural academic language in the test questions

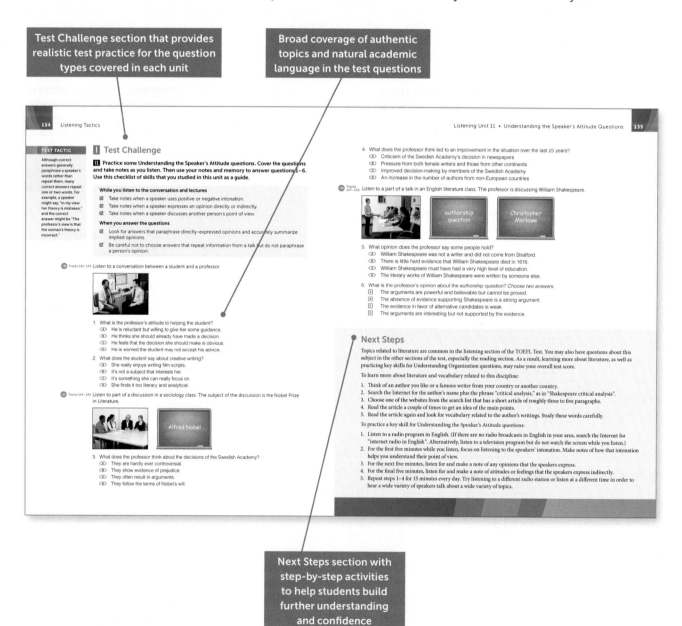

Next Steps section with step-by-step activities to help students build further understanding and confidence

Unique Vocabulary Index Helps Students Learn and Use Key Expressions for TOEFL

Tactics for the TOEFL iBT® Test also has a **unique Vocabulary Index** of all the useful words used in the book. The index is color-coded to show the category to which a word belongs—an academic discipline, campus vocabulary, or academic word list—and includes each word's part of speech to help students understand how to use it.

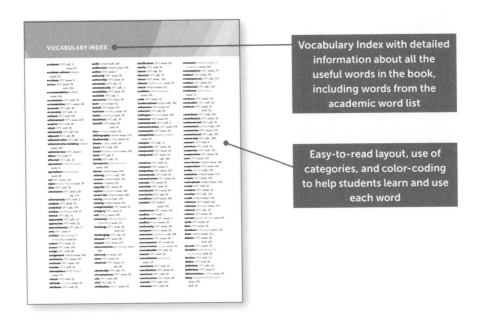

Vocabulary Index with detailed information about all the useful words in the book, including words from the academic word list

Easy-to-read layout, use of categories, and color-coding to help students learn and use each word

Online Practice Site Provides Additional Lessons to Help Students Achieve Success in the TOEFL Test Quickly and Effectively

Students will also have access to a practice website offering more than 150 online lessons designed to complement the material in the student book. In total, the lessons will provide an estimated 100 hours of additional practice.

The website will have three types of lessons. **Language focus lessons** will expand students' knowledge and understanding of useful vocabulary and expressions. **Skills focus lessons** will help students to build key skills to answer specific question types that appear in the TOEFL test. And **Test focus lessons** will provide additional authentic test practice.

The online lessons will include plenty of new material, but will also recycle content from the student book in innovative ways. The vocabulary and subject focus of the online lessons will match the focus of the content units in the student book.

Online practice site with more than 150 lessons covering three areas: language, skills, and test practice

Full Pack Version Includes Answer Key, Audio Scripts, and All Audio Material

The Pack version of *Tactics for the TOEFL iBT® Test* includes all the student book material as well as the Audio Script and Answer Key Booklet, and the Audio on CD.

The **single CD has all of the audio files** in convenient MP3 format. When listening to the audio files, students will hear the same range of accents—including speakers from North America, Great Britain, Australia, and New Zealand—that they will hear in the actual TOEFL test.

The audio files have been designed to provide the most flexible experience for students and teachers. This makes it easy to listen again to individual lectures or even individual questions. There are even audio tracks for the speaking and writing responses.

Students will also be able to read the **complete Audio Scripts** in order to gain maximum understanding of what the speakers say. The audio scripts include plenty of examples of key vocabulary from each unit as well as expressions from the academic word list.

An **Answer Key** provides quick access to the right answers for each task. An extended answer key that provides explanations for why each answer is right or wrong as well as sample responses for speaking and writing questions is available on the companion website.

Audio files in MP3 format that are split into multiple tracks for ease of use by teachers and students

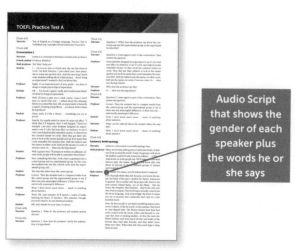

Audio Script that shows the gender of each speaker plus the words he or she says

Answer Key with clear solution to all questions that have a definite answer, and suggested answers to questions that require short responses from students

Companion Website Offers Comprehensive Support for Teachers, Students Working Independently, and Tutors

Users who purchase the Pack version for *Tactics for the TOEFL iBT® Test* will also have **access to a companion website** designed for teachers and students studying independently. The website will offer detailed teaching notes and self-study suggestions that include ideas for extending individual activities in the book. The website will also include an extended answer key that provides explanations for why each answer is right or wrong as well as sample responses for speaking and writing questions.

Companion site for teachers and students with additional ideas for using the book and an extended Answer Key

About the Test

The TOEFL Test measures your ability to read, listen to, speak, and write English in an academic setting. It is a computer-based test that is delivered via the Internet. The name TOEFL stands for Test of English as a Foreign Language, and iBT stands for Internet-based Test. More than 9,000 universities, colleges, governments, and employers around the world request that people take the TOEFL Test in order to demonstrate their ability to communicate effectively using English. The TOEFL Test is developed by Educational Testing Service (ETS).

How to Register for the Test

There are three ways you can register for the TOEFL iBT:

- Online – visit www.ets.org/toefl/ibt/register.
- Telephone – call your Regional Registration Center (visit www.ets.org/toefl/ibt/register for the telephone number).
- Mail – send the application form to your Regional Registration Center (visit www.ets.org/toefl/ibt/register for the mailing address).

You cannot register in person by walking into a TOEFL Test Center, but in some locations you might be able to register in person at a TOEFL iBT Resource Center. In general, however, registering online is the easiest and most convenient option.

If you choose to register online or by telephone, you can register for tests eight days before the test date. For an additional fee you can register for a test four days before the test date. If you choose to register by mail, you will be assigned a test date, time, and location based on information you provide on your application.

When you take the TOEFL Test, you can choose up to four universities or other institutions to receive your official TOEFL score automatically. You can select these institutions for free when you register. Alternatively, you can select them by logging in to your TOEFL account after you have registered. The deadline for selecting the institutions is one day before your test. After that time, you will have to pay a fee of about $20 (USD) to select each institution. You can also pay this fee if you wish to select more than four institutions. Note that you cannot select institutions to receive your TOEFL score at the test center on your test day.

TEST TACTIC

TOEFL iBT is a computer-based test, so before you take the test, train yourself to be comfortable reading passages on a computer screen, listening to English using headphones, speaking into a microphone, and using a mouse and keyboard.

NOTES ABOUT REGISTRATION

- You can take the TOEFL iBT an unlimited number of times. However, you cannot take the test more than once every 12 days.
- You should register as early as possible to make sure that you get your most convenient time, date, and location.
- When you register successfully, you will get a registration confirmation number. You will need this number when you take the test, so do not lose it.
- The price to register for the TOEFL iBT varies depending on the country in which you are planning to take the test. Typically, it ranges from $160–$250 (USD). For the current fees for your location, visit www.ets.org/toefl/ibt/about/fees/.

For more detailed information about registering for the TOEFL iBT, visit www.ets.org/toefl/ibt/about/bulletin and download the current version of the TOEFL iBT Registration Bulletin. There is also a document with specific advice about registering online that you can download at www.ets.org/Media/Tests/TOEFL/pdf/4677_TOEFL_Reg_Guide.pdf.

Test Day

The following information will explain what you can expect on the day of your test. For more detailed information or to watch a short video about the test day experience, visit www.ets.org/toefl/ibt/test_day/expect/. Two other links that might be helpful are www.ets.org/toefl/ibt/test_day/bring and www.ets.org/toefl/ibt/faq/. Visit these websites for information about what to bring to the test and answers to questions that students frequently ask about TOEFL.

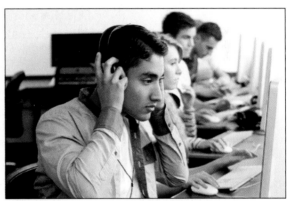

BEFORE THE TEST BEGINS

- You should arrive at least 30 minutes before the scheduled start time of your test. If you arrive late, you may not be able to take the test, and you will not receive a refund.
- When you arrive, show your photo identification, such as your passport, and registration confirmation number to the test administrator. That person will confirm your identity and explain the procedures. ETS has specific rules about which photo identification documents are acceptable. Visit www.ets.org/toefl/ibt/register/id for up-to-date details.
- For security reasons, a digital photograph of you will be taken. You will also be asked to write and sign a confidentiality agreement.
- A few minutes before the test begins you will be assigned a seat in the testing room. You cannot choose where to sit. You will be given some scratch paper and pencils that you can use to take notes. You may not use your own paper or pencil.
- At your seat you will see a computer monitor, a keyboard, a mouse, and a pair of headphones with a built-in microphone. You may not bring in any personal items, including food or drink, to the testing room except for your photo identification.

DURING THE TEST

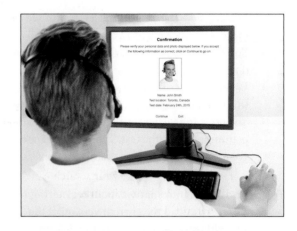

- You will first see your photograph and personal information on the screen. For security reasons, you will need to confirm that the picture is you and the information is correct.
- You will then see several screens that give you general information about the TOEFL Test including regulations about taking the test. You will also see a confidentiality agreement on the screen that you must accept.
- Next the test will begin. The test has four sections. Each section has special directions that you will see and/or hear. Each section lasts a different amount of time:

Section	Notes
Reading Section	About 62 or 82 minutes (including directions and time to read and answer the questions)
Listening Section	About 62 or 92 minutes (including directions and time to listen and answer the questions)
10 minute break	
Speaking Section	About 20 minutes (including directions and time to prepare for and respond to the questions)
Writing Section	About 60 minutes (including directions and time to prepare for and respond to the questions)

The length of the reading and listening sections depends on how many passages you see in the reading section. If you see three reading passages, the reading section will take about 62 minutes and the listening section will take about 92 minutes. If you see four reading passages, the reading section will take about 82 minutes and the listening section will take about 62 minutes.

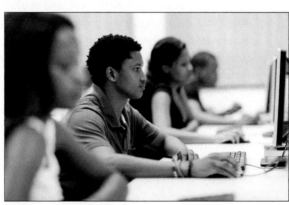

- If you have a problem at any time during the test, raise your hand and a testing center administrator will help you. Note that the administrator can only help you with problems related to the test, such as a problem with your computer; he or she cannot help you by answering or explaining any of the questions on the test.
- Also raise your hand if you need new scratch paper on which to take notes. A testing center administrator will take back your used scratch paper and replace it with new scratch paper.
- Every student taking the TOEFL Test at the same test center as you will start at a slightly different time and may answer the questions more quickly or more slowly than you. This means that you are likely to hear background noise while you are taking the test from other people listening to lectures or responding to speaking tasks. You will need to learn to ignore this noise.
- If you need to use the bathroom at any time, you will need to raise your hand and alert a testing center administrator. Note that the clock will not stop while you are out of the room.

TEST TACTIC

You may want to wear the headset throughout the whole test. This will help you focus by blocking out background noise in the test center.

AT THE END OF THE TEST

- At the end of the test you will have a chance to report or cancel your test scores. If you choose to report your scores, you will be sent a personal score report and your scores will be sent to the institutions that you selected when you registered for the test. If you choose to cancel your scores, your scores will not be calculated. Note that if you cancel your scores you will not get your money back.

- After you have chosen to report or cancel your scores, you will need to hand in your scratch paper and pencils to the testing center administrator, and then sign out. After that, you are free to leave.

- In rare cases, there are technical problems when students take the TOEFL Test that make it difficult for a student to do his or her best. If you experience such a problem, report it to a testing center administrator before you leave the test center. You may be asked to fill out a report form. In some cases, you may be allowed to reschedule your test without charge.

AFTER THE TEST

- About 10 days after your test date you will receive an email letting you know that your test results are available. You can then check your scores online.

- You will also receive a printed score report by mail. This usually arrives between 14 and 20 days after your test date. The printed score report will give your scores for each section of the test as well as information about your level and likely ability in each section.

- If your test results are good and you have not selected any institutions to receive your score automatically, you can choose to send your scores to institutions at this time for an additional fee of about $20 (USD). If your test results are not as good as you hoped, you can choose to register again for the TOEFL iBT.

- If your speaking and/or writing scores are very close to the scores you need and you have not selected any institutions to receive your score automatically, you can choose to have either or both of these sections rescored. However, you should be aware that rescoring is expensive – $80 (USD) for rescoring one section or $160 (USD) for rescoring both speaking and writing – and your score may not change (or may even go down). For more information about how to apply to have your test rescored, visit www.ets.org/toefl/ibt/scores/cancel/.

Overview

The reading section measures your ability to understand university-level academic texts. You will see:

- Directions for the reading section   about 2 minutes
- Three or four reading passages, each approximately 700 words long, with 12–14 questions after   60 or 80 minutes
  each passage (36–42 questions in total for three passages or 48–56 questions for four passages)

Your answers will be scored by a computer and your raw score will be converted to a scaled score from 0–30.

NOTES

- The reading passages on the TOEFL Test come from university-level textbooks and often introduce a subject or topic. You will not need any previous knowledge about these subjects: all the information you need to answer the questions is mentioned in the passage.
- You may see three different types of passages: expositions, which explain a single topic; arguments, which express and support a point of view; and historical or biographical narratives, which describe a past event or somebody's life. Expository passages are the most common type.
- Some passages contain difficult words or phrases. These expressions are underlined in the passage, and clicking on them will bring up a definition of the word in the lower left part of the screen.
- You may see up to ten different types of questions in the reading section, divided into three categories: basic information questions, inferencing questions, and reading to learn questions.
- If you see four passages, the questions about one of the passages may NOT count towards your raw score. However, there is no way to know which of the passages will not count, so you should answer all questions as well as you can.

Detailed Guide

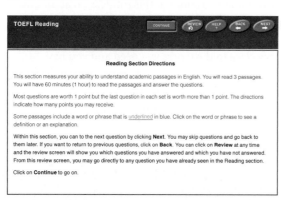

When you begin the reading section of the TOEFL Test, the first screen you see will be the directions for the reading section.

When you are ready, click the button labeled **Continue** in the top right of the screen to begin the reading section.

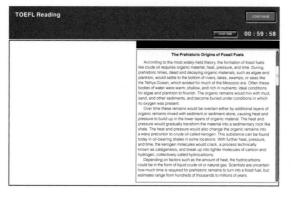

TEST TACTIC

If you find it hard to answer all the questions in 20 minutes, save time by scrolling to the end of the passage without reading it. You can read the relevant parts of the passage later when you answer each question.

Next you will see a reading passage on the right side of the screen and a blank area on the left side of the screen. The timer will begin counting down.

The passage will be too long to fit on the screen. To see the final paragraphs of the passage you will need to scroll to the bottom using the scrollbar to the right of the passage. After you scroll to the bottom of the passage you will be able to click the **Continue** button to see the questions.

After you click **Continue**, you will see the first question. You will also see a toolbar with various buttons at the top right of the screen. Each button has a different function.

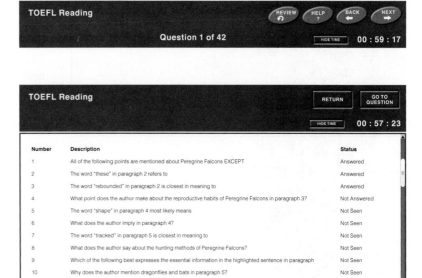

When you click the **Review** button, you will see a screen that shows the status of all the questions about the current passage. Questions you have looked at will be marked "Answered" or "Not Answered." Questions you have not looked at yet will be marked "Not Seen."

You can use the Review screen to jump to any question you have already answered. This is a useful tool to save time and make sure you have answered all of the questions. Note that the timer will continue to count down while you look at the Review screen.

Clicking the **Help** button gives you helpful information about how to answer the questions and use the onscreen buttons. Note that the timer will continue to count down while you look at the Help screen. Also note that the Help screen will NOT give you specific advice about the correct answer for a question, only general advice about how to answer the questions.

Clicking the **Back** button will take you back to previous questions. You can review and change your answer to any question that you have already answered. You can also answer any questions that you skipped. If you are currently looking at the first question about a passage, clicking **Back** will take you to the last question about the previous passage, if there is one.

In most cases, clicking the **Next** button will show you the next question about the current passage. If the current question is the last question about the current passage, clicking **Next** will take you to the next passage. If the current question is the last question about the last passage, clicking **Next** will show a message on the screen.

The message will explain that while there is time remaining, you can answer any questions that you skipped, or change your answers to any of the questions. If you choose to continue on to the Listening section, you will not be able to return to the Reading section.

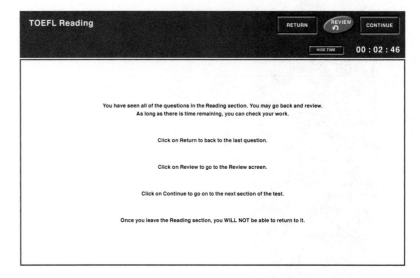

1. According to paragraph 3, what method has been used to try to control mountain pine beetles?

◯ other insects

◯ predators

◯ viruses

⬤ pesticides

Paragraph 3 is marked with an arrow ➤.

Select the TWO answer choices that describe cities in which René Descartes lived in the early 1630s.

To receive credit, you must select TWO answers.

☐ Amsterdam

☒ Leiden

☒ Utrecht

☐ Santpoort

Most questions in the reading section ask you to choose one answer from four choices.

To choose your answer, click on the answer or on the oval next to it. To change your answer, click on a different answer choice.

After you have chosen your answer, click on the **Next** button to go on to the next question.

Rarely, you might see a question that requires you to choose more than one answer. These questions have special directions.

To choose your answers, click on the squares next to them. To change an answer, click on the square next to a different answer choice and the most recently selected answer will be canceled.

You need to click on the required number of answers to get credit for these questions. If you select too many answers, you will see a warning message.

Look at the four squares [■] that indicate where the following sentence can be added to the passage.

Published in 1882, these were very popular and Abbey's career flourished.

Where would the sentence best fit?

Click on a square [■] to add the sentence to the passage.

American painter Edwin Austin Abbey was born in Philadelphia, Pennsylvania. ■ He first gained a reputation as an illustrator while working in the art department of Harper & Brothers publishing in New York. ■ In 1878 he moved to the UK and produced illustrations for the poems of Robert Herrick. ■ He later became closely identified with the art life of England, and received various awards, including election to the prestigious Royal Academy. ■

American painter Edwin Austin Abbey was born in Philadelphia, Pennsylvania. ■ He first gained a reputation as an illustrator while working in the art department of Harper & Brothers publishing in New York. ■ In 1878 he moved to the UK and produced illustrations for the poems of Robert Herrick. **Published in 1882, these were very popular and Abbey's career flourished.** He later became closely identified with the art life of England, and received various awards, including election to the prestigious Royal Academy. ■

Some questions – called Insert Text questions – require you to add a sentence to the passage at one of four locations marked by black squares. These questions have special directions in a gray box.

In the passage you will see four black squares (■). To choose your answer, click on the black square at the position where you think the new sentence should be added. The square will disappear and the sentence will be added at that position in **bold text**.

To change your answer, click on a different square. You can change your answer as often as you need.

Some questions – called Prose Summary questions – require you to choose three answers from six choices and add them to a summary of the passage. These questions have special directions in a gray box.

To choose an answer, click on it with your mouse. Keep the mouse button held down and drag the answer to an empty space in the answer box. The answer will be added to the box. Do this twice more to choose all three answers. It does not matter in which order you add the three answers.

You can change your answers as often as you wish. To change an answer, click on it or drag it outside of the answer box. The answer will return to its original position among the six answer choices.

Prose Summary questions take up the whole screen, so you will not be able to see the reading passage at the same time. To view the passage, click on the **View Text** button at the top right of the screen. The text on the button will change to **View Question**, and you will see the passage. When you want to see the question again, click on **View Question**.

Some questions – called Fill in a Table questions – require you to choose five answers from six or more choices. You will see two or three categories, each with space for one, two, or three answers. No answer matches more than one category, and at least one answer does not match any category. These questions have special directions in a gray box.

You can choose and change your answers for Fill in a Table questions in the same way as for Prose Summary questions.

Fill in a Table questions take up the whole screen in the same way as Prose Summary questions, so you must click the **View Text** button if you want to see the passage to help you decide on your answers.

Directions: An introductory sentence for a brief summary of the passage is provided below. Complete the summary by selecting the THREE answer choices that express the most important ideas in the passage. Some sentences do not belong in the summary because they express ideas that are not presented in the passage or are minor ideas in the passage. **This question is worth 2 points.**

Drag your answer choices to the spaces where they belong.
To remove an answer choice, click on it. To review the passage, click **VIEW TEXT**.

When first discovered, antibiotics represented a significant advance in healthcare.

-
- Over-prescription of antibiotics has led to the a rise in bacteria resistant to multiple drugs.
-

Answer Choices

Drug resistant bacteria are the cause of widespread environmental problems.

Superbugs such as MRSA cause thousands of people to fall sick each year.

Research conducted in the US has shown that veterinarians like prescribing antibiotics.

Scientists are studying various ways to combat the threat of antibiotic resistance.

Patients who have surgical procedures need antibiotics to avoid getting infections.

TOEFL Reading

VIEW TEXT REVIEW HELP ? BACK NEXT

Question 14 of 42   HIDE TIME   00 : 42 : 31

Directions: Select the answers that correctly describe the treasure found as part of each hoard. One of the answers will NOT be used. **This question is worth 3 points.**

Drag your answer choices to the spaces where they belong.
To remove an answer choice, click on it. To review the passage, click **VIEW TEXT**.

Answer Choices

Silver tableware

Pepper pots

Gold coins and jewelry

Dishes with pedastals

Inscribed rings

Mildenhall Treasure
-
-

Hoxne Hoard
-
- A broken handle in the shape of a tiger
-

TEST TACTIC

If a question is taking a long time to answer, select your best idea, make a note of the question number on your scratch paper, and go on to the next question. If you have time remaining at the end, click the **Review** button to go back to these questions.

Scoring

Your answers for the reading section will be scored by computer. For most questions, you will get 1 point for a correct answer. For Prose Summary questions (see Reading Unit 7), you can get 1 or 2 points depending on how many answers you get right. For Fill in a Table questions (also Reading Unit 7), you can get 1–3 points depending on how many answers you get right.

The computer will add up all of your correct answers to get your raw score. The maximum raw score depends on how many passages you had and on the types of questions you saw. In general, though, for three passages, the maximum raw score is roughly 45 points. For four passages, the maximum raw score is around 60 points.

After your raw score has been calculated, the computer will convert it to a scaled score from 0–30. ETS does not give specific information about how your raw score is converted. However, it is likely that your raw score is calculated as a percentage of the maximum raw score, and your scaled score is then calculated as the same percentage of 30 (the maximum scaled score). So, for example, if your raw score is 36 points out of a maximum of 45 points, your percentage of correct answers is 80%. This would give you a scaled score of 80% of 30, or 24 points.

This chart shows an estimate of how many answers you need to get right in order to get a scaled score of 15–30.

Percentage Correct	Raw Score (three passages)	Raw Score (four passages)	Scaled Score
99–100%	39	52	30
95–98%	37–38	49–51	29
92–94%	36–37	48–49	28
89–91%	35	46–47	27
85–88%	33–34	44–46	26
82–84%	32–33	43–44	25
79–81%	31–32	41–42	24
75–78%	29–30	39–41	23
72–74%	28–29	37–38	22
69–71%	27–28	36–37	21
65–68%	25–27	34–35	20
62–64%	24–25	32–33	19
59–61%	23–24	31–32	18
55–58%	21–23	28–30	17
52–54%	20–21	27–28	16
49–51%	19–20	25–27	15

TEST TACTIC

Most questions are worth one point, but Prose Summary and Fill in a Table questions are worth two or three points. Be sure to leave enough time to answer these questions because they can have a big effect on your score.

When you receive your score from the TOEFL Test, you will get a score report. The report will give your scaled score in reading from 0–30, your reading level (High, Intermediate, or Low), plus a short description of the typical performance of students at that level.

Here are the levels and descriptions for reading:

Level (Scaled Score)	Your Performance
High (22–30)	Test takers who receive a score at the HIGH level, as you did, typically understand academic texts in English that require a wide range of reading abilities regardless of the difficulty of the texts. Test takers who score at the HIGH level, typically: • have a very good command of academic vocabulary and grammatical structure; • can understand and connect information, make appropriate inferences, and synthesize ideas, even when the text is conceptually dense and the language is complex; • can recognize the expository organization of a text and the role that specific information serves within the larger text, even when the text is conceptually dense; and • can abstract major ideas from a text, even when the text is conceptually dense and contains complex language.
Intermediate (15–21)	Test takers who receive a score at the INTERMEDIATE level, as you did, typically understand academic texts in English that require a wide range of reading abilities, although their understanding of certain parts of the texts is limited. Test takers who receive a score at the INTERMEDIATE level typically: • have a good command of common academic vocabulary, but still have some difficulty with high-level vocabulary; • have a very good understanding of grammatical structure; • can understand and connect information, make appropriate inferences, and synthesize information in a range of texts, but have more difficulty when the vocabulary is high level and the text is conceptually dense; • can recognize the expository organization of a text and the role that specific information serves within a larger text, but have some difficulty when these are not explicit or easy to infer from the text; and • can abstract major ideas from a text, but have more difficulty doing so when the text is conceptually dense.
Low (0–14)	Test takers who receive a score at the LOW level, as you did, typically understand some of the information presented in academic texts in English that require a wide range of reading abilities, but their understanding is limited. Test takers who receive a score at the LOW level typically: • have a command of basic academic vocabulary, but their understanding of less common vocabulary is inconsistent; • have limited ability to understand and connect information, have difficulty recognizing paraphrases of text information, and often rely on particular words and phrases rather than a complete understanding of the text; • have difficulty identifying the author's purpose, except when that purpose is explicitly stated in the text or easy to infer from the text; and • can sometimes recognize major ideas from a text when the information is clearly presented, memorable, or illustrated by examples, but have difficulty doing so when the text is more demanding.

Source: www.ets.org/Media/Tests/TOEFL/pdf/TOEFL_Perf_Feedback.pdf

Directions

This reading diagnostic test is intended to help you find out your strengths and weaknesses in reading. You will have 40 minutes to read two passages and answer 25 questions (worth 28 points). The passages and questions are designed to be at the same level as the ones you will see on the TOEFL Test. When you have finished, check your answers with your instructor or against the Answer Key. Then use the conversion chart on page 19 to convert your raw score to your likely score on the TOEFL Test.

Test

Read the two passages and answer questions 1–25. You have 40 minutes.

Peregrine Falcons

Peregrine Falcons, which are commonly known as Duck Hawks in North America, are medium-sized birds of prey with dark blue or slate-gray feathers on their backs and wings, often with darker bands. Their underparts are pale with dark bars. They have a dark head and cheeks with a pale neck and throat. Peregrines range in size from 35–50 centimeters (14–20 inches) with a wingspan of 100–110 centimeters (39–43 inches) and a body weight between 500 and 1,600 grams (roughly 18–56 ounces), which makes them among the largest of the falcons. Like other falcons they are members of the family *Falconidae* and exhibit sexual dimorphism in that males are smaller than females.

Peregrines live in an extremely broad range of habitats, including in many cities, and are found on all continents with the exception of Antarctica. They are not just the most widespread raptor, or bird of prey, but also the bird with the broadest range of natural habitats. During the 1960s and 1970s Peregrine populations declined sharply as a result of the use of pesticides for farming and other purposes. Since the employment of these was reduced, numbers have rebounded strongly, and Peregrines are now considered in no danger of extinction.

Peregrine Falcons typically mate for the first time when they are two or three years old. The nesting pair then mate for life and even return to the same nesting location each year. The nest is usually a hollow on a cliff edge protected by an overhang; in cities, Peregrines regularly make nesting sites on bridges or skyscrapers. In most cases, a female will lay between one and five eggs a year, with three to four being average. Chicks hatch after about one month, and leave the nest after a further six to seven weeks. Peregrine eggs and chicks are regularly predated by eagles and other large raptors.

Peregrines typically prey on other birds and bats while they are in flight. Occasionally they will also hunt small but abundant terrestrial mammals such as rats, mice, voles, and shrews. When hunting, they usually fly high and then look down for potential prey. When they see a target, Peregrines launch into a steep and extremely fast dive to catch their prey. When diving, they regularly reach speeds of 320 kilometers per hour (200 miles per hour), but have been measured traveling as fast as 389 km/h (242 mph), which makes them the fastest animals in the world. They strike their prey in mid-flight with a foot, either killing it outright or stunning it, and then catch it before it falls to the ground. Peregrines exhibit a number of physical adaptations that allow them to reach such speeds. They have nictitating membranes – sometimes called third eyelids – to protect their eyes while still allowing them to see. They also have bony projections on their nostrils that shape the flow of air around them in such a way that pressure from the air does not damage their lungs.

Until recently, scientists were uncertain how Peregrines tracked prey species when hunting. An innovative study that involved outfitting the birds with miniature video cameras, however, has shed interesting light on their methods. Scholars had theorized that Peregrines might use one of two methods, either diving straight towards their prey or following a flight path that kept the prey at a 45-degree angle in the Peregrine's vision – the angle at which Peregrines can see most sharply. The video evidence showed that Peregrines actually used a strategy called *motion camouflage* that scholars first identified when analyzing the hunting methods of bats and dragonflies. A hunting Peregrine predicts the point at which it will meet its target and dives towards that spot making sure it keeps its prey at a constant angle in its field of view. The advantage of this approach is that the prey species may be fooled into thinking the raptor is not a threat – until it is too late – because it does not seem to be coming closer. The disadvantage, and it is a significant one, is that if the target changes direction, the Peregrine's real position will be obvious and the target can easily take evasive measures.

1. All of the following points are mentioned about Peregrine Falcons EXCEPT:
   - (A) They are medium-sized falcons.
   - (B) They have both dark and light feathers.
   - (C) Female birds are larger than male ones.
   - (D) They are able to live in most environments.

2. The word "these" in paragraph 2 refers to
   - (A) purposes
   - (B) pesticides
   - (C) populations
   - (D) habitats

3. The word "rebounded" in paragraph 2 is closest in meaning to
   - (A) turned out
   - (B) come back
   - (C) fallen off
   - (D) opened up

4. What point does the author make about Peregrine Falcons in paragraph 3?
   - (A) Most Peregrines are physically able to mate every six to seven weeks.
   - (B) Peregrines prefer not to protect their young from other birds of prey.
   - (C) Peregrines prefer artificial nesting sites like bridges to natural cliffs.
   - (D) The same male and female birds mate with each other each year.

5. The word "shape" in paragraph 4 most likely means
   - (A) shelter
   - (B) prevent
   - (C) influence
   - (D) pattern

6. What does the author imply in paragraph 4?
   - (A) Peregrines would not be able to fly so fast if they did not have bony nostril projections or nictitating membranes.
   - (B) Peregrines rarely fly as fast as 389 km/h because the flow of air at that speed can cause damage to their lungs.
   - (C) Peregrines need to be able to fly very fast because most of their prey species are also capable of extreme speed.
   - (D) Peregrines are able to catch stunned targets before they reach the ground because they can fly and dive so quickly.

7. The word "tracked" in paragraph 5 is closest in meaning to
   - (A) modified
   - (B) copied
   - (C) selected
   - (D) followed

8. What does the author say about the hunting methods of Peregrine Falcons?
   - (A) They use a technique that allows them to trick potential targets into believing there is no immediate danger.
   - (B) They adopt several methods to help them easily catch targets that are attempting to take evasive measures.
   - (C) They tend to dive directly towards a target and then maintain a flight path at a sharp but constant angle.
   - (D) They are more effective at hunting when it is light because they can more easily identify specific targets.

9. Which of the following best expresses the essential information in the highlighted sentence in paragraph 5? Incorrect choices change the meaning in important ways or leave out essential information.
   - (A) The two most popular theories of how Peregrine Falcons dive towards their prey were found to be incorrect after the angle of most dives was measured at 45 degrees.
   - (B) Scientists expected that Peregrines would dive towards prey in a way that either allowed them to see it best or reach it most directly.
   - (C) Scholars found that most Peregrines dive straight towards their prey at an angle that allows them to see as many other birds as possible.
   - (D) Peregrines that follow a flight path when diving typically use two different methods and diving angles to catch prey depending on how sharp their vision is.

10. Why does the author mention dragonflies and bats in paragraph 5?
   - (A) To point out that the results of analysis of hunting methods are hard to predict
   - (B) To explain that scientists who study Peregrines often study other animals, too
   - (C) To imply that other animals that hunt while in flight use motion camouflage
   - (D) To give an example of some common animals that Peregrine Falcons prey upon

11. Look at the four squares (■) that indicate where the following sentence could be added to the passage.

In fact, the video footage shows that close to three-fourths of all Peregrine hunting dives end in failure.

Where would the sentence best fit? Choose position **A**, **B**, **C**, or **D**.

The video evidence showed that Peregrines actually used a strategy called motion camouflage that scholars first identified when analyzing the hunting methods of bats and dragonflies. **A** A hunting Peregrine predicts the point at which it will meet its target and dives towards that spot making sure it keeps its prey at a constant angle in its field of view. **B** The advantage of this approach is that the prey species may be fooled into thinking the raptor is not a threat because it does not seem to be coming closer. **C** The disadvantage, and it is a significant one, is that if the target changes direction, the Peregrine's real position will be obvious and the target can easily take evasive measures. **D**

12. **Directions:** An introductory sentence for a brief summary of the passage is provided below. Complete the summary by selecting the THREE answer choices that express the most important ideas in the passage. Some sentences do not belong in the summary because they express ideas that are not presented in the passage or are minor ideas in the passage. **This question is worth 2 points.**

> **Peregrine Falcons are medium-sized raptors with a broad geographical range.**
>
> •
>
> •
>
> •

- Ⓐ Peregrines rarely hunt mammals like rats or mice because these animals are difficult to catch.
- Ⓑ Mating pairs of Peregrines typically have three or four offspring yearly, not all of which survive.
- Ⓒ Peregrines mainly hunt and catch prey in flight using a fast dive as their main hunting method.
- Ⓓ Physical adaptations allow Peregrines to live and reproduce in a wide range of different habitats.
- Ⓔ Peregrines were briefly threatened during the 1960s and 1970s, but are no longer in danger.
- Ⓕ A photographic study of Peregrines helped scientists understand the hunting methods of birds.

Intellectual Property Protection

Intellectual property refers to any kind of work that is the result of human creativity and intelligence. These works include inventions, processes, designs, names, symbols, manuscripts, and musical works, among others. The owner or creator of the property has the exclusive legal right to use it for business purposes. To prevent others from infringing on their exclusive rights, businesses that operate in the United States have three broad options for protecting their intellectual property depending on the type of property it is: copyright, trademarks, and patents.

Copyright is a form of intellectual property protection that is granted to the creator of an original work of authorship, which typically includes written, musical, artistic, and theatrical or cinematic works. Copyright gives a property owner the exclusive right to benefit financially from a work through its use, reproduction, or distribution. In most nations the default period of copyright protection is the life of the named author plus an additional 50 or 70 years. For works published under no name or a fake name, the default period is usually 50 or 70 years from the date of publication. In cases where different countries grant different periods of copyright protection, nations may follow the rule of the shorter term. Under this rule, the maximum length of copyright for a work is the maximum term in the country of origin if that term is shorter.

It is important to note that copyright protects the form of expression, not the subject matter of a work. If, say, a photograph of the Grand Canyon is copyrighted, the creator of that photograph is the only entity with the right to sell, distribute, or benefit from it in any way. However, there is nothing to stop a different entity from taking a photograph of the same scene and selling or distributing that, provided the second work is distinguishable from the first. And copyright protection does allow users of a copyrighted work to make "fair use" of it. Generally this means users may copy at least part of a copyrighted work for personal use, though the precise definition of what constitutes fair use is rarely given.

A trademark is a word, name, symbol, or design that companies use to indicate the source of goods or services. When used for the latter, the term *servicemark* is sometimes used in place of the more general term. Unlike copyrights or patents, trademarks can last indefinitely if the owner continues to use the mark commercially, although in most countries the mark must be renewed periodically. Trademarks grant businesses the exclusive right to sell or distribute a particular product or service under a particular name or brand. Other businesses can sell or distribute similar products and services under a trademark that is clearly different, or can sell or distribute different products and services under a similar mark. To illustrate, a private business offering educational services using the name Yale might violate the trademark of Yale University, a car wash business would safely be able to use the name Yale, however, because the service being offered is in no way similar to the services offered by a university.

A patent works differently from copyright and trademarks. Whereas the latter two give the owner of an intellectual property exclusive rights to that property, a patent grants the owner the right to prevent others from making, using, or selling an invention, idea, or design. A patent's term is typically 20 years from the date when the application is filed. In some cases this can be extended.

In the United States, inventors may file for three types of patents. Utility patents cover new or useful improvements to processes, machines, or manufacturing methods. Design patents cover original new designs for manufactured products. And plant patents cover inventions or discoveries of new or distinct types of plants. A common element to all types of patents is that the invention must exhibit novelty. Patents for inventions that have already been described or are known to exist in the world are usually not granted. Patents for inventions that are new but obvious are rarely granted either. For instance, a patent would not be given for an invention that is merely a larger or smaller version of an existing product.

13. What feature do the three different kinds of intellectual property protection have in common?
    (A) They give the owner of an intellectual property an advantage in business.
    (B) They prevent non-owners of an intellectual property from using it in any way.
    (C) They allow owners of one or more creative works to sell those works to others.
    (D) They give certain exclusive rights to the owner of a work of the human mind.

14. The word "infringing" in paragraph 1 is closest in meaning to
    (A) unloading
    (B) disregarding
    (C) excavating
    (D) defending

15. The author makes all of the following points in paragraph 2 EXCEPT:
    (A) Works by named authors get longer copyright protection than works by unnamed authors.
    (B) Property owners can apply to extend the default copyright period for between 50 and 70 additional years.
    (C) Countries may apply a shorter period of copyright protection for works originating in another country.
    (D) Only the owner of a copyrighted intellectual property should get a monetary advantage from that work.

16. What does the author imply in paragraph 3?
    (A) "Fair use" would not apply to commercial uses of copyrighted works.
    (B) Photographs of natural scenes like the Grand Canyon are often copyrighted.
    (C) Copyright laws provide ineffective protection for owners of copyrighted works.
    (D) The subject matter of copyrighted works affects how people can use them.

17. The word "precise" in paragraph 3 is closest in meaning to
    (A) prolific
    (B) useful
    (C) specific
    (D) conscious

18. The word "periodically" in paragraph 4 most likely means
    (A) in the short term
    (B) with great care
    (C) after due process
    (D) from time to time

19. Which of the following best expresses the essential information in the highlighted sentence in paragraph 4? Incorrect choices change the meaning in important ways or leave out essential information.
    (A) Businesses operate under different trademarks so they can sell and distribute different products from their competitors.
    (B) Companies with similar names can do business provided they offer dissimilar products or services from each other.
    (C) Other companies can operate a different business using a similar name or a similar business using a different name.
    (D) Businesses with a trademark similar to one owned by another company must provide a variety of different services.

20. Why does the author mention Yale University in paragraph 4?
   - (A) To give an example of a specific case of trademark violation
   - (B) To clarify the way in which trademark protection works
   - (C) To argue that trademarks offer little intellectual property protection
   - (D) To demonstrate how companies can use trademarks safely

21. The word "this" in paragraph 5 refers to
   - (A) application
   - (B) date
   - (C) term
   - (D) design

22. The word "novelty" in paragraph 6 is closest in meaning to
   - (A) originality
   - (B) navigation
   - (C) popularity
   - (D) sentiment

23. What does the author say about patent applications?
   - (A) In some cases a patent may be granted for something that a person discovered rather than invented.
   - (B) Design and utility patents are only granted when they are for new and useful manufacturing methods.
   - (C) There are three times more applications for patents in the United States than in other countries.
   - (D) The term of protection that a patent provides is 20 years from the date the application is approved.

24. Look at the four squares (■) that indicate where the following sentence could be added to the passage.

The duration of copyright protection is generally limited.

Where would the sentence best fit? Choose position **A**, **B**, **C**, or **D**.

A Copyright is a form of intellectual property protection that is granted to the creator of an original work of authorship, which typically includes written, musical, artistic, and cinematic works. **B** Copyright gives a property owner the exclusive right to benefit financially from a work through its use, reproduction, or distribution. **C** In most nations the default period of copyright protection is the life of the named author plus an additional 50 or 70 years. **D** For works published under no name or a fake name, the default period is usually 50 or 70 years from the date of publication. In cases where different countries grant different periods of copyright protection, nations may follow the rule of the shorter term. Under this rule, the maximum length of copyright for a work is the term in the country of origin if that term is shorter.

25. **Directions:** Select the phrases that correctly describe each type of intellectual property protection. One of the phrases will NOT be used. **This question is worth 3 points.**

> **Copyright or Trademarks**
>
> *
>
> *

> **Patents**
>
> *
>
> *
>
> *

- Ⓐ   Protection may continue after the owner's death.
- Ⓑ   Protection lasts no more than 50 years unless renewed.
- Ⓒ   Protection is only available for non-obvious inventions.
- Ⓓ   Protection applies to works of art and literature or product names.
- Ⓔ   Protection can be applied for in one of several categories.
- Ⓕ   Protection allows owners to stop others from using a product.

Score Conversion

Check your answers to questions 1–25. Then use this conversion chart to find out your approximate reading score range on the TOEFL Test.

Raw Score (out of 28)	Probable Level	Approximate Score Range
26–28	High	28–30
23–25	High	25–27
20–22	High	22–24
18–20	Intermediate	19–21
14–17	Intermediate	15–18
10–13	Low	11–14
6–9	Low	7–10
3–6	Low	3–6
0–2	Low	0–2

Unit Focus

There are ten types of reading questions in the TOEFL Test, including two similar question types called Factual Information and Negative Factual Information questions. Factual Information questions ask about specific information mentioned in part of the reading passage. They are one of the most common questions in the test; you can expect three to six Factual Information questions after every passage. Negative Factual Information questions ask about details NOT mentioned in the passage. They are less common than Factual Information questions; you can expect zero to two such questions after each passage. The skills you need to answer both of these question types are the same. These skills include:

- recognizing key phrases in the question and answer choices.
- recognizing whether answer choices paraphrase or contradict part of a reading passage.
- recognizing whether answer choices are mentioned or not mentioned in a reading passage.

The vocabulary focus is on academic words and phrases related to:

- paleontology, the study of plants and animals that lived on Earth a long time ago, but are now all dead.

A Warm-up

A1 **Which of the three fields of paleontology that are mentioned in this passage would you most like to study? Why? Share your reasons with other students.**

The science of paleontology involves the study of prehistoric life. It first began as an academic discipline in the eighteenth century and over the years it has developed as human knowledge and technological ability have increased. There are now several fields within the discipline including paleobotany, the study of ancient plants, paleoclimatology, the study of changes in the Earth's climate, and paleoecology, the study of interactions among ancient animals and plants.

B Academic Vocabulary

B1 **Use the letter clues to help you choose the best answer to complete missing words 1–8 in this passage. Then use a dictionary to check your answers. One answer has been done for you.**

Living things such as plants, animals, or even bacteria are known as 1. ___organisms___. Scientists use the term 2. s_____ to describe organisms that look similar to each other and have essentially the same DNA. The word 3. _____l is used to describe species, such as dogs, that have warm blood and give birth to live babies, while species like snakes that have cold blood and lay eggs are known as 4. r_____. When a mammal, reptile, or other organism dies, the dead body is called its 5. r_____. If the remains of an organism are buried and then turned to stone as a result of heat and pressure over a long period of time, the remains are known as a 6. _____l. Scientists have discovered many fossils of species that are now extinct, which means they have all died out, including fossils of extinct reptiles from 7. _____t____ times before humans were alive. These reptiles, which were often very large, are known as 8. _____s. You can see specimens, or examples, of prehistoric fossils in certain museums.

dinosaurs	mammal	prehistoric	reptiles
fossil	organisms	remains	species

C Analyzing Factual Information Questions

All Factual Information questions ask you about specific points that are mentioned in part of the reading passage. Factual Information questions may be written in one of several ways, as in these examples:

According to paragraph 3, which of the following is true about _____?

What does the author say about _____ in paragraph 4?

What event caused _____?

The author explains that _____ led to

According to paragraph 6, _____ most likely happened because

For many Factual Information questions, the paragraph number in which the answer can be found is mentioned in the question. This paragraph will be indicated on the computer screen by an arrow.

The correct answer to Factual Information questions:

- restates information that is mentioned in the passage.
- may include information from two different parts of the relevant section or paragraph.

In contrast, incorrect answers:

- often restate or repeat information from the passage, but do not answer the question.
- may use words from the passage to express an idea that is not actually mentioned in the passage.
- sometimes change a detail from the passage or contradict information mentioned in the passage.

C1 Answer Factual Information questions 1 and 2. Then discuss your answers with a partner.

One of the most effective ways of dating fossils is through the use of so-called index, or guide, fossils. These are fossils of organisms that lived during a specific period of time, but which are easily recognizable and commonly found over a wide area. These three characteristics allow scientists to date other fossils found in the same sedimentary layer. For example, if a fossil to be dated is found in the same rock layer as some index fossils, it can be assumed that the undated fossil and the index fossils all lived at roughly the same time. Among the most useful index fossils are certain species of corals, trilobites, and ammonites. Tiny microfossils, such as radiolarians and foraminifera, are more numerous but harder to identify, even for experts. They are useful for providing more precise dates than larger index fossils.

1. According to the author, which of these is a characteristic of index fossils?
   A They are found in at least two different rock layers.
   B They typically have a broad geographical distribution.
   C They are usually tiny microfossils, such as ammonites.
   D They are formed from organisms that lived in rock layers.

2. What point does the author make about microfossils?
   A They are more abundant than larger fossils.
   B They include fossil trilobites, ammonites, and corals.
   C Radiolarians are more abundant than foraminifera.
   D They are rarely difficult for experts to recognize.

TEST TACTIC

Factual Information questions are one of the two most common types of reading question in the TOEFL Test. As a result, becoming better at answering these questions accurately and quickly is likely to have a positive effect on your reading score.

C2 Match the wrong answers from exercise C1 to the correct description. Work with a partner. One answer has been done for you.

1. This answer is mentioned in the passage, but does not answer the question.	2B
2. These answers describe something that is not mentioned in the passage.	
3. These answers contradict or change information in the passage.	

D Mastering Factual Information Questions – Recognizing Key Phrases

An important skill for answering Factual Information questions is recognizing key phrases in the questions and answers. Noting these key phrases can help you find the right part of the passage as well as recognize the right answer more easily.

D1 Complete this explanation about key phrases by choosing the best phrase from A–F to fill blanks 1–6. One answer has been done for you.

Key phrases in the question and answer choices can help you identify where in the passage you will find the answer. For example:

- If a question includes the key phrase *paragraph 2*, you can be sure the answer will only be found in that paragraph.
- If a question contains the key phrase 1. _after the bones were discovered_ , you can be sure the answer will be found in the part of the passage that focuses on events that happened after the discovery.

Other key phrases in the question or answer choices will help you identify the correct answer. For example:

- If a key phrase is a name or specific term like 2. _____ or *go extinct*, a number like *100*, or a time reference like 3. _____, you should be able to identify a name or specific term, number, or time reference in the passage that has the same meaning.
- If a key phrase is an adjective like *many* or *fewer*, an adverb like *still* or 4. _____, or a noun phrase that refers to a specific thing, person, or place, such as 5. _____ or *paleontologists*, you should look for an adjective, adverb, or noun phrase with the same meaning.

Paying close attention to these key phrases can help you choose the right answer or to eliminate wrong ones. If a particular phrase is omitted or changed, it will make an answer choice incorrect.

Of course, not every phrase in the question and answer choices is a key phrase. For example, phrases like 6. _____ or *what does the writer say* are not likely to be helpful. Similarly, if a reading passage is about fossils, the word *fossils* is not likely to be a useful key phrase because it will appear in the passage so often.

A according to the author
B after the bones were discovered
C Carboniferous period

D several million years
E these days
F prehistoric North America

D2 Use information from D1 to complete tasks 1 and 2 about the Factual Information question below. Work with a partner.

1. Discuss why the highlighted phrases in the Factual Information question below are key phrases.
2. Discuss why the words "dinosaur" and "fossils" are NOT highlighted as key phrases.

According to paragraph 2, why do many dinosaur fossils sell for high prices at auction houses?
   A Rare items such as dinosaur fossils are usually expensive.
   B Fossils are becoming increasingly fashionable as works of art.
   C There are more buyers for fossils these days than 100 years ago.
   D Dinosaur fossils are often found in valuable rocks like marble.

D3 Work with a partner to highlight the key phrases in this example Factual Information question and answer choices. One key phrase has been highlighted for you.

1. What is one factor that probably led to the large size of sauropod dinosaurs?
   A They had relatively few natural predators.
   B Like other dinosaurs, they had hollow bones.
   C They lived in lakes and rivers that supported their weight.
   D They spent little of their energy raising their children.

E Mastering Factual Information Questions – Recognizing Right and Wrong Answers

Another important skill for answering Factual Information questions is recognizing right and wrong answers. Most right or wrong answers follow certain patterns. Knowing these patterns will help you to choose the right answer and avoid errors.

E1 Read the passage and answer the Factual Information question. Then complete the table. One answer in the table has been done for you.

Probably the most famous hoax in paleontology is that of the Piltdown Man. In 1912, fragments of what appeared to be a prehistoric human skull were apparently dug out of the ground near Piltdown in England. The bones initially caused great excitement because of what they suggested about the development of modern humans. After 40 years, however, scientists realized that the bone fragments came from two separate species: part of a human skull and an orangutan jawbone. Both bone fragments were relatively modern, but had been stained to look much older.

What does the author say about the Piltdown Man? *Choose two answers.*

A A prehistoric human skull found in England turned out to be fake.
B The Piltdown bones seemed to explain aspects of human development.
C The Piltdown bone fragments included an orangutan jawbone and skull.
D Relatively modern bones can be stained to look older than they are.

This answer paraphrases or simplifies an idea mentioned in the passage.	Right	
This answer paraphrases information from two parts of the passage.	Right	Answer A
This answer paraphrases part of the passage, but does not answer the question.	Wrong	
This answer looks similar to the passage, but contradicts a point or detail.	Wrong	

E2 Choose the statement, A or B, that answers Factual Detail questions 1–4. Then work with a partner to decide why each statement is right or wrong.

The woolly mammoth died out around the time of the last glacial retreat about 10,000 years ago. The reasons for its extinction are unclear. Climate change has been suggested, but several previous climate changes had not had an effect. Another hypothesis is that hunting by bands of humans put the mammoth population under severe pressure.

1. According to the author, woolly mammoths might have gone extinct because of
   A the actions of groups of humans.
   B several periods of climate change.

One of the most ambitious works of modern scholarship is the *Treatise on Invertebrate Paleontology.* When originally conceived in the 1950s, the assumption was that it would require three volumes totaling perhaps 3,000 pages. In fact, even though it is still a work-in-progress, the treatise currently comprises 50 volumes containing hundreds of thousands of words.

2. Which of the following statements about the *Treatise on Invertebrate Paleontology* is true?
   A It was originally thought scholars would finish it in the 1950s.
   B It contains many more words than people originally expected.

TEST TACTIC

Most wrong answers to Factual Information questions are not completely wrong. It is common for a wrong answer to include some words that match the passage and only a few words – sometimes just one word – that make the answer wrong. Keep this point in mind when you are analyzing the answer choices.

Scientists have various techniques for dating rocks and materials. These include several different radiometric dating methods. The basic principle of all radiometric dating methods is the same, but they differ in terms of their accuracy and time frame. Radiocarbon dating, for example, can be used to date materials up to 60,000 years old, whereas uranium-lead dating can be used for objects between 1 million and 4.5 billion years old.

3. What does the author say about radiometric dating?
    A   The only two reliable methods are radiocarbon dating and uranium-lead dating.
    B   Some methods are more useful than others for dating younger rocks and materials.

The term *fossils* generally refers to the petrified remains of parts of an organism's body, but paleontologists also study *trace fossils*, such as fossilized footprints or droppings, to learn about the behavior of prehistoric creatures.

4. What does the author say about trace fossils?
    A   They can help paleontologists understand how ancient organisms acted.
    B   They are the petrified remains of organisms studied by paleontologists.

E3 Which of these statements does NOT correctly describe at least one of the wrong answers in exercise E2?

A   Wrong answers typically repeat a few of the words and phrases that are used in the passage.
B   Wrong answers sometimes include a word that refers to an idea not mentioned in the passage.
C   Wrong answers generally describe something that is unrealistic or unlikely to be true in real life.
D   Wrong answers may include a different form of a word from the passage, such as move instead of movement.

E4 Use the techniques you just learned to answer the Factual Information questions below.

Studies of prehistoric climate data show that until approximately 2.5 billion years ago, Earth's atmosphere held almost no oxygen. After that time, levels of atmospheric oxygen began to rise as a by-product of photosynthesis by cyanobacteria. This event, known as the Great Oxidation, or sometimes the Great Oxygenation Event, was arguably the most significant climate event in history. Oxygen was poisonous to most species of bacteria living at the time, and the Great Oxidation was thus responsible for a mass extinction. But oxygen in the atmosphere also gave rise to the development of multi-cellular organisms, which use oxygen to power biological processes. In that sense, the Great Oxidation was a prerequisite for all modern life forms. The Great Oxidation also led to climate change. Free oxygen in the atmosphere reacted with and reduced levels of atmospheric methane. As methane is a greenhouse gas that helps maintain warm surface temperatures, reduced levels led to lower surface temperatures that eventually resulted in a prolonged ice age known as the Huronian Glaciation. One final change attributed to the Great Oxidation is a dramatic increase in the diversity of minerals found on Earth. Research has suggested that hundreds of new minerals were formed when existing minerals were oxidized, a process that, as its name suggests, requires oxygen.

1. What effect did the Great Oxygenation Event have?
    A   An increase in the number and diversity of cyanobacteria
    B   The creation of several new mineral-forming processes
    C   A rise in the level of methane in the atmosphere
    D   The poisoning of many existing species of bacteria

2. What does the author say about the Huronian Glaciation?
    A   It reduced surface temperatures exactly 2.5 billion years ago.
    B   It caused levels of several atmospheric greenhouse gases to fall.
    C   It lasted for a short time until surface temperatures warmed.
    D   It resulted from increased levels of free atmospheric oxygen.

F Analyzing Negative Factual Information Questions

Negative Factual Information questions ask you to decide which point is not mentioned in the reading passage. They are easy to recognize because they include the word NOT or EXCEPT in capital letters, as these examples show:

According to paragraph 3, which of the following is NOT true about _____?

In paragraph 6, the author makes all of the following points EXCEPT

What point does the author NOT make about _____?

The correct answer to Negative Factual Information questions:

- may contradict or change information that is mentioned in the passage.
- may express an idea that is not mentioned anywhere in the passage (although it may seem likely to be true).
- can usually be found by reading just one paragraph, but may require looking at two or more paragraphs.

In contrast, incorrect answers:

- restate, summarize, or simplify information that is stated in the passage.

Remember that Negative Factual Information questions are the opposite of Factual Information questions in that the right answer is the one that you cannot find in the passage and the wrong answers are the ones that you can find.

F1 Answer Negative Factual Information questions 1 and 2. Then discuss your answers with a partner.

A popular story type in fantasy literature involves the idea of prehistoric animals surviving to the present-day in remote or underground areas. The earliest story of this type, Jules Verne's *Journey to the Center of the Earth*, was published in 1864. In this tale, some travelers descend into a volcano and find an underground world filled with prehistoric plants and animals, including a herd of mastodons, a type of elephant that in the real world went extinct roughly 12,000 years ago. Almost five decades after Verne, Sir Arthur Conan Doyle, most famous now for his series of tales about the fictional detective Sherlock Holmes, wrote a novel titled *The Lost World*. In the story, some scientists discover a remote plateau in the South American rainforest. Upon reaching the top of the plateau, they are attacked by pterosaurs and dinosaurs. They also encounter various reptiles and prehistoric mammals that are now extinct before escaping from the plateau and reaching safety.

> **TEST TACTIC**
>
> Reading passages in the TOEFL Test may include unfamiliar vocabulary. Many students waste time trying to understand every unknown word, but usually this is unnecessary. You can often answer questions just by focusing on the words you know.

1. The author mentions all of the following about Jules Verne's *Journey to the Center of the Earth* EXCEPT:
   A The story is set in a world that exists under the Earth's surface.
   B It was the first story to be published of a popular type of genre.
   C The events of the story take place more than 10,000 years ago.
   D The characters in the story encounter prehistoric creatures.

2. What does the author NOT say about *The Lost World* by Sir Arthur Conan Doyle?
   A Its author is mostly known as a writer of detective stories.
   B It was published shortly after the story by Jules Verne was written.
   C The characters in the story are attacked by various creatures.
   D The story is set in a distant part of the jungle in South America.

F2 Work with a partner to answer questions 1 and 2.

1. Which right answer in exercise **F1** contradicts or changes information in the passage?
2. Which right answer in **F1** expresses an idea that might be true but is not mentioned anywhere in the passage?

G Mastering Negative Factual Information Questions – Analyzing the Answer Choices

The skills for answering Factual Information questions also work for Negative Factual Information questions, especially recognizing incorrect answer choices that either contradict the passage or introduce an idea that is not mentioned in the passage.

G1 Decide if statements 1–6 Restate the passage, Contradict the passage, or are Not mentioned in the passage. One answer has been done for you.

Tyrannosaurus rex is arguably the best known dinosaur among the general population, in part due to its reputation as a fearsome predator. But was *T. rex* actually so deadly? Among paleontologists there has been a long-running, and sometimes heated, debate about how tyrannosaurs acquired food. Some have argued that their relatively slow speed of movement and tiny, weak forearms mean they weren't efficient killers, but rather they must have acted as scavengers, feeding off dinosaurs that had died from natural causes or been killed by other predators. Others have claimed they were active hunters that would attack other species including hadrosaurs such as *Edmontosaurus*, and possibly even huge sauropods like *Diplodocus*. The recent discovery of a fossil *Edmontosaurus* with part of a *T. rex* tooth completely embedded in its bone sheds new light on the issue. The only explanation is that the tooth became stuck in the bone, which then healed around the tooth. And the only scenario that accounts for this is the *Edmontosaurus* being attacked by a *Tyrannosaurus* while alive and, crucially, not just surviving the attack, but living long enough afterwards for its bones to heal. This evidence strongly supports the idea that tyrannosaurs were active hunters because the *Edmontosaurus* was alive when attacked and scavengers do not typically attack live prey. However, this evidence neither shows how often *T. rex* attacked live prey nor proves that it never acted as a scavenger.

1. It is not clear why *Tyrannosaurus rex* is so well known.
   ☐ Restate ☑ Contradict ☐ Not mentioned
2. Some scientists believe *T. rex* ate already dead dinosaurs.
   ☐ Restate ☐ Contradict ☐ Not mentioned
3. Others paleontologists claim *T. rex* hunted sauropods but not hadrosaurs.
   ☐ Restate ☐ Contradict ☐ Not mentioned
4. *Diplodocus* moved more slowly than *T. rex* because of its huge size.
   ☐ Restate ☐ Contradict ☐ Not mentioned
5. The evidence of the tooth supports the idea that *T. rex* hunted live prey.
   ☐ Restate ☐ Contradict ☐ Not mentioned
6. Additional evidence is likely to prove whether *T. rex* ever scavenged food.
   ☐ Restate ☐ Contradict ☐ Not mentioned

TEST TACTIC

Answering some Negative Factual Information questions takes time because you must find the three choices that paraphrase the passage before you know the right choice. If time is running out, guess the answer to remaining Negative Factual Information questions and save your time for questions you can answer more quickly.

H Test Challenge

H1 Answer Factual Information and Negative Factual Information questions 1–10 on the next page. Try to answer all of the questions in 15 minutes or less in order to get realistic practice for the test. The following checklist of skills that you learned in this unit may help you.

☑ Look for key phrases in the answer choices that are paraphrased in the passage.

☑ Eliminate answer choices that contradict the passage or are not mentioned in it.

Lazarus Species and Living Fossils

Paleontologists analyze fossils to determine when a particular species went extinct. When fossils of a species no longer appear in the fossil record after a particular geological period, it is generally safe to assume the species died out during that period. In rare cases, however, fossils of a species are sometimes found in the fossil record after a long absence. Such species are called Lazarus species. If living specimens of the Lazarus species are found that are barely changed from fossil specimens, the species may also be called a living fossil. An example of a species that meets the criteria for both names is the Wollemi Pine. The first fossils of this species appear in the fossil record dating from the middle of the Mesozoic era roughly 200 million years ago, but no fossils have been found younger than two million years old. Scientists therefore believed that the species had gone extinct at around this time. However, living Wollemi Pines were found in 1994 in a remote area of Wollemi National Park in southeastern Australia.

1. According to the author, a living fossil is
   - (A) an organism that is only known from its fossil record
   - (B) a species that does not have any gaps in its fossil record
   - (C) a species that has existed for more than 200 million years
   - (D) a living species that looks almost the same as its fossils

2. The author mentions all of the following about the Wollemi Pine EXCEPT:
   - (A) Scientists thought it had died out two million years ago.
   - (B) It is both a living fossil and a Lazarus species.
   - (C) It last appeared in the fossil record in the Mesozoic era.
   - (D) It was discovered in an isolated part of Australia.

Dinosaur Sounds

Modern technology has helped scientists learn an increasing amount of information from fossils. In a fascinating study, scientists at the New Mexico Museum of Natural History and Sandia National Laboratories simulated the sound of a living dinosaur. They first used a medical scanner to view the interior of a well-preserved skull of a *Parasaurolophus*, a dinosaur that lived about 75 million years ago. They then used powerful computers to analyze the scanner data and create a software model of the air passages inside a long, bony crest on the skull. This model let the scientists establish the frequency of the sound waves the dinosaur could produce. The software also simulated blowing air through the skull to produce sounds. The noise produced was a loud, low-frequency rumble that could change in pitch. *Parasaurolophus* roamed in huge herds grazing the land, and paleontologists speculate that the dinosaurs may have used the sound to warn other members of the herd of danger or as a means of socializing.

3. Which of these steps did scientists NOT follow when simulating the sound made by *Parasaurolophus*?
   - (A) Using medical technology to preserve the skull well
   - (B) Scanning and analyzing the interior of the skull
   - (C) Creating a model of air passages within the skull
   - (D) Simulating the movement of air through the skull

4. Why do scientists think that *Parasaurolophus* made sounds?
   - (A) To locate other herds of large dinosaurs
   - (B) To recognize nearby sources of nutrition
   - (C) To have social interactions with other species
   - (D) To advise herd members of potential hazards

The Prehistoric Origins of Fossil Fuels

According to the most widely-held theory, the formation of fossil fuels like crude oil requires organic material, heat, pressure, and time. During prehistoric times, dead and decaying organic materials, such as algae and plankton, would settle to the bottom of rivers, lakes, swamps, or seas like the Tethys Ocean, which existed for much of the Mesozoic era. Often these bodies of water were warm, shallow, and rich in nutrients; ideal conditions for algae and plankton to flourish. The organic remains would mix with mud, sand, and other sediments, and become buried under conditions in which no oxygen was present.

Over time these remains would be overlain either by additional layers of organic remains mixed with sediment or sediment alone, causing heat and pressure to build up in the lower layers of organic material. The heat and pressure would gradually transform the material into a sedimentary rock like shale. The heat and pressure would also change the organic remains into a waxy precursor to crude oil called kerogen. This substance can be found today in oil-bearing shales in some locations. With further heat, pressure, and time, the kerogen molecules would crack, a process technically known as catagenesis, and break up into lighter molecules of carbon and hydrogen, collectively called hydrocarbons. Depending on factors such as the amount of heat, the hydrocarbons could be in the form of liquid crude oil or natural gas. Scientists are uncertain how much time is required for prehistoric remains to turn into a fossil fuel, but estimates range from hundreds of thousands to millions of years.

5. All of the following are required for the formation of fossil fuels EXCEPT
   - (A) sand or mud
   - (B) available oxygen
   - (C) heat and pressure
   - (D) organic remains

6. According to paragraph 2, what is kerogen?
   - (A) A mixture of mud, sand, and dead organic material
   - (B) A wax-like material that can turn into crude oil
   - (C) Lighter hydrocarbon molecules like natural gas
   - (D) Organic remains fossilized in sedimentary rock

7. According to the passage, what is one factor that influences whether catagenesis leads to oil or gas?
   - (A) The amount of pressure
   - (B) The location of the kerogen
   - (C) The temperature
   - (D) The amount of time

Baron Georges Cuvier

The French scientist Georges Cuvier was one of the fathers of modern paleontology. He is most famous now for his work on vertebrate paleontology and for establishing the fundamental principles of biostratigraphy, which involves using fossils to assign relative ages to strata, or layers of rock, in Earth's crust. During his lifetime, he was even more famous than he is now, and accrued many academic and professional honors. He was made a French peer in 1819 for his contributions to science, after which he was known by his title Baron Cuvier.

Cuvier was born in eastern France, close to the border with Switzerland, in 1769. He was a gifted child who excelled at school, but after graduation his family circumstances initially made it hard for him to get an academic position. By the age of 27, however, he was working as a lecturer in Paris. In 1796 he delivered an important paper that analyzed bones from African and Indian elephants as well as fossilized bones from mammoths and another elephant-like species.

In his paper he proved not only that African and Indian elephants were distinct species, but also that the fossilized bones were from two other different species. As these other species no longer existed, Cuvier argued that the animals must have gone extinct. This was an important argument because many scientists at that time did not believe that species could die out. Cuvier's paper, along with another paper he delivered later the same year in which he identified and named the species *Megatherium*, an extinct prehistoric sloth, effectively ended the debate and forced other scientists to accept the reality of species extinction.

8. Which of these events did NOT occur during the life of Georges Cuvier?
   - (A) He accepted the idea of extinction as a result of work by other scientists.
   - (B) He delivered a paper discussing several different species of elephant.
   - (C) He produced work that led to the development of biostratigraphy.
   - (D) He received numerous professional awards, as well as being given a title.

9. According to paragraph 2, what is true of Cuvier's childhood?
   - (A) His family moved from Switzerland to Paris.
   - (B) He did not enjoy school and failed to graduate.
   - (C) He delivered several important academic papers.
   - (D) His intelligence made him an excellent student.

10. What point does the author make in paragraph 3?
   - (A) Cuvier's work proved the existence of fossils of *Megatherium*.
   - (B) Some scholars did not accept that species could become extinct.
   - (C) Cuvier had a debate with other scientists about *Megatherium*.
   - (D) Cuvier's academic theories made it hard for him to find work.

TEST TACTIC

Every time you get a Factual Information or Negative Factual Information question wrong, learn from your mistake. First, understand why the right answer is right and your answer is wrong. Next, understand why you chose the wrong answer. Finally, think about how to avoid making similar mistakes in the future.

Next Steps

Topics related to paleontology are common in the reading section of the TOEFL Test. You may also have topics about this subject in the other sections of the test. As a result, learning more about paleontology, as well as practicing key skills for Factual Information and Negative Factual Information questions, may raise your overall test score.

To learn more about paleontology and vocabulary related to this discipline:

1. Read an article in your language about one aspect of paleontology to get some background knowledge about this topic.
2. Read an English article about the same topic to understand the main ideas, but do not try to understand every word.
3. Read the English article again. When you see an unfamiliar word, try to understand the word from its context and write a definition. Then check your dictionary. If your definition was wrong, study the context again to understand your error. After checking your dictionary, decide if the word is useful; if it is, study the word carefully and find other examples of it.

To practice key skills for Factual Information and Negative Factual Information questions:

Factual Information questions, which are also called detail questions or comprehension questions, are probably the most common type of reading comprehension question for all types of reading materials. As a result, you can find thousands of such questions in books or online. You can practice these questions to build useful skills for the TOEFL Test.

1. Find a source of a large number of reading questions that you think are too easy for you.
2. Keep answering exercises from this source until you have answered 20 questions in a row perfectly.
3. When you have completed 20 questions in a row perfectly, find a new source with harder exercises and repeat step 2.

Many students make careless mistakes when they answer reading questions. You can train yourself to avoid making careless mistakes by trying to answer more difficult questions *only* after you have answered 20 easier questions in a row perfectly.

Unit Focus

There are ten types of reading questions in the TOEFL Test, including Vocabulary questions. These questions test if you can understand the meaning of a word or phrase as it is used in a specific part of the passage. Vocabulary questions usually ask about words that are common in general or academic English, not words related to a specific academic subject. They are one of the most common questions in the reading section, and you will usually have from three to five Vocabulary questions after every passage. Several key skills can help you answer Vocabulary questions effectively, including:

- recognizing context clues in the passage that help you understand the meaning of a word.
- recognizing clues to the meaning of a word in the word itself.

The vocabulary focus is on academic words and phrases related to two similar academic subjects:

- history and ancient history, the study of events, situations, and people from earlier times to the recent past.

A Warm-up

A1 Read these sayings about history. Then work with a partner to complete tasks 1–3.

> "Study history if you want to know the future."
> "If you don't know history, you are certain to repeat it."
> "History is a set of lies that people have agreed on."

1. Do you think each saying about history is true? Why or why not?
2. Use the sayings as a guide to make up your own saying about history.
3. Share your saying from task 2 with others and vote on the best three sayings in the class.

B Academic Vocabulary

B1 Choose the best definition, A–H, for each word to complete this table of useful words related to history and ancient history. One answer has been done for you.

Word	Definition	Synonym
civilization (noun)	1.	society
conflict (noun)	2. a disagreement between groups that leads to fighting	war
conquest (noun)	3.	invasion
found (verb)	4.	establish
monarch (noun)	5.	sovereign
reign (verb)	6.	rule
settlement (noun)	7.	community
territory (noun)	8.	kingdom

A a disagreement between groups that leads to fighting
B a place where people live, such as a village or town
C a region that is governed and controlled by a ruler
D a society with a high level of culture and organization
E an attack on a region that leads to control of that region
F the person who rules over a kingdom or empire
G to be the head of a territory or nation for a period of time
H to start something, especially a settlement or colony

C Analyzing Vocabulary Questions

Vocabulary questions ask you about the meaning of a word or phrase as it is used in the passage. The key word or phrase will be highlighted in both the question and the passage:

The word "_____" in paragraph 3 is closest in meaning to

The phrase "_____" in the passage most likely means

In stating that "_____" the author means that

Remember that Vocabulary questions only ask about the meaning of the highlighted word or phrase *as it used in the passage*. If the highlighted word has several meanings, be careful. Make sure that the answer you choose matches the meaning used in the passage, not another meaning of that word. For example, the most common meaning of the word "company" is "business," but in the phrase "a company of soldiers," the meaning of "company" is "group" not "business."

The correct answer to Vocabulary questions:

- will have the same meaning as the highlighted expression as it is used in the passage.
- can replace the highlighted expression in the passage without changing the meaning of the passage.

In contrast, incorrect answers:

- never have the same meaning as the highlighted expression as it is used in the passage. However, if the highlighted expression has several meanings, an incorrect answer may match one of the other meanings.
- sometimes mean the opposite of the highlighted expression as it is used in the passage.
- may look similar to the highlighted expression, such as by having similar spelling or the same beginning or ending.

TEST TACTIC

Every answer choice for Vocabulary questions is grammatically possible. You only need to decide whether each choice has the same meaning as the highlighted word, not whether it is grammatically correct.

C1 Answer Vocabulary questions 1 and 2. Then compare answers with a partner.

Despite its being an extraordinarily complex issue, many believe that President Abraham Lincoln handled the emancipation question in a comparatively successful fashion.

1. The word "fashion" in the passage is closest in meaning to
   A trend
   B manner
   C faction
   D design

The rise of Octavian, later known as Augustus Caesar, to the leadership of the Roman state ended years of civil war and brought order to Roman politics for the first time in decades.

2. The word "order" in the passage is closest in meaning to

   A demand
   B ordeal
   C turmoil
   D stability

C2 Match the wrong answers from exercise C1 to the correct description, 1, 2, or 3. Use a dictionary if necessary. Then compare answers with a partner. One answer has been done for you.

1. Wrong answers that have the same meaning as a different meaning of the highlighted word	1A
2. Wrong answers that have the opposite meaning of the highlighted word	
3. Wrong answers that look similar in some way to the highlighted word	

D Mastering Vocabulary Questions – Using Context Clues from the Passage

The context – the sentence in which the highlighted word is used as well as nearby sentences – often contains information that can help you understand the meaning of the highlighted word. For instance, in the phrase "the event was deferred until later instead of being canceled", "until later" and "canceled" are context clues which suggest that "deferred" probably means "delayed."

D1 **Use the underlined context clues in these passages to help you answer questions 1–4.**

A major epidemic popularly called the Black Death occurred in the mid-fourteenth century. It caused the deaths of up to 60% of the population of affected areas as doctors were able to provide almost no help to those who became sick.

1. The word "epidemic" most likely means
   A outbreak of disease
   B natural disaster

The Bayeux Tapestry, which despite its name is actually an embroidered cloth, was completed around 1077 A.D. and depicts the events that led to the Norman conquest of England. It also shows the people involved in those events.

2. The word "depicts" is closest in meaning to
   A explains
   B illustrates

During the Heian period of Japanese history, there was an emphasis on art and works of fiction. Indeed, during this time the first Japanese novels and poems were published, such as The Tale of Genji, which is widely considered a masterpiece.

3. The phrase "works of fiction" means
   A imagination
   B literature

Unlike the League of Nations, which endured for just 27 years and never had more than 58 members, the United Nations has existed since 1945 and has seen a steady increase in membership from 51 initially to nearly 200 today.

4. The word "endured" probably means
   A continued
   B suffered

D2 **Fill in the blanks with the correct answer. When you have finished, compare your answers with a partner. One answer has been done for you.**

Clues that you can find in the passage are called context clues. These clues can help you understand the meaning of highlighted expressions in the TOEFL Test. You may see four common types of context clues:

- As seen in passage ___4___ in exercise **D1**, the highlighted word may be contrasted with other words or phrases.

- As seen in passage _____, the context might include a word or phrase that is a synonym of the highlighted word.

- As seen in passage _____, an example in the context might make the meaning of the highlighted word clear.

- As seen in passage _____, the context may include other words that suggest the meaning of the highlighted word.

D3 Work with a partner to answer questions 1–4. If neither answer is correct, write your own.

One of the defining acts of Thomas Jefferson's presidency was the Louisiana Purchase, in which the United States of America acquired a vast area from France for $15 million. The purchase effectively doubled the size of the United States, making it by far the largest territorial gain in US history. There was broad domestic opposition before the Purchase was completed because it was felt the Constitution did not allow for the acquistion of land. However, a vote by members of the House of Representatives narrowly approved the sale by a count of 59 in favor to 57 against.

1. The word "vast" in the passage probably means
   A useful   B valuable   C _your answer_

2. The word "domestic" in the passage is closest in meaning to
   A national   B commercial   C _your answer_

There are several myths about the founding of Rome. In the most well-known story, twin brothers Romulus, after whom the city was named, and Remus established the city in 753 B.C. on the Palatine Hill. In reality, archaeological data suggests that humans began dwelling in the area thousands of years before the traditional founding date and that the city developed from crude settlements on the Palatine and Quirinal hills. Not every scholar accepts this interpretation of the evidence, however.

3. The word "dwelling" in the passage most likely means
   A dating   B traveling   C _your answer_

4. The word "interpretation" in the passage is closest in meaning to
   A occupation   B viewpoint   C _your answer_

D4 Choose the best word from A–L to complete blanks 1–10 in these sentences. Two of the words do NOT match any of the blanks. One answer has been done for you.

Prehistoric humans used 1. ____fire____ for many purposes, including providing heat, keeping away dangerous 2. _____, cooking food, and making tools.

Scholars estimate that the various 3. _____ and towns that formed the Indus Valley Civilization, one of the world's earliest and largest urban cultures, might have had a maximum 4. _____ of almost 5 million people.

Less is known about the Dark Ages, which spanned the sixth to thirteenth centuries A.D., than either earlier or later times because relatively few written 5. _____ have survived from this 6. _____.

During the Second Barons' War, the first major 7. _____ at Lewes in southern England was fought between an army of 8. _____ led by Baron Simon de Montfort and another led by King Henry III.

In the 1930s, the Netherlands, like many other 9. _____ around the world, experienced a severe economic crisis known as the Great Depression, though the 10. _____ happened later there than in many places.

A battle	E documents	I period
B cities	F experience	J population
C creatures	G fire	K soldiers
D decline	H nations	L strengths

D5 Underline the words and phrases in exercises D3 and D4 that helped you choose each answer. Work with a partner.

E Mastering Vocabulary Questions – Using Clues from the Highlighted Word

In addition to context clues from the passage, clues from the highlighted word itself such as its prefix (beginning) or word root (main part) may help you understand its meaning. For example, the word *submarine* has the prefix *sub*, which means "under," and the word root *mar*, which means "sea." These clues suggest that *submarine* means "under (the) sea."

E1 Choose the best answers to complete blanks 1–10 in these tables of common prefixes and word roots. One answer has been done for you.

Common Prefix	Meaning	Example Word
auto–	self	**auto**matic (adj.)
bi–	1. two/twice	**bi**lingual (adj.)
co– (also col–, com–, con–, cor–)	2.	**com**municate (verb)
contra– (also contr–)	3.	**contr**ast (noun/verb)
inter–	between	**inter**national (adj.)
mis–	wrong/bad	**mis**take (noun/verb)
post–	after	**post**pone (verb)
pre–	4.	**pre**paration (noun)
re–	5.	**re**peat (noun/verb)
trans–	across	**trans**late (verb)

again/back
before
opposite/against
together/with
two/twice

Common Word Root	Meaning	Example Word
cede (also ceed, cess)	go	pre**cede** (verb)
dict	speak	contra**dict** (verb)
labor	6.	coll**abor**ate (verb)
memor (also mem)	7.	misre**mem**ber (verb)
nect	8.	intercon**nect** (verb)
nomy	law	auto**nomy** (noun)
nov	9.	re**nov**ate (verb)
port	10.	trans**port** (noun/verb)
script	write	post**script** (noun)
sect	cut/divide	bi**sect** (verb)

carry
join/bind
new
remember
work

E2 Work with a partner to write a definition of each example word listed in the table of word roots. Use the example below as a guide. When you finish, check your definitions in a dictionary and correct any mistakes.

Example   *"Precede" probably has a meaning similar to "go before."*

E3 Choose the best example words from the tables in exercise E1 to complete sentences 1–5. Compare answers with a partner when you finish. One answer has been done for you.

1. Sir Arthur Evans is justly famous for discovering the remains of Bronze Age palaces on the island of Crete, though his decision to _____renovate_____ the ruined buildings has been criticized by many scholars.
2. The roots of the American War of Independence lay in the desire of Americans to create laws themselves rather than be ruled by Great Britain; to have _____, in other words.

3. In 1648, representatives from Spain and the Dutch Republic signed a series of treaties that not only formally ended both the Thirty Years' War and the Eighty Years' War but also provided a foundation for modern _____ relations.

4. During the Bronze Age in Ancient Greece, battles were fought in the heroic style described in Homer's epic poems the *Iliad* and *Odyssey*. Ritual insults and duels between individual warriors would often _____ the general battle.

5. In 1990, scientists from multiple countries, including the US, the UK, Japan, and France, began to _____ on a joint venture called the Human Genome Project. It was expected that this project would take 15 years to finish, but in fact it was completed ahead of schedule in 2003.

E4 **Complete tasks 1–3 with a partner. When you have finished, share your lists with the rest of the class.**

1. The prefix *bi–* means "two or twice." Make a list of other number prefixes, such as *tri–*. Include examples of each prefix.

2. The prefix *mis–* has a negative meaning. Make a list of other negative prefixes that you know. Include examples.

3. Make a list of additional examples for every prefix and word root in the two tables in exercise **E1**.

E5 **Answer questions 1–5. Underline any word clues or context clues from the passage that help you.**

Marco Polo spent 24 years traveling from Europe to Asia and back. When he returned to Venice in 1295 A.D., he was imprisoned for four years. He used the time productively, though, by dictating his memoirs to another prisoner.

1. The word "memoirs" in the passage most likely means

   A reason for a journey   B story of a person's life   C trouble with the law

In December, 1901, the Italian inventor Guglielmo Marconi claimed to have sent a broadcast by radio across the Atlantic Ocean from southwest England to Newfoundland, Canada, a distance of approximately 3,500 kilometers.

2. The word "broadcast" in the passage is closest in meaning to

   A passage   B transmission   C signature

The 1383–1385 Crisis is the name given to the period when Portugal had no ruling monarch. It began when King Ferdinand I died without a son and ended after much civil unrest with the crowning of King John I after the Battle of Aljubarrota.

3. The word "period" in the passage is closest in meaning to

   A perquisite   B governance   C interval

The first threshing machine was invented by Andrew Meikle in 1784 and allowed farmers to separate grain from stalks and husks easily and cost-effectively. Until its invention, this laborious task could only be done by hand.

4. The word "laborious" in the passage is closest in meaning to

   A studious   B mistimed   C challenging

The Code of Ur-Nammu from the Sumerian city-state of Ur is the oldest known surviving law code. It predates the better-known Code of Hammurabi from Babylon by at least 300 years. Scholars know that the full version of the Code includes 57 separate offenses. However, the Code is written on stone tablets that are more than 4,000 years old and only 40 of the laws have been reconstructed. Each offense is listed with the punishment that a guilty person should receive after the verdict was handed down.

5. The word "predates" in the passage is closest in meaning to

   A maintained for   B lasted until   C existed before

TEST TACTIC

To avoid being distracted by the highlighted word, imagine that the question and passage have a blank instead of a highlighted word. Then think "Which of these answers is the best choice to fill in the blank?"

F Test Challenge

F1 Answer Vocabulary questions 1–8. Try to finish in 12 minutes or less so as to get realistic practice for the test. Use the checklist of skills that you learned in this unit as a guide.

☑ Look for context clues in the passage that help you understand the meaning of the highlighted expression

☑ Look for clues within the highlighted word itself such as its prefix or its word root

---

The Delian League

The Delian League, founded in 478 B.C., was an alliance of 150 to 170 city-states under the leadership of Athens, which had the most powerful navy. The aim of the League was to offer its members mutual protection against the Persian Empire, which had made a number of attacks on Greek city-states. The League's name derives from the island of Delos where the treasury was housed and where meetings of the member states took place. Within a few years of the League's founding, Athens began taking advantage of its strength and forced the other member states to continue making financial contributions even after fighting with Persia had ended. As members were not allowed to secede from the League, this resulted in some city-states becoming poorer and weaker. This behavior led to conflict between Athens and the less influential members of the League, and in due course prompted the outbreak of the Peloponnesian War in 431 B.C.

---

1. The word "derives" in the passage most likely means
   - Ⓐ delivers
   - Ⓑ occurs
   - Ⓒ comes
   - Ⓓ causes

2. The phrase "secede from" in the passage is closest in meaning to
   - Ⓐ repay
   - Ⓑ leave
   - Ⓒ impede
   - Ⓓ support

3. The word "influential" in the passage is closest in meaning to
   - Ⓐ affluent
   - Ⓑ controversial
   - Ⓒ automatic
   - Ⓓ powerful

4. The phrase "in due course" in the passage is closest in meaning to
   - Ⓐ pragmatically
   - Ⓑ eventually
   - Ⓒ occasionally
   - Ⓓ optionally

King George III

George III was the monarch of Great Britain and Ireland from 1760 until his death in 1820. Numerous conflicts occurred during his reign, including the Seven Years' War, the American Revolutionary War, and campaigns against Napoleon. During his rule, George III suffered from episodes of mental illness. These occurred more frequently and became more severe in the later years of his reign, and by 1810 it was felt that he was no longer able to perform his duties as monarch, so his son, George IV, was made regent. At the time, the cause of and best way to cure his problem baffled doctors, but a recent review of medical reports from the time and analysis of samples of preserved hair from George III suggest that he was possibly suffering from arsenic-induced porphyria, a disease of the blood that can cause neurological symptoms.

5. The word "episodes" in the passage most likely means
   - Ⓐ stories
   - Ⓑ epics
   - Ⓒ periods
   - Ⓓ doubts

6. The word "severe" in the passage is closest in meaning to
   - Ⓐ fallible
   - Ⓑ serious
   - Ⓒ austere
   - Ⓓ periodic

7. The word "regent" in the passage is closest in meaning to
   - Ⓐ ruler
   - Ⓑ advisor
   - Ⓒ creator
   - Ⓓ caregiver

8. The word "baffled" in the passage most likely means
   - Ⓐ interested
   - Ⓑ puzzled
   - Ⓒ treated
   - Ⓓ dominated

Next Steps

Topics related to history and ancient history are common in the reading section of the TOEFL Test. You may also have topics about these subjects in other sections of the test. As a result, learning more about these subjects, as well as practicing key skills for Vocabulary questions, may raise your overall test score.

To learn more about history and ancient history, and vocabulary related to these disciplines:

1. Read an article in your language about one aspect of history to get some background knowledge about this topic.
2. Read an English article about the same topic to understand the main ideas, but do not try to understand every word.
3. Read the English article again. When you see an unfamiliar word, check its meaning in your dictionary. If the word has a useful prefix or word root, make a note of it and think of or find three other words with the same prefix or root. (You can find useful lists of word roots and prefixes online. Try searching for "learn word roots" or "useful academic prefixes".)

To practice key skills for Vocabulary questions:

1. If you see an unfamiliar word or phrase when you are reading, try to understand its meaning from the context.
2. Write one word or phrase that you think has the same meaning and another word or phrase that means the opposite.
3. Check your ideas in a dictionary and, if they are not a good synonym or antonym for the word, look again at the context.
4. Using a dictionary, thesaurus, or the Internet, learn one more synonym and one more antonym for each word.

Unit Focus

There are ten types of reading questions in the TOEFL Test, including Rhetorical Purpose questions. These questions test how well you can understand why the author mentions specific information in one paragraph or in the whole passage. Typically, you will get between zero and two Rhetorical Purpose questions after each passage. To answer these questions accurately, you need to practice and use several key skills that you will learn in this unit, including:

- comparing infinitives used in the answer choices with the function of the passage.
- recognizing answers that contradict information in the passage.
- recognizing answers that describe information not mentioned in the passage.

The vocabulary focus is on academic words and phrases related to:

- marine biology, the scientific study of plants and animals that live in the ocean.

A Warm-up

A1 Write short paragraphs to complete statements 1–3. Write about only one of the two options in each statement. Include a reason and example in each response. When you have finished, exchange answers with a partner and give each other feedback.

1. I would be interested / not be interested in studying marine biology because ...
2. One type of seafood that I like / dislike is ... because ...
3. My favorite / least favorite type of sea creature is ... because ...

B Academic Vocabulary

B1 Choose a highlighted word from the passage to complete each definition, 1–8. One answer has been done for you.

Marine biology is the study of organisms that live in the oceans, including fish, mammals, reptiles, birds, and plants and algae. Some marine biologists study organisms that live in shallow waters near the shore or in coastal environments that, depending on the level of the tide, are sometimes under water and sometimes above water. Others study submarine creatures found in deep water zones or even on the seabed at the bottom of the ocean. Marine biologists also study how environmental factors such as ocean currents, water temperature, and levels of pollution affect marine organisms.

1. Stable movements of water in one direction _____ currents _____
2. Organisms that are similar to plants _____
3. Related to the oceans _____
4. The area where the land meets the sea _____
5. The bottom of the ocean _____
6. The daily change in the level of the ocean _____
7. The opposite of deep _____
8. Under the water _____

C Analyzing Rhetorical Purpose Questions

Rhetorical Purpose questions focus on the reason why the author mentions something. These questions often include a phrase like "in order to," "function," or "purpose," as in the examples below. Some Rhetorical Purpose questions ask about a specific detail within a paragraph. If a word or phrase is highlighted in the question, it will also be highlighted in the passage.

The author discusses _____ in order to

Why does the author mention "▓▓▓▓▓▓▓▓" in paragraph 2?

You may also see Rhetorical Purpose questions that ask about the purpose of a whole paragraph, as in these examples:

What is the main function of paragraph 3?

What purpose does paragraph 4 serve in the passage as a whole?

The correct answer to Rhetorical Purpose questions:
- will not be directly stated in the passage, so you will have to use indirect evidence to recognize the author's purpose.
- will describe the most likely reason why the author mentions a specific detail or the most likely purpose of a paragraph.
- typically paraphrases words and phrases from the passage rather than repeating them.

In contrast, incorrect answers often paraphrase, summarize, or repeat information from the passage, but:
- may describe a purpose that paraphrases some words from the passage, but does not match the passage.
- may describe a purpose that matches a different part of the passage than the question asks about.
- may describe a purpose that is contradicted by other information in the relevant part of the passage.

C1 Answer Rhetorical Purpose questions 1 and 2. Then discuss your answers with a partner.

Brightly-colored clownfish live in warm, shallow areas of the Pacific and Indian oceans where they form symbiotic relationships with a few species of sea anemone. When predators are nearby, clownfish gain protection by swimming among the anemone's tentacles, which are poisonous to other species. The tentacles also provide a safe nesting site. It is believed that clownfish are immune to the toxin because of a slimy coating on their skin. Clownfish will also eat both bits of food left over from the anemone's meal and individual tentacles that have died. In return, the waste products of clownfish are of value to sea anemones because they provide nutrients like nitrogen that are believed to promote tissue growth and regeneration. Clownfish also defend anemones from predators, keep them clean by consuming the remains of meals, and their bright colors may even lure small fish that anemones eat.

1. What is the main function of this paragraph?
   A To compare the feeding habits of clownfish with those of sea anemones
   B To discuss the ways in which clownfish benefit from being brightly colored
   C To describe the mutually beneficial relationship of sea anemones and clownfish
   D To disprove a theory about why clownfish are immune to sea anemone poison

2. The author mentions "waste products" in order to
   A suggest that clownfish get both benefits and disadvantages from sea anemones
   B argue that the only benefit sea anemones get from clownfish is access to food
   C explain how sea anemones and clownfish protect each other from predatory attacks
   D introduce an example of an advantage that clownfish bring to sea anemones

C2 Work with a partner to explain why each wrong answer to exercise **C1** is wrong. One example has been done for you.

Example   Answer 1A paraphrases some information from the passage but it is wrong because it describes a function that does not match the passage.

D Mastering Rhetorical Purpose Questions – Analyzing Infinitives in the Answer Choices

The answer choices to Rhetorical Purpose questions often begin with a full infinitive (such as *to argue*) or a bare infinitive (*argue*). Focusing on these words can help you eliminate choices that do not describe the function of the author's words.

D1 Complete this table by choosing the best infinitive from answers A–F. One answer has been done for you.

Common functions	Common infinitives in Rhetorical Purpose questions		Example phrase
make a point directly	1. *argue*	state	*
make a point indirectly	suggest	imply	*
introduce an example	2.	give an example	such as …
say how two things differ	compare	4.	compared with …
discuss a point in detail	explain	describe	in addition, …
stress an important idea	3.	point out	most important …
show that an idea is right	demonstrate	prove	this shows that …
argue against an idea	contradict	5.	however, …
describe a (new) concept	define	6.	known as …

* These two functions are common, but there are no specific example phrases that can help you recognize them.

A contrast   C emphasize   E introduce
B disprove   D illustrate   F argue

D2 Choose one of the common functions from exercise **D1** to describe the function of passages 1–5. Work with a partner. One answer has been done for you.

Large areas of the ocean that have a high density of anchored kelp are known as kelp forests. Such areas form ecosystems that are both extremely productive and dynamic.

1. The function of this passage is to _____ *describe a (new) concept* _____.

Some intertidal zones, such as those found on Pacific islands with a narrow tidal range, form just a thin strip of land.

2. The function of this passage is to _____

_____.

Scientists had long considered the coelacanth to be extinct. The discovery and identification of a specimen of the fish off the coast of South Africa in 1938, however showed that, although it was rare, the species did in fact still exist.

3. The function of this passage is to _____

_____.

Dolphins and porpoises are both cetaceans, but they differ in several ways. Compared with dolphins, porpoises tend to be smaller and stouter. They also have blunt jaws with square teeth instead of beak-like jaws with conical teeth.

4. The function of this passage is to _____

_____.

D3 Underline the words and phrases in each passage that helped you answer exercise **D2**. When you have finished, compare your ideas with a partner.

D4 Choose the best infinitive from answers A−F to complete statements 1−5. One of the answers does NOT match any of the statements. One answer has been done for you.

Herman Melville's *Moby-Dick* tells the story of an attempt to hunt down and kill a giant sperm whale of the same name. When first published in 1851 it was criticized strongly and, as a consequence, had poor sales. It was not until the early decades of the twentieth century that critics began to recognize the power of Melville's writing. Indeed, many critics now rank the work with books like Mark Twain's *Adventures of Huckleberry Finn* as a great American novel.

1. The purpose of this paragraph is to _____contrast_____ critical opinions about Herman Melville's novel *Moby-Dick*.
2. The author mentions *Adventures of Huckleberry Finn* to _____ another well-regarded American novel.

Marine snow is the name given to the remains of dead or dying animals or plants and other organic matter that continuously descends from the upper layers of the ocean to its depths. Deep-sea organisms live at depths where sunlight cannot penetrate, so they cannot directly rely on the sun for energy. Because the composition of marine snow is largely organic, it forms the basis of an important source of energy and nutrients for such organisms.

3. The purpose of this paragraph is to _____ the concept of marine snow.
4. The author mentions "the sun" in order to _____ some oceanic organisms rely on it for energy.
5. The author mentions the "composition of marine snow" to _____ its value for some organisms.

A give an example of
B introduce
C contrast
D emphasize
E suggest
F explain

D5 Answer questions 1 and 2. Compare answers with a partner when you have finished.

Algal blooms occur when there is a rapid increase in the number of algae in a body of water, most likely as a result of increased levels of nutrients in the water. Changes in the level of nutrients may be a natural phenomenon caused by the movement of ocean currents, or may be the result of human activities like farming or industry that cause chemicals to enter the water. Algal blooms have often been noted in areas with declining populations of oysters and other shellfish that feed by filtering nutrients from the water, which implies another possible contributing factor.

Some blooms are harmful to marine organisms like dolphins and sea turtles. Such blooms are popularly known as red tides because of the characteristic reddish-brown color of the algae that cause them, although they are not tidal and do not always color the water red. In fact, blooms may change the color of the water to various hues of green, red, or brown, depending on the species of algae causing the bloom.

1. Why does the author mention "oysters and other shellfish" in paragraph 1?
   A To suggest a point indirectly
   B To contrast one point with another
   C To define a new concept

2. The author mentions "sea turtles" in paragraph 2 in order to
   A argue against an idea
   B introduce an example
   C discuss a point in detail

TEST TACTIC

When two or three answer choices have the same infinitive (or different infinitives with the same meaning), one of those answers is often correct. As a result, you should focus on those answer choices first.

E Mastering Rhetorical Purpose Questions – Analyzing the Answer Choices

Some Rhetorical Purpose questions have answers that do not include infinitives, or have several answers with infinitives that have the same meaning. For these questions, an important skill is analyzing an answer choice to recognize if it paraphrases (restates) the passage, contradicts the passage, or makes a point that is not mentioned in the passage.

E1 **Match statements A–H to the correct category. One answer has been done for you.**

Until 1960, many scientists believed that the conditions found in the deepest parts of the ocean – extreme cold and pressure more than 1,000 times the pressure at sea level – were too harsh for life. In that year, however, during a submarine voyage to the bottom of the Mariana Trench – the deepest point on Earth – living organisms were seen.

A   Challenging conditions exist at the deepest point of the oceans.
B   Scientists expected to find life at the bottom of the Mariana Trench.

King crabs are a high-value fishery. Red king crabs have the most-prized meat, followed by blue king crabs. However, populations of both these species have remained low for decades, so many fishermen focus on golden king crabs. Scarlet king crabs also have delicious meat, but are not fished commercially owing to their small size and rarity.

C   Populations of red and blue king crabs have been increasing for decades.
D   Golden king crabs are easier to catch than red or blue king crabs.

Seaweeds, like plants, derive energy from the sun through the process of photosynthesis. Despite this, biologists classify them as algae, not plants since, among other things, they have no need for tissues with specialist functions such as roots, leaves, or a vascular system for transporting nutrients, water, and other resources.

E   Unlike seaweeds, plants have tissues that have specialist functions.
F   Seaweeds grow in warm waters to obtain more energy from the sun.

Swordfish are named for the characteristic sword-shaped bill that extends a meter or more beyond their body, and which they use to kill prey such as squid, fish, and crustaceans. Like other billfish, swordfish are large, predatory fish – up to 4 meters in length or more – and exhibit sexual dimorphism in that females grow bigger than males. They are found in all of the world's oceans at depths above 500 meters or so, which is another trait shared by other billfish.

G   Swordfish resemble other kinds of billfish.
H   Female swordfish are not as large as males.

Answers that paraphrase the passage

- *Challenging conditions for life exist at the deepest points of the oceans.*
-
-

Answers that contradict the passage

-
-
-

Answers that are not mentioned in the passage

-
-

E2 Rewrite the answers to exercise **E1** that contradict the passage so that they paraphrase the passage. Compare your rewritten answers with a partner when you have finished.

E3 Answer questions 1–5. If neither answer A nor B is correct, write your own answer.

Pinnipeds, the scientific name for seals, sea lions and fur seals, and walruses, are classified as a superfamily of marine mammals. They are semi-aquatic, meaning they spend time both on land and in the water. Like other mammals that sleep in water, only one hemisphere of the brain of a pinniped sleeps at a time. This allows them to maintain a sufficient level of consciousness to breathe and detect and avoid predators. Recent analyses of the brains of sleeping seals have suggested that a specific neurotransmitter, a chemical that affects the brain, may be responsible for the different level of consciousness of each hemisphere. As the neurotransmitter in question, acetylcholine, is found in many organisms, there is a possibility that this finding will enable better understanding of sleep mechanisms in other species, including humans.

1. What is the main function of this passage?
   A To explain the lifestyle of pinnipeds
   B To explain the way that pinnipeds sleep
   C _____ *your answer*

2. Why does the author mention "acetylcholine"?
   A To identify a substance that may explain pinniped sleep patterns
   B To identify a cause of consciousness in pinnipeds and other species
   C _____ *your answer*

Reefs form in shallow, coastal waters when individual coral polyps become attached to a submarine rock or the seabed. When the polyps die, their exoskeleton of calcium carbonate – the same material as limestone – remains. Over time, additional polyps attach themselves to these skeletal remains and the reef grows. The health and growth of coral reefs require specific water conditions. The water must be clean, warm but not too warm (roughly 20–29 degrees Celsius, which is 68–84 degrees Fahrenheit), and clear enough for sunlight to reach the coral. If any of these conditions are not met, corals either grow slowly or become damaged and eventually die, as is happening now in many places.

It has been estimated that about 10% of coral reefs are already dead with at least 60% more at risk. Several general factors are thought to be the cause, including warmer waters caused by a rise in global temperatures. Climate change has also caused a rise in sea levels, which is another factor. Higher levels of CO_2 in the atmosphere mean more CO_2 is taken up by the oceans, leading to more acidic water that can dissolve the calcium carbonate of the coral polyps' skeletons.

3. Why does the author mention "limestone" in paragraph 1?
   A To clarify the meaning of a scientific expression
   B To clarify the type of rock coral polyps attach to
   C _____ *your answer*

4. The author mentions water temperatures in paragraph 1 in order to
   A give an example of a condition that can kill coral polyps
   B give an example of how sunlight warms the oceans
   C _____ *your answer*

5. What purpose does paragraph 2 serve in the passage as a whole?
   A To describe conditions that cause coral reefs to grow slowly
   B To describe the factors that are affecting climate change
   C _____ *your answer*

E4 Which words in the passages, questions, and answers helped you complete exercise **E3**? Discuss with a partner.

TEST TACTIC

When a question asks about the function of a specific highlighted phrase, the information that gives you the answer is often found either in the sentence that contains the specific phrase, or in the sentence just before or after it.

F Test Challenge

F1 **Answer Rhetorical Purpose questions 1–6. Try to finish in 9 minutes or less so as to get realistic practice for the test. Use the checklist of skills you learned in this unit as a guide.**

☑ Analyze infinitives in the answer to eliminate answers that do not match the function of the passage

☑ Eliminate answer choices that contradict the passage or include details not mentioned in the passage

TEST TACTIC

If time is running out, eliminate as many answers as you can based on the infinitive, then pick the choice that is most closely related to the title of the passage from the remaining answers. This will give you a chance to get the question right without taking much time.

Octopus Defenses

Octopuses can employ a number of defensive behaviors when threatened. They have a hard beak with which to bite predators, and many, if not all, species of octopus are venomous, so this bite can be fatal. However, octopuses usually prefer to avoid confrontations and when threatened they usually either hide or try to escape. When they need to move quickly, octopuses can suck in and then expel water in the form of a jet. It is a seldom-used, energy-intensive method of movement, but it allows them to move fast and with great acceleration when threatened.

Probably the most well-known defensive strategy of the octopus is to expel ink. The ink contains mucus and melanin, a natural color-forming pigment found in most organisms. If an octopus expels a lot of ink, it spreads out in the water and forms a dark cloud that hides the octopus from its attacker. In other cases, an octopus might expel a smaller quantity of ink that contains a higher concentration of mucus, allowing the ink to hold its form for longer and make a cloud that can be similar in shape to the octopus itself. This can confuse a predator into attacking the ink, not the octopus.

1. The primary purpose of paragraph 1 is to
   - (A) explain why the bite of octopuses is venomous
   - (B) describe how octopuses try to avoid being attacked
   - (C) describe where octopuses usually hide from danger
   - (D) illustrate different methods of octopus locomotion

2. Why does the author mention "melanin" in paragraph 2?
   - (A) To suggest that many organisms can produce ink
   - (B) To emphasize that octopus ink is very colorful
   - (C) To imply that melanin is the main component of ink
   - (D) To explain the reason why octopus ink is colored

3. Why does the author discuss the concentration of mucus in octopus ink in paragraph 2?
   - (A) To explain why predators prefer attacking ink clouds instead of octopuses
   - (B) To clarify why some expelled ink clouds retain their structure for longer
   - (C) To argue that predators are confused when the ink contains little melanin
   - (D) To explain why the ability of octopuses to expel ink is so well-known

Scientific Nomenclature

In biology, all life is classified according to shared physical characteristics, with international scientific authorities recognizing seven main ranks. The ranks are hierarchical in that top level ranks are more general and contain fewer members than each successive lower level. The first rank is the kingdom, which describes whether an organism is an animal, a plant, a fungus, and so on. The two ranks below kingdom are phylum (in zoology) or division (in botany) and then class. Below class are order, family, and then genus and species, the two most basic ranks. The binomial, or two-part, scientific name of a species is a combination of its genus name and its species name.

The way this system works can be seen by looking at the classification of two marine organisms. The blue whale is a member of the class Mammalia, or mammals, the order Cetacea, or whales, dolphins, and porpoises, and the family Balaenopteridae, or baleen whales. Its genus and species are *Balaenoptera* and *Balaenoptera musculus* respectively. The blue shark, on the other hand, is classified as belonging to the class Chondrichthyes, meaning cartilaginous fish, the order Carcharhiniformes, and the family Carcharhinidae, which includes 51 other species of requiem sharks as they are informally, but commonly, known in English. The genus name is *Prionace* and the species name is *Prionace glauca*.

4. What is the main function of paragraph 1?
   (A) To compare different kinds of organisms
   (B) To define a method for ranking kingdoms
   (C) To describe a scientific classification system
   (D) To illustrate the benefits of classifying organisms

5. The author mentions zoology and botany in order to
   (A) emphasize how these subjects differ from one another
   (B) demonstrate how the number of scientific ranks can differ
   (C) explain the usage of two different but equivalent rank names
   (D) imply that botanists and zoologists rarely talk to each other

6. In paragraph 2, the author's primary purpose is to
   (A) give specific examples of the biological classification of organisms
   (B) contrast the scientific names of whales, dolphins, porpoises, and sharks
   (C) explain why the color of an animal is not reflected in its scientific name
   (D) give a general overview of the ways in which whales and sharks differ

Next Steps

Topics related to marine biology are common in the reading section of the TOEFL Test. You may also have topics about this subject in the other sections of the test. As a result, learning more about this subject, as well as practicing key skills for Rhetorical Purpose questions, may raise your overall test score.

To learn more about marine biology and vocabulary related to this discipline:

1. Read widely about marine biology in your language. This will give you useful background knowledge of the subject.
2. Read an English article about a topic related to marine biology several times until you understand the main concepts.
3. Read the English article again and make a list of unfamiliar words related to marine biology. Then do an Internet search for each word on your list and note the number of times it can be found on the Internet. (Most search engines list the number of results at the top of the page.) Then study and learn the ten most common words.

To practice key skills for Rhetorical Purpose questions:

1. Find a short article about marine biology (or another subject) online and choose one paragraph from the article.
2. Write a short, simple description of the purpose of every sentence in the article. For example, you might describe a sentence in an article by writing "This sentence defines bioluminescence." or "This sentence compares crabs and lobsters."
3. Next, use your descriptions of the function of each sentence to write a simple description of the function of the whole paragraph. For example, you might write "This paragraph describes how marine creatures use bioluminescence," or "This paragraph discusses the economic importance of crab and lobster fishing."
4. If possible, compare your sentence and paragraph descriptions with those written by a study partner and discuss any differences of opinion.

Unit Focus

There are ten types of reading questions in the TOEFL Test, including Inference questions. These questions test how well you can recognize ideas and points that are suggested by the author, but not directly stated in the passage. Typically, you will see one or two Inference questions after each reading passage. To answer Inference questions accurately, you need to be able to "read between the lines," which involves using several key skills that you will learn in this unit, including:

- recognizing key phrases in the question that will help you find the right information in the passage.
- distinguishing between ideas that are stated directly in the passage and ideas that are mentioned indirectly.

The vocabulary focus is on academic words and phrases related to:

- ecology, the scientific study of the connections among plants, animals, people, and the environment.

A Warm-up

A1 Work with a partner. Deliver a short speech in response to topics 1 and 2. Organize your answers well and speak for up to 45 seconds. After each speech, give your partner feedback.

1. Some people think that humans are the biggest threat (danger) to the environment. Do you agree or disagree with this idea? Why? Support your opinion with details and examples.
2. What is one thing that you think everybody in your country could do to protect the environment? Support your position with details and examples.

B Academic Vocabulary

B1 Choose the word from answers A–H that best completes the definitions of the highlighted words in sentences 1–8. One answer has been done for you.

1. Biodiversity, or biological diversity, is the term used to describe the _____ variety _____ of all forms of life found in a certain habitat.
2. A large, naturally-occurring ecological _____ of plants and animals in a particular habitat is known as a biome.
3. Conservation is the act of providing _____ to endangered species so that they survive. Preservation is a synonym.
4. Deforestation occurs when many of the trees in a heavily-wooded _____ are cut down but not replanted.
5. Scientists define an ecosystem as a group of organisms that interact with one another and with their _____.
6. In ecology, the word habitat has the specific meaning of the natural conditions and environment in which _____ live.
7. A predator, such as a wolf or lion, is a(n) _____ that actively hunts and kills other organisms in order to survive.
8. A prey species is one that is eaten by a(n) _____ species. Typically, prey species are more numerous than predators.

A community	C organism	E protection	G species
B environment	D predator	F region	H variety

C Analyzing Inference Questions

Inference questions ask about ideas that are indirectly mentioned in the passage. They typically include words like "infer," "imply," "conclude," or "suggest," as these examples show. Most inference questions either state the paragraph in which the answer can be found, or include a specific reference that allows you to find the paragraph(s) easily:

What can be inferred from paragraph 2 about _____?

What does the author imply about _____ described in paragraph 3?

What can be concluded from paragraph 4 about the recent actions of _____?

What does the author suggest might happen to _____ if _____ were to occur?

The correct answer to Inference questions:
- must be suggested in the passage rather than directly stated.
- is generally related to the main idea of the passage and/or the main topic of the relevant paragraph.

In contrast, incorrect answers:
- may seem to restate an idea from the passage, but actually contradict information in the passage.
- may seem like a reasonable answer to the question, but are neither mentioned nor implied in the passage.

TEST TACTIC

If two of the answer choices for an Inference question have opposite or very different meanings, there is a chance that one of those two answers is correct. If you focus on those two choices first, you might be able to save time.

C1 Answer Inference questions 1 and 2. When you have finished, discuss your answers with a partner.

The modern discipline of ecology began in the latter part of the nineteenth century with the publication of works first by German biologist Ernst Haeckel and then by Danish botanist Eugen Warming. Haeckel gave the discipline its name in a work written in 1866, while Warming was the first to write a textbook and teach a university course on the subject. This is not to say that the concepts and principles of ecology were unknown before Haeckel and Warming. Many previous scholars, including Aristotle and Theophrastus in classical times, van Leeuwenhoek and Bradley in the early part of the 1700s, and then Lamarck, von Humboldt, and Darwin, developed and wrote about various concepts – including soil nutrient, cycles, food chains, and population regulation – that are now considered aspects of ecology.

1. Which of these statements can be inferred from the passage?
   A Warming's textbook on ecology was published in 1866, the same year as Haeckel's work.
   B Haeckel's work in 1866 described several concepts that are now considered aspects of ecology.
   C Warming's first university course on the discipline of ecology was popular among students.
   D Scientists studied ecological ideas before 1866, but did not describe their subject as ecology.

2. What can be concluded from the passage?
   A Darwin and von Humboldt worked together to develop their concepts.
   B Lamarck's work came after that of van Leeuwenhoek and Bradley.
   C Darwin's ideas about ecology were based on work by von Humboldt.
   D Aristotle and Theophrastus knew of each other's work on ecology.

C2 Match the wrong answers from **C1** to description 1 or 2. Work with a partner. One answer has been done for you.

1. The answer choice seems to restate the passage, but contradicts, adds, or omits a key detail.	1A
2. The answer choice seems like a reasonable answer, but is not mentioned or implied in the passage.	

D Mastering Inference Questions – Analyzing the Question

An important skill for answering Inference questions is recognizing key phrases in the question. Recognizing these key phrases can help you more easily find the sentences in the passage where the answer will be implied.

D1 **Match the underlined phrases in this example Inference question to the correct description. One answer has been done for you.**

What can be <u>inferred</u> from <u>paragraph 4</u> about the <u>effects of wildfires</u>?
             A

A This word or phrase tells you that this is an Inference question.
B This phrase tells you in which paragraph of the passage you should look for the answer.
C This phrase tells you to look for sentences in the passage that are related to this specific topic.

D2 **Work with a partner to explain why the underlined phrases in example Inference questions 1–4 are key phrases. Use the descriptions from exercise D1 as a guide.**

1. What can be <u>inferred</u> from <u>paragraph 2</u> about <u>food webs</u>?
2. In <u>paragraph 3</u>, what does the author <u>imply</u> about the <u>keystone species model</u>?
3. What can be <u>concluded</u> from <u>paragraph 4</u> about the <u>recent actions of conservationists</u>?
4. What does the author <u>suggest</u> might happen to <u>European oak trees</u> if <u>moderate climate change</u> were to occur?

D3 **Underline the key phrases in example Inference questions 1–4. Be prepared to say why you think each phrase is a key phrase.**

1. What does the author imply about biodiversity in paragraph 1?
2. What does the author suggest about the role of earthworms in maintaining soil fertility?
3. What can be understood about the difference between biotic and abiotic environments?
4. What can be inferred from paragraph 3 about the importance of honeybees to agriculture?

D4 **Identify the key phrases in questions 1–4. Then underline the sentence(s) in the passage that give information about the key phrases. When you have finished, compare your underlined sentences with a partner.**

Although they were once considered to be purely destructive events to be prevented if possible, modern ecologists view wildfires as a natural disturbance that shapes habitats much like floods, storms, or landslides do. Indeed, several ecosystems rely on regular wildfires to ensure their ongoing vitality just as other species depend on other natural events. Within these ecosystems, species may be fire dependent, meaning they rely on fires to change the local environment in beneficial ways. Other species are fire adapted, meaning they have traits that allow them to survive fires, such as fire-resistant bark, the ability to grow rapidly after a fire, or seeds that need intense heat to germinate.

1. What does the author suggest about the effects of natural disturbances like wildfires?
2. What can be concluded about how fire-dependent and fire-adapted organisms differ?

Two books were published in 1962 – *Our Synthetic Environment* by Murray Bookchin using the pen-name Lewis Herber, and *Silent Spring* by Rachel Carson – that are generally considered to have begun the modern movement to protect the environment. At first, the movement focused on limiting the use of chemical pesticides, but over time other issues have become more important, including nuclear power, acid rain, and now climate change. The widespread use of expressions with *eco-* as a prefix, including eco-friendly, eco-awareness, and eco-tourism, show how mainstream the movement has become.

3. What can be inferred about the author of the book *Our Synthetic Environment*?
4. What is implied about how the environmental protection movement has changed?

TEST TACTIC

In general, the correct answer can be found in or close to the sentence(s) that match key phrases in the question. If you think the correct answer is implied in a sentence that is not close to the relevant sentence(s), you might have made a mistake.

D5 Use the three steps to help you answer questions 1–4. Then compare answers with a partner.

Step 1	Identify the key phrases in question 1. Then scan the passage to find sentence(s) that include these key phrases.
Step 2	Read the sentence(s) in the passage that you found in task 1. Then answer question 1.
Step 3	Repeat steps 1 and 2 for questions 2, 3, and 4.

Estimates vary, but it is likely several billion Passenger Pigeons lived in North America at the start of the nineteenth century. Yet several factors caused them to go extinct in just over 100 years. The birds depended on hardwood forests for food as well as for nesting and roosting sites. Massive deforestation meant the birds not only had fewer places to nest and roost but also had to turn to farmers' fields for food, which led to farmers shooting the birds to protect their crops. Professionals also began killing the birds on an industrial scale as a source of cheap, easy-to-hunt meat. The flocks were so enormous that bands of hunters were frequently able to kill 50,000 or more birds a day for months at a time. Eventually, the twin pressures of habitat destruction and hunting reduced the number of survivors significantly. At this point, the bird's behavior became a factor in its own decline. Passenger Pigeons were a communal species, meaning they were only able to breed when part of a large flock. As the population continued to fall, flocks became too small for optimum breeding, and fewer and fewer young hatched each year until, by the 1890s, the bird had almost completely died out. The final Passenger Pigeon is believed to have died in the Cincinnati Zoo in 1914.

1. What does the author imply about Passenger Pigeons at the start of the nineteenth century?
   A The number of birds had declined since the eighteenth century.
   B There were so many birds it was impossible to count them accurately.

2. What can be concluded about the feeding habits of Passenger Pigeons?
   A They found food in the same place they nested and slept.
   B They preferred agricultural crops to other food sources.

3. What does the author suggest about the hunting of Passenger Pigeons?
   A There were only a few professional hunters.
   B Hunting the birds was not a difficult task.

4. What can be inferred from this paragraph about the extinction of Passenger Pigeons?
   A The last pigeon was not killed as a direct result of hunting or habitat loss.
   B The species went extinct because the surviving birds could no longer breed.

E Mastering Inference Questions – Recognizing Implied Information

Another key skill for Inference questions is distinguishing between information that is stated directly in the passage and information that is implied. It is also useful to recognize answers that express an idea that is not mentioned in the passage.

 Track 1   **E1** Listen to part of a TOEFL class. The teacher and students are talking about Inference questions. Complete this summary of the ideas they discuss by adding the correct example, A or B, to 1 and 2.

Information that is directly stated in the passage can help you make a conclusion. For example, 1. _____. Another technique is to imagine some words are missing from the passage. If those words are added, the indirect meaning becomes direct. For example, 2. _____

A if a writer says "there was no rain and many animals died," it is possible to imagine adding the explanation "because they had no water" to make the writer's idea direct.
B if a passage says a book was published in 1962, we can conclude that the author of that book was born before 1962.

E2 Practice recognizing inferences by reading these passages and then answering questions 1–4.

A very simple example of the often complex feeding relationships among different species can be seen with foxes and rabbits. The former feed on rabbits, which in turn eat grasses and other plants, which ultimately derive energy from the sun. This kind of linear sequence in which one species depends for food on another species is called a food chain, or, when all the interlinked food chains in an ecological community are considered together, a food web.

1. Which answer can be inferred from the passage?
   A Food chains usually include only three species.
   B Food webs are more complex than food chains.

2. Which highlighted phrase in the passage helps you answer question 1?
   A grasses and other plants, which ultimately derive energy from the sun
   B the interlinked food chains in an ecological community are considered together, a food web

The keystone species model lends itself to computer simulation. In simple terms, a keystone species is one that plays an essential role in maintaining an ecological community even though it is not very abundant. The classic example of a keystone species can be seen in simulations like "fox and rabbit" in which a small population of foxes controls the number of rabbits in a simplified ecosystem. By varying the conditions of the simulation, such as the size of the initial population of foxes or rabbits, or the availability of food plants, different outcomes can be observed. If the initial conditions of the simulation lead to a decline in the number of ■ the keystone species, the number of rabbits may keep rising until all their food plants have been eaten, which in turn leads to a crash in their population.

3. What can be concluded from the passage?
   A Foxes are sometimes considered a keystone species.
   B Simulations of the keystone species model are accurate.

4. Which phrase could be added to the passage at the square (■) so that the answer to question 3 is stated directly?
   A foxes, which are
   B simulations of

E3 Read these passages. Then check (✓) the box to indicate if each statement is **Stated directly, Implied, or Not mentioned. Compare your answers with a partner when you have finished. One answer has been done for you.**

In the natural world, all organisms interact with other organisms. Two male deer of the same species fighting each other during breeding season, for instance, is an example of intraspecific competition. Other kinds of intraspecific interaction include cooperation and antagonism. Interspecific interactions, in contrast, occur when two different species interact in some way, such as when a bee pollinates a flower.

1. Intraspecific interactions occur among individuals of the same species.
   ☐ Stated directly   ☑ Implied   ☐ Not mentioned
2. An interspecific interaction occurs between two species.
   ☐ Stated directly   ☐ Implied   ☐ Not mentioned

Amensalism is the name given to a type of biological interaction in which the behavior or a product of one organism has no effect on that organism but a detrimental effect on other organisms. The classic example is the black walnut tree which secretes a chemical called juglone into the soil that harms most other species of plants living nearby and can also affect humans who come into contact with it. Commensalism is the opposite of amensalism.

3. Black walnut trees are unaffected by juglone.
   ☐ Stated directly   ☐ Implied   ☐ Not mentioned
4. Animals living near black walnut trees are harmed by juglone.
   ☐ Stated directly   ☐ Implied   ☐ Not mentioned

E4 Use the skills you have learned to answer questions 1 and 2.

Mutualism occurs when two organisms interact in a way that benefits both individuals. Cooperation differs from mutualism in that it occurs between two individuals of the same species. Mutualism can be classified according to the nature of the relationship. In resource-resource interactions, the most common type, each individual provides a resource, such as nutrients, that benefits the other. In a service-resource interaction, one species provides a service to the other and in return gets access to a resource. The Oxpecker, for example, is a bird that eats disease-causing ticks and other parasites that live on the skin of some species of large mammals. Service-service interactions are the final, and rarest, type of mutualism. In such interactions, both species give and receive a beneficial service, such as protection from predators. Most service-service relationships also have a service-resource or even a resource-resource aspect.

1. What can be inferred about mutualistic relationships? *Choose two answers.*
   A They are the most common interaction between species.
   B They occur between individuals of different species.
   C Relatively few species practice such relationships.
   D They involve a mutually advantageous exchange.

2. What is implied about service-resource interactions? *Choose two answers.*
   A They are rarer than resource-resource relationships.
   B They benefit some species more than others.
   C They commonly involve an exchange of nutrients.
   D One species may protect the other from illness.

F Test Challenge

F1 Answer Inference questions 1–8. Try to finish in 12 minutes or less so as to get realistic practice for the test. Use the checklist of skills you learned in this unit as a guide.

☑ Read the question carefully and note key words that will help you choose the right answer.

☑ Find the key sentence(s) in the passage that include the key words. Read these sentences carefully.

☑ Compare the answer choices with the key sentence(s) and select the answer that implies the same idea.

TEST TACTIC

If an Inference question is hard, try thinking about it as a Rhetorical Purpose question. For example, change the question "What is implied about prey species" into "Why does the author mention prey species?" This might help you recognize the implication more easily.

Conservation of California Condors

California Condors first received protection in 1967 under the US Endangered Species Preservation Act and were then formally identified and protected as part of the US Endangered Species Act of 1972. The California Condor Recovery Plan was passed in 1975 with the aim of increasing the number of birds by preserving their natural habitat. The Plan was revised in 1979 with a continued focus on habitat preservation, plus a project to breed Condors in captivity for release into the wild. A further revision in 1984 recognized that the continued decline in Condor numbers made more intensive and urgent action necessary, especially efforts to increase the low reproductive rates of the birds. By 1986 the Condor was on the brink of extinction, with just 22 birds still alive, only three of which were in the wild. A decision was made that the only hope for the species was to capture the last remaining wild birds and focus on captive breeding.

Initial efforts to breed the birds in captivity met with limited success, but by 1992 researchers felt confident enough to try reintroducing the species into the wild; there were problems, however, and a decision was made in 1994 to recapture the released birds. Another attempt at releasing captive birds into the wild was made in 1995, again in southern California, but this time with more success. In 1996 the California Condor Recovery Plan was revised again with a continued emphasis on captive breeding and a new aim of reintroducing the species into the wild. Further release sites in Arizona, central California, and northwestern Mexico were chosen in 1996, 1997, and 2002 respectively. The results of these conservation efforts and plans have been very successful.

The International Union for the Conservation of Nature (IUCN) lists the California Condor as critically endangered still, a status reserved for those species most at risk of extinction, but the number of birds alive now is estimated at more than 400, with more than 200 of those living in the wild. Despite this success, a review of the California Condor Recovery Plan in 2008 argued that without sustained investment and human intervention, the species might again become extinct in the wild. As the total cost of the conservation efforts to date is roughly $40 million, and ongoing costs are likely to run to several million dollars per year, continued investment and intervention cannot be assured.

1. What does the author suggest about efforts to preserve the habitat of California Condors?
   - (A) They began in 1972 when the US Endangered Species Act passed.
   - (B) Optimum habitat conditions for California Condors are hard to find.
   - (C) They were not successful at increasing the number of Condors.
   - (D) They were effective after the California Condor Recovery Plan was revised.

2. The author implies that the first release of captive Condors into the wild
   - (A) took place in the southern part of California
   - (B) was more successful than people had expected
   - (C) occurred after the successful release of other species
   - (D) led to the creation of a new conservation plan

3. What can be concluded about the IUCN?
   - (A) It lists the conservation status of numerous bird species.
   - (B) It has out of date information about the number of Condors.
   - (C) It played an important role in the conservation of Condors.
   - (D) It only records how many of a given bird species live in the wild.

4. What can be inferred about future of the California Condor?
   - (A) It is highly unlikely that the bird will become extinct in the wild.
   - (B) It will cost approximately $40 million to preserve the species.
   - (C) Condors are no longer in danger because of past conservation work.
   - (D) The cost of continued conservation efforts might be too high.

Tropical Rainforests

Tropical rainforests are found in equatorial regions. They are characterized by high average temperatures of 24 degrees Celsius or more, annual rainfall in excess of 8,000 millimeters, and relatively little seasonal change in weather. Examples of this type of biome can be found in southeast Asia, Africa, and Central and South America. Another defining characteristic is their incredible biodiversity. To take one example, a typical temperate forest may have just a handful of species of trees in total; a tropical rainforest may have close to 500 species of trees in just 10,000 square meters. Tropical rainforests are the most biologically diverse ecosystems on the planet, containing perhaps 50% of all species of animals and plants, many of which have still not been given a scientific classification.

The products of these biomes are essential to modern society. More than 3,000 commonly eaten foods are originally from tropical rainforests, including avocados, citrus fruits, bananas, tomatoes, corn, potatoes, rice, chocolate, ginger, coffee, and some nuts. In addition, tropical rainforests are a valuable source of medicines. Up to a quarter of modern pharmaceuticals derive from tropical rainforests. Just a fraction of tropical rainforest plants have been surveyed for their medicinal value, and scientists working for universities, governments, and drug companies are convinced that additional compounds of medical value will be found among such species. Sadly, industries like cattle ranching and logging are causing considerable deforestation resulting in the extinction of an estimated 100-plus species daily.

5. What can be concluded about temperate forests from paragraph 1?
- (A) They receive about as much rain as tropical rainforests.
- (B) They are usually smaller than tropical rainforests.
- (C) They have less biodiversity than tropical rainforests.
- (D) They are found in the same regions as tropical rainforests.

6. Which of the following can be inferred from paragraph 1?
- (A) A total of about 500 species of trees can be found in tropical rainforests.
- (B) Species found in tropical rainforests look very different from one another.
- (C) A number of species in tropical rainforests have not been identified.
- (D) About half of all species in tropical rainforests are animals or plants.

7. Which of these ideas does the author suggest about drugs in paragraph 2?
- (A) Medically-useful compounds may be found in unsurveyed plant species.
- (B) Most species that provide medically useful drugs have already been surveyed.
- (C) Tropical rainforests are a less useful source of drugs than other ecosystems.
- (D) Common food items may contain drugs that could become valuable medicines.

8. What does the author imply about deforestation? *Choose two answers.*
- [A] It does not yet affect medically-useful species.
- [B] It is caused by human activities.
- [C] It may cause the loss of valuable species.
- [D] It is sad, but necessary for modern society.

Next Steps

Topics related to ecology are common in all four sections of the TOEFL Test. As a result, learning more about this subject, as well as practicing key skills for Inference questions, may raise your overall test score.

To learn more about ecology and vocabulary related to this discipline:

1. Read an article in your language about one aspect of ecology to get some background knowledge about this topic.
2. Read again and make a list of useful words for ecology. Use a dictionary to find the English translation for these words.
3. Read an English article about the same topic. First, understand the main ideas. Then read again in order to identify which of the words you studied in step 2 are used in the English article.

To practice a key skill for Inference questions:

Find an article in English about ecology (or another subject you find interesting). Read the article and find an opinion, idea, or point that the writer states directly. Decide how to change this section of the article so that the opinion, idea, or point is implied not stated. For example, you might have to cut some words or phrases from the original article, or rewrite some phrases using less direct language. By learning how to change direct statements into indirect ones, you will improve your ability to recognize and understand implied ideas in both the reading and listening sections of the TOEFL Test.

Unit Focus

There are ten types of reading questions in the TOEFL Test, including Sentence Simplification questions. These questions ask you to look at a highlighted sentence in the passage and choose the answer that paraphrases the major ideas in that sentence. Typically, you will get one Sentence Simplification question after each passage, but some passages may not have this type of question. To answer Sentence Simplification questions accurately, you need to learn and practice several key skills, including:

- recognizing answer choices that either restate or simplify a sentence from the passage.
- recognizing the function of sentences from the passage and the answer choices to the question.
- recognizing answer choices that leave out or change essential information.

The vocabulary focus is on academic words and phrases related to two academic disciplines:

- anthropology, the study of human cultures, and archaeology, the study of human history by analyzing found objects.

A Warm-up

A1 Which of the books described below would you NOT like to read? Give a speech explaining your opinion and reason.

A number of classic but controversial works of anthropology were published in the twentieth century, including *Coming of Age in Samoa* (1928), by Margaret Mead, a book about the lives of teenagers on the Pacific island of Ta'u; *The Chrysanthemum and the Sword* (1946), by Ruth Benedict, which discusses Japanese culture; and *Yanomamö: the Fierce People* (1968), by Napoleon Chagnon, which is about a group living in the Amazon rainforest.

B Academic Vocabulary

B1 Complete this table with one of the definitions, A–H. Check your answers with a partner when you have finished. One answer has been done for you.

Word	Part of speech	Prefix, suffix, or word root		Definition
1. artifact	noun	fac	*make / do*	F
2. ceremony	noun	—		
3. decipher	verb	cipher	*a code / mystery*	
4. descend	verb	de	*down / from*	
5. excavation	noun	ex	*out of / away* from	
6. indigenous	adjective	gen	*race / kind*	
7. inherit	verb	—		
8. kinship	noun	ship	*relation between*	

A   to come from a particular ancestor (a relative who lived in the past)
B   to receive something when a person, usually a relative, dies
C   a formal ritual event, such as a marriage or funeral
D   a relationship, either by birth or marriage, to other people
E   describing people who come from a particular place
F   a historically important object made by humans
G   to make sense of an unknown code or writing system
H   the act of digging something out from the ground

C Analyzing Sentence Simplification Questions

Sentence Simplification questions test how well you can recognize answers that restate or simplify a highlighted sentence in the passage. These questions always have the same directions:

Which of the following best expresses the essential information in the highlighted sentence in paragraph 2? Incorrect choices change the meaning in important ways or leave out essential information.

Note that Sentence Simplification questions focus on one highlighted sentence only. To answer them, you do not need to spend any time reading the other, non-highlighted sentences in the passage.

The correct answer to Sentence Simplification questions:

- almost always paraphrases the ideas from the highlighted sentence rather than using the same words.
- may simplify the highlighted sentence, but will not omit any of the major ideas in that sentence.
- usually has the same function as the highlighted sentence, such as contrasting two ideas or giving the cause of a particular situation.

In contrast, incorrect answers usually include some words from the highlighted sentence, but may:

- change key information from the highlighted sentence or include an idea not in that sentence.
- summarize only part of the highlighted sentence and leave out an essential idea or detail.
- change the function of the highlighted sentence by, for example, describing the effect of a situation, not its cause.

TEST TACTIC

Sometimes the highlighted sentence includes a word or phrase like "it" or "this project" that refers to an idea in the previous sentence. In these cases, you should read the previous sentence quickly to understand the reference.

C1 Answer the following Sentence Simplification question. When you have finished, discuss with a partner.

The aim of participant observation, a traditional data-collection technique used by anthropologists, is to gain a deep, first-hand understanding of a group of people by spending time with them in their cultural environment. Several levels of participant observation have been identified: passive, moderate, and active. In passive participation, the researcher closely watches, but does not engage with, the group being studied. Moderate participation includes more involvement with the group, but the researcher still preserves some distance from it to remain emotionally detached and objective. Active participation requires the researcher to accept and adopt completely the customs and behaviors of the group to gain the most complete understanding possible.

1. Which of the following best expresses the essential information in the first highlighted sentence? Incorrect choices change the meaning in important ways or leave out essential information.

   A Anthropologists seek to observe an environment in which a group of people spend time.

   B Collecting data about various groups of people allows anthropologists to understand those people's traditions.

   C An established way for anthropologists to understand a group is to spend time in its environment.

   D By observing a group for a period of time, anthropologists aim to become part of its cultural environment.

2. Which of the following best expresses the essential information in the second highlighted sentence? Incorrect choices change the meaning in important ways or leave out essential information.

   A Moderate participation requires the researcher both to participate with the group and to retain objectivity.

   B The researcher must stay emotionally separate from the group when engaging in moderate participation.

   C The objective of moderate participation is to allow the group being studied to become involved in the research.

   D An increased level of engagement with the group by the researcher is a feature of moderate participation.

C2 Match the wrong answers from **C1** to description 1 or 2. Work with a partner. One answer has been done for you.

1. The answer choice changes some essential information from the highlighted sentence.	1A
2. The answer choice leaves out some essential information from the highlighted sentence.	

D Mastering Sentence Simplification Questions – Recognizing Restated and Simplified Answers

A key skill for answering Sentence Simplification questions accurately is recognizing the answer choice that either restates or simplifies the essential ideas from the highlighted sentence.

D1 Which answer, A or B, restates the essential information in the highlighted sentence in these short passages? The incorrect choice changes the meaning in important ways.

In one model of human social development used by anthropologists, societies are organized in one of four ways. In order of increasing complexity and size, these are called bands, tribes, chiefdoms, and states. In the modern world, most societies are states; in earlier times, however, bands, tribes, and chiefdoms were more common.

1A. Bands, tribes, chiefdoms, and states are all large and increasingly complex types of organized human society.

1B. When ranked from simplest to most complex and smallest to largest, societies can be bands, tribes, chiefdoms, or states.

Bands, the simplest form of human society, are typically made up of a group of related individuals, usually numbering no more than 100. They are often egalitarian, with decisions being shaped by informal leaders and agreed upon by consensus. Every band that has been studied has practiced hunting and gathering.

2A. Bands usually do not have formal chiefs and each member has the same amount of authority to make decisions.

2B. Members of a band often act informally and rarely make decisions unless they agree that the decision makes sense.

Tribes are more difficult to define, but in general terms, tribal societies are formed from bands that are politically integrated under a formal leader or council of elders. Each member of the tribe usually shares the same language, culture, and ideology. The term ethnic group is now often used in preference to tribe.

3A. Although it is hard to define the term, tribes are usually composed of bands under the political control of a leader.

3B. Tribes are formally defined as a band that is led by a group of politically-integrated elders or chiefs.

Chiefdoms typically consist of a number of communities under the permanent control of a chief or group of leaders. Usually the community in which the chief lives is the dominant community; smaller subsidiary communities, each with their own leader who is subservient to the overall chief, often form part of the chiefdom, too.

4A. The leaders of each community in a chiefdom usually move to the dominant community from subsidiary communities.

4B. Chiefdoms often have one main community in which the chief resides, plus other smaller, less important communities.

States, which control a society composed of numerous communities located within a territory, are highly organized. States are politically autonomous with a centralized government that can collect taxes, enact and enforce laws, and attack or enter into treaties with other states. Unlike other forms of society, states are not based on kin relationships.

5A. States with a central government collect taxes and perform other functions automatically.

5B. The central government of a state can use its political power in several ways.

D2 Read these two passages. Then work with a partner to complete tasks 1 and 2.

In 1836 the Danish scholar Christian Jürgensen Thomsen proposed that early human history could be divided into three ages: the Stone Age, Bronze Age, and Iron Age. Other scholars had previously suggested systems for classifying history based on the materials used to make tools and weapons, but their systems did not allow for these objects to be dated. Thomsen's system not only allowed for the relative dating of objects, but also led to a greater understanding of human cultural development, and became one of the foundations of modern archaeology.

1. Choose three answers from A–D to complete this restatement of the first passage. One of the answers does NOT match any of the blanks. One answer has been done for you.

Christian Jürgensen Thomsen proposed dividing 1. _____human prehistory_____ into the Stone Age, Bronze Age, and Iron Age. He was not the first scholar to suggest a 2. _____, but all previous such systems had flaws. Modern archaeology is based on Thomsen's system, which let scholars date objects and better comprehend 3. _____.

A classification system
B cultural development
C human prehistory
D tools and weapons

Ground-penetrating radar (GPR) allows archaeologists to see below the earth without the need to excavate, and thus destroy, surface features of the site. High frequency radio waves from a GPR device are sent into the earth and any subsurface features, spaces, materials, or artifacts will reflect the waves back to the device. Typically, GPR is useful at depths of up to 10 meters and is often used to find artificial and natural features like buried objects, buildings, roads, or rivers.

2. Choose three answers from E–H to complete this restatement of the second passage. One of the answers does NOT match any of the blanks.

GPR gives archaeologists the opportunity to see what lies beneath the earth without destroying 4. _____. The device works by emitting radio waves into the ground that bounce back off features or 5. _____. Commonly used to locate both natural and manmade features, GPR devices work best above a 6. _____.

E certain depth
F excavation work
G objects of interest
H surface structures

D3 Put five sentences from A–F in order to form a paragraph that restates this passage. One of the sentences does NOT belong in the restated paragraph.

A key principle of archaeology is the importance of context in fully understanding an excavated object. Context can be defined as the specific locale – even down to the soil layer – in which an artifact is found. Context also includes the other objects or materials found with, nearby, or in the same soil layer as the artifact. Context allows scholars to better understand the purpose of an object and the culture of the people who made it. For example, a sword might be understood as having either a military or ceremonial purpose depending on the context in which it was found.

A Another aspect of context is the other items found in the same location as the object.
B Without a clear sense of an object's context, less information can be known about it.
C Context includes the precise location where a buried object was discovered.
D An important idea in archaeology is how context helps scholars understand an artifact.
E Whether a sword was used for war or another purpose might be unclear without knowledge of its context.
F When archaeologists know an artifact's context, they can better understand it and the culture that made it.

E Mastering Sentence Simplification Questions — Recognizing the Function of a Sentence

Another valuable skill for Sentence Simplification questions is recognizing the function of both the highlighted sentence and the answer choices. Incorrect answers sometimes have a different function than the highlighted sentence.

 Track 2 **E1** **Listen to an experienced teacher discuss some common functions in Sentence Simplification questions. Put the functions in the order that the teacher mentions them. One answer has been done for you.**

1. Compare or contrast two ideas
2.
3.
4.
5.

A   Describe all or part of a process
B   Explain a cause, reason, or result
C   Compare or contrast two ideas
D   Summarize some information or an idea
E   Describe a problem with something

E2 **Which sentence, 1–5, is an example of the common functions described in E1? Discuss your ideas with a partner.**

1. Although Heinrich Schliemann made several astonishing discoveries, he is widely criticized by modern archaeologists for his destructive methods and his fanciful interpretations of his finds.
2. After identifying a potential site, archaeologists survey the area to learn as much as possible before starting to excavate.
3. Archaeology is regarded as a branch of anthropology in the US, whereas in Europe it is considered a separate academic discipline.
4. Many of the burial sites of Egyptian pharaohs were looted by thieves before they were discovered and excavated by archaeologists, meaning little of value remained.
5. The law of superposition, which states that, in general, older material is found below younger material, is a key axiom in archaeology and some other sciences.

E3 **Use information from these passages to answer questions 1 and 2.**

Ethnography is the study of a recent or existing culture. Its principal focus is on how people from that culture think and act as determined through direct observation and interviews with living individuals. Social systems are often studied, including marriage customs, political and economic organization, religious beliefs, and art and music. Ethnography should not be confused with ethnology, which entails a comparative study of more than one culture.

1. Which answer, A or B, has both the same meaning and the same function as the highlighted sentence?
    A   Studying ethnology can be confusing because it requires comparing a number of diverse cultures.
    B   Ethnology involves looking at how several cultures are similar and dissimilar, and as such it differs from ethnography.

Ethnocentrism, that is the judging of another culture by the standards of one's own culture, is considered a natural part of human psychology. Notwithstanding this, anthropologists working in the first part of the twentieth century including Franz Boas and Bronisław Malinowski saw ethnocentrism as a barrier to understanding. Boas developed the principle of cultural relativism – exemplified by the idea that all cultures are relative and ideas that hold true for one culture may not be true for other cultures – as a way to overcome ethnocentric viewpoints.

2. Which answer, A or B, has both the same meaning and the same function as the highlighted sentence?
    A   The principle of cultural relativism was developed as a way to counter ethnocentricity.
    B   The idea of cultural relativism differs markedly from commonly-held ethnocentric opinions.

F Mastering Sentence Simplification Questions – Recognizing Distractors

A further skill for Sentence Simplification questions is recognizing and avoiding distractors – that is, answer choices that may look similar to the highlighted sentence, and may even paraphrase one part of that sentence, but which are incorrect.

F1 Compare each pair of sentences, 1–4. In each case, sentence B does NOT correctly restate sentence A. Put a check (✓) in the correct column to indicate the problem with sentence B. One answer has been done for you.

1A. The Yanomamö are a group of roughly 20,000 people living in villages of up to 400 people in the Amazon rainforest in the border region between Brazil and Venezuela.

1B. The Amazon rainforest between Brazil and Venezuela is home to around 20,000 small villages of Yanomamö people.

2A. Although non-invasive techniques exist for learning about an archaeological site, in most cases, excavation remains the primary method for acquiring data.

2B. Archaeologists acquire the majority of information about archaeological sites through excavating them.

3A. Numerous ancient writing systems have been discovered by archaeologists, including Linear B, which has been deciphered, and Linear A, which has not.

3B. Archaeologists have discovered and deciphered a number of ancient writing systems, including Linear A and Linear B.

4A. The Kula ring is a complex ceremonial exchange system that occurs among communities living on islands northeast of Papua New Guinea.

4B. People that live on islands to the north and east of Papua New Guinea exchange complex items with communities on that island.

	1B	2B	3B	4B
Sentence B changes the function of Sentence A.				
Sentence B changes essential information in Sentence A.	✓			
Sentence B leaves out essential information from Sentence A.				

> **TEST TACTIC**
>
> Some distractors paraphrase the highlighted sentence but leave out an essential detail. These can be difficult to recognize because they correctly restate part of the highlighted sentence. To avoid choosing these wrong answers, make sure you look at all four answer choices before selecting your final answer.

G Test Challenge

G1 Answer Sentence Simplification questions 1–6. Try to finish in 9 minutes or less so as to get realistic practice for the test. Use the checklist of skills that you learned in this unit as a guide.

☑ Eliminate answers that change essential details from the highlighted sentence

☑ Eliminate answers that leave out essential information from the highlighted sentence

☑ Eliminate answers that change the function of the highlighted sentence

Kinship and Descent

Because it is a key organizing principle of many traditional societies, kinship is an important and often-studied concept in anthropology. In broad terms, kinship can be understood as one's relationships with family members either by blood – known as consanguinity – or marriage – known as affinity. This definition of kinship does not account for adoptive kin or fictive kin, but has the benefit of being both simple and applicable to most cultures and situations.

The kinship ties that an individual can claim depend on the system of descent employed by his or her society. This system is important because in many cultures an individual's duties, eligibility to join certain groups, and rights of inheritance and residence may all follow kinship lines. Anthropologists have identified several descent systems.

The most common system is unilineal kinship, in which descent is either patrilineal (through the father) or matrilineal (mother). Double descent, also called double unilineal or bilineal, describes kinship in which patrilineal ties are considered in some contexts and matrilineal ties in others. Bilateral descent describes cultures in which an individual is considered to descend equally from both the patrilineal and matrilineal sides of the family. Ambilineal descent, which like bilateral descent is a form of cognatic descent, gives individuals the chance to choose whether to trace descent from their mother or father, or, in some cultures, from their mother-in-law or father-in-law.

TEST TACTIC

If time is running out, count the number of ideas in the highlighted sentence. In general, the correct answer will either have the same number of ideas as the highlighted sentence or one idea less. Incorrect answers, however, may include more ideas or two ideas less.

1. Which of the following best expresses the essential information in the highlighted sentence in paragraph 1? Incorrect choices change the meaning in important ways or leave out essential information.
   - (A) Adoptive kin and fictive kin have advantages in some cultures and situations that the definition does not include.
   - (B) Most cultures prefer to use a simple and widely applicable definition of kinship that does not account for all kin types.
   - (C) Although is easy to understand and relevant to most situations, the definition does not include every form of kinship.
   - (D) Some types of kin cannot be included in a simple definition of kinship because they do not exist in most cultures.

2. Which of the following best expresses the essential information in the highlighted sentence in paragraph 2? Incorrect choices change the meaning in important ways or leave out essential information.
   - (A) An important system of descent is one that adopts the kinship lines that a culture follows with relation to eligibility.
   - (B) The system of kinship descent that a culture adopts affects an individual's status and rights within that culture.
   - (C) Many societies limit the duties, eligibility, and rights of individuals according to the system of descent he or she follows.
   - (D) Certain cultures may limit what an individual is allowed to do based on where that individual chooses to reside.

3. Which of the following best expresses the essential information in the highlighted sentence in paragraph 3? Incorrect choices change the meaning in important ways or leave out essential information.
   - (A) Ambilineal descent allows individuals to select the relative from whom they descend.
   - (B) Cognatic forms of descent are flexible systems because individuals have more choice.
   - (C) The system known as ambilineal descent is traced from an individual's parents and in-laws.
   - (D) Under ambilineal descent, the choice of kinship connection depends on the culture.

Underwater Archaeology

A common misconception is that underwater archaeology, which, as its name implies, deals with the excavation, analysis, and interpretation of sites or objects of historical interest found at the bottom of a body of water, always involves the exploration of shipwrecks. In fact, any human settlement, artifact, or structure that was once on land but is now submerged may be the object of study, including sites from prehistorical, classical, historical, and industrial times.

Underwater archaeology shares the same principles, methodologies, and even many of the same techniques as dry-land archaeology, but is inevitably more complex, dangerous, and costly owing to the challenging environment in which it occurs. Many sites can only be reached by diving, which requires specialist equipment and training and limits how much time divers can spend at the site. Furthermore, study of some locations can be affected by currents, tides, and severe weather.

One of the most ambitious underwater archaeology projects was the excavation of the *Mary Rose*, a British warship dating from the time of King Henry VIII. The ship sank during a battle in 1545, but was rediscovered in 1971 at which time a plan to salvage the wreck was proposed. From 1979 to 1982, divers spent more than 20,000 hours exploring the site. In 1982 archaeologists and project leaders were able to overcome some major technical obstacles and raise the ship from the bottom of the sea for preservation and exhibition in a museum.

4. Which of the following best expresses the essential information in the highlighted sentence in paragraph 1? Incorrect choices change the meaning in important ways or leave out essential information.
   - (A) As the name underwater archaeology implies, it is common for shipwrecks to be excavated.
   - (B) Sites and objects of historical interest such as shipwrecks can even be found under water.
   - (C) People misinterpret shipwrecks because the concept of underwater archaeology is unclear.
   - (D) Many do not realize that underwater archaeology may encompass studying any submarine site or artifact.

5. Which of the following best expresses the essential information in the highlighted sentence in paragraph 2? Incorrect choices change the meaning in important ways or leave out essential information.
   - (A) It uses the same methods as land archaeology, so the cost, danger, and challenge of underwater archaeology are high.
   - (B) The difficulties and techniques of underwater archaeology are effectively the same as those of dry-land archaeology.
   - (C) The challenge that underwater archaeology provides is balanced by its use of the same techniques and ideas as other branches of archaeology.
   - (D) Despite the challenging environment in which underwater archaeology takes place, it is similar in many ways to dry-land archaeology.

6. Which of the following best expresses the essential information in the highlighted sentence in paragraph 3? Incorrect choices change the meaning in important ways or leave out essential information.
   - (A) Archaeologists and leaders overcame obstacles in 1982 when the *Mary Rose* project ended.
   - (B) After the *Mary Rose* was raised from the sea bed, archaeologists preserved it in a museum.
   - (C) Despite challenges, the *Mary Rose* was successfully raised for conservation and viewing.
   - (D) A 1982 exhibition highlighted the difficulties archaeologists faced in raising the *Mary Rose*.

Next Steps

Topics related to anthropology and archaeology may appear in any section of the TOEFL Test. As a result, learning more about these subjects and practicing key skills for Sentence Simplification questions may raise your overall test score.

To learn more about anthropology, archaeology, and vocabulary related to these disciplines:

1. Read an article in your language about one aspect of anthropology or archaeology to get some background knowledge.
2. Read an English article about the same topic several times until you understand all of the main ideas. When you see an unfamiliar word, try to understand the word from its context and write a definition. Check your definition in a dictionary and correct any mistakes. Then decide if the word is useful for anthropology or archaeology; if it is, study it in more detail.

To practice a key skill for Sentence Simplification questions:

1. Find two news articles about the same story and read each article once. (Stories about academic discoveries are ideal.)
2. Look for sentences in the second article that accurately paraphrase sentences in the first article.
3. Look for sentences in the second article that paraphrase sentences in the first article, but leave out or change a detail.

Unit Focus

There are ten types of reading questions in the TOEFL Test, including Insert Text questions and Reference questions. Insert Text questions ask you to decide the best position at which to add a new sentence into the passage. Reference questions, on the other hand, ask you to identify the phrase in the passage that a highlighted word or phrase refers to. You will usually see an Insert Text question after every reading passage in the TOEFL Test, but Reference questions are not as common. Insert Text and Reference questions are different, but the same skills can help you answer both question types. These skills include:

- recognizing the function of a sentence and the most likely position where a sentence of that function comes.
- recognizing words and phrases in a sentence that match context clues in the passage.
- recognizing coherence and cohesion in a passage to decide where best to add a sentence.

The vocabulary focus is on academic words and phrases related to:

- botany, the scientific study and categorization of plants.

A Warm-up

A1 Complete tasks 1–3.

1. Make a list of three important food crops that grow in your country or in another country that you know about.
2. Share your list with other students. Then listen to other students and add the crops they mention to your list.
3. What are the three most important crops on your list? Discuss why they are so important.

B Academic Vocabulary

B1 Complete definitions 1–8 with words from the passages. One answer has been done for you.

Trees have a hard, outer layer. This is known as bark. The bark protects trees from pests, which are organisms such as insects that can cause damage. Not all insects are pests. Some perform the vital function of transferring reproductive material between the male and female parts of a plant, a process known as pollination.

1. The word "bark" is defined in the passage as the _____hard, outer layer_____ of trees.
2. The word "pests" is defined as _____, such as insects.
3. "Pollination" occurs when _____ is transferred between male and female parts of a plant.

Most plants grow in soil – the upper layer of earth that is usually a mixture of dead organisms, small pieces of rock, and mud. Their roots spread underground in the soil to anchor the plant. They also absorb water and nutrients, the substances that all organisms need to survive.

4. The word "soil" is defined as a mixture of _____ that forms the upper layer of earth.
5. A plant's "roots" absorb water and vital substances, and _____ in the soil.
6. The word "nutrients" is defined as _____ require for survival.

Plants have various types of specialist tissues, which are groups of cells with a similar form and function. Among the most important tissues are those that can convert the sun's energy into sugars, a process called photosynthesis

7. The word "tissues" is defined as groups of cells that share a _____.
8. "Photosynthesis" is the process by which plant tissues turn _____.

C Analyzing Insert Text Questions

All Insert Text questions follow the same pattern. On the screen you will see one or two paragraphs from the passage. The paragraph(s) will contain four squares at the start or end of some sentences. Usually, these sentences are next to each other in the paragraph(s). You will also see a new sentence in bold and the question will ask you which is the best square in the passage at which to add the new sentence, as in this example:

> Look at the four squares [■] that indicate where the following sentence could be added to the passage.
>
> **You will see a sentence in bold font here that can be added to the passage.**
>
> Where would the sentence best fit?
>
> Click on a square [■] to add the sentence to the passage.

When you click on one of the squares with your mouse, the screen will change to show you the new sentence added at that position in the paragraph. You can change your answer as many times as you like by clicking on a different square.

If the new sentence is added to the passage at the correct position:

- phrases in the new sentence will logically relate or refer to words or phrases in the sentence before and/or after it.
- the whole paragraph will show cohesion – each sentence will logically follow from the previous sentence.

If the new sentence is added to the passage at one of the three incorrect positions:

- phrases in the new sentence will not relate or refer to matching words or phrases in the previous or next sentence.
- the cohesion of the paragraph may be lost – the new sentence may break a connection between two sentences that are logically related to one another.

C1 **Answer Insert Text question 1 based on the reading passage below. Then discuss your answer with a partner.**

A Swedish scholar Carl Linnaeus is most famous now for developing and popularizing the scientific system of naming known as binomial nomenclature. **B** During his lifetime, however, Linnaeus was better known for his many publications (most of which were written in Latin) on botany in general and the plants of Scandinavia in particular. **C** Among these are *Fundamenta Botanica* (first published in 1736), *Genera Plantarum* and *Flora Lapponica* (both 1737), *Flora Svecica* (1745), *Philosophica Botanica* (1751), and *Species Plantarum* (1753). **D**

1. Look at the four squares (■) that indicate where the following sentence could be added to the passage.

   This system allows a species to be scientifically classified by assigning it a two-part name.

   Where would the sentence best fit? Choose position **A**, **B**, **C**, or **D**.

C2 **Write in the letter of the position, A–D, that completes these reasons why the wrong answers are incorrect. One answer has been done for you.**

- Position __A__ is not the best position at which to add the new sentence because the phrase "This system" in the new sentence refers to something already mentioned, but this position is at the start of the paragraph, so nothing has already been mentioned.
- The new sentence cannot be added at position _____ because the sentences before and after this position are linked and should not be separated: the sentence before includes "publications" and the sentence after includes "published."
- Position _____ is not where the new sentence should be added because no word or phrase in the new sentence relates to a word or phrase in the sentence before this position.

D Mastering Insert Text Questions – Recognizing the Function of a Sentence

Sentences with different functions are more likely or less likely at certain positions within a paragraph. If you can recognize the function of a sentence, you may be able to answer Insert Text questions more easily and quickly.

Track 3 **D1** **Take notes as you listen to an experienced teacher talk about Insert Text questions. Then use your notes to answer questions 1 and 2.**

1. What does the teacher NOT say about using sentence functions to answer Insert Text questions?
   A The function of a sentence may help you decide likely positions for the answer, but not the exact position.
   B Some types of sentences are much more common in the TOEFL test than other types.
   C Any type of sentence can appear anywhere in a paragraph, but some positions are unlikely.
   D If the function of a sentence is not obvious, try to answer the question using other strategies.

2. The teacher discusses likely positions within a paragraph for sentences with a particular function. Indicate which positions the teacher says are common for each function. One answer has been done for you.

Function	Near start of paragraph	Middle of paragraph	Near end of paragraph
Adding a detail or example			
Comparing or contrasting ideas			
Defining a term or concept			
Expressing a conclusion			
Introducing a topic	✓		

D2 **Work with a partner to complete tasks 1–3.**

1. Five functions of a sentence are shown in exercise **D1**. Make a list of some other sentence functions you know.
2. Look at your list of functions from task 1 and say at which position(s) in a paragraph they are commonly found.
3. Share your list of functions and common positions with other students. Then listen to their lists and take notes.

D3 **What function, A–E, matches each sentence, 1–5? Work with a partner. One answer has been done for you.**

1. Infections like these can affect the economy, so it can be seen that plant pathology is an important field of study. __D__
2. Rice ragged stunt virus and bacterial leaf blight, for instance, are both pathogens that can affect rice crops. ____
3. Many insects and other pests also affect the health of plants, but plant pathologists do not study these factors. ____
4. Various types of disease-causing pathogens affect plants, including fungi, parasites, viruses, and bacteria. ____
5. Plant pathology is the name given to the study of diseases that are caused by such organisms. ____

A Adding a detail or example   D Expressing a conclusion
B Comparing or contrasting ideas   E Introducing a topic
C Defining a term or concept

D4 **Put the sentences from exercise D3 in the correct order to make a logically-organized paragraph about plant pathology. Work with a partner.**

E Mastering Insert Text Questions – Focusing on Context Clues

The new sentence and the sentences marked by the four squares (■) will contain words or phrases – context clues – that can help you decide the best position at which to add the new sentence. Finding context clues in the new sentence that match or refer to clues in the passage is a key skill for answering Insert Text questions accurately.

E1 Which word or phrase in these paragraphs does each highlighted phrase refer to? Underline the word or phrase and draw an arrow connecting it to the matching highlighted phrase. One answer has been done for you.

The plant kingdom can be divided into two broad groups of seed-bearing plants: angiosperms and gymnosperms. The former differ from the latter in several ways, most notably in having an enclosed seed and in having flowers. There are almost 250,000 species of angiosperms in total, many of which are important sources of food, resources such as wood, or medicine.

The plant kingdom also contains some species that do not bear seeds. These include bryophytes, such as mosses, and pteridophytes, such as ferns. These species reproduce using spores, which are capsules of genetic information with a protective coating. They are carried by the wind or transported in some other way to a different location. When a spore lands in a suitable one, it begins to grow, creating a copy of the parent organism.

E2 Answer questions 1–5 about sentences A–F. Work with a partner.

1. Which words in sentence B refer to "trees" in sentence A? Find two answers.
2. Which phrase in sentence C gives an example of "leaf shape" mentioned in sentence B?
3. Which word in sentence D refers to "Coniferous trees" in sentence C?
4. Which adjectives in sentence E contrast with the word "thin" in sentence C? Find two answers.
5. Could you move sentence F to position E, and sentence E to position F? Why or why not?

A Typically, trees are defined as a plant with a long woody stem, called a trunk, that supports branches and leaves.
B Common ways of classifying them are by leaf shape and by the hardness or softness of their wood.
C Coniferous trees typically keep their thin, needle-like leaves throughout the year.
D They also typically produce light-colored soft wood that is easily worked.
E Broadleaf trees have broader, flatter leaves that, except in tropical climates, usually fall to the ground in autumn.
F They typically have hard, dense wood that is strong and durable but difficult to work with.

E3 Use context clues to help you choose the best answer from the box to fill the blanks at positions A–H. One answer has been done for you.

Plants are both affected by and affect their **A** _____environment_____ in various ways. Plants turn sunlight into energy through the process of photosynthesis. As such, the availability of **B** _____ is a significant environmental factor. Only certain species can grow on **C** _____ floors, for example, which receive little illumination from the sun because of the surrounding trees. Soil is another critical factor. Factors that affect which plants can grow, such as the quantity of nutrients and pH value, all differ from one type of **D** _____ to another. Finally, climate has a big impact, too, with average **E** _____ and rainfall being particularly important factors. In terms of how they impact their environs, some plants produce chemicals that can influence which other **F** _____ of plants can grow nearby. And because carbon dioxide is taken up and **G** _____ is emitted during photosynthesis, plants have an effect on the global **H** _____, too.

atmosphere   forest   oxygen   species
environment   light   soil   temperature

F Mastering Insert Text Questions – Recognizing Cohesion and Coherence

Well-written paragraphs are coherent – each sentence logically follows from the previous one – and cohesive – words in one sentence refer back or forward to words in other sentences. Recognizing coherence and cohesion is a valuable skill for Insert Text questions as it can help you decide where best to add the new sentence.

F1 Use context clues and the coherence and cohesion of each passage to decide the best place to add each bold sentence. Then discuss your answers with a partner. One answer has been done for you.

1. The best position in the passage at which to add this sentence is position ___*c*___.

   Scientific analysis of resin shows that it contains compounds that are toxic to a variety of organisms that eat plant tissues.

   A Natural resin is a sticky liquid secreted by various species of plants, especially coniferous trees like pines, firs, and cedars, that hardens and becomes solid over time. **B** Its specific function is uncertain, but it is likely that, at least in part, resin serves to protect the plant from pests. **C**

2. The best position in the passage at which to add this sentence is position _____.

   There are two types of sap: phloem sap, which flows from sources of carbohydrate to tissues that require them, and xylem sap, which moves from the roots of the plant to its leaves.

   A Plant sap is a watery fluid that transports water and nutrients throughout the tissues and organs of vascular plants. **B** Some xylem saps are used by humans as a source of food, including maple syrup, which is the processed xylem sap of certain species of maple tree. **C**

3. The best position in the passage at which to add this sentence is position _____.

   There is strong evidence that latex has a defensive function.

   A Around one in ten flowering plants produce latex, a milky liquid composed of proteins, sugars, oils, and other substances. **B** It is often produced when a plant suffers tissue damage, such as when an insect begins consuming it, and it contains levels of defensive compounds much greater than other tissues. **C**

4. The best position in the passage at which to add this sentence is position _____.

   Mucilage, a thick, glue-like liquid produced by plants, is often used either as a base for adhesives or in food and medicine.

   A In the plant kingdom, some carnivorous plants use the stickiness of mucilage to trap insects. **B** In other plants its functions include storing water or food, helping seeds to germinate or disperse, or protecting damaged tissues. **C**

F2 Work with a partner to complete this table of reasons why the sentences in exercise F1 cannot be added at some positions in the passage. Note that one wrong position is wrong for two reasons. Two answers have been done for you.

Reason why the new sentence cannot be added at some positions	Position
It adds details about a topic *before* the topic has been introduced or defined.	1A
It introduces or defines a topic *after* details about that topic have been mentioned.	
It separates two sentences that are coherent and logically related.	1B

G Analyzing Reference Questions

Reference questions ask you to identify which word or phrase in the passage refers to a highlighted word. The key word will be highlighted in the question, too. The key word or phrase may be a pronoun (such as "they" or "it"), a determiner (such as "the other" or "several"), or a noun phrase (such as "that idea" or "the situation").

> The word "_____" in the passage refers to
>
> The phrase "_____" in the passage refers to
>
> The phrase "_____" in the passage refers to the concept of

The correct answer to Reference questions:

- will make sense, be correct English, and will not change the meaning of the passage if it replaces the highlighted word.

In contrast, incorrect answers:

- will not make sense, or will make sense, but change the meaning of the passage if they replace the highlighted word.

G1 **Answer Reference questions 1 and 2. Then discuss your answers with a partner.**

Piper nigrum is a flowering vine native to certain countries in South Asia that bears clusters of fruit which are called peppercorns when dried. Once so valuable that they were known as black gold and sometimes used as a form of money, peppercorns are still widely used in the cuisine of many cultures.

1. The word "they" in the passage refers to
   A countries
   B clusters
   C peppercorns
   D cultures

When Columbus set sail from Spain in 1492 on the journey that resulted in the discovery of the American continent, his intention and that of his financial backers was actually to find a westward route to the Indies – as the lands of South and Southeast Asia were known – which were the only known source of valuable spices like pepper and cloves that were eagerly sought by European consumers. Columbus' hope was that finding a westward route would make trading these commodities easier and therefore more profitable.

2. The phrase "these commodities" in the passage refers to
   A consumers
   B spices
   C lands
   D backers

G2 **Indicate which phrases, 1–8, from the passages in exercise G1 helped you answer that exercise. One answer has been done for you.**

1. a flowering vine   ☐ Helpful   ☒ Not helpful
2. when dried   ☐ Helpful   ☐ Not helpful
3. so valuable   ☐ Helpful   ☐ Not helpful
4. black gold   ☐ Helpful   ☐ Not helpful
5. set sail from Spain   ☐ Helpful   ☐ Not helpful
6. the American continent ☐ Helpful   ☐ Not helpful
7. westward route   ☐ Helpful   ☐ Not helpful
8. pepper and cloves   ☐ Helpful   ☐ Not helpful

H Mastering Reference Questions – Focusing on Context Clues and Cohesion

As with Insert Text questions, a key skill for answering Reference questions is recognizing cohesion and context clues in the passage. These can help you decide which answer the highlighted word or phrase refers to.

H1 **Circle the expressions in passages 1–4 that either refer to or give an example of the highlighted word. One answer has been done for you.**

1. The study of fungi – (mushrooms, yeasts, and molds) – is often considered a subfield of botany even though (they) are not classified as plants. One major difference is that (their) cell walls are made from chitin, not cellulose like plants.

2. A number of common foods are technically fruits even though they are often considered to be vegetables. Among these items are avocados, eggplants, which are actually a type of berry, cucumbers, which are from the same family as melons, tomatoes, and even olives, which means that, strictly speaking, olive oil is a fruit juice.

3. Bamboo, which is native to every populated continent except Europe, is the largest member of the grass family. It grows extremely quickly and many species are both strong and durable, factors that have led to its use for a wide variety of purposes including as a construction material, as a food or medicine, and as a raw material for making paper and textiles. The plant also has a symbolic role in many Asian cultures.

4. *The Day of the Triffids* by John Wyndham is a classic science fiction story from the 1950s. The triffids referred to in the title are a fictional species of large, venomous, mobile plant that often attacks humans. The tale describes the efforts of a small group of people who have survived a natural disaster to find a place to live that is safe from triffids.

H2 **Use context clues and cohesion clues to answer questions 1–4. If none of the answers is correct, write your own.**

Several species of acacia trees in Africa and Central America have developed symbiotic relationships with ants. The insects live in hollow thorn-like appendages on the branches of the tree. They also acquire nutrients from the tree. In return, they provide the tree with some measure of protection against predation by other insects or herbivorous organisms. Some species of ants will also attack the leaves of plants that are growing near acacias and that might compete with them for resources.

1. The word "they" in the passage refers to
   A nutrients
   B branches
   C insects
   D _your answer_

2. The word "them" in the passage refers to
   A ants
   B leaves
   C plants
   D _your answer_

A genus of plants known as seed ferns (scientific name *Glossopteris*) evolved during the Permian period, which lasted from roughly 299 to 252 million years ago. Fossil discoveries show they were woody, seed-bearing, grew up to 30 meters (33 yards) in height, and had broad, tongue-shaped leaves. They became a dominant species during the Permian but went extinct at the end of that period. Seed fern fossils have been discovered in every southern continent. This evidence led several scholars to suggest that all of the world's landmasses were once joined as one massive supercontinent known as Gondwana before separating and moving to their current positions on the surface of the Earth, a theory that is now known to be correct.

3. The word "They" in the passage refers to
   A years
   B discoveries
   C leaves
   D *your answer*

4. The phrase "This evidence" in the passage refers to
   A the extinction of seed ferns at the end of the Permian
   B the discovery of seed fern fossils on many continents
   C the joining of all Earth's landmasses into a single continent
   D *your answer*

Test Challenge

I1 **Practice Insert Text and Reference questions by answering questions 1–10. Try to finish in 15 minutes or less so as to get realistic practice for the test. Use this checklist of skills that you studied in this unit as a guide.**

For Insert Text questions

☑ Decide which positions are likely and unlikely based on the function of the new sentence.

☑ Find words or phrases in the new sentence that match context clues in the passage.

☑ Look for cohesion and coherence in the passage to decide where best to add the new sentence.

For Reference questions

☑ Focus on context clues, cohesion, and coherence to decide which answer matches the highlighted expression.

Carnivorous Plants

All plants derive energy from sunlight through the process of photosynthesis, but must get vital nutrients from their surroundings. Carnivorous plants typically live in nutrient-poor soils and, as a result, have evolved a number of ways to trap insects and other small organisms that are a good source of these minerals. Two types of carnivorous plants, sundews and butterworts, have leaves covered with sticky mucilage that glistens in sunlight. Insects that are attracted to the shimmering light become trapped on the leaves. **A** Pitcher plants are another type of carnivorous plant. They attract insects with bright colors and sweet nectar or water at the bottom of a pitcher-shaped leaf that traps the insect and prevents it from escaping. **B** Bladderworts are aquatic carnivorous plants that capture small organisms through the use of suction powered by differential pressure: when a prey species brushes against special membranes, a trapdoor opens that sucks in both the prey and the surrounding water. **C** The final type of carnivorous plant is the venus flytrap, which has specialist leaves that snap closed when an insect touches them and remain closed until it dies. **D**

---

1. The phrase "these minerals" in the passage refers to
   Ⓐ small organisms
   Ⓑ nutrient-poor soils
   Ⓒ carnivorous plants
   Ⓓ vital nutrients

2. Look at the four squares (■) that indicate where the following sentence could be added to the passage.

   In all cases, once the prey has been trapped, carnivorous plants digest it and obtain its nutrients.

   Where would the sentence best fit? Choose position **A**, **B**, **C**, or **D**.

TEST TACTIC

For Reference questions, the answers are listed in the order they appear in the passage. In most cases answer A will be the answer that is farthest away from the highlighted expression. Knowing that the answers are in order may help you find them more quickly and save time.

Miracle Fruit

Three different types of plant that have the capacity to alter taste perception in humans are known colloquially as "miracle fruit." **A** All three plants are being studied by food scientists to learn more about their active ingredients and to determine if these are suitable for being used as food additives or as medicines. **B** The most widely known of these is *Synsepalum dulcificum*, a berry that grows in parts of tropical West Africa. **C** It contains a protein molecule called miraculin, which activates sweet receptors on the tongue in the presence of acid. **D** Miraculin makes sour foods and beverages taste sweet for up to an hour after consumption. Chewing the seeds of the fruit of *Thaumatococcus danielli* has the same effect. Their covering contains a protein called thaumatin, which is approximately 3,000 times sweeter than sugar and which affects the tongue so that sour flavors taste sweet until the effect wears off. *Gymnema sylvestre*, an herb native to India and Sri Lanka, also sometimes goes by the name "miracle fruit," although this is a misnomer as its leaves rather than its fruit affect taste. Unlike the other two species, *G. sylvestre* suppresses sweet tastes.

3. Look at the four squares (■) that indicate where the following sentence could be added to the passage.

   The berry itself does not have a high sugar content, however, and does not taste particularly sweet when eaten.

   Where would the sentence best fit? Choose position **A**, **B**, **C**, or **D**.

4. The word these in the passage refers to
   - Ⓐ three plants
   - Ⓑ food scientists
   - Ⓒ active ingredients
   - Ⓓ food additives

5. The word this in the passage refers to
   - Ⓐ name
   - Ⓑ India
   - Ⓒ herb
   - Ⓓ tongue

Tree Trunks

A The trunk of a tree is made up of five basic layers. **B** From the outside to the inside, these are the outer and inner bark, the vascular cambium layer, the sapwood, and the heartwood. **C** Together they provide protection, structural support, and transportation of water, nutrients, and food to all of its branches, leaves, and cells. **D**

Outer bark consists of dead cells that protect against moisture loss as well as environmental damage from weather, natural phenomena, and pests. Inner bark, the cells of which die and become outer bark as they are pushed outwards by a tree's growth, is a layer of tube-shaped cells called phloem. These act as pipes for the transportation of carbohydrates from the leaves, where they are made during photosynthesis, to the rest of the tree.

Beneath the inner bark is the vascular cambium layer, the only part of the trunk that grows. The cambium cells continually divide inward to form new wood and outward to form new bark. **E** This is regulated by growth hormones called auxins that are released by leaf buds each spring. **F**

The two inner layers of the trunk are collectively known as the xylem. **G** Sapwood is the newly-created wood formed by the cambium. **H** It consists of living cells that conduct water and minerals from the roots to the leaves, branches, and upper parts of a tree. As the cambium continues to produce new sapwood, the older, inner layers of that material die and are converted into heartwood. This layer is usually darker than the sapwood and consists of cellulose fibers bound with a complex compound called lignin. Lignin provides enough strength for the heartwood cells to continue supporting mature trees from within even though they are no longer alive.

6. Look at the four squares (■) that indicate where the following sentence could be added to the passage.

   The latter is named for its location at the center of the trunk and not because it is any more important to the tree than the other layers; indeed, some species of trees do not form heartwood at all.

   Where would the sentence best fit? Choose position **A**, **B**, **C**, or **D**.

7. The word "its" in the passage refers to
   - Ⓐ layer
   - Ⓑ bark
   - Ⓒ tree
   - Ⓓ trunk

8. The word "This" in the passage refers to
   - Ⓐ the death of inner bark cells caused by growth
   - Ⓑ the transportation of carbohydrates from the leaves
   - Ⓒ the division of cells in the cambium layer
   - Ⓓ the release of auxins from leaf buds each year

9. Look at the four squares (■) that indicate where the following sentence could be added to the passage.

   After release these are transported to the rest of the tree's cells along with sugars via the phloem layer.

   Where would the sentence best fit? Choose position **E**, **F**, **G**, or **H**.

10. The word "they" in the passage refers to
    - Ⓐ mature trees
    - Ⓑ heartwood cells
    - Ⓒ cellulose fibers
    - Ⓓ inner layers

Next Steps

Topics related to botany are common in the reading section of the TOEFL Test. You may also have questions about these subjects in the other sections. As a result, learning more about botany, as well as practicing key skills for Insert Text and Reference questions, may raise your overall test score.

To learn more about botany and vocabulary related to this discipline:

1. Find an online museum (sometimes called a virtual museum) that has exhibitions or tours related to botany. Useful search phrases that may help you find interesting sites are "virtual museum plants" and "online museum botany".
2. Use your computer to visit or tour the online exhibition. When you hear or see an unfamiliar word on the site, use your dictionary to check its meaning. If you think the word is likely to be useful for botany, study it in more detail.

To practice a key skill for Insert Text and Reference questions:

1. Find an academic or news article in English related to botany (or another subject that you find interesting).
2. Read the article once to understand the main ideas, but do not worry about the meaning of every word.
3. Read the first paragraph of the article again and highlight the first pronoun or determiner that you find.
4. Now scan the first paragraph and look for words or phrases that the highlighted word refers to.
5. Repeat steps 3 and 4 for the other pronouns and determiners in the first paragraph and again for the other paragraphs.

Unit Focus

There are ten types of reading questions in the TOEFL Test, including two types of "reading to learn" questions: Fill in a Table questions and Prose Summary questions. These questions test your understanding of how ideas in the passage are related to other ideas. Fill in a Table questions ask you to match answer choices to one of several categories, and Prose Summary questions ask you to choose the answers that accurately summarize key ideas in the passage. Unlike other reading questions, which are worth just one point, reading to learn questions are worth up to three points. You need to learn and practice several key skills to answer these questions, including:

- recognizing answers that restate or contradict ideas in the passage.
- recognizing answers that look similar to the passage, but are not mentioned in it.
- distinguishing between answers that restate major and minor ideas from the passage.

The vocabulary focus is on academic words and phrases related to:

- Earth science, the scientific study of Earth, including sub-disciplines like geography and geology.

A Warm-up

A1 Complete tasks 1 and 2 with a partner.

1. Write the name of one geographical landform, like a lake, river, mountain, or desert, from each continental area, A–F.

   A Africa   C Australasia   E North America
   B Asia   D Europe   F South America

2. Share your list and knowledge of each landform with other students. Then listen to their lists.

B Academic Vocabulary

B1 Choose the best definition, A–H, for words 1–8, which are related to Earth science. When you have finished, check your answers in a dictionary. One answer has been done for you.

1. atmosphere _____ *the mixture of gases, including oxygen and nitrogen, that surrounds Earth* _____
2. climate _____
3. continent _____
4. erosion _____
5. eruption _____
6. glacier _____
7. precipitation _____
8. sediment _____

A a large area of land that may be divided into two or more countries
B a mass of ice that often moves slowly and does not fully melt each year
C fine material that slowly sinks to the bottom of a sea, lake, or river
D the weather that occurs in a region over a period of time
E drops or crystals of water in the atmosphere that fall to Earth
F the mixture of gases, including oxygen and nitrogen, that surrounds Earth
G the gradual wearing down of rock or soil by water, wind, or other causes
H the violent release of materials such as lava, rocks, ash, and gas from a volcano

C Analyzing Fill in a Table Questions

You can recognize Fill in a Table questions from their detailed directions, as in this example:

Directions: Select the phrases that correctly describe _____ and _____.
Two of the phrases will NOT be used. **This question is worth 3 points.**

Below the directions you will see two or three categories and space for five answers. You will also see a list of six or more answer choices, at least one of which will not match any of the categories. Each correct answer choice will match only one of the categories.

Fill in a Table questions are worth up to 3 points. To get 3 points, you need to choose all five correct answers and assign them to the correct category. To get 2 points, you must choose and correctly assign four answers, and to get 1 point you must choose and correctly assign three answers. Choosing and assigning zero to two correct answers is not worth any points.

The five correct answers to Fill in a Table questions:

- restate ideas that are mentioned in the passage and that match one of the category headings.

In contrast, the one or two answers that are incorrect and should not be used:

- might use words from the passage, but express an idea that is not mentioned in the passage.
- might restate an idea from the passage, but not an idea that matches any of the categories.
- might look similar to an idea from the passage, but contradict or change one or more key details.

TEST TACTIC

In some reading passages, key ideas are discussed in separate paragraphs, but in other passages key ideas are compared and contrasted within the same paragraph. Recognizing how a passage or paragraph is organized can help you find the answers to Fill in a Table questions more quickly and easily.

C1 **Read the passage. Then select the phrases that correctly describe each category. One of the phrases will NOT be used.**

Scientists use one scale to measure earthquakes, and a different one for volcanic eruptions. The Moment Magnitude Scale (MMS), which was developed in the 1970s as a replacement for the older Richter Scale, assigns a value from 1 to 10 according to how much energy an earthquake releases. The scale is logarithmic, meaning that each point on the scale represents ten times less energy than the point above it. The Volcanic Explosivity Index (VEI) measures the power of a volcanic eruption on a nine-point scale from 0 to 8. From VEI 0 to VEI 2, each level represents 100 less power than the one above it. From VEI 2 to VEI 8, the scale is logarithmic like the MMS. An eruption's VEI level is determined both by how long it lasts and how powerful it is in terms of how much material is ejected.

Moment Magnitude Scale

-
-

Volcanic Explosivity Index

-

Both Moment Magnitude Scale and Volcanic Explosivity Index

-
-

A   The scale was designed as a substitute for an older scale.
B   The scale measures only how much energy is released by an event.
C   The scale can help scientists decide when an event is likely to occur.
D   All or most points on the scale represent ten times the power of the point below.
E   The scale can be used to measure nine or more levels of event.
F   The scale measures both the duration and intensity of an event.

D Mastering Fill in a Table Questions – Analyzing the Answer Choices

To answer Fill in a Table questions, you need to practice several key skills. These include recognizing answers that are not mentioned in the passage, recognizing answers that restate or contradict the passage, and deciding which category an answer matches.

 Track 4   **D1** **Take notes as you listen to an experienced teacher discuss Fill in a Table and Prose Summary questions. Then use your notes to answer questions 1 and 2.**

1. What does the teacher say about Fill in a Table and Prose Summary questions? *Choose two answers.*
   A   They are worth several points so it is important to save time to answer them well.
   B   They are harder than other questions, so students should answer them carefully.
   C   Fill in a Table questions are not as common as Prose Summary questions.
   D   Most students find it difficult to improve their ability to answer these questions.

2. The teacher discusses some strategies for answering Fill in a Table questions. Put the strategies in the order that the teacher mentions them. One answer has been done for you.

1.
2.
3.
4. Eliminate this answer choice if it contradicts the information in the relevant section of the passage.
5.

A   Eliminate this answer choice if it contradicts the information in the relevant section of the passage.
B   Skim and scan the passage to find the relevant section that matches one of the answer choices.
C   Scan the relevant section to decide which category the answer matches and then select your answer.
D   Eliminate this answer choice if the information is not mentioned anywhere in the passage.
E   Decide if the answer choice restates or contradicts the information in the relevant section.

D2 **Use skimming and scanning to decide if each statement, 1–4, is Mentioned or Not mentioned in this passage. One answer has been done for you.**

Valleys are formed when the flowing waters of a river or stream cut down through the underlying rock and soil over thousands of years. They typically have a V shape when seen in cross-section, although a valley that forms in an arid area with hard underlying rock may form a steep-sided canyon. If the climate later becomes cold enough for glaciers to form and one moves downhill along the path of a typical river valley, the shape of the valley changes significantly. The glacier erodes the gentle slopes of the valley making them steeper. The floor of the valley is also affected and becomes wider than before. If the glacier then melts, the former V shape will have become the characteristic U shape of a glaciated valley. Some of the glacial meltwater may remain in the bottom of the valley, forming one or more ribbon lakes, which are named for their long, thin shape.

1. V-shaped valleys are neither as steep nor as wide as U-shaped valleys.
   ☑ Mentioned   ☐ Not mentioned
2. Canyons may form when a river runs through a dry area with hard rock.
   ☐ Mentioned   ☐ Not mentioned
3. Most V-shaped valleys eventually become U-shaped valleys.
   ☐ Mentioned   ☐ Not mentioned
4. Erosion caused by glaciers may lead to the formation of rivers.
   ☐ Mentioned   ☐ Not mentioned

D3 Use skimming and scanning to decide if each statement, 1–4, Restates or Contradicts this passage. One answer has been done for you. When you have finished, rewrite the statements that contradict the passage so that they restate it.

Scientists distinguish several different kinds of precipitation. The term *drizzle* is used when drops of water in the atmosphere with a diameter less than 0.5 millimeter fall as precipitation. Drizzle is the most frequent form of precipitation over wide areas of the planet, though the drops of water that form drizzle are often so small that the precipitation evaporates before reaching the ground. Another form of precipitation is rain, which makes up a significant part of the moisture that forms the planet's water cycle. When the temperature is cold, several different varieties of precipitation may form. Sleet is one, although the meaning of the term depends on location. In some countries, sleet means snow mixed with rain that partially melts when it falls to Earth. In other regions, sleet is a mixture of snow, ice pellets, and freezing rain. When atmospheric water vapor freezes to form ice crystals, it is called snow. If the water vapor forms irregular lumps of ice at least 5 millimeters across instead of crystals, it is known as hail, while graupel, or soft hail, is the name given to precipitation composed of smaller ice pellets mixed with tiny ice crystals.

1. Drizzle may not always fall to Earth's surface.
    ☑ Restates   ☐ Contradicts
2. Rain is the most common form of precipitation.
    ☐ Restates   ☐ Contradicts
3. Precipitation in the form of rain constitutes a small part of the water cycle.
    ☐ Restates   ☐ Contradicts
4. Sleet, snow, hail, and graupel all form under cold conditions.
    ☐ Restates   ☐ Contradicts

D4 Match these statements to their category by choosing the correct heading for categories 1 and 2 from A–D.

The Mississippi River is the longest river in the United States, and one of the three or four longest rivers in the world. Its source is Lake Itasca in north-central Minnesota, and from there it wends in a generally southward direction to its delta on the Gulf of Mexico. The Mississippi is divided into Upper, Middle, and Lower portions, with the divisions occurring at its confluences with the Missouri River and Ohio River respectively. Other tributaries include the Red, Arkansas, and Tennessee Rivers. A number of large settlements are located along the river and depend on it economically to a greater or lesser extent, including St. Louis, Memphis, and New Orleans.

1. _____

    •   Its source is in northern Minnesota.
    •   It flows southwards past some major cities.
    •   It meets the ocean at the Gulf of Mexico.

2. _____

    •   The Middle Mississippi starts where the Mississippi River meets the Missouri River.
    •   The Lower Mississippi runs from the confluence with the Ohio River to the Gulf Mexico.

A   Main divisions of the Mississippi River
B   Major rivers in the United States of America
C   Physical characteristics of the Mississippi River
D   The general route of the Mississippi River

TEST TACTIC

Be careful with answer choices to Fill in a Table questions that both restate the passage clearly and match one of the categories very obviously. Obvious answers like these sometimes contradict a detail in the passage, so make sure you read all the answers carefully to avoid making mistakes.

D5 Use the skills you have learned to answer this Fill in a Table question by selecting the answers, A–G, that correctly describe each category. Two of the answers will NOT be used. One answer has been done for you.

When a volcano erupts, hot liquid rock called lava is often produced. Three broad classes of lava are known: mafic, felsic, and intermediate. Mafic lava is rich in iron and magnesium and erupts at very hot temperatures. It has a low viscosity, so eruptions of mafic lavas may flow long distances. Mafic lavas with very high levels of magnesium that erupt at temperatures as high as 1,600 degrees Celsius are called ultramafic. Felsic lavas are rich in elements including silica and aluminum, and are usually highly viscous and may erupt at temperatures 300 degrees lower than mafic lavas. Because of their viscosity, they typically do not flow for long distances except when they erupt at higher-than-usual temperatures. Intermediate lavas, as their name implies, possess characteristics halfway between felsic and mafic lavas. Chemically they contain fairly high levels of iron, magnesium, silica, and aluminum and erupt at temperatures between 750 and 950 degrees Celsius. They also have a viscosity level between that of the other two types of lava.

Mafic and ultramafic lavas

- *Their low level of viscosity means they may flow for long distances.*
-

Felsic or intermediate lavas

-
-
-

A   Their low level of viscosity means they may flow for long distances.
B   They erupt at low temperatures because they are rich in magnesium and iron.
C   They may be formed when lava eruptions from two types of volcano combine.
D   They contain high levels of the elements aluminum and silica.
E   They contain a wider variety of chemical elements than other types of lava.
F   They typically erupt at higher temperatures than other lavas.
G   Eruptions that occur under normal conditions rarely flow great distances.

E Analyzing Prose Summary Questions

You can also recognize Prose Summary questions from their detailed directions:

Directions: An introductory sentence for a brief summary of the passage is provided below. Complete the summary by selecting the THREE answer choices that express the most important ideas in the passage. Some sentences do not belong in the summary because they express ideas that are not presented in the passage or are minor ideas in the passage. **This question is worth 2 points.**

Below the directions you will see a sentence summarizing a key idea from the passage and space for three other sentences. You will also see a list of six answer statements, three of which also summarize a key idea from the passage. You will get 2 points for choosing all three right answers, 1 point for two right answers, and 0 points for one or zero right answers.

The three correct answers to Prose Summary questions:
- restate major ideas from the passage (sometimes by combining information from two paragraphs).
- are related to the overall main idea of the passage, which you can easily recognize from the title of the passage.

In contrast, the three incorrect answers:
- may restate a minor idea from the passage.
- may restate a point from the passage, but contradict one or more key details.
- may use words from the passage, but express an idea that is not mentioned in the passage.

E1 **Answer this Prose Summary question. Discuss your answers with a partner when you have finished.**

Portolan charts are a type of map intended for marine navigation. They were first made in Italy in the late thirteenth century, and then later in Spain and Portugal, and were in use from roughly 1275 to 1500 A.D. They differ in several ways from earlier maps. For one thing, portolans typically show specific marine regions in detail, often the coasts of the Mediterranean, Black Sea, or Atlantic Ocean, whereas many other maps showed the whole world (such maps are collectively known as *mappae mundi*) or one region, but with a focus on countries, not seas. In addition, portolans were drawn by pilots or navigators with first-hand knowledge of a region. Other maps were generally drawn by scholars who had never visited the places they were depicting. Further, portolans were designed for real-world navigation and depicted coastal features realistically as well as compass directions and, sometimes, typical wind directions. The Carta Pisana, the oldest surviving portolan, shows the Black Sea and Mediterranean coasts in enough detail that it could be used today even though it was made over 700 years ago. At the time of their creation and use, portolans provided information that was very valuable because it allowed sailors and traders to travel safely. They were so valuable, in fact, that the Spanish and Portuguese governments apparently considered them to be state secrets.

Directions: An introductory sentence for a brief summary of the passage is provided below. Complete the summary by selecting the THREE answer choices that express the most important ideas in the passage. Some sentences do not belong in the summary because they express ideas that are not presented in the passage or are minor ideas in the passage.

> **Portolan charts were a type of map intended to be used for safe sea travel.**
>
> •
>
> •
>
> •

A Portolan charts were drawn by scholars and professional map-makers.
B Individual portolan charts often show the coastlines of multiple bodies of water.
C The information shown on portolan charts was considered to be of great value.
D Old maps that depict the whole world are known as *mappae mundi*.
E Portolans include information of use to sailors such as wind directions.
F Portolan charts accurately show the features of the coasts they depict.

E2 **Complete descriptions 1–3 of the *wrong* answers from exercise E1. One answer has been done for you.**

1. Answer _____*A*_____ is wrong because it contradicts a key detail from the passage.
2. Answer _____ is wrong because it summarizes a minor idea from the passage.
3. Answer _____ is wrong because it describes a point that is not mentioned in the passage.

F Mastering Prose Summary Questions – Analyzing the Answer Choices

As with Fill in a Table questions, a key skill for answering Prose Summary questions is recognizing whether answers contradict or restate the passage. Another skill is recognizing if an answer restates a major or minor idea in the passage.

Track 5   F1 **Take notes as you listen to an experienced teacher. Then use your notes to choose the best statement, A–C, to complete the steps for answering Prose Summary questions.**

Step 1	First, skim and scan the _____
Step 2	Next, compare the _____
Step 3	Finally, re-read the _____

A   relevant section and decide if the answer choice is a major or minor idea in the passage. If it is a minor idea, eliminate this answer. If it is a major idea, choose this answer.

B   answer choice to the relevant section of the passage and decide if the answer restates or contradicts the passage. If it contradicts the passage, eliminate this answer.

C   passage to find the section that gives information about an answer choice. If you cannot find a relevant section, eliminate this answer choice.

F2 **Match each answer choice, A–E, to the correct category. Then compare answers with a partner. One answer should NOT be chosen because it describes information that is not mentioned in the passage.**

Gaius Plinius Caecilius Secundus, or Pliny the Younger, was a Roman lawyer and writer. He is famous mainly for writing a large number of letters that constitute an excellent historical record of important events in Roman history. For geographers, two of Pliny's letters written to his friend the famous Roman historian Tacitus are especially interesting because they give a detailed account of the eruption of Mount Vesuvius in the year 79 A.D. This eruption apparently caused the death of Pliny's uncle, the noted Roman writer Pliny the Elder.

In these two letters, Pliny gives a clear, detailed account of the eruption. He describes the shape, height, and color of the ash cloud formed by the eruption. He also details the fall of hot ash, pumice, and rocks blackened by heat. He describes how the ash began to pile up "like snowdrifts" and reduced visibility and made breathing difficult. He also references numerous earthquakes that followed the eruption. Pliny's account is so vivid and accurate that modern volcanologists use the term Plinian eruption to describe volcanic eruptions of this type.

Answers that restate information in the passage
•
•

Answers that contradict information in the passage
•
•

A   The eruption of Mount Vesuvius caused hot ash and heated rocks to fall to the ground.

B   Unlike his uncle, Pliny the Younger did not see the eruption of Vesuvius himself.

C   Pliny the Younger's account of the eruption was imprecise in a number of ways.

D   Pliny the Younger knew many well-known Romans including the historian Tacitus.

E   According to Pliny the Younger, people felt earthquakes after Vesuvius erupted.

F3 Decide if statements 1–8 summarize a Major point or Minor point about the following passages. Major points usually match the overall main idea (as shown by the title of the passage) and describe a general point rather than a specific detail. One answer has been done for you.

Soil Formation

Soil is formed from parent materials that are weathered, transformed, transported, and then deposited to make the soil. Parent material can be classified as residual, transported, or cumulose. Residual materials are minerals that are formed from the original bedrock. Transported materials have been moved from one place and deposited in another place by the action of water, wind, ice, or gravity. And cumulose materials are organic parent materials that have grown in place and then accumulated to form a soil.

1. Soils are formed from up to three types of parent material.   ☑ Major   ☐ Minor
2. Ice and liquid water can relocate parent materials of soil.   ☐ Major   ☐ Minor

Sedimentary Rocks

Sedimentary rocks are formed when particles of material are deposited within bodies of water, such as oceans and lakes, or at the Earth's surface. Over time, the level of deposited material builds up, and pressure from the mass of the overlying material transforms the lowest-lying sediments into solid layers of rock. Although different types of sedimentary rocks, including sandstones, limestones, shales, and conglomerates, cover a large proportion of Earth's crust, they are underlain by igneous and metamorphic rocks, and scientists generally estimate that sedimentary rocks account for less than 10% of the total volume of the crust.

3. Pressure transforms particles and sediment into rock layers.   ☐ Major   ☐ Minor
4. Sedimentary rocks form a small proportion of Earth's crust.   ☐ Major   ☐ Minor
5. Scientists have to estimate some data about sedimentary rocks.   ☐ Major   ☐ Minor

Ansel Adams

Ansel Adams was among the most important and influential American photographers of the twentieth century. He photographed a wide variety of subjects, but he is best-known for his high-contrast, wide-format black and white landscape pictures with a wide tonal range. Many of his most famous pictures, such as *The Tetons and the Snake River* and *Monolith, the Face of Half Dome*, show natural features like rock cliffs, granite domes, mountain peaks and ranges, forested river valleys and bare rock slopes, and lakes, waterfalls, rivers, and streams.

6. Ansel Adams is best known for his landscape photographs.   ☐ Major   ☐ Minor
7. Ansel Adams' photographs sometimes depict bare rock.   ☐ Major   ☐ Minor
8. Black and white photographs can have a wide range of tones.   ☐ Major   ☐ Minor

G Test Challenge

G1 Answer these Fill in a Table and Prose Summary questions. Try to finish in 12 minutes or less so as to get realistic practice for the test. Use this checklist of skills that you studied in this unit as a guide.

For Fill in a Table questions

☑ Eliminate answer choices that are not mentioned in the passage or that contradict it.

☑ Eliminate answers that paraphrase the passage but do not match any of the categories.

☑ Decide which category each of the remaining answers matches.

For Prose Summary questions

☑ Eliminate answer choices that are not mentioned in the passage or that contradict it.

☑ Decide if the remaining answers restate a major or minor idea in the passage; then choose the three major points.

TEST TACTIC

If you are not sure whether an answer choice restates a major or minor point in the passage, imagine deleting that point. If the passage still makes sense and the author's arguments are still clear, the answer probably describes a minor point.

TEST TACTIC

For Prose Summary questions, if two answer choices express opposite ideas, often one of those choices is right and one is wrong. For Fill in a Table questions, if two answers express opposite ideas, one might be right and one wrong, or the two choices might match different categories.

Glacial Inlets

The formation of glacial inlets occurs when a glacier melts and its characteristic U-shaped valley is submerged by a rise in sea level. Depending on the size and weight of the glacier that caused them, these glacial inlets may be significantly deeper than the floor of the adjacent sea, although the depth is usually less near the mouth of the inlet.

Two main types of glacial inlet are recognized by scientists, with names that come from the same linguistic root and so are extremely similar: fjords (or fiords) and fjards (fiards). Förden are a third type of glacial inlet that are found in one part of Germany and Denmark. These inlets share many characteristics, but also differ in several ways.

Fjords are typically found in mountainous areas and may have very high, steep sides. For example, the sides of Sognefjord in Norway rise vertically from the water for almost one thousand meters along parts of its length. The channel of the fjord may be relatively straight, but is more commonly winding, and often splits to form several branches, one of which is usually wider than the others. Fjords tend to be longer and narrower than fjards or förden. The longest fjord in the world, Scoresby Sund in Greenland, is over 350 kilometers in length.

Fjards are typically found in areas of lower relief and thus tend to be lower and less steep than fjords. Because of their low relief, fjards are often associated with features like salt marshes and mud flats that are not characteristic of fjords. They are usually irregular in shape and deep – though generally not as deep as fjords – with a shallow mouth.

1. **Directions:** Select the phrases that correctly describe each type of glacial inlet. One of the phrases will NOT be used. **This question is worth 3 points.**

Fjords
•
•

Fjards
•

Fjords and fjards
•
•

- Ⓐ   Inlet channels may be shallower in some parts than others.
- Ⓑ   Inlets are usually short and straight with few branches.
- Ⓒ   Inlets may occur near low-relief features like mud flats.
- Ⓓ   Channels are often steep-sided, winding, and branched.
- Ⓔ   Inlets are formed when a glacial valley is submerged.
- Ⓕ   Inlets typically occur in mountainous regions.

Naming Landforms

English has a huge number of words that either derive from or are loaned from other languages. One area of the language where this is especially true is names for natural features and landforms. Many of these words are English words originally, of course, but there are also words for landforms from languages as diverse as Arabic, Russian, Italian, Irish Gaelic, Greenlandic, and Old Norse.

There are several reasons for this inclusion in English of words from such a range of languages. Many natural features are found in some regions but not in others. English has words for features that are found in the British countryside, such as rivers, lakes, hills, mountains, cliffs, sand dunes, and so on. But to describe features that are less common or which do not occur at all, words from other languages are often used. For example, glaciers sometimes form concave depressions in mountains. These are relatively rare in England, but are common in other regions and can be called either a *cirque*, from French, a *corrie*, from Scottish Gaelic, or a *cwm*, pronounced /coom/, from Welsh. In a similar way, the names for types of lava like *a'a* and *pahoehoe* come from the Hawaiian language because these lavas are commonly found in the volcanic Hawaiian Islands.

During the period when the fields of geography and geology were becoming more scientific, these subjects were widely studied and taught in various European countries, including France, Germany, Spain, and Italy. As a result, if a scholar from one of those countries was the first to describe a landform in detail, words from that scholar's language may be used to name the landform even if it can be found in Britain. Examples include the Spanish word *cuesta* to describe a ridge with one gentle and one steep slope, the German word *dreikanter* to describe a rock shaped by wind-blown sand, and the French word *levee* to describe a natural or artificial embankment that controls river levels.

Finally, as with many academic subjects, scholars working in the Earth sciences often use classical languages to name features that are new to science, for which no local name could be determined, or which were described in classical sources. The word archipelago, meaning a chain of islands, comes from two Greek words meaning *chief* and *sea*. The name for metamorphic rocks also derives from Greek, in this case from a word meaning *to transform*, which describes the process that metamorphic rocks undergo; the names for igneous and sedimentary rocks, however, both come from Latin words that mean, respectively, *fiery* and *settling* or *sinking down*.

2. **Directions:** An introductory sentence for a brief summary of the passage is provided below. Complete the summary by selecting the THREE answer choices that express the most important ideas in the passage. Some sentences do not belong in the summary because they express ideas that are not presented in the passage or are minor ideas in the passage. **This question is worth 2 points.**

> **Many geographical landforms have names that come from languages other than English.**
>
> •
>
> •
>
> •

    ⓐ Scholars turn to ancient languages to name previously unknown landforms.

    ⓑ Mountainous regions that contain concave glacial depressions are not found in England.

    ⓒ Some names come from the European language that was first used to describe them.

    ⓓ Metamorphic rocks, whose name comes from Greek, have undergone a transformation.

    ⓔ Levees are a common feature along the banks of a number of rivers in France.

    ⓕ Names may come from a language native to the region where a landform is common.

TEST TACTIC

If you are running out of time to answer a Prose Summary question, quickly choose the three answers that are most directly related to the title of the passage and most general (rather than specific). This will often give you at least 1 point without taking much time.

Continental Drift

Looking at a map of the world, the shapes of some continents seem as if they fit together like a kind of giant puzzle. The first person to suggest in print that the continents had originally been joined and then had moved to their present locations was the Flemish map-maker and geographer Abraham Ortelius near the end of the sixteenth century. Other notables who suggested similar theories are the explorer Alexander von Humboldt, and geographer and scientist Antonio Snider-Pellegrini, both in the nineteenth century. A book by Snider-Pellegrini published in 1858 even included maps showing his impression of how the American and African continents had once been joined.

However, the idea was not taken seriously by scholars until Alfred Wegener, a German meteorologist and polar researcher, published the same idea in a 1912 article and 1915 book. Wegener's theory, which mirrored some similar, earlier theories though he developed his ideas independently, described what he termed *Kontinentalverschiebung*, which translates into English as "continental drift." In his works, in addition to noting the close 'fit' of the continents with one another, Wegener gave geological evidence. He noted that sedimentary rocks that share the same attributes are found in South America, Africa, Antarctica, India, and Australia. Wegener also noted that fossils of the same plants and reptiles could be found widely distributed over these same continental areas. Wegener argued that, when taken as a whole, his evidence strongly suggested that the current continents had once all been joined as one huge continent but had later separated and moved to their present positions on the surface of the Earth.

From the beginning, a few people accepted his ideas, but the predominant reaction was critical, with a number of influential geologists like Harold Jeffreys and George Gaylord Simpson attacking Wegener's views. In general, critics were not convinced by his evidence, which was viewed as being circumstantial rather than conclusive. Further, the forces that Wegener proposed as strong enough to move the continents – including pseudo-centrifugal force from the Earth's rotation – were calculated to be too weak to do so and no other mechanism that might be able to move continents was accepted. It has also been suggested there was bias against Wegener because he was mainly a meteorologist not a geologist and did not follow certain standard practices of the latter discipline.

By the 1950s, however, evidence from new discoveries began to change people's minds. Some rocks contain minerals like hematite that are magnetized by the Earth's magnetic field when they are formed. The polarity, strength, and orientation of the magnetism in these minerals can be used to determine when and where the rock was formed. Analysis of such minerals from rocks in India showed that they had been formed in the southern hemisphere and then moved north of the equator as Wegener had proposed. Additional paleomagnetic evidence suggested that the positions of Europe and North America, too, had changed. Then in the 1960s it became clear that the Earth was spreading apart at mid-ocean ridges where new crustal material was being formed. This process of seafloor spreading finally provided a mechanism for how continents move and proved Wegener's theory to most people's satisfaction. Sadly, Wegener died in 1930 and did not live to see his ideas widely accepted.

3. **Directions:** Select the phrases that correctly describe evidence relating to the theory of continental drift. Two of the phrases will NOT be used. **This question is worth 3 points.**

Evidence that Wegener initially presented

-
-
-

Evidence that persuaded other scientists

-
-

(A) Proof that Europe and North America had once been in the same location
(B) Information about the magnetic polarity of certain minerals in rocks
(C) Rocks found in diverse locations that share the same characteristics
(D) The way in which the shape of some continents seem to fit together well
(E) Recognition that Wegener's theories were previously suggested by other scholars
(F) The discovery that the seafloor is spreading and new crustal material is being formed
(G) Widely distributed fossilized remains from various species of organism

4. **Directions:** An introductory sentence for a brief summary of the passage is provided below. Complete the summary by selecting the THREE answer choices that express the most important ideas in the passage. Some sentences do not belong in the summary because they express ideas that are not presented in the passage or are minor ideas in the passage. **This question is worth 2 points.**

Note that in the real TOEFL Test, you will never have both a Prose Summary and Fill in a Table question about the same passage.

> **Alfred Wegener's theory of continental drift was not accepted at first but was later proved correct.**
>
> •
>
> •
>
> •

(A) New scientific discoveries in the 1950s and 1960s led to Wegener's theory being accepted.
(B) Wegener's theory was criticized because it did not adequately explain how continents move.
(C) Alfred Wegener died before his theory of continental drift was widely accepted.
(D) Wegener's ideas were put forward in two works – an article and a book.
(E) A few people wrote books in support of Wegener's theory of continental drift.
(F) Alfred Wegener provided several geological examples in support of his theory.

Next Steps

Topics related to Earth science are very common in both the TOEFL reading and listening sections, so learning more about this subject, as well as practicing key skills for Fill in a Table and Prose Summary questions, may help you increase your overall test score.

To learn more about Earth science and vocabulary related to this discipline:

1. Read an article in your language about one aspect of Earth science to get some background knowledge about this topic.
2. Read an English article about the same topic to understand the main ideas, but do not try to understand every word.
3. Read the English article again and make a list of up to ten unfamiliar words that are directly related to the topic and that you think are important. If the article is about glaciers, for example, your list might include words like *moraine* or *crevasse* but not a word like *ice*, which is a familiar word, or *process*, which is not directly related to the topic of glaciers.

To practice key skills for Fill in a Table and Prose Summary questions:

1. Choose two articles in English about the same aspect of Earth science.
2. Pick one of the articles – call this article A – and scan it to find five major points and five minor points.
3. Read article B to see if it restates the major and minor points that you noted from article A.
4. Next, look for ideas in either article A or B that are not mentioned in the other article.
5. Finally, look for points in either article A or B that are contradicted in the other article.

Directions

This reading review test is intended to help you find out your strengths and weaknesses in reading. You will have 40 minutes to read two passages and answer 25 questions (worth 28 points). The passages and questions are designed to be at the same level as the ones you will see on the TOEFL Test. When you have finished, check your answers with your instructor or against the Answer Key. Then use the conversion chart on page 90 to convert your raw score to your likely score on the TOEFL Test.

Test

Read the two passages and answer questions 1–25. You have 40 minutes.

Parasites

Parasites are organisms that have specialized adaptations allowing them to live within (as endoparasites) or on (as ectoparasites) a much larger host organism for an extended period of time. This lifestyle benefits the parasite, typically by providing it with access to something it needs, such as nutrients or other vital resources. Traditionally, all parasite infections were believed to be non-mutual in that the relationship was detrimental to the host organism. Recent research studies, however, have provided evidence that in some cases parasites may actually confer health advantages on their hosts, too. Parasites are typically classified according to their life cycle and how they interact with their hosts.

Macroparasites have two main defining characteristics. As their name suggests, they tend to be large enough to be seen with the naked eye. In addition, their life cycle involves at least two different hosts: a primary host in which they reach maturity and may reproduce, and a secondary host in which the parasites complete one or more developmental stages in their life cycle. For example, schistosomiasis is caused by several species of parasitic trematodes, a kind of flatworm. The worms reach maturity in humans, who catch the infection after being exposed to water contaminated with freshwater snails. These snails act as the secondary host for the parasite. Some macroparasites, such as tapeworms, have even more complex life cycles and must complete various developmental stages in a sequence of different hosts. And in some cases, such as with the roundworm that causes trichinosis, the host may have both mature and juvenile parasites in different internal organs, thereby functioning as both the primary and secondary host to the parasite.

In contrast with macroparasites, microparasites are too small to be seen without a microscope. In addition, they typically live out their life cycle within a single host organism, and are usually transmitted directly between hosts of the same species without going through a secondary host. The main classes of microparasites are bacteria, protozoa, and fungi, all of which are single-celled organisms, as well as viruses, which are non-cellular. The bacterium that causes salmonella poisoning, for instance, is a microparasite. Based on size, the plasmodium protozoan that causes malaria is a microparasite, yet it shares a feature of macroparasites in that it needs two hosts: a mosquito and human or other animal.

In addition to their differences in size and typical life cycle, macroparasites and microparasites cause different kinds of infections. Those resulting from macroparasites tend to be chronic and develop slowly because of the relatively long generation times – measured in weeks or even months – of those organisms. Hosts that recover from an infection rarely develop immunity to it, although this can happen if a particular host has a very high parasite burden. By contrast, infections resulting from microparasites are often acute and come on quickly because of the much shorter generation time and higher reproductive rate of these parasites. Hosts that are infected and then recover from infections by microparasites often develop protective immunity against further infections in the future.

One further class of parasitic organism is the parasitoid. These organisms share many of the characteristics of true parasites – they live on or within a host organism, for instance, and require that host to complete part of their life cycle. However, a parasitoid infection often requires the death of the host organism. The ichneumon wasp is an example. Female wasps lay eggs on or inside a host. When the eggs hatch the larva feed on the host's dying or dead body until they mature and become adults. It is true that certain parasites do sometimes cause acute infections that are fatal to their host organisms, but this is not a required part of their life cycle. Indeed, when its host dies, a parasite typically dies, too.

1. Which of the following best expresses the essential information in the highlighted sentence in paragraph 1? Incorrect choices change the meaning in important ways or leave out essential information.
   - Ⓐ Host organisms can live for an extended period when parasites have not adapted to them.
   - Ⓑ Larger organisms can typically live with parasitic organisms for longer periods of time.
   - Ⓒ Parasitic organisms have adapted to living on or inside a different organism called a host.
   - Ⓓ The special adaptations of some organisms allow them to be ectoparasites or endoparasites.

2. The word "detrimental" in paragraph 1 most likely means
   - Ⓐ communal
   - Ⓑ beneficial
   - Ⓒ detailed
   - Ⓓ harmful

3. In paragraph 2, the author states that macroparasites usually
   - Ⓐ have complex life cycles
   - Ⓑ use snails as secondary hosts
   - Ⓒ live within a host's internal organs
   - Ⓓ reach maturity in humans

4. The word "juvenile" in paragraph 2 is closest in meaning to
   - Ⓐ flexible
   - Ⓑ young
   - Ⓒ divisive
   - Ⓓ paternal

5. The author mentions all of the following about microparasites EXCEPT:
   - Ⓐ They are all single-celled organisms.
   - Ⓑ They are not visible to the naked eye.
   - Ⓒ They typically do not need a secondary host.
   - Ⓓ They mainly cause acute problems in their host.

6. Why does the author mention the plasmodium protozoan in paragraph 3?
   - Ⓐ To explain why microparasites which are bacteria, fungi, or viruses do not require two hosts
   - Ⓑ To give an example of a parasite that can live within a single host or within more than one host
   - Ⓒ To suggest that microparasites cause diseases in humans more often than macroparasites do
   - Ⓓ To demonstrate that the categories of macroparasite and microparasite are not exclusive

7. What point does the author make about parasitic infections in paragraph 4?
   - Ⓐ In general, macroparasitic infections do not affect their host rapidly.
   - Ⓑ Infections caused by microparasites often last for weeks or even longer.
   - Ⓒ Parasites with shorter generation times only rarely cause infections.
   - Ⓓ Parasitic infections are likely to be less of a problem in the future.

8. The word "immunity" in paragraph 4 is closest in meaning to
   - Ⓐ capacity
   - Ⓑ imbalance
   - Ⓒ danger
   - Ⓓ resistance

9. What does the author imply in paragraph 5?
   - Ⓐ Severe parasitic infections usually kill the host.
   - Ⓑ Parasitoids do not die when their host does.
   - Ⓒ Mature parasitoids are generally not dangerous.
   - Ⓓ All parasitoid species infect a host by laying eggs.

10. The word "their" in paragraph 5 refers to
   - Ⓐ host organisms
   - Ⓑ acute infections
   - Ⓒ certain parasites
   - Ⓓ female wasps

11. Look at the four squares (■) that indicate where the following sentence could be added to the passage.

   More than 200 million people around the world are thought to suffer from schistosomiasis, making it a disease with significant socioeconomic effects.

   Where would the sentence best fit? Choose position Ⓐ, Ⓑ, Ⓒ, or Ⓓ.

   Macroparasites have two main defining characteristics. As their name suggests, they tend to be large enough to be seen with the naked eye. In addition, their life cycle involves at least two different hosts: a primary host in which they reach maturity and may reproduce, and a secondary host in which the parasites complete one or more developmental stages in their life cycle. ▐A For example, schistosomiasis is caused by several species of parasitic trematodes, a kind of flatworm. ▐B The worms reach maturity in humans who catch the infection after being exposed to water contaminated with freshwater snails. ▐C These snails act as the secondary host for the parasite. ▐D Some macroparasites, such as tapeworms, have even more complex life cycles and must complete various developmental stages in a sequence of different hosts. And in some cases, such as with the roundworm that causes trichinosis, the host may have both mature and juvenile parasites in different internal organs, thereby functioning as both the primary and secondary host to the parasite.

12. **Directions:** Select the phrases that correctly describe each type of parasitic organism. One of the phrases will NOT be used. **This question is worth 3 points.**

Macroparasites
•
•

Microparasites
•
•

Parasitoids
•

A　Gain health benefits from their host

B　Reproduce at a rapid rate

C　Reach adulthood in their primary host

D　Have a life cycle that is often fatal to their host

E　Usually cause chronic infections in a host

F　May be one of four classes of organism

Machu Picchu

Machu Picchu is the site of a ruined Inca city in the mountains of Peru roughly 80 kilometers (50 miles) from the city of Cusco, the ancient Incan capital. Archaeologists believe Machu Picchu was built during the period when the Incan Empire was at its strongest, most likely around 1450 A.D. It is not known for certain why the site was built, but the most widely accepted theory is that Pachacuti, the ninth ruler of the Incas, had it built as a royal estate. Evidence suggests that the site was occupied by a permanent population of around 300 people, but may have housed as many as 1,000 when the emperor visited. Machu Picchu was mostly abandoned in the 1530s or 1540s during the Spanish Conquest of the Incas, though the Spanish soldiers likely did not visit or know about the site. Archaeological data suggests that a few people may have continued to occupy the site until 1572, the year when the last Incan capital city was captured.

After it was abandoned, the site was forgotten except by local people. It became widely known only in the early years of the twentieth century when American academic Hiram Bingham III discovered and reported it as part of an expedition sponsored by Yale University. Bingham's name has become closely associated with the site, though it is possible that Machu Picchu was actually rediscovered as early as the 1860s or 1870s by two Germans, businessman Augusto Berns and engineer J. M. von Hassel. At least one map dating from 1874, for example, makes reference to the site. There are also claims that two British missionaries, Thomas Payne and Stuart McNairn, climbed up to Machu Picchu five years before Bingham first visited the site.

The layout and architecture of the site follow the natural terrain of the mountain on which Machu Picchu is built, with the site divided into two sectors, a heavily-terraced agricultural sector divided into upper and lower zones in the southeastern part of the site, and an urban sector in the northeastern part. The terraces allowed more of the mountain slopes to be devoted to farming; they also helped reduce the impact of soil erosion and protect against landslides. The fields had cleverly engineered channels to provide irrigation, with the water coming from natural springs. The agricultural setup ensured that the site was self-sufficient, with scholars estimating that farmers would have been able to grow enough food to feed several times the maximum number of people who ever lived at the site.

The urban sector has roughly 200 buildings situated around a large central square. The buildings to the west of the square mostly had a ceremonial or spiritual function, while those to the east were predominantly residential. The most famous buildings at the site include the Temple of the Sun, the Temple of Three Windows, the Temple of the Condor, and the Hitching Post of the Sun, or the Intihuatana Stone. These names are the ones given by modern scholars; the original names by which the Inca knew these structures, and indeed their original purpose, are not known. The urban sector also includes palatial homes for the rich as well as simpler homes for lower-class residents, fountains, storehouses, workshops, and possibly royal tombs.

One of the most striking features of Machu Picchu is its construction. The primary building material is granite blocks cut from nearby quarries. Granite is a hard rock that is difficult to cut to exact specifications even with modern tools. The Inca clearly did not have those, or even a system of writing, yet the stones were cut to exact measurements and then fitted to other stones using a technique called *ashlar* in which no mortar, a material normally used to bind bricks or blocks of stone together, was used. Buildings constructed using ashlar are generally extremely durable, an important point because the area where Machu Picchu is located is prone to earthquakes. At the time it was constructed, the Inca did not have draft animals like horses or donkeys, and there is no evidence that they used wheeled vehicles, so it is believed that all of the stones were cut, moved, and placed by teams of hundreds of workers.

13. Why was Machu Picchu probably built?
  - Ⓐ To provide homes for 1,000 people
  - Ⓑ To defend against attacking armies
  - Ⓒ As a place where a ruler could stay
  - Ⓓ To be a capital of the Incan Empire

14. The word "abandoned" in paragraph 1 is closest in meaning to
  - Ⓐ deserted
  - Ⓑ allocated
  - Ⓒ assembled
  - Ⓓ supported

15. What point does the author NOT make in paragraph 2?
  - Ⓐ Hiram Bingham III was the first person to spread news about Machu Picchu widely.
  - Ⓑ German businessmen tried to make money from Machu Picchu in the 1870s.
  - Ⓒ For a long time the only people who knew about Machu Picchu were the ones living near it.
  - Ⓓ Evidence suggests that Hiram Bingham III was not the first person to rediscover Mach Picchu.

16. The word "terrain" in paragraph 3 is closest in meaning to
  - Ⓐ opportunity
  - Ⓑ construction
  - Ⓒ environment
  - Ⓓ settlement

17. Select the TWO answer choices that describe the functions of the terraces mentioned in paragraph 3. *To receive credit you must select two answers.*
  - Ⓐ To give protection against natural processes
  - Ⓑ To create channels for transporting water
  - Ⓒ To provide additional land for agriculture
  - Ⓓ To increase the impact of human engineering

18. Which of the following best expresses the essential information in the highlighted sentence in paragraph 3? Incorrect choices change the meaning in important ways or leave out essential information.
  - Ⓐ Farmers could grow enough food for themselves, but were not set up to grow sufficient food for the groups of scholars.
  - Ⓑ The site at Machu Picchu did not have sufficient land or agricultural resources for the estimated maximum population.
  - Ⓒ There was enough agricultural land and water to provide food for a larger population than could live at the site.
  - Ⓓ Even when the maximum population lived at the site, experts believe farmers were able to feed them several times.

19. What does the author imply in paragraph 4?
  - Ⓐ The Inca who lived at Machu Picchu built houses with many windows because the sun was important to them.
  - Ⓑ Some buildings that are called temples by modern scholars may not originally have had a religious function.
  - Ⓒ The palatial homes for rich residents of Machu Picchu are located to the west of the large central square.
  - Ⓓ Most residences in the urban sector were constructed as close as possible to the large central square.

20. The word "those" in paragraph 5 refers to
   - Ⓐ   granite blocks
   - Ⓑ   nearby quarries
   - Ⓒ   exact specifications
   - Ⓓ   modern tools

21. The word "bind" in paragraph 5 most likely means
   - Ⓐ   pressure
   - Ⓑ   occupy
   - Ⓒ   denote
   - Ⓓ   connect

22. Why does the author mention the lack of horses and donkeys in paragraph 5?
   - Ⓐ   To emphasize the impressive nature of the construction of Machu Picchu
   - Ⓑ   To suggest that the construction of Machu Picchu proceeded rather slowly
   - Ⓒ   To give an example of something that would have helped with construction
   - Ⓓ   To explain why there is no evidence that the Inca used vehicles with wheels

23. The phrase "is prone to" in paragraph 5 is closest in meaning to
   - Ⓐ   rapidly protects
   - Ⓑ   largely avoids
   - Ⓒ   hardly develops
   - Ⓓ   often experiences

24. Look at the four squares (■) that indicate where the following sentence could be added to the passage.

   These were fed by the abundant rains the site received annually, particularly between October and April.

   Where would the sentence best fit? Choose position **A**, **B**, **C**, or **D**.

   The layout and architecture of the site follow the natural terrain of the mountain on which Machu Picchu is built, with the site divided into two sectors, a heavily-terraced agricultural sector divided into upper and lower zones in the southeastern part of the site, and an urban sector in the northeastern part. **A** The terraces allowed more of the mountain slopes to be used for farming; they also helped reduce the impact of soil erosion and protect against landslides. **B** The fields had cleverly-engineered channels to provide irrigation, with the water coming from natural springs. **C** The agricultural setup ensured that the site was self-sufficient, with scholars estimating that farmers would have been able to grow enough food to feed several times the maximum number of people who ever lived at the site. **D**

25. **Directions:** An introductory sentence for a brief summary of the passage is provided below. Complete the summary by selecting the THREE answer choices that express the most important ideas in the passage. Some sentences do not belong in the summary because they express ideas that are not presented in the passage or are minor ideas in the passage. **This question is worth 2 points.**

> **Machu Picchu is an important Inca site in the mountains of Peru.**
>
> •
>
> •
>
> •

- Ⓐ An American university sponsored expeditions to discover Machu Picchu in the 1860s and 1870s.
- Ⓑ Traditional Inca building methods could not be used at Machu Picchu because of the danger of earthquakes.
- Ⓒ Machu Picchu did not become known to the wider world until the early part of the twentieth century.
- Ⓓ The site at Machu Picchu has two zones, one for food production and one for housing and other purposes.
- Ⓔ Soldiers from Spain could not attack Machu Picchu because too many people were living at the site.
- Ⓕ The methods of construction used to build Machu Picchu are impressive given the technology at the time.

Score Conversion

Check your answers to questions 1–25. Then use this conversion chart to find out your approximate reading score range on the TOEFL Test.

Raw Score (out of 28)	Probable Level	Approximate Score Range
26–28		28–30
23–25	High	25–27
20–22		22–24
18–20	Intermediate	19–21
14–17		15–18
10–13		11–14
6–9	Low	7–10
3–6		3–6
0–2		0–2

Overview

The listening section measures your ability to understand conversations and lectures spoken in English. You will see and/or hear:

• Instructions to put on your headphones	less than 1 minute
• Directions for adjusting the volume of the sound you will hear through your headphones	about 1 minute
• Directions for the listening section	about 2 minutes
• Either two conversations and four lectures with 34 questions (if you had four passages in the reading section), or three conversations and six lectures with 51 questions (if you had three passages in the reading section)	60–90 minutes

Your answers will be scored by a computer and your raw score will be converted to a scaled score from 0–30.

NOTES

- The conversations and lectures are divided into sets, with each set having one conversation and two lectures. You will have ten minutes to answer the 17 questions in each set. The clock does not count down while you are listening to the conversation and lectures.
- Each conversation lasts three minutes or longer. The speakers may be a student and a professor, or a student and a person who works at a college. The conversations are about typical issues for students, such as taking classes, using the library, or paying college fees.
- Each lecture lasts four minutes or longer. You may hear a monologue, in which only a professor speaks. You may also hear interactive lectures in which you will hear a professor plus comments and questions from one or two students. Monologues are often the first lecture in a set, and interactive lectures are often the second lecture in a set. Topics for lectures include typical subjects that students study at college.
- You may see up to eight different types of questions in the listening section, divided into three categories: basic comprehension questions, pragmatic understanding questions, and connecting information questions.
- If you have three sets (in other words, three conversations and six lectures), it is possible that the questions about one of the conversations and two of the lectures will NOT count towards your raw score. However, there is no way to know which conversation and lectures will not count, so you should answer all questions to the best of your ability.
- Most speakers in the listening section will speak with a North American accent, but you may also hear speakers from Australia, Great Britain, or New Zealand. These speakers will not have strong accents.

Detailed Guide

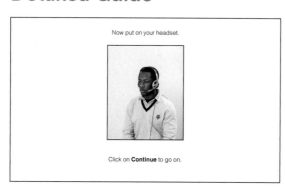

Now put on your headset.

Click on **Continue** to go on.

Before you begin the listening section you will see a screen telling you to put on your headset. You must use the headset in order to hear the conversations and lectures.

After you have put on your headphones, click on the button labeled **Continue**.

Next you will see instructions for changing the volume. Follow the instructions and adjust the volume so that you can hear the speaker clearly through your headset.

When you have set the volume at a comfortable level, click on the button labeled **Continue**. The speaker will keep repeating the message until you click this button.

When you begin the listening section of the TOEFL Test, you will first see the directions for the whole section. You will hear a narrator read the directions aloud. You can change the volume while the narrator is speaking by clicking on the **Volume** button in the top right corner of the screen.

When you are ready to begin the test, click the button marked **Continue**.

Next you will see a picture of two people on the screen, such as a student and a professor, or a student and a college librarian. A narrator will say who the people are and tell you to listen to their conversation.

The conversation will usually last at least three minutes. You will see a bar below the picture that shows how much longer the conversation will last. You may take notes while you listen to the conversation.

Usually the picture on the screen does not change during the conversation. However, in rare cases you might see a picture of a notebook with some words written on it.

After the conversation you will see a screen telling you to get ready to answer some questions. This screen will disappear automatically after a few seconds.

Then a question will appear on the screen and the narrator will read it aloud. Next the answer choices will appear. The timer will begin to count down as soon as the answer choices appear.

In total you will see five questions after each conversation. After you answer one question, the next one will appear and you will not be able to go back and change your answer to the previous question. When you have answered all five questions, the timer will stop and you will hear a lecture.

Changing the Volume

To change the volume, click on the **Volume** icon at the top of screen. The volume control will appear. Move the volume indicator to the left or to the right to change the volume.

To close the volume control, click on the Volume icon again.

You will be able to change the volume during the test if you need to.

> *You may now change the volume.*
> *When you are finished, click on Continue.*

Listening Section Directions

This section measures your ability to understand conversations and lectures in English.

The Listening section is divided into 2 separately timed parts. In each part you will listen to one conversation and two lectures. You will each conversation or lecture only **one** time.

After each conversation or lecture, you will answer some questions about it. The questions typically ask about the main idea and supporting details. Some questions ask about a speaker's purpose or attitude. Answer the questions based on what is stated or implied by the speakers.

You may take notes while you listen. You may use your notes to help you answer the questions. Your notes will **not** be scored.

If you need to change the volume while you listen, click on the **Volume** icon at the top of the screen.

In some questions, you will see this icon: 🎧 This means that you will hear, but not see, part of the question.

Some of the questions have special directions. These directions appear in a gray box on the screen.

Most questions are worth 1 point. If a question is worth more than 1 point, it will have special directions that indicate how many points you can receive.

You must answer each question. After you answer, click on **Next**. Then click on **OK** to confirm your answer and go on to the next question. After you click on **OK**, you cannot return to previous questions.

Now get ready to answer the questions.

You may use your notes to help you answer.

TOEFL Listening   VOLUME   HELP ?   OK   NEXT ➡

Question 1 of 17   HIDE TIME   00 : 09 : 46

Why does the student visit her professor?

◯ To get help with an assignment

◯ To submit a late piece of work

◯ To return a book he borrowed

◯ To explain that she will be absent

History

Before each lecture you will see a screen with the name of an academic subject, such as "History" or "Marine Biology." The narrator will then tell you to listen to a lecture from a class about this subject.

Then the screen will change and you will see a picture of a professor on the screen. The professor will speak about an academic topic, usually for at least four or five minutes but sometimes for longer. Sometimes you will hear comments or questions from a student, too. You will see a bar below the picture that shows how much longer the lecture will last.

You may take notes while you listen to the professor or other speakers.

convection

During the lecture the picture on the screen might change. If a student asks a question or makes a comment, the picture will usually show a close up of the student.

If the professor mentions an important detail, such as a name or date, you might see a picture of a chalkboard with this detail written on it. And if the professor explains a complex process or different aspects of a topic, you might see a diagram.

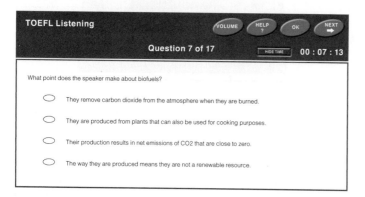

After each lecture you will see a screen telling you to get ready to answer some questions. This screen will disappear automatically after a few seconds.

Then a question will appear on the screen and the narrator will read it aloud. Next the answer choices will appear. The timer will begin to count down as soon as the answer choices appear.

In total you will see six questions after each lecture. After you answer one question, the next one will appear and you will not be able to go back and change your answer to the previous question.

When you have answered all six questions, the timer will stop and you will either hear the next lecture or see a screen telling you that this part of the listening section is finished. If you see this screen, You will have to click **Continue** to go on to the next part of the listening or the next part of the test.

TEST TACTIC

When the picture on the screen changes, it is usually a sign that the speaker is discussing a key point. So if the picture changes, concentrate hard, listen carefully, and take effective notes.

Most questions in the listening section ask you to choose one answer from four choices. To choose your answer, click on the answer or on the oval next to it. To change your answer, click on a different answer choice.

After you have chosen your answer, click on the **Next** button and then the **OK** button at the top right of the screen. After you have clicked **OK**, you will see the next question and you will not be able to go back or change your answer.

You cannot go on to the next question until you select an answer choice.

Some questions that ask you to choose one answer from four choices are replay questions. For these questions you will first see a message telling you to listen again to part of the conversation or lecture. Then you will see the picture of the speaker or speakers again and listen to part of the conversation or lecture. Next you will see a question on the screen plus an icon of some headphones. Finally you will listen again to a short part of the replayed part of the conversation or lecture. You will then see the answer choices and be able to answer the question in the normal way.

For some replay questions you will not see the picture of the speaker or speakers again, and you will only hear a replayed part of the conversation or lecture once.

Note that the time to answer questions will not count down while you listen to replayed parts of the conversation or lecture.

Some questions require you to choose two or three answers from four to six choices. These questions have special directions shown in a gray box.

To choose your answers, click on the box next to them. If you need to choose a different answer, click on the box next to an answer you have already selected to deselect it. Then click on the box next to a different answer.

You will only be able to go to the next question when you have chosen the required number of answers. If you choose too many or too few answers and then click on the **Next** and **OK** buttons, you will see a warning message.

In the lecture, the professor discusses who had the right to vote in Athens in the fifth century B.C. Indicate whether these groups had the right to vote.

Click in the correct box for each answer.		
	Yes	No
Women who were married to male citizens		✓
Male citizens who had completed military training		
Male citizens of other city states in Greece		
Foreigners who had been granted citizenship of Athens		

Some questions ask you to decide which answers match which categories. These questions also have special directions shown in a gray box.

To mark your answers, click in the correct column. A check (✓) will appear. If you wish to change an answer, click again in the same column to clear your answer and then click in another column. You can change answers as often as you wish.

For most of these questions, each answer choice matches only one category. In some cases, however, an answer choice may match two categories.

You must assign every answer to a category before you will be able to click on the **Next** and **OK** buttons.

The professor mentions the typical stages in the flight of a model rocket. Put the stages in the correct order.

Drag the answer choices to the spaces where they belong. To remove an answer choice, click on it.

1	
2	
3	Coasting flight
4	
5	

- Powered ascent
-
- Slow descent
- Ejection charge
- Lift off

Some questions ask you to put events or steps in a process in order. These questions also have special directions shown in a gray box.

To answer these questions, drag the answer choices into the correct order. If you wish to change an answer, drag a different answer into the same space, or drag the original answer away from the table. You can change answers as often as you wish.

You must assign every answer to a position before you will be able to click on the **Next** and **OK** buttons.

After you have answered all of the questions in the listening section, you will have a break for ten minutes.

TEST TACTIC

Try to use some of your time during the ten-minute break after the listening section to prepare yourself for the speaking section. For example, you could think about the steps you need to follow to answer each type of speaking question.

Scoring

Your answers for the listening section will be scored by computer. For most questions, you will get 1 point for a correct answer, but some questions may have specific directions that say they are worth 2 or 3 points.

The computer will add up all of your correct answers to get your raw score. The maximum raw score depends on how many questions you had. The maximum raw score may be 34 points (if you listened to two conversations and four lectures) or 51 questions (if you listened to three conversations and six lectures).

After your raw score has been calculated, the computer will convert it to a scaled score from 0–30. ETS does not give specific information about how your raw score is converted to a scaled score from 0–30. However, it is likely that your raw score is calculated as a percentage of the maximum raw score, and your scaled score is then calculated as the same percentage of 30 (the maximum scaled score). So, for example, if your raw score is 24 points out of a maximum of 34 points, your percentage of correct answers is 70%. This would give you a scaled score of 70% of 30, or 21 points.

This chart shows an estimate of how many answers you need to get right in order to get a scaled score of 14–30.

Percentage Correct	Raw Score out of 34	Raw Score out of 51	Scaled Score
99–100%	34	50–51	30
95–98%	32–33	48–50	29
92–94%	31–32	47–48	28
89–91%	30–31	45–46	27
85–88%	29–30	43–45	26
82–84%	28–29	42–43	25
79–81%	27–28	40–41	24
75–78%	26–27	38–40	23
72–74%	24–25	37–38	22
69–71%	23–24	35–36	21
65–68%	22–23	33–35	20
62–64%	21–22	32–33	19
59–61%	20–21	30–31	18
55–58%	19–20	28–29	17
52–54%	18	27–28	16
49–51%	17	25–26	15
45–48%	15–16	23–24	14

When you receive your score from the TOEFL Test, you will get a score report. The report will give your scaled score in listening from 0–30, your listening level (High, Intermediate, or Low), plus a short description of the typical performance of students at that level.

Here are the levels and descriptions for listening that you might see on your score report:

Level (Scaled Score)	Your Performance
High (22–30)	Test takers who receive a score at the HIGH level, as you did, typically understand conversations and lectures in English that present a wide range of listening demands. These demands can include difficult vocabulary (uncommon terms, or colloquial or figurative language), complex grammatical structures, abstract or complex ideas and/or making sense of unexpected or seemingly contradictory information. When listening to lectures and conversations like these, test takers at the HIGH level typically can: • understand main ideas and important details, whether they are stated or implied; • distinguish more important ideas from less important ones; • understand how information is being used (for example, to provide evidence for a claim or describe a step in a complex process); • recognize how pieces of information are connected (for example, in a cause-and-effect relationship); • understand many different ways that speakers use language for purposes other than to give information (for example, to emphasize a point, express agreement or disagreement, or convey intentions indirectly); and • synthesize information, even when it is not presented in sequence, and make correct inferences on the basis of that information.
Intermediate (14–21)	Test takers who receive a score at the INTERMEDIATE level, as you did, typically understand conversations and lectures in English that present a wide range of listening demands. These demands can include difficult vocabulary (uncommon terms or colloquial or figurative language), complex grammatical structures and/or abstract or complex ideas. However, lectures and conversations that require the listener to make sense of unexpected or seemingly contradictory information may present some difficulty. When listening to conversations and lectures like these, test takers at the INTERMEDIATE level typically can: • understand explicitly stated main ideas and important details, especially if they are reinforced, but may have difficulty understanding main ideas that must be inferred or important details that are not reinforced; • understand how information is being used (for example, to provide support or describe a step in a complex process); • recognize how pieces of information are connected (for example, in a cause-and-effect relationship); • understand, though perhaps not consistently, ways that speakers use language for purposes other than to give information (for example, to emphasize a point, express agreement or disagreement, or convey intentions indirectly); and • synthesize information from adjacent parts of a lecture or conversation and make correct inferences on the basis of that information, but may have difficulty synthesizing information from separate parts of a lecture or conversation.

TEST TACTIC

Some listening question types are more common than others. To improve your listening score, focus on becoming better at answering Detail questions (see Unit 9), Gist questions (Unit 8), and Making Inferences questions (Unit 14) in that order.

Low (0–13)	Test takers who receive a score at the LOW level, as you did, typically understand the main idea and some important details of conversations. However, test takers at the low level may have difficulty understanding lectures and conversations in English that involve abstract or complex ideas and recognizing the relationship between those ideas. Test takers at this level also may not understand sections of lectures and conversations that contain difficult vocabulary or complex grammatical structures. Test takers at the LOW level typically can: • understand main ideas when they are stated explicitly or marked as important, but may have difficulty understanding main ideas if they are not stated explicitly; • understand important details when they are stated explicitly or marked as important, but may have difficulty understanding details if they are not repeated or clearly marked as important, or if they are conveyed over several exchanges among different speakers; • understand ways that speakers use language to emphasize a point or to indicate agreement or disagreement, but generally only when the information is related to a central theme or is clearly marked as important; and • make connections between the key ideas in a conversation, particularly if the ideas are related to a central theme or are repeated.

Source: www.ets.org/Media/Tests/TOEFL/pdf/TOEFL_Perf_Feedback.pdf

Directions

This listening diagnostic test is intended to help you find out your strengths and weaknesses in listening. You will listen to two conversations and two lectures and answer 22 questions about them. The conversations and lectures are designed to be at the same level as the ones on the TOEFL Test. You may take notes while you listen. After each conversation, take 3.5 minutes to answer the questions. After each lecture, take 4.5 minutes to answer the questions. When you have finished, check your answers with your instructor or against the Answer Key. Then use the conversion chart on page 103 to find out your likely score on the TOEFL Test.

Test

◁)) Tracks 6–11   Listen to a conversation between a student and a university employee.

1. Why does the woman go to see the man?
    - Ⓐ   To resolve an issue with her resident advisor
    - Ⓑ   To apply for a new student identity card
    - Ⓒ   To arrange to move in with a new roommate
    - Ⓓ   To complain about issues in her residence

2. What can be inferred about the man when he says this?
    - Ⓐ   He is surprised at what the woman's resident advisor said to her.
    - Ⓑ   He thinks the woman misunderstood her resident advisor's words.
    - Ⓒ   He did not realize there was no waiting list for campus residences.
    - Ⓓ   He thinks the woman is using humor to discuss her resident advisor.

3. Listen again to part of the conversation. Why does the student say this?
    - Ⓐ   She is concerned that she might not be able to switch rooms.
    - Ⓑ   She wants the man to come with her to McMaster Residence.
    - Ⓒ   She feels that the man was not listening to her carefully.
    - Ⓓ   She thinks her explanation might have confused the man.

4. What do the speakers say about McMaster Residence? *Choose two answers.*
    - Ⓐ   Some students have had issues using their computers in the residence.
    - Ⓑ   The residence is coeducational, but individual floors are segregated by gender.
    - Ⓒ   It has a more convenient location than the woman's current residence.
    - Ⓓ   All of the students who live there share a room with a roommate.

5. How soon could the woman move into her new residence?
    - Ⓐ   By the end of the day
    - Ⓑ   Before the weekend
    - Ⓒ   After five or six days
    - Ⓓ   By the end of the year

Tracks 12–18   Listen to part of a lecture in a sports science class.

6. What does the professor mainly discuss?
    Ⓐ The reasons why runner's high affects some people but not others
    Ⓑ The origin and causes of the physical sensation called runner's high
    Ⓒ The effects of some naturally produced chemicals on runners' brains
    Ⓓ The ways in which runner's high reduces physical and psychological pain

7. The professor discusses some effects of runner's high. Indicate which of these effects he mentions.

	Yes	No
Feelings of happiness		
Improved brain activity		
Increased levels of doubt		
Reduced sensitivity to pain		

8. Listen again to part of the lecture. What does the professor imply?
    Ⓐ Non-runners can experience runner's high.
    Ⓑ Runner's high can lead to physical pain and discomfort.
    Ⓒ Certain chemicals can block the effects of runner's high.
    Ⓓ Low intensity activity can cause runner's high.

9. What point does the professor make about psychological factors?
    Ⓐ Scientists have proven that they help people achieve exercise goals.
    Ⓑ There is some doubt whether they are affected by runner's high.
    Ⓒ They are hard to evaluate scientifically because they are subjective.
    Ⓓ They are unrelated to the physical factors that runners experience.

10. What does the professor say about persistence hunting? *Choose two answers.*
    Ⓐ It still occurs among certain societies of hunter-gatherers.
    Ⓑ It reinforces traditional methods of hunting and foraging.
    Ⓒ Animals that are adapted for running often engage in it.
    Ⓓ It involves hunting prey for a long time over long distances.

11. Listen again to part of the lecture. Why does the professor say this?
    Ⓐ To indicate that the point he is about to make is not proven
    Ⓑ To suggest that nobody has a likely theory about runner's high
    Ⓒ To emphasize that scientists are still researching the topic
    Ⓓ To argue that some theories make more sense than others

Tracks 19–24   Listen to a conversation between a student and his professor.

12. What do the speakers mainly discuss?
    - (A) Ideas that the man does not understand
    - (B) Why the man has fallen behind in class
    - (C) How the man can study more effectively
    - (D) Some reading that the professor assigned

13. What does the man say about the teaching assistant?
    - (A) Her response was not very helpful.
    - (B) She is not available to see him.
    - (C) She asked him to wait a few days.
    - (D) She is worried about his work.

14. Listen again to part of the conversation. Why does the professor say this?
    - (A) She thinks the man has been studying in the wrong way.
    - (B) She is worried that the man will not accept her advice.
    - (C) She wants to encourage the man to think in a positive way.
    - (D) She does not want the man to think she is criticizing him.

15. What does the man say about his study habits? *Choose two answers.*
    - [A] He enjoys discussing ideas with others.
    - [B] He does not like to study in silence.
    - [C] He only rarely studies in the library.
    - [D] He usually prefers to learn on his own.

16. What is the student likely to do next?
    - (A) Discuss his theories with the professor
    - (B) Speak to the teaching assistant
    - (C) Start or join a study group
    - (D) Visit the campus medical center

Tracks 25–31   Listen to part of a talk in an Earth sciences class.

17. What does the professor mainly discuss?
    - (A) The development of knowledge about volcanoes
    - (B) Effects of the eruption of volcanoes on villagers
    - (C) Mexican volcanoes that erupted in the 1940s
    - (D) The chronology of the eruption of one volcano

18. The professor discusses the eruption of a volcano. Put the events in the order in which they occurred.

First	
Second	
Third	
Fourth	

    Ⓐ The eruption caused a fissure to form in a farmer's field.
    Ⓑ Volcanic material formed a cone approximately 50 meters tall.
    Ⓒ Local people heard the sounds of subterranean earthquakes.
    Ⓓ Very high clouds of ash and smoke formed in the sky.

19. What does the professor say about the eruption of Parícutin?
    Ⓐ It lasted approximately 52 years from start to finish.
    Ⓑ The first year of the eruption was the most explosive.
    Ⓒ It was more violent than 90% of other volcanoes.
    Ⓓ Its quiet phase lasted for approximately six months.

20. What can be inferred about the professor when she says this?
    Ⓐ She is surprised that airlines diverted flights to let passengers view the eruption.
    Ⓑ She imagines that airline passengers were not happy when their flights were diverted.
    Ⓒ She does not believe airline passengers would have had a good view of the eruption.
    Ⓓ She feels that airline passengers these days would not be interested in seeing an eruption.

21. What point does the professor make about the data collected about Parícutin?
    Ⓐ Data collected early in the eruption was more valuable than later data.
    Ⓑ The photographic data was especially useful as a tool for detailed analysis.
    Ⓒ The data enhanced scientific understanding of volcanoes in general.
    Ⓓ The data became helpful when scientists analyzed it with a computer.

22. What does the professor imply when she says this?
    Ⓐ Parícutin is an example of a cinder cone volcano.
    Ⓑ Scientists from around the world studied Parícutin.
    Ⓒ Scholars reached few conclusions about Parícutin.
    Ⓓ Cinder cone volcanoes are not very common.

Score Conversion

Check your answers to questions 1–22. Give yourself one point for each fully correct answer. Then use this conversion chart to find out your approximate listening score range on the TOEFL Test.

Raw Score (out of 22)	Probable Level	Approximate Score Range
20–22		28–30
18–20	High	25–27
16–18		22–24
13–16	Intermediate	18–21
10–13		14–17
7–10		10–13
4–7	Low	5–9
0–3		0–4

Unit Focus

There are seven types of listening questions in the TOEFL Test. These include gist questions, which are classified as "basic comprehension" questions. You will see two types of gist questions in the TOEFL Test: Gist-content questions ask you about the main idea of the conversation or lecture; and Gist-purpose questions ask you the reason why the speakers are having a conversation or, sometimes, why a professor mentions a particular idea during a lecture. You will see a gist question after almost every conversation or lecture, often as the first question. You will learn several key skills to answer gist questions in this unit, including:

- listening and taking notes about the main ideas of a conversation or talk.
- recognizing why the speaker or speakers are discussing a particular topic.
- analyzing answer choices to decide if they are likely or unlikely.

The vocabulary focus is on campus and academic words and phrases related to:

- doing, submitting, and getting a grade for coursework that a professor has assigned.
- biology, the study of living organisms, and related sub-disciplines like biochemistry.

A Warm-up

A1 Work with a partner to complete tasks 1–3. Spend three minutes on each task.

1. Make a list of topics that a student might discuss with a professor, a librarian, a sports coach, and a study counselor.
2. Make a list of reasons why a student might visit a tutor's office, a university cafeteria, a bookstore, and a computer lab.
3. Share your lists with another pair of students and listen to their ideas.

B Campus Vocabulary

B1 Read this article giving advice to new college students. Then answer questions 1–6 about the highlighted expressions.

Advice for New Students

Life at college can be wonderful. There are so many people to meet and things to do that it can be hard to focus on your studies. However, studying is your reason for going to college, so it is important to maintain a good grade point average (GPA) by working hard and submitting your work by the due date. If you do not understand how to do an assignment, discuss the issue with your tutor during his or her office hours. If you need more time to research and finish a term paper, your tutor might be willing to give you an extension. If there is a serious medical reason why you need additional time, you might be eligible for an incomplete, which will give you until the middle of the next semester to submit your work.

1. Which highlighted expressions mean a task that students need to complete for homework? *Choose two answers.*
2. Which highlighted expression means the date or time by which homework or coursework must be handed in?
3. Which highlighted expressions mean extra time to finish homework beyond the original deadline? *Choose two answers.*
4. Which highlighted expression means the average of all the final marks a student has received for completing college courses?
5. Which highlighted expression means a period when students do not need an appointment to speak to a professor?
6. Which highlighted expression means to read and study a subject in order to write or give a presentation about it?

C Analyzing Gist-content and Gist-purpose Questions

All gist questions focus on the gist, that is, the main idea or main purpose, of the listening, but the two types of gist questions look slightly different. Gist-content questions ask about the main subject of the conversation or lecture and usually begin with *What,* as in these examples. Gist-content questions are common after both conversations and lectures:

> What do the speakers mainly discuss?
>
> What is the main topic of the lecture?
>
> What aspect of _____ does the professor mainly discuss?

Gist-purpose questions, on the other hand, ask why the two speakers are talking or why a professor mentions a particular idea. They usually begin with *For what reason* or *Why,* as in these examples. Gist-purpose questions are common after conversations, but less common after lectures:

> For what reason does the man visit _____?
>
> Why does the student visit the _____?
>
> Why does the professor mention _____?

The correct answer to Gist-content and Gist-purpose questions usually:

- describes something that was either discussed throughout the conversation or lecture or mentioned several times.
- paraphrases information from the conversation or lecture rather than repeating the speakers' words.

In contrast, incorrect answers to both types of gist questions often:

- repeat or restate words from just one part of the conversation or lecture.
- include words from the conversation or lecture, but incorrectly summarize its main point.

> **TEST TACTIC**
>
> The main topic of conversations is often about how to solve a minor problem that the student has. When you listen, take careful notes whenever one speaker discusses a problem or a solution to a problem. Often these notes will help you answer a Gist-content or Gist-purpose question.

C1 **Read this script from a conversation between a student and her professor. Then complete tasks 1 and 2.**

Student	Professor? Could I check two things about the assignment for Biology 208? The paper should be 1,000 words and you need it next Friday, right?
Professor	No, and no. There's a term paper due at the end of the semester that needs to be 1,000 words, but this assignment should only be 500 words. And the due date is actually this Friday, not next Friday.
Student	*This* Friday? I'm not sure I can finish by then ... er, could I get an extension?
Professor	Sorry, Jodie, but no. I don't give extensions unless a student is sick and, well, you seem pretty healthy... Besides, it's only Tuesday, so you've got a few days.

1. Why did the student go to see her professor?
   A To receive an assignment
   B To confirm some information
   C To ask for an extended due date
   D To explain that she is sick

2. Underline words in the script that helped you answer question 1. Work with a partner.

C2 **Complete these descriptions of the wrong answers from exercise C1 by writing in the letter of each wrong answer.**

1. The student did not know she needed extra time before going to see her professor, so answer _____ cannot be right.
2. Answer _____ cannot be correct as the student does not mention this and because the professor says she is healthy.
3. The student asks her professor about an assignment she has already received, so answer _____ must be wrong.

D Mastering Gist-content and Gist-purpose Questions – Recognizing Topic Markers

Sometimes a speaker may use a phrase (called a topic marker) to introduce the main point of the lecture or conversation. Recognizing topic markers is a valuable skill for gist questions because after using the topic marker phrase, the speaker usually goes on to discuss the main idea in more detail.

🔊 Tracks 32–37 **D1** Listen to excerpts (short parts) from six conversations and lectures. In which excerpt, 1–6, does a speaker use each topic marker, A–F? One answer has been done for you.

Topic marker	Excerpt
A I wanted to find out…	
B I was hoping to …	1
C Let's continue our discussion of …	
D Now let's turn to …	
E Today we're going to talk about …	
F We're going to be covering …	

🔊 Tracks 32–37 **D2** Listen again to the excerpts from exercise **D1** and take notes. Then use your notes to answer questions 1–6.

1. In excerpt 1, why does the man go to see his professor?
    A To get some help with an assignment   B To submit a paper before the deadline

2. In excerpt 2, what does the professor say the main topic of the lecture will be?
    A An important molecule   B Common names in biology

3. In excerpt 3, what does the professor say she will mainly discuss?
    A How the heart, lungs, and liver differ   B The functions of internal organs

4. In excerpt 4, why does the woman talk to the man?
    A To ask for information about her grades   B To request a new student ID number

5. In excerpt 5, what does the professor say the main topic of the lecture will be?
    A Genetic material   B The cell nucleus

6. In excerpt 6, what does the professor say he will mainly discuss?
    A Different methods of reproduction   B How mammals and birds differ

E Mastering Gist-content and Gist-purpose Questions – Listening for Repeated Information

The gist of a conversation or lecture is something that the speakers discuss several times throughout the conversation or lecture. As a result, recognizing and making a note of repeated information may help you to recognize the right answer to Gist-content and Gist-purpose questions.

TEST TACTIC

Sometimes the reason why a student visits a professor and the main topic they discuss differ. For example, a student might visit his tutor to borrow a book, but their conversation might focus on an assignment, not the book. To avoid errors, listen both for topic markers and repeated information.

E1 Use these notes about a lecture to answer question 1 (a Gist-content question) and question 2 (Gist-purpose).

cell division → two types for cells with nucleus
1 meiosis for reproduction of organism
     step one – parent cell copies mixed up DNA
                 parent cell divides into two
     step two – DNA in new cells changes
                 both cell and DNA split
                 daughter cells get ½ of DNA

2 mitosis for reproduction of cells
     parent cell copies DNA in own nucleus
     parent cell divides = usually 100% copy
         errors rare

also binary fission for cells <u>without</u> nucleus
     read about bf before next week's class

1. What does the professor mainly discuss? (The answer will be something mentioned throughout the notes.)
   A   The reproduction of cells and organisms
   B   Complex changes to DNA within cells
   C   Two processes by which cells divide
   D   How parent and daughter cells differ

2. Why does the professor mention binary fission? (The answer will be mentioned in just one part of the notes.)
   A   To introduce the topic of the next class
   B   To contrast it with mitosis and meiosis
   C   To explain the process of binary fission
   D   To describe the function of a cell nucleus

Track 38   **E2**   **Take notes as you listen to a student talk with his professor. Then use your notes to answer questions 1 and 2.**

1.   How often do the speakers discuss each of these things? Put a check (✓) in the correct column.

	Once	Twice	Multiple Times
An assignment that the professor gave			
The due date of the assignment			
A recommended article			
An extension of the assignment's deadline			
A failing grade for the assignment			
A visit to the Study Skills Center			

2.   Why did the student go to see his professor? (The answer will be something the speakers discuss multiple times.)
   A   To ask her opinion of the Study Skills Center
   B   To understand why he failed an assignment
   C   To ask for extra time to complete a paper
   D   To get a suggestion for which article to read

F   Mastering Gist-content and Gist-purpose Questions – Recognizing Unlikely Answers

Sometimes an answer choice expresses an idea that is not likely to be the main idea or purpose of the conversation or lecture. If you can recognize these unlikely answers, you will find it easier to choose the correct answer to gist questions.

F1   **Check (✓) the box if you think each answer to example gist questions 1 and 2 is Likely or Unlikely. Note that you do not need to listen to anything to complete this task. One answer has been done for you.**

1. Why does the student go to see her professor?
   A   To ask the professor to do some research for her   ☐ Likely   ☑ Unlikely
   B   To ask for advice about how to write a term paper   ☐ Likely   ☐ Unlikely
   C   To discuss a difficult academic theory   ☐ Likely   ☐ Unlikely
   D   To talk about the professor's new office   ☐ Likely   ☐ Unlikely

2. What does the professor mainly discuss in the lecture?
   A   The results of an important biological experiment   ☐ Likely   ☐ Unlikely
   B   Why the government should invest in biotechnology   ☐ Likely   ☐ Unlikely
   C   The best way for students to complete an assignment   ☐ Likely   ☐ Unlikely
   D   Several important concepts in biotechnology   ☐ Likely   ☐ Unlikely

F2 Match each Unlikely answer from exercise **F1** to one of descriptive reasons 1–4. One answer has been done for you.

Reasons

1. It is unlikely a student would visit a professor in order to have a whole conversation about this topic.
2. It is unlikely that a student would ask a professor for this, and unlikely that a professor would agree to it.
3. In lectures in the TOEFL Test, professors rarely express personal views about political or social topics.
4. Professors typically give lectures to discuss academic theories, concepts, and so on, not to explain homework.

Answer A from question 1 in exercise F1 matches reason 2.

G Mastering Gist-content and Gist-purpose Questions – Analyzing the Answer Choices

The correct answer to a gist question usually paraphrases or summarizes the words that the speaker(s) use. Incorrect answers, on the other hand, often repeat words that the speaker(s) use. So being able to recognize answers that restate the listening is an important skill for answering Gist-content and Gist-purpose questions correctly.

G1 Read these partial scripts from a conversation and a lecture. Then answer questions 1 and 2 by choosing the answer choice that restates or summarizes the professor's words.

Professor	Come in, Ben. I wanted to talk to you about the paper you handed in. I'm afraid I can't give you a grade because you didn't cite the sources for your ideas.
Student	What do you mean? I included a bibliography like you requested.
Professor	There's a bibliography, yes, but you didn't say which ideas came from which sources. It's not enough just to give a list of the books you read, you also need to attribute ideas to the person who came up with them.
Student	You mean that if an idea comes from the writer of one book, I need to say that it comes from her?
Professor	Exactly ... Can you add that information and resubmit the paper by tomorrow?

1. Why did the professor ask to see the student?
   A To ask him to add a bibliography to his paper
   B To get him to explain his ideas in more detail
   C To suggest some useful sources of ideas to him
   D To have him say where his arguments came from

| Professor | Last week we discussed DNA. Today we're going to talk about another nucleic acid – ribonucleic acid, or RNA. First let's see how RNA and DNA differ. You all remember that DNA is a double helix, right? Well RNA is a single-stranded molecule not a double-stranded one. Another difference is that RNA's four bases are guanine, cytosine, and adenine, but instead of having thymine like DNA, RNA has uracil. And finally, as its name suggests, RNA contains the monosaccharide ribose rather than deoxyribose, which is in DNA. OK, so let's move on to discuss the vital roles that RNA plays within the body. |

2. What is the main purpose of this part of the talk?
   A To describe the bases that make up DNA and RNA
   B To compare two different kinds of nucleic acid
   C To talk about the vital roles of RNA in the body
   D To remind students about the structure of DNA

TEST TACTIC

The academic subject of the talk may help you decide if an answer choice is likely or unlikely. For example, the main idea of a lecture about physics might be Einstein's scientific theories, but is unlikely to be Einstein's personal relationships because those are unrelated to physics.

Track 39 **G2** **Listen to part of a lecture in a biochemistry class and choose one word from answers A–F to fill blanks 1–6 in these notes.**

```
elements → 92 natural / 25 essential for living  1.
      plants + animals need different  2.
4 elements most important → 95% of most organisms
      hydrogen, carbon, nitrogen, oxygen
      carbon in every cell → organic  3.
7 elements major importance
      phosphorus, sulfur, calcium, potassium
      sodium, magnesium, chlorine
trace elements → only need in tiny  4.
      organisms need them for  5.
      e.g., humans have 75mg of copper (less than single grain rice)
      too little →  6.                   / too much → poison
```

A amounts
B elements
C health
D heart disease
E molecules
F organisms

G3 **Use the notes from exercise G2 to answer questions 1 and 2.**

1. What does the professor mainly discuss?
    A How many and which elements exist naturally
    B Which substances are necessary for life
    C How to recognize which molecules are organic

2. Why does the professor mention copper?
    A To illustrate the importance of trace elements for health
    B To show that not every species requires every trace element
    C To define trace elements in a way students will understand

H Academic Vocabulary

H1 **Look at these partial scripts from some of the lectures you have heard in this unit. Answer questions 1–8 with a word from each script.**

Professor   Today we're going to talk about the most important molecule in biology. It's sometimes referred to as "hydrogen oxide" …

1. Which noun in the partial script above means a group of atoms that are bonded together?

Professor   We're going to be covering the functions of the major internal organs of mammals, such as the heart, lungs, and liver …

2. Which noun means body parts of plants or animals that have a specific function?

Professor   Carbon can be found in all living cells: it is, after all, the element that determines whether a molecule is organic, meaning related to life, or inorganic …

3. Which noun means the smallest units of an organism that have a structure and specific function?
4. Which noun means a substance like carbon that cannot be changed into another substance?

Professor   Let's continue our discussion of the nucleus of the cell. Last class we talked about its structure – the outer membrane, the pores, the genetic material inside it …

5. Which noun means the central part of a living cell?
6. Which adjective describes material that is related to genes and DNA?

Professor   Now let's turn to methods of reproduction that animals use. There are two basic methods – giving birth to live offspring, as almost all mammals and a few fish do …

7. Which noun means the action of producing a child?
8. Which noun means the child of a person or animal?

TEST TACTIC

Wrong answers to gist questions may be too general or specific. For example, if a lecture is about eagles, an answer that gives the main idea as birds is probably too general to be right and an answer that gives the main idea as Golden Eagles is probably too specific.

I Test Challenge

I1 Practice some Gist-content and Gist-purpose questions. While you listen, cover the questions and take notes. Then use your notes and memory to answer questions 1–6. Use this checklist of skills that you studied in this unit as a guide.

While you listen to the conversations and lectures

☑ Listen for topic marker phrases and make careful notes of what the speakers say immediately after you hear one.

☑ Take notes when you hear repeated information, especially information that is mentioned throughout the talk.

When you answer the questions

☑ Avoid answers that describe an idea that is unlikely to be the main idea or purpose of the talk.

☑ Remember that answers that repeat several words from the talk are often distractors.

🔊 Tracks 40–41 Listen to a conversation between a student and a university employee.

1. Why does the man go to see the university employee?
   - Ⓐ To ask for help with a minor medical problem
   - Ⓑ To get formal approval to miss an upcoming exam
   - Ⓒ To learn whether his exam is on Thursday or Friday
   - Ⓓ To pick up a letter about his student record

🔊 Tracks 42–43 Listen to a talk in a biology class.

K-selection
r-selection

2. What main topic does the professor discuss?
   - Ⓐ What students should study for a midterm exam
   - Ⓑ The level of parental care that species provide
   - Ⓒ Different strategies for reproductive success
   - Ⓓ Environmental selection among mammals

🔊 Tracks 44–45 Listen to part of a lecture in a history of science class.

3. What is the professor mainly discussing?
   - Ⓐ Scientific discoveries in the early twentieth century
   - Ⓑ The importance of Crick and Watson's theory
   - Ⓒ The use of X-rays to take pictures of molecules
   - Ⓓ The history of the discovery of DNA's structure

Tracks 46–47 Listen to a conversation between a student and her professor.

4. What do the two speakers mainly discuss?
   - Ⓐ The student's part-time job
   - Ⓑ The student's attitude in class
   - Ⓒ Why the student has poor grades
   - Ⓓ Ways to gain academic confidence

Tracks 48–49 Listen to part of a talk in a biotechnology class.

5. Why does the professor talk about farming?
   - Ⓐ To describe an overlooked aspect of biotechnology
   - Ⓑ To recommend a number of uses of biotechnology
   - Ⓒ To discuss successful methods biotechnologists have used
   - Ⓓ To give an example of the dangers of biotechnology

Tracks 50–51 Listen to a lecture in an introduction to biological sciences class.

6. What is the main purpose of the lecture?
   - Ⓐ To contrast the characteristics of plants and animals
   - Ⓑ To explain how living cells respond to the environment
   - Ⓒ To give a clear definition of respiration and organization
   - Ⓓ To describe the characteristics of living organisms

Next Steps

Topics related to biology are common in the listening section of the TOEFL Test. You may also have questions about this subject in the other sections of the test. As a result, learning more about biology, as well as practicing key skills for Gist-content and Gist-purpose questions, may raise your overall test score.

To learn more about biology and vocabulary related to this discipline:

1. Do an Internet search for "key concepts in biology" and choose a topic that sounds interesting from the search results.
2. Read an article about this topic just once. After reading, make a list of questions about this topic that are unclear to you.
3. Read a different article about the same topic just once. Write answers to as many of the questions on your list as you can. Then make a new list of questions that are unclear (or still unclear) to you.
4. Read other articles about the same topic until you can write answers to all of the questions on your list.
5. Review the answers that you wrote to your questions and make a list of vocabulary you used in your written answers. Study these words in detail until you are confident that you will remember the meaning and normal usage of each word.

To practice a key skill for Gist-content and Gist-purpose questions:

1. Listen once to a television or radio news broadcast, such as a story about business, politics, sports, or science.
2. Take notes as you listen. Focus on noting down information that is repeated throughout the broadcast.
3. Review your notes. Then use your notes and your memory to write a one or two-sentence summary of the broadcast. For example, if you listened to a news story about a woman who helped some people in trouble, your summary might be: *A woman helped some people escape from a burning building. Police officers said she probably saved several lives.*

Unit Focus

There are seven types of listening questions in the TOEFL Test. These include Detail questions, which are the most common question type. You will see one to three Detail questions, which are classified as "basic comprehension" questions, after each lecture and conversation. Detail questions test your comprehension of major points from the listening. For most questions you must choose one correct answer from four choices, but sometimes you will have to choose two or three correct answers from four to six choices. You will learn several key skills to answer Detail questions in this unit, including:

- listening for information in a conversation or lecture that answers a question like *who*, *where*, or *what*.
- listening for the way in which various points in a conversation or lecture are related to one another.
- recognizing and taking notes about the major points of a conversation or lecture.

The vocabulary focus is on campus and academic words and phrases related to:

- people who hold academic and administrative positions that students often meet and deal with at college.
- astronomy, the scientific study of objects in space (beyond Earth's atmosphere) and the universe as a whole.

A Warm-up

A1 **Work with a partner to complete tasks 1–3.**

1. Write four questions that ask something about astronomy or space that you would like to know. For example, you might write *How old is the universe?* or *What are stars made of?* Work together to write grammatically correct questions.
2. Listen to the questions that other students wrote. If you can answer any of their questions, share your knowledge.
3. Read your questions to other students. Take notes as you listen to their answers.

B Campus Vocabulary

B1 **Choose the best phrase from answers A–H to complete sentences 1–8. Each sentence helps you understand the meaning of one of the highlighted expressions. One answer has been done for you.**

1. Speak to your academic advisor if you need answers to academic ___questions___ such as which classes to take.
2. If you want to play college _____, the coach is the person who will decide if you are good enough and train you.
3. Visit a counselor if you are having personal _____ and want some advice about how to solve or deal with them.
4. If you ever need to speak to the person in _____ of academic matters at your college, that person is the dean.
5. All of the instructors at a college or in a particular _____ at a college are known collectively as the faculty.
6. When you attend _____ and seminars, make sure that you listen carefully to the points that the professor makes.
7. In order to find out information about your academic _____ or how to register for classes, speak to a registrar.
8. If you need help understanding a _____ that an instructor discussed in class, speak to the teaching assistant.

A charge	C lectures	E questions	G sports
B department	D problems	F record	H theory

C Analyzing Detail Questions

Detail questions ask you about major ideas that the speaker or speakers discuss in the conversation or lecture:

What does the professor say about _____?

Why did the _____ begin?

According to the woman, how was _____ formed?

Some Detail questions ask you to choose two or three correct answers from four to six choices, as in this example:

What are the effects of _____? *Choose two answers.*

The correct answer to a Detail question usually:

- describes a major idea from the conversation or lecture rather than a minor point.
- paraphrases information from the conversation or lecture rather than repeating the speakers' words.

In contrast, incorrect answers to Detail questions:

- may paraphrase or repeat words that describe a minor point from the conversation or lecture.
- sometimes use words from the conversation or lecture but describe information that was not mentioned by any speaker.
- may contradict information that a speaker mentions during the conversation or lecture.
- may restate a major or minor point from the conversation or lecture that does not answer the question.

> **TEST TACTIC**
>
> If a Detail question asks you to choose two or three answers, you cannot move on to the next question until you have chosen that many answers. As a result, it is not possible to get a question wrong because you did not notice that you needed to choose multiple answers.

C1 **Read this script from a lecture in an art history class. Then answer question 1.**

Professor   As we discussed last week, Vincent Van Gogh was fascinated, obsessed even, with depicting color on the canvas. He also went through a period where he was particularly interested in the effects of night and the nocturnal on light and color. Several of his more famous works are paintings of the night sky, including *Starry Night Over the Rhone* and *The Starry Night*. He painted the first of these by night and described it in a letter to his brother using phrases like "the aquamarine field of the sky" and "sparkling green and pink stars." Even though it was painted from life, Van Gogh used a bit of artistic license. The painting depicts the constellation Ursa Major, but in fact he was looking south when he painted it and this constellation would only have been visible to the north. Unlike *Starry Night Over the Rhone*, Van Gogh painted *The Starry Night* from memory. As such, it's not intended to be an accurate portrayal of the night sky. Despite this, some have noted that parts of the painting resemble actual features found in space such as a whirlpool galaxy or interstellar gas cloud. Van Gogh almost certainly knew nothing about these features, however, so again they should be attributed to artistic license.

1. What points does the professor make about Van Gogh? *Choose three answers.*
   A He was inspired to paint night scenes after reading letters from his brother.
   B He sometimes painted nocturnal scenes from life, sometimes from memory.
   C He used his imagination to portray the features and colors of the night sky.
   D He believed that painting images of the night sky would make him famous.
   E He painted night scenes because of his interest in how night affects colors.
   F He lived and worked in a region where the sky to the north was rarely visible.

C2 **Underline clues in the wrong answers that help you recognize why that answer is wrong. Then work with a partner to write short explanations as in this example:**

Example   The phrase "letters from his brother" is a clue because the lecture says Van Gogh sent letters to his brother, not received letters from him.

D Mastering Detail Questions – Recognizing Details as You Listen

Detail questions typically begin with words like *what, who, where, when,* and so on. As you listen to the conversations and lectures, you may notice that a speaker is talking about what happened, who did something, or where or when something began. Make a note of information like this that seems to answer a question, as it may help you answer Detail questions.

D1 Look at these example notes from a lecture and conversation. Which question, A–F, does each circled point answer?

Hubble (space telescope → orbiting Earth) since 1990
many problems before and after launch
    original plan to launch in 1983 (but delayed
    new plan to launch in 1986 (but shuttle disaster
    launched in 1990 but (mirror had wrong shape)
    astronauts had to fix mirror in space
Hubble now (produces amazing images of planets + stars)
    estimate (of $400 million wrong = actually $10 billion+)

A	How much has it cost?
B	What does it do?
C	What will somebody do?
D	What problems occurred?
E	What is it and where is it?
F	When was it given?

Woman   need extra time to do assignm about Hubble
Man   why? (Assignment set 2 weeks ago)
W   sorry but play for college softball team
         (will play in final of softball tournament
         team traveling 2 days before deadline)
         coach said must get permission from prof to play
M   understand + give permission + good luck!

🔊 Tracks 52–55 **D2** Take notes as you listen to some excerpts (short parts) from conversations and talks. Then use your notes to answer questions 1–4. To get realistic practice for the test, cover the questions and answers while you listen.

1. What information does the woman give in Excerpt 1?
   A What the man should say to the dean
   B Who the man's academic advisor is
   C How the man can attend the conference
   D Why the man is not able to see the dean

2. What does the man discuss in Excerpt 2? *Choose two answers.*
   A How gas giant planets are formed
   B What Saturn's rings are made of
   C Which planets have ring systems
   D Why Saturn's rings are well developed

3. What does the woman talk about in Excerpt 3? *Choose two answers.*
   A What happened during the Space Race
   B Which country won the Space Race
   C When and why the Space Race ended
   D What benefits the Space Race brought

4. What do the speakers discuss in Excerpt 4?
   A The purpose of the staff training session
   B Why an office on campus is currently closed
   C The time when the woman's training will finish
   D When the woman will meet the registrar

E Mastering Detail Questions – Noticing How Ideas Are Connected

Detail questions sometimes focus on how two points or ideas are related, so a key skill for detail questions is to listen for and make a note of information that explains the relationship between two ideas. To do this effectively, listen for expressions that introduce common relationships between ideas.

E1 Work with a partner to complete tasks 1 and 2.

1. Add expressions A–H to the correct column in the table. One answer has been done for you.
2. Add at least one more expression to each of the four categories.
3. Add the title "Example" to the blank column. Then add matching expressions like "such as".

Cause or Effect	Contrast	Similarity	Sequence	
The reason is … … because of …	but … … unlike … However, …	Similarly, … Another …	After that, … Then, …	

A However, …   C In the same way, …   E As a result of …   G A related point …

B Until finally, …   D To begin, …   F due to …   H Instead of …

E2 Take notes as you listen to some excerpts from conversations and talks. Then use your notes to answer questions 1–4 by checking (✓) the right box. One answer has been done for you.

1. Which relationship between ideas does the woman discuss in Excerpt 1?
   ☐ Contrast   ☑ Similarity
2. Which relationship between ideas does the woman discuss in Excerpt 2?
   ☐ Example   ☐ Cause/Effect
3. Which relationship between ideas does the man discuss in Excerpt 3?
   ☐ Similarity   ☐ Time
4. Which relationship between ideas does the speaker woman in Excerpt 4?
   ☐ Cause/Effect   ☐ Contrast

F Mastering Detail Questions – Noticing Details Mentioned as Part of a List

Some Detail questions ask you to choose two or three answers that are mentioned during a conversation or talk. These questions may ask about information that is mentioned as part of a list even though this information may describe minor points from the talk. A useful skill for Detail questions is listening and making a note of information that is mentioned as part of a list.

F1 Take notes as you listen to excerpts from a conversation and lecture. Then use your notes to answer questions 1 and 2.

1. What help can the International Student Center provide? *Choose two answers.*
   A Study guidance geared towards overseas students
   B Information about how to do assignments more quickly
   C Advice on how to make friends with other students
   D Suggestions for dealing with feelings of homesickness

2. According to the man, what is found in the vacuum of space? *Choose two answers.*
   A Particles called neutrinos
   B Atoms of hydrogen
   C High-density particles
   D Many kinds of matter

G Mastering Detail Questions – Recognizing Major and Minor Points

The majority of Detail questions ask about major details from the conversations and lectures, not minor points. So a useful skill for answering Detail questions is deciding whether information that a speaker mentions is a major or minor point.

 Tracks 52–55   **G1** **Listen again to some excerpts you have already heard. As you listen, take notes. Then use your notes to answer questions 1–4. Use the checklists to help you.**

Major points	☑	may be discussed for a period of time.
	☑	may be mentioned more than once.
	☑	are often related to the main idea of the talk.
Minor points	☑	may be important if mentioned as part of a list.
	☑	are often discussed just once and for a short time.
	☑	may be unrelated or weakly related to the main idea.

1. Which of these points from excerpt 1 is a major point, and which is a minor point?
   A The man needs to see the dean.
   B The man has an academic advisor.

2. Which of these points from excerpt 2 is a major point, and which is a minor point?
   A Several planets are surrounded by rings.
   B Planetary rings are formed of dust and ice.

3. Are these two points from excerpt 3 both major points or both minor points?
   A Government spending on the Space Race was high, but had positive benefits.
   B The Space Race was a period of competition between the US and the USSR.

4. Are these two points from excerpt 4 both major points or both minor points?
   A The woman is uncertain why the registrar's office is not open.
   B There was no sign on the door of the registrar's office.

H Mastering Detail Questions – Analyzing the Answer Choices

Most correct answers to listening questions in the TOEFL Test, including Detail questions, paraphrase what the speaker(s) say. Therefore, recognizing answers that restate words from the conversations and lectures is a key listening skill.

 Tracks 56–59   **H1** **Take notes as you listen again to some of the excerpts from conversations and lectures that you have already heard. Then use your notes to answer questions 1–4.**

1. What major point does the woman make in excerpt 1?
   A Hearing deeper sounds makes people think colors are darker.
   B Redshift changes how light moves towards or goes past objects.
   C When the wavelength of light is longer its color looks more red.

2. What does the professor say about larger optical telescopes in excerpt 2?
   A They are not an important tool for astronomers these days.
   B They have proportionally smaller lenses than other telescopes.
   C They can gather more light than smaller instruments.

3. According to excerpt 3, what happens when a star dies? *Choose two answers.*
   A After first getting smaller, a dying star gets larger.
   B During the red giant phase, carbon and helium separate.
   C The planetary nebula phase causes the star to contract.
   D In its final stages, the star will get smaller and cooler.

4. What point does the speaker make in excerpt 4?
   A Astronomers need formal training to make significant observations.
   B Simple tools and techniques can be used to do useful work in astronomy.
   C Major discoveries in astronomy require the use of costly equipment.

Tracks 56–59 **H2** **Listen again to the excerpts from exercise H1 and complete tasks 1–5. One answer has been done for you.**

1. In excerpt 1, does the woman repeat or paraphrase the words "looks more red?"
   ☐ Repeat ☑ Paraphrase

2. In excerpt 2, does the woman repeat or paraphrase the words "smaller instruments?"
   ☐ Repeat ☐ Paraphrase

3. In excerpt 3, does the man repeat or paraphrase the words "dying star?"
   ☐ Repeat ☐ Paraphrase

4. Also in excerpt 3, does the man repeat or paraphrase the words "smaller and cooler?"
   ☐ Repeat ☐ Paraphrase

5. In excerpt 4, does the woman repeat or paraphrase the words "simple tools?"
   ☐ Repeat ☐ Paraphrase

I Academic Vocabulary

I1 **Choose the correct phrase, A–H, to complete definitions 1–8 of some useful highlighted words related to astronomy. One answer has been done for you.**

1. A constellation is a group of stars that, as seen from Earth, forms a _____*pattern*_____ or shape that has meaning for humans.
2. A massive cluster of _____, planets, satellites, dust, and gas is a galaxy. The universe has billions of galaxies.
3. Gravity is the force that a heavy object, that is one with large mass, exerts on a nearby _____ with less mass.
4. Gravity causes planets to go around, or orbit, stars; it also causes stars to orbit the _____ of their galaxies.
5. Planets are bodies in space – made of _____ or gas – that orbit a star but do not shine with internal light
6. A satellite is a body in space, like a moon or _____, that orbits a larger body. Many satellites have elliptical orbits.
7. The _____ plus the planets like Earth, Mars, and Jupiter that orbit it are collectively known as the solar system.
8. Astronomers view the universe through a device known as a telescope. Many different _____ of telescopes exist.

A centers	C object	E rock	G stars
B kinds	D pattern	F spacecraft	H sun

J Test Challenge

J1 Practice answering these Detail questions. While you listen, cover the questions and take notes. Then use your notes and memory to answer questions 1–8. Use this checklist of skills that you studied in this unit as a guide.

While you listen to the conversation and lectures

☑ Listen for and make a note of information in the talks that answers questions like *who*, *where*, *how*, *what*, or *why*.

☑ Make a note when one of the speakers discusses information that explains how two ideas are connected.

☑ Listen for and make a note of major points from the talk – these are often points that are related to the main idea.

When you answer the questions

☑ Be careful of answers that describe a minor point from the talk, unless the question asks you to choose two or three answers.

☑ Remember that correct answers often paraphrase the words and phrases that you heard in the talks.

🔊 Tracks 61–63 Listen to a conversation between a student and a university employee in a Careers Office on campus.

1. What does the man want?
   Ⓐ A high-paying job for just a few weeks
   Ⓑ Information about getting a good job after graduation
   Ⓒ A part-time job on campus for a few hours each week
   Ⓓ A job that gives him a chance to travel

2. What kind of experience does the man have? *Choose two answers.*
   Ⓐ He has worked in the Housing Office.
   Ⓑ He has lived overseas for several years.
   Ⓒ He can speak more than one language.
   Ⓓ He has impressive computer skills.

🔊 Tracks 64–67 Listen to part of a talk in an astronomy class.

3. What are two characteristics of the terrestrial planets? *Choose two answers.*
   Ⓐ All four planets are close to each other in size.
   Ⓑ They are low in mass but have a high density.
   Ⓒ They are found in the outer solar system.
   Ⓓ They do not have many natural satellites.

4. What point does the professor make about Ganymede?
   Ⓐ It has more than 60 natural satellites.
   Ⓑ It is surrounded by a planetary ring system.
   Ⓒ It is like a terrestrial planet in some ways.
   Ⓓ It is located close to the planet Mercury.

5. What does the professor say about dwarf planets? *Choose two answers.*
   - [A] Before 2006 they were known by a different classification.
   - [B] They are typically 25% smaller than true planets.
   - [C] Not all astronomers agree on how to classify them.
   - [D] They orbit gas giant planets rather than the sun.
   - [E] A number of them have been discovered recently.

 Tracks 68–71 Now listen to part of a talk in an astronomy class.

Fermi paradox

6. What is the Fermi paradox?
   - (A) An important discussion about the nature of nuclear physics
   - (B) An argument among astronomers about the size of a galaxy
   - (C) An estimate of the time it would take to travel between stars
   - (D) A question about why humans have not met intelligent aliens

7. What does the professor say about Earth?
   - (A) It is similar to some planets that orbit other stars.
   - (B) It is an average planet that orbits an average star.
   - (C) It might have conditions for life that are out of the ordinary.
   - (D) It is a rare planet because multi-cellular life is common.

8. What points does the professor make about the search for intelligent life? *Choose two answers.*
   - [A] Humans are not spending enough time and money on the search.
   - [B] Humans have not been searching for intelligent life for very long.
   - [C] Humans may not be searching for the right types of evidence.
   - [D] Humans are not intelligent enough to recognize hidden evidence.

Next Steps

Topics related to astronomy are common in the listening section of the TOEFL Test. You may also have questions about this subject in the other sections of the test, especially the reading section. As a result, learning more about astronomy, as well as practicing key skills for Detail questions, may raise your overall test score.

To learn more about astronomy and vocabulary related to this discipline:

1. Choose a science fiction movie or a documentary about space or space exploration that sounds interesting to you. Make sure that the movie you choose has English subtitles.
2. While you are watching, make a note of any unfamiliar words you see in the subtitles. Pause the movie if necessary.
3. After watching, check the unfamiliar words in your dictionary. If they are related to astronomy, study them carefully.

To practice a key skill for Detail questions:

1. Listen once to a television or radio news broadcast, such as a story about space, business, politics, sports, or astronomy.
2. Take notes as you listen. Focus on taking notes about the major points of the story and how those points are connected.
3. Read a news article about the same story. Compare the details in the article with your notes. Give yourself two points for every correct detail in your notes, but take away one point for each wrong detail. Write down your final points total.
4. Repeat steps 1–3 with a different news story. Try to increase your points total each time you do this self-study activity.

Unit Focus

There are seven types of listening questions in the TOEFL Test. These include Understanding the Function of What Is Said questions, which are classified as "pragmatic understanding" questions. Function questions test if you can recognize a speaker's motivation, or reason, for saying something. The motivation will not be stated directly, so you will have to use indirect clues to choose the correct answer. You will have a Function question after most conversations and lectures. This unit will teach you several key skills to answer Function questions, including:

- listening for expressions that tell you why a speaker is talking.
- using contextual information to understand why a speaker is talking.
- evaluating answer choices and eliminating unlikely options.

The vocabulary focus is on campus and academic words and phrases related to:

- the cost of studying and living at a university in North America and other words related to students' finances.
- art, including architecture, painting, and sculpture, and art history, the study of how art has developed over time.

A Warm-up

A1 Work with a partner to complete tasks 1–3.

1. Think of an artist from your country or one whose work you admire. Tell your partner some information about this artist.
2. Listen to your partner tell you some information about an artist. Take notes as you listen.
3. Share the information that your partner told you with the rest of the class. Then listen to other students talk. Finally, tell your partner which artist interests you most and why.

B Campus Vocabulary

B1 Read this article giving financial advice to new college students. Then answer questions 1–8.

These financial tips and reminders will help you enjoy a stress-free time while you are a student here at Fillmore Tech College. First, remember you will need to pay tuition for your classes and fees for other college services. You will also need $8,000–$12,000 per year for living expenses like housing, food, transportation, utilities, entertainment, and so on. We offer various types of financial aid for students in financial need, including a limited number of scholarships: check our website for more details. Staff in the bursar's office can also help you apply for a student loan and work out a repayment schedule, or provide information about work-study programs that offer a guaranteed part-time position on campus.

1. Which word in the article means a university official whose office has responsibility for dealing with financial matters?
2. Which word means money that students have to pay to a college for general services rather than for tuition?
3. Which phrase is a general name for financial support that students can receive if they cannot afford to pay for college fully?
4. Which phrase describes additional expenses related to living at college that students have?
5. Which phrase means money that college students who need funds can borrow, but must repay later?
6. Which word means financial support that students in need can apply for, but do not need to repay later?
7. Which word means the payment that students make in order to be allowed to attend classes?
8. Which phrase describes a program that helps college students find a job working on campus?

C Analyzing Function Questions

Function questions ask why a speaker said something. Most of these questions are replay questions. This means you will listen to an excerpt (short part) of the whole conversation or lecture you have just heard. Next you will see a question on the screen. You will then hear all or part of the excerpt again. Here are some examples of the question you will see on the screen before part of the conversation or lecture is replayed:

Why does the professor say this?

Why does the woman ask this?

What does the student mean when she says this?

Some Function questions are not replay questions. These questions describe and ask about a specific part of the conversation or lecture, as in these examples:

Why does the student mention having to visit _____?

Why does the professor mention the difficulty of _____?

The correct answer to Function questions:

- describes the most likely reason why the speaker said something.
- rarely includes the same words or phrases that the speaker used.

In contrast, incorrect answers to Function questions:

- may describe an unlikely reason for the speaker to say something.
- may restate the literal meaning of the speaker's words, but not explain why he or she used those words.
- often repeat the same words or phrases that the speaker said.

TEST TACTIC

The correct answer to Function questions is usually not something a speaker expresses directly. So, for example, if a man says, "I'm late for class," the function of his words is probably to say that he must leave soon, not to say that he is late.

C1 Read this script from a conversation between a student and his professor. Then answer questions 1 and 2.

Student	Do you have a minute, Professor? I wanted to ask you about our seminar last Monday. I didn't really understand the argument you made about vanishing points.
Professor	Well, I guess I can explain again, but I'm curious why you didn't ask me in class. I can appreciate your not wanting to interrupt a lecture, but the whole purpose of a seminar is to discuss ideas and clear up things you don't understand.
Student	I thought I understood it in class, but then I did some of the reading you assigned, and realized that actually I had the wrong idea.
Professor	OK, now I get why you didn't ask me before. I'll gladly help you, but I've got an appointment in a few minutes, so could you come back at 12 o'clock?
Student	Oh, actually, today's Wednesday, isn't it? I was going to attend Professor Cheung's talk on Chinese narrative paintings at 12, so could I come see you after that?
Professor	Oh, right, the talk is today. I'm going as well, so seeing you after would be ideal.

1. What does the professor mean when she says the highlighted words?
   A She thinks the student does not know the difference between seminars and lectures.
   B She does not want the student to interrupt either lectures or seminars with questions.
   C She appreciates the student's interest in asking questions and discussing the subject.
   D She suggests that the student should have asked for clarification during the class.

2. Why does the student say the highlighted words?
   A To ask the professor what day it is
   B To suggest he had forgotten a plan
   C To tell the professor his daily schedule
   D To remind the professor about a talk

D Mastering Function Questions – Listening for Functional Expressions

Sometimes a speaker will use an expression that helps you understand why he or she is speaking. For instance, if a speaker says, "the reason is that" or "because," it is clear that he or she is giving a reason for something. Recognizing these and other functional expressions and taking notes when you hear them are both key skills for Function questions.

◁))) Track 72   **D1** **Take notes as you listen to an experienced teacher talk about Function questions. Then use your notes and memory to put answers A–F in the order the teacher says them. The first answer has been done for you.**

Common Function	Functional Expressions
1. give an example	
2.	
3.	
4.	
5.	
6	

A clarify information
B compare or contrast
C define something
D give a reason
E give an example
F give some advice

◁))) Track 72   **D2** **Complete tasks 1 and 2.**

1. Use your notes and memory to add the example functional expressions the teacher mentions to the table in exercise **D1**.
2. Listen again to the experienced teacher's talk and correct your answers to task 1.

◁))) Tracks 73–78   **D3** **Listen to some excerpts from conversations and lectures. After each excerpt, add the functional expression you hear to the table in exercise D1.**

D4 **Work with a partner to think of other functional expressions that match each common function listed in exercise D1. Add the expressions to the table. Then share your ideas with other students.**

E Mastering Function Questions – Recognizing the Function from Context

The context, or situation, in which a speaker is talking can also help you recognize the function of his or her words. The context may be the main idea of the whole conversation or lecture, information a speaker has just mentioned, or even the academic subject the lecture is about.

E1 **Add at least three of the functions from exercise D1 that you think are likely functions a speaker would have in contexts 1-4. Then discuss your ideas with a partner. One answer has been done for you.**

Context	Likely Functions
1. A university employee tells a student how to get financial aid.	clarify information, give a reason, give some advice
2. A professor discusses art movements in the twentieth century.	
3. A professor talks about the influence of the Bauhaus school.	
4. A professor explains how to recognize Islamic and Buddhist art.	

◀) Tracks 79–82 **E2** **Listen to excerpts from two conversations and two lectures. After each excerpt, use the context to help you decide what the speaker is likely to do next. Then discuss your answers with a partner. One question has been answered for you.**

1. Listen to part of a conversation in a college library. What is the man likely to do next?
   - A Advise the woman not to study at cafés in town in the future ☐ Likely ☑ Unlikely
   - B Tell the woman she has to buy a replacement copy of the lost book ☑ Likely ☐ Unlikely
   - C Suggest that the woman telephone the café where she lost the book ☑ Likely ☐ Unlikely

2. Listen to part of a lecture in an art history class. What is the woman likely to do next?
   - A Describe other paintings like *The Night Watch* that are known to be by Rembrandt ☐ Likely ☐ Unlikely
   - B Explain what terms to use when a work cannot definitely be attributed to an artist ☐ Likely ☐ Unlikely
   - C Discuss how Rembrandt and other artists created their most famous paintings ☐ Likely ☐ Unlikely

3. Listen to part of a conversation in a finance office. What is the woman likely to do next?
   - A Talk about other financial aid options the man has ☐ Likely ☐ Unlikely
   - B Explain why the student was not eligible to apply ☐ Likely ☐ Unlikely
   - C Ask the student to describe his academic record ☐ Likely ☐ Unlikely

4. Listen to part of a lecture in a geology class. What is the professor likely to do next?
   - A Discuss different artists who used lapis lazuli ☐ Likely ☐ Unlikely
   - B Compare natural and artificial paint colors ☐ Likely ☐ Unlikely
   - C Talk about ways lapis lazuli is used these days ☐ Likely ☐ Unlikely

◀) Tracks 83–86 **E3** **Listen to longer excerpts from the conversations and lectures in exercise E2. Take notes and decide whether answer A, B, or C, is the correct answer to each question in that exercise.**

F Mastering Function Questions – Recognizing Why a Speaker Says Something

Listening to the words a speaker uses and thinking about the context can help you understand a speaker's reason for saying something. To do this more effectively, ask yourself questions as you listen, such as *Why is the speaker saying this?* or *What does the speaker want the listener(s) to understand?*

◀) Tracks 87–90 **F1** **Listen to excerpts from two conversations and two lectures. As you listen to each excerpt, think about why the speaker is talking and what he or she wants the listener(s) to understand. Then answer the question.**

1. Listen to excerpt 1. What does the man mean?
   - A He is sorry for missing an important deadline.
   - B It is too late to submit a financial aid application.

2. Listen to excerpt 2. Why does the woman say this?
   - A To explain why she lives on campus
   - B To recommend living off-campus

3. Listen to excerpt 3. Why does the man say this?
   - A To give examples of well-known buildings
   - B To contrast two meanings of a particular term

4. Listen to excerpt 4. Why does the woman say this?
   - A To encourage students to attend an event
   - B To compare the works of several famous artists

🔊 Tracks 91–94 **F2** **Listen to some excerpts from different conversations and lectures. As you listen, think about why the speaker is saying this and what he or she wants the listener(s) to understand. Then write down your ideas. One answer has been done for you.**

1. Listen to excerpt 1. Why does the man ask this? _____ *to clarify information*
2. Listen to excerpt 2. Why does the woman say this?_____
3. Listen to excerpt 3. Why does the woman say this?_____
4. Listen to excerpt 4. Why does the man say this?_____

🔊 Tracks 95–98 **F3** **Listen to longer versions of the conversations and lectures from exercise F2. Take notes and check your answers to that exercise.**

G Mastering Function Questions – Evaluating the Answer Choices

A key skill for Function questions is to recognize common reasons why answer choices are wrong. If you can recognize these reasons, you can avoid choosing incorrect answers. Another key skill is using common sense to decide if an answer choice is likely or unlikely to be correct.

🔊 Tracks 99–105 **G1** **Listen to excerpts from a conversation and two lectures. Then mark each answer as Correct or Incorrect. One answer has been done for you.**

Listen to a conversation in the Finance Office.

1. Listen again to part of the conversation. What does the man mean?
   A He does not like the words the woman uses.   ☐ Correct ☑ Incorrect
   B His grades are not as good as he would like.   ☑ Correct ☐ Incorrect
   C He would rather apply for a part-time job.   ☐ Correct ☑ Incorrect

Listen to part of a discussion in an art history seminar.

2. Why does the speaker talk about the meanings of the name of the painting?
   A To give additional supporting evidence for his point of view   ☐ Correct ☐ Incorrect
   B To suggest that students should study Italian and French   ☐ Correct ☐ Incorrect
   C To help students understand which painting he is discussing   ☐ Correct ☐ Incorrect

Listen to part of a lecture about Chinese art.

3. Listen again to part of the lecture. Why does the woman say this?
   A To suggest that bamboo represents the summer   ☐ Correct ☐ Incorrect
   B To contrast how quickly bamboo and other plants grow   ☐ Correct ☐ Incorrect
   C To explain why bamboo is both strong and flexible   ☐ Correct ☐ Incorrect

4. Listen again to part of the lecture. What does the woman mean?
   A People are usually surprised when plum blossoms appear.   ☐ Correct ☐ Incorrect
   B During winter, people look forward to the arrival of spring. ☐ Correct ☐ Incorrect
   C Cold weather and snow cause plum trees to produce blossoms.   ☐ Correct ☐ Incorrect

🔊 Tracks 106–111 **G2** **First decide if the answers to questions 1–3 are likely or unlikely. Then listen to three excerpts and choose the right answer to each question.**

1. What reason does the student have for saying this to her professor?
   A To motivate her professor to give her more information
   B To tell her professor to read a particular book
   C To ask her professor for more information about a topic

2. What reason does the professor have for saying this to his students?
   A To define the meaning of an unfamiliar expression
   B To say something interesting to prevent boredom
   C To contrast aspects of two different cultures

3. What reason does the professor have for saying this to her student?
   A She wants the students to study the topic more after class.
   B She needs to clarify the meaning of a question before answering it.
   C She feels she should apologize for not speaking more clearly.

H Academic Vocabulary

H1 Choose the best highlighted word from definitions A–H to complete descriptions of three famous artworks. One answer has been done for you.

This work, part of the cave paintings at the famous Lascaux Caves in southwestern France, shows a typical scene of horses, deer, and cattle. The animals are painted in mineral 1. ___pigments___ like red and yellow ochre as well as 2. _____. The cave art at Lascaux is believed to have been painted more than 17,000 years ago.

Da Vinci's *Mona Lisa* is arguably the most famous example of a painting in the portraiture genre. It was most likely painted between 1503 and 1506 during the 3. _____. The 4. _____ was painted in oil on a wooden panel and is believed to be an image of Lisa Gherardini, the wife of a Tuscan merchant.

Monet's *Impression, Sunrise* painted in oil on 5. _____ in the year 1872 is a 6. _____ painting of the harbor at Le Havre in northern France. The small ship in the 7. _____ contrasts with the expanse of sea and sky painted in the loose brush strokes typical of Impressionism. Indeed, the Impressionist 8. _____ was named for this work.

A A canvas is a piece of stretched fabric – usually linen or cotton – on which artists paint using oil or acrylic paints.

B In art, charcoal can refer either to a black or dark gray form of carbon used for drawing, or a drawing done in charcoal.

C The foreground is the part of a painting, photograph, or view that appears closest to the observer.

D A painting or other work of art that shows a wide view of a natural scene is called a landscape.

E A style of art adopted by a group of artists who agree on certain artistic principles is called a movement.

F Pigments are substances that can be added to a liquid such as ink or paint to give it color.

G A portrait is a work of art such as a painting or photograph that focuses on the subject's face.

H The Renaissance was a movement in Europe from the fourteenth to seventeenth centuries marked by cultural and artistic changes.

I Test Challenge

I1 Practice some Understanding the Function of What Is Said questions. While you listen, cover the questions and take notes. Then use your notes and memory to answer questions 1–6. Use this checklist of skills that you studied in this unit as a guide.

While you listen to the conversation and lectures

☑ Listen for functional expressions like "for example" or "in my view" that tell you a speaker's reason for speaking.

☑ Ask yourself questions while you listen such as *Why is she saying this?* to better understand the speaker's motivation.

When you answer the questions

☑ Remember that wrong answers often repeat a speaker's words or paraphrase the literal meaning of his or her words.

☑ Use common sense to judge which answers are likely based on the context of the talk and based on real life.

TEST TACTIC

Many Function questions have answers that begin with infinitives (e.g., "to explain" or "to describe"). In some cases you can quickly eliminate an answer because it has an infinitive that obviously does not match the conversation or lecture.

Tracks 112–114 Listen to a conversation between a student and his professor.

1. Listen again to part of the conversation. What does the professor mean when she says this?
   - (A) The student's behavior is likely to cause trouble.
   - (B) The student has missed the deadline to cancel.
   - (C) It is a shame the student will not be able to help.
   - (D) The art show will be successful without his help.

2. Listen again to part of the conversation. Why does the professor say this?
   - (A) To describe the organization of the committee to the man
   - (B) To explain why she cannot guarantee a job for the man yet
   - (C) To clarify some important information the man did not know
   - (D) To imply that she needs help dealing with the committee

Tracks 115–117 Listen to part of a lecture in an art history class.

3. Listen again to part of the lecture. Why does the professor say this?
   - (A) To remind students they should read their course books before class
   - (B) To imply the names of the Group of Seven members are unimportant
   - (C) To let students know they do not need to copy down all of the names
   - (D) To encourage students to listen to his views more carefully

4. Listen again to part of the lecture. Why does the professor say this?
   - (A) To emphasize the typical subject of Group of Seven paintings
   - (B) To explain why most Group of Seven paintings show Algonquin Park
   - (C) To give an example of a typical painting by the Group of Seven
   - (D) To suggest Algonquin School is a better name than Group of Seven

Tracks 118–120 Listen to part of a talk in a paleontology class. The professor is discussing prehistoric art.

5. Listen again to part of the lecture. What does the woman mean?
   - Ⓐ Most caves have images of human figures as well as predators.
   - Ⓑ She is shocked that images of predatory animals were painted.
   - Ⓒ There is no such thing as a typical prehistoric cave painting.
   - Ⓓ Caves with prehistoric art rarely have paintings of predators.

6. Why does the professor discuss DNA analysis of horse bones and teeth?
   - Ⓐ To prove that the majority of artists at Chauvet Cave were female
   - Ⓑ To support the argument that cave artists painted actual animals
   - Ⓒ To explain why horses are painted more often than other animals
   - Ⓓ To demonstrate that scientific analysis can explain artistic techniques

Next Steps

Topics related to art and art history are common in the TOEFL Test, especially in the reading and listening sections. As a result, learning more about these subjects, as well as practicing key skills for Understanding the Function of What Is Said questions, may raise your overall test score.

To learn more about art and art history and vocabulary related to these disciplines, create some word chains:

1. Think of a basic word you know that is related to art or art history. For example, you might choose the word "paint."
2. Write the word at the top of a piece of paper. Also write its definition and its part of speech, such as noun or verb.
3. Think of a word that is connected to the previous word in the chain. For example, a word connected to "paint" might be "brush." (If you cannot think of a word connected to the previous word, do some research.)
4. Write this new word on the paper below the previous word. Include its definition and grammar information, too.
5. Repeat steps 3 and 4 until you have filled up the paper. If you do this every day, you will soon build your vocabulary.

To practice key skills for Understanding the Function of What Is Said questions:

1. Choose a short article or advertisement in a newspaper or magazine and try to understand the function of each sentence. For example, is the writer trying to express an opinion, suggest an action, give an example, or something else?
2. Repeat step 1 with different texts until you are confident you can recognize the function of most written sentences.
3. Watch a movie in English and pause it every few minutes. Think about what the speaker has just said and try to understand the function of his or her words.
4. Repeat step 3 with different movies until you are confident you can recognize the function of most spoken sentences.
5. Listen to academic lectures about art or another subject. You can find free lectures using the Internet. Pause the lecture every few minutes. Think about what the speaker has just said and think about the function of his or her words.

Unit Focus

There are seven types of listening questions in the TOEFL Test. These include Understanding the Speaker's Attitude questions, which are classified as "pragmatic understanding" questions. Attitude questions test how well you can recognize the opinion, attitude, or feelings of a speaker from his or her words and tone of voice. You will see several Attitude questions when you take the TOEFL Test, though you will probably not have one after every conversation or lecture. You will learn several key skills to answer Attitude questions in this unit, including:

- recognizing whether a speaker's tone of voice is positive or negative.
- recognizing and taking notes on directly and indirectly stated opinions and preferences.
- listening for and taking notes when a speaker discusses the opinion of somebody else.

The vocabulary focus is on campus and academic words and phrases related to:

- choosing which classes to take, and attending required and optional classes.
- literature, the study of written works that have artistic value including novels, short stories, poems, and dramas.

A Warm-up

A1 First add two emotions to this list. Then write down as many situations as possible in which you might feel emotions 1–8. Work with a partner. When you have finished, share your list with other students.

1. anxious
2. apologetic
3. disappointed
4. doubtful
5. interested
6. optimistic
7. _your idea_
8. _your idea_

A2 Complete sentences 1–4 using words from exercise **A1** or other words you know that describe how people feel. When you have finished, share your answers with other students and listen to their answers.

1. Last time I bought something expensive I felt _____ because _____
2. When I have to do homework I usually feel _____ because _____
3. Next time I take the TOEFL Test I think I will feel _____ because _____
4. If they have to talk in public, a lot of students feel _____ because _____

B Campus Vocabulary

B1 Choose the best word from choices A–H to complete definitions 1–8. Use a dictionary to check the meaning of any unfamiliar words.

1. The academic subject that a student at university chooses to specialize in studying is called a(n) _____.
2. A(n) _____ is an academic field that college students study which requires taking fewer courses than a major.
3. To get a degree, students must take a number of required _____ in subjects like English, math, and science.
4. Unlike core classes, which are compulsory, _____ classes are ones that students can choose to take.
5. Some classes have _____ courses which students must take before they can enroll in those specific classes.
6. _____ are classes for a small number of students who are expected to share ideas and participate actively.

7. When students pass a class they receive a certain number of _____ that are needed in order to graduate.

8. To _____ a class means to attend lectures, but not to do assignments, take exams, or receive credits.

A audit	C credits	E major	G prerequisite
B core classes	D elective	F minor	H seminars

C Analyzing Attitude Questions

Attitude questions typically ask about the opinion, attitude, or feelings of a speaker as in the examples below.

What is the student's opinion about _____?

How does the student feel about _____?

What can be inferred about the professor's attitude towards _____?

What point of view does the professor express about _____?

A few Attitude questions are replay questions, meaning you will hear an excerpt (short part) of the conversation or lecture again. In rare cases, an Attitude question may ask how certain a speaker is about something.

The correct answer to an Attitude question:

- may paraphrase an opinion that a speaker mentions directly.
- may summarize an opinion that a speaker expresses indirectly.
- matches a speaker's intonation – positive opinion for a positive tone of voice, for example.

In contrast, incorrect answers to Attitude questions may:

- repeat some of the words that a speaker used but not summarize or paraphrase his or her opinion.
- describe an opinion that is expressed by a person other than the person the question mentions.
- refer to a speaker's attitude towards a different idea than the one that the question asks about.

TEST TACTIC

Speakers may express opinions and feelings either directly or indirectly. Attitudes may be expressed directly, too, but it is more common for them to be expressed using indirect language or through a speaker's tone of voice.

C1 **Use these scripts from a conversation and a lecture to answer questions 1 and 2.**

Student	Excuse me, Professor? I really appreciate your agreeing to let me audit your modern poetry class, but I've decided not to audit the class after all. I'm taking a lot of credits this semester as it is, you see, and I don't want to overstretch myself.
Professor	I see. Well, it sounds like you've made the decision for a good reason.
Student	Thanks, Professor. I thought you might be mad at me for changing my mind.

1. How did the student feel before visiting his professor?
   A Concerned
   B Agreeable
   C Reasonable
   D Sorrowful

Professor	I'd like to continue our discussion of classic English novels by talking about one of my favorite books, *The History of Tom Jones, a Foundling* by English novelist Henry Fielding. It's told in the first person, which gives it an immediacy that is still fresh even though it was published in 1749. It's a picaresque novel, so it doesn't have much of a plot compared to modern novels, but it's an exciting work that tells of the amusing adventures of the main character – named Tom Jones, obviously.

2. What is the professor's opinion of the novel *Tom Jones*?
   A She feels it is not as enjoyable as modern novels because it has no plot.
   B She believes that certain aspects of the story are too obvious.
   C She thinks it is an enjoyable work with several positive qualities.
   D She considers it to be a humorous story that is no longer popular.

D Mastering Attitude Questions – Recognizing Positive and Negative Intonation

A speaker's tone of voice can help you understand his or her opinion, attitude, or feelings about something. As a result, listening for and taking notes when a speaker uses positive or negative intonation is a key skill that can help you answer Understanding the Speaker's Attitude questions.

Tracks 121–122 **D1** Follow the notes below as you listen to excerpts from a conversation and a lecture. Circle and label the notes when you hear a speaker use either positive or negative intonation. One example has been done for you.

Woman	Modern *positive* (poetry seminar sounds good) → want take next semester
	Not taken prerequisite class
	Researched modern poetry in high school + will major in literature
	Want permission to take the class
Man	Not possible to take seminar without prerequisite
	Students without prereq have difficult time no permission
	Woman can audit class if she wants
Woman	Not thought about audit but good idea → thanks

Plot devices → situation / event / object / character moves story forward
    Necessary and found in every story BUT can be too obvious and not believable
Deus ex machina (DEM) = plot device with bad reputation
    Miraculous event that saves lives of protagonists e.g., arrival of hero
    DEM often criticized because not believable / natural / creative
    May be accepted by readers (or not noticed) if DEM follows from story
    Rescue of children in Lord of the Flies is natural example of DEM

Tracks 123–126 **D2** Listen to some excerpts from conversations and lectures. Does each speaker use positive or negative intonation?

1. Speaker 1   ☐ Positive   ☐ Negative
2. Speaker 2   ☐ Positive   ☐ Negative
3. Speaker 3   ☐ Positive   ☐ Negative
4. Speaker 4   ☐ Positive   ☐ Negative

Tracks 127–128 **D3** Listen to an excerpt from a conversation and lecture. As you listen, take notes about the speakers' intonation. After the first excerpt, answer questions 1 and 2. After the second excerpt, answer questions 3 and 4.

1. In excerpt 1, what is the professor's attitude to the student's question?
   A Disappointed
   B Apologetic

2. In excerpt 1, how does the student sound at the end of the conversation?
   A Confused
   B Surprised

3. In excerpt 2, how does the professor sound when he first mentions *Animal Farm*?
   A Critical
   B Interested

4. In excerpt 2, how does the professor sound at the end of the lecture?
   A Frustrated
   B Enthusiastic

E Mastering Attitude Questions – Recognizing Directly-Stated Opinions

In conversations and lectures in the TOEFL Test, speakers sometimes directly state their opinions or preferences about a subject. It is important to recognize and take accurate notes when a speaker expresses an opinion or preference because these notes may help you choose the correct answer to Attitude questions.

 Tracks 129–134 **E1** **Listen to six speakers use common expressions to state their feelings directly. As you listen, put a check (✓) in the column to show who uses each expression. Note that speakers 4 and 6 use two expressions. One answer has been done for you.**

	Speaker 1	Speaker 2	Speaker 3	Speaker 4	Speaker 5	Speaker 6
1. It seems to me that ...						
2. For me, ...						
3. My view is that ...						
4. From my point of view, ...						
5. My preference is for ...	✓					
6. In my experience, ...						
7. I'd say that ...						
8. I'm convinced that ...						

E2 **Make a list of other common expressions for stating your opinion or preference. Work with a partner. When you have finished, share your ideas with other students.**

 Tracks 135–136 **E3** **Listen to an excerpt from a conversation and lecture and take notes about opinions that the speakers express. Then use your notes and memory to answer questions 1–5. Choose the answers that restate the speakers' opinions.**

1. In excerpt 1, what is the professor's opinion of the student?
   A She would be successful if she decided to focus on literature.
   B She has recently begun to ask excellent questions in class.
   C She needs to participate more actively during lessons.

2. In excerpt 1, what is the student's attitude when the professor gives his opinion about her ability?
   A She is disappointed.
   B She is overjoyed.
   C She is surprised.

3. In excerpt 1, what is the professor's opinion of the student's essay?
   A It has both good points and bad points.
   B It is well organized but not long enough.
   C It deserves a higher grade than a B minus.

4. In excerpt 2, what is the professor's opinion about the *Satyricon* and *Golden Ass*?
   A They should not be classified as novels.
   B The works are very different from each other.
   C The works are shorter than other novels.

5. In excerpt 2, what is the professor's opinion about the novel *Don Quixote*?
   A It differs from modern picaresque novels.
   B It is an interesting, influential work.
   C It is the best book ever written.

F Mastering Attitude Questions – Recognizing Implied Opinions

In some conversations and lectures speakers imply their opinions rather than stating them directly. It is important both to recognize opinions that are mentioned indirectly and to take accurate notes when you hear one because some Attitude questions ask about indirectly-expressed opinions.

F1 Use the underlined phrases in this partial script to answer question 1.

Professor	I wanted to talk to you about our seminar class. <u>At the beginning of the semester your assignments were great, and you participated actively and made some great points in class, and, well, I was wondering what's changed.</u>
Student	I'm sorry, Professor. I had to start doing a part-time job about a month ago, and since then I've been tired all the time and it's been much harder to make time to prepare adequately for class and do the assignments.
Professor	I had a feeling it was something like that. <u>Look, I don't want to worry you, but this is a core class and unless you can find a better way to balance your time, you might have to take this class again next semester.</u>

1. What two opinions does the professor express indirectly? *Choose two answers.*
   A The student should find a full-time job not a part-time one.
   B There is a chance that the student might fail the class.
   C The student's participation has not been good recently.
   D The student makes good choices about balancing her time.

TEST TACTIC

Sometimes a speaker's words and tone of voice might contradict each other. For example, a speaker might say, "Well, that's just great," but use a tone of voice that indicates frustration. In general, tone of voice is more likely to indicate a speaker's true feelings.

F2 Use this partial script from an academic lecture to answer question 1. Then underline the words and phrases that helped you choose the answers. Compare your ideas with a partner when you have finished.

Professor	Epic poems, such as Homer's *Odyssey* and *Iliad* and Virgil's *Aeneid*, are long narrative poems that tell of heroic deeds. Classical epics share five conventions, but before I discuss them, let me clarify a couple of points. You'll see complicated lists of additional characteristics in some of the articles on your reading list, but the five conventions are the core of what defines an epic. Also, my focus is on Greek and Latin epics, so you won't be able to apply all of these ideas to epics in other languages, such as Sumerian or Akkadian epics like *Gilgamesh* or Sanskrit epics like *Mahabharata*, OK?

1. What two opinions does the speaker express indirectly? *Choose two answers.*
   A Not all epic poems are narrative poems that tell heroic stories.
   B Some scholars give a complicated definition of epic poems.
   C Epic poems in Greek are better than epics in other languages.
   D Not all epic poems share the same set of conventions.

 Tracks 137–138 **F3** Listen to an excerpt from a conversation and a lecture. As you listen, take notes about the opinions that the speakers imply. Then use your notes and memory to answer questions 1 and 2.

1. What two opinions does the woman express indirectly in excerpt 1? *Choose two answers.*
   A The man should speak to his professor about the situation.
   B The problem will permanently affect the man's academic record.
   C The man's professor has not filled out records for the class.

2. What two opinions does the man express indirectly in excerpt 2? *Choose two answers.*
   A The *kigo*, or seasonal reference, in haiku poems is usually not a poetic phrase.
   B Syllables in English do not always match syllables in Japanese.
   C The concept of a *kireji*, or cutting word, may not be clear to listeners.

G Mastering Attitude Questions – Recognizing Different People's Opinions

In some conversations and lectures, two different speakers express opinions, or one speaker mentions the opinions of other people as well as his or her own point of view. Attitude questions may ask about the opinions of various people, not just the speaker, so being able to recognize which person holds which opinion is a key skill for these questions.

 Tracks 139–140

G1 **Listen to excerpts from two lectures. As you listen, take notes about opinions that the speakers discuss and about who holds those opinions. Then use your notes and memory to answer questions 1 and 2.**

1. Listen to excerpt 1 and take notes. Then put a check (✓) in the correct column to show who holds each opinion. One answer has been done for you.

Opinions about *The Love Song of J. Alfred Prufrock* by T.S. Eliot	Reviewers	Student	Professor
It is emotionally powerful.			✓
It is shocking and non-poetic.			
It causes feelings of discomfort.			

2. Listen to excerpt 2 and take notes. Then match each opinion to the person who holds or held it.

Opinions about French author Jules Verne	Contemporary critics	European academics	Professor
Jules Verne was a serious writer worthy of academic study.			
The works of Jules Verne were popular, but not high quality.			
Verne's writing style was new, but influenced other writers.			

H Academic Vocabulary

H1 **Which answer, A–H, best completes definitions 1–8 of the highlighted words, which are all related to literature? One answer has been done for you.**

1. In literature, criticism can be defined ____ *as discussion about the qualities of a novel, poem, or play.*
2. A narrative is the account or story _____
3. Novels are long works _____
4. The plot of a story is the sequence _____
5. Poetry is the general name given _____
6. The term prose describes writing that is similar _____
7. The protagonist is the main character _____
8. When a book is published, it is made available _____

A   as discussion about the qualities of a novel, poem, or play.
B   for distribution and sale in printed or electronic form.
C   in a fictional narrative such as a novel, epic poem, or drama.
D   of a sequence of events told in the order that they occurred.
E   of events in a fictional work, such as a story, play, or movie.
F   of imaginative fiction that often have a complicated plot.
G   to literary works written in verse rather than in prose.
H   to normal spoken language, such as an essay or news article.

I Test Challenge

I1 Practice some Understanding the Speaker's Attitude questions. Cover the questions and take notes as you listen. Then use your notes and memory to answer questions 1–6. Use this checklist of skills that you studied in this unit as a guide.

While you listen to the conversation and lectures

☑ Take notes when a speaker uses positive or negative intonation.

☑ Take notes when a speaker expresses an opinion directly or indirectly.

☑ Take notes when a speaker discusses another person's point of view.

When you answer the questions

☑ Look for answers that paraphrase directly-expressed opinions and accurately summarize implied opinions.

☑ Be careful not to choose answers that repeat information from a talk but do not paraphrase a person's opinion.

🔊 Tracks 141–143 Listen to a conversation between a student and a professor.

1. What is the professor's attitude to helping the student?
    Ⓐ He is reluctant but willing to give her some guidance.
    Ⓑ He thinks she should already have made a decision.
    Ⓒ He feels that the decision she should make is obvious.
    Ⓓ He is worried the student may not accept his advice.

2. What does the student say about creative writing?
    Ⓐ She really enjoys writing film scripts.
    Ⓑ It's not a subject that interests her.
    Ⓒ It's something she can really focus on.
    Ⓓ She finds it too literary and analytical.

🔊 Tracks 144–146 Listen to part of a discussion in a sociology class. The subject of the discussion is the Nobel Prize in Literature.

Alfred Nobel

3. What does the professor think about the decisions of the Swedish Academy?
    Ⓐ They are hardly ever controversial.
    Ⓑ They show evidence of prejudice.
    Ⓒ They often result in arguments.
    Ⓓ They follow the terms of Nobel's will.

4. What does the professor think led to an improvement in the situation over the last 25 years?
   - Ⓐ Criticism of the Swedish Academy's decision in newspapers
   - Ⓑ Pressure from both female writers and writers from other continents
   - Ⓒ Improved decision-making by members of the Swedish Academy
   - Ⓓ An increase in the number of authors from non-European countries

 Listen to a part of a talk in an English literature class. The professor is discussing William Shakespeare.

5. What opinion does the professor say some people hold?
   - Ⓐ William Shakespeare was not a writer and did not come from Stratford.
   - Ⓑ There is little hard evidence that William Shakespeare died in 1616.
   - Ⓒ William Shakespeare must have had a very high level of education.
   - Ⓓ The literary works of William Shakespeare were written by someone else.

6. What is the professor's opinion about the authorship question? *Choose two answers.*
   - Ⓐ The arguments are powerful and believable but cannot be proved.
   - Ⓑ The absence of evidence supporting Shakespeare is a strong argument.
   - Ⓒ The evidence in favor of alternative candidates is weak.
   - Ⓓ The arguments are interesting but not supported by the evidence.

Next Steps

Topics related to literature are common in the listening section of the TOEFL Test. You may also have questions about this subject in the other sections of the test, especially the reading section. As a result, learning more about literature, as well as practicing key skills for Understanding Organization questions, may raise your overall test score.

To learn more about literature and vocabulary related to this discipline:

1. Think of an author you like or a famous writer from your country or another country.
2. Search the Internet for the author's name plus the phrase "critical analysis," as in "Shakespeare critical analysis".
3. Choose one of the websites from the search list that has a short article of roughly three to five paragraphs.
4. Read the article a couple of times to get an idea of the main points.
5. Read the article again and look for vocabulary related to the author's writings. Study these words carefully.

To practice a key skill for Understanding the Speaker's Attitude questions:

1. Listen to a radio program in English. (If there are no radio broadcasts in English in your area, search the Internet for "internet radio in English". Alternatively, listen to a television program but do not watch the screen while you listen.)
2. For the first five minutes while you listen, focus on listening to the speakers' intonation. Make notes of how that intonation helps you understand their point of view.
3. For the next five minutes, listen for and make a note of any opinions that the speakers express.
4. For the final five minutes, listen for and make a note of attitudes or feelings that the speakers express indirectly.
5. Repeat steps 1–4 for 15 minutes every day. Try listening to a different radio station or listen at a different time in order to hear a wide variety of speakers talk about a wide variety of topics.

Unit Focus

There are seven types of listening questions in the TOEFL Test. These include Understanding Organization questions, which are classified as "connecting information" questions. Organization questions test how well you can recognize either the organization of a lecture or the relationship between one concept and the main idea of the conversation or lecture. These questions are more common after lectures than conversations, but you will probably not see one after every lecture. This unit will teach you several key skills to answer Organization questions, including:

- recognizing why a speaker mentions a particular idea, point, or detail.
- recognizing how a particular idea, point, or detail relates to the whole conversation or lecture.
- recognizing common ways in which academic lectures are organized.
- taking effective notes and using those notes to eliminate incorrect answers.

The vocabulary focus is on campus and academic words and phrases related to:

- names for students at different stages of their education and for different categories of students.
- sociology, the study of human societies in general as well as individuals and groups within society.

A Warm-up

A1 Complete sentences 1–5, which describe topics commonly studied by sociologists, with the correct ending, A–E.

1. The study of crime _____
2. The study of education _____
3. The study of the family _____
4. The study of health _____
5. The study of technology _____

A focuses on issues like marriage and divorce, raising children, and relationships with relatives.
B involves identifying why people break the law and how society prevents or deals with law-breaking.
C focuses on understanding how things like illness, disability, and aging populations affect society.
D includes investigating the ways in which computers and the Internet have an impact on society.
E deals with issues like how learning both impacts and is impacted by the norms of a society.

B Campus Vocabulary

B1 Use information from this passage to complete definitions 1–8 of the highlighted expressions. Two answers have been done for you.

Undergraduate students at North American colleges typically study for four years to earn a degree. Undergraduates in their first year of study are called freshmen. Students in the other years of study are called sophomores, juniors, and seniors, respectively. Students who are taking graduate-level classes are usually called grad students. Students who originally enrolled at one college but are now studying at a different one are called transfer students, while exchange students are visiting from another college temporarily, usually for a semester or year.

1. An undergraduate is a student who _____ has not yet earned a degree.
2. A freshman is a student who _____ is in his or her first year of study.
3. A sophomore is a student who _____
4. A junior is a student who _____
5. A senior is a student who _____
6. A grad student is studying _____
7. A transfer student originally _____
8. An exchange student is _____

C Analyzing Organization Questions

There are two kinds of Organization questions. The most common kind asks you how one idea, example, or point that a speaker discusses is related to the whole lecture or conversation, as in these examples:

Why does the student mention _____?

Why does the lecturer talk about _____?

Why does the professor discuss _____?

The other kind of Organization question asks how all or part of a lecture is organized:

How does the professor organize her lecture?

How does the professor introduce the concept of _____?

The correct answer to an Organization question:

- usually describes how one idea, example, or point relates to the main idea of the conversation or lecture.
- may describe the way that the whole lecture is organized.
- will not be stated explicitly by any of the speakers during the conversation or lecture.

In contrast, incorrect answers to Organization questions:

- may summarize one idea, example, or point rather than explain how it relates to the whole conversation or lecture.
- may incorrectly describe the organization of the whole lecture.
- typically repeat or restate words from the conversation or lecture.

TEST TACTIC

The first kind of Organization question looks similar to Understanding the Function of What Is Said questions (see Unit 10). They differ in that Organization questions ask how the speaker's words relate to the subject of the talk, but Function questions ask how listeners would understand the speaker's words.

C1 Use these scripts from a conversation and a lecture to answer questions 1 and 2.

Woman	Excuse me? A professor told me that a book I need for an assignment is on the special reserve list, but I'm a transfer student and the special reserve system here is different from the one at my previous college.
Man	Oh, it's pretty simple. Instructors can put a book that many students are likely to need on special reserve. That means you can borrow it, but only for three days, and you'll have to go to the reserve desk to do so.
Woman	OK. Thanks, for the explanation. I'll go over to the reserve desk right now.

1. Why does the woman mention she is a transfer student?
   A To emphasize that it is important she gets a copy of the book soon
   B To explain why she doesn't understand the special reserve system
   C To point out that the library's systems are confusing for some students
   D To explain that she needs to borrow the book for longer than three days

| Professor | Although many of the major concepts and techniques of modern sociology have been known and used for thousands of years, sociology is a relatively modern discipline. French philosopher Auguste Comte felt that science could be used to analyze and understand the social world, and in 1838 he coined the name sociology. Later in the same century, three other influential thinkers – Karl Marx, Max Weber, and, especially, Emile Durkheim – developed the ideas that became the foundations of modern sociology. |

2. How does the professor organize his talk?
   A He contrasts different ideas about a subject.
   B He talks about events in the order they occurred.
   C He mentions problems and then gives solutions.
   D He discusses what led to acceptance of a theory.

D Mastering Organization Questions – Recognizing Why a Speaker Says Something

Most Organization questions ask why a speaker mentions a specific point. As a result, key skills to answer Organization questions include being able to recognize why a speaker mentions something, and identifying how a speaker's point is related to the whole conversation or lecture. As with all listening questions, taking effective notes is also important.

◁))) Track 150 **D1** **Take notes as you listen to an experienced teacher talk about answering Organization questions. Then use your notes to put points A–E in the order the teacher discusses them. One answer has been done for you.**

1. Take notes when a speaker gives a detailed example
2.
3.
4.
5.

A Take notes when a speaker compares two things
B Take notes when a speaker makes a digression
C Ask "What is the speaker likely to talk about next?"
D Take notes when a speaker gives a detailed example
E Ask "Why is the speaker saying this information?"

◁))) Tracks 151–155 **D2** **Listen to five excerpts (short parts) from conversations and lectures and take notes. After each excerpt, answer the question. One answer has been done for you.**

1. What does the man do in excerpt 1?
   ☐ Gives an example   ☑ Compares two things   ☐ Makes a digression
2. What does the woman do in excerpt 2?
   ☐ Gives an example   ☐ Compares two things   ☐ Makes a digression
3. What does the man do in excerpt 3?
   ☐ Gives an example   ☐ Compares two things   ☐ Makes a digression
4. What does the woman do in excerpt 4?
   ☐ Gives an example   ☐ Compares two things   ☐ Makes a digression
5. What does the man do in excerpt 5?
   ☐ Gives an example   ☐ Compares two things   Makes a digression

D3 **Use these notes from part of a lecture to answer questions 1 and 2.**

Longitudinal study → observation of same data over period of time
Used in sociology to study events in life of people / organizations
     Same people / organizations observed throughout study
Studies provide accurate results → easy to see changes over time
     + Results unaffected by cultural differences unlike other methods
Studies are expensive → sample size often small
Also take long time → participants drop out (attrition)

TEST TACTIC

While you are listening to a conversation or lecture, it can also be helpful to ask "How are the speaker's words connected to the main idea?" If you can recognize this connection, it may help you answer an Organization question.

1. Why does the speaker talk about cultural differences?
   A To explain why one type of study takes a long time to do
   B To compare one type of sociology study with other types

2. Why does the speaker mention the sample size of many longitudinal studies?
   A To point out that cost and sample size are related
   B To explain why these studies are rarely conducted

D4 **Take notes as you listen to four excerpts from conversations and lectures. Then use your notes to answer questions 1–8.**

Listen to part of a conversation between a student and his academic advisor. Then answer questions 1 and 2.

1. Why does the woman mention the lack of specialists in industrial sociology?
   A To emphasize the man should soon make a decision about what to specialize in
   B To explain why she thinks the student should apply to study at a different university

2. What is the woman likely to talk about next?
   A Faculty members at her university who specialize in industrial sociology
   B Colleges that offer good graduate programs in industrial sociology
   C Reasons why certain classes are offered at some schools but not others

Listen to part of a lecture in a sociology class. Then answer questions 3 and 4.

3. Why does the man mention the background of an author?
   A He wants to explain why students should be careful about accepting the theories in a book.
   B He wants students to know that the ideas in a book may not be expressed in familiar terms.

4. What is the man likely to discuss next?
   A He will probably explain what caused Jared Diamond to change from studying physiology to geography.
   B He is likely to summarize the main arguments in Jared Diamond's book *Guns, Germs, and Steel*.
   C He will most likely describe another book that he wants his students to read before the next class.

Listen to part of a lecture in an introductory social sciences class. Then answer questions 5 and 6.

5. Why does the professor mention several social science disciplines?
   A To highlight the importance of participant observation as a methodological tool
   B To argue that participant observation is both widely-used and simple to understand

6. What might the woman talk about next? *Choose two answers.*
   A Examples of well-known participant observation studies
   B Different types of research tools associated with anthropology
   C Examples of types of behavior researchers choose to observe

Listen to part of a discussion in a sociology seminar. Then answer questions 7 and 8.

7. Why does the woman mention developing regions?
   A To give an example of the types of societies that sociologists generally study
   B To clarify which types of families are more usual in which types of societies

8. What are the speakers likely to discuss next?
   A Possible causes and effects of a recent social development
   B Different ways sociologists study nuclear and extended families
   C How growing up with a single parent can have an effect on children

 D5 **Listen again to the excerpts from exercise D4 and complete tasks 1 and 2.**

1. Underline phrases with two or more words in the answer choices to exercise **D4** that repeat what a speaker says. For example, in excerpt 1 the woman says "make a decision," so you should underline these words in question 1, answer A.

2. In general, do right answers or wrong answers more often repeat phrases that a speaker says? Why do you think this is? Discuss with a partner. Then share your ideas with other students.

E Mastering Organization Questions – Recognizing Common Ways to Organize Lectures

Some Organization questions ask you how all or part of a lecture is organized. To answer these questions, it is important to know and be able to recognize common ways in which academic lectures are organized.

E1 Choose the answer, A–E, that matches each description of a way to organize a lecture. Then compare answers with a partner. One answer has been done for you.

Ways to organize lecture	Description
1. Cause and effect	
2. Chronological	
3. Problem and solution	
4. Contrast	The professor compares two different things or two aspects of one subject.
5. Topical	

A The professor compares two different things or two aspects of one subject.
B The speaker discusses events in the order they occurred, usually from earliest to latest.
C The professor talks about several different aspects of a single topic or theory.
D The lecturer focuses on the events or actions that made other events or actions happen.
E The speaker discusses negative issues and how these issues might be resolved.

E2 Look at these notes from two academic lectures. Then answer questions 1 and 2.

TEST TACTIC

Typically, ideas that are connected are discussed close together. For example, if a man discusses both crime and poverty in the middle of a lecture, these topics are probably connected. However, if he discusses crime early in the lecture and poverty at the end, the topics are probably unconnected.

Questionnaires → common sociology research tool to get data
Two broad types of questionnaire used in sociology
1 Structured (also called closed → focus on closed questions)
        Good for quantitative info (e.g., how much / how often)
2 Unstructured (open → focus on open questions)
        Good for qualitative info (e.g., why / how / how feel)
Both types of questionnaire have advantages + disadvantages

1. How is the lecture about questionnaires organized?
    A The professor describes the causes of a particular activity.
    B The lecturer discusses events in the order they occurred.
    C The speaker compares two different aspects of one topic.

Structural functionalism → important theory in sociology
        Different aspects of society work together like organs in a body
        Body is strong + stable with each organ / weak + unstable without
Theory developed over time → Comte first suggested in mid 19 century
Developed more by Spencer and Durkheim in late 19 C
Theory refined in early / mid 20 C by Parsons (social action theory)
Modern refinements by Davis + Moore / Merton / Almond + Powell

2. What organization does the lecture about structural functionalism have?
    A Contrast
    B Chronological
    C Problem and solution

E3 Which way of organizing lectures from exercise **E1** would be the best way to organize lectures on academic topics 1–5? Why? Discuss with a partner.

1. Topic: the importance of the family in both industrial and agricultural societies
2. Topic: how government policies on prohibition led to a sharp increase in crime rates
3. Topic: the different roles and functions that several types of educational institutions have
4. Topic: the impact of aging populations on societies and ways to improve the situation
5. Topic: the growth of online communities since the development of the Internet

Tracks 160–164 **E4** Take notes as you listen to excerpts from five lectures. Then use your notes and memory to answer questions 1–10. Two answers have been done for you.

1. How is the lecture in excerpt 1 probably organized?
   ☑ Problem and solution   ☐ Cause and effect
2. What phrases from the lecture helped you answer question 1?
   bias and other problems / one solution
3. How is the talk in excerpt 2 probably organized?
   ☐ Topical   ☐ Contrast
4. What phrases helped you answer question 3?
5. How is the discussion in excerpt 3 probably organized?
   ☐ Chronological   ☐ Cause and effect
6. What phrases helped you answer question 5?
7. How is the talk in excerpt 4 probably organized?
   ☐ Contrast   ☐ Problem and solution
8. What phrases helped you answer question 7?
9. How is the lecture in excerpt 5 probably organized?
   ☐ Topical   ☐ Chronological
10. What phrases helped you answer question 9?

F Academic Vocabulary

F1 Read this passage about sociology. Use information from the passage to decide which word, A–H, best completes definitions 1–8. One answer has been done for you.

Like other social sciences, sociology is a broad discipline. At the micro level, it focuses on interactions among individuals, as well as on how the behavior of individuals both affects and is affected by society. Also important are concepts like agency and structure. On a larger scale, sociology is concerned with such things as social trends, cultural traditions and norms, bias against minority groups, the effects of technology on society, and interactions among groups, cultures, and organizations. Sociologists use various methods to gather data. For example, observers can measure and record events that occur, or researchers might conduct questionnaires, interviews, or experiments.

1. ____Bias____ means either an irrational preference for or dislike of something or someone.
2. A specific person who is distinct from others in a group or society is a(n) _____.
3. _____ can be defined as a movement towards or away from some idea over time.
4. Specific ways of doing something – such as carrying out a plan or researching a topic – are called _____.
5. A(n) _____ occurs when two or more individuals, groups, or other institutions act with or talk to each other.
6. Sets of questions, usually with a choice of answers, designed to gather information about a subject are _____.
7. _____ is the way that a person acts in a particular situation, especially in terms of interacting with others.
8. A person who watches events or situations but usually does not participate in them is called a(n) _____.

A behavior	C individual	E methods	G questionnaires
B bias	D interaction	F observer	H trends

G Test Challenge

G1 Practice some Understanding Organization questions. While you listen, cover the questions and take notes. Then use your notes and memory to answer questions 1–6. Use this checklist of skills that you studied in this unit as a guide.

While you listen to the conversation and lectures

☑ Ask questions about what the speakers are saying, such as *Why is she saying this?* or *What will he say next?*

☑ Take notes when a speaker gives a detailed example, compares ideas, or talks about an idea that seems unrelated to the previous topic of discussion.

☑ Listen for how lectures are organized – does the speaker discuss various aspects of one topic, the causes or effects of something, or the chronological order in which events happened, for example?

When you answer the questions

☑ Remember that incorrect answers often paraphrase or repeat the words and phrases that you heard, but do not correctly describe the organization of the talk.

🔊 Tracks 165–167 Listen to a conversation between a student and a university official.

1. Why does the woman talk about credit hours?
   - Ⓐ To point out that most grad students are not eligible to become an exchange student
   - Ⓑ To explain why students with a weak academic record cannot become an exchange student
   - Ⓒ To remind the man to speak to his academic advisor before applying to the exchange program
   - Ⓓ To explain the main criterion for eligibility for applying to become an exchange student

2. Why does the woman mention London?
   - Ⓐ To say that the man would need permission if he wanted to apply there
   - Ⓑ To give an example of an exchange program for which good grades are needed
   - Ⓒ To point out that the man's grade point average is too low to apply there
   - Ⓓ To suggest that the man should think seriously about applying there

🔊 Tracks 168–170 Listen to part of a lecture in an introductory sociology class.

TEST TACTIC

In rare cases, Organization questions might be replay questions, which means which you will hear part of the lecture again. To answer these questions, you can use the same techniques as for Understanding the Function of What Is Said questions (see Unit 10).

3. How does the professor organize the lecture?
   - Ⓐ He contrasts the benefits of one theory with those of another theory.
   - Ⓑ He gives specific examples from society to support two arguments.
   - Ⓒ He defines two key concepts and then describes how they are related.
   - Ⓓ He introduces two phenomena and explains how one caused the other.

4. Why does the professor mention a sport team?
   - Ⓐ To make a complex distinction easier for students to follow
   - Ⓑ To argue that playing sports, like work, is an everyday activity
   - Ⓒ To point out that rules and other structures control agency
   - Ⓓ To clarify the relationship between work and physical activity

 Tracks 171–173 Listen to part of a talk in a media studies class. The professor is discussing documentary films.

social issues documentaries

5. How is the lecture organized?
   - Ⓐ The professor compares successful documentary films with unsuccessful ones.
   - Ⓑ The professor discusses one kind of documentary and then questions its social impact.
   - Ⓒ The professor introduces a problem with documentaries and then describes a solution.
   - Ⓓ The professor explains why documentaries have increased in popularity recently.

6. Why does the professor mention *The Thin Blue Line* by Errol Morris?
   - Ⓐ To give an example of a documentary film that had a clear and measurable impact
   - Ⓑ To demonstrate how a documentary can be supported by a social action campaign
   - Ⓒ To explain why films by Michael Moore and Morgan Spurlock have not been effective
   - Ⓓ To argue that even popular documentary films rarely influence other film-makers

Next Steps

Topics related to sociology are common in the listening section of the TOEFL Test. You may also have questions about this subject in the other sections of the test, especially the speaking section. As a result, learning more about sociology, as well as practicing key skills for Organization questions, may raise your overall test score.

To learn more about sociology and vocabulary related to this discipline:

1. Think of a topic related to society, such as crime, education, family, health, technology, tourism, work, and so on.
2. Make a list of words in your language that are related to this topic. Then use a dictionary to find the English translations.
3. Find a short Internet article about this topic in English and search the article for the words you translated in step 2.
4. Make a note of each word that you found in the article in step 3. Then study these words and learn how to use them.
5. Repeat steps 3 and 4 several times. Then think of a new topic related to society and repeat steps 2–4.

To practice a key skill for Understanding Organization questions:

1. Find some free academic lectures about sociology (or another subject that interests you) on the Internet. (The search phrases "free sociology lectures" or "free podcasts about sociology" should help you find some good sources of lectures.)
2. Begin listening to one of the lectures. If you find the speaker too difficult to understand, try a different lecture.
3. Take notes as you listen to the lecture. Then, after 60 to 90 seconds, pause the lecture.
4. While the lecture is paused, think about what the speaker just said. Then ask yourself these questions: (1) Why did the speaker say this? (2) How is the lecture organized? and (3) What is the speaker about to say next?
5. Repeat steps 3 and 4 until the lecture ends. (If the lecture is long, stop after 10–15 minutes and continue the next day.)

Doing this every day for 10 to 15 minutes will help you build key listening skills not only for Understanding Organization questions but also for other types of listening questions.

Unit Focus

There are seven types of listening questions in the TOEFL Test. These include Connecting Content questions, which are classified as "connecting information" questions. Connecting Content questions test how well you can recognize the relationship between ideas that a speaker discusses. You will see several of these questions when you take the TOEFL Test, but you will probably not have one after every conversation or lecture. You will learn and practice several key skills to answer Connecting Content questions in this unit, including:

- understanding how ideas, points, or details in a conversation or lecture are related to each other.
- making a note when a speaker assigns a concept or detail to a category.
- making a note when a speaker uses positive or negative language.
- making a note of events or steps in a process that a speaker mentions.

The vocabulary focus is on campus and academic words and phrases related to:

- living on campus in university-owned housing or off campus in privately-owned housing.
- political science, the study and analysis of government systems, political activity, and international relations.

A Warm-up

A1 **Complete tasks 1 and 2 with a partner. Spend about five minutes on each task.**

1. Make a list of words and phrases that describe politicians. Use a dictionary if you wish.
2. Are your words mostly positive or negative? Why do you think this is? Discuss with other students.

B Campus Vocabulary

B1 **Choose a word or phrase from this notice to complete each sentence, 1–8. One answer has been done for you.**

Important Announcements about Student Accommodation

- Beginning next term, every campus dormitory that is currently female-only or male-only will become coeducational. Resident advisors in each dorm will soon be holding information sessions to answer questions about this change.
- As requested, students in off-campus housing may now purchase a meal plan.
- The popular "roommate swap" board in the Housing Office is now available to access online at www.statecollege.educ/swap.

---

1. A building where students live and sleep when they are at college is called a ___dormitory___ (or dorm).
2. A dormitory where both male and female students live can be described as _____ (or coed).
3. _____ (or RAs) live in a dorm and provide help to other students living there.
4. Places where students live that are not located on the grounds of a college are known as _____.
5. A general word for all types of places to live, including dormitories and off-campus housing, is _____.
6. Students who need to discuss accommodation issues should go to the _____.
7. A _____ is a system that allows students to pay in advance for food they will eat at campus facilities.
8. A person who lives and sleeps in the same room, apartment, or house as somebody else is a _____.

C Analyzing Connecting Content Questions

There are three types of Connecting Content questions. In the first type, you will see a table with two categories – either *Yes* and *No*, or *Included* and *Not Included* – and four or five answer choices. Each answer matches only one category.

The second type of Connecting Content question is similar to the first type, but it may have more than two categories and the category names will vary according to the subject of the conversation or lecture. The speaker or speakers will mention the category names when they speak. In rare cases, one answer may match more than one category.

The third type of Connecting Content question usually asks you to put events or people in order from the earliest (or first) to the latest (or last). Sometimes you may have to put the steps in a process in the correct order. Note that for this third type of question, occasionally you will see instructions which state that one of the answer choices should not be used.

In general, you can correctly answer Connecting Content questions if you:

- take notes about the information and the category each time a speaker mentions an idea connected to a category.
- listen carefully for and make a note of positive and negative expressions when a speaker introduces a new idea.
- listen carefully and take notes when a speaker mentions the order in which steps or events should happen.

 Track 174 **C1** **Take notes as you listen to two students discuss a homework assignment. Then use your notes to answer questions 1–3.**

1. The speakers discuss the two Houses of the United States Congress. Indicate which statement describes each House.

	Lower House	Upper House
Each member serves a six-year term and may be re-elected.		
Different states have different numbers of members.		
The usual name is the House of Representatives.		

2. The speakers discuss Congress. Indicate which statements correctly describe the Senate.

	Yes	No
The number of senators per state does not depend on population.		
Senators meet in the south wing of the United States Capitol.		
There are 435 members in total.		

3. The speakers discuss the construction of the United States Capitol. Put the events in the order in which they occurred.

First	
Second	
Third	
Fourth	

- Government officials began meeting in the Capitol building before construction was complete.
- The Capitol building was used for government functions as well as church services.
- A competition was held to encourage designs for expansions to the Capitol building.
- The United States Congress met in locations including Philadelphia and New York.

C2 **Which question in exercise C1 matches each type of Connecting Content question described at the top of this page?**

TEST TACTIC

Most answers to Connecting Content questions match just one category. An answer that matches "Yes" obviously cannot also match "No." In some cases, however, an answer might match two categories. For example, a politician might match both "Nineteenth Century Leaders" and "Twentieth Century Leaders."

D Mastering Connecting Content Questions – Recognizing Categories

One key skill for Connecting Content questions is recognizing and making a note when a speaker introduces a category. The speaker may name the category before discussing it, or give information about the category first and then name it.

D1 **Look at this script from part of a conversation. Then answer questions 1–3. One answer has been done for you.**

Student	I'm living in a dormitory, but my roommate is noisy and I can't study well, so I was thinking about moving.
Employee	OK, well, there are a few things you could do. The simplest option would probably be to transfer to a different dorm. That typically takes between one and two weeks. You could also transfer into a shared apartment on campus, but there's already a very long waiting list for those, so it might be months before you could do that. Your other option would be to move off-campus and find a place in town.
Student	If I wanted to move into off-campus housing, how long would that take?
Employee	Once you find a place you like, we can usually get the paperwork sorted out in two to three business days.

1. What is the first option that the employee mentions to the student? _transfer to a different dorm_
2. What is the second option that the employee mentions to the student? _____
3. What is the final option that the employee mentions to the student? _____

🔊 Tracks 175–178 **D2** **Take notes as you listen to excerpts (short parts) from two conversations and two lectures. After each excerpt, use your notes to answer one of questions 1–4.**

1. In excerpt 1, which assignments does the woman say the man must do? One answer has been done for you.

	Yes	No
Give a presentation		✓
Produce a case study		
Write a term paper		

2. In excerpt 2, which meal plans do the speakers discuss?

	Yes	No
Block plan		
Limited plan		
Value plan		

3. In excerpt 3, which types of trade agreement does the professor discuss?

	Yes	No
Bilateral agreements		
Multilateral agreements		
Trilateral agreements		
Unilateral agreements		

4. In excerpt 4, which of these political systems does the professor discuss?

	Yes	No
Authoritarianism		
Democracy		
Federalism		
Monarchy		

E Mastering Connecting Content Questions – Matching Details to a Category

Another key skill that will help you answer Connecting Content questions quickly and accurately is recognizing and making a note when a speaker mentions either general information or specific details that are connected to a category.

E1 Look again at the script from part of a conversation in exercise **D1**. Then answer the Connecting Content question.

The speakers discuss options the student has for moving out of her current accommodation. Indicate how long each option would take. One answer has been done for you.

	Transfer to a different dormitory	Transfer into an on-campus apartment	Move out of university accommodation
Less than one week			✓
From one to two weeks			
More than four weeks			

Tracks 179–182 **E2** Listen again to the excerpts that you heard in exercises **D2** and add to the notes you already made. Then answer questions 1–4.

1. In excerpt 1, the speakers discuss assignments for a class. Indicate which details match each assignment.

	Term paper	Case study
Should be less than 1,000 words		
Must be submitted by week six of the course		
Can be delivered in the form of a presentation		

2. In excerpt 2, the speakers discuss meal plan options. Indicate which details match each kind of meal plan.

	Block plan	Value plan
Students can eat in any restaurant on campus.		
Students are limited to 10 plan meals per week.		
Students can eat as much as they like per meal.		

3. In excerpt 3, the professor discusses trade agreements. Indicate which description matches each type of agreement.

	Unilateral	Bilateral	Multilateral
Only one nation benefits from the agreement.			
All signing nations benefit from the agreement.			
The agreement applies only to the export of goods.			
The agreement applies both to imports and exports.			

4. In excerpt 4, the professor discusses different kinds of political systems. Indicate which description matches each system.

	Authoritarianism	Democracy	Monarchy
Some groups may have fewer rights than others.			
The government holds all of the power.			
Individual people have power to change government.			
The ruler has power as a result of his or her parents.			

F Mastering Connecting Content Questions – Recognizing Positive or Negative References

Another key skill for Connecting Content questions is to recognize and take notes when a speaker uses positive or negative words to describe an idea. This can help you decide whether the speaker includes or excludes this idea from a category.

Tracks 183–184   **F1** Listen to a short conversation and a lecture and take notes. Then use your notes to answer questions 1 and 2.

1. In the conversation, the speakers discuss the man's plans. Indicate which of these opinions the man holds. One answer has been done for you.

	Yes	No
He thinks some of the professor's colleagues are public law experts.		✓
He really enjoyed taking the professor's class last year.		
His term paper for the professor's class was very good.		
His family might be unhappy if he chose to study political science.		

2. In the lecture, the speaker discusses plurality voting. Indicate which of these points he makes.

	Yes	No
Citizens generally find plurality voting systems harder to understand than other systems.		✓
One criticism of plurality voting is that the winning party may not have majority support.		
With plurality voting, some citizens may feel that a vote for a minority party is a wasted vote.		
Roughly 40% of countries have adopted a proportional representation voting system.		
Countries with a proportional representation system tend to have few political parties.		

TEST TACTIC

Take notes when a speaker mentions a date connected with an idea, person, or event. If the speaker gives several dates, you may see a Connecting Content question that asks you to put answers in order. Taking careful notes when you hear dates will make such questions easier.

F2 Look at the answers to exercise **F1**. Match each *No* answer to one of reasons 1–3. One answer has been done for you.

Reasons	*No* answers
1. A different person said this answer, not the person asked about in the question.	• Question 1, first answer •
2. This answer contradicts (says the opposite of) what the speaker actually said.	• •
3. This answer includes some of a speaker's words, but adds ideas he or she did not say.	• •

G Mastering Connecting Content Questions – Recognizing the Order of Events

To answer Connecting Content questions accurately, it may also be helpful to recognize and make a note when the speaker discusses either the order in which events occur or the order of steps in a process.

G1 Read these lecture notes. Then look at question 1. This question has already been answered, but some of the answers are in the wrong order. Work with a partner to put the answers in the right order.

TOPIC = women's suffrage (WS) = right to vote
often public <u>demo</u>nstrations before WS was allowed
first demo in France in late eighteenth century
  (C18)
<u>camp</u>aign in C19 in USA by Susan B Anthony and
  others
  – neither polit camp successful at giving WS
WS in C18 + C19 in few places but limited +
  temporary
  – Sweden, Finland, few US states, Sierra Leone
New Zealand 1893 = first nation to give full WS
  – because of camp led by Kate Sheppard
  from 1891

Australia gave full WS in 1902 in federal elections
  – limits for aboriginal women in some states
Finland, Norway and Denmark first European
  countries
  – 1907, 1913, and 1915 respectively for full WS
after end World War I, many nations granted WS
  – UK in 1918 but only women over 30
  (men over 21)
  – USA 1920 / Spain 1931 / France + Japan
  1945
almost all countries now WS but limited some
  places

1. The professor describes the history of women's right to vote. In which order did these events occur?

First	Unsuccessful demonstrations for women's suffrage were held.
Second	A campaign led to the first nation granting full women's suffrage.
Third	Women were granted limited voting rights in some regions.
Fourth	Numerous countries chose to give women the right to vote.
Fifth	Several European countries gave women full voting rights.

G2 Discuss questions 1 and 2 with a partner.

1. What abbreviations (short ways of writing something) are used in the notes for exercise **G1**?
2. What other words or phrases in the notes could be abbreviated?

Tracks 185–186 **G3** **Listen to a conversation and lecture and take notes. Then use your notes to answer questions 1 and 2.**

1. The speakers discuss applying to become a resident advisor. Put the steps in the application process in order. One step should NOT be included. One answer has been done for you.

First	Attend an information session
Second	
Third	
Fourth	

- Attend an individual training session
- Attend an information session
- Attend a group interview
- Fill out and submit the application
- Wait for the application to be assessed

2. The professor discusses how laws are passed in the United States. Put the legislative steps in the correct order.

First	
Second	
Third	
Fourth	

- A committee discusses the bill and approves or rejects it.
- A member of Congress sponsors a bill or measure.
- If the bill is enrolled, the president can accept or veto it.
- Members of both chambers of Congress debate the bill.

H   Academic Vocabulary

H1 **Work with a partner to decide which definition, A–H, matches the highlighted words in statements 1–6.**

1. A bilateral agreement between two states
2. A coalition of bureaucrats and military leaders
3. During an election citizens cast their vote
4. Legislation giving women the right to vote
5. Representatives elected to serve different regions
6. Senators vote to override the president's veto

A A contract between two (or more) people or countries is a(n) _____.
B An organized event at which people vote for a candidate is a(n) _____.
C A temporary political union between two or more parties is a(n) _____.
D Laws written and passed by an official body or government is _____.
E Nations or regions within a nation with their own government are _____.
F Non-elected officials who work for a government department are _____.
G Elected politicians whose role is to act on behalf of citizens are _____.
H The political power to reject a decision, law, or proposal is a(n) _____.

 Tracks 187–192 **H2** **Listen to some short excerpts from conversations and lectures you have already heard. Which highlighted word from exercise H1 do you hear in each excerpt? One answer has been done for you.**

Excerpt 1 _____representatives_____   Excerpt 4 _____

Excerpt 2 _____   Excerpt 5 _____

Excerpt 3 _____   Excerpt 6 _____

I Test Challenge

11 **Practice some Connecting Content questions. While you listen, cover the questions and take notes. Then use your notes and memory to answer questions 1–6. Use this checklist of skills that you studied in this unit as a guide.**

TEST TACTIC

Usually one or two answers are easier than others. If you do these answers first, the harder answers are often easier to add to the table. For example, if you assigned two answers to the "Yes" column, at least one of the remaining answers must be in the "No" column.

While you listen to the conversation and lectures

☑ Listen carefully and take notes when a speaker mentions a category or a detail connected to a category.

☑ Listen carefully and take notes when a speaker expresses positive or negative ideas about something.

☑ Concentrate and take notes when a speaker discusses the order of events or steps in a process.

When you answer the questions

☑ Use your notes and memory to choose the correct categories or correct sequence for each answer.

Tracks 193–195 Listen to a conversation between a student and a university employee.

1. The speakers discuss a newly constructed dormitory. Indicate which benefits of this dormitory the speakers mention.

	Yes	No
The large number of available rooms		
The techniques used in its construction		
The relatively inexpensive cost of living there		
The convenience of its location for the man		

2. The speakers discuss two alternative housing options for the student. Indicate what the speakers say about each option.

	On-campus accommodation	Off-campus accommodation
Prices tend to be expensive		
Not constructed recently		
No coed accommodations		
Less convenient location		

Tracks 196–198 Listen to part of a lecture in an international relations class.

3. The speaker discusses the League of Nations. Indicate which of these answers were goals of the League of Nations.

	Yes	No
Find a way to end World War I quickly		
Maintain peace throughout the world		
Solve international disputes diplomatically		
Cooperate with governments to promote trade		

4. The speaker describes the events that led to the founding of the United Nations. Put the events in the order that they happened.

First	
Second	
Third	
Fourth	

- The League of Nations was founded to promote world disarmament.
- The United Nations Charter was drafted and signed in San Francisco.
- Members of the UN Security Council ratified the United Nations Charter.
- A group of allied countries discussed and signed the Atlantic Charter.
- Governments discussed and founded several international organizations.

Tracks 199–201 Listen to a lecture in an introduction to world literature class.

5. The professor discusses political satire. Indicate which of these traits the professor includes in her definition of satire.

	Included	Not included
Being humorous		
Being critical		
Being ironic		
Being indirect		

6. The professor mentions some examples of political satire. Put the names of these satirical authors in order of when they were writing, from the earliest time to the most recent.

First	
Second	
Third	
Fourth	

- Aristophanes
- Jonathan Swift
- Maurice Joly
- Niccolò Machiavelli

Next Steps

Topics related to political science are common in the listening section of the TOEFL Test. You may also have questions about this subject in the other sections of the test. As a result, learning more about political science, as well as practicing key skills for Connecting Content questions, may raise your overall test score.

To learn more about political science and vocabulary related to this discipline:

1. Read a few articles in your language about political science to get some background knowledge about this topic.
2. Search the Internet for websites that let you watch or listen to free academic lectures about political science. For example, you could search for "free political science lectures" or "free online political science videos".
3. Listen to each lecture several times and make a note of words and phrases that the speaker uses frequently.
4. Check these words in your dictionary and study and learn the most useful words related to political science.

To practice key skills for Connecting Content questions:

1. Watch an Internet video in which somebody compares or contrasts two or three things.
2. As you listen, make notes about the positive and negative points the speaker makes about each thing.
3. After you have watched the video, create two tables that summarize the positive and negative aspects of each thing.
4. You can also watch "how to" videos in which a speaker gives a step-by-step explanation of how to do something. Make notes while you watch. Then after the video finishes, use your notes to write a short summary of the process.

Unit Focus

There are seven types of listening questions in the TOEFL Test. These include Making Inferences questions, which are one type of "connecting information" questions. In Making Inferences questions, you have to understand or make a conclusion about something that a speaker mentions indirectly. These questions are relatively common, and you will probably have at least one Making Inferences question after each conversation and lecture. This unit will teach you several key skills to answer Making Inferences questions, including:

- recognizing how and when a speaker is expressing an idea indirectly.
- drawing a conclusion from ideas a speaker mentions or a conclusion about what a speaker is likely to do.
- recognizing whether an answer choice is mentioned directly, indirectly, or not mentioned at all.

The vocabulary focus is on campus and academic words and phrases related to:

- using textbooks as well as borrowing books and using the services of a university library.
- economics, the study and analysis of the production, distribution, and consumption of goods and services.

A Warm-up

A1 This diagram shows a simplified economic cycle. Label each box with one answer from A–D. (Check the meaning of those words in a dictionary, if necessary.) One answer has been done for you.

1. Recovery	

A Depression
B Downturn
C Prosperity
D Recovery

B Campus Vocabulary

B1 Read the definitions of these highlighted expressions. Then choose the best expression to complete each blank in the conversation. One answer has been done for you.

A bibliography is a list of the books and articles that a student used for research while writing an assignment.

The list of all the books, journals, and other materials in a library that a user can borrow or consult is called the catalog.

The main book that students are assigned to read when they take a particular course is the coursebook or textbook.

An interlibrary loan is when a user requests a book from a different library because it is unavailable at his or her library.

A journal is a type of magazine that publishes specialist articles and information about one academic discipline.

The list of books and articles that a professor asks students to read for a course is called a reading list.

Professors can put books that are likely to be required by many students on a special reserve list in the library.

In a library, the stacks are the shelves where all of the books, journals, and other materials are stored.

Student	Could I talk to you about the grade you gave me for this paper, Professor? It was lower than I expected.
Professor	I gave you a low grade because your paper was half-finished, Joe. The only book listed in your 1. <u>bibliography</u> is the 2. _____, so it looks like you didn't read any of the titles from the 3. _____ that I gave you.
Student	I wanted to do the reading, but I couldn't find the books from the list in the library 4. _____. And I couldn't read the 5. _____ article that you mentioned because that journal's not in the library's 6. _____. I requested the journal via 7. _____, but it didn't arrive from the other library in time.
Professor	The books are not in the stacks because I placed them on the 8. _____ list. I mentioned that in class, remember? I also said that I had copies of the journal article available in my office.
Student	Oh. I missed two classes because of illness, and I guess I missed some important information. Sorry.

C Analyzing Making Inferences Questions

Making Inferences questions ask you about information that is not directly stated by a speaker. Most Making Inferences questions include a word that refers to indirect information like "conclude," "imply," or "infer," as in these examples:

What can be concluded about the woman?

What does the professor imply about _____?

What can be inferred about _____?

Some Making Inferences questions are replay questions. This means you will hear an excerpt (short part) of the whole conversation or lecture you have just heard. Next you will see a question on the screen like one of the examples below. In most cases, you will then hear all or part of the excerpt again:

What does the student imply when he says this?

What does the professor imply about _____ when she says this?

The correct answer to Making Inferences questions:
- correctly describes an idea that one or both speakers mentioned indirectly.
- rarely repeats the same words or phrases that the speaker used.
- may describe how two or more details from the conversation or lecture are related.

In contrast, incorrect answers to Making Inferences questions:
- often repeat the same words or phrases that the speaker said.
- may restate or repeat an idea that one or both speakers mentioned directly.

TEST TACTIC

The right answer to Inference questions is usually related to the main idea or purpose of the talk. If you are unsure which answer to choose, ask "What's the main idea?" and "Which answer is most closely related to it?" These questions may help you choose the right answer.

C1 Read these partial scripts from a conversation and a lecture. Then answer questions 1 and 2.

Student	Excuse me, Professor. I'm not sure how to answer the assignment you set.
Professor	Have you done all the reading that I assigned?
Student	I read the chapters in the coursebook, but there are two titles on the reading list I haven't looked at yet.
Professor	Well, then your next step is clear, I think.

1. The professor implies that the student should
   A answer more clearly
   B complete the reading
   C return to the library
   D hand in the homework

Professor There's a famous quotation by Adam Smith, the Scottish scholar who's often called the "father of modern economics," that I'd like to discuss. I don't remember Smith's exact words, I'm afraid, but he said something like, "What's prudent conduct for every private family is scarcely folly for a great kingdom." Now Smith was writing this over 220 years ago, at a time when the style was to convey one's ideas in a roundabout way, but his message is actually simple: ideas that make economic sense for a family also make economic sense for a country.

2. What does the professor imply about Adam Smith?
   A It is not important to know his exact words.
   B His ideas are interesting but old-fashioned.
   C His words do not express his concept directly.
   D He believed great kingdoms were rarely prudent.

D Mastering Making Inferences Questions – Listening and Taking Notes Effectively

The answers to Making Inferences questions are not stated directly during the conversations or lectures, so a key skill for answering these questions is to listen effectively and take notes when you think a speaker is expressing an idea indirectly.

Tracks 202–205 **D1 Listen to four students talk about listening for inferences. Then match each person to the point they make, A–D. One answer has been done for you.**

Ahmed	Miki	Jorgen	Rosa
Point _c_	Point _____	Point _____	Point _____

A Some speakers express an idea indirectly by discussing an opposite idea.
B Some speakers express an idea indirectly by mentioning various points, but not explicitly stating a conclusion.
C Some speakers express an idea indirectly by talking about an idea that is related to the implied point.
D Some speakers express an idea indirectly by using a specific tone of voice.

Tracks 206–208 **D2 Listen to some excerpts from conversations and lectures. Take notes as you listen. Then use your notes and memory to answer questions 1–6.**

1. In excerpt 1, what point does the woman make indirectly?
   A The reading list from her professor is hard to find.
   B A book she needs is not available in her college library.

2. How does she express this point?
   A She discusses an idea that is related to her implied point.
   B She mentions various points, but does not explicitly state a conclusion.

3. In excerpt 2, what does the man imply?
   A The prices of products and services do not generally go up.
   B If demand for a product decreases, its price often decreases, too.

4. How does he express this point?
   A He expresses an opposite idea.
   B He uses a specific tone of voice.

5. In excerpt 3, what point does the man make indirectly?
   A Books are not easy to find in the library's stacks.
   B He did not expect to be able to search the catalog.

6. How does he express this point?
   A He talks about an idea that is related to his implied point.
   B He uses a specific tone of voice.

D3 Use these notes from a conversation and lecture to answer questions 1 and 2. Then compare answers with a partner.

Prof   How help?
Student Not follow ideas in coursebook
P   Whole book?
S   No – chapters 3 + 4
P   Please remind me
S   About Chicago school of economics
P   Like to help but very broad topic

Difficult to develop economic theories based on real data
Real-world economic data often complicated + "messy"
Economic models → easier to understand but limited
Usually include variables / use mathematics + logic
e.g., Leontief's input-output model (won Nobel prize)
Types = stochastic (quantitative) / non-stochastic
Different types have different limitations

1. What can be inferred from the conversation? *Choose two answers.*
   A The professor thinks the student should read the whole coursebook more carefully.
   B The professor does not remember the contents of each chapter of the coursebook.
   C The professor thinks the student is asking a question that is too general.
   D The professor is not familiar with the ideas of the Chicago school of economics.

2. What does the professor imply in the lecture? *Choose two answers.*
   A Non-stochastic economic models are not quantitative.
   B People who use an economic model often win a Nobel prize.
   C Models are developed by mathematicians, not by economists.
   D Economists use models because real-world data is so complex.

🔊 Tracks 209–211 **D4** Take notes as you listen to excerpts from a conversation and two lectures. After each excerpt use your notes and memory to answer questions 1–3.

1. What can be inferred from excerpt 1? *Choose two answers.*
   A The process of applying for an interlibrary loan is complicated.
   B The man already has scheduled activities on the weekends.
   C The man needs a job that pays more than minimum wage.
   D Jobs at the university library are popular among students.

2. What can be inferred from excerpt 2? *Choose two answers.*
   A The depression phase occurs before the recovery phase.
   B Some models of the business cycle are more complex than others.
   C The name "economic cycle" is less common than "business cycle."
   D Economic optimism is necessary for the recovery stage to begin.

3. What can be inferred from excerpt 3? *Choose two answers.*
   A The professor asked the students to do some reading before class.
   B A person's level of risk aversion determines how often he or she invests.
   C A risk-seeking investor looks for high-risk, high-return investments.
   D The students do not fully understand the concept of risk aversion.

TEST TACTIC

If you think a speaker is making a point indirectly, try underlining that section of your notes (or putting a sign in the margin of your notes). This will help you find implied ideas more easily later, and may help you reach conclusions based on the speaker's words.

E Mastering Making Inferences Questions – Reaching Conclusions

For some Making Inferences questions you will need to make a conclusion based on what you hear. You might have to come to a conclusion about a situation or theory, about a speaker's opinion, or about what a speaker is likely to do next. Typically, you will hear at least two pieces of information during a conversation or lecture to help you draw a conclusion.

E1 Read this script from part of a lecture. Then complete tasks 1 and 2 with a partner.

Professor   During a property bubble, real estate prices continue rising until they become so high that buyers can no longer afford them. The financial crisis of 2007–2012 was caused when property bubbles around the world burst. The "Lost Decade" in Japan, when the economy grew at a very slow rate, was also caused by a burst bubble, though in that case the bubble was related to the price of many assets, not just real estate.

1. What conclusions can you draw from the script? *Choose two answers.*
   A Property bubbles can cause economic problems.
   B Property bubbles can occur in any country.
   C Slow economic growth rates can cause property bubbles.
   D It is a good idea to buy a home during a property bubble.

2. Underline the words and phrases in the script that helped you answer task 1.

◁ Tracks 212–214 E2 Listen to some excerpts from a conversation and two lectures. After each excerpt, answer the questions.

Listen to part of a conversation. Can you make the following conclusion from the conversation?

1. The man's bibliography for an assignment included books he did not read.   ☐ Yes   ☐ No

Listen to part of a lecture about normative economics. Can you reach the following conclusions from the lecture?

2. Positive economics focuses on what actually happens in the economy, not on what should happen.   ☐ Yes   ☐ No

3. Social choice is the most important theory based on normative economics.   ☐ Yes   ☐ No

Listen to part of a lecture about import quotas. Can you come to the following conclusions from the lecture?

4. Without import quotas, domestic producers of a product cannot be successful.   ☐ Yes   ☐ No

5. Import quotas do not benefit either overseas producers or domestic consumers.   ☐ Yes   ☐ No

TEST TACTIC

It is relatively common for speakers to mention an indirect idea more than once and in more than one way. So when you look at your notes after listening, look for ideas that are repeated: these might indicate an implied idea.

F Mastering Making Inferences Questions – Analyzing the Answer Choices

The right answer to a Making Inferences question must describe an idea that the speaker implied, but the wrong answers often paraphrase an idea that the speaker directly states, or repeat some of the speaker's words but express an idea the speaker does not mention. Recognizing these different types of wrong answers is a key skill for Making Inferences questions.

F1 Read these scripts for two Making Inferences questions that replay part of the talk. Then answer questions 1 and 2.

Narrator   Listen again to part of the conversation. What does the student imply when she says this?

Student   I'm finding your economics class stimulating, but the reading list is longer than I expected. I had to get a part-time job this semester, and with my hours there plus the other classes I'm taking, there's never enough time.

Narrator   Listen again to part of the lecture. What does the professor imply when he says this?

Professor   I'd like to define some expressions that, judging from your recent papers, seem to be confusing to some of you. Economists typically use the word *monetary* when talking about things like the amount of money in circulation in the economy. They typically use *fiscal* when referring to government expenditures and tax revenues. In contrast, they generally use *financial* when the discussion is related to raising capital or providing funds. I hope that's clear and that you'll use these terms correctly in the future.

1. Put a check (✓) in the correct column to indicate which ideas the student implies and which she states directly.

	Implies	States directly
The woman is enjoying an economics class that she is taking.		
The woman needed to make some extra money this semester.		
Doing the reading for her economics class requires a lot of time.		

2. Put a check (✓) in the correct column to indicate which ideas the professor implies and which he states directly.

	Implies	States directly
Some of his students used some economics terms incorrectly in their assignments.		
The word *fiscal* is most often used to refer to government expenses and incomes.		
Economists generally use the words *fiscal* and *financial* with different meanings.		

Tracks 215–217 **F2** **Listen to some excerpts from a two conversations and a lecture. After each excerpt, answer the questions.**

Listen to part of a conversation. Does the man Imply, State, or Not mention ideas 1 and 2?

1. He thinks the price of the coursebook is expensive.
   ☐ Imply   ☐ State   ☐ Not mention

2. He will go to an off-campus bookshop to buy a used book.
   ☐ Imply   ☐ State   ☐ Not mention

Listen to part of a lecture. Does the woman Imply, State, or Not mention ideas 3 and 4?

3. GDP is the value of goods and services used by the population of a country.
   ☐ Imply   ☐ State   ☐ Not mention

4. Countries with a low GDP most likely do not have a healthy economy.
   ☐ Imply   ☐ State   ☐ Not mention

Listen to part of a conversation. Does the woman Imply, State, or Not mention ideas 5 and 6?

5. The library has been having problems with its computerized catalog recently.
   ☐ Imply   ☐ State   ☐ Not mention

6. The man will not be able to search the library catalog for about two hours.
   ☐ Imply   ☐ State   ☐ Not mention

G Academic Vocabulary

Track 218 **G1** **Listen to a speaker define these useful highlighted words related to economics. As you listen, fill in the missing phrases. One answer has been done for you.**

1. The word capital often means __money or property__ that can be used to purchase or invest in something.
2. A consumer, like a customer, can be defined as a person who buys or uses _____.
3. Demand refers to the level of desire among consumers in _____ for specific goods and services.
4. Items that a company has produced in order for _____ them are called goods.
5. Productivity generally refers to how _____ and efficiently a business can produce goods.
6. A recession is defined as a relatively short period of time when the economy experiences a _____.
7. Resources, such as oil, water, capital, or workers, are the _____ assets a country or company has.
8. Supply typically refers to how much of a particular good or service is available in one market at a _____.

G2 **Discuss tasks 1–5 with one or two partners. When you have finished, share your ideas with other students.**

1. What is the relationship between the words *capital* and *capitalism*?
2. What are the verb forms of the words consumer, demand, productivity, and supply?
3. The words *goods* and *services* are often used together as a phrase. How do services differ from goods?
4. What word is used to describe a recession that is both long and serious?
5. What are some of the most important resources in your country? Why are they important?

H Test Challenge

TEST TACTIC

Do not choose an answer that you feel is true only because of your common sense or your existing knowledge of a subject. Unless an answer choice is supported by something that a speaker says or implies, it is unlikely to be correct.

H1 **Practice some Making Inferences questions. While you listen, cover the questions and take notes. Then use your notes and memory to answer questions 1–6. Use this checklist of skills that you studied in this unit as a guide.**

While you listen to the conversation and lectures

☑ Listen for signs that a speaker may be expressing an idea indirectly – such as describing an opposite idea, making several related points but not explicitly stating a conclusion, and so on – then take notes on what you hear.

When you answer the questions

☑ Use your notes and memory to draw conclusions from two or more related points that a speaker mentioned.

☑ Remember that incorrect answers often paraphrase or repeat a speaker's words and may express an idea that a speaker did not mention.

Tracks
219–221 Listen to a conversation in a university library.

1. Listen again to part of the conversation. What does the woman imply when she says this?
   - Ⓐ Undergraduates can borrow more than four interlibrary loan books.
   - Ⓑ The man should register as a student at the university to get library access.
   - Ⓒ Only university alumni can borrow books through interlibrary loan.
   - Ⓓ The problem does not affect students at other universities.

2. What is the student likely to do next? *Choose two answers.*
   - Ⓐ Apply to become a student at a distance-learning institution
   - Ⓑ Apply for some books through the interlibrary loan scheme
   - Ⓒ Apply for access to the library at Eastern State University
   - Ⓓ Apply for a special card that lets him borrow up to six books

Tracks
222–224 Listen to part of a lecture in a European history class. The professor is talking about trade policies.

3. Listen again to part of the conversation. What does the woman imply when she says this?
   - Ⓐ Politicians focused on gaining increased personal wealth.
   - Ⓑ Voters supported politicians who wanted balanced trade.
   - Ⓒ Opportunities for trade were limited by political policies.
   - Ⓓ Politicians made decisions favoring economic gain.

4. What does the professor imply about mercantilism?
   - Ⓐ Mercantilist policies were the cause of a majority of European wars between 1652 and 1784.
   - Ⓑ Mercantilism led to the creation of profitable trading links between major European powers.
   - Ⓒ Some nations that were once colonies still suffer the effects of former mercantilist policies.
   - Ⓓ Not all governments understood the links between mercantilism and wealth accumulation.

Tracks 225–227 Listen to part of a talk in an economics class. The professor is discussing economic goals.

full employment

economic growth

economic stability

5. What does the author imply about economic goals?
   - Ⓐ In reality, governments are not likely to be able to achieve them.
   - Ⓑ In most cases, they are difficult to define, understand, and measure.
   - Ⓒ Microeconomic goals are often reached later than macroeconomic goals.
   - Ⓓ In general, governments care about them more than individuals do.

6. What can be inferred about economic stability?
   - Ⓐ Nations that have achieved it tend to experience fluctuations in production.
   - Ⓑ Achieving it gives both governments and individuals confidence in the future.
   - Ⓒ It is most often achieved by societies that adopt long-term economic plans.
   - Ⓓ Achieving it requires a focus on reducing the rates of inflation and deflation.

Next Steps

Topics related to economics are common in every section of the TOEFL Test, especially the reading, listening, and speaking sections. As a result, learning more about economics, as well as practicing key skills for Making Inferences questions, may raise your overall test score.

To learn more about economics and vocabulary related to this discipline:

1. Read a story related to business, finance, or economics in a newspaper or magazine. Highlight any unfamiliar words.
2. After you finish, make a list of the ten highlighted words that are used most frequently in the article.
3. Use an English-English dictionary to find out what these words mean and how they are typically used.
4. Search the Internet for articles that have the first word on your list *in their title*. (If you are using Google, you can do this by typing "intitle:" plus the word you want to find; for example, "intitle: distribution".)
5. Read some of the articles to see how the word is used. Then repeat step 4 with the other nine words on your list.
6. Repeat steps 2–5 about a different story related to business, finance, economics, and so on.

To practice key skills for Making Inferences questions:

1. Watch a television program in which a presenter interviews somebody such as a politician, actor, and so on.
2. As you watch, note down what the interviewee says. When he or she says something indirectly, underline your notes.
3. At the end of the interview, review your notes and write a summary of ideas that the interviewee expressed indirectly.
4. Repeat steps 1–3 with a different television program until you are confident that you can recognize inferences well.
5. Repeat steps 1–4, but this time either do not watch the screen while you listen, or listen to a radio interview.

Directions

This listening review test is intended to help you find out your strengths and weaknesses in listening. You will listen to two conversations and two lectures and answer 22 questions about them. The conversations and lectures are designed to be at the same level as the ones on the TOEFL Test. You may take notes while you listen. After each conversation, take 3.5 minutes to answer the questions. After each lecture, take 4.5 minutes to answer the questions. When you have finished, check your answers with your instructor or against the Answer Key. Then use the conversion chart on page 167 to find out your likely score on the TOEFL Test.

Test

Tracks 228–233 Listen to a conversation between a student and one of his instructors.

1. Why does the student visit his instructor?
   - (A) To find out when her office hours are
   - (B) To ask about a class he did not attend
   - (C) To get her advice about his study plans
   - (D) To explain why he will stop taking a class

2. What does the man say about the woman's class? *Choose two answers.*
   - [A] He finds the workload too heavy.
   - [B] It is not one of his core classes.
   - [C] The class is very interesting.
   - [D] He was unable to register for it.

3. Listen again to part of the conversation. What does the student imply when he says this?
   - (A) He feels like he has too much work to do.
   - (B) He registered for too many classes by mistake.
   - (C) He will register for more classes next semester.
   - (D) He is not sure whether to take the class or not.

4. Why does the instructor mention her time as an undergraduate?
   - (A) To point out that many students experience similar issues
   - (B) To emphasize that it is important to make decisions quickly
   - (C) To explain why many students do not feel fully motivated
   - (D) To suggest that the student's plan might not be the best one

5. What will the student most likely do next?
   - (A) He will think about which class he should drop.
   - (B) He will attend the professor's class.
   - (C) He will find out about his core requirements.
   - (D) He will drop the psychology class he is taking.

Tracks 234–240 Listen to part of a lecture in a United States History class.

William Henry Harrison

Martin Van Buren

Tippecanoe and Tyler too

6. What is the main purpose of the lecture?
   - Ⓐ To highlight the military career of William Henry Harrison
   - Ⓑ To give the reasons for William Henry Harrison's death
   - Ⓒ To describe William Henry Harrison's main political opponents
   - Ⓓ To note some effects of William Henry Harrison's presidency

7. The professor discusses events in the life of William Henry Harrison. Put the events in the order in which they occurred.

First	
Second	
Third	
Fourth	
Fifth	

   - Ⓐ He resigned his post as commander of an army.
   - Ⓑ He lost and then won elections to become president.
   - Ⓒ He became the governor of Indiana Territory.
   - Ⓓ He held office as a senator of the United States.
   - Ⓔ He retired from public life and settled on a farm.

8. What were some results of Harrison's time as governor of Indiana Territory? *Choose two answers.*
   - A The Territory lost a battle at Tippecanoe.
   - B The size of the Territory increased.
   - C Several officials resigned their posts.
   - D Hostility with Native Americans grew.

9. On what points was Martin Van Buren criticized during the 1840 presidential campaign?
   Choose two answers.
   - A His use of negative slogans
   - B His impact on the economy
   - C His affluent mode of life
   - D His violent military record

🎧 10. Listen again to part of the lecture. What does the professor imply?
   - Ⓐ Slogans are a common feature of modern political campaigns.
   - Ⓑ Relatively few wealthy politicians are successful at winning elections.
   - Ⓒ Both Martin Van Buren and William Henry Harrison had nicknames.
   - Ⓓ Martin Van Buren was unable to criticize William Henry Harrison's policies.

11. What happened to Vice President John Tyler after Harrison's death?
   - Ⓐ He was president of the United States for almost four years.
   - Ⓑ He became a respected member of Congress in 1841.
   - Ⓒ He lost an emergency election to become the president.
   - Ⓓ He held the post of acting president until Congress convened.

Tracks 241–246 Listen to a conversation between a student and a university employee.

12. For what reason does the woman visit the man's office?
- Ⓐ To ask about vegetarian meal options
- Ⓑ To learn about different meal plans
- Ⓒ To request a cancellation and refund
- Ⓓ To pay the fees for her meal plan

13. What do the speakers say about the café in the Student Center? *Choose two answers.*
- Ⓐ It is being remodeled, but will reopen soon.
- Ⓑ It offers good meal options for vegan students.
- Ⓒ Students with a meal plan cannot eat there.
- Ⓓ It is a popular meeting place for students.

14. Listen again to part of the conversation. What does the student imply?
- Ⓐ Her current diet is negatively affecting her health.
- Ⓑ The man does not know how vegan differs from vegetarian.
- Ⓒ She worries that the café will not offer salad every day.
- Ⓓ Most dining locations offer a poor selection for vegans.

15. Listen again to part of the conversation. What can be inferred about the student?
- Ⓐ She is not happy about what the man has told her.
- Ⓑ She thinks the man has given her wrong information.
- Ⓒ She believes the renovations are taking too long.
- Ⓓ She has changed her mind about the cancellation.

16. What will the student probably do next?
- Ⓐ Pay the administration fee
- Ⓑ Tell the man her decision
- Ⓒ Speak to her parents
- Ⓓ Apply for financial support

Tracks 247–253 Listen to part of a talk in a psychology class. The professor is discussing stress.

17. Listen again to part of the talk. What does the professor imply when she says this?
- Ⓐ Students may have forgotten that their exam is coming up.
- Ⓑ Students should study hard for the two weeks before their exam.
- Ⓒ Students might feel stress because their exam is coming up.
- Ⓓ Students are unlikely to have questions about stress on their exam.

18. What factors make a life change more stressful? *Choose three answers.*
   - [A] How large the change is
   - [B] How many people the change affects
   - [C] How often the change happens
   - [D] How long the change lasts
   - [E] How unexpected the change is
   - [F] How costly the change is to manage

19. What theory does the male student suggest about why change causes stress?
   - (A) The brain equates change with potential danger.
   - (B) People feel stress when they cannot focus on today.
   - (C) Changes are not predictable, so people rarely feel safe.
   - (D) Human bodies react when things change from good to bad.

20. The professor mentions three types of stressors. Indicate which characteristics match each type.

	Ambient stressors	Life stressors	Traumatic stressors
Are caused by things like work or relationships			
Are often unexpected and may involve violence			
May be caused by negative or positive events			
Affect multiple people at the same time			

21. What example of a routine stressor does the professor give?
   - (A) Noise caused by construction work
   - (B) Having a dispute with a manager
   - (C) Driving to and from a hospital
   - (D) Getting married and having a baby

22. Listen again to part of the talk. What does the professor imply when she says this?
   - (A) There are three causes of traumatic stressors.
   - (B) Traumatic stressors cause high levels of stress.
   - (C) Traumatic stressors have several characteristics.
   - (D) Few people experience multiple traumatic stressors.

Score Conversion

Check your answers to questions 1–22. Give yourself one point for each fully correct answer. Then use this conversion chart to find out your approximate listening score range on the TOEFL Test.

Raw Score (out of 22)	Probable Level	Approximate Score Range
20–22		28–30
18–20	High	25–27
16–18		22–24
13–16	Intermediate	18–21
10–13		14–17
7–10		10–13
4–7	Low	5–9
0–3		0–4

Overview

The speaking section measures your ability to speak English effectively in academic settings. You will see and/or hear:

• Directions for adjusting the recording level of the microphone	about 1 minute
• Directions for the speaking section	about 2 minutes
• Independent Task 1 about a familiar topic, with 15 seconds to prepare and 45 seconds to respond	about 1 minute
• Independent Task 2 about a familiar topic, with 15 seconds to prepare and 45 seconds to respond	about 1 minute
• Integrated Task 3 about a campus situation, with 45 seconds to read a text, about 75 seconds to listen to a conversation, 30 seconds to prepare, and 60 seconds to respond	about 3.5 minutes
• Integrated Task 4 about academic course content, with 45 seconds to read a text, about 120 seconds to listen to a lecture, 30 seconds to prepare, and 60 seconds to respond	about 4.5 minutes
• Integrated Task 5 about a campus situation, with about 90 seconds to listen to a conversation, 20 seconds to prepare, and 60 seconds to respond	about 3 minutes
• Integrated Task 6 about academic course content, with about 120 seconds to listen to a lecture, 20 seconds to prepare, and 60 seconds to respond	about 3.5 minutes

Your spoken responses will be recorded and sent as digital files to human raters for grading. After all of your responses have been graded, your raw scores will be converted to a scaled score from 0–30.

NOTES

- Most speakers that you hear will speak with a North American accent, but you may also hear speakers from Australia, Great Britain, or New Zealand in some questions. These speakers will not have strong accents.
- Your responses will be recorded automatically. You do not need to press any buttons to start recording.

Detailed Guide

TEST TACTIC

Use the time when you are setting up your microphone to warm up your voice. Record yourself several times until you feel confident that you are speaking clearly and fluently. This might help you deliver better responses.

Before the speaking section begins you will need to set up the microphone you are using. The microphone will be connected to the headset, so you should wear your headset to get the best quality recording. Setting up the microphone will allow your voice to be recorded accurately and clearly.

To do this you will be asked to answer a practice question. Your answer to this question will not be scored.

When you answer, follow the directions on the screen and speak clearly but not too loudly or quietly. After recording, listen to your voice. If you are satisfied that your voice is clear and easy to hear, click the button marked **Continue**. If you want to record your voice again, click **Record Again**.

When you begin the speaking section of the TOEFL Test, you will first see the directions for the whole section. You will hear a narrator read the directions aloud. You can change the volume while the narrator is speaking by clicking on the **Volume** button in the top right corner of the screen.

When you are ready to begin the test, click the button marked **Continue**.

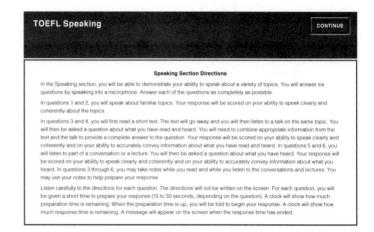

Before you see the first question, you will see a picture of a student wearing a headset and you will hear a narrator explain Speaking Task 1. You will not see the explanation on the screen. When the narrator finishes the explanation, this screen will disappear automatically.

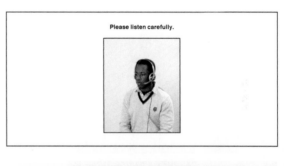

Next you will see the question for Speaking Task 1. A narrator will read the question aloud. Then a second voice will tell you to begin preparing your response. After that you will have 15 seconds to prepare. The amount of preparation time remaining will be shown on the screen.

After your preparation time is up, the second voice will tell you to begin speaking. You will have 45 seconds to speak. When you speak, make sure your voice is clear and you are speaking into the microphone. The amount of time remaining will be shown on the screen while you are speaking. When the time is up, the computer will automatically go on to the next question.

Next you will hear but not see an explanation of Speaking Task 2. Then you will see the Speaking Task 2 question on the screen. As with Task 1, you will hear a narrator saying the question. You will also hear a second voice telling you to begin preparing and then to begin speaking. You will have the same amount of preparation and response time for Speaking Task 2 as you do for Task 1.

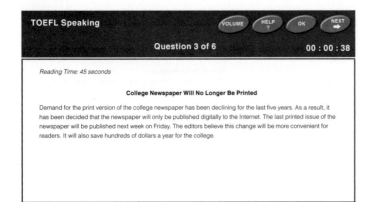

Next you will hear but not see an explanation of Speaking Task 3. Then you will see a short reading passage on the screen. The passage will describe a situation at a college campus. The narrator will briefly introduce the passage and tell you to read it.

You will usually have 45 seconds to read, but if the passage is shorter or longer than usual, you may have 40 seconds or 50 seconds. You may take notes about the passage while you read.

Next you will see a picture of two students on the screen and the narrator will tell you to listen to their conversation. The students will express their opinions about the situation described in the reading passage. One of the students will give detailed reasons for his or her views.

The conversation will usually last 60–90 seconds. You will see a bar below the picture of the people that shows how much longer the conversation will last. You may take notes while you listen to the conversation.

After the conversation you will first see a screen telling you to get ready to answer the question. This screen will disappear automatically after a few seconds. You will see this screen before Speaking Tasks 4, 5, and 6, too.

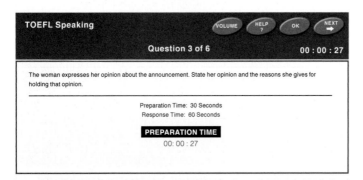

Then you will see the Speaking Task 3 question on the screen. The narrator will read the question aloud. Then a second voice will tell you to begin preparing your response. After that you will have 30 seconds to prepare. The amount of preparation time remaining will be shown on the screen. Then the second voice will tell you to begin speaking. You will have 60 seconds to speak. The amount of speaking time remaining will be shown on the screen.

Next you will hear but not see an explanation of Speaking Task 4. Then you will see a short reading passage on the screen. The passage will give general information about an academic topic. The narrator will briefly introduce the passage and tell you to read it.

You will usually have 45 seconds to read, but if the passage is shorter or longer than usual, you may have 40 seconds or 50 seconds. You may take notes about the passage while you read.

Next you will see a picture of a professor on the screen and the narrator will tell you to listen to a lecture on the same topic as the passage. The professor usually gives specific information, such as examples or details, about the general topic described in the passage.

The lecture will usually last 60–90 seconds but may be longer. You will see a bar below the picture of the professor that shows how much longer the lecture will last. You may take notes while you listen to the lecture.

After the lecture you will see a question on the screen. As with Task 3, you will hear a narrator saying the question. You will also hear a second voice telling you to begin preparing and then to begin speaking. You will have the same amount of preparation and response time for Speaking Task 4 as you do for Task 3.

TOEFL Speaking VOLUME HELP? OK NEXT

Question 4 of 6 00 : 00 : 22

Using points and examples from the talk, explain how people can alleviate the symptoms of panic disorder.

Preparation Time: 30 Seconds
Response Time: 60 Seconds

RESPONSE TIME
00: 00 : 22

Next you will hear but not see an explanation of Speaking Task 5. Then you will see a picture of two people on the screen and the narrator will tell you to listen to their conversation. The speakers may be two students or one student and a professor or university employee. The speakers will discuss a problem that one or both of them have plus two possible solutions to the problem.

The conversation will usually last 60–90 seconds. You will see a bar below the picture of the people that shows how much longer the conversation will last. You may take notes while you listen to the conversation.

After the conversation you will see a question on the screen. The narrator will read the question aloud. Then a second voice will tell you to begin preparing your response. After that you will have 20 seconds to prepare. The amount of preparation time remaining will be shown on the screen. Then the second voice will tell you to begin speaking. You will have 60 seconds to speak. The amount of speaking time remaining will be shown on the screen.

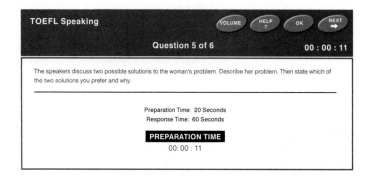

TOEFL Speaking VOLUME HELP? OK NEXT

Question 5 of 6 00 : 00 : 11

The speakers discuss two possible solutions to the woman's problem. Describe her problem. Then state which of the two solutions you prefer and why.

Preparation Time: 20 Seconds
Response Time: 60 Seconds

PREPARATION TIME
00: 00 : 11

Next you will hear but not see an explanation of Speaking Task 6. Then you will see a picture of a professor on the screen. The narrator will tell you to listen to a lecture on an academic topic. The professor usually gives a general introduction to a topic and then discusses specific details or examples about it.

The lecture will usually last 90–120 seconds but may be longer. You will see a bar below the picture of the professor that shows how much longer the lecture will last. You may take notes while you listen to the lecture.

After the lecture you will see a question on the screen. As with Task 5, you will hear a narrator saying the question. You will also hear a second voice telling you to begin preparing and then to begin speaking. You will have the same amount of preparation and response time for Speaking Task 6 as you do for Task 5.

Scoring

Your six responses will be recorded and sent to ETS's Online Scoring Network. Your responses will be graded by three to six trained raters. No personal data is sent with each response, so the raters will not know your name, nationality, previous scores on the TOEFL Test, or any other personal details. The raters will not communicate with each other in any way about your responses.

Each rater will listen to your response and grade it holistically by focusing on the quality of your whole response. The rater will especially focus on your delivery, your language use, and how well you developed the topic. The rater will assign your response a grade from 0–4. The rater can only assign whole grades like 3, not half grades like 3.5.

When judging the quality of your delivery, the raters will focus on the following criteria for Speaking Tasks 1–6:

Score	Delivery – Speaking Tasks 1–6
4	The speech must be clear, fluent, and well-paced. There may be a few minor issues with intonation or pronunciation that do not affect the listener's ability to understand easily.
3	The speech must be generally clear and mostly fluent. There may be minor but obvious issues with intonation, pronunciation, and pacing. The listener may need to make an effort to understand.
2	The speech must be understandable if the listener concentrates. There may be serious issues with pronunciation, intonation, fluency, and pace. The listener may not understand all of the ideas.
1	The speech will have consistent problems with pronunciation, intonation, and pacing. There are likely to be long and frequent pauses within sentences and between sentences

TEST TACTIC

While you are speaking, other students at the test center will be speaking, too. To get used to this background noise, practice speaking at home with the television or radio on in the background.

When judging the quality of your language use, the raters will focus on the following criteria for Speaking Tasks 1–6:

Score	Language Use – Speaking Tasks 1–6
4	The speech must include a variety of simple and complex grammar structures and use vocabulary expressions effectively. If there are errors, they should be minor and must not confuse the listener.
3	The speech must use grammar and vocabulary effectively and automatically most of the time. The use of grammar and vocabulary may be limited to relatively simple structures, and may include errors that cause minor confusion for the listener.
2	The speech will demonstrate a limited ability to use grammar and vocabulary. The listener will usually understand simple ideas, but complex ideas will cause confusion or misunderstanding.
1	The speech will use a very limited range of grammar and vocabulary. The listener may not understand even simple ideas.

When judging the quality of your topic development, the raters will use slightly different criteria for Speaking Tasks 1 and 2 compared with Speaking Tasks 3–6:

Score	Topic Development – Speaking Tasks 1 and 2
4	The response must be well developed. Ideas should follow a logical sequence or be clearly related to each other.
3	The response must be reasonably well developed although the relationship between ideas may not be obvious. The development of some ideas may be limited, and general rather than specific.
2	The response should be connected to the topic but the development of ideas will be limited and sometimes unclear. There may be a lot of repetition, and the relationship between ideas may be unclear.
1	The response may seem unconnected to the topic except for very basic ideas. There may be a lot of repetition, including repetition of words and phrases from the question.

Score	Topic Development – Speaking Tasks 3–6
4	The response must be well developed. The ideas should be clearly relevant to the task and include specific details. Some details may be incorrect or omitted.
3	The response must be reasonably well developed. The ideas should be relevant to the task, but may be inaccurate, incomplete, or general rather than specific.
2	The response must include some relevant information, but will have obvious mistakes and missing information. Key details will be missing, unclear, or wrong. Ideas may not be clearly connected to each other.
1	The response will have very little relevant information. Most ideas will be unclear, wrong, or too general. There may be a lot of repetition, including repetition of words and phrases from the question.

To achieve a score of 4 points, a response must match all three descriptions at level 4 for delivery, language use, and topic development. To achieve 1, 2, or 3 points, a response must match or exceed at least two of the descriptions at that level. So, for example, a response that is at level 4 for delivery, level 4 for language use, but level 3 for topic development would score 3 points. And a response that is at level 2 for delivery, but level 3 for language use and topic development would also score 3 points.

Responses that are not in English or that are completely off the topic will receive a score of zero.

Your raw scores for each response are then converted to a scaled score from 0 to 30 points. ETS does not explain in detail how the raw scores are converted to a scaled score. However, this table, which is adapted from information published by ETS, shows how some example final scores would be converted to the 0–30 scale:

Scores for Individual Speaking Tasks						Average of all Speaking Tasks	Scaled Score
Task 1	Task 2	Task 3	Task 4	Task 5	Task 6		
4	4	4	4	4	4	4.00	30
4	4	4	4	4	3	3.83	29
4	4	4	4	3	3	3.66	28
4	4	4	3	3	3	3.50	27
4	4	3	3	3	3	3.33	26
4	3	3	3	3	3	3.16	24
3	3	3	3	3	3	3.00	23
3	3	3	3	3	2	2.83	22
3	3	3	3	2	2	2.66	20
3	3	3	2	2	2	2.50	19
3	3	2	2	2	2	2.33	18
3	2	2	2	2	2	2.16	17
2	2	2	2	2	2	2.00	15

When you receive your score from the TOEFL Test, you will get a score report. The report will give your scaled score in speaking from 0–30, your speaking level (Good, Fair, Limited, or Weak), plus a short description of the typical performance of students at that level. The descriptions will cover the three types of responses: Speaking about Familiar Topics (Speaking Tasks 1 and 2), Speaking about Campus Situations (Tasks 3 and 5), and Speaking about Academic Course Content (Tasks 4 and 6).

Here are the level descriptions for responses about familiar topics (Speaking Tasks 1 and 2):

Level	Your Performance
Good (3.5–4.0)	Your responses indicate an ability to communicate your personal experiences and opinions effectively in English. Overall, your speech is clear and fluent. Your use of vocabulary and grammar is effective with only minor errors. Your ideas are generally well developed and expressed coherently.
Fair (2.5–3.0)	Your responses indicate you are able to speak in English about your personal experiences and opinions in a mostly clear and coherent manner. Your speech is mostly clear with only occasional errors. Grammar and vocabulary are somewhat limited and include some errors. At times, the limitations prevent you from elaborating fully on your ideas, but they do not seriously interfere with overall communication.
Limited (1.5–2.0)	Your responses indicate some difficulty speaking in English about everyday experiences and opinions. Listeners sometimes have trouble understanding you because of noticeable problems with pronunciation, grammar and vocabulary. While you are able to respond partially to the questions, you are not able to fully develop your ideas, possibly due to limited vocabulary and grammar.
Weak (0–1.0)	Your responses are incomplete. They contain little or no content and are difficult for listeners to understand.

Here are the level descriptions for the responses about campus situations (Speaking Tasks 3 and 5):

Level	Your Performance
Good (3.5–4.0)	Your responses indicate an ability to speak effectively in English about reading material and conversations typically encountered by university students. Overall, your responses are clear and coherent, with only occasional errors of pronunciation, grammar or vocabulary.
Fair (2.5–3.0)	Your responses demonstrate an ability to speak in English about reading material and experiences typically encountered by university students. You are able to convey relevant information about conversations, newspaper articles and campus bulletins; however, some details are missing or inaccurate. Limitations of grammar, vocabulary and pronunciation at times cause difficulty for the listener. However, they do not seriously interfere with overall communication.
Limited (1.5–2.0)	Your responses indicate that you have some difficulty speaking in English about information from conversations, newspaper articles, university publications and so on. While you are able to talk about some of the key information from these sources, limited grammar and vocabulary may prevent you from fully expressing your ideas. Problems with pronunciation make it difficult for listeners to understand you at times.
Weak (0–1.0)	Your responses are incomplete. They include little or no information about the topic. Your speech is often difficult for listeners to understand, and the meaning is unclear.

And here are the level descriptions for the responses about academic course content (Speaking Tasks 4 and 6):

Level	Your Performance
Good (3.5–4.0)	Your responses demonstrate an ability to communicate effectively in English about academic topics typical of first-year university studies. Your speech is mostly clear and fluent. You are able to use appropriate vocabulary and grammar to explain concepts and ideas from reading or lecture material. You are able to talk about key information and relevant details with only minor inaccuracies.
Fair (2.5–3.0)	Your responses demonstrate that you are able to speak in English about academic reading and lecture material, with only minor communication problems. For the most part, your speech is clear and easy to understand. However, some problems with pronunciation and intonation may occasionally cause difficulty for the listener. Your use of grammar and vocabulary is adequate to talk about the topics, but some ideas are not fully developed or are inaccurate.
Limited (1.5–2.0)	In your responses, you are able to use English to talk about the basic ideas from academic reading or lecture materials, but, in general, you include few relevant or accurate details. It is sometimes difficult for listeners to understand your responses because of problems with grammar, vocabulary and pronunciation. Overall, you are able to respond in a general way to the questions, but the amount of information in your responses is limited and the expression of ideas is often vague and unclear.
Weak (0–1.0)	Your responses are incomplete. They include little or no information about the topic. Your speech is often difficult for listeners to understand, and the meaning is unclear.

Source: www.ets.org/Media/Tests/TOEFL/pdf/TOEFL_Perf_Feedback.pdf

TEST TACTIC

In general, it is better to use a variety of simple grammar and vocabulary structures accurately than to use complex grammar and vocabulary structures incorrectly. You are more likely to use unnatural language or make confusing errors when using complex structures.

Directions

This speaking review test is intended to help you learn your speaking strengths and weaknesses. You will answer six speaking tasks that are designed to be at the same level as the ones on the TOEFL Test. For some tasks you will listen to one or two speakers. You may take notes while you listen. For the most realistic practice, cover the questions when you listen, and record your answers when you speak.

Test

Tracks 254–255 **TASK 1 – SPEAKING ABOUT A FAMILIAR TOPIC**

Talk about a place that was important to you when you were a child. Describe the place and say why it was important to you. Give reasons and details to support your answer.

Preparation Time: 15 Seconds   Response Time: 45 Seconds

Tracks 256–257 **TASK 2 – SPEAKING ABOUT A FAMILIAR TOPIC**

Some college students prefer studying for assignments with other people. Other students prefer working on their own when they have an assignment. Which way do you prefer? Why?

Preparation Time: 15 Seconds   Response Time: 45 Seconds

Tracks 258–261 **TASK 3 – SPEAKING ABOUT A CAMPUS SITUATION**

A student wrote a letter to the university newspaper about a problem. Read the letter. You have 45 seconds to read the letter. Begin reading now.

Office Hours Problem

I've noticed a trend recently with regard to office hours. Not only do instructors seem to be reducing how much time they are available to see students, but often they come to their office late when they have office hours scheduled. I think the university should institute a policy to force all teaching staff to do a minimum number of office hours per week and find a way to enforce the policy. I'm sure I'm not the only student who feels frustrated by this situation.

Now listen to two students as they discuss the letter.

The man/woman expresses his/her opinion about the letter. State his/her opinion and explain the reasons he/she gives for holding that opinion.

Preparation Time: 30 Seconds   Response Time: 60 Seconds

Tracks 262–265 **TASK 4 – SPEAKING ABOUT ACADEMIC CONTENT**

Now read the passage about the conduction of heat. You have 45 seconds to read the passage.

The Conduction of Heat

In simple terms, heat conduction is the movement of heat (in the form of thermal energy) from one area to another. Heat naturally flows from a region of higher temperature to one of lower temperature until both areas reach roughly the same temperature, a condition known as thermal equilibrium. Conduction takes place in solids, liquids, and gases. It occurs when atoms and molecules interact with other atoms and molecules, transferring some of their energy in the form of heat. Conduction is the most significant means of heat transfer between solid objects. It is less significant between solids and liquids, and even weaker between solids and gases.

Now listen to a lecture on this topic in an introductory science class.

Using points and examples from the lecture, explain the conduction of heat between solids, liquids, and gases.

Preparation Time: 30 Seconds   Response Time: 60 Seconds

 Tracks 266–269 **TASK 5 – SPEAKING ABOUT A CAMPUS SITUATION**

Now listen to a conversation between a man and a woman.

The speakers discuss two possible solutions to a problem. Describe the problem. Then state which of the two solutions you prefer and why.

Preparation Time: 20 Seconds   Response Time: 60 Seconds

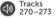 Tracks 270–273 **TASK 6 – SPEAKING ABOUT ACADEMIC CONTENT**

Now listen to part of a talk in a biology class.

Using points and examples from the talk, summarize the two definitions of comorbidity that the professor discusses.

Preparation Time: 20 Seconds   Response Time: 60 Seconds

Score Conversion

Ask a teacher or native speaker to evaluate each response from 0–4. (If necessary, you can evaluate your responses yourself. See pages 172–175 of the Speaking Reference unit for the criteria for scoring.) Then add up the scores for each response to find your raw score and use this conversion chart to find out your approximate speaking score range on the TOEFL Test.

Raw Score (out of 24)	Probable Level	Approximate Score Range
21–24	Good	26–30
15–20	Fair	19–25
9–14	Limited	11–18
1–8	Weak	1–10

Unit Focus

In the speaking section of the TOEFL Test you will have six tasks. Speaking Task 1 is one of two independent tasks about familiar topics. The question will typically ask you to express an opinion about a person, place, object, activity, or event that you know. You will have 15 seconds to prepare your response and 45 seconds to speak. In this unit you will learn and practice several key skills to answer Speaking Task 1 questions effectively, including:

- learning and using a model answer that matches all Speaking Task 1 questions.
- thinking of and expressing relevant opinions and reasons clearly and directly.
- thinking of and talking about detailed examples that support your reasons.
- speaking clearly, fluently, and confidently without long pauses.

The vocabulary focus is on practical words and phrases related to:

- describing people, places, objects, activities, and events.

A Warm-up

A1 Work with a partner. Answer three speaking tasks from this chart each. When you answer, try to speak for up to 45 seconds without any long pauses. After each speech, give your partner some helpful feedback.

Describe one	helpful person relaxing place useful object enjoyable activity popular event	that you know and say why	he she it	is so	helpful. relaxing. useful. enjoyable. popular.

B Practical Vocabulary

B1 Choose the best answer, A–F, to complete this chart of descriptive adjectives that would be useful for answering Speaking Task 1 questions. Check a dictionary if any of the words have unfamiliar meanings.

Descriptive Adjective	Synonym	Antonym
1.	compassionate	Unkind
economical	inexpensive	2.
3.	inspiring	Boring
relaxing	4.	5.
time-saving	6.	Inefficient

A calming
B caring
C convenient
D costly
E exciting
F stressful

C Analyzing Speaking Task 1

There are four types of Speaking Task 1 questions that you might see in the TOEFL Test. These question types look slightly different from each other, but you can answer all of them in the same way.

The first type, which is the most common, asks you to talk positively about a person, place, object, event, or activity, as in this example:

Choose a _____ you enjoyed and say why you enjoyed it. Include examples and details in your response.

The second type of question is similar to the first type, but it asks you to talk negatively about someone or something:

> What is one _____ that you do not enjoy? Give a reason and specific examples in support of your answer.

The third type asks you to talk about one option from a list of several choices:

> Do you prefer _____ , _____ , or _____ ? Why? Provide specific details and examples in your answer.

The final type of question asks you to say what advice or recommendation you would give to another person:

> A friend has asked your advice about _____ . What specific advice about _____ would you give your friend? Why? Include examples and details in support of your answer.

When the question appears on the screen, an announcer will read it. After that a second announcer will tell you to begin preparing your response. After 15 seconds, the second announcer will tell you to begin your response. The screen will show both the question and how much time remains during your preparation and speaking time.

To answer a Speaking Task 1 question effectively and get a good score, your response should:

- use language well – you need to use grammar and vocabulary naturally and effectively with few mistakes.
- be delivered well – your speech should be clear and fluent, with good pronunciation and few long pauses.
- develop the topic well – you need to give a well-organized response that directly answers the question.

Common problems when answering Speaking Task 1 questions that are likely to reduce your score include:

- poor language use – frequent mistakes, or vocabulary and grammar that are unnatural.
- poor delivery – unclear pronunciation or intonation, frequent or long pauses, or lack of fluency.
- poor topic development – a response that is disorganized, repeats ideas, or does not answer the question.

C1 **Match questions 1–4 to one of the four types of Speaking Task 1 questions described above.**

1. A friend is planning to visit your hometown. How would you recommend that your friend travel there? Why?
2. Would you prefer to attend a university in your hometown, one in another part of your country, or one overseas? Why?
3. What is one gift you received that you really liked? Describe the gift and say why you liked it.
4. What is one event you attended recently that you did not enjoy? Describe the event and say why you did not enjoy it.

C2 **Look at this response to a Speaking Task 1 question. Then complete tasks 1–3.**

It's hard to choose just one gift that I really like. However, if I had to pick one, it would be a tablet computer that my parents gave me. ~~This tablet is the gift that I like most.~~ The main reason is that my tablet is useful for studying. For example, with my tablet I can read books or connect to the Internet wherever I am. This means I can study at home, at a café, or at a friend's house, which is very convenient. ~~It is useful and convenient to study wherever I want.~~ So that's why I really like my tablet.

1. Which of the Speaking Task 1 questions from exercise **C1** does the response answer?
2. What is the problem with the two crossed out sentences (~~like this~~) in the response?
3. Practice saying the response until you can say it confidently and fluently. Do not say the crossed out sentences.

TEST TACTIC

The opinions, reasons, and supporting examples that you talk about in your responses to Speaking Task 1 questions do not have to be true. The rater will assign your score based on how well you answer the question and use English, not based on whether your answer is true or not.

D Mastering Speaking Task 1 – Preparing an Effective Response

Thinking of and choosing an opinion, reason, and example that are all easy to talk about will help you get a good score for Speaking Task 1. However, you only have 15 seconds to prepare your response, so it is essential to make good decisions and to use your time effectively.

D1 **Summarize the opinion, reason, and example from this response to a Speaking Task 1 question. One answer has been done for you.**

> Choose a book you enjoyed reading and say why you enjoyed it. Include examples and details in your response.

It's hard to choose just one book that I enjoyed. However, if I had to pick one, it would be a book that helped me learn English effectively. The main reason is that this book helped me gain confidence. For example, before I got this book I thought I would fail an English exam that I had to take. But reading the book helped me understand English better and I became more confident, so I passed the exam with a high score. So that's why this book is one that I enjoyed reading.

Opinion _____

Reason _____

Example _The speaker was worried about failing an English exam but a book gave her confidence and she passed._

D2 **Look at this checklist for preparing an effective response for Speaking Task 1 questions. Then complete tasks 1 and 2.**

> ☑ Your opinion, reason, and example should be familiar ideas that you have talked about before in English.
>
> ☑ You should be able to discuss the opinion, reason, and example using simple, easy-to-pronounce words.
>
> ☑ The opinion, reason, and example should directly answer the question and be connected to each other.

1. Do the opinion, reason, and example from exercise **D1** match each point in the checklist? Discuss with a partner.
2. Work with a partner to think of another opinion, reason, and example for the Speaking Task 1 question in exercise **D1**. Use the checklist as a guide.

D3 **Complete tasks 1–5.**

1. Take 15 seconds to think of an opinion, reason, and example for question A below.
2. After 15 seconds, use the checklist from exercise **D2** to judge your opinion, reason, and example. If you are satisfied that your ideas match each point in the checklist, go on to task 3; if not, repeat task 1.
3. Quickly write down the opinion, reason, and example that you thought of in task 1. Write in notes, not full sentences.
4. Repeat tasks 1–3 for Speaking Task 1 questions B–D below.
5. Share your ideas for Speaking Task 1 questions A–D with other students. Then listen to their ideas. Which are the best ideas? Why are they the best ideas?

A What is one subject that you do not enjoy studying? Give a reason and specific examples in support of your answer.

B Describe one person who has helped you in your life. Say who the person is and how he or she has helped you.

C A friend has asked your advice about an interesting topic to learn about. What topic would you recommend? Why?

D Do you prefer studying at home, in a café, or at a library? Why? Provide specific details and examples in your answer.

TEST TACTIC

If you want to make a note of your opinion, reason, and example during the 15 seconds of preparation time, that is OK. However, most people find that 15 seconds is enough time to think of ideas, but not enough time to write ideas down.

E Mastering Speaking Task 1 – Delivering a High-Quality Response

All Speaking Task 1 questions can be answered in the same way. As a result, using a template – a well-organized model answer that uses natural language – will help you avoid mistakes and deliver an effective, quality response in 45 seconds.

E1 What information, A–E, does each highlighted phrase in this template introduce? Use the response in exercise **D1** as a guide. One answer has been done for you.

It's hard to choose ...   1. _____ *a summary of the question* _____

However, if I had to pick one, it would be ...   2. _____

The main reason is that ...   3. _____

For example, ...   4. _____

So that's why ...   5. _____

A   a detailed supporting example
B   an easy-to-write-about opinion
C   a paraphrase of your opinion (optional)

D   a summary of the question
E   a clear and relevant reason

E2 Write in the highlighted phrases from exercise **E1** to complete this response to a Speaking Task 1 question. One answer has been done for you.

> Choose a book you enjoyed reading and say why you enjoyed it. Include examples and details in your response.

1. *It's hard to choose* _____ only one book that I really liked. 2. _____ a book about choosing a career from my parents. 3. _____ this book helped me decide what to do with my life. 4. _____, when I was a high school student I wanted to work with cars, so I was planning to get a job as a mechanic. However, after reading the book I decided that working with cars would be tedious, so I changed my plan. 5. _____ I really enjoyed the book about choosing a career.

🔊 Track 274 **E3** Complete tasks 1 and 2.

1. Listen to a high-level student say the full response from exercise **E2** sentence by sentence. Repeat each sentence after you hear it. Try to match the speaker's intonation, rhythm, and pronunciation. Keep practicing until you can say the response confidently and fluently.
2. Work with a partner to practice saying the full response from **E2**. Each time your partner speaks, give him or her useful feedback about intonation, rhythm, and pronunciation.

E4 Write in the best answer, A–D, to complete blanks 1–4 in this Speaking Task 1 response. When you have finished, practice saying the completed response until you can say it fluently and confidently in 45 seconds or less.

> Describe one place you would like to go for a vacation. Support your answer with details.

It's hard to choose 1. _____. However, if I had to pick one, it would be 2. _____. The main reason is that 3. _____. For example, when I was a student at high school and university, 4. _____. I would love to go and see the real buildings in Rome and learn more about the history and culture of that city. So that's why I would choose to visit Rome.

A   taking a trip to Rome in Italy
B   I read about the old buildings in Rome

C   only one place to go for a vacation
D   I find Roman history very stimulating

E5 **Write a full response to this Speaking Task 1 question.**

What is one event you attended recently that you did not enjoy? Describe the event and say why you did not enjoy it.

It's hard to choose _____

However, if I had to pick one, it would be _____

The main reason is that _____

For example, _____

So that's why _____

E6 **Practice saying your response from exercise E5 until you can say it fluently and confidently in 45 seconds or less.**

E7 **Work with a partner to complete tasks 1–5. Use some of the words you studied in exercise B1 in your responses.**

1. Prepare a response to one of the Speaking Task 1 questions in this chart:

Describe one	person place object activity *your idea*	that you would like to that you do not want to you would recommend that a friend	meet. visit. buy. do. *your idea.*

2. Listen to the response that your partner prepared. Take notes if you like.
3. After listening, put checks (✔) in the YES or NO columns of the table below. Then give your partner feedback.
4. Say the response you prepared and get your partner's feedback. Try to get perfect feedback – YES in every column.
5. Fix any mistakes in your response that your partner noticed. Then repeat tasks 1–5 with several different partners.

Did your partner	YES	NO
Give an opinion that clearly and directly answers the question?		
Mention a reason that is directly relevant to the topic of the question?		
Give a supporting example that logically follows from the reason?		
Finish his or her response in less than 45 seconds?		
Use the template phrases accurately?		
Speak clearly, fluently, and confidently without long pauses?		

E8 **How confident are you about answering Speaking Task 1 questions? Complete this short survey.**

1. I think that I will be able to prepare my response well in 15 seconds.
   ☐ Yes ☐ Maybe ☐ No
2. I think that I will be able to remember the model language from the template.
   ☐ Yes ☐ Maybe ☐ No
3. I think that I will be able to add my own opinion, reason, and example to the template.
   ☐ Yes ☐ Maybe ☐ No
4. 4. I think that I will be able to deliver my speech fluently and confidently in 45 seconds.
   ☐ Yes ☐ Maybe ☐ No

E9 **For each question in exercise E8 that you answered Maybe or No, discuss with other students how you can improve and become more confident so that you could answer Yes.**

TEST TACTIC

If you find that you cannot complete all five sections of the template in 45 seconds, do not worry about step 5. A concluding sentence is optional provided that your opinion, reason, and supporting example are clear.

F Test Challenge

 Tracks 275–282 **F1** **Answer** *two* **of questions 1–4. For each question, take 15 seconds to prepare and speak for no more than 45 seconds in order to get realistic practice for the test. Use this checklist of skills that you learned in this unit as a guide.**

> Note that in this book you will hear a beep at the end of your speaking time. In the TOEFL Test you will not hear this final beep; instead, you will see how much time is left on the screen.

- ☑ Make sure your opinion, reason, and example are familiar, match the topic, and logically support each other.
- ☑ Follow the template as closely as you can – this will help you deliver a well-organized, effective, natural response.

1. Describe an important event from your childhood. Explain why this event is important to you. Include specific examples.
2. Talk about a place you have visited that you did not like very much. Explain why you disliked this place.
3. Which of the following do you use most often: a digital camera, a cell phone, or a computer? Why? Give details and examples to support your response.
4. Your friend has asked for advice about how to become healthier. What advice would you give your friend? Support your answer.

F2 **Prepare responses to the two questions from exercise F1 that you have not answered yet. Say your responses to a partner in 45 seconds and give and receive feedback to help each other deliver better responses.**

Next Steps

Descriptive adjectives are useful for answering Speaking Task 1, Speaking Task 2, and Writing Task 2 questions. You may also see or hear these words in the reading and listening sections of TOEFL. As a result, learning more descriptive words, as well as practicing key skills for Speaking Task 1 questions, may help you increase your TOEFL score.

To learn more descriptive adjectives:

1. Read an article in English once to understand the main ideas, but do not try to understand every word.
2. Read the article again and make a list of adjectives in the article that describe a person, place, idea, situation, or event.
3. Write sentences using the adjectives on your list, and then say your sentences aloud in a clear, confident voice. Writing and then saying the sentences will help you remember the adjectives.

To practice key skills for Speaking Task 1 questions:

1. Spend two minutes to make a list of as many different people as you can think of.
2. For the first person on your list, spend 15 seconds thinking of reasons and examples either why you like that person, why you dislike that person, or why you think another person should speak to that person. (Your reasons and examples do not have to be true, but they do have to be easy to talk about.)
3. Then take 45 seconds to give a speech based on your reasons and examples. Use the template from exercise **E1**.
4. Repeat steps 2 and 3 for the other people on your list.
5. Repeat steps 1–4, but this time make a list of places, objects, activities, or events.

Unit Focus

In the speaking section of the TOEFL Test you will have six tasks. Speaking Task 2 is one of two independent tasks about familiar topics. The question will ask you to express an opinion about a general topic like education, work, health, or free time activities. The topic will include two contrasting points of view, and you will need to say which one you think is better. You will have 15 seconds to prepare your response and then 45 seconds to speak. In this unit you will learn and practice key skills to answer Speaking Task 2 questions effectively, including:

- learning and using a model answer that matches all Speaking Task 2 questions.
- thinking of and expressing relevant opinions and reasons clearly and directly.
- thinking of and talking about detailed examples that support your reasons.
- speaking clearly, fluently, and confidently without long pauses.

The vocabulary focus is on practical words and phrases related to:

- education, work, health, and free time.

A Warm-up

A1 **How many reasons can you think of that answer questions 1–4? Share your answers with other students and listen to their ideas. Which are the best ideas?**

1. Do you prefer studying alone or with your friends? Why?

   I prefer studying with my friends because _____ *your reasons* _____

2. Which is better, working for a large company or working for a small company? Why?

   I think that working for a large company is better because _____ *your reasons* _____

3. Do you agree or disagree that regular exercise is the best way to maintain your health? Why?

   I agree that exercising often is the best way to stay healthy because _____ *your reasons* _____

4. Would you rather spend your free time watching television or reading a book? Why?

   I would rather relax in front of the television because _____ *your reasons* _____

B Practical Vocabulary

B1 **Copy answers A–H to the category they match. One answer has been done for you.**

Expressions related to education		Expressions related to free time activities	
•		•	
•		•	
Expressions related to health		**Expressions related to work**	
•		• earn a good salary	
•		•	

A earn a good salary
B stay in good shape
C take a few days off

D submit an assignment
E spend time with friends
F maintain my health

G get good grades
H find a good job

C Analyzing Speaking Task 2

There are three types of Speaking Task 2 questions that you might see on the TOEFL Test. These question types look different from each other, but you can answer all of them in the same way.

For the first type of question, which is the most common, you must state which idea you prefer from two contrasting ideas and say why this is your preference. Here is an example of this type of question:

Some people like to do _____. Other people like to do _____. Which do you prefer? Why? Support your answer with details and examples.

To answer the second type of question you must explain why you agree or disagree with a particular statement:

Do you agree or disagree that _____? Why? Support your answer.

For the third type of question, you must say which of two contrasting ideas is better for other people and explain why you think so:

Some people believe students should _____. Other people think students should _____. Which option do you think is better for students? Why?

When the question appears on the screen, an announcer will read it. After that a second announcer will tell you to begin preparing your response. After 15 seconds, the second announcer will tell you to begin your response. The screen will show both the question and how much time remains during your preparation and speaking time.

To answer a Speaking Task 2 question effectively and get a good score, your response should:
- use language well – you need to use grammar and vocabulary naturally and effectively with few mistakes.
- be delivered well – your speech should be clear and fluent, with good pronunciation and few long pauses.
- develop the topic well – you need to give a well-organized response that directly answers the question.

Common problems when answering Speaking Task 2 questions that are likely to reduce your score include:
- poor language use – frequent mistakes, or vocabulary and grammar that are unnatural.
- poor delivery – unclear pronunciation or intonation, frequent or long pauses, or lack of fluency.
- poor topic development – a response that is disorganized, repeats ideas, or does not answer the question.

TEST TACTIC

Lack of fluency – which often happens if you worry too much about grammar and vocabulary – is likely to affect your score, but minor language mistakes are not. So keep speaking, even if you realize that you have made a few small errors.

C1 Match questions 1–3 to one of the three types of Speaking Task 2 questions described above.

1. Some schools require students to wear a uniform. Other schools allow students to wear their own clothes. Which do you think is better for students? Why?
2. Some people enjoy spending free time alone. Others prefer to spend it with friends. What is your preference? Why?
3. Do you agree or disagree that speaking more than one language is a useful skill for people who work in a store? Why?

C2 Look at this response to a Speaking Task 2 question. Then complete tasks 1–3.

There are some advantages to spending _____ time with others. However, overall I feel that enjoying leisure time alone is better. The main reason is that I can save money. For example, when I am on my own I can do _____ activities like walking in the park or reading a library book. Doing _____ things is important for me these days because I don't have much money. In contrast, if I hang out with friends, usually we go out and I have to buy things like food, coffee, or movie tickets. So that's why I prefer spending my _____ time by myself.

1. Which word completes the response? (The same word is missing from all four blanks.)
2. Which of the Speaking Task 2 questions from exercise **C1** does the response answer?
3. Practice saying the response (with the missing word added to the blanks) until you can say it confidently and fluently.

D Mastering Speaking Task 2 – Preparing an Effective Response

Thinking of and choosing an opinion, reason, and example that are all easy to talk about will help you get a good score for Speaking Task 2. However, you only have 15 seconds to prepare your response, so it is essential to make good choices and use your time effectively.

Track 283 **D1** **Listen to two students discuss preparing for Speaking Task 2 questions. What advice does the woman give the man? Check (✓) the correct column. One answer has been done for you.**

	Yes	No
Choose the opinion that is easier to talk about even if it is not your real opinion.	✓	
Use stock reasons that match many topics, such as education, time, work, or health.		
Think of two contrasting examples – one that is positive and one that is negative.		
Make sure one example is about a person you know well, like a family member or friend.		

D2 **Match each opinion and reason, A–D, to either question 1 or 2. One answer has been done for you.**

1. Some people enjoy watching TV when they have free time. Others like going for walks. Which do you enjoy more? Why?
2. Some people learn best by reading books. Others prefer reading articles on a computer. What is your preference? Why?

A opinion – books / reason – slower to read on screen so books save time ___matches question 2___
B opinion – computers / reason – computer skills are essential for getting good job _____
C opinion – watching TV / reason – learn useful facts by watching documentaries _____
D opinion – walking / reason – walking is good exercise to stay healthy _____

D3 **Complete tasks 1–3 with a partner.**

1. Which two answers from A–D in exercise **D2** would be easiest for you to talk about? Why?
2. Which stock reason – education, time, work, or health – matches each reason given in answers A–D in **D2**?
3. Make a list of other reasons (including stock reasons) that would match each opinion in **D2**. Then share your ideas with the class. Which are the best reasons? Why are they the best reasons?

D4 **Look at this example from a response to a Speaking Task 2 question. Then complete tasks 1 and 2.**

For example, when I was a child I often read articles on a computer and this helped me develop excellent computer skills. Because of these skills, now I have a great job with a good salary. However, my friend only read books and did not develop good computer skills. Even though he is very smart and has a lot of academic knowledge, he does not have a good job.

1. Which opinion and reason – A, B, C, or D – from exercise **D2** does the example match?
2. With a partner, write three examples that match the other opinions and reasons from **D2**. Try to include a positive example that supports the opinion and a negative one about the other choice.

D5 **Complete steps 1–5.**

Step 1   Take 15 seconds to think of an opinion, reason, and example for question 1 below.
Step 2   Then decide if you are satisfied with your ideas. If yes, go to step 3; if not, repeat step 1.
Step 3   Quickly note down the opinion, reason, and example that you thought of in step 1.
Step 4   Repeat steps 1–3 for question 2 below.
Step 5   Share your ideas for questions 1 and 2 with other students. Then listen to their ideas. Which are the best ideas? Why are they the best ideas?

1. Some people want a job that pays well. Others would rather have a job that gives them plenty of time off. What kind of job would you prefer? Why?
2. Do you agree or disagree that universities teach students the skills they need to be successful in their careers? Why?

E Mastering Speaking Task 2 – Delivering a High-Quality Response

All Speaking Task 2 questions can be answered in the same way. As a result, using a template – a well-organized model answer that uses natural language – will help you avoid mistakes and deliver an effective, quality response in 45 seconds.

E1 **What information, A–E, does each highlighted phrase in this template introduce? One answer has been done for you.**

There are some advantages to …   1. _____ *a summary of the opinion you reject* _____

However, overall I feel that …   2. _____

The main reason is that …   3. _____

For example, …   4. _____

So that's why …   5. _____

A   a paraphrase of your opinion (optional)
B   a detailed supporting example
C   a summary of the opinion you reject

D   a clear and relevant reason for your opinion
E   a summary of the opinion you choose

E2 **Write in the highlighted phrases from exercise E1 to complete this response to a Speaking Task 2 question. One answer has been done for you.**

Some people believe children should learn how to use a computer at school. Other people think young children should focus on learning academic subjects. Which do you think is better for children? Why?

1. _____ There are some advantages to _____ children concentrating on academic subjects.
2. _____ children should learn computer skills at school.
3. _____ computer skills may help them get a good job in the future. 4. _____ my sister had computer lessons at school and because her computer skills are good, she easily got a great job after graduating from university. In contrast, my cousin didn't learn about computers at school and he lacks good computer skills. For this reason, he can't find a good job now even though he's very smart. 5. _____
I think schools should teach children about computers.

🔊 Track 284   **E3** **Complete tasks 1 and 2.**

1. Listen to a high-level student say the full response from exercise **E2**. Repeat each sentence after you hear it. Try to match the speaker's intonation, rhythm, and pronunciation. Keep practicing until you can say each sentence confidently and fluently.
2. Work with a partner to practice saying the full response. Each time your partner speaks, give him or her feedback about intonation, rhythm, and pronunciation.

E4 Use your own words to complete two opposite responses to this Speaking Task 2 question. Then practice saying each response until you can say it confidently and fluently in 45 seconds or less.

> Some people like to have a job with a high salary. Other people would rather get a job that gives them lots of free time. Which type of job would you like? Why? Support your answer.

TEST TACTIC

If you cannot think of both a positive example about your opinion and a negative example about the other opinion, make the example that you *can* think of longer by adding specific details such as names, numbers, dates, and so on.

There are some advantages to having a job that pays well. However, overall I feel that getting a job which allows me plenty of time off is preferable. The main reason is that _____

_____

_____

_____ So that's why I would rather have a job that gives me lots of free time, not one with a high salary.

There are some advantages to a job that lets me have plenty of time off. However, overall I feel that a position that comes with a good salary is better. The main reason is that _____

_____

_____

_____ So that's why I would prefer a job that pays well to one that offers a lot of free time.

E5 Work with a partner to complete tasks 1–5. Use some of the words you studied in exercise **B1** in your responses.

1. Prepare a response to *one* of these Speaking Task 2 questions:
   - Some students like to learn about science. Others would rather study literature or art. Which do you prefer? Why?
   - Do you agree or disagree that having several part-time jobs is better than having one full-time position? Why?
   - Some students choose to eat only fruits and vegetables. Others like eating meat and fish, too. Which do you prefer?
   - Some children like to spend free time watching movies. Others prefer to play with friends. Which is better? Why?

2. Listen to the response that your partner prepared. Take notes if you like.
3. After listening, put checks (✔) in the YES or NO columns of the table below. Then give your partner feedback.
4. Say the response you prepared and get your partner's feedback. Try to get perfect feedback – YES in every column.
5. Fix any mistakes in your response that your partner noticed. Then repeat tasks 1–5 with several different partners.

Did your partner	YES	NO
Give an opinion that clearly matches one of the choices from the question?		
Mention a reason that is directly relevant to the topic of the question?		
Give a supporting example that logically follows from the reason?		
Finish his or her response in less than 45 seconds?		
Use the template phrases accurately?		
Speak clearly, fluently, and confidently without long pauses?		

F Test Challenge

F1 **Answer *two* of questions 1–4. For each question, take 15 seconds to prepare and speak for no more than 45 seconds in order to get realistic practice for the test. Use this checklist of skills that you learned in this unit as a guide.**

Tracks 285–292

> ☑ Make sure your opinion, reason, and example are familiar, match the topic, and logically support each other.
>
> ☑ Follow the template as closely as you can – this will help you deliver a well-organized, effective, natural response.

This book uses a beep to indicate your speaking time is up. Remember that you will not hear this beep in the real test.

1. Some college students work part-time while they are studying. Others choose not to work so they can concentrate on their studies. Which do you think is better for students? Explain why.

2. Some people prefer doing outdoor activities in their free time. Others prefer spending their free time indoors. Which do you prefer? Include details and examples in your explanation.

3. At some colleges, students study just one subject in order to get a deep knowledge of that subject. At other colleges, students study various subjects in order to get a broad knowledge of many subjects. Which is better for students? Why?

4. Do you agree or disagree that it is healthier to live in a small town than in a big city? Why? Support your answer.

F2 **Prepare responses to the two questions from exercise F1 that you have not answered yet. Say your responses to a partner in 45 seconds and give and receive feedback to help each other deliver better responses.**

Next Steps

Expressions related to education, work, health, and free time are especially useful for answering Speaking Task 1, Speaking Task 2, and Writing Task 2 questions. These words may also appear in the other sections of TOEFL. As a result, learning other useful expressions related to these topics, as well as practicing key skills for Speaking Task 2 questions, may help you increase your overall TOEFL score.

To learn more expressions related to study, work, health, and free time:

1. Do an Internet search for "study tips", "work advice", "how to stay healthy", or "fun free time activities".
2. Read one of the articles that you find. While you read, make a list of words and phrases related to the topic.
3. Write sentences using these words and phrases. Then practice saying your sentences in a clear, confident voice. Writing and then saying the sentences will help you remember the words and phrases.

To practice key skills for Speaking Task 2 questions:

1. Spend a few minutes to make a list of pairs of opposite ideas. For example, your list might include things like summer and winter, or actions like working part-time and full-time.
2. Choose one pair of ideas from your list. Think of a reason and detailed supporting example why you like one of the items in the pair. Then think of a reason with supporting example why you dislike the opposite idea.
3. Use the template for Speaking Task 2 to give a 45-second response using the ideas you thought about in step 2. Record your speech. Then listen to the recording. If you are not satisfied for some reason, keep practicing until you feel satisfied.
4. Repeat steps 2 and 3 for the other pairs of opposite ideas on your list.

Unit Focus

In the speaking section of the TOEFL Test you will have six tasks. Speaking Task 3 is one of two integrated tasks about common campus situations that college students experience. You will first read a short passage about a situation at college. Then you will listen to two students discussing the same situation. After that you will be asked to summarize the opinion and supporting reasons of one of the students. In this unit you will learn and practice several key skills to answer Speaking Task 3 questions effectively, including:

- taking notes when you read a passage and listen to a conversation.
- using your preparation time effectively to organize your response.
- learning and using a template to deliver a clear, organized, effective response.
- speaking clearly and confidently, with natural pauses and emphasis.

The vocabulary focus is on campus words and phrases related to:

- places at college where students spend time.

A Warm-up

A1 Write a short response to questions 1–3. Use the example as a guide.

How would you feel if your college announced that
1. students could use the library 24 hours a day, seven days a week?
2. students would be charged $250 to pay for a new computer center?
3. students would no longer be allowed to use cell phones on campus?

Example   I would be unhappy if my college let students use the library 24 hours a day, seven days a week. The main reason is that I think my college would probably increase tuition fees to pay for it.

B Campus Vocabulary

B1 Use words from this conversation to complete sentences 1–8. One answer has been done for you.

Woman	Excuse me, I need to go to the International Student Office. I've got a map, but I'm new on campus and I'm not even sure where I am now.
Man	We're between the Student Center and the fitness center, which are, uh, these buildings on your map. See? So to get to the International Student Office, you'll need to go past the music auditorium, which is here on the map, and then the Health Services Center, here. OK?
Woman	Yeah, I see. And after that it looks like I just need to go a little bit farther past the dining hall and the Administrative Building. Thank you for the help.

1. The ___administrative building___ is where a student might go to collect administrative documents.
2. An _____ is a building where students can attend concerts or other events.
3. The _____ of a university is where all of the academic and administrative buildings are.
4. When students are hungry, they can eat at a _____, cafeteria, or restaurant.
5. A student who wants to work out could go for a run or go to the _____.
6. A doctor or nurse who works at a college probably sees patients at the _____.
7. If a student from another country has a problem, he or she should go to the _____.
8. A central place on campus where students can relax with friends is the _____.

C Analyzing Speaking Task 3

For Speaking Task 3 questions, you will first see a short reading passage on the screen and an announcer will briefly summarize the main idea of the passage. The passage, which may be an announcement, a newspaper article, or a letter, will discuss a new or changed situation at a college. The passage will include either reasons for or opinions about the new situation. You will usually have 45 or 50 seconds to read the passage, depending on its length.

After you read, the announcer will introduce a conversation in which a man and woman discuss the situation described in the passage. Both people will give their opinion, but one person – the main speaker – will give a longer opinion with more detailed reasons and supporting ideas. While you listen, take notes about the main speaker's opinion, reasons, and supporting examples.

After listening, you will see the question on the screen and the announcer will read it aloud. The question will look like this:

> The man expresses his opinion about _____. State his opinion and explain the reasons he gives for holding that opinion.

A second announcer will then tell you to begin preparing your response. You will have 30 seconds to prepare. The amount of preparation time remaining will be shown on the screen. After the preparation time, the second announcer will tell you to start speaking. You will have 60 seconds to speak. The amount of time remaining will be shown onscreen.

To answer a Speaking Task 3 question effectively and get a good score, your response should:

- use language well – you need to use grammar and vocabulary naturally and effectively with few mistakes.
- be delivered well – your speech should be clear and fluent, with good pronunciation and few long pauses.
- develop the topic well – you need to summarize the situation mentioned in the passage, state the main speaker's opinion, and summarize his or her supporting reasons.

Common problems when answering Speaking Task 3 questions that may reduce your score include:

- poor language use – frequent mistakes, or vocabulary and grammar that are unnatural.
- poor delivery – unclear pronunciation or intonation, frequent or long pauses, or lack of fluency.
- poor topic development – a response that does not clearly summarize the main speaker's point of view.

TEST TACTIC

Speaking Task 3 questions ask you to discuss only the main speaker's opinion and reasons. If you discuss other opinions, including *your* opinion, you will probably not have time to answer the question completely, which will reduce your score.

C1 Answer questions 1–4 by summarizing this passage and script. After you have summarized, say each answer clearly. One answer has been done for you.

The college is pleased to announce a series of free lectures to be held in the auditorium. The lectures will cover a range of non-academic topics, including politics, business, music, and art. There will be a lecture at 8 p.m. every Thursday in October.

Man	Great news about these new lectures in the auditorium, isn't it?
Woman	Really? They're not about academic subjects, so …
Man	Even though I'm not studying politics or business, I'm still interested, especially if I can learn about them for free. And I know *you're* interested in music and art. Plus, it's great the college is offering these events. Last year, a lot of people were unhappy because there were so few events on campus. If we go to these lectures, maybe the college will offer more events.
Woman	Hmmm. Good point. Maybe I'll go to one or two of them.

1. What does the college announce? _____ <u>The college announces some free lectures.</u> _____
2. How does the man feel about the announcement? _____
3. What is the first reason he gives for his feeling? _____
4. What is the second reason he gives? _____

D Mastering Speaking Task 3 – Reading the Passage

When you read the passage, you need to find and make a note of the main point of the passage plus any reasons, opinions, or details that support or explain the main point. If you have time, it can also be helpful to think about how students might react to the situation described in the passage.

D1 **These notes about the reading passage below mention the type of document, main idea, and supporting points. Underline the section(s) of the passage that match each point in the notes. One answer has been done for you.**

> student thinks procedure to start student clubs not good
> — should not have to be full-time student to start
> — should not have to find 50 members before start
> student wants college to change policy to start clubs

New Registration Procedure Needed for Student Clubs

I like chess so when I found there was no student chess club at the college, I wanted to start one. However, the procedure for registering student clubs makes that impossible. According to college policy, new clubs can only be founded by full-time students, and clubs will not be approved unless at least 50 students are interested in joining. I can see no reason why part-time students like me cannot start a club, and why must a club find potential members *before* it can be registered? I hope other students will join me in asking the college to reconsider its policy.

D2 **Work with a partner to predict how students might react to this passage. Use the examples as a guide. When you have finished, share your ideas with other students.**

Examples   I think students would support the writer because finding 50 interested students is too many.
            Students might oppose the writer because part-time and full-time students should not have the same rights.

D3 **Complete tasks 1 and 2.**

1. Read these announcements and take notes. Use the sample notes in exercise **D1** as a guide.
2. Predict how students might react to the information in the announcements. When you have finished, discuss your predictions with a partner.

Improvements to Campus Exercise Facilities

The college is pleased to announce that the new fitness center in Murrow Hall is now complete and will be open starting March 1. The college now has state-of-the-art sporting facilities that are open 24 hours a day, seven days a week for use by academic staff, administrative staff, and students who have an athletic scholarship. Students without an athletic scholarship can either gain access to the new facilities by applying for a "Gym Access" card for just $50 per semester, or use existing exercise facilities at no charge.

New Bulletin Boards in Student Center

Last Monday students in the Student Center on campus were surprised to see that several new bulletin boards had been erected. At first the boards were empty, but within hours the first notices had been posted. When asked for comment, a college spokesperson said that the college hoped the bulletin boards would provide a central place for students to put up notices and advertisements. The spokesperson also said the bulletin boards would help make the campus look cleaner because notices posted elsewhere on campus would be taken down.

D4 Now use your notes and predictions from exercise **D3** to answer questions 1–6. Speak clearly and use full sentences when you answer.

1. What is the main situation described in the first passage?
2. What is the first supporting reason, opinion, or detail mentioned in the first passage?
3. What is the second supporting reason, opinion, or detail mentioned in the first passage?
4. What is the main situation described in the second passage?
5. What is the first supporting reason, opinion, or detail mentioned in the second passage?
6. What is the second supporting reason, opinion, or detail mentioned in the second passage?

E Mastering Speaking Task 3 – Listening to the Conversation

The conversation will typically last 60 to 80 seconds. While you are listening, take clear notes about both speakers' ideas, as well as the reasons and details they give. If you are confident you have recognized whether the main speaker is the man or woman, focus only on his or her words.

E1 Read these notes about a conversation in which two students discuss the letter about student clubs from exercise **D1**. Match each underlined abbreviation (short way to write something) to the full word, A–L. One answer has been done for you.

M	see letter about <u>stdnt</u> clubs?
W	saw it
M	agree <u>w/</u> stdnt = <u>cllg</u> should change policy
	cllg rule = <u>ft</u> + <u>pt</u> stdnts must be <u>eql</u>
	current club policy against cllg rules
W	not know rule
M	not make sense clubs need 50 stdnts <u>B4</u> registered
	clubs not cost cllg <u>$</u> so <u>#</u> members not matter
W	good point

A   and   _____
B   before   _____
C   college   _____
D   (are) equal _____
E   full-time   _____
F   man   ___M___
G   money   _____
H   number (of) _____
I   part-time   _____
J   student   _____
K   with   _____
L   woman   _____

🔊 Track 293 **E2** Take notes as you listen to two students discussing the letter about student clubs from exercise **D1**. Then complete tasks 1–3 with a partner.

1. Listen to the conversation to check your answers to exercise **E1**. Then compare answers.
2. What other words in the notes could be abbreviated? How would you abbreviate them?
3. What other abbreviations do you use when you take notes? Share your ideas with other students.

🔊 Track 294 **E3** Take notes as you listen to two students discussing the announcements from exercise **D3**. Then use your notes to write full sentences in answer to questions 1–4.

1. Who is the main speaker?
2. What is his or her opinion about the announcement?
3. What is the first reason the main speaker gives for his or her opinion?
4. What is the second reason that the main speaker gives?

🔊 Track 295 **E4** Take notes as you listen to two students discussing the newspaper article about bulletin boards in exercise **D3**. Then use your notes to answer questions 1–4. Speak clearly and use full sentences when you answer.

1. Who is the main speaker?
2. What is his or her opinion about the announcement?
3. What is the first reason the main speaker gives for his or her opinion?
4. What is the second reason that the main speaker gives?

F Mastering Speaking Task 3 – Preparing Your Response

Use your preparation time to circle and label the key points in the notes you made while reading the passage and listening to the conversation. This will help you deliver a well-organized response. If you have enough time, either add details to your notes from your memory or rehearse your speech.

F1 Label these notes by matching the correct label, D1–R2, with each circled point. One answer has been done for you.

student thinks procedure to start student clubs not good
– should not have to be full-time student to start
– should not have to find 50 members before start
(student wants college to change policy to start clubs)

M see letter about <u>stdnt</u> want start chess club?
W saw it
M (agree w/ stdnt) = cllg should change policy
   (cllg rule = ft + pt stdnts must be eql)
   (current club policy against cllg rules)
W not know rule
M (not make sense clubs need 50 stdnts B4 registered)
   (clubs not cost cllg $ so # members not matter)
W good point

D1 (supporting detail 1)
D2 (supporting detail 2)
MP (main point)
OP (main speaker's opinion)
R1 (main speaker's reason 1)
R2 (main speaker's reason 2)

F2 Circle the key points in your notes from exercises **E3** and **E4** and label them D1, D2, MP, OP, R1, and R2.

G Mastering Speaking Task 3 – Delivering Your Response

All Speaking Task 3 questions follow a similar pattern. This means that using a template – a well-organized model answer that includes natural language – will help you save time, avoid mistakes, and deliver an effective, high-quality response.

G1 This response to a Speaking Task 3 question uses a template. Which labeled key point from your notes follows each highlighted template phrase: D1, D2, MP, OP, R1, or R2? One answer has been done for you.

The man expresses his opinion of the arguments in the letter about college policy for registering a student club. State his opinion and the reasons he gives for holding that opinion.

The two people discuss 1. __MP__ a letter by a student about a changed policy for starting student clubs.

The man supports 2. _____ the student's viewpoint.

First, he states that 3. _____ the college has a rule that full-time and part-time students should be treated equally.

He then adds that 4. _____ the current policy about registering student clubs is against this rule.

Next, the man says that 5. _____ he doesn't understand why clubs need 50 potential members before being registered.

He goes on to say that 6. _____ clubs don't cost the college money, so the number of members doesn't matter.

Track 296 **G2** **Listen to a high-level student say this response and complete tasks 1–4.**

The two people discuss a letter by a student about changing the policy for starting student clubs. **The man supports** the student's viewpoint. **First, he states that** the college has a rule that full-time and part-time students should be treated equally. **He then adds that** the college's policy about registering student clubs is against this rule. **Next, the man says that** he doesn't think clubs need fifty potential members before they can be registered. **He goes on to say that** student clubs don't cost the college any money, so the number of members doesn't matter.

1. Mark the speaker's pauses on the response. Use / for a short pause and // for a longer pause.
2. Underline the words in the response that the speaker emphasizes (says strongly).
3. Note the pronunciation of difficult words. Practice saying these words until you are confident you can say them correctly.
4. Practice saying the response with a partner. Each time your partner speaks, give him or her useful feedback about pronunciation, pausing, and emphasis.

G3 **Complete tasks 1 and 2.**

1. Look at your notes from exercises **D3** and **E4** about the college fitness center. Use your notes to write a full response using the template. Two sentences have been written for you.
2. Practice saying your completed response until you can say it fluently and confidently in 60 seconds or less.

The man expresses his opinion of the announcement about the new fitness center. State his opinion and the reasons he gives for holding that opinion.

The two people discuss 1. _____ *an announcement about a new fitness center.* _____

The *man/woman supports/opposes* 2. _____ *the decision of the college.* _____

First, *he/she* points out that 3. _____

He/She then adds that 4. _____

Next, the *man/woman* says that 5. _____

He/She finishes by saying that 6. _____

G4 **Look at your notes from exercises D3 and E4 about the bulletin boards in the Student Center. Use your notes to prepare a spoken response to this question.**

The woman expresses her opinion about the addition of bulletin boards to the Student Center. State her opinion and the reasons she gives for holding that opinion.

G5 **Work with a partner to complete tasks 1–4.**

1. Listen to the response that your partner prepared in exercise **G4**. Take notes if you like.
2. After listening, put checks (✓) in the YES or NO columns of the table below. Then give your partner feedback.
3. Say the response you prepared and get your partner's feedback. Try to get perfect feedback – YES in every column.
4. Fix any mistakes in your response that your partner noticed. Then repeat tasks 1–4 with several different partners.

Did your partner	YES	NO
Clearly describe the main point of the reading passage?		
Clearly state the main speaker's opinion?		
Mention the main speaker's first reason with supporting details?		
Mention the main speaker's second reason with supporting details?		
Finish his or her response in less than 60 seconds?		
Use the template phrases accurately?		
Speak clearly, fluently, and confidently without long pauses?		

TEST TACTIC

If you have a few extra seconds during the preparation time, try warming up your voice by saying something like, "Hello, my name is ... It's nice to meet you." This may help your voice sound more powerful and confident when you start speaking.

This book uses a beep to indicate your speaking time is up. Remember that you will not hear this beep in the real test.

H Test Challenge

H1 Answer Speaking Task 3 questions 1–3. Take 45 seconds to read the passage. Then listen to the conversation. After listening, spend 30 seconds preparing your response and speak for no more than 60 seconds in order to get realistic practice for the test. Use the checklist of skills that you learned in this unit as a guide.

- ☑ Read the passage and take notes about the main idea plus supporting reasons and/or details.
- ☑ Listen to the conversation and note the main speaker's opinion and supporting reasons and ideas.
- ☑ Use the preparation time to circle and label key information in your notes.
- ☑ Use the template to make sure your response is well-organized and natural, and speak clearly and fluently.

1. State University is planning to upgrade its library facilities. Read an announcement from the university about this plan.

Announcement from the University President

State University has decided to upgrade the library facilities available on campus. Over the next year, a new library will be constructed that will have double the number of books available for borrowing compared with the current library, as well as state-of-the-art computer facilities. It will also have over 500 individual study rooms that will be available for student use. Because the cost of constructing the new library will be high, all full-time students will be charged a one-time Library Improvement Fee of $100.

🔊 Tracks 297–300 Now listen to two students as they discuss the announcement.

The man/woman expresses his/her opinion about the announcement. State his/her opinion and explain the reasons he/she gives for holding that opinion.

2. A student wrote a letter to City College's newspaper about a suggested improvement to the college. Read the letter.

New Food Options Needed on Campus

I've studied at City College for two years and basically it's a great place to study. However, there's one area that could really be improved, and that's the quality of food served at the restaurants and cafeterias available on campus. Currently, students only have access to dining halls serving fast food. They're cheap, but the food's unhealthy, low-quality, and almost every dish has meat. I think that a modern college should offer students healthier options like salad bars, vegetarian cafés, and juice bars. I'd also like to see the dining halls serving dishes from other countries.

🔊 Tracks 301–304 Now listen as two students discuss the letter.

The man/woman expresses his/her opinion about the suggestion in the letter. State his/her opinion and explain the reasons he/she gives for holding that opinion.

3. A university is changing the hours of operation at its Health Services Center. Read the notice about these changes.

Change to Hours of Operation at the Health Services Center

In response to rising costs and falling demand, the university has decided to slightly reduce the hours when the Health Services Center will operate. Instead of offering evening services on Mondays, Wednesdays, and Thursdays, evening services will now be offered on Fridays only. In addition, the Health Services Center will no longer be open on the weekend. These changes are effective immediately. Students who need medical assistance when the Health Services Center is closed have the choice of attending several clinics located in town, details of which are available at the Health Services Center.

 Tracks 305–308 Now listen to two students as they discuss the notice.

The man/woman expresses his/her opinion about the decision stated in the notice. State his/her opinion and explain the reasons he/she gives for holding that opinion.

Next Steps

Speaking Task 3 questions often focus on places that students go to on campus. You may also hear vocabulary related to these places in Speaking Task 5 or during conversations in the listening section. As a result, learning words related to campus places, as well as practicing key skills for Speaking Task 3, may help you increase your overall test score.

To learn more about vocabulary related to campus locations:

1. Visit the website of a college and search for "campus map". Print out the map (or look at it on the screen if you prefer).
2. For each place on the campus map, make a list of people who might work there or go there.
3. Make a second list of what the people who work or go to that place would do when they are there.
4. Then think about possible changes to that place and how those changes might affect students positively or negatively. For example, if the place is a Computer Center, one possible change is that the computers would be upgraded. This would benefit students because upgraded computers work faster. Another change is the hours of operation might be reduced. This would be bad for students because the Computer Center might be closed when they needed to go there.

To practice key skills for Speaking Task 3 questions:

1. Listen to a radio broadcast in which people can phone in to give their opinion about a topic. (You can use the Internet to search for "phone-in radio shows" in your area or phone-in radio shows that you can listen to online.)
2. When somebody gives an opinion about a topic, listen and take notes on the person's opinion and reasons.
3. Spend 30 seconds reviewing your notes. Then give a spoken summary of the opinion and reasons that you heard. If you repeat this activity often, you should find your ability to answer Speaking Task 3 questions will improve.

UNIT 18
SPEAKING • Integrated Speaking Task 4

Unit Focus

In the speaking section of the TOEFL Test you will have six tasks. Speaking Task 4 is one of two integrated tasks about academic content. You will first read a short passage about one aspect of an academic topic. Then you will listen to a professor discussing the same topic. After that you will be asked to explain how the professor's words relate to the reading. In this unit you will learn and practice several key skills to answer Speaking Task 4 questions effectively, including:

- taking notes when you read a passage and listen to a conversation.
- using your preparation time effectively to organize your response.
- learning and using a template to deliver clear, organized, effective responses.
- speaking clearly and confidently, with natural pronunciation and intonation.

The vocabulary focus is on academic words and phrases related to:

- psychology, the scientific study of how the human mind functions and how humans behave in different situations.

A Warm-up

A1 Read this short description of two types of motivation. Then complete tasks 1 and 2.

In psychology, extrinsic motivation describes external factors that make people act, such as peer pressure, parental pressure, or desire for money. An example would be a person learning how to use a computer in order to get a better job. Intrinsic motivation, on the other hand, is motivation that comes from within. So a person choosing to learn about computers because of an innate, or natural, interest in technology would be an example of intrinsic motivation.

1. Write about a time when you did something as a result of extrinsic motivation. Explain what you did and why you did it. Then write about a time when you did something because of intrinsic motivation. Again, say what you did and why.
2. Read your answers to the class. Then listen to other students' answers. What motivating factors are most common?

B Academic Vocabulary

B1 Write in the best answer, A–H, to complete definitions 1–8 of the highlighted words. Then compare answers with a partner. One answer has been done for you.

1. To analyze something, like why a person behaves in a _certain way, is to examine it carefully in order to explain it_ .
2. Characteristics, also known as traits, are the recognizable _____
3. A conscious action is one that a person is deliberately doing; _____
4. A strong wish to do something, especially if that wish occurs _____
5. A person who plays an active part in an event, activity, or _____
6. The word perception is used to describe using one's senses, _____
7. A rational belief is one that is based on logic and clear thinking; _____
8. A person's values, or beliefs, are the emotional principles and _____

A an irrational one is based on emotions and feelings.
B an unconscious action is one that a person is unaware of.
C certain way, is to examine it carefully in order to explain it.
D experiment is called a participant.
E features of an individual's personality.
F standards that are very important to that person.
G such as the sense of sight, to understand something.
H suddenly, is called an impulse.

C Analyzing Speaking Task 4

For Speaking Task 4 questions, you will first see a reading passage on the screen and an announcer will mention its main topic. The passage often gives an overview of one aspect of an academic subject, such as defining an idea or introducing a topic. Depending on the length of the passage, you will have 45 or 50 seconds to read it and take notes.

Next, the announcer will introduce a lecture about the same topic. The person giving the lecture will typically give some specific examples that illustrate the general idea or situation mentioned in the passage. While you listen, take notes about the points, details, and examples that the speaker discusses.

After listening, you will see the question on the screen and hear the announcer say it. The question will be similar to one of these examples:

Using points and examples from the lecture, explain how _____ affects _____.

Using examples the speaker mentions, explain how _____ can cause _____.

Using examples from the talk, explain how _____ and _____ are related.

A second announcer will then tell you to begin preparing your response. You will have 30 seconds to prepare. The amount of preparation time remaining will be shown on the screen. After the preparation time, the second announcer will tell you to start speaking. You will have 60 seconds to speak. The amount of time remaining will be shown onscreen.

To answer a Speaking Task 4 question effectively and get a good score, your response should:
- use language well – you need to use grammar and vocabulary naturally and effectively with few mistakes.
- be delivered well – your speech should be clear and fluent, with good pronunciation and few long pauses.
- develop the topic well – you need to answer the question clearly and discuss details and examples from the lecture.

Common problems when answering Speaking Task 4 questions that are likely to reduce your score include:
- poor language use – frequent mistakes, or vocabulary and grammar that are unnatural.
- poor delivery – unclear pronunciation or intonation, frequent or long pauses, or lack of fluency.
- poor topic development – not talking about specific aspects of the topic, or not answering each part of the question.

TEST TACTIC

If you notice a word in the passage that is used frequently, think about its pronunciation and say it in your mind several times. This will help you hear and understand this word during the lecture. It will also help you say that word accurately and naturally during your response.

C1 Read this short passage and script. Then answer questions 1–4. Speak clearly and in full sentences when you answer.

Peer pressure is the name given to the influence that members of a social group or individuals can have on others. This influence may cause a person to act in certain ways or adopt certain values, even if those actions and values are not what that person would normally do or believe.

Professor We tend to think of peer pressure as exerting a negative influence, and often it does, but sometimes it's positive. Let me give you an example. I read about a small town near the college where over 95% of household waste is recycled. Why? Well, apparently a few families began recycling more, which made their neighbors feel that they should recycle more, which caused other neighbors to recycle even more, until the whole town was recycling almost everything possible. Without the peer pressure exerted by their neighbors, it's likely that the residents of this town would recycle at a level closer to the national average of just 34% of household waste.

1. Does the reading passage give a general or specific description of peer pressure?
2. Does the professor talk about an example of positive or negative peer pressure?
3. According to the professor, how and why did people in the small town change their behavior?
4. According to the professor, how would people in the town probably act if they did not experience peer pressure?

D Mastering Speaking Task 4 – Reading the Passage

When reading the passage, you need to make a note of its main point. Typically, this is a definition or explanation of an academic principle or theory. You also need to take notes on any specific details that add information about the main point. Remember to leave room on your note paper so you can take notes from the lecture, too.

D1 Read this passage from a typical Speaking Task 4 question. Then answer questions 1 and 2.

Confirmation Bias

When people are presented with a theory, argument, or opinion that is in line with their own views, they are more likely to read or listen to it, accept it as true, and remember it. Conversely, people typically ignore, reject, or forget theories, arguments, or opinions that they personally oppose. These tendencies, known as confirmation bias, are stronger for emotional issues and for beliefs that people hold deeply. Confirmation bias can cause people to make poor decisions if they ignore, reject, or forget evidence that their opinion is not the best one.

---

1. Which summary, A–C, of the main point of the passage is too general, which one is too detailed, and which one is good?

    A   Confirmation bias (CB) = people accept ideas or arguments they read or hear when they match something they already believe but ignore ideas, theories, and so on they do not personally believe
    B   Confirmation bias (CB) = people easily accept opinions they believe but reject ones they don't
    C   Confirmation bias (CB) = people usually accept some opinions but not others

2. Which of these notes, A–E, about the passage are useful? Check (✔) the correct box. Then compare your answers with a partner and discuss why each note is either useful or not useful.

A People can read or listen to theories, arguments, and opinions	☐ Useful	☐ Not useful
B CB stronger about emotional topics	☐ Useful	☐ Not useful
C CB stronger about issues people believe strongly	☐ Useful	☐ Not useful
D People with CB can make poor decisions because of CB	☐ Useful	☐ Not useful
E People may ignore, reject, or forget opinions and evidence	☐ Useful	☐ Not useful

D2 Take notes about the main points and supporting details of these two passages from Speaking Task 4 questions. When you have finished, compare notes with a partner.

The NIMBY Principle

In principle, people tend to support development projects, such as the construction of a railway line, which they feel would benefit their community. However, if the development will affect them directly because it will occur close to where they live, they often oppose it. This is known as the NIMBY principle, with "NIMBY" standing for "not in my back yard." Construction projects likely to be opposed as a result of the NIMBY principle are factories or other industrial buildings, power stations, prisons, airports, and even projects that seem positive like schools or hospitals.

Social Psychology

Broadly speaking, the focus of social psychology is the study of how and under what conditions human thoughts, drives, beliefs, and behaviors are affected by other people. Social pyschologists also focus on related ideas such as the ways in which human perception and interaction are influenced by other people and by society. Social psychology theories are based on empirical, experimental data and cover a broad range of topics including individual and group behavior, and both positive and negative aspects of social behavior including leadership, conformity, and prejudice.

E Mastering Speaking Task 4 – Listening to the Lecture

In the lecture, which usually lasts from 75 to 90 seconds but may be longer, the speaker usually gives specific examples of the idea described in the reading passage, or explains how the idea applies to specific situations. While listening, take well-organized notes about the speaker's points on the same piece of paper as your notes about the reading passage.

TEST TACTIC

Before listening, think of an abbreviation for the main point of the passage. For example, you might use *CB* if the main point is confirmation bias, or *PP* for peer pressure. When you listen, write this abbreviation when the lecturer makes a point that directly relates to the reading.

E1 Read this short passage about taking notes for Speaking Task 4 questions. Then discuss questions 1–3 with a partner.

Effective Note-taking for Speaking Task 4 Questions

- You will not have time to write down every word you hear, so focus on writing only key words.
- If you can recognize how an idea is related to the main point of the reading passage, mention it in your notes.
- Use abbreviations – short ways to write words, like + for *and* or *bc* for *because* – to save time.
- Use arrows to show how two points are related to each other, such as to show that one thing caused another thing.
- Indent (leave space at the left edge) notes that are related to a note above them so the connection is easy to see later.

1. Which of the suggestions about note-taking from the passage do you already do?
2. Which *two* of the suggestions do you think are the most useful? Why?
3. Are these suggestions useful for other TOEFL questions, not just Speaking Task 4? Why or why not?

E2 Look at these reading and listening notes from part of a Speaking Task 4 lecture. Then complete tasks 1 and 2 with a partner.

READING	LISTENING
confirmation bias (CB) = people accept opinions they believe but reject ones they don't	prof + wife discuss vacation plans
CB stronger about emotional topics	wife suggest go NYC but prof not want NYC bc ngtv opin
CB stronger about issues people believe strongly	→ emotional experience as child
People with CB make poor decisions due to it	wife showed brochures + told recommendations
	prof reject pstv points + focus on ngtv = CB

1. The listening notes contain eight different abbreviations. Circle each abbreviation and write the full word.
2. The notes contain some unabbreviated long words like *emotional, experience, brochures,* and *recommendations.* How could you abbreviate these words?

🔊 Track 309–310   **E3**   **Listen to the lecture that the notes in exercise E2 are about and complete tasks 1 and 2.**

1. Read the listening notes as you listen to part one of the lecture. Listen carefully for the full form of each abbreviation.
2. Complete the notes as you listen to part two of the lecture.

🔊 Track 311   **E4**   **Look at your notes from the passage about the NIMBY principle in exercise D2. Then listen to a lecture on the same topic and take notes on the same piece of paper. Then use your notes to complete tasks 1 and 2.**

1. Did you use abbreviations when you took notes? Why or why not?
2. Overall, were you satisfied with the notes you took? Why or why not?

🔊 Track 312   **E5**   **Look at your notes from the passage about social psychology in exercise D2. Then listen to a lecture on the same topic and take notes on the same piece of paper.**

F   Mastering Speaking Task 4 – Preparing Your Response

Unlike questions for Speaking Task 3 and Speaking Task 5, questions for Speaking Task 4 do not follow a standard pattern. For this reason, you need to analyze the question carefully in order to understand what you need to say and how best to organize your response. After reading the question, use the remaining time to circle and label key points in your notes.

F1   **Write a description for how to answer Speaking Task 4 questions 1–3. Use the example as a guide.**

Using points and examples from the lecture, explain how confirmation bias affects the decisions people make.

Example   To answer this question, I would need to:
- Use information from the lecture in my response.
- Explain how confirmation bias influences people's decisions.

1. Using examples from the lecture, explain how confirmation bias affects people's behavior and how people can overcome this bias.
2. Using points and examples from the talk, explain how intrinsic and extrinsic motivation differ.
3. Using the example of recycling from the talk, explain what peer pressure is and how it affects people's behavior.

F2   **The key points in this Speaking Task 4 response have been underlined and labeled KP1–KP8 (KP stands for "key point"). Work with a partner to circle and label the notes below that match each key point. One answer has been done for you.**

Using points and examples from the lecture, explain how confirmation bias affects the decisions people make.

The reading introduces the concept of <u>confirmation bias</u>.[KP1] In summary, this is when <u>people prefer information that matches their opinions</u>[KP2] and <u>make bad decisions because of this preference</u>.[KP3] The professor gives <u>a personal example</u>[KP4] of this concept. First, he says that <u>his wife wanted a vacation in New York, but he did not want to go there because of a negative experience in New York when he was a child</u>.[KP5] Next, he mentions that <u>he rejected information about New York that did not match his negative opinion of that city</u>.[KP6] Finally, he states that <u>he and his wife vacationed in Miami instead of New York, but this was a bad decision</u>.[KP7] This example shows how <u>confirmation bias affected the professor's decision</u>.[KP8]

READING

KP1

(confirmation bias) (CB) = people accept opinions they
      believe but reject ones they don't

CB stronger about emotional topics

CB stronger about issues people believe strongly

People with CB make poor decisions due to it

LISTENING

prof + wife discuss vacation plans
      wife suggest go NYC but prof not want NYC bc ngtv opin
      → emotional experience as child

wife showed brochures + told recommendations

prof reject pstv points + focus on ngtv points = CB

couple go Miami not NYC → bad experience

too hot + storm → stay in hotel

F3 Analyze Speaking Task 4 questions 1 and 2 to understand what you need to do and how to organize your answers. Then circle and label key points in the notes you made about the NIMBY principle and social psychology from exercises **E4** and **E5**.

1. Explain how the examples that are mentioned by the professor demonstrate the NIMBY principle.
2. The speaker describes an experiment by Solomon Asch. Explain why this is a typical social psychology experiment.

G Mastering Speaking Task 4 – Delivering Your Response

Using a template – a well-organized model answer that includes natural language – will help you save time and deliver an effective, high-quality response for Speaking Task 4 questions. The Task 4 template has to be more flexible than for some other speaking questions, however, because Speaking Task 4 questions do not follow a standard pattern.

G1 Choose the function, A–E, that matches each highlighted template phrase in this response. Note that one function matches three phrases. One answer has been done for you.

The reading introduces the concept of ...   1.   _introduce the main point from the reading passage._

In summary, this is ...   2. _____

The professor gives a personal example of this concept.   3. _____

First, he says that ...   4. _____

Next, he mentions that ...   5. _____

Finally, he states that ...   6. _____

This example shows how ...   7. _____

A   Summarize the main point from the reading passage.
B   Summarize a point from the lecture that answers the question.
C   Give a very general overview of the focus of the lecture.
D   Introduce the main point from the reading passage.
E   Summarize how the example from the lecture answers the question.

TEST TACTIC

When you are delivering your response, it is OK to paraphrase the words of the lecturer, summarize his or her words, or even repeat his or her exact words. Use whichever method is easiest for you.

Track 313 **G2** **Complete tasks 1 and 2.**

1. Listen to a high-level student say the full response from exercise **F2** sentence by sentence. Repeat each sentence after you hear it. Try to match the speaker's intonation, rhythm, and pronunciation. Keep practicing until you can say the response confidently and fluently.
2. Work with a partner to practice saying the full response from exercise **F2**. Each time your partner speaks, give him or her useful feedback about intonation, rhythm, and pronunciation.

G3 **Work with a different partner to answer questions 1–5.**

1. How would you change the template phrases in exercise **G1** if the professor were a woman?
2. How would you change the first template phrase if the reading passage defined an idea?
3. How would you change the third template phrase if the speaker gave a non-personal example?
4. How would you change the third and last template phrases if the speaker gave two examples?
5. What would you do if the speaker mentioned two points or four points instead of three?

G4 **Write a full response to this Speaking Task 4 question. Use the notes you made and labeled in exercise F3. Then practice saying your completed response until you can say it fluently and confidently in 60 seconds or less.**

Explain how the examples that are mentioned by the professor demonstrate the NIMBY principle.

The reading introduces the concept of _____

In summary, this is _____

The professor gives a personal example of this concept. _____

First, she says that _____

Next, she mentions that _____

Finally, she states that _____

This example shows how _____

G5 **Prepare a full response to this Speaking Task 4 question. Use the template and the notes you made and labeled in F3.**

The speaker describes an experiment by Solomon Asch. Explain why this is a typical social psychology experiment.

G6 **Work with a partner to complete tasks 1–4.**

1. Listen to the response that your partner prepared in exercise **G5**. Take notes, if you like.
2. After listening, put checks (✓) in the YES or NO columns of the table below. Then give your partner feedback.
3. Say your response from exercise **G5** and get your partner's feedback. Try to get perfect feedback – YES in every column.
4. Fix any mistakes in your response that your partner noticed. Then repeat tasks 1–3 with several different partners.

Did your partner	YES	NO
Clearly introduce and summarize the main point of the reading passage?		
Give a general overview of the focus of the lecture?		
Summarize points from the talk that answer the question?		
State explicitly how information from the talk answers the question?		
Finish his or her response in less than 60 seconds?		
Use the template phrases accurately?		
Speak clearly, fluently, and confidently without long pauses?		

H Test Challenge

H1 **Answer Speaking Task 4 questions 1–3. Take 45 seconds to read the passage. Then listen to the lecture. After listening, spend 30 seconds preparing your response and then speak for no more than 60 seconds in order to get realistic practice for the test. Use this checklist of skills that you learned in this unit as a guide.**

☑ Read the passage and take notes about the main point plus supporting reasons and/or details.

☑ Listen to the talk and make a note of the points that the speaker makes, especially if they relate to the passage.

☑ Use the preparation time to analyze the question and then circle and label key points in your notes.

☑ Speak clearly and fluently, and use the template to make sure your response is well-organized.

1. Now read the passage about sunk-cost bias. You have 45 seconds to read the passage. Begin reading now.

This book uses a beep to indicate your speaking time is up. Remember that you will not hear this beep in the real test.

Sunk-cost Bias

Past investments of time or money that cannot be recovered are known as sunk costs. People tend to think about sunk costs when making decisions, but this can lead to poor decisions because of so-called sunk-cost bias. A person who has already invested time or money in a project, for example, may decide to continue investing so as not to waste the initial, non-recoverable investment. This is fine when continued investment is likely to be beneficial, but in cases where continued investment is a bad risk, the rational decision would be to stop investing.

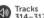 Tracks 314–317 Now listen to a lecture on this topic in a business studies class.

Using points and examples from the talk, explain how sunk-cost bias can cause people to make irrational decisions.

2. Now read the passage about defense mechanisms. You have 45 seconds to read the passage. Begin reading now.

Defense Mechanisms

Sigmund Freud, often known as the father of psychoanalysis, developed the theory of defense mechanisms. These are psychological strategies that allow people to function normally by protecting them from situations and events that could cause emotional distress and anxiety. Defense mechanisms may also protect people against inappropriate impulses. Typically, defensive strategies are unconscious – the brain adopts them automatically rather than as a result of conscious thought – but in some cases people will consciously choose to use one or more strategies

Tracks 319–321 Now listen to part of a lecture on this topic in a psychology class.

Using details from the talk, explain why denial and rationalization are examples of defense mechanisms.

3. Now read the passage about the halo effect. You have 45 seconds to read the passage. Begin reading now.

The Halo Effect

If one characteristic of an individual, such as his physical appearance or behavior, is viewed positively, people are very likely to assume – without any evidence – that the same individual has other positive characteristics, such as kindness or intelligence. The reverse holds true as well: individuals with one less desirable trait are often seen as having other negative characteristics, again despite there being no evidence for that. This cognitive bias is called the halo effect, and it applies not just to individuals, but to organizations, countries, and products, too.

 Tracks 322–325 Now listen to a lecture on the same topic in a marketing class.

Using points and examples from the talk, explain how companies try to take advantage of the halo effect.

Next Steps

Speaking Task 4 and Task 6 questions are often about some aspect of psychology. This topic is also very common in the reading and listening sections of the TOEFL Test. As a result, learning words related to psychology, as well as practicing key skills for Speaking Task 4, may help you increase your overall test score.

To learn more vocabulary related to psychology:

1. Search the Internet for an online dictionary of psychological terms. (Search for "psychology dictionary" or similar.)
2. Read the definitions to find one that describes something you would like to learn more about.
3. Search the Internet for a longer article about the definition that sounds interesting. As you read the article, make a list of words related to psychology that are important for understanding the article.
4. Repeat steps 1–3 a few times each week. (When you are satisfied that your knowledge of psychology vocabulary has improved, try searching for an online dictionary about a different academic subject and then repeat the steps.)

To practice key skills for Speaking Task 4 questions:

1. Listen to one of the lectures from the listening section of this book that you have already studied. Take notes as you listen. Pause the audio after about 90 seconds.
2. Quickly look at your notes and number the points you want to summarize in the order you will say them.
3. Give a speech in which you summarize what the speakers said. Use phrases from steps 3–6 of the Speaking Task 4 template in your summary.
4. Repeat steps 1–3 for the next 90 seconds of the lecture. Then repeat again for the rest of the lecture.

Unit Focus

In the speaking section of the TOEFL Test you will have six tasks. Speaking Task 5 is one of two integrated tasks about common campus situations that college students experience. You will first listen to a conversation between two people. They will discuss a minor problem that one or both of them are having as well as possible solutions to the problem. Then you will be asked to summarize the problem and say which of the possible solutions you think is better and why. In this unit you will learn and practice several key skills to answer Speaking Task 5 questions effectively, including:

- taking clear, effective notes when you listen to a conversation.
- using your preparation time effectively to organize your response well.
- learning and using model phrases to deliver a clear, natural response.
- speaking clearly and confidently, with natural pronunciation and intonation.

The vocabulary focus is on campus words and phrases related to:

- important events, times, and periods during a typical academic year.

A Warm-up

A1 **What would you do if you had problems 1–4? Write one solution for each problem. Use the example as a guide. When you have finished, compare answers with other students.**

1. I find it hard to study because my roommate listens to loud music all the time.
2. I make a lot of mistakes in English when I write an essay or speak to my professors.
3. I eat too much unhealthy food because there are only fast-food restaurants on campus.
4. I live a long way from campus and it takes me more than one hour each day to get to class by bus.

Example   *I would ask my roommate to play music less often and more quietly.*

B Campus Vocabulary

B1 **Match one of the definitions, A–H, to each phrase, 1–8. One answer has been done for you.**

1. career fair
2. field trip
3. graduation
4. midterm
5. semester
6. spring break
7. student orientation
8. summer session

A a ceremony at which students receive a degree for successfully completing their studies

B a period of 15–18 weeks (one half of an academic year) during which students attend college

C an academic period when students can choose to take classes instead of taking a long vacation

D a trip made by students or researchers in order to get firsthand knowledge about a place

E a vacation from college that typically lasts one week when some students go away with friends

F an event at which new students can learn important information about life at college

G an event at which students can meet prospective employers and learn about job opportunities

H an exam that takes place approximately halfway through an academic semester or term

C Analyzing Speaking Task 5

For Speaking Task 5 questions, you will first hear a conversation between two people – either two students or a student and a university employee such as a tutor, professor, or administrator. The people will first talk about a problem that one or both of them are having. Then they will discuss two possible solutions to the problem. While you listen, takes notes about the problem and the two solutions. The conversation is usually between 60 and 90 seconds in length.

After listening, you will see the question on the screen and an announcer will read it aloud. The question will look like this:

> The students discuss two possible solutions to their problem. Describe the problem. Then state which of the two solutions you prefer and explain why.

A second announcer will then tell you to begin preparing your response. You will have 20 seconds to prepare. The amount of preparation time remaining will be shown onscreen. After the preparation time, the second announcer will tell you to begin speaking. You will have 60 seconds to deliver your response. The amount of time remaining will be shown onscreen.

To answer a Speaking Task 5 question effectively and get a good score, your response should:
- use language well – you need to use grammar and vocabulary naturally and effectively with few mistakes.
- be delivered well – your speech should be clear and fluent, with good pronunciation and few long pauses.
- develop the topic well – you need to summarize the problem and both state and explain the solution you prefer.

Common problems when answering Speaking Task 5 questions that may reduce your score include:
- poor language use – frequent mistakes, or vocabulary and grammar that are unnatural.
- poor delivery – unclear pronunciation or intonation, frequent or long pauses, or lack of fluency.
- poor topic development – not summarizing the problem or not explaining the reasons for your preferred solution.

TEST TACTIC

One speaker will often begin the conversation by asking the other speaker something like "Are you OK?" or "Is everything alright?" Then one of the speakers will introduce the problem. Sometimes, however, a speaker will begin discussing the problem right away. Be prepared for either possibility when you begin listening.

C1 Use information from this script of a conversation from Speaking Task 5 to write full sentences in answer to questions 1–5 below. One sentence has been written for you.

Woman	Hi, James. Everything OK?
Man	Oh, hi, Maria. I've got a midterm on Friday, and I agreed to join a review session with a couple of classmates on Thursday. But I've just learned that one of my professors has organized a field trip on the same day.
Woman	So you're not sure whether to go on the field trip or join the study session?
Man	Right. I considered asking my friends to do a study session on Wednesday not Thursday, but I know they'd both need to miss classes in order to do that.
Woman	Well, there'll be other field trips later in the year, won't there? You could join the study session this time and go on the next field trip.
Man	Hmm... it's worth thinking about, but this field trip is to a place I'd really like to visit. It's really unlikely my professor will arrange another field trip to the same place.

1. What is the problem?   The man's problem is that a study session and field trip are at the same time.
2. Which option should he take?   In my view, he should _____
3. Why should he do this?   The main reason is that _____
4. Which option should he reject?   In contrast, I don't think he should _____
5. Why should he reject it?   This is because _____

C2 Practice saying your sentences from exercise **C1**. Keep practicing until you can say them fluently and confidently.

D Mastering Speaking Task 5 – Listening to the Conversation

The conversation will typically last between 60 and 90 seconds. First, the speakers will describe a problem. Then they will discuss two suggestions for how to solve the problem. While you listen, take well-organized notes on the problem, the suggestions for solving the problem, and any positive or negative comments a speaker makes about each suggestion.

Tracks 326–329 **D1** Take notes as you listen to four conversations from Speaking Task 5 questions. Then use your notes to complete this table. One answer has been done for you.

	Who has the problem?	What is the problem?
Conversation 1	☐ Man ☑ Woman ☐ Both	She wants to go away with friends but has to do some schoolwork
Conversation 2	☐ Man ☐ Woman ☐ Both	
Conversation 3	☐ Man ☐ Woman ☐ Both	
Conversation 4	☐ Man ☐ Woman ☐ Both	

Tracks 326–329 **D2** Listen again to the conversations from exercise **D1** and take notes. Then answer questions 1 and 2.

1. Indicate in which conversation a speaker uses each expression to introduce a suggestion. Place a check (✓) in the correct box. One answer has been done for you.

	Conversation 1	Conversation 2	Conversation 3	Conversation 4
Have you thought about				
Maybe we could				
What I would do is				
Why don't you	✓			

2. Indicate in which conversation a speaker makes each suggestion. Place a check (✓) in the correct box. One answer has been done for you.

	Conversation 1	Conversation 2	Conversation 3	Conversation 4
Do her assignments and then take a break	✓			
Find out dates and times for other orientations				
Try to start the internship later				
Visit the Housing Office				

Track 330 **D3** Listen to a conversation from a Speaking Task 5 question and fill in the missing details in these notes.

W prof asked two people help at conf on Mon + Tue
   [1. _____] per day → want to?
M cannot → already volun at [2. _____] orientation
W volun just one day + conf other day?
M other people [3. _____] → not want to do same
W ask orientation organizer for payment?
M organizer complains about small event [4. _____]

D4 Use the notes from exercise **D3** to answer questions 1–6. When you have finished, compare answers with a partner.

1. What is the problem and who has it?
2. What is the first suggestion the woman makes?
3. What does the man say about this suggestion?
4. What is the woman's second suggestion?
5. What does the man say about this suggestion?
6. The word "professor" is abbreviated to "prof." What other words are abbreviated in the notes?

Tracks
331–332 **D5** Listen to two more Speaking Task 5 conversations. Take notes as you listen. Use the notes in exercise **D3** as a guide.

E Mastering Speaking Task 5 – Preparing Your Response

Use your 20 seconds of preparation time first to circle and label up to five key points in your notes: the problem, the two suggestions, and any reaction that a speaker has about either suggestion. Then decide which of the two suggestions you will choose to be the preferred suggestion you discuss in your response.

E1 Label the five circled key points in these notes with one label from A–E. One answer has been done for you.

W	prof asked two people help at conf on Mon + Tue		**prob**	The problem the speakers discuss
	$100 per day → want to?		**S1**	The first suggestion by a speaker
M	cannot → already volun at student orientation		**S2**	The second suggestion by a speaker
W	volun just one day + conf other day?		**R1**	Reaction about the first suggestion
M	other people drop out → not want to do same		**R2**	Reaction about the second suggestion
W	ask orientation organizer for payment?			
M	organizer complains about small event budget			

Track 333 **E2** Take notes as you listen to a man and woman talking. Then match suggestions 1–4 to the person who makes them. One answer has been done for you.

1. If one suggestion is on a familiar topic you have talked about before, choose that suggestion.
   ☑ Man   ☐ Woman
2. If you have better notes about one suggestion than the other, choose that suggestion.
   ☐ Man   ☐ Woman
3. If you do not understand one suggestion well, choose the other suggestion.
   ☐ Man   ☐ Woman
4. If it might take a long time to talk about one suggestion, choose the other suggestion.
   ☐ Man   ☐ Woman

E3 Complete tasks 1 and 2.

1. Look at the notes from exercise **E1**. Choose one of the two suggestions as your preferred suggestion. Label your preferred suggestion either "S1+" or "S2+."
2. Tell a partner why you would choose this suggestion as your preferred suggestion.

E4 Complete tasks 1–5.

1. Look at the first set of notes you made in exercise **D5**. Circle five key points in those notes.
2. Label the key points *prob, S1, S2, R1,* and *R2,* for problem, suggestion 1, and so on.
3. Decide which one of the two suggestions is your preferred suggestion. Label it *S1+* or *S2+.*
4. Tell a partner why you would choose this suggestion as your preferred suggestion.
5. Repeat tasks 1–4 about the second set of notes you made in exercise **D5**.

E5 Work with a partner to think of *both* a positive and a negative reason for each solution for problems 1 and 2. When you have finished, share your ideas with other students. One answer has been done for you.

If neither speaker gives a reaction to one of the suggestions or if your notes about the speakers' reactions are not clear, it may be helpful to think of your own reasons why a suggestion is a good idea or a bad idea. You can then use your reasons instead of the speakers' reasons in your response.

Problem 1	A student needs a full-time summer job to make money but also needs to attend summer session.
Solution 1	Get a part-time job instead of a full-time job • Positive – She can make some money and still study • Negative – She might not make enough money
Solution 2	Get a full-time job and take evening classes during the summer • •

Problem 2	A student wants to attend a career fair, but doesn't have time to type up an updated resume.
Solution 1	Go to the career fair with an out-of-date resume and mention his latest experience in person • •
Solution 2	Type up an updated resume quickly on the morning of the career fair and go to the fair late • •

F Mastering Speaking Task 5 – Delivering Your Response

All Speaking Task 5 questions follow a similar pattern. This means that using a template – a well-organized model answer that includes natural language – will help you save time, avoid mistakes, and deliver an effective, high-quality response.

F1 Choose the best answer from A–E to complete this partial response to a Speaking Task 5 question. The template phrases in the response are highlighted. One answer has been done for you.

The speakers discuss two possible solutions to the man's problem. Describe his problem. Then state which of the two solutions you prefer and why.

The man has a problem because 1. _____

The speakers discuss a couple of possible solutions to this problem.

In my view, the man should 2. _____

The main reason is that 3. _____

In contrast, I don't think he should 4. _____   drop out as a volunteer (S1)   _____

This is because 5. _____

A   drop out as a volunteer. (S1)
B   even though the event budget is small, he might get some money. (R2)
C   he volunteered at an orientation so he cannot work at a conference. (prob)
D   other people have dropped out and the man does not want to do the same thing. (R1)
E   speak to the organizer of the student orientation and try to get paid for his time. (S2+)

Track 334 **F2** **Listen several times to a high-level student say this response. As you listen, complete tasks 1–4.**

The man has a problem because he volunteered at an orientation so he cannot work at a conference. The speakers discuss a couple of possible solutions to this problem. In my view, the man should speak to the organizer of the student orientation and try to get paid for his time. The main reason is that even though the event budget is small, he might get some money. In contrast, I don't think he should drop out as a volunteer. This is because other people have dropped out and the man does not want to do the same thing.

1. Mark the speaker's pauses on the response. Use / for a short pause and // for a longer pause.
2. Underline the words in the response that the speaker emphasizes (says strongly).
3. Note the pronunciation of difficult words. Practice saying these words until you are confident you can say them correctly.
4. Practice saying the response with a partner. Each time your partner speaks, give him or her useful feedback about pronunciation, pausing, and emphasis.

F3 **Work with a partner to complete tasks 1 and 2.**

1. Rewrite the response from exercise **F2** using the other suggestion as the preferred suggestion. One sentence has been written for you.

The man has a problem because _____

The speakers discuss a couple of possible solutions to this problem.

In my view, the man should _____ drop out as a volunteer. _____

The main reason is that _____

In contrast, I don't think he should _____

This is because _____

2. Say the new response to your partner. Give each other useful feedback about pronunciation, pausing, and emphasis.

F4 **Complete tasks 1–3.**

1. Use your notes from conversation 1 of exercise **D4** to write a full response to the question below. One sentence has been written for you.
2. Practice saying your completed response until you can say it fluently and confidently in 60 seconds.
3. Say your response to a partner and listen to his or her feedback. Then listen to his or her response and give feedback.

   The speakers discuss two possible solutions to the man's problem. Describe his problem. Then state which of the two solutions you prefer and why.

The man has a problem because _____ he cannot focus on studying for his midterm exams. _____

The speakers discuss a couple of possible solutions to this problem.

In my view, the man should _____

The main reason is that _____

In contrast, I don't think he should _____

This is because _____

F5 Use your notes from conversation 2 of exercise **D5** to write a full response to this question. One sentence has been written for you.

The speakers discuss two possible solutions to a problem the woman has. Describe the problem. Then state which of the two solutions you think she should adopt. Explain why.

The woman has a problem because _she has made plans and cannot go on a field trip that interests her._

The speakers discuss a couple of possible solutions to this problem.

In my view, the woman should _____

The main reason is that _____

In contrast, I don't think she should _____

This is because _____

F6 Work with a partner to complete tasks 1–4.

1. Listen to the response that your partner prepared in exercise **F5**. Take notes, if you like.
2. After listening, put checks (✓) in the YES or NO columns of the table below. Then give your partner feedback.
3. Say your response from exercise **F5** and get your partner's feedback. Try to get perfect feedback – YES in every column.
4. Fix any mistakes in your response that your partner noticed. Then repeat tasks 1–3 with several different partners.

Did your partner	YES	NO
Clearly and correctly state who has the problem?		
Clearly and correctly describe the problem?		
Explain which suggestion he or she prefers and why?		
Explain which suggestion he or she does not prefer and why?		
Finish his or her response in less than 60 seconds?		
Use the template phrases accurately?		

G Test Challenge

G1 Answer Speaking Task 5 questions 1–3. After listening, spend 20 seconds preparing your response and speak for up to 60 seconds in order to get realistic practice for the test. Use the checklist of skills that you learned in this unit as a guide.

☑ Listen to the conversation and take notes on the problem, the suggestions, and comments about the suggestions.

☑ Use the preparation time to decide which suggestion you prefer and to circle and label key information in your notes.

☑ Speak clearly and fluently, and use the template to make sure your response is well organized and natural.

🔊 Tracks 335–338 1. Listen to a conversation between two students.

The speakers discuss two possible solutions to a problem. Describe the problem. Then state which of the two solutions you prefer and why.

Tracks 339–342   2. Listen to a conversation between a man and a woman.

The speakers discuss two possible solutions to a problem. Describe the problem. Then state which of the two solutions you prefer and why.

Tracks 343–346   3. Listen to a conversation between a student and a professor.

The speakers discuss two possible solutions to a problem. Describe the problem. Then state which of the two solutions you prefer and why.

Next Steps

Speaking Task 5 questions often deal with important events and times during the academic year. You may also hear vocabulary related to this topic in Speaking Task 3 and during conversations in the listening section. As a result, learning words related to this topic, as well as practicing key skills for Speaking Task 5, may help you increase your overall test score.

To learn more vocabulary related to important events, times, and periods during a typical academic year:

1. Visit the website of a university or college that you are interested in attending or that you know about.
2. Use the search feature of that website to find articles that include some of the campus vocabulary from exercise **B1** on page 208 of this unit.
3. Read the articles and see how the words from **B1** are used. Then find other words in the article that are related to important events and times during the academic year. Study these words in order to understand their meaning and usage.

To practice key skills for Speaking Task 5 questions:

1. Search the Internet for "problems students have at university" or "common problems for college students".
2. Read one of the articles you find and take notes about the problems and two possible solutions to each problem. (If you cannot find two solutions in the article, think of possible solutions yourself.)
3. Imagine a person is having a problem that you researched in step 2. Use the template for Speaking Task 5 to make a speech that describes the problem, explains your preferred solution, and explains why another solution is not as good.
4. Repeat steps 1–3 often so that you become confident talking about problems using the template for Speaking Task 5.

Unit Focus

In the speaking section of the TOEFL Test you will have six tasks. Speaking Task 6 is one of two integrated tasks about academic content. You will first hear a short lecture about one aspect of an academic topic. Then you will be asked to summarize the key ideas from the lecture. In this unit you will learn and practice several key skills to answer Speaking Task 6 questions effectively, including:

- taking clear, effective notes when you listen to an academic lecture.
- using your preparation time effectively to organize your response well.
- learning and using model phrases to deliver a clear, natural response.
- speaking clearly and confidently, with natural pronunciation and intonation.

The vocabulary focus is on academic words and phrases related to:

- business studies, including the study of economics, finance, management, and marketing.

A Warm-up

◄))) Track 347 **A1** **Listen to parts of several academic lectures and take notes. Then use your notes to complete statements 1–5. You can either paraphrase or repeat each speaker's words. One answer has been done for you.**

Macroeconomics is concerned with 1. _____ _the performance of the whole economy._
Microeconomics, on the other hand, focuses on 2. _____
_____

Loss leaders are 3. _____

Direct marketing involves 4. _____

A sole proprietorship is a business 5. _____

B Academic Vocabulary

B1 **Which answer, A–H, matches each highlighted word in sentences 1–4? Compare answers with a partner when you have finished. Then use a dictionary to confirm your answers.**

1. In a typical recession, consumers try to save money by spending less and by choosing cheaper alternatives to luxury brands.
2. In highly competitive industries, the difference between making a profit and losing money may come down to how much marketing a company does and to the loyalty of its customers.
3. There is a great deal of competition in business these days, but small, family-run businesses can succeed if they offer services that consumers really want.
4. In theory, the stockholders in a corporation have the power to hire and fire executives, although in practice, stockholders almost always approve the recommendations of the corporation's board members about hiring and firing.

A products that are sold under a particular name
B Work that is done by employees to help customers
C Making products sound attractive to increase sales
D Senior business managers with a lot of responsibility
E A financial benefit from selling or doing something
F People who buy goods or services from a company
G People who have partial ownership in a corporation
H The act of trying to be or do better than someone else

C Analyzing Speaking Task 6

For Speaking Task 6 questions, an announcer will first introduce a lecture about an academic topic. During the lecture, the speaker will usually explain a theory or idea, discuss a problem and its causes or solutions, or describe a process. The speaker will also generally give specific examples that make his or her points clear and easy to understand.

After listening to the lecture, you will see the question on the screen and hear the announcer say it. The question will be similar to one of these examples:

> Using the examples mentioned by the speaker, explain how _____ and _____ differ.

> Using points and examples from the lecture, compare the two kinds of _____ that the professor discusses.

> Using the example of _____, explain the concept of _____ and say why _____.

A second announcer will then tell you to begin preparing your response. You will have 20 seconds to prepare. The amount of preparation time remaining will be shown onscreen. After the preparation time, the second announcer will tell you to begin speaking. You will have 60 seconds to deliver your response. The amount of time remaining will be shown onscreen.

To answer a Speaking Task 6 question effectively and get a good score, your response should:

- use language well – you need to use grammar and vocabulary naturally and effectively with few mistakes.
- be delivered well – your speech should be clear and fluent, with good pronunciation and few long pauses.
- develop the topic well – you need to answer the question clearly by mentioning details and examples from the lecture.

Common problems when answering Speaking Task 6 questions that are likely to reduce your score include:

- poor language use – frequent mistakes, or vocabulary and grammar that are unnatural.
- poor delivery – unclear pronunciation or intonation, frequent or long pauses, or lack of fluency.
- poor topic development – paraphrasing information from the talk poorly, or not answering each part of the question.

C1 Answer questions 1–4 based on this script from a Speaking Task 6 lecture. Write full sentences when you answer. One answer has been done for you.

Professor	Inflation can be defined as a continuing increase in the price of goods or services over a period of time. If the rate of inflation is low, inflation may be viewed positively as it signifies a growing economy. Indeed, some economists believe a permanently low and stable inflation rate may reduce the risk and seriousness of recessions. If the rate is high, however, its effects become increasingly severe because people's earnings do not increase at the same level as inflation. So although goods and services cost more than they used to, people have about the same amount of money as they did before. Obviously, they cannot buy as many goods and services if those goods and services are more expensive, so demand goes down, making a recession likely.

1. How does the professor define inflation?
   The professor defines inflation as a continuing increase in the price of goods and services over a period of time.

2. What level of inflation is viewed positively? Why?

   _____

3. What level of inflation is viewed negatively? Why?

   _____

4. How might inflation lead to a recession?

   _____

D Mastering Speaking Task 6 — Listening to the Lecture

The lecture usually lasts 75 to 90 seconds. As you listen, take clear, well-organized notes about key ideas, concepts, theories, details, and examples that the speaker discusses.

Track 348 **D1** **Take notes as you listen to an experienced teacher talk about Speaking Task 6. Then use your notes to put suggestions A—D in the order the teacher says them. One answer has been done for you.**

First	Always make a note when the speaker defines or explains concepts, theories, principles, or issues
Second	
Third	
Fourth	

A Take notes about information that explains how one thing has had an effect on another thing.
B Make a note of information about how two things are different from each other or how one thing has changed over time.
C Always make a note when the speaker defines or explains concepts, theories, principles, or issues.
D Pay close attention to words that signal that the speaker is about to give an example or supporting detail.

Track 348 **D2** **Listen again to the experienced teacher's advice. Take notes as you listen. Then write in missing expressions 1—4.**

Expressions that explain how one thing has had an effect on another thing	• as a result of … • 1.
Expressions that show how two things are different or how one thing has changed	• at first …, but later … • 2.
Expressions that indicate definitions or explanations of important ideas	• this can be defined as … • 3.
Expressions that signal the speaker is giving an example or supporting details	• to illustrate … • 4.

D3 **Complete tasks 1 and 2 with a partner.**

1. Add some other expressions to the categories in exercise **D2**.
2. Share your ideas from task 1 with other students and listen to their ideas. Make a note of any expressions not in your list.

D4 **Use this script from a Speaking Task 6 lecture to fill in missing details 1—6 in the notes on the next page. Work with a partner.**

Professor   In business, "integration" typically means creating efficiency. Today I'll discuss two distinct types of integration. First is vertical integration, which is when one company controls two or more steps in the production process of an item. For example, a global company might control three steps in the production of clothes: first, the clothes are made in its own factories. Next, the clothes are shipped using its own transportation company. And finally, the clothes are sold to customers in its own stores. Typically, businesses get an advantage from vertical integration because it allows them to reduce costs and avoid delays in the supply chain. Horizontal integration, on the other hand, is when one company controls two or more companies that offer the same, or a very similar, product. So, for instance, a manufacturing company might sell two brands of televisions in different ways. It might sell one brand of TVs, call them brand A, in retail stores, and sell another brand, brand B, only through online channels. Companies usually engage in horizontal integration to get more market share.

```
integ = create efficiency = 2 types
┌─────────────────────┐
│ 1.                  │
└─────────────────────┘
       = one company controls 2+ steps in production of item
       eg global comp controls 3 steps in producing clothes
          (1) make clothes in ┌──────────────┐ / (2) transportation / (3) sell in shops
                              │ 2.           │
                              └──────────────┘
          → advantages: reduced ┌──────────────┐ and fewer delays
                               │ 3.           │
                               └──────────────┘
┌─────────────────────┐
│ 4.                  │
└─────────────────────┘
       = one comp controls 2+ comp selling same product
       eg manuf comp sells 2 brands of ┌──────────────┐
                                       │ 5.           │
                                       └──────────────┘
          (1) brand A in stores / (2) brand B online
          → advantages: increased ┌──────────────┐ share
                                  │ 6.           │
                                  └──────────────┘
```

D5 Write the full form of these abbreviations (short ways to write something) that are used in the notes in exercise **D4**. One answer has been done for you.

1. integ _____integration_____
2. 2+ _____

3. comp _____
4. manuf _____

D6 Discuss with a partner the best way to abbreviate words 1–6 from the notes in **D4**.

1. production
2. global
3. transportation

4. advantages
5. reduced
6. increased

Track 349 **D7** Read these partial notes about a Speaking Task 6 lecture. Then listen to the lecture and add missing notes 1–5.

```
stagflation = combine stagnation + inflation
stag  = high inflat + low econ growth = ┌──────────────┐
                                       │ 1.           │
                                       └──────────────┘
      = global stag in 70s (caused by increased oil prices)
         → led to ┌──────────────┐
                 │ 2.           │
                 └──────────────┘
stag  = historically hard for governments to break out
      = few policies against inflat ┌──────────────┐
                                    │ 3.           │
                                    └──────────────┘
      = policies that do work ┌──────────────┐
                             │ 4.           │
                             └──────────────┘
      = global stag from 70s ┌──────────────┐
                            │ 5.           │
                            └──────────────┘
```

D8 Read this short passage. Then complete tasks 1–4 with a partner.

Taking notes is a key skill both for the listening section of the TOEFL Test and the Integrated Speaking and Writing questions. Like most skills, the more you practice it, the easier it will become and the more you will improve. Research shows that boring practice is less effective than enjoyable practice, so when you practice taking notes, try to do so in an interesting, creative, fun, or unusual way to get the best possible results.

1. Make a list of some interesting, creative, fun, or unusual ways to practice taking notes.
2. Decide which are the three most interesting or useful ideas on your list.
3. Share your best three ideas with other students and listen to their ideas. Take notes as you listen.
4. Choose the note-taking ideas that are the most interesting for you, and practice them as often as you can.

TEST TACTIC

When you are taking notes, pay close attention to the beginning of the lecture. The speaker usually discusses the main subject or purpose of the talk within the first 10–15 seconds and then typically goes on to discuss two aspects of this topic.

E   Mastering Speaking Task 6 – Preparing Your Response

You only have 20 seconds to prepare your response, so you will not have time to write out a detailed plan for your speech. First you should analyze the question carefully to understand what information a well-organized response should include. Use the remaining time to circle the key points in your notes that you will talk about and to label those points in the order you will mention them.

E1   Analyze Speaking Task 6 questions 1–3. What information do you need for an effective response to each question? Some answers have been done for you. Use these answers as a guide.

1. Using points and examples from the talk, compare the two types of business integration that the professor discusses.

   To deliver a good response to this question, I should:
   - ☑ Mention and define business integration, which is the main topic of the lecture.
   - ☑ Introduce and define the first type of integration that the speaker mentions.
   - ☑ Summarize details and / or examples about the first type of integration.
   - ☑ Introduce and define the second type of integration that the speaker mentions.
   - ☑ _____

2. Using the examples mentioned by the professor, say how sole proprietorships and partnerships are different.

   To deliver a good response to this question, I should:
   - ☑ Mention and define two types of businesses, which is the main topic of the lecture.
   - ☑ Define what a sole proprietorship is.
   - ☑ _____
   - ☑ Contrast the definition of a partnership with the definition of a sole proprietorship.
   - ☑ _____

3. Using points and examples from the lecture, explain the ways in which direct marketing benefits organizations.

   To deliver a good response to this question, I should:
   - ☑ Mention and define direct marketing, which is the main topic of the lecture.
   - ☑ _____
   - ☑ _____
   - ☑ Introduce the second benefit of direct marketing that the speaker mentions.
   - ☑ _____

E2   The notes about integration on the next page have nine circled Key Points (labeled KP1–KP9). Match the Key Points to the steps required to deliver a good response to question 1 in exercise **E1**. One answer has been done for you.

1. _____   ☑ Mention and define business integration, which is the main topic of the lecture.
2. _KP2 / KP3_   ☑ Introduce and define the first type of integration that the speaker mentions.
3. _____   ☑ Summarize details and/or examples about the first type of integration.
4. _____   ☑ Introduce and define the second type of integration that the speaker mentions.
5. _____   ☑ Summarize details and/or examples about the second type of integration.

KP1 integ = create efficiency = 2 types
KP2 vertical
KP3   = one company controls 2+ steps in production of item
         eg global comp controls 3 steps in producing clothes
KP4   (1) make clothes in factories / (2) transportation / (3) sell in shops
KP5   → advantages: reduced costs and fewer delays
KP6 horizontal
KP7   = one comp controls 2+ comp selling same product
         eg manuf comp sells 2 brands of TVs
KP8   (1) brand A in stores / (2) brand B online
KP9   → advantages: increased market share

E3 Look at these notes and Speaking Task 6 question. Then complete tasks 1 and 2.

stagflation = combine stagnation + inflation
stag   = high inflat + low econ growth = bad for econ
        = global stag in 70s (caused by increased oil prices)
          → led to recession in many countries
stag   = historically hard for governments to break out
        = few policies against inflat work against stag
        = policies that do work take money + time
        = global stag from 70s lasted over 10 years

Using points and examples from the lecture, explain what stagflation is and say how it can affect the economy.

1. Analyze the question and decide what information you need to include in your response to the question about stagflation. (You will not have time to write out your ideas as you did in exercise **E1**, but thinking about the information before you speak will help you deliver an organized response.)
2. Circle and label information in the notes that you think should be a Key Point.

F Mastering Speaking Task 4 – Delivering Your Response

It is not always possible to use a template – a well-organized model answer that includes natural language – for Speaking Task 6 questions because the questions vary. However, if you prepare a well-organized response, in most cases you can use model phrases to deliver effective, high-quality responses to Speaking Task 6 questions.

F1 Which Key Points, KP1–KP9, from the notes in exercise **E2** are summarized in each sentence of this response? Some sentences include information from two Key Points. One answer has been done for you.

KP1 ____ The professor discusses two types of integration, which helps businesses be efficient.
____ First, she talks about vertical integration, which is when a company controls several steps in producing an item.
____ She gives the example of a company that controls three steps in the production of clothes.
____ She goes on to say that vertical integration reduces costs and delays.
____ Next, she discusses horizontal integration, which is when a company controls companies selling the same product.
____ She mentions the case of a company that controls two companies that both sell televisions.
____ She then points out that horizontal integration increases market share.

Track 350 **F2** **Complete tasks 1 and 2.**

1. Listen to a high-level student say the model answer from exercise **F1**. Repeat each sentence after you hear it. Try to match the speaker's intonation, rhythm, and pronunciation. Keep practicing until you can say each sentence confidently.

2. Work with a partner to practice saying the full response from exercise **F1** several times. After your partner speaks, give him or her useful feedback about intonation, rhythm, and pronunciation.

F3 **Use the notes about stagflation from exercise E3 to write a response to this Speaking Task 6 question.**

Using points and examples from the lecture, explain what stagflation is and say how it can affect the economy.

The professor discusses _____

He defines this as _____

First, he talks about _____

He goes on to explain that _____

Next, he discusses _____

He then points out that _____

F4 **Work with a partner to complete tasks 1–4.**

1. Listen to the response that your partner prepared in exercise **F3**. Take notes, if you like.
2. After listening, put checks (✓) in the YES or NO columns of the table below. Then give your partner feedback.
3. Say your response from exercise **F3** and get your partner's feedback. Try to get perfect feedback – YES in every column.
4. Fix any mistakes in your response that your partner noticed. Then repeat tasks 1–3 with several different partners.

Did your partner	YES	NO
Summarize the main purpose of the lecture?		
Give a detailed paraphrase of key points from the lecture?		
Finish his or her response in less than 60 seconds?		
Use model phrases from the model answer accurately?		
Speak clearly, fluently, and confidently without long pauses?		
Organize his or her answer in a clear, logical way?		

G Test Challenge

G1 **Answer Speaking Task 6 questions 1–3. After listening, spend 20 seconds preparing your response and speak for up to 60 seconds in order to get realistic practice for the test. Use the checklist of skills that you learned in this unit as a guide.**

☑ Listen to the talk and make clear, detailed, well-organized notes of the points that the speaker makes.

☑ Use the preparation time to analyze and understand the question. Then circle and label key details in your notes.

☑ Speak clearly and fluently, and use the model phrases to make sure that your response sounds natural.

This book uses a beep to indicate your speaking time is up. Remember that you will not hear this beep in the real test.

Tracks
351–354   1. Now listen to part of a lecture in a business studies class.

Using points and examples from the lecture, describe the two types of free software that the professor discusses.

Tracks
355–358   2. Now listen to part of a talk in a marine biology course.

Using points and examples from the talk, explain what fish farming is and say why cobia is a suitable species for farming.

Tracks
359–362   3. Now listen to part of a discussion in a law seminar.

Using points and examples from the seminar, describe the legal responsibilities of a corporation.

Next Steps

Speaking Task 6 questions are often about some aspect of business or marketing. These topics are common in the other sections of the TOEFL Test, too. As a result, learning words related to business and marketing, as well as practicing key skills for Speaking Task 6, may help you increase your overall test score.

To learn more about vocabulary related to business and marketing:

1. Read the headline of a newspaper article about business or marketing.
2. Based on the headline, predict some words you will see in the article.
3. Read the article once to understand the main ideas. Then read it again and search for the words you predicted.
4. Read the article again and search for words related to business you did not predict you would see.
5. Study the words you found in steps 3 and 4. Learn their meanings as well as how to use them.

To practice key skills for Speaking Task 6 questions:

1. Listen to about 90 seconds of a radio broadcast or online talk about business (or any other subject that interests you).
2. As you listen, take clear, detailed, well-organized notes of the points that the speaker makes.
3. After listening for about 90 seconds, spend 20 seconds labeling your notes and preparing to speak.
4. Then deliver a 60-second talk using the model phrases that you learned in this unit. Your talk should summarize the main purpose of the broadcast and paraphrase the points that the speaker discusses. Record yourself giving the talk.
5. After you have finished, listen to the recording of your speech. Make a note of things you could improve next time.
6. Repeat steps 1–4. Try to avoid making the same mistakes that you noticed in step 5 when you listened to your recording.

Directions

This speaking review test is intended to help you learn your speaking strengths and weaknesses. You will answer six speaking tasks that are designed to be at the same level as the ones on the TOEFL Test. For some tasks you will listen to one or two speakers. You may take notes while you listen. For the most realistic practice, cover the questions when you listen, and record your answers when you speak.

Test

🔊 Tracks 363–364 **TASK 1 – SPEAKING ABOUT A FAMILIAR TOPIC**

What is one food that you do not enjoy eating? Why? Support your answer with specific details and examples.

Preparation Time: 15 Seconds   Response Time: 45 Seconds

🔊 Tracks 365–366 **TASK 2 – SPEAKING ABOUT A FAMILIAR TOPIC**

Some people like going out to a theater to watch a movie. Other people prefer watching movies at home. Which way of watching movies do you prefer? Why? Support your response.

Preparation Time: 15 Seconds   Response Time: 45 Seconds

🔊 Tracks 367–370 **TASK 3 – SPEAKING ABOUT A CAMPUS SITUATION**

State University is canceling events on campus. Read the notice about this cancellation. You have 45 seconds to read the notice. Begin reading now.

Campus Events Canceled

Two students were taken to hospital last week because of trouble at an event on campus. In response to this situation, the university has decided to cancel all events on campus until further notice. The university council feels that this action, which is effective immediately, is necessary to ensure the safety of all students. The university council will meet with the student association and representatives from student clubs and organizations in November to discuss the situation and find a permanent solution.

Now listen as two students discuss the notice.

The man/woman expresses his/her opinion about the notice. State his/her opinion and explain the reasons he/she gives for holding that opinion.

Preparation Time: 30 Seconds   Response Time: 60 Seconds

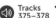**TASK 4 – SPEAKING ABOUT ACADEMIC CONTENT**

Now read the passage about geoarchaeology. You have 45 seconds to read the passage. Begin reading now.

Geoarchaeology

Geoarchaeology is a collaborative, interdisciplinary approach to the study of archaeology. It involves the use of analytical techniques and theoretical and practical concepts from multiple disciplines such as geography, geology, and even sciences like chemistry or physics to answer questions and solve problems in archaeology. These questions and problems include such issues as the human and environmental factors that are involved in site formation, the reconstruction of ancient climates and environments, the use of chronometric tools to date artifacts, and the sourcing of materials and artifacts.

Now listen to part of a lecture on this topic in an archaeology class.

Using the example of obsidian artifacts that the professor discusses, explain how trace element analysis helped answer an archaeological question.

Preparation Time: 30 Seconds   Response Time: 60 Seconds

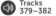**TASK 5 – SPEAKING ABOUT A CAMPUS SITUATION**

Now listen to a conversation between a man and a woman.

The speakers discuss two possible solutions to a problem. Describe the problem. Then state which of the two solutions you prefer and why.

Preparation Time: 20 Seconds   Response Time: 60 Seconds

TASK 6 – SPEAKING ABOUT ACADEMIC CONTENT

Now listen to part of a talk in a public health class.

Using points and examples from the talk, say what vaccination is. Then say how attitudes towards vaccination have changed over time.

Preparation Time: 30 Seconds   Response Time: 60 Seconds

Score Conversion

Ask a teacher or native speaker to evaluate each response from 0–4. (If necessary, you can evaluate your responses yourself. See pages 172–175 of the Speaking Reference unit for the criteria for scoring.) Then add up the scores for each response to find your raw score and use this conversion chart to find out your approximate speaking score range on the TOEFL Test.

Raw Score (out of 24)	Probable Level	Approximate Score Range
21–24	Good	26–30
15–20	Fair	19–25
9–14	Limited	11–18
1–8	Weak	1–10

Overview

The writing section measures your ability to write English in an academic setting. You will see and/or hear:

• General directions for the writing section	about 2 minutes
• Specific instructions for the first writing task based on reading and listening	about 2 minutes
• Integrated Writing Task 1 based on reading and listening, with three minutes to read a passage, 2–3 minutes to listen to a lecture about the same topic, and 20 minutes to type your response	about 26 minutes
• Independent Writing Task 2 based on knowledge and experience	30 minutes

Your typed responses will be recorded and sent as digital files to human raters for grading. After both of your responses have been graded, your raw scores will be converted to a scaled score from 0–30.

NOTES

- You must type your responses. Handwritten answers are not allowed.
- You will not be able to continue working on your responses after the time is up.
- Your responses will be saved automatically when your time is up. You do not need to do anything to save your work.

Detailed Guide

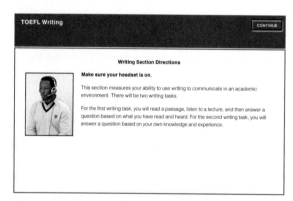

When you begin the writing section of the TOEFL Test, you will first see the directions for the whole section. You will hear a narrator read the directions aloud. You can change the volume of the narrator's voice while he is speaking by clicking on the **Volume** button in the top right corner of the screen.

When you are ready to go on, click the button marked **Continue**.

Next you will see specific directions for Writing Task 1. You will hear a narrator read the directions aloud. You can change the volume of the narrator's voice if you wish.

When you are ready to begin the writing test, click the button marked **Continue**.

TEST TACTIC

Because you must type your responses, learning to type quickly and accurately using a computer keyboard is a key skill for the TOEFL Test. You can find many effective, free typing tools on the Internet.

After the directions, you will see a reading passage on the left side of the screen. The passage typically has 230–300 words. You will have three minutes to read this passage. You can take notes on your scratch paper while you are reading.

A timer in the top right corner of the screen will show you how much reading time is left.

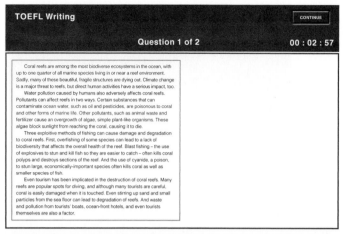

Next the reading passage will automatically disappear and you will see a picture of a professor on the screen. The narrator will tell you to listen to a lecture on the same topic as the reading passage. Then you will hear a professor deliver a lecture. The lecture will typically last between two and three minutes. You will see a bar below the picture that shows how much longer the lecture will last. You will only hear the lecture one time. You can take notes while you are listening.

While the professor is talking, you can change the volume, if necessary.

After the lecture, you will see a screen telling you to get ready to answer the question. This screen will disappear automatically after a few seconds.

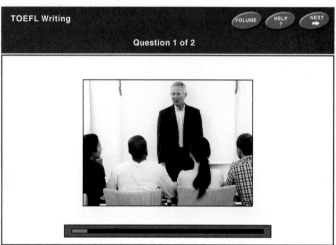

Then the screen will change and you will see the reading passage again. You will see the writing question on the screen, too, and the narrator will read the question aloud.

You will then have 20 minutes to plan and type a response to the question. While you are typing, you will be able to refer to your notes and see the reading passage, but you will not be able to listen again to the lecture.

As you type your response, your words will appear on the right side of the screen next to the reading passage. The number of words you have written will appear above your response. Generally, an effective response to Writing Task 1 will contain 150–225 words.

Both sources discuss threats to coral reefs

You will see several on-screen buttons that you can click to perform copy and paste functions. To use the **Cut** button, first select some text with your mouse. Then click the button. The selected text will be deleted from the screen and copied in the computer's memory. You can then click the **Paste** button to insert this copied text at a different position in your response.

If you make a mistake at any point, such as deleting a word or phrase, you can click the **Undo** button. This may help you recover from the mistake.

At the top of the screen you will see a toolbar with various buttons as well as the time remaining. You can choose to hide the amount of time remaining, if you prefer, by clicking the **Hide Time** button. If you change your mind, click the **Show Time** button.

Clicking the **Help** button will give you information about how to use the writing tools. If you click this button, the timer will count down while you look at the help information.

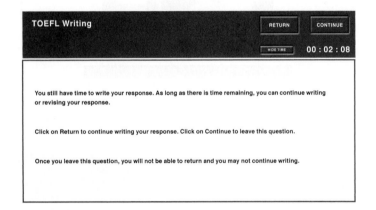

The Next button allows you to finish your response to Writing Task 1 and go on to Writing Task 2. If you click this button, you will see a warning message. You will have a choice of clicking **Return** to continue writing your response, or **Continue** to go on to the next task. Note that your time will continue to count down while you look at this message.

When your response time is over, the computer will automatically show you the directions for Writing Task 2.

Finishing Writing Task 1 early will not give you extra time for Task 2. If you finish either task early, use the remaining time effectively by making sure your response is clearly written, well organized, and free of obvious errors.

When your time is up for Writing Task 1, you will see the directions for Writing Task 2. You will not hear a narrator read these directions aloud.

When you are ready to go on, click the **Continue** button in the top right corner of the screen to begin the task.

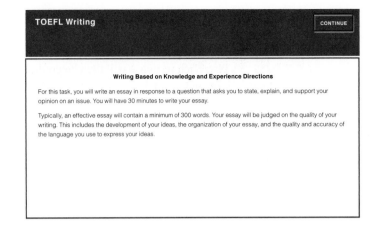

After the directions, the screen will change and you will see the question for Writing Task 2 on the screen. You will not hear a narrator read the question aloud.

You will then have 30 minutes to plan and type a response to the question. The time remaining will be shown at the top right of the screen below the **Next** button.

Typing your response to Writing Task 2 works the same as for Writing Task 1. You will see a count of how many words you have typed. Typically an effective response to Task 2 questions will have close to 300 words. You will have access to the same tools – **Cut**, **Paste**, and **Undo** – as well as the **Help** button.

If you finish typing your response before the 30 minutes is over, you can click on the **Next** button to finish the test. If there is still time remaining you will see the same warning message as for Writing Task 1 and you will be asked to confirm that you wish to end the test by clicking the **Continue** button.

When the test is over you will see a screen showing the end of the test. You will then have a chance to submit your score or cancel it.

Scoring

Your two responses will be sent electronically to ETS, the organization that develops the TOEFL Test. Each response will then be graded by a certified human rater and by a computerized automated scoring system.

Your responses to the integrated writing task and independent writing tasks will be sent to different human raters. No personal data is sent with either response, so the raters will not know your name, location, gender, previous scores on the TOEFL Test, or other personal details. The raters will not communicate with one other in any way about your responses.

After receiving your response, the rater will grade it holistically by focusing on the quality of your whole response. Typically, he or she will spend 60 to 90 seconds reading and evaluating your response. The rater will use the scoring rubrics described below to assign a grade from 0–5. The rater can only assign whole grades like 4, not half grades like 4.5.

When judging your response to the integrated writing task based on reading and listening, the rater will focus on the following criteria:

Score	Integrated Writing Task 1
5	A response at this level: • explains clearly how the main information from the lecture relates to information in the reading. • is typically well organized and fully developed. • generally has no more than a few minor errors that do not confuse the rater.
4	A response at this level: • should explain how most of the main ideas from the lecture relate to the reading, although some details may be missing, or slightly inaccurate or unclear. • may have frequent or obvious minor mistakes in grammar and vocabulary, although these mistakes should not seriously confuse the rater.
3	A response at this level: • typically summarizes some key details from the lecture and explains how they relate to the reading, but details are often incorrect or missing, and connections between the two sources are frequently unclear. • may have numerous obvious grammar and vocabulary mistakes that make it somewhat hard for the rater to understand the writer's ideas.
2	A response at this level: • may summarize some relevant information from the lecture, but many details are likely to be missing, very unclear, or very inaccurate. In addition, details of how the lecture and passage are related may be unclear. • may have numerous major problems with grammar and vocabulary that make it hard for the rater to understand the writer's ideas.
1	A response at this level: • generally includes very little information from the lecture, and does not show how the lecture and passage are connected. • typically has so many errors of all kinds that it is extremely hard for the rater to understand any of the writer's ideas.

A score of zero is given to blank responses, ones that are not written in English, ones that only copy words from the reading passage, or ones that only present the student's opinion about the topic, not the opinions in the passage and the lecture.

When judging your response to the independent writing task based on knowledge and experience, the rater will focus on the following criteria:

Score	Integrated Writing Task 2
5	A response at this level: • answers the question effectively with ideas that are clearly explained and fully developed. • is typically well organized and includes explanations and supporting examples that are coherent. • uses a variety of vocabulary expressions and grammar structures well and naturally, though it may have a few minor errors that do not confuse the rater.
4	A response at this level: • answers the question reasonably well, though some ideas may not be fully developed. • is generally well organized and supports ideas with effective explanations and examples, although some connections between ideas may not be clear. • uses a range of vocabulary expressions and grammar structures well, though it will likely have some obvious mistakes that are unlikely to confuse the rater.
3	A response at this level: • answers the question but is unlikely to be fully developed. • is reasonably well organized and includes some supporting details and examples, but ideas may not be clearly explained or connected to each other. • may use a limited range of accurate vocabulary and grammar structures, but is also likely to use language inconsistently and make mistakes that sometimes confuse the rater.
2	A response at this level: • usually has limited development and does not fully answer the question. • is not well organized and does not provide enough supporting details and examples. • has numerous obvious grammar and vocabulary mistakes that are likely to confuse the rater.
1	A response at this level: • is under developed and does not answer the question effectively. • is not organized and includes little or no detail relevant to the topic. • has serious and frequent errors.

A score of zero is given to blank responses, ones that are not written in English, or ones that are completely off topic.

TEST TACTIC

The scoring criteria do not specify that you need to use advanced grammar or vocabulary to get a good score. In fact, unless you are a very high-level student, using advanced language will probably reduce your score because you are more likely to make errors that confuse the reader.

In addition to certified human raters, your two responses will be assessed by a computerized scoring system called the e-rater engine developed by ETS. Like the human raters, e-rater will assign a score for each response from 0–5 but can only assign whole grades, not half grades. E-rater works in the following way:

The e-rater engine predicts essay scores based on features related to writing quality, including grammar, usage, mechanics, style, organization, and development. The computational methodology underlying the system is NLP (natural language processing), which identifies and extracts linguistic features from electronic text.
Source: www.ets.org/Media/Home/pdf/AutomatedScoring.pdf

Next, your scores for each response from the human rater and e-rater are compared. In most cases, the score from the human rater and from e-rater are the same or within one point of each other. So, for example, the human rater might assign a score of 4 points and e-rater might assign a score of 3, 4, or 5 points. In these cases, your final score for this response will be the average of the two scores. So, for example, if the human rater assigned a score of 4 points for your integrated writing response and e-rater assigned a score of 5 points, your final score for this task would be 4.5 points.

In rare cases, the scores from the human rater and e-rater differ by two or more points. So, for example, the human rater might assign a score of 3 points, but e-rater might assign a score of 5 points. In these cases, a second human rater will grade your response, and your final score for this task will be the average of all three scores. So, for instance, if the two human raters both assigned a score of 3 points for your independent writing response but e-rater assigned a score of 5 points, your final score for this task would be 3.67 points.

Your final score for the writing section is the average of the final scores for your two responses. So, for example, if you received an averaged final score of 3.5 points for the integrated task and an averaged final score of 4.0 points for the independent task, your final raw score for the writing section would be 3.75 points. This score is then converted to a scaled score from 0 to 30 points.

ETS does not explain in detail how the raw scores are converted to a scaled score. However, this table shows how some example final scores would be converted to the 0–30 scale:

Final Score – First Task	Final Score – Second Task	Final Score – Average	Scaled Score
5.00	5.00	5.00	30
4.50	5.00	4.75	29
4.50	4.50	4.50	28
4.00	4.50	4.25	27
3.50	4.50	4.00	25
3.50	4.00	3.75	24
3.00	4.00	3.50	22
3.00	3.50	3.25	21
2.50	3.50	3.00	20

TEST TACTIC

As with most skills, regular practice is one key to becoming better at writing for the TOEFL Test. If you have enough time, write a TOEFL essay each day. If your time is limited, write three perfect sentences every day. That means sentences with no grammar, vocabulary, or spelling errors.

When you receive your score from the TOEFL Test, you will get a score report that not only gives your scaled score in writing from 0–30, but also describes your performance for the two written responses (Good, Fair, or Limited). The report will also give a short description of the typical performance of students at that level.

Here are the levels and descriptions for the integrated writing task based on reading and listening:

Level	Scaled Score	Your Performance
Good (4.0–5.0)	24–30	You responded well to the task, relating the lecture to the reading. Weaknesses, if you have any, might have to do with: • slight imprecision in your summary of some of the main points; and/or • use of English that is occasionally ungrammatical or unclear.
Fair (2.5–3.5)	17–23	You responded to the task, relating the lecture to the reading, but your response indicates weaknesses such as: • an important idea or ideas may be missing, unclear, or inaccurate; • there may be unclarity in how the lecture and the reading passage are related; and/or • grammatical mistakes or vague/incorrect uses of words may make the writing difficult to understand.
Limited (1.0–2.0)	1–16	Your response was judged as limited due to: • failure to understand the lecture or reading passage; • deficiencies in relating the lecture to the reading passage; and/or • many grammatical errors and/or very unclear expressions and sentence structures.

And here are the levels and descriptions for the independent writing task based on knowledge and experience:

Level	Scaled Score	Your Performance
Good (4.0–5.0)	24–30	You responded with a well-organized and developed essay. Weaknesses, if you have any, might have to do with: • use of English that is occasionally ungrammatical, unclear or • unidiomatic, and/or • elaboration of ideas or connection of ideas that could have been stronger.
Fair (2.5–3.5)	17–23	You expressed ideas with reasons, examples and details, but your response indicated weaknesses, such as: • you may not provide enough specific support and development for your main points; • your ideas may be difficult to follow because of how you organize your essay or because of the language you use to connect your ideas; and/or • grammatical mistakes or vague/incorrect uses of words may make the writing difficult to understand.
Limited (1.0–2.0)	1–16	You attempted to express your opinion, but your response indicates notable deficiencies, such as: • your response contains insufficient detail; • your ideas and your connections of ideas are difficult to understand because of many grammatical errors and/or very unclear expressions and sentence structure; and/or • your response is only marginally related to the question that was asked.

Source: www.ets.org/Media/Tests/TOEFL/pdf/TOEFL_Perf_Feedback.pdf

Directions

This writing diagnostic test is intended to help you find out your strengths and weaknesses in writing. You will complete two writing tasks in 50 minutes. The total time required for the test is approximately 56 minutes. The tasks are designed to be at the same level as the ones you will see on the TOEFL Test. For the first task you will listen to a lecture. For the most realistic practice, cover the question when you listen. You may take notes while you listen. If possible, type your answers. When you have finished, ask a teacher to evaluate both responses from 0–5 or do it yourself. Then use the conversion chart on page 235 to convert your raw scores to your likely score on the TOEFL Test.

Test

TASK 1 – WRITING BASED ON READING AND LISTENING

For this task, you will read a passage about an academic topic. You will have three minutes to read. You may take notes on the passage while you read. You will then listen to a lecture about the same topic. While you listen you may also take notes. You may use your notes to help you answer the question.

You will then write a response to a question that asks you about the relationship between the lecture you heard and the reading passage. Try to answer the question as completely as possible using information from the reading passage and the lecture. The question does not ask you to express your personal opinion. Your response will be judged on the quality of your writing and on the completeness and accuracy of the content. Typically, an effective response will be 150 to 225 words.

Now read this passage. You have three minutes to read.

According to popular belief, in 1271 Italian merchant Marco Polo, together with his father and uncle, began a 24-year round-trip journey to China. After his return to Venice in 1296, Marco Polo wrote an influential account of his travels. Analysis of those writings, however, suggests that he might not have visited China at all, and that the details of his journey described in the book were copied from other sources.

One point that suggests Marco Polo did not visit China is his silence on aspects of Chinese culture that would have been surprising to Europeans. For example, his book does not make any reference to drinking tea, using chopsticks to eat, printed books, the Chinese system of logographic writing, or the use of trained sea birds to catch fish.

Polo's book is also silent on massive construction projects that would have amazed European travelers. The Great Wall of China existed at the time when Polo visited China, but his book makes no mention of it at all.

One final point is that Marco Polo says he and his relatives held important roles in the Mongol court. However, there are no references to Marco Polo or his father or uncle in Chinese documents from that time, a surprising omission because important officials were often mentioned in court documents. So again, it is hard to avoid the conclusion that Marco Polo did not, in fact, visit China.

Tracks 383 Now listen to a lecture on the topic you just read about.

You now have 20 minutes to plan and write your response. You may see the reading passage again while you write.

Summarize the points made in the lecture you just heard, being sure to specifically explain how they cast doubt on points made in the reading passage.

TASK 2 – WRITING BASED ON KNOWLEDGE AND EXPERIENCE

In this task you will demonstrate your ability to write an essay in response to a question that asks you to express and support your opinion about a topic or issue. Your essay will be scored on the quality of your writing. This includes the development of your ideas, the organization of your essay, and the quality and accuracy of the language you use to express your ideas. Typically, an effective essay will contain a minimum of 300 words.

Read the question below. You have 30 minutes to plan, write, and revise your essay.

Do you agree or disagree with the following statement?

Clear, effective communication is the most important element of any successful relationship between people.

Support your answer with reasons and specific details.

Score Conversion

Ask a teacher or native speaker to evaluate both responses from 0–5. (If necessary, you can evaluate your responses yourself. See pages 230–233 of the Writing Reference unit for the criteria for scoring.) Then add up the score for each response to find your raw score and use this conversion chart to find out your approximate writing score range on the TOEFL Test.

Raw Score (out of 10)	Probable Level	Approximate Score Range
10	Good	30
9		27
8		24
7	Fair	21
6		18
5		15
4	Limited	12
3		8
2		6
1		3

Unit Focus

In the writing section of the TOEFL Test you will have two tasks. Task 1 is called the integrated writing task. There are three types of Task 1 questions that all require a slightly different response. For Challenge questions, the most common type, you will need to explain how information from a lecture contrasts with information from a reading passage. In this unit you will learn key skills and a model answer that will help you write effective responses to Challenge questions, including:

- taking notes about the main points when you first see the reading passage.
- taking detailed notes about ideas in the lecture that are related to ideas in the reading.
- learning natural model phrases to write an effective introduction and three body paragraphs.
- avoiding common problems like copying phrases directly from the reading passage.

The vocabulary focus is on academic words and phrases related to:

- different aspects of society.

A Warm-up

A1 Do you agree or disagree with these quotations about society? Write your opinion and reason. Then talk with a partner and summarize his or her opinion and reason. Discuss each quotation with a different partner.

"The saddest aspect of life … is that science gathers knowledge faster than society gathers wisdom."
ISAAC ASIMOV

1. I _____agree / disagree_____ with this quotation about society because _____give the reason_____.
   My partner _____agrees / disagrees_____ with Isaac Asimov's words because _____give the reason_____.

"I think the teaching profession contributes more to … society than any other single profession."
JOHN WOODEN

2. I _____agree / disagree_____ with this quotation about society because _____give the reason_____.
   My partner _____agrees / disagrees_____ with John Wooden's words because _____give the reason_____.

B Academic Vocabulary

B1 Choose the best word from answers A–H to complete sentences 1–8. If necessary, check the meaning of the words in a dictionary. One answer has been done for you.

1. A commercial or business activity that many people do is often described as a(n) _____industry_____.
2. A(n) _____ is something, such as a lack of money or place to live, that causes difficulty for somebody.
3. A(n) _____ is an organization or place such as a university or bank that plays an important role in society.
4. A situation, especially one that affects society, that people are concerned about is called a(n) _____.
5. A person's _____ towards something or somebody is how he or she feels about that thing or person.
6. _____ is the condition of not having enough money to pay for basic needs like food or clothing.
7. A program of action or plan that a government or group follows to change a situation is called a(n) _____.
8. _____ is the condition of accepting other people's views about subjects like religion or politics.

A attitude	C industry	E issue	G poverty
B hardship	D institution	F policy	H tolerance

c Analyzing Writing Task 1 – Challenge Questions

For Writing Task 1, you will first see a reading passage on the screen. The passage will be between 230 and 300 words long and will present three ideas, arguments, theories, or examples related to an academic topic. You will have three minutes to read the passage and take notes.

After three minutes, the passage will disappear from the screen and an announcer will tell you to listen to a lecture on the same topic. The lecture will last two to three minutes, and you will only have one chance to listen to it, so you should take notes as you listen. In almost every case, the speaker will discuss ideas, arguments, theories, or examples that challenge the three ideas from the passage. In these cases you will have a Challenge question like one of the examples below.

After listening, the writing task will appear on the screen and the announcer will read it aloud. You will then have exactly 20 minutes to prepare and type your response. During this time you will be able to see the passage again.

Challenge questions usually include a specific word or phrase like "challenge" or "different from" that makes it clear that the ideas in the passage and the lecture contrast with each other, as in these examples:

> Summarize the points made in the lecture, explaining how they contrast with arguments made in the reading passage.

> Summarize the points made in the lecture you just heard, being sure to explain how they are different from the points made in the reading passage.

Occasionally, however, a Challenge question may include the phrase "respond to," as in this example:

> Summarize the points made in the lecture, explaining how they respond to specific points in the reading passage.

To answer Writing Task 1 Challenge questions effectively and get a good score, it is important to:
- paraphrase, summarize, or quote the ideas and supporting details that the speaker discusses in the lecture.
- give a clear, detailed explanation of how each point from the lecture differs from a point in the reading passage.
- use model paragraphs with natural phrases so your response is well-organized and has few mistakes.

One common problem that can reduce your score when answering all types of Writing Task 1 questions is:
- copying sentences from the reading passage rather than paraphrasing or summarizing the ideas in the passage.

C1 Circle the word or phrase in Writing Task 1 questions 1–5 that tells you each question is a Challenge question. One answer has been done for you.

1. Summarize the points made in the lecture, being sure to explain how they (challenge) the points made in the reading.
2. Summarize the points made in the lecture you just heard, explaining how they oppose specific points made in the reading passage.
3. Summarize the points made in the lecture you just heard, being sure to specifically explain how they cast doubt on points made in the reading passage.
4. Summarize the speaker's points from the lecture, being sure to explain how they differ from the points made in the reading passage.
5. Summarize the points made in the lecture you just heard, being sure to state how they contradict specific points made in the reading passage.

TEST TACTIC

In general, it is best to paraphrase or summarize the reading passage in your response. However, if you often make mistakes when paraphrasing or summarizing, or are slow at doing it, you will probably not reduce your score if you copy a few words and phrases directly from the reading.

D Mastering Writing Task 1 – Reading the Passage

A key skill is to recognize information in the passage that will help you understand the lecture. You will see the passage again after the lecture, so you do not need to understand every word when you first see it. However, you *do* need to make a note of the writer's main view about the topic (usually given in paragraph 1) as well as the three main points that he or she makes (usually given in the final three paragraphs). When you take notes, use abbreviations to save time.

D1 Reading passages for Writing Task 1 questions are usually organized in the same way as this example. Answer questions 1–4 after reading the example passage.

> We read a great deal these days about a crisis in American education, and statistics do show that American students are often no better than average at things like reading, ability to use technology, and knowledge of science and mathematics. A reason often given for this is that low pay for teachers means the quality of many teachers is not as good as it could be. One way to solve this crisis would be to pay teachers based on their ability and performance.
>
> The current system of experience-based pay means that teachers know they will get paid the same whether they put in a lot of work or a little work in any given year. This leads to a situation where some teachers do the minimum amount of work. Performance-based pay would lead to enhanced effort and performance by teachers.
>
> Further, there is a direct and measurable link between the quality of instruction that students receive and their results as measured by how much they have learned. If teachers work harder and teach better because doing so will improve their pay, students are going to learn more and show improved levels of performance and achievement.
>
> Another issue is that many smart people do not choose to become teachers because pay and conditions for teachers are not very good. Offering teachers higher pay for better performance would undoubtedly attract higher numbers of good quality, smart people into the profession, and this would improve student results, too.

1. Which answer describes how the reading passage is organized?
    A   The first two paragraphs give the writer's opinions about the topic; the last two paragraphs give other people's opinions.
    B   The first paragraph gives the author's opinion; the other paragraphs discuss specific details related to the author's view.

2. Which paragraph explains why some intelligent people do not go into teaching?
    Paragraph   ☐ 1   ☐ 2   ☐ 3   ☐ 4

3. Which paragraph notes a link between teacher effort and student performance?
    Paragraph   ☐ 1   ☐ 2   ☐ 3   ☐ 4

4. Which paragraph explains why some teachers do not work as hard as they could?
    Paragraph   ☐ 1   ☐ 2   ☐ 3   ☐ 4

TEST TACTIC

After you finish taking notes about the three main points in the passage, use any remaining time to predict what the speaker might say in the lecture. Most Writing Task 1 questions are Challenge questions, so the best idea is to focus on how the speaker might challenge the reading.

D2 Look at these notes about the reading passage in exercise **D1**. Then discuss and answer questions 1–5 with a partner.

MV	crisis in US educ = only average perf by students (S) performance-based pay (PBP) for teachers (T) would solve
P1	PBP → more effort + better perf by T
P2	PBP → improved perf + achievem by S
P3	PBP → more good quality people become T

1. What abbreviations (short ways to write something) are used in the notes to mark the writer's main view and the three main points?
2. What abbreviations are used in the notes for the words *education*, *performance*, and *achievement*?
3. What do the abbreviations *S*, *PBP*, and *T* in the notes stand for? How do you know?

D3 Read this passage and take notes. Use the notes in exercise **D2** as a guide. Complete the task in three minutes.

> Poverty is a global issue, and some have argued that a financial transaction tax – often called a Robin Hood tax – is the answer. Such a tax would involve levying a small fee of about 0.05% on all transactions between financial institutions. It is claimed that this tax might raise billions of dollars in revenue each year that could be used to fight poverty around the world. Reducing poverty is a worthwhile goal, to be sure, but a financial transaction tax is not the way to achieve it.
>
> First, a financial transaction tax would reduce profits of pension and other retirement funds, so retired people who rely on these funds would see a reduction in their income. In other words, a tax intended to reduce poverty would make some of society's most vulnerable people poorer.
>
> It is also argued that a financial transaction tax would only affect financial institutions, not consumers. However, history shows that businesses usually pass on higher costs to customers. So if such a tax were introduced, customers would see price increases for bank services, which again would lead to financial hardship for many.
>
> Finally, a financial transaction tax would probably lead to job losses in the finance industry. Cities like New York where finance is a major source of employment could also see job losses in industries that support the financial sector. A recent study suggests 1% of all private sector jobs might be lost. So again, a Robin Hood tax would contribute to poverty, not reduce it.

E Mastering Writing Task 1 — Listening to the Lecture

While you listen to the lecture, take detailed notes about the speaker's points. You will not have time to note every word the speaker says, so focus on ideas that relate to the three main points in the reading passage. Use abbreviations to save time.

E1 Read this script from a lecture about performance-based pay for teachers. Then decide if statements 1–6 are true or false. Rewrite the answers you mark false so that they are correct. One answer has been done for you.

Professor   People claim there's an education crisis these days and that giving teachers higher pay for better performance will solve it. But a closer look suggests that performance-based pay may not be such a good idea.

Think back to the reading. The writer says that teachers would work harder under a system of merit-based pay. It's possible this is true, but impossible to be sure since no studies have been done to prove it. However, numerous studies have shown that offering more money is generally a poor way to motivate people to work harder.

The writer also argues that performance-based pay for teachers will lead to better student results. Students might perform better, but not necessarily due to better teaching. Why? Well, offering workers more money for better results makes some people "cheat" the system and find ways to get better results without doing better work. There's every reason to think the teaching profession would be the same.

Finally, studies have shown that many people become teachers to help others and be creative, not for monetary gain. So performance-based pay is likely to mean that many people who care more about money than about inspiring students decide to become teachers. But teachers like that are unlikely to solve the education crisis.

1. The lecture has the same organization as the reading passage in exercise **D1**.   ☒ True   ☐ False
2. The speaker's overall opinion about the topic is given at the end of the lecture.   ☐ True   ☐ False
3. The speaker's opinion about the topic is opposite to the opinion in the reading.   ☐ True   ☐ False
4. In the lecture, the speaker never mentions the reading passage directly.   ☐ True   ☐ False
5. The speaker discusses the same points as the reading and in the same order.   ☐ True   ☐ False
6. The speaker disagrees with some points from the reading, but agrees with others.   ☐ True   ☐ False

🔊 Track 384 **E2** **Listen to an experienced teacher talk about Writing Task 1. In which order does the teacher mention each point about taking notes? One answer has been done for you.**

> When you take notes while listening to the lecture, it is a good idea to:
>
> ☑ Use abbreviations to take notes more quickly and use the time more effectively   _____
>
> ☑ Copy the speaker's words directly or paraphrase them, whichever is easier for you   _____
>
> ☑ Take as many notes as you can about ideas that are related to points in the reading   _First_

🔊 Track 385 **E3** **Listen to the first half of the lecture about performance-based pay for teachers. As you listen, read the notes below. Then answer questions 1–3.**

MV	Some think PBP will solve educ crisis, but not good idea
P1	Possible T work harder if get PBP but no studies prove it
	Other studies show more $ does not motiv people work harder

1. Do the notes mainly paraphrase the lecture or copy the speaker's words directly?
2. What abbreviations used in the notes are also used in the reading notes in exercise **D2**?
3. What abbreviations for "money" and "motivate" are used in the notes?

🔊 Track 386 **E4** **Complete tasks 1 and 2. Use the checklist in exercise E2 and the partial notes in exercise E3 as a guide.**

1. Listen to the second half of the lecture from exercise **E3**. Complete the notes in **E3** as you listen.
2. Listen to a lecture about a financial transaction tax. Take notes as you listen.

F Mastering Writing Task 1 – Writing an Effective Response

TEST TACTIC

For Writing Task 1, there is generally no need to plan how you will answer the question. The model paragraphs you will learn in this unit are designed to have a logical structure, and the ideas you mention should follow the order of the ideas in the reading and lecture.

Your response should begin with an introduction and then have three body paragraphs, one for each matching point in the passage and lecture. You do not need a conclusion. Writing Task 1 questions follow a standard pattern. As a result, it is possible to use the same standard body paragraph three times with only minor changes.

F1 **Read this sample response to the reading passage and lecture about performance-based pay for teachers. Then write short answers to questions 1–8.**

Both sources discuss the issue of giving performance-based pay to teachers. This piece of writing will summarize how the points that the writer discusses are challenged by the speaker.

The writer first claims that teachers would work harder if they received performance-based pay. The speaker states that no academic studies prove that this is true. He goes on to state that other studies show that paying people more money is often not a good way to motivate them to work. This is one way that the lecture challenges the reading.

The writer next says that student results would improve if teachers got merit-based pay because teachers would teach better. The speaker argues that results would not improve because of better teaching. He continues by arguing that some teachers may find ways to cheat. This is another way that the lecture casts doubt on the reading.

The writer then asserts that more smart people will become teachers if they receive performance-based pay. The speaker makes the point that few people become teachers because they want a high salary. He then says that performance-based pay might cause people who love money to become teachers. This is the final way that the lecture contradicts the reading.

1. The introduction (first paragraph) has two sentences. Which sentence is a transition sentence?
2. In the introduction, which sentence describes how the ideas in the lecture relate to ideas in the passage?

3. In the introduction, which sentence gives a short summary of the main idea of the passage and lecture?
4. Body paragraph 1 has four sentences. Which sentence describes how the lecture relates to the passage?
5. In body paragraph 1, which sentence summarizes a point from the reading passage?
6. In body paragraph 1, which sentence summarizes the speaker's view about the point from the reading passage?
7. In body paragraph 1, which sentence gives information that supports the speaker's view?
8. Do body paragraphs 2 and 3 have the same organization as body paragraph 1?

F2 **Complete this response to a Writing Task 1 Challenge question using either the notes below or your own notes from exercise D3 (reading) and task 2 of exercise E4 (lecture).**

Reading Notes	Lecture Notes
MV Robin Hood tax (RHT) = 0.05% on financial transactions	MV RHT has advans
RHT → raise money to reduce world poverty but disadvantages	P1 RHT is only 0.05% so low cost to retired people Couple with $5000 per month have just $25 less
P1 RHT → reduce pension profits → retired people become poor	P2 Not all banks would increase costs / customers could switch banks
P2 RHT → banks increase costs → customers have financial problems	Also conditions of RHT could say banks not allowed pass on costs
P3 RHT → financial industry cuts jobs → other industries cut jobs too	P3 Any new tax leads to job losses, but usu temporary situation Governm could use $ raised by RHT tax to help people who lose jobs

Summarize the points made in the lecture, being sure to explain how they challenge the points made in the reading passage.

Both sources discuss _____
This piece of writing will summarize how the points that the writer discusses are challenged by the speaker.

The writer first claims that _____
The speaker states that _____
She goes on to state that _____
This is one way that the lecture challenges the reading.

The writer next says that _____
The speaker argues that _____
She continues by arguing that _____
This is another way that the lecture casts doubt on the reading.

The writer then asserts that _____
The speaker makes the point that _____
She then points out that _____
This is the final way that the lecture contradicts the reading.

G Mastering Writing Task 1 – Avoiding Common Problems

In your response, you need to refer to the reading passage as well as the lecture, but copying phrases and ideas directly from the reading may reduce your score. As a result, learning how to paraphrase ideas from the passage is a key skill.

G1 **Study the three examples of paraphrasing on the next page. Then use the examples to help you paraphrase the two short reading passages. One answer has been done for you.**

TEST TACTIC

If there is a phrase you will need to type often, like "performance-based pay," carefully type it once. Then highlight it with the mouse and click the Cut button. Then you can quickly Paste it where you need it, which will help you save time and avoid typing mistakes.

☑ A paraphrasing technique that rarely leads to mistakes is changing the order of clauses or phrases within a sentence.

Example   There is a crisis in American education.
       → American education is in crisis.

☑ Another technique that does not lead to many mistakes is changing the grammatical form of words in the original.

Example   Merit-based pay for teachers would lead to better performance.
       → Teachers would perform better if they were paid based on their merit.

☑ A final effective paraphrasing technique, but one that can lead to errors, is using synonyms for words in the original.

Example   There is a link between quality of instruction and students' results.
       → There is a connection between teaching quality and learners' grades.

There are three reasons why bullying is a less serious problem these days than it was in the past. First, many schools have implemented a zero-tolerance policy on bullying, so bullies may be expelled from school for a first offense. Second, educators receive much better training these days, so they can stop or prevent bullying before it happens. And third, social attitudes towards bullying have changed, which means that fewer people think it is acceptable or do it.

1. The writer first claims that <u>people who bully can be made to leave school because of zero-tolerance policies.</u>
2. The writer next says that _____
3. The writer then asserts that _____

Frankly, it's ridiculous to argue there is less bullying now than in the past. First, studies have shown that zero-tolerance policies have had almost no impact on how much bullying occurs. Second, more bullying is taking place away from school where educators can do nothing to stop it no matter how much training they have. And third, social attitudes have always been against bullying, but a comparison of data from 1970, 1990, and 2010 shows that bullying is actually on the rise.

4. The writer first claims that _____
5. The writer next says that _____
6. The writer then asserts that _____

H   Test Challenge

H1   **Practice writing a Challenge question by completing the Writing Task 1 question on page 243. First spend three minutes reading the passage at the top of that page. Then listen to the lecture. Finally, take exactly 20 minutes to write or type your response. Use the checklist of skills you studied in this unit as a guide.**

Before you begin writing

☑ Scan the passage and make a note of the main view and the three points, ideas, or theories that the writer gives.

☑ Listen to the lecture and take notes; focus especially on points that are related to the three points from the reading.

While you are writing

☑ Write an introduction that summarizes the topic of the reading and lecture, and the relationship between the sources.

☑ Write three body paragraphs that describe in detail how points discussed in the lecture relate to ideas in the reading.

Although there are relatively few of them on the roads currently, electric cars offer a range of benefits both for individuals and for society. As a result, it would make sense for governments to offer subsidies to auto makers to produce electric vehicles, and for auto makers to prioritize the manufacture of these vehicles.

A key benefit of electric vehicles is their low cost of operation. The average journey by car in the United States is about ten miles. According to one study, the cost to drive a gasoline-powered car that distance is around $1.60, but the cost of a ten-mile trip in an electric car is under 50 cents. An average driver would save hundreds of dollars a year with an electric car.

Another benefit for individuals is the convenience offered by electric cars. All types of cars need to be refueled, but electric cars can easily be refueled simply by plugging them in and recharging their batteries. This can be done at home. Refueling a gasoline-powered car, on the other hand, requires going to the gas station, a trip which itself burns fuel.

And the environmentally-friendly nature of electric vehicles is well known. Unlike gasoline-powered vehicles, electric ones do not burn fossil fuels for energy, and release no harmful gases like carbon monoxide or carbon dioxide into the atmosphere. These gases have been linked to climate change and health issues, so electric cars are both cleaner and safer.

🔊 Track 388 Now listen to a lecture on the topic you just read about.

Summarize the points made in the lecture you just heard, being sure to specifically explain how they cast doubt on points made in the reading passage.

Next Steps

You may have questions and topics related to society in every section of the TOEFL Test. In consequence, learning more vocabulary about this topic, as well as practicing key skills for Writing Task 1 questions, may raise your overall test score.

To learn and practice more vocabulary related to society:

1. Make a list of things you like and things you dislike about your society.
2. Do some research in English to compare the things you like about your society with the same things in other societies.
3. Do some research in English to come up with ideas for improving the things you dislike about your society.
4. While you are doing your research, make a note of and study any new words and expressions that you notice.

To practice a key skill for Writing Task 1 questions:

1. Listen to a talk that is about three minutes long. (If a talk is too long, listen to part of it.) Take notes as you listen.
2. Use your notes to write five sentences that accurately repeat what the speaker says in the talk. Listen again, if necessary, so you can write the sentences perfectly.
3. Write paraphrases of the five sentences. Use the three paraphrasing techniques that you learned in this unit.
4. If you repeat steps 1–3 every day, you will become better at paraphrasing, which is a key skill for all three types of Writing Task 1 questions and several speaking questions, too.

Unit Focus

In the writing section of the TOEFL Test you will have two tasks. Task 1 is called the integrated writing task. There are three types of Task 1 questions that all require a slightly different response. For Problem-Solution questions, you will need to explain how a lecture gives solutions to problems or answers to questions mentioned in a reading passage. In this unit you will learn key skills and a model answer that will help you write effective responses to Problem-Solution questions, including:

- taking notes about the main points when you first see the reading passage.
- taking detailed notes about ideas in the lecture that are related to ideas in the reading.
- learning natural model phrases to write an effective introduction and three body paragraphs.
- avoiding common problems like incorrectly summarizing information from the lecture.

The vocabulary focus is on academic words and phrases related to:

- the environment.

A Warm-up

A1 Complete tasks 1–4.

1. Spend three minutes making a list of some environmental problems that affect your country or that you know about.
2. Share your list with a partner. Then listen to your partner's list and take notes about any problems not on your list.
3. With your partner, discuss and make a note of some possible solutions to the environmental problems on your lists.
4. Share your list of problems and possible solutions with other students. Then listen to their list of problems and solutions.

B Academic Vocabulary

B1 Expressions A–H are defined below. Work with a partner to choose the best expressions to complete statements 1–4. Two answers have been done for you.

1. Some studies show the use of pesticides in __agriculture__ to stop insects destroying crops may harm local _____.
2. Many people argue that burning __fossil fuels__ for energy may lead to a global increase in the average daily _____.
3. As the _____ of a city grows, the amount of light, noise, and atmospheric _____ those people generate also grows.
4. When people cut down trees and other _____, research shows that nearby _____ are more likely to flood.

A agriculture – the practice of farming, including growing crops
B fossil fuels – sources of energy like coal and oil that are buried in the ground
C pollution – something that makes air or water dirty or unsafe
D population – the number of people who live in a city or region
E temperature – how hot or cold the weather is at a particular time
F vegetation – plants, such as trees, bushes, grasses, and so on
G waterways – a body of water like a river that boats can travel on
H wildlife – a general word for the wild animals that live in a region

C Analyzing Writing Task 1 – Problem-Solution Questions

For Writing Task 1, you will first see a reading passage on the screen. The passage will be between 230 and 300 words long and will present three ideas, arguments, theories, or examples related to an academic topic. You will have three minutes to read the passage and take notes.

After three minutes, the passage will disappear from the screen and an announcer will tell you to listen to a lecture on the same topic. The lecture will last two to three minutes, and you will only have one chance to listen to it, so you should take notes as you listen. In some cases, the speaker will present solutions to problems that the reading passage discusses, or answers to questions that the reading passage asks. In these cases you will have a Problem-Solution question like one of the examples below.

After listening, the writing task will appear on the screen and the announcer will read it aloud. You will then have just 20 minutes to prepare and type your response. During this time you will be able to see the passage again.

Problem-Solution questions typically include a phrase like "address the problems" or "answer the questions," as in these examples:

> Summarize the points made in the lecture you just heard, being sure to specifically explain how they address the problems discussed in the reading passage.

> Summarize the points made in the lecture, being sure to say how they answer the questions raised in the reading passage.

To answer Writing Task 1 Problem-Solutions questions effectively and get a good score, it is important to:
- paraphrase, summarize, or quote the ideas and supporting details that the speaker discusses in the lecture.
- give a detailed explanation of how each point from the lecture responds to a question or problem in the passage.
- use model paragraphs with natural phrases so your response is well-organized and has few mistakes.

One common problem that can reduce your score when answering all types of Writing Task 1 questions is:
- incorrectly summarizing points from the lecture either by making language errors or by misunderstanding the speaker's views.

TEST TACTIC

In rare cases, a Problem-Solution question may use a phrase like "respond to issues." This can be confusing because "respond to" is also used in Challenge questions. However, if the passage discusses problems or asks questions, and the lecture mentions solutions or gives answers, it is a Problem-Solution question.

C1 Decide if Writing Task 1 questions 1–5 are Problem-Solution questions or Challenge questions (see Writing Unit 21). One answer has been done for you.

1. Summarize the points made in the lecture, explaining how they respond to specific issues in the reading passage.
☑ Problem-Solution   ☐ Challenge

2. Summarize the points made in the lecture you just heard, being sure to specifically explain how they cast doubt on points made in the reading passage.
☐ Problem-Solution   ☐ Challenge

3. Summarize the points made in the lecture, being sure to explain how they oppose specific points made in the reading passage.
☐ Problem-Solution   ☐ Challenge

4. Summarize the points made in the lecture you just heard, being sure to explain how they offer solutions to problems discussed in the reading passage.
☐ Problem-Solution   ☐ Challenge

5. Summarize the points made in the lecture you just heard, making sure you explain how they answer issues mentioned in the reading passage.
☐ Problem-Solution   ☐ Challenge

D Mastering Writing Task 1 – Reading the Passage

A key skill is to recognize information in the passage that will help you understand the lecture. You will see the passage again after the lecture, so you do not need to understand every word when you first see it. However, you *do* need to make a note of the writer's main view about the topic (usually given in paragraph 1) as well as the three main points that he or she makes (usually given in the final three paragraphs). When you take notes, use abbreviations to save time.

D1 Read the checklist, the passage about the urban heat island effect, and the notes about the passage. Then discuss questions 1 and 2 with a partner.

When you take notes from the reading passage, you should:

☑ Label your notes so you can easily recognize the writer's main view and three main points

☑ Note only the writer's main view and three main points, not background information or supporting details

☑ Use abbreviations (short ways to write something) in your notes in order to save time

A phenomenon known as the urban heat island effect means cities are often significantly warmer than surrounding areas, especially at night. This is because the materials like concrete and steel used in the construction of city buildings trap heat during the day and release it at night. This phenomenon has a number of environmental effects.

As many cities are hotter than surrounding areas, residents of those cities use more electricity during the summer to keep cool. The cost of this usage – for fans, air conditioners, and refrigerators – may be as much as $100 million per year in a city like Los Angeles. And as energy production is rarely pollution-free, there is an environmental cost, too.

The urban heat island effect can also have a harmful effect on bodies of water within and near cities. When rain falls on a city, stored heat is transferred to the water. This warmed water flows into streams, rivers, and lakes and raises their temperature, which can stress or even kill wildlife. In one example, rainfall over Cedar Rapids, Iowa led to a large increase in the temperature of water in a nearby stream that killed many fish.

In addition to the environmental impact, the urban heat island effect can cause summer heat waves to last longer and be more severe. This leads to health issues, including an increase in the mortality rate – that is, the number of deaths. This issue is particularly significant in cities with a large seasonal variation in weather like Chicago and New York.

MV urban heat island effect (UHIE) → effects on environm
UHIE caused by city construction materials trapping heat
P1 UHIE → more use of elec → high annual $ / more pollut
P2 UHIE → nearby rivers etc. → raises temp → harms wildlife
P3 UHIE → heat waves longer + hotter → increases deaths

1. What information in the notes is unnecessary because it gives background information?
2. What abbreviations are used in the notes? What does each abbreviation stand for?

D2 Read this passage and take notes. Use the checklist in exercise **D1** as a guide. Complete the task in three minutes.

A cultural symbol in many places, lions are currently listed as a vulnerable species by the International Union for the Conservation of Nature. Since the 1950s, it is estimated that the number of lions in Africa has fallen by a factor of ten to 20. If the situation does not improve, the species may face extinction.

A major cause of the decline in population of lions is hunting. Some of the hunting is done by local farmers protecting their livestock, but the bigger problem is hunting for trophy specimens by wealthy foreign tourists who are willing to pay significant amounts to shoot a lion. And because tourist dollars are an important source of income for many people in the regions where lions live, the rate at which lions are hunted for sport is only likely to increase.

Another cause is habitat loss. Growing human populations mean people are living and farming in areas that were previously uninhabited. This means less space both for lions and their prey. Unlike other big cats, lions only do well in areas with a high prey density. In areas with lower prey density, lion populations become fragmented and shrink.

A final problem facing lions is related to the first two issues. As lion populations and habitats are affected by hunting and human settlements, and as individual groups of lions become isolated from one another, the genetic diversity of each group of lions becomes more limited. Over time this leads to a so-called population bottleneck, meaning that the number of animals left for breeding may be too small for the species as a whole to survive.

TEST TACTIC

Even if you find the reading passage hard to understand, do not worry. You will see the passage again during the 20 minutes of writing time. During the first three minutes of reading time, focus on finding and noting the three main points, ideas, questions, or problems.

E Mastering Writing Task 1 — Listening to the Lecture

While you listen to the lecture, take detailed notes about the speaker's points. You will not have time to note every word the speaker says, so focus on ideas that relate to the three main points in the passage. Use abbreviations to save time.

Track 389 **E1** Listen to three students talk about strategies they use when taking notes. Match each speaker, A–C, to one strategy.

Strategy 1	The three points the speaker discusses in Writing Task 1 will be in the same order as the points in the reading. This knowledge helps you predict what the speaker will discuss next.	Speaker _____
Strategy 2	Just after the lecture finishes, you might have a good memory of the speaker's words. If so, do not start writing immediately, but take a little time to add to your lecture notes before your memory fades. This will help you summarize the lecture more effectively.	Speaker _____
Strategy 3	Although note-taking is difficult, the more you practice it, the easier it will become. So practice taking notes often, such as when you watch TV or listen to the radio.	Speaker _____

Track 390 **E2** Take notes as you listen to a lecture about the urban heat island effect. Then copy three answers from A–D to complete these unfinished notes. One of the answers does not match the unfinished notes.

MV   UHIE affects people + environm BUT ways to reduce
P1   1. _____
      Painting roofs light color also reduces
P2   2. _____
      Also use green roofs to soak up H_2O before
P3   3. _____
      Many cities have places for cooling and education

A Reducing heat in city reduces danger for people
B Planting trees + grass reduces heat in city
C Teaching people about cost of elec reduces effect
D Use materials to let H_2O cool before flow into river

Track 391 **E3** Take notes as you listen to a lecture about the declining population of lions. Use the checklist below and the notes in exercise **E2** as a guide.

You will only have one chance to listen to the lecture, so you should

☑ Take as many notes as you can about ideas that are related to points in the reading

☑ Use abbreviations (short ways to write something) in your notes in order to save time

☑ Copy the speaker's words directly or paraphrase them, whichever is easier for you

F Mastering Writing Task 1 – Writing an Effective Response

Your response should begin with an introduction and then have three body paragraphs, one for each matching point in the passage and lecture. You do not need a conclusion. Problem-Solution questions are similar to Challenge questions, so you can use the same standard paragraphs you learned for Challenge questions with only minor changes to four sentences.

F1 **Look at this outline response to a Writing Task 1 Challenge question (see Writing Unit 21). Then use the example in the first paragraph of the response as a guide to complete tasks 1 and 2.**

Both sources discuss _____. This piece of writing will summarize how the points that the writer discusses ~~are challenged by the speaker.~~ are addressed by the speaker

The writer first claims that _____. The speaker states that _____. He/She goes on to state that _____. This is one way that the lecture challenges the reading.

The writer next says that _____. The speaker argues that _____. He/She continues by arguing that _____. This is another way that the lecture casts doubt on the reading.

The writer then asserts that _____. The speaker makes the point that _____. He/She then points out that _____. This is the final way that the lecture contradicts the reading.

1. Cross out a phrase in each paragraph that is suitable for Challenge questions but not for Problem-Solution questions.
2. Replace the crossed out phrase with one of these phrases. (It does not matter which answer replaces which phrase.)
   - addresses issues from the reading
   - answers questions in the reading
   - takes up points in the reading

F2 **Complete sentences 1, 3, and 5 in this unfinished response by paraphrasing information from the passage or notes in exercise D1. Then complete sentences 2, 4, and 6 by summarizing the notes in exercise E2. Work with a partner.**

Both sources discuss the environmental impact of the urban heat island effect. This piece of writing will summarize how the points that the writer makes are addressed by the speaker.

The writer first claims that 1. _____. The speaker states that planting trees in cities can reduce the urban heat island effect. She goes on to state that 2. _____. This is one way that the lecture addresses issues from the reading.

The writer next says that 3. _____. The speaker argues that using special construction materials can cool water before it reaches rivers. She continues by arguing that 4. _____. This is another way that the lecture answers questions in the reading.

The writer then asserts that 5. _____. The speaker says that 6. _____. She then says that many cities have locations where residents can stay cool, which reduces the effect on mortality. This is the final way that the lecture takes up points in the reading.

F3 Complete this response to a Writing Task 1 Problem-Solution question using either the notes below or your own notes from exercise **D2** (reading) and exercise **E3** (lecture).

Reading Notes
MV lion popul decreasing (LPD)
  → may go extinct
P1 LPD cause = hunting by wealthy
   foreigners for trophies
P2 also habitat loss (HL) due to human
   popul growth also
P3 also popul bottleneck (PB) caused
   by low popul + isolation

Lecture Notes
MV   Lions (L) go extinct is pessimistic view / simple actions
     can remove threat
P1   make L endangered species in hunter's countries
     also ban trophy imports → likely to reduce hunting of L
P2   national parks (NP) in Africa = L + other animals
     protected
     HL continue outside NP, but with NP, HL not too bad
P3   Conservationists can move female L to new regions
     Reduces PB and lets L survive not go extinct

Summarize the points made in the lecture, being sure to explain how they address the problems discussed in the reading.

Both sources discuss _____.
This piece of writing will summarize how the points that the writer makes are addressed by the speaker.

The writer first claims that _____
_____.

The speaker states that _____
_____.

She goes on to state that _____
_____.
This is one way that the lecture addresses issues from the reading.

The writer next says that _____
_____.

The speaker argues that _____
_____.

She continues by arguing that _____
_____.
This is another way that the lecture answers questions in the reading.

The writer then asserts that _____
_____.

The speaker says that _____
_____.

She then says that _____
_____.
This is the final way that the lecture takes up points in the reading.

TEST TACTIC

If you often run out of time when typing your response, write body paragraphs with only three sentences: one to summarize the passage, one to summarize the talk, and one to explain how the two are related. This shorter response is quicker to write, but is still likely to get a good score.

G Mastering Writing Task 1 – Avoiding Common Problems

Correctly and clearly summarizing the ideas that the speaker discusses in the lecture is an essential skill for Writing Task 1. As a result, summarizing the lecture incorrectly or incompletely is likely to reduce your score.

Tracks 392–394 **G1** **Listen to excerpts (short parts) from three lectures and complete tasks 1–3. When you have finished, compare answers with a partner. Then listen again to confirm your answers.**

1. Listen to excerpt 1 and take notes. Then use your notes and memory to correct any mistakes in this summary of the two solutions to the problem of rising sea levels that the speaker discusses.

   The speaker states that climate change is the main cause of rising sea levels so stopping climate change might reduce sea level rise. He goes on to state that another way to deal with rising oceans would be to build a small system of earthworks, similar to the ones in Holland, to hold back the sea.

2. Listen to excerpt 2 and take notes. Then use your notes and memory to correct any mistakes in this summary of the two ways of reducing pollution caused by incineration that the speaker discusses.

   The speaker argues that the amount of pollution from incineration can be reduced by filtering the waste gases after they are released into the atmosphere. She continues by arguing that another way to reduce pollution levels in waste gases is to force them through a liquid called a scrubber before they are released.

3. Listen to excerpt 3 and take notes. Then use your notes and memory to correct any mistakes in this summary of the two ways that consumers can avoid paying high prices for organic produce that the speaker discusses.

   The speaker says that organic food that is in season in the local area typically costs more than fruits and vegetables that are grown using conventional methods. He then says that consumers can also buy organic food from grocery stores because prices there are generally cheaper than at farmer's markets.

H Test Challenge

H1 **Practice writing a Problem-Solution question by completing the Writing Task 1 question on page 251. First spend three minutes reading the passage. Then listen to the lecture. Finally, take exactly 20 minutes to write or type your response. Use the checklist of skills you studied in this unit as a guide.**

TEST TACTIC

To save time when typing your response, first type the model phrases for the first body paragraph. Use your mouse to highlight the paragraph. Then click the Cut button once and the Paste button three times. Finally, change the second and third body paragraphs so they match the model phrases.

Before you begin writing

☑ Scan the passage and make a note of the main view and the three points, ideas, or theories that the writer gives.

☑ Listen to the lecture and take notes; focus especially on points that are related to the three points from the reading.

While you are writing

☑ Write an introduction that summarizes the topic of the reading and lecture and the relationship between the sources.

☑ Write three body paragraphs that describe in detail how points discussed in the lecture relate to ideas in the reading.

Different nations and institutions have a different definition of what constitutes food waste, but regardless of how it is defined, food waste is a serious and growing global problem. A study conducted by the International Congress in 2011 estimates that approximately one-third of all food produced for human consumption gets lost or wasted and that this happens at every stage of the food supply chain. Let's look at three specific problems common in developed nations.

One issue that results in food waste is overproduction. Agricultural producers contractually agree on quantities of food to deliver to retailers. They may produce more than necessary to be sure they can fulfil their contract despite bad weather or other adverse factors. In many cases where farmers have produced too much, the excess is left to rot in the ground.

So-called appearance quality standards are another cause of food waste. Supermarkets in developed countries have strict standards about the shape, color, size, weight, and appearance of crops. Items not meeting those standards may be sold as animal feed, but are often simply discarded. For some crops, the waste may be up to 30 percent of the harvest.

In industrialized countries, food is often processed before being sold during which loss and wastage can occur. The processing includes cutting, cleaning, and packaging so that the processed food has the right look and size. Food that is damaged or not up to quality is often thrown out even though it would be safe to eat, as disposal is cheaper than the alternatives.

🔊 Track 395 Now listen to a lecture on the topic you just read about.

Summarize the points made in the lecture you just heard, being sure to specifically explain how they address issues raised in the reading passage.

Next Steps

You may have questions and topics related to the environment in every section of the TOEFL Test. As a result, learning more vocabulary about this topic, as well as practicing key skills for Writing Task 1 questions, may raise your overall test score.

To learn and practice more vocabulary related to the environment:

1. Do an Internet search for "news stories about the environment."
2. Read one of the stories and make a list of words in the story that are related to the environment.
3. Study the new words carefully and learn their meanings and how they are used.
4. Repeat steps 1–3, but this time do an Internet search for "news stories about <word>", replacing <word> with one of the words related to the environment that you learned in steps 2 and 3.

To practice a key skill for Writing Task 1 questions:

1. Find some sources of academic lectures that have a script of the speaker's words. You can find these in textbooks on academic English or academic listening such as the *Lecture Ready* series by Oxford University Press, or on the Internet.
2. Choose a lecture that sounds interesting. Then do some basic research on the topic of the lecture before you listen to it.
3. Listen to the lecture and take detailed notes. After listening for 2–3 minutes, pause the lecture.
4. Compare your notes to the script of the lecture. For each word in the script that you accurately noted, give yourself one point. (You should give yourself one point even if you used an abbreviation when you noted the word.)
5. Repeat steps 1–4 with a different lecture (or the next 2–3 minutes of the same lecture). Challenge yourself to get a higher points total each time.

Unit Focus

In the writing section of the TOEFL Test you will have two tasks. Task 1 is called the integrated writing task. There are three types of Task 1 questions that all require a slightly different response. For Support questions, you will need to explain how information from a lecture supports or adds to information mentioned in a reading passage. In this unit you will learn key skills and a model answer that will help you write effective responses to Support questions, including:

- taking notes about the main points when you first see the reading passage.
- taking detailed notes about ideas in the lecture that are related to ideas in the reading.
- learning natural model phrases to write an effective introduction and three body paragraphs.
- avoiding common problems like making too many basic grammar, vocabulary, and spelling mistakes.

The vocabulary focus is on academic words and phrases related to:

- technology.

A Warm-up

A1 Choose two phrases from the box or think of your own ideas to complete the first part of sentences 1–4. Then think of and add an example to support each statement.

1. In my opinion, technology has _____. For example, _____.
2. In my view, technology has _____. For instance, _____.
3. I think that technology has _____. To give an example, _____.
4. It is my belief that technology has _____. To illustrate, _____.

changed	had an effect on	affected	influenced
how I learn	my health	my social life	my hobbies

B Academic Vocabulary

B1 Choose the best words from A–H to complete these paragraphs about technology. One answer has been done for you.

A 1. ___*device*___ is a tool or machine that has been designed to perform a particular function. For example, a computer hard disk is a device designed for the 2. _____ of data. In the modern world, many devices are 3. _____, meaning they contain computer chips that give them specific capabilities. A rice cooker with numerous programmable settings, for instance, is an electronic device.

A computer system typically comprises equipment like a central processing unit, screen, disk storage, and so on, that are collectively known as 4. _____. For computer hardware to be useful, it must run 5. _____. This is the code, or 6. _____, that allows a computer user to perform functions as diverse as accessing data from a 7. _____, playing a game, browsing the Internet, or writing a report. When hardware is out of date, it must be replaced with a more advanced device; when software is out of date, however, a user can often 8. _____ it to the latest version, usually by downloading a file from the Internet.

A database	C electronic	E program	G storage
B device	D hardware	F software	H upgrade

C Analyzing Writing Task 1 – Support Questions

For Writing Task 1, you will first see a reading passage on the screen. The passage will be between 230 and 300 words long and will present three ideas, arguments, theories, or examples related to an academic topic. You will have three minutes to read the passage and take notes.

After three minutes, the passage will disappear from the screen and an announcer will tell you to listen to a lecture on the same topic. The lecture will last two to three minutes, and you will only have one chance to listen to it, so you should take notes as you listen. In rare cases, the speaker might discuss information that supports or adds to the ideas, arguments, theories, or examples from the reading passage. In these cases you will have a Support question like one of the examples below.

After listening, the writing task will appear on the screen and the announcer will read it aloud. You will then have exactly 20 minutes to prepare and type your response. During this time you will be able to see the passage again.

Support questions typically include a word like "support" or "strengthen," as in these examples:

> Summarize the points made in the lecture, being sure to explain how they support the points in the reading passage.

> Summarize the points made in the lecture, being sure to explain how they strengthen specific arguments made in the reading passage.

To answer Writing Task 1 Support questions effectively and get a good score, it is important to:

- paraphrase, summarize, or quote the ideas and supporting details from the lecture.
- give a detailed explanation of how each point from the lecture supports or adds to a point in the reading passage.
- use model paragraphs with natural phrases so your response is well-organized and has few mistakes.

One common problem that can reduce your score when answering all types of Writing Task 1 questions is:

- making too many grammar, vocabulary, or spelling errors by being careless or using language that is too hard for you.

TEST TACTIC

Remember that your task when responding to any type of Writing Task 1 question is to explain how the lecture relates to the reading. If you express your own opinion about the topic, you may not have enough time to write an effective response, which will reduce your score.

C1 Choose the best answer from A–C to fill in blanks 1–3 in the questions below.

Support Questions

- Summarize the points in the lecture, being sure to explain how they confirm the points in the reading.
- Summarize the points made in the lecture you just heard, being sure to specifically explain how they 1. _____ for the points made in the reading passage.

Challenge Questions (see Writing Unit 21)

- Summarize the points in the lecture, taking care to explain how they contradict points made in the reading.
- Summarize the points made in the lecture you just heard, being sure to state how they 2. _____ specific points made in the reading passage.

Problem-Solution Questions (see Writing Unit 22)

- Summarize the points made in the lecture, being sure to explain how they address the questions raised in the passage.
- Summarize the points made in the lecture, making sure you explain how they 3. _____ mentioned in the reading.

A cast doubt on   B give supporting evidence   C solve the problems

D Mastering Writing Task 1 – Reading the Passage

A key skill is to recognize information in the passage that will help you understand the lecture. You will see the passage again after the lecture, so you do not need to understand every word when you first see it. However, you *do* need to make a note of the writer's main view about the topic (usually given in paragraph 1) as well as the three main points that he or she makes (usually given in the final three paragraphs). When you take notes, use abbreviations to save time.

D1 Underline the writer's main view and three main points in this reading passage from a Writing Task 1 question. When you have finished, compare ideas with a partner. One answer has been done for you.

The Internet has only been a global phenomenon for around 20 years, but many could not imagine life without it. We use the Internet for so many things – education, work, friendship, entertainment – that it has become a vital part of everyday life for many. People are now starting to realize, however, that <u>the Internet has negative effects</u>, too.

One issue that is often mentioned is how the Internet is eroding people's ability to communicate well in writing. In many forms of written communication on the Internet, correct spelling, grammar, and use of punctuation are not expected. So, many young people develop bad writing habits that can lead to problems when they attend college or begin work.

The Internet has also had an impact on people's physical health. Browsing sites, playing games, chatting with friends, watching videos, and all the other activities that people typically engage in while using the Internet are all sedentary activities, meaning that they can be done without any physical exertion. People who spend many hours each day not moving are at risk for weight gain and all the many health problems associated with obesity.

Another problem relates to what could be called intellectual laziness. Several books have been written describing how the Internet affects not just people's willingness to read lengthy texts, but also, over time, their ability to do so. An abbreviation sometimes seen in user-posted comments on the Internet is "tldr," standing for "too long, didn't read."

D2 Look at these notes about the reading in exercise **D1**. Which set of notes is better: A or B? Why? Discuss with a partner.

A Notes
MV internet (IN) phenomenon for 20 years +
 used for many things
  vital part of everyday life for many
  people but sometimes negative
P1 people bad at spelling etc. because not
 attend college or get a job
P2 IN is fun (games, chat, videos) but people
 should exercise more
P3 Intellectual laziness is caused by IN

B Notes
MV internet (IN) used for many good things
 BUT has bad effects
P1 IN = bad spell/grammar/punc → prob at
 univ/job because poor writing
P2 IN activities = no movement → gain weight
 + health prob
P3 people not willing / able read long articles
 on IN → intellectual laziness

D3 Read this passage and take notes. Use the better set of notes in exercise **D2** as a guide. Complete the task in three minutes.

The use of cloud computing has become a major trend in computing over the past decade because of the advantages it offers to businesses. Cloud computing is the use of a network, usually the Internet, to access computing resources that are stored remotely. In other words, a user in one location can access computer hardware or software in a different location via the network.

Cost efficiency is one of the major advantages of cloud computing. Using the cloud, businesses can typically get access to business applications like word processing, spreadsheets, and databases, far cheaper than if they had to purchase individual licenses for these programs for every employee. Paying for data storage on the cloud is also typically much cheaper than purchasing physical storage devices.

Another huge advantage of cloud computing for many businesses and their employees is continuous access to data. Provided they have access to a network, users can access their work data from anywhere, anytime, and on almost any device. This gives employees the option to work from home – a practice often known as telecommuting. It also allows employees to work together on shared documents easily.

One more benefit of cloud computing is data safety. Backing up data to and restoring or recovering it from physical backup drives is typically an expensive and time-consuming process. Cloud service providers, however, typically offer data backup, data restoration, and data recovery services. This gives businesses the peace of mind to know that should anything go wrong, they will easily be able to access or restore backup data and even recover lost data.

E Mastering Writing Task 1 – Listening to the Lecture

While you listen to the lecture, take detailed notes about the speaker's points. You will not have time to note every word the speaker says, so focus on ideas that relate to the three main points in the passage. Use abbreviations to save time.

Tracks 396–399 **E1** Listen to some excerpts (short parts) from academic lectures and take notes. Then use your notes to write responses to tasks 1–3. One response has been written for you.

1. Summarize the examples of tool use among animals that the speaker mentions.
   The speaker mentions that several species of animals use tools to find food and for other basic needs.

2. Summarize the information about Luddites that the speaker gives.

   _____

3. Summarize the details about ENIAC that the speaker discusses.

   _____

Track 400 **E2** Look at these partial notes from a lecture about the negative effects of the Internet. Then listen to the lecture and take notes about the other two points the speaker discusses.

> MV   agree IN great but causes prob
> P1   IN also affect spoken communic as IN communic usu written
>   people not good + uncomfortable at face-face conversations

Track 401 **E3** Listen to a lecture about cloud computing. Take notes as you listen. Use the partial notes in exercise **E2** as a guide.

E4 Check (✓) Yes or No in response to statements 1–5 about listening to the lecture and taking notes.

1. I am generally able to recognize and note the speaker's main view.   ☐ Yes   ☐ No
2. In most cases I can recognize and note the speaker's three main points.   ☐ Yes   ☐ No
3. I am confident that the notes I take are clear and have enough detail.   ☐ Yes   ☐ No
4. In general, I find it easy to use abbreviations when I am taking notes.   ☐ Yes   ☐ No
5. I never lose concentration in the middle of the lecture when taking notes.   ☐ Yes   ☐ No

TEST TACTIC

Before you begin Writing Task 1, fold your note paper into eight sections: use the four left sections to note the main idea and three main points from the passage, and the four right sections for the main idea and points from the talk. This will help you easily find related points when typing your response.

E5 Complete tasks 1–3 about your responses to exercise **E4**.

1. Find one or two partners who have roughly the same number of "No" responses as you.
2. For each "No" response, discuss how to improve that aspect of listening or note-taking.
3. Share your ideas from task 2 with other students in the class. Then listen to their ideas.

F Mastering Writing Task 1 – Writing an Effective Response

Your response should begin with an introduction and then have three body paragraphs, one for each matching point in the passage and lecture. You do not need a conclusion. Support questions are similar to the other question types, so you can use the standard paragraphs you learned for Challenge and Problem-Support questions as long as you change the last sentence of each paragraph.

F1 Complete blanks 1–10 in this response about the passage in exercise **D1** and the lecture in **E2** by copying answers from A–J. One answer has been done for you.

Both sources discuss 1. __how the Internet can negatively affect people__. This piece of writing will summarize how the points that 2. _____
_____.

The writer first claims that the Internet has affected people's ability to write well. The speaker states that 3. _____
_____.

She goes on to state that many people find it difficult and uncomfortable to have a conversation with someone. 4. _____
_____.

The writer next says that 5. _____
_____.

The speaker argues that the Internet can also make people's eyes become tired and stressed. She continues by arguing that 6. _____
_____.

7. _____
_____.

The writer then asserts that 8. _____
_____.

The speaker makes the point that 9. _____
_____.

She then points out that 10. _____
_____.

This is the final way that the lecture endorses the reading.

A using the Internet can affect people's health because they do not move.
B the Internet has also affected people's ability to talk to each other.
C many people accept opinions without thinking about problems with a writer's ideas.
D the writer makes are supported by the speaker.
E a study shows that more people than 30 years ago cannot see distant things clearly.
F the Internet makes people intellectually lazy because they dislike reading long articles.
G people are also intellectually lazy about thinking about what they read.
H This is one way that the lecture supports the reading.
I how the Internet can negatively affect people.
J This is another way that the lecture confirms ideas in the reading.

F2 Complete this unfinished response to a Writing Task 1 Support question using either the notes below or your own notes from exercise **D3** (reading) and exercise **E3** (lecture).

Reading Notes	Lecture Notes
MV cloud computing (CC) = trend → advans for businesses (B)	MV CC has many advans for B like writer said
P1 cost efficiency = cheaper access to B software (SW) + data	P1 low cost is advan = small business upgrade SW for employees is $2000 CC license for SW just $100 / year
P2 data access = users can access data from anywhere and share files	P2 data access is benefit = people want quality of life + balance of work/life employees want work from home → CC lets B attract good workers
P3 data safety = CC makes easy to back up/restore/recover data	P3 most people know should back up data but never do it CC → data backup is automatic so huge benefit to B

Summarize the points made in the lecture, being sure to explain how they support the points mentioned in the reading.

Both sources discuss _____.

This piece of writing will summarize how the points that the writer makes are supported by the speaker.

The writer first claims that _____.
The speaker states that _____.
He goes on to state that _____.
This is one way that the lecture challenges the reading.

The writer next says that _____.
The speaker argues that _____.
He continues by arguing that _____.
This is another way that the lecture casts doubt on the reading.

The writer then asserts that _____.
The speaker makes the point that _____.
He then points out that _____.
This is the final way that the lecture contradicts the reading.

F3 Challenge questions (see Writing Unit 21) are more common in the TOEFL Test than Support questions. Complete tasks 1 and 2 to get some extra practice at writing Challenge questions.

Track 402 1. Listen to a new lecture about cloud computing. Take notes as you listen.
2. Use your reading notes from exercise **D3** (or the reading notes from exercise **F2**) and your lecture notes from task 1 to write or type a response to the Writing Task 1 Challenge question below. Complete the task in 20 minutes.

Summarize the points made in the lecture you just heard, being sure to specifically explain how they cast doubt on points made in the reading passage.

G Mastering Writing Task 1 – Avoiding Common Problems

Using standard paragraphs can help you get a good score for Writing Task 1. Avoiding basic grammar, vocabulary, and spelling errors will also help. Making a few basic mistakes may not affect your score, but if there are too many errors, your score is likely to be reduced.

G1 A teacher has circled and noted the errors in this response to a Writing Task 1 Challenge question. Work with a partner to decide how to correct each mistake. Then write out a corrected copy of the response in your notebook.

Both sources discuss the cloud computing trend. This piece of writing will summarize how the points that the writer discusses are challenged by the speaker.

The writer first claims that cloud computing **helped** [TENSE] businesses **due to** [CONJ] it gives them cost efficiency. The speaker states that cloud computing may help big corporations which have offices in many locations and numerous workers. He goes on to state that smaller companies with **less** [WW] employees may not save **the money** [ART] by using cloud computing. This is one way that the lecture challenges the reading.

The writer next says that cloud computing is convenient because users can **access to** [PREP] their data any time they want, using any device they want. The speaker argues that cloud computing is only **convenience** [WF] when there are no network **problem.** [PL] He continues by arguing that every cloud service provider has had network issues which make it impossible for **employee** [PL] to access data. This is another way that the lecture casts doubt on the reading.

The writer then asserts that cloud computing is safe because data can be backed up and restored **easy.** [WF] The speaker makes the point that data stored in the cloud is not safe and can easily be lost, stolen, deleted, or **copyed.** [SP] He then points out that we **hear often** [WO] news stories about businesses that lost customer data **stored** [PREP] the cloud. This is the final way that the lecture contradicts the reading.

Error Codes ART – missing or incorrect article / CONJ – missing or incorrect conjunction / PL – this word should or should not be plural
PREP – missing or incorrect preposition / SP – incorrect spelling / TENSE – incorrect tense
WF – incorrect word form (e.g., noun instead of adjective) / WO – incorrect word order / WW – wrong word

---

TEST TACTIC

If you do not have good notes about one of the three main points from the reading or lecture, try writing a body paragraph with only three sentences about that point: one sentence to summarize the passage, one to summarize the talk, and one to explain how they are related.

H Test Challenge

H1 Practice writing a Support question by completing the Writing Task 1 question on page 259. First spend three minutes reading the passage. Then listen to the lecture. Finally, take exactly 20 minutes to write or type your response. Use the checklist of skills you studied in this unit as a guide.

Before you begin writing

☑ Scan the passage and make a note of the main view and the three points, ideas, or theories that the writer gives.

☑ Listen to the lecture and take notes; focus especially on points that are related to the three points from the reading.

While you are writing

☑ Write an introduction that summarizes the topic of the reading and lecture and the relationship between the sources.

☑ Write three body paragraphs that describe in detail how points discussed in the lecture relate to ideas in the reading.

For a number of years, people have been debating the merits of electronic voting systems. There are many arguments against such systems, but as electronic voting technology matures, the strength of those arguments weakens.

One criticism of electronic voting is that it might lead to fewer votes because some people would choose not to vote from fear of technology. In fact, electronic voting would likely lead to higher voter turnout. In surveys, most voters 18 to 30 – an age group with historically low voting rates – say they would be more likely to vote if they could vote online. And only a small proportion of those over 30 say they would be less likely to vote if electronic voting were introduced.

A related issue is concern that voters might make mistakes when voting, such as accidentally voting for a candidate they do not endorse, or voting for too many candidates, because they are unfamiliar with computer technology. In practice, however, electronic voting systems can be designed so that these kinds of errors become either impossible or extremely unlikely.

Another aspect of electronic voting that is commonly criticized is whether the results can be trusted. The worry is that an error in the computer program that counts the votes for each candidate could lead to incorrect results. Again, it is likely that electronic voting will lead to more accurate results, not less trustworthy ones. The vote counting software can be tested an unlimited number of times on sample data to ensure it works correctly under all circumstances.

🔊 **Track 403** Now listen to a lecture on the topic you just read about.

Summarize the points made in the lecture you just heard, being sure to explain how they support the points in the reading.

Next Steps

You may have questions and topics related to technology in every section of the TOEFL Test. As a consequence, learning more vocabulary about this topic, as well as practicing key skills for Writing Task 1 questions, may raise your overall test score.

To learn and practice more vocabulary related to technology:

1. Make a list of the ten most important examples of technology that you use regularly. For example, your list might include "the Internet" and "smartphone."
2. Read articles or listen to lectures about the "history of" or the "development of" the first item on your list. For example, if the first item on your list is "television," you would learn about the "history of television." You can find articles or lectures about most topics on the Internet.
3. As you read or listen, make a note of new vocabulary related to technology. Then study these words and try using them.
4. Repeat steps 2 and 3 with the other nine items on the list you made in step 1.

To practice a key skill for Writing Task 1 questions:

1. Write ten sentences every day. Focus on writing perfect sentences with no grammar, vocabulary, or spelling mistakes.
2. Show your sentences to a teacher or native speaker of English and ask that person to underline any mistakes. Ask that person not to correct or explain the mistakes.
3. Look at all of the underlined mistakes in your sentences, and find out what your mistake is and why it is a mistake.
4. Rewrite each sentence with mistakes ten times correctly. By writing the corrected form of each mistake ten times, you will fix the correct grammar, vocabulary, or spelling in your memory. This will help you avoid the same mistake in the future.

Unit Focus

In the writing section of the TOEFL Test you will have two tasks. Task 2 is called the independent writing task. There are three types of Task 2 questions. For Single Opinion questions, which are the most common type, you will have to express one opinion about a familiar topic and support that opinion with two different reasons. In this unit you will learn key skills and a model answer that will help you write effective responses to Single Opinion questions, including:

- thinking of relevant ideas and planning an effective response.
- learning natural model phrases to write an introduction, two body paragraphs with examples, and a conclusion.
- avoiding common problems like making too many basic grammar, vocabulary, and spelling mistakes.

The vocabulary focus is on practical words and phrases related to:

- having a job or working.

A Warm-up

A1 **Work with a partner to complete tasks 1–4.**

1. Write a list of characteristics of good and bad jobs. For example, you might write "good pay" or "too much stress."
2. Share your ideas with other students. Then listen to their ideas and add new points to your lists.
3. What is one job that you would love to have in the future? Why? Support your answer.
4. What is one job that you would never like to do? Why? Give detailed reasons.

B Practical Vocabulary

B1 **Answer questions 1–8 by looking at headlines A–D about work. Check your answers with a partner when you have finished. One answer has been done for you.**

A
Many workers socialize with colleagues, but not supervisors

B
Survey: Perfect position has high salary, plenty of time off

C
Retail workers want less overtime, opportunities for promotion

D
Report says employees average 9.3 hours per day at workplace

1. Which word in headline A is a synonym for *bosses*? _____supervisors_____
2. Which word in headline A means the same as *coworkers*? _____
3. Which word in headline B means *money paid for doing work*? _____
4. Which word in headline B has basically the same meaning as *job*? _____
5. Which word in headline C means *extra time spent working after normal hours*?_____
6. Which word in headline C means *a move up to a more senior position at a job*? _____
7. Which word in headline D is a synonym for *staff* or *workers*? _____
8. Which word in headline D means *the place, such as an office, where a person works*? _____

C Analyzing Writing Task 2 — Single Opinion Questions

In Writing Task 2, you will have 30 minutes to prepare and type a response to a question. You will not have a choice of questions. There are three different question types, with Single Opinion questions being the most common. To answer these questions you need to give one opinion about a familiar topic and support your opinion with two different reasons and examples.

Some Single Opinion questions describe two opinions about a topic and ask which of the two opinions you have, as in this example:

> Some people think _____ is good. Others feel that _____ is better. Which do you prefer? Support your answer with detailed reasons.

Other Single Opinion questions ask whether you agree or disagree with a statement, as in this example:

> Do you agree or disagree with the following statement? It is beneficial to _____. Give reasons and examples to support your point of view.

The final kind of Single Opinion questions ask whether you would like to do something or not, as in this example:

> Would you like to _____? Why or why not? Support your answer.

Notice how all three examples ask you to express an opinion about one of two options: in the first example, either the option that "Some people think" or the one that "Others feel," in the second example, either agreeing or disagreeing with the statement, and in the third example, either explaining why or why not.

To answer Single Opinion questions effectively and get a good score, it is important to:
- plan your response by thinking of at least two ideas with examples that support your opinion and reasons.
- use model paragraphs with natural phrases so your response is well organized and has few mistakes.
- write clear sentences that express ideas which are directly related to the question.

One common problem that can reduce your score when answering all types of Writing Task 2 questions is:
- making too many grammar, vocabulary, or spelling errors by being careless or using language that is too hard for you.

TEST TACTIC

It is possible to answer a Single Opinion question by discussing both sides of the topic. However, doing this is more difficult than focusing on just one side of the topic, so you will probably make more mistakes. The reader may also find it harder to understand your response.

C1 **Summarize the two options you could express an opinion about from questions 1–4. One answer has been done for you.**

1. Would you like to get a job in another country or would you prefer to work in your country? Why?

   Option 1 ___get a job in another country___   Option 2 ___get a job in my country___

2. Do you think it is a good idea for students to work part time while they attend university? Why or why not?

   Option 1 _____   Option 2 _____

3. Do you agree or disagree that workers need good computer skills in order to get a job? Why? Support your answer.

   Option 1 _____   Option 2 _____

4. Some people are happy to work overtime in order to make extra money. Others prefer not to work overtime because they want to enjoy their free time. What is your preference? Why?

   Option 1 _____   Option 2 _____

D Mastering Writing Task 2 – Planning an Effective Response

For all types of Writing Task 2 questions, learning how to plan your response effectively is a key skill for the TOEFL Test.

🔊 Track 404 **D1** **Listen to an experienced teacher discuss preparing for a Writing Task 2 essay. Which ideas does the teacher express? One answer has been done for you.**

1. As there are only 30 minutes to answer Writing Task 2 questions, planning a response is not necessary. ☐ Yes ☑ No

2. Planned answers are generally better organized, have less repetition, and achieve a better score. ☐ Yes ☐ No

3. In general, if you decide to plan your response, you should finish your planning in two minutes or less. ☐ Yes ☐ No

4. Learning how to plan a response quickly and effectively is a key skill for doing well on the TOEFL Test. ☐ Yes ☐ No

5. The ideas and examples you come up with when you plan your response do not have to be true. ☐ Yes ☐ No

🔊 Track 405 **D2** **Listen to the teacher explain how to plan a Writing Task 2 essay. As you listen, underline the words in steps 1–3 that the teacher does NOT say. What words does she say instead of these words? Two answers have been done for you.**

Step 1	Read the question carefully and ~~notice~~ [recognize] the two ~~choices~~ [options] from the question that you could write about.
Step 2	Make a note of two reasons with detailed examples why you might choose each option from the question.
Step 3	Look at the reasons and examples you noted and decide which of the two options is easier to write about.

D3 **Look at these planning notes for a Writing Task 2 question. Then do tasks 1–4. The first task has been done for you.**

Would you like to get a job in another country or would you prefer to work in your country? Why?

(1 get job overseas)	(2 get job in my country)
more money → salaries in my country low	less stress → not have to learn new language / new culture
new experiences → new country / new people / new ideas	easy to get job → lots of jobs in my country now

1. Circle the two options in the notes that summarize the two options from the question.
2. Circle the first reason and supporting example for the first option.
3. Circle the second reason and supporting example for the second option.
4. Which of the two options would you find easier to write about? Why? Discuss with a partner.

D4 **Plan a response to Writing Task 2 questions 1–3. Follow the steps listed in D2.**

1. Do you agree or disagree that workers need good computer skills in order to get a job? Why?
2. Some people feel work is the most important part of their life. Others think friends and family are more important than work. What do you think? Why?
3. Do you agree or disagree with the following statement? Success only comes through hard work. Support your opinion with reasons and examples.

E Mastering Writing Task 2 — Writing an Effective Introduction

After planning your response, you need to type it. Every response should begin with an introduction in which you state your opinion about the question. You do not have to express your real opinion. Using a model introduction paragraph that is suitable for all Single Opinion questions is an effective way to write your introduction quickly and without errors.

E1 **Choose the best description, A–D, for each sentence of this example introduction. One of the descriptions does NOT match any of the sentences.**

> Would you like to get a job in another country or would you prefer to work in your country? Why?

I can see why some might feel that finding work in a foreign country has advantages.
On the whole, however, it is my opinion that getting a job in my country is preferable.
This piece of writing will explain my views on this topic in more detail.

The first sentence of the introduction _____

The second sentence _____

The third sentence _____

A   Contrasts the first opinion with your view about the topic
B   Introduces a detailed reason with a supporting example
C   Gives an opinion about the topic that is not your opinion
D   Gives a general description of the rest of your essay

E2 **Complete these introductions by copying phrases from the example introduction in exercise E1. Note that the missing phrases are the same for both introductions. One answer has been done for you.**

Do you think it is a good idea for students to work part time while they attend university? Why or why not?

_____ _I can see why some might feel that_ _____ university students should not work part time.
_____ students benefit when they work part time. _____
_____ .

Do you agree or disagree that workers need good computer skills in order to get a job? Why? Support your answer.

_____ good computer skills are useful but not necessary to find work.
_____ without such skills, finding a job is very hard _____
_____ .

E3 **Write introductions to Writing Task 2 questions 1 and 2. Use this checklist as a guide.**

- ☑ Use a phrase from the example introduction you studied in exercise **E1** to begin each sentence of your introduction.

- ☑ Use ideas from the notes that you made when you did exercise **D5** to complete each sentence of your introduction.

1. Some people feel work is the most important part of their life. Other people think other aspects of life are more important. What do you think? Why?
2. Do you agree or disagree with the following statement? Success only comes through hard work. Support your opinion.

F Mastering Writing Task 2 – Writing Effective Body Paragraphs

After your introduction, you need two body paragraphs. Each paragraph should give a clear, direct reason for your opinion, and support that reason with a detailed example. Your reason, details, and examples do not have to be true. Using model body paragraphs that are suitable for all Single Opinion questions is an effective way to write quickly and with few errors.

F1 Read this example response to a Writing Task 2 question. Then complete the description of how to organize body paragraphs 1 and 2 by matching the three steps to statements A, B, and C. One answer has been done for you.

Would you like to get a job in another country or would you prefer to work in your country? Why?

INTRODUCTION
I can see why some might feel that working overseas has advantages. On the whole, however, it is my opinion that getting a job in my country is preferable. This piece of writing will explain my views on this topic in more detail.

BODY PARAGRAPH 1
First of all, I am reasonably sure that working in my country would be less stressful than working overseas. Recently, I read an interesting article about this subject. According to what I read, living and working in another country causes most people to feel stress, which can lead to health problems like heart disease. The article also mentioned that there are three main reasons for this stress: difficulty communicating in a foreign language, difficulty dealing with different customs, and not being able to see friends and family.

BODY PARAGRAPH 2
In addition, I am completely confident that I could find a job in my country more easily and more quickly than a position in another country. In my experience, these days many companies in my country are hiring new workers, but companies in other countries are not hiring so many employees. To give an example, my sister and her friends recently graduated from college and all of them found a job within a few weeks, but my friend who lives in another country says it is not very likely that he will find a job soon.

Step 1	_Give a reason for your point of view that is clear, simple, and direct._
Step 2	_____
Step 3	_____

A Mention supporting information from your experience or an article you read.
B Give a reason for your point of view that is clear, simple, and direct.
C Add one or more additional supporting details from your experience or from the article.

F2 Rewrite the response from exercise **F1** to express the opposite point of view. Use the notes in exercise **D3** to help you, if necessary. Some parts of the response have been written for you.

I can see why some might feel that _____
On the whole, however, it is my opinion that _____
This piece of writing will explain my views on this topic in more detail.

First of all, _____
Recently, I read an interesting article about this subject. According to what I read, _____
_____
The article also mentioned that _____

In addition, _____
In my experience, _____
To give an example, _____

F3 Plan a response to Writing Task 2 questions 1 and 2 below. (Review section **D**, if necessary.) Then use your plans to write an introduction and two body paragraphs in response to each question. Use the model phrases from exercise **F2**.

1. Do you agree or disagree with the following statement? Education is the key to success at work. Support your opinion.
2. Some people want a job that has a high salary. Other people want a job that gives them plenty of time off. Which type of job would you prefer? Why? Give reasons and details to support your answer.

G Mastering Writing Task 2 — Writing an Effective Conclusion

The last paragraph of your response should be a short conclusion. The conclusion should paraphrase your opinion about the topic and then express a hope, plan, or possibility related to your opinion and the topic. As with the introduction and body paragraphs, it is a good idea to use a model conclusion paragraph that is suitable for all Single Opinion questions.

G1 Choose the answer, A–C, that best describes the two sentences in this example conclusion. One of the answers does NOT describe either sentence.

Would you like to get a job in another country or would you prefer to work in your country? Why?

In conclusion, for the reasons given, my preference would be to find work in my country.

In the future, my plan is to apply for jobs in my country rather than positions overseas.

The first sentence of the conclusion	_____
The second sentence	_____

A   gives a further reason for your point of view
B   expresses a future possibility, hope, or plan
C   paraphrases your opinion about the topic

G2 Put phrases A–F in order to make conclusions for Writing Task 2 questions 1 and 2. You should use some phrases twice. Use the example conclusion from exercise **G1** as a guide.

1. Do you think it is a good idea for students to work part time while they attend university? Why or why not?
2. Do you agree or disagree that workers need good computer skills in order to get a job? Why? Support your answer.

A   I feel that it is better for students to work part time
B   improve my computer skills before I apply for a job
C   In conclusion, for the reasons given,
D   good computer skills make finding a job easier
E   In the future, my plan is to
F   get a part-time job when I attend college

H Mastering Writing Task 2 — Using Natural Expressions

Planning your response well and using model paragraphs can help you get a good score for Writing Task 2. Using natural expressions to give your view about whether something is likely or unlikely may also help you write an effective response.

H1 Do the highlighted phrases in sentences 1–4 suggest that something is likely or not likely to happen? Check the box (✓) to mark your answer. One answer has been done for you.

1. In the future, I think there is a slim chance that my boss will give me a promotion.
   □ Likely to happen ☑ Not likely to happen
2. I am reasonably sure that in the future I will apply for a job working with technology.
   □ Likely to happen □ Not likely to happen
3. Because I dislike selling, I am completely confident that I will never work in a store.
   □ Likely to happen □ Not likely to happen
4. It is doubtful that I will apply for any jobs abroad because I would be homesick.
   □ Likely to happen □ Not likely to happen

H2 Write some sentences using the highlighted phrases from exercise **H1** to describe some things that you are likely or unlikely to do. Then show your sentences to a partner and give each other useful feedback.

▌ Mastering Writing Task 2 – Avoiding Common Problems

Avoiding basic grammar, vocabulary, and spelling errors will help you get a good score in Writing Task 2. Making a few basic mistakes may not affect your score, but if there are too many errors, your score is likely to be reduced.

I1 A teacher has circled and noted the errors in this response to a Single Opinion question. Work with a partner to decide how to correct each mistake. Then write out the corrected response in your notebook.

Would you like a career as a teacher? Explain why or why not and give details and examples to support your answer.

I can see why some might feel that being a teacher would not be enjoy. On the whole, however, it is my opinion that getting a job as a teacher would have many advantage. This piece of writing will explain my views on this topic in more detail.

First of all, as a teacher I would be able to make a lot of money because teachers in my country earned a high salary. Recently, I read an interesting article about this subject. According to what I read, even inexperienced teachers who have just graduated from the college get above-average salaries. The article also mentioned that teachers get a pay increase every years. These days, buying food, clothes, and renting or buying a place to live is expensive in my city, so I want to earn as much money than possible when I get a job.

In addition, as a teacher I would get plenty of paid vacation time each year. In my experience, teachers in my country get more than 12 weeks of time off each year. To give an example, my uncle is a teacher and he gets six weeks of vacation time on the summer and two weeks in spring, fall, and winter. Because of he has a high salary he can afford to travel new places each year. I love traveling, and it would be great to have so many time off so that I can travel to many new places.

In conclusion, for the reasons given, I would be definitely interested in training as a teacher. In the future, there is a chance that I will majer in education at university and become a teacher.

Error Codes ART – missing or incorrect article / CONJ – missing or incorrect conjunction / PL – this word should or should not be plural
PREP – missing or incorrect preposition / SP – incorrect spelling / TENSE – incorrect tense
WF – incorrect word form (e.g., noun instead of adjective) / WO – incorrect word order / WW – wrong word

---

J Test Challenge

TEST TACTIC

To get the most realistic practice for the TOEFL Test, type your response on a computer. Before you begin, turn off spelling check and grammar check if your software has them.

J1 Practice Writing Task 2 by answering either question 1 or 2. Plan and write or type your response in exactly 30 minutes in order to get realistic practice for the TOEFL Test. Use this checklist of skills that you studied in this unit as a guide.

Before you begin writing

Remember that in the TOEFL Test you will not get a choice of Writing Task 2 questions. You will have just one question, and the first step in planning your response should be to recognize what type of question it is: Single Opinion, Double Opinion (see Writing Unit 25), or Contrast Opinion (see Writing Unit 26).

☑ For Single Opinion questions, first read the question and recognize the two options that you could write about.

☑ Think and make a note of reasons with supporting examples why you might choose each option.

☑ Look at your reasons and examples and decide which of the two options is easier for you to write about.

While you are writing

☑ Write an introduction, two body paragraphs, and a conclusion using the model phrases you learned in this unit.

☑ Use natural phrases to make additional points or express contrasting ideas.

☑ Take care to avoid basic grammar, vocabulary, and spelling mistakes.

1. Do you agree or disagree with the following statement? A good supervisor should be friendly, but not a friend. Support your answer.
2. Some people want a workplace where they can wear casual clothes. Others are happy to work at a company where they have to wear professional clothes. Which kind of workplace do you like? Why? Support your answer.

Next Steps

You may see questions and topics related to working and having a job in all sections of the TOEFL Test. As a result, learning more vocabulary related to working, as well as practicing key skills for Writing Task 2 Single Opinion questions, may raise your overall test score.

To learn and practice more vocabulary related to working or having a job:

1. Search online job advertisements and find an advertisement for a position that looks interesting.
2. Read the advertisement carefully and make a list of words in the advertisement you do not know.
3. Learn the meanings of these words as well as how to use them in a sentence.
4. Write a cover letter as if you were applying for the position in the ad. Use the words you learned in your letter. (If you are not confident about how to write a cover letter, search the Internet for "sample cover letters".)

To practice key skills for Writing Task 2 Single Opinion questions:

1. Look again at the job advertisement you found from step 1 above. Do some research about the job, such as learning what kinds of duties and responsibilities it requires or what salary is typical. Then decide if you would like to do the job or not.
2. Write an essay that states whether or not you would like to do the job, gives two reasons for your opinion, and supports each reason with a detailed example. Use the model phrases that you learned in this unit in your essay.

Unit Focus

In the writing section of the TOEFL Test you will have two tasks. Task 2 is called the independent writing task. There are three types of Task 2 questions. For Double Opinion questions, you will have to express two related opinions about a familiar topic and support each opinion with a different reason. In this unit you will learn key skills and a model answer that will help you write effective responses to Double Opinion questions, including:

- thinking of relevant ideas and planning an effective response.
- learning natural model phrases to write an introduction, two body paragraphs with examples, and a conclusion.
- avoiding common problems like writing too many simple sentences.

The vocabulary focus is on practical words and phrases related to:

- health.

A Warm-up

A1 Answer questions 1–3. For each question, write at least three different answers.

1. What are some good things to do in order to stay healthy?
2. What are some of the most common effects of catching a cold?
3. What are some things that people should *not* do when they are sick?

A2 Complete tasks 1–4.

1. Share your answers to question 1 from exercise **A1** with a partner.
2. Listen to your partner's answers to question 1 from **A1**. Add your partner's ideas to your list.
3. Look at your list of answers to question 1 in **A1**. Decide which two answers would be easiest for you to write about if you had to write an essay on that topic.
4. Repeat tasks 1–3 for the other questions in **A1**. For each question, work with a different partner.

B Practical Vocabulary

B1 Answer questions 1–7 by looking at statements A–C about healthcare. Check your answers with a partner when you have finished. One answer has been done for you.

1. Which word in statement A means *people who see a doctor because of a medical problem*?
    _____patients_____
2. Which word in statement A is a synonym for *doctors*? _____
3. Which word in statement A means *actions or medicines that help a sick person get better*?
    _____

TEST TACTIC

Using statistics – such as *seven out of ten*, *twice as many*, and *40 percent of* – in your written and spoken responses is an effective way to make them more natural and detailed. Your statistics do not have to be true.

4. Which *two* words in statement B describe kinds of medical problems? _____
5. Which word in statement B is a more formal word for *drugs*? _____
6. Which word in statement C means *an unexpected event that must be dealt with urgently*? _____
7. Which word in statement C is a synonym for the word *operations*? _____

A According to a national survey, almost seven out of ten patients say their physicians prescribe effective treatments.

B Compared with twenty years ago, roughly twice as many conditions and diseases can be treated with medicines.

C Nearly 40 percent of surgeries performed in some hospitals are emergency procedures; the rest are planned operations.

C Analyzing Writing Task 2 – Double Opinion Questions

In Writing Task 2, you will have 30 minutes to prepare and type a response to a question. You will not have a choice of questions. Some questions are Double Opinion questions. Unlike Single Opinion questions (see Writing Unit 24), to answer Double Opinion questions effectively you need to express two opinions about the topic, and support each opinion with a different reason and example.

Most Double Opinion questions include a plural noun like *causes, effects, factors, qualities, reasons*, or *ways*, as in the examples below. This plural noun makes it clear that you need to write about more than one cause, effect, factor, quality, reason, or way:

> These days, people have more _____ than they did in the past. What are the causes of this phenomenon? Support your opinion with reasons and details.

> In your opinion, what are the qualities of a good _____? Support your opinion with reasons and detailed examples.

> In what ways has _____ had an effect on _____? Give reasons and examples to support your response.

Some Double Opinion questions ask about current situations or about what people could do. These questions may include a plural noun that is specific to the question, such as *problems* or *advantages*, but often will not have a plural noun:

> _____ is a problem in some countries. What similar problems exist in your country? Support your opinion.

> What can people do to make _____ better? Give details and examples that support your answer.

To answer Double Opinion questions effectively and get a good score, it is important to:

- plan your response by thinking of at least two opinions with supporting examples that answer the question.
- use model paragraphs with natural phrases so your response is well organized and has few mistakes.
- write clear sentences that express ideas which are directly related to the question.

One common problem that can reduce your score when answering all types of Writing Task 2 questions is:

- using too many simple sentences instead of a variety of simple, compound, and complex sentences.

C1 Summarize what you would need to do to answer Double Opinion questions A–D. One answer has been done for you.

1. To answer question A, I would need to discuss two <u>factors that have led to people living longer lives</u> <u>than in the past</u> .
2. To answer question B, I would need to discuss two _____
3. To answer question C, I would need to discuss two _____
4. To answer question D, I would need to discuss two _____

A These days, many people live longer lives than they did in the past. What factors are responsible for this situation?

B People visit a doctor when they are sick. In your view, what are the qualities of a good physician? Support your opinion.

C In what ways has technology affected people's health? Give reasons and examples to support your response.

D Obesity (being overweight) is a problem in some countries. What health problems are common in your country?

D Mastering Writing Task 2 – Planning an Effective Response

For all types of Writing Task 2 questions, responses that are planned are generally more effective and get a higher score than ones that are unplanned. As a result, learning how to plan your response effectively is a key skill for the TOEFL Test. However, it is important to remember that the ideas and examples you think of while planning do not have to be true.

D1 **Copy answers A–C into the correct space to complete the descriptions of the three steps in planning an effective response to Double Opinion questions.**

Step 1	First, decide _____
Step 2	For Double Opinion questions, think _____
Step 3	Finally, look _____

A of and make a note of at least three ideas (each with an example) that answer the question.
B if the question is Single Opinion (see Writing Unit 24), Double Opinion (this unit), or Contrast Opinion (Writing Unit 26).
C at your ideas and examples from the second step and choose the two easiest ideas to write about.

D2 **Read this advice about how to think of ideas for Double Opinion Writing Task 2 questions. Then answer questions 1–6. When you answer, try to paraphrase the passage rather than copy it. One answer has been done for you.**

In general, good ideas that match Writing Task 2 questions need three characteristics. First, they should be familiar ideas. This means ideas you have spoken or written about before in English. The reason is that when you write about familiar ideas, you will usually write more quickly and make fewer mistakes.

Second, good ideas for Writing Task 2 questions need to be simple ideas, not complex ones. The reason is that simple ideas are easy for you to explain – so you can write them more quickly – and easy for the reader to understand – so he or she is not likely to get confused. A good way to recognize whether an idea is simple is to think whether a child could easily understand the idea.

And third, good ideas for Writing Task 2 questions should be directly related to the topic. As with the other two characteristics, this is because ideas that are directly related to the topic are easier to write about. For example, if a Writing Task 2 question asks you about the best ways to stay healthy, you might have two ideas – exercise regularly and listen to music. The first idea is directly related to the topic – everyone knows that exercise is good for health – so it would be easy to write about. The second idea, however, is not directly related to the topic. You could explain that stress causes many health issues and listening to music can reduce stress so it is good for health, but this is more difficult, so it will take longer to write about it, and there is a greater chance that you will make mistakes and confuse the reader.

1. What is the first characteristic of a good idea for Writing Task 2 questions?
   A good idea that matches a Writing Task 2 question should be a familiar idea.

2. How can you recognize whether an idea is familiar or not?
   A familiar idea is one that you _____

3. What are two advantages of thinking of familiar ideas?
   Two advantages are _____

4. What is the second characteristic that good ideas need and why is it important?
   Second, good ideas should _____
   The reason is that _____

5. How can you judge whether one of your ideas has this characteristic?

You can ask yourself if _____

6. What is the final characteristic of good ideas for Writing Task 2 questions? Why?

Finally, good ideas should because _____

D3 Look at these planning notes for a Double Opinion Writing Task 2 question. Then complete tasks 1–4.

> People do many different things to maintain their health. In your view, what are the best ways to stay healthy? Why?

(exercise regularly)	e.g., running or walking → cheap way to lose weight
get different job	e.g., most stress from job → if different job, maybe less stress
visit doctor often	e.g., doctor does tests → tests show problems → doctor gives medicine
eat more vegetables	e.g., vegetables have vitamins → good for body

1. Read and circle the four ideas in the notes that match the question. The first idea has already been circled.
2. Put a check (✓) next to each idea if it is a familiar idea for you, or an X if it is unfamiliar for you.
3. Put a second check next to each idea if it is simple and direct, or an X if it is complex and indirect.
4. Tell a partner which two of the ideas you would choose to write about and why.

D4 Look at these partial planning notes for a Double Opinion Writing Task 2 question. Then complete tasks 1–4.

> What are the most important qualities of a nurse? Use details and examples to explain why these qualities are important.

friendly	e.g., hospitals are stressful places → feel less stress if people friendly
good at communicating	_____
careful	_____

1. Only one of the ideas has a supporting example. Think of and add supporting examples for the other two ideas.
2. There are only three ideas that match the question. Think of and add at least one more idea with a supporting example.
3. Decide which of the ideas are most familiar to you. Also decide which of the ideas are the most simple and direct.
4. Tell a partner which two of the four ideas you would choose to write about and why.

D5 Plan responses to Writing Task 2 questions 1–4. Follow the steps to planning listed in exercise **D1**. Focus on coming up with ideas that are familiar, simple, and direct.

1. In general, people's health is better than it was in the past. What are some reasons for this situation?
2. Becoming a doctor, nurse, or other medical professional typically requires years of training. Why do you think some people choose to become a medical professional? Give details and examples that support your answer.
3. In many countries, the number of elderly people in the population is rising. What are some causes of this phenomenon?
4. Nowadays food is easier to prepare than it was in the past. How has this change improved people's quality of life? Support your ideas.

TEST TACTIC

To save time, use one of the ideas that you thought about while planning, but did not choose as your opinion, as the idea that you write about in the first sentence of your introduction.

E Mastering Writing Task 2 – Writing an Effective Response

After planning your response, you need to type it. Every response needs an introduction, two body paragraphs, and a conclusion. To produce an effective response with few errors, it is a good idea to use model paragraphs. The model paragraphs that you learned for Single Opinion questions in Writing Unit 24 are also suitable for Double Opinion questions.

E1 **Read this response to a Double Opinion Writing Task 2 question. Then complete the table below by copying the answer, A–K, that best describes each part of the response. Two answers have been done for you.**

> People do many different things to maintain their health. In your view, what are the best ways to stay healthy? Why?

I can see why some might feel that making regular appointments to see a doctor is a good way to stay healthy. **On the whole, however, it is my opinion that** there are more effective ways to maintain my health. **This piece of writing will discuss my views on this topic in more detail.**

First of all, I feel that eating healthy food, especially fruits and vegetables, is a great way to become healthy and stay healthy. **Recently I read an interesting article about this subject. According to what I read,** fresh fruits and vegetables like apples, bananas, and carrots contain vitamins and other things that are good for my body. **The article also mentioned that** people who regularly eat fresh fruits and vegetables are sick 47% less often than people who rarely eat these things.

In addition, I think that exercising regularly is one of the best, easiest, and cheapest ways to stay in good health. **In my experience,** there are many places where people can work out and many activities that people can easily do without spending a lot of money. **To give an example,** there is a park near my home where I can easily run, play tennis with my friends, or just walk. These activities do not cost any money, which is good for me because I do not have a job these days.

In conclusion, for the reasons given, I think doing regular exercise and eating foods that are good for me are the best ways to stay healthy. **In the future,** I will exercise every day and eat more fruits and vegetables for lunch and dinner.

Introduction	Part 1	
	Part 2	
	Part 3	
Body paragraph 1	Part 1	Give a simple, familiar, and direct first opinion and reason
	Part 2	
	Part 3	
Body paragraph 2	Part 1	
	Part 2	
	Part 3	Add a supporting example to your personal experience
Conclusion	Part 1	
	Part 2	

A Give a simple, familiar, and direct first opinion and reason
B Add a supporting example to your personal experience
C Give an opinion about the topic that some people have
D Introduce a personal experience that supports your view
E Give a simple, familiar, and direct second opinion and reason

F   Contrast the first opinion with your views about the topic
G   Introduce information from an article you recently saw
H   Express a hope, idea, plan, or possibility for the future
I   Give a general description of the rest of your essay
J   Paraphrase (or summarize) your views about the topic
K   Describe additional supporting details from the article

E2 Compare the response to a Double Opinion question in exercise **E1** with the response to a Single Opinion question in exercise **I1** in Writing Unit 24 (page 266). Which statement, A, B, or C, accurately describes how the two responses differ?

A   The two body paragraphs in the Single Opinion response use different model phrases than the two body paragraphs in the Double Opinion response.
B   The introduction and conclusion in the Single Opinion response have a different organization than the introduction and conclusion in the Double Opinion response.
C   In the Single Opinion response, body paragraphs 1 and 2 discuss the same opinion, but in the Double Opinion response, body paragraphs 1 and 2 discuss different opinions.

E3 Look at this unfinished response to a Double Opinion Writing Task 2 question. Finish the second body paragraph and write a conclusion based on the notes below. Use the model response in exercise **E1** as a guide.

friendly	e.g., hospitals are stressful places → feel less stress if people are friendly
good at communicating	e.g., can explain things to patients and doctors well → good communication avoids mistakes
careful	e.g., patients get better when nurse careful / medical mistakes caused by careless nurses

What are the most important qualities of a nurse? Use details and examples to explain why these qualities are important.

I can see why some might feel that nurses should be good communicators. On the whole, however, it is my opinion that there are two more important qualities that nurses should have. **This piece of writing will explain my views on this topic in more detail.**

First of all, it is my belief that being careful is a very important quality that nurses need. **Recently I read an interesting article about this subject. According to what I read,** patients get better quickly when they have nurses who are careful to make sure that their patients get the right medicine and the right treatment. **The article also mentioned that** roughly one third of all medical mistakes are caused by a medical professional, like a doctor or nurse, making a careless mistake.

In addition, from my point of view another key quality for nurses is being friendly. _____

_____

_____

_____

_____

_____

_____

_____

_____

_____

F Mastering Writing Task 2 – Using Natural Expressions

Planning your response well and using model paragraphs can help you get a good score for Writing Task 2. It is also a good idea to use multi-word expressions when you write about your ideas and express your opinions. This will not only make your writing seem more natural, but it will increase the word count of your response as well.

F1 **Put the words in order to make five natural expressions for giving your opinion. One answer has been done for you.**

1. of view, / my / from / point _____ *From my point of view,* _____
2. of the / that / I am / opinion _____
3. belief / it is / my / that _____
4. seems / that / to me / it _____
5. thinking, / to my / of / way _____

F2 **Write a sentence in response to questions 1–5. Begin each sentence with one of the expressions from exercise F1.**

1. Do you think doctors and nurses should be paid more money?
2. What do you think about the quality of hospitals in your country?
3. Do you believe that children or the elderly need more medical care?
4. Should your government spend more on healthcare, on education, or on sports?
5. Do you think it is more important for physicians to be friendly or good at communicating?

G Mastering Writing Task 2 – Avoiding Common Problems

Planning your response well and using model paragraphs can help you get a good score for Writing Task 2. It is also a good idea to avoid common problems like writing a response with too many simple sentences. To get a good score for Writing Task 2, your response should include a variety of simple, compound, and complex sentences.

G1 **Practice writing some complex sentences. Combine each pair of sentences, 1–4, using the given relative pronoun (*which* or *who*). One answer has been done for you.**

1. Obesity is definitely a problem in my country. It can have several serious effects on people's health. *(which)*
   Obesity, which can have several serious effects on people's health, is definitely a problem in my country.

2. Stress is another health problem that many people in my country have. Stress can lead to problems like heart disease. *(which)*
   _____
   _____

3. Medical research is one factor that has helped people live longer lives. The research includes finding better treatments for dangerous diseases. *(which)*
   _____
   _____

4. Another factor that has helped people live longer in my country is improved medical training for physicians. They must now study for six years before they get a medical license. *(who)*
   _____
   _____

TEST TACTIC

ETS, the organization that develops TOEFL, says effective Writing Task 2 responses typically have 300 words. However, shorter responses that are well organized and answer the question directly can still get the maximum score. The sample response in section E of in this unit is a good example of a high-scoring short response.

H Test Challenge

H1 Practice Writing Task 2 by answering either question 1 or 2. Plan and write or type your response in exactly 30 minutes in order to get realistic practice for the TOEFL Test. Use this checklist of skills that you studied in this unit as a guide.

Before you begin writing

Remember that in the TOEFL Test you will not get a choice of Writing Task 2 questions. You will have just one question, and the first step in planning your response should be to recognize what type of question it is: Single Opinion (see Writing Unit 24), Double Opinion, or Contrast Opinion (Writing Unit 26).

☑ For Double Opinion questions, think and make a note of at least three ideas with supporting examples that answer the question.

☑ Look at your ideas and choose the two ideas that are the easiest for you to write about.

While you are writing

☑ Write an introduction, two body paragraphs, and conclusion that use the model phrases you learned in this unit.

☑ Use natural phrases to express your opinion clearly and directly.

☑ Try to write a variety of sentences, including complex sentences that use relative pronouns.

1. In what ways does exercise affect people's health? Use reasons and specific examples to support your answer.
2. Why do you think some people have habits that are bad for their health? Support your opinion.

Next Steps

You may have questions and topics related to health and medicine in all sections of the TOEFL Test. As a result, learning more vocabulary about this topic, as well as practicing key skills for responding to Writing Task 2 Double Opinion questions, may raise your overall test score.

To learn and practice more vocabulary related to health and medicine:

1. Make a list of illnesses and medical problems that you or someone you know has had. If necessary, use a dictionary or the Internet to find the English name for each medical condition.
2. For the first medical condition on your list, do an Internet search for "history of [condition]". For example, you might search for "history of the flu". Read some of the articles that you find, and make a list of useful vocabulary in the articles.
3. Repeat step 2, but this time do a search for "cures for [condition]". (For example, search for "cures for the flu".)
4. Review your list of useful vocabulary from steps 2 and 3 and study the words carefully. Then repeat steps 2 and 3 for the other conditions on your list from step 1.

Do the following steps each day to practice key skills for Writing Task 2 Double Opinion questions:

1. Come up with your own Double Opinion questions by replacing the underlined phrase in questions A and B below with a different phrase. For example, instead of *dentist* in question A, you could put *nurse*, *friend*, and so on.
2. Plan and type a response to your Double Opinion question. Use the strategies and expressions you learned in this unit.
3. Wait a few days and then review your essay. Fix all the mistakes you can find, including sentences that are too simple.

A What are the qualities of a good underlined dentist? Why are these qualities important? Support your answer.
B What are the best ways to become healthy? Give detailed reasons and examples to support your view.

WRITING • Independent Writing Task 2 — Contrast Opinion Questions

Unit Focus

In the writing section of the TOEFL Test you will have two tasks. Task 2 is called the independent writing task. There are three types of Task 2 questions. For Contrast Opinion questions, you will have to express two contrasting opinions about a familiar topic and support each opinion with a different reason. In this unit you will learn key skills and a model answer that will help you to write effective responses to Contrast Opinion questions, including:

- thinking of relevant ideas and planning an effective response.
- learning natural model phrases to write an introduction, two body paragraphs with examples, and a conclusion.
- avoiding common problems like writing a response that is too short.

The vocabulary focus is on practical words and phrases related to:

- transportation and travel.

A Warm-up

A1 Complete tasks 1 and 2.

1. Make a list of many different ways of traveling. For example, you might list vehicles like trains or cars, or traveling alone or with friends.
2. Share your list with a partner. Work together to write comparison sentences about every way of traveling on your lists. Use the example as a guide.

Example   *To my way of thinking, cars and trains are equally good when you need to travel a long distance.*

B Practical Vocabulary

B1 Choose the best answer from A–H to complete definitions 1–8 of expressions related to transportation and travel. One answer has been done for you.

1. _____Distance_____ is the number of miles or kilometers (or other system for measuring length) between two places.
2. Taking a _____ involves traveling between two places, especially two places that are located some distance apart.
3. _____ are machines, often with wheels, that can be used to transport people or goods from one place to another.
4. Many cities have a _____ system of buses, trains, and subways that residents use to travel around.
5. The way a bus or other public transportation vehicle travels between its starting and end points is called its _____ .
6. The last station or stop on the route of a train, bus, streetcar, or airplane is known as the final _____ .
7. The people who travel on public transportation (or on other forms of mass transit like airplanes) are called _____ .
8. When there is bad weather, airplanes may experience a _____ and passengers may arrive at their destination late.

A delay	C distance	E public transportation	G route
B destination	D journey	F passengers	H vehicles

TEST TACTIC

The example responses in this book do not use contractions (e.g., *don't*). Using contractions in your TOEFL responses is not wrong, but contractions are not common in formal writing. As a result, writing without contractions will mean your responses look natural.

C Analyzing Writing Task 2 — Contrast Opinion Questions

In Writing Task 2, you will have 30 minutes to prepare and type a response to a question on the computer screen. You will not have a choice of questions. There are three different question types, including Contrast Opinion questions. To answer Contrast Opinion questions effectively you need to give two contrasting opinions about a familiar topic and support each opinion with a different reason and example. You may also need to say which of the two opinions you prefer.

Most Contrast Opinion questions include phrases like "compare and contrast," "like and dislike," or "advantages and disadvantages," as in these examples:

Compare and contrast _____ with _____. Which do you think is better? Why?

What do you like and dislike about _____? Why? Give details and reasons to support your opinions.

Other Contrast Opinion questions mention two methods of doing something or two ways of thinking about a situation and then ask you to compare or discuss the two methods or ways, as in these examples:

Some people like _____. Other people prefer _____. Compare the advantages of _____ and _____. Which do you prefer? Why?

Some think _____ are good. Others feel _____ are better. Discuss these views.

To answer Contrast Opinion Writing Task 2 questions effectively and get a good score, it is important to:

- plan your response by thinking of ideas with supporting examples for both aspects of the question.
- use model paragraphs with natural phrases so your response is well organized and has few mistakes.
- write clear sentences that express ideas which are directly related to the question.

One common problem that can reduce your score when answering all types of Writing Task 2 questions is:

- writing a response that is too short.

C1 Are Writing Task 2 questions 1–4 examples of Single Opinion, Double Opinion, or Contrast Opinion questions? (If necessary, review page 261 of Writing Unit 24 and page 269 of Writing Unit 25.) One answer has been done for you.

1. What are the best ways for visitors to travel around your hometown? Why?
   ☐ Single Opinion   ☑ Double Opinion   ☐ Contrast Opinion
2. Would you like to work as an airline pilot or flight attendant? Why or why not?
   ☐ Single Opinion   ☐ Double Opinion   ☐ Contrast Opinion
3. What do you like and dislike about visiting a foreign country? Support your views.
   ☐ Single Opinion   ☐ Double Opinion   ☐ Contrast Opinion
4. What are some of the benefits and problems of driving to work each day?
   ☐ Single Opinion   ☐ Double Opinion   ☐ Contrast Opinion

C2 Add your own travel-related words to the blanks to complete Contrast Opinion questions 1–4. Work with a partner. When you have finished, share your ideas with other students. One answer has been done for you.

1. Compare _taking a train_ with _taking a bus_. Which way of traveling do you prefer? Why?
2. What are the advantages and disadvantages of _____? Support your opinion with details and examples.
3. What do you like and dislike about _____? Why? Give reasons in support of your view.
4. Some people feel _____. Other people think _____. Compare these views. Then explain your view.

D Mastering Writing Task 2 – Planning an Effective Response

For all types of Writing Task 2 questions, responses that are planned are generally more effective and get a higher score than ones that are unplanned. As a result, learning how to plan your response effectively is a key skill for the TOEFL Test. However, it is important to remember that the ideas and examples you think of while planning do not have to be true.

D1 Read the information about planning a response to Contrast Opinion questions. Then decide which statement, A–C, paraphrases which step, 1–3, in the information. One answer has been done for you.

Step 1	First, decide if the Task 2 question is Single Opinion (see Writing Unit 24), Double Opinion (Writing Unit 25), or Contrast Opinion (this unit).
Step 2	For Contrast Opinion questions, think of several ideas for each aspect of the question.
Step 3	Choose the ideas you will mention for each aspect of the question, and the order you will write about them.

A Decide which ideas to write about and how to organize them.
   This answer paraphrases   ☐ Step 1   ☐ Step 2   ☐ Step 3
B Recognize the type of question that you need to answer.
   This answer paraphrases   ☐ Step 1   ☐ Step 2   ☐ Step 3
C Come up with ideas that match each part of the question.
   This answer paraphrases   ☐ Step 1   ☐ Step 2   ☐ Step 3

D2 Choose the best title, A–C, for these two strategies for planning effective responses to Writing Task 2 questions. One title does NOT match either of the strategies.

1. _____

   - Stock reasons are familiar reasons that match many Writing Task 2 topics.
   - Examples of stock reasons include money, time, health, work, relationships, and education.
   - Using stock reasons regularly can help you to save time and avoid mistakes.

2. _____

   - Detailed supporting examples are a good way to improve your Writing Task 2 responses.
   - One effective way to add details to your examples is to answer unspoken questions.
   - Some unspoken questions you could answer are *when*, *where*, *who*, and *how much*.

A Method for improving the quality of your supporting examples
B Technique for coming up with effective reasons for your ideas
C Strategy for developing more effective academic arguments

D3 Look at these planning notes for Contrast Opinion Writing Task 2 questions 1 and 2. Match each circled reason to one of the stock reasons listed in exercise D2.

1. Compare and contrast traveling around your country by bus and by airplane. Which way of traveling around your country do you think is better? Why?

bus	(very slow)	e.g., takes hours even for short distances = waste of time
	(hard to study)	e.g., have exams soon, but hard to read or study during journey
airplane	(expensive)	e.g., even ticket to nearby cities usually costs more than $200
	(stressful)	e.g., newspaper article → most people are stressed by flying

2. Some people like traveling to different cities when they have free time. Other people prefer to stay home. Compare the advantages of these different ways of spending free time. Which view do you support? Why?

different cities (learn new things)   e.g., can visit local museums to learn about local history
                  (make new friends)   e.g., traveled to new city last year and made very good friends
stay home   (can work if needed) e.g., job is busy now, so boss often asks me to do extra hours
                  (less stress)   e.g., newspaper article → travel to new places is very stressful

D4 **Look again at the planning notes in exercise D3 and answer questions 1–5. One answer has been done for you.**

1. Which example answers the unspoken question "How much?" ___First example about airplanes in question 1___
2. Which example answers the unspoken question "How long?" _____
3. Which three examples answer the unspoken question "When?" _____
4. Which two examples answer the unspoken question "Where?" _____
5. Which two examples answer the unspoken question "Why?" _____

E Mastering Writing Task 2 – Writing an Effective Introduction

After planning your response, you need to type it. Every response should begin with an introduction. For Contrast Opinion questions, you will have to learn a slightly different final sentence from the model introduction paragraph you learned for Single Opinion and Double Opinion questions (see Writing Units 24 and 25).

E1 **Choose the best answers from A–D to complete the introduction paragraphs for Writing Task 2 questions 1 and 2. One answer has been done for you.**

1. What do you like and what do you dislike about traveling by airplane? Explain your opinions.

I can see why some might feel that 1. _____there is nothing to dislike about traveling by plane_____.

On the whole, however, it is my opinion that 2. _____

This piece of writing will explain my views on both aspects of this topic in more detail.

2. Some believe bicycles are the best vehicle for traveling short distances. Others think cars are better. Discuss these views.

I can see why some might feel that 3. _____

On the whole, however, it is my opinion that 4. _____

This piece of writing will explain my views on both aspects of this topic in more detail.

A bicycles are definitely the better choice for short journeys.
B there is nothing to dislike about traveling by plane.
C airplane travel actually has both good points and bad points.
D both automobiles and bicycles have good points for short journeys.

E2 **Now write an introduction for this Contrast Opinion Writing Task 2 question. Use the bold model phrases in the example introductions in exercise E1 in your response.**

Discuss the advantages and disadvantages of using public transportation to travel around a city that you know. Support your views.

F Mastering Writing Task 2 – Writing Effective Body Paragraphs

After writing your introduction, you need to type two body paragraphs. For Contrast Opinion questions, each body paragraph should discuss one part of the question. For this reason, you will have to learn different first sentences for the two model body paragraphs you learned for Single Opinion and Double Opinion questions (see Writing Units 24 and 25).

F1 Read these two body paragraphs in response to a Contrast Opinion question. Then answer questions 1 and 2.

What do you like and what do you dislike about traveling by airplane? Explain your opinions.

Thinking about the first aspect of this topic, one thing I like about air travel is that it is a quick, convenient, and safe way to visit foreign destinations. Recently I read an interesting article about this subject. According to what I read, traveling by airplane is much safer than traveling by another method such as by automobile or train. The article also mentioned that air travel is both faster and more convenient than traveling to another country by road, rail, or ship.

In contrast, one thing I dislike about air travel is how expensive it is. In my experience, traveling by plane usually costs at least twice as much as traveling by car, train, or bus. For example, even though I can fly from my home in France to Spain, Portugal, the UK, or other places in less than 90 minutes, the cost of an airline ticket is usually several hundred dollars. Taking a train to these destinations would be slower, but the price would be less than $100, which is more affordable.

1. Which answer, A or B, best describes the organization of both body paragraphs in the response?
   A Each paragraph mentions one or two points that answer the question.
   B Both paragraphs discuss positive ideas that are related to the question.

2. Complete this table by matching model phrases A–H to the correct question type and paragraph. (If necessary, review section **F** in Writing Unit 24 and Writing Unit 25.) Use some answers twice. One answer has been done for you.

Single Opinion and Double Opinion Questions	Contrast Opinion Questions
Body Paragraph 1 • First of all, ... • •	**Body Paragraph 1** • • •
Body Paragraph 2 • • •	**Body Paragraph 2** • • •

A First of all, ...
B In addition, ...
C In contrast, ...
D In my experience, ...

E Recently I read an interesting article about this subject. According to what I read, ...
F The article also mentioned that ...
G Thinking about the first aspect of this topic, ...
H To give an example, ...

F2 Work with a partner to write two body paragraphs for this Contrast Opinion question by putting sentences A–F on the next page in the correct order.

Some believe cars are the best vehicles for traveling short distances. Others think bicycles are better. Discuss these views.

A   Thinking about the first aspect of this topic, in most cases cars are a very fast and convenient way to carry out daily activities like going to a shopping mall or visiting a friend who lives nearby.

B   In contrast, bicycles are a great choice for short journeys for people who want to become healthy.

C   In my experience, riding a bicycle helps me stay fit and healthy but driving a car makes me gain weight because I am not doing any exercise.

D   Recently I read an interesting article about this subject. According to what I read, journeys by car take less than 17 minutes on average, but journeys by other vehicles like bicycles or buses take much longer.

E   The article also mentioned that people prefer cars for many short trips because they offer protection from the weather.

F   To give an example, in the winter I rarely ride my bicycle because it is cold and I usually feel unhealthy and overweight, but in the summer I ride my bicycle as often as I can when I am traveling somewhere close, so I feel healthy and strong.

F3 **Now write body paragraphs for this Contrast Opinion Writing Task 2 question. Use the model phrases from exercise F1 in your response.**

Discuss the advantages and disadvantages of using public transportation to travel around a city that you know. Support your views.

G Mastering Writing Task 2 – Writing an Effective Conclusion

The last paragraph of your response should be a conclusion. For Contrast Opinion questions, you can use the model conclusion you learned for Single Opinion and Double Opinion questions with a different final sentence that expresses your preference for one of the two aspects of the topic.

G1 **Copy the best answers from A–E to complete the conclusion paragraphs for Writing Task 2 questions 1 and 2. One of the answers does NOT belong in either conclusion.**

1. What do you like and what do you dislike about traveling by airplane? Explain your opinions.

    In conclusion, for the reasons given, _____

    Overall, however, _____

2. Some believe bicycles are the best vehicle for traveling short distances. Others think cars are better. Discuss these views.

    In conclusion, for the reasons given, _____

    Overall, however, _____

A   I think the advantages of air travel outweigh the disadvantages.

B   my feeling is that the situation will definitely change in the future.

C   I feel that both bicycles and cars have some advantages, depending on the situation.

D   I think the advantages of traveling by bicycle outweigh the advantages of going by car.

E   I believe there are both good points and bad points about air travel.

G2 **Write a conclusion for this Contrast Opinion question. Use the model phrases from exercise G1 in your response.**

Discuss the advantages and disadvantages of using public transportation to travel around a city that you know. Support your views.

TEST TACTIC

The conclusion is important for Contrast Opinion questions because it is the only place in which you state your opinion about the topic. If you think you will not have enough time to finish the conclusion, write your paragraphs in this order: introduction, conclusion, body paragraph 1, body paragraph 2. That way you will definitely have a clear conclusion even if you cannot finish your second body paragraph.

H Mastering Writing Task 2 – Using Natural Expressions

Planning your response well and using model paragraphs can help you get a good score for Writing Task 2. It is also a good idea to use multi-word expressions to support your examples with specific, detailed statistics. This will not only make your writing seem more natural, but it will increase the word count of your response as well.

H1 Match each expression, A–F, to one of the three categories. One answer has been done for you.

Expressions between 0% and 33%	Expressions between 34% and 66%	Expressions between 67% and 100%
• •	• •	• about seven in every ten •

A   about seven in every ten
B   just under one quarter of

C   nearly 20 percent of
D   something like half of all

E   almost two thirds of
F   around 90 out of 100

H2 Write a sentence in response to questions 1–4. If you do not know the answer, make one up. Begin each sentence with one of the expressions from exercise H1. When you have finished, compare sentences with a partner.

1. What proportion of the journeys that people make in your country are by train?
2. How many people in your country take vacations overseas every year?
3. What percentage of the people you know prefer traveling with friends?
4. How many employees who work in your country's capital city take public transportation each day?

I Mastering Writing Task 2 – Avoiding Common Problems

It is possible to get a perfect score for a Writing Task 2 response that has fewer than 300 words if the response is well organized and answers the question directly. However, in general longer responses tend to be better than shorter ones.

I1 Complete tasks 1 and 2. Work with a partner on task 1.

1. Rewrite each sentence, 1–8, so that it has the same meaning but uses more words. Use the examples as a guide.
2. When you have finished, share your answers with other students. Make a note of the longest, clearest answers.

Examples   I dislike walking.
→ In general, I do not enjoy walking very much.

Bus journeys in my city are slow.
→ Using a bus to travel around my city usually takes a long time.

Many people buy insurance before traveling.
→ A lot of people choose to buy travel insurance before they take a trip.

1. Traveling by train is expensive.
2. I recently traveled by boat.
3. Many people dislike flying.
4. Bicycles are good for short journeys.

5. Ticket prices have increased.
6. I dislike waiting at airports.
7. Visiting another country can be fun.
8. Some vehicles cause pollution.

J Test Challenge

J1 **Practice Writing Task 2 by answering either question 1 or 2. Plan and write or type your response in exactly 30 minutes in order to get realistic practice for the TOEFL Test. Use this checklist of skills that you studied in this unit as a guide.**

Before you begin writing

In the TOEFL Test you will not get a choice of Writing Task 2 questions. You will have just one question, and the first step in planning your response should be to recognize what type of question it is: Single Opinion (see Writing Unit 24), Double Opinion (Unit 25), or Contrast Opinion.

☑ For Contrast Opinion questions, think of several reasons for each aspect of the question. Thinking of stock reasons – money, time, health, work, relationships, and education – is usually a good idea.

☑ Look at your reasons and decide which ones you will write about and in which order you will write about them.

While you are writing

☑ Write an introduction, two body paragraphs, and conclusion that use the model phrases you learned in this unit.

☑ Give detailed supporting examples by answering unspoken questions and by using natural phrases to add statistics.

☑ Try to write clear, direct sentences which match the topic and which are neither too short nor too long.

1. Compare and contrast traveling long distances by train with traveling long distances by airplane. Give details to support your points.
2. Discuss the advantages and disadvantages of traveling somewhere with friends and traveling somewhere alone. Which method of traveling do you prefer? Why?

TEST TACTIC

TOEFL does not give you tools such as bold text, spell check, or a built-in dictionary. If you are used to tools like these, you may find it hard to type your response in the test. To overcome this problem, turn off all tools like these when you practice typing at home.

Next Steps

You may have questions and topics related to transportation and travel in every section of the TOEFL Test. As a result, learning more vocabulary related to traveling, as well as practicing key skills for Writing Task 2 Contrast Opinion questions, may raise your overall test score.

To learn and practice more vocabulary related to transportation and travel:

1. Make a list of all the vehicles that you know. Start with the word "trains."
2. Write "Things I Did Not Know about Trains" at the top of a blank sheet of paper.
3. Do some research about trains. When you find something you did not know about trains, paraphrase it on your sheet of paper. Continue researching until you have paraphrased at least ten new pieces of information about trains.
4. Review the information you did not know about trains to find and learn useful vocabulary related to transportation or travel.
5. Repeat steps 2–4 for the other vehicles on your list from step 1.

To practice key skills for Writing Task 2 Contrast Opinion questions, practice either of these tasks every day:

1. Think of a person, place, object, activity, or event. Then spend two minutes making a list of several advantages or things you like about it and another two minutes making a list of disadvantages or things you dislike. Repeat the task five times.
2. Write two contrasting opinions about a topic, such as "Computers are convenient tools" and "Computers are too expensive." Then take 30 minutes to write an essay that compares these two viewpoints and expresses your own view.

Directions

This writing review test is intended to help you find out your strengths and weaknesses in writing. You will complete two writing tasks in 50 minutes. The total time required for the test is approximately 56 minutes. The tasks are designed to be at the same level as the ones you will see on the TOEFL Test. For the first task you will listen to a lecture. For the most realistic practice, cover the question when you listen. You may take notes while you listen. If possible, type your answers. When you have finished, ask a teacher to evaluate both responses from 0–5 or do it yourself. Then use the conversion chart on page 285 to convert your raw scores to your likely score on the TOEFL Test.

Test

TASK 1 – WRITING BASED ON READING AND LISTENING

For this task, you will read a passage about an academic topic. You will have three minutes to read. You may take notes on the passage while you read. You will then listen to a lecture about the same topic. While you listen you may also take notes. You may use your notes to help you answer the question.

You will then write a response to a question that asks you about the relationship between the lecture you heard and the reading passage. Try to answer the question as completely as possible using information from the reading passage and the lecture. The question does not ask you to express your personal opinion. Your response will be judged on the quality of your writing and on the completeness and accuracy of the content. Typically, an effective response will be 150 to 225 words.

Now read this passage. You have three minutes to read.

Coral reefs are among the most biodiverse ecosystems in the ocean, with up to one quarter of all marine species living in or near a reef environment. Sadly, many of these beautiful, fragile structures are dying out. Climate change is a major threat to reefs, but direct human activities have a serious impact, too.

Water pollution caused by humans adversely affects coral reefs. Pollutants can affect reefs in two ways. Certain substances that can contaminate ocean water, such as oil and pesticides, are poisonous to coral and other forms of marine life. Other pollutants, such as animal waste and fertilizer, cause an overgrowth of simple plant-like organisms called algae. These algae block sunlight from reaching the coral, causing it to die.

Three exploitive methods of fishing can cause damage and degradation to coral reefs. First, overfishing of some species can lead to a lack of biodiversity that affects the overall health of the reef. Blast fishing – the use of explosives to stun and kill fish so they are easier to catch – often kills coral polyps and destroys sections of the reef. And the use of cyanide, a poison, to stun large, economically-important fish species often kills both coral and smaller species of fish.

Even tourism has been implicated in the destruction of coral reefs. Many reefs are popular spots for diving, and although many tourists are careful, coral is easily damaged when it is touched. Even stirring up sand and small particles from the sea floor can lead to the degradation of reefs. And waste and pollution from tourists' boats, ocean-front hotels, and even tourists themselves are also a factor.

Track 406 Now listen to a lecture on the topic you just read about.

You now have 20 minutes to plan and write your response. You may see the reading passage again while you write.

Summarize the points made in the lecture you just heard, being sure to specifically explain how they support points made in the reading passage.

TASK 2 – WRITING BASED ON KNOWLEDGE AND EXPERIENCE

In this task you will demonstrate your ability to write an essay in response to a question that asks you to express and support your opinion about a topic or issue. Your essay will be scored on the quality of your writing. This includes the development of your ideas, the organization of your essay, and the quality and accuracy of the language you use to express your ideas. Typically, an effective essay will contain a minimum of 300 words.

Read the question below. You have 30 minutes to plan, write, and revise your essay.

In the last 20 years, technology has become both more advanced and more available. In what ways has greater access to advanced technology affected the way people work? Use specific reasons and details to support your answer.

Score Conversion

Ask a teacher or native speaker to evaluate both responses from 0–5. (If necessary, you can evaluate your responses yourself. See pages 230–233 of the Writing Reference unit for criteria for scoring.) Then add up the score for each response to find your raw score and use this conversion chart to find out your approximate writing score range on the TOEFL Test.

Raw Score (out of 10)	Probable Level	Approximate Score Range
10		30
9	Good	27
8		24
7		21
6	Fair	18
5		15
4		12
3	Limited	8
2		6
1		3

PHOTO CREDITS

2 Dejan Stanisavljevic/Shutterstock; 3 © iStock/Sol Stock; 3 Courtesy of English Center Constanta; 4 Audrey Popov/Shutterstock; 4 Daniel Ernst/iStock/Thinkstock; 4 Thinkstock/Hongqi Zhang; 5 vvoe/Shutterstock; 24 sarkao/Shutterstock; 26 © iStock/CowboyRoy; 32 Thinkstock/Photos.com; 33 © iStock/GeorgiosArt; 39 © iStock/viridis; 42 NA image/Shutterstock; 46 Thinkstock/iStock; 49 Panaiotidi/Shutterstock; 57 OPIS Zagreb/Shutterstock; 62 Thinkstock/iStock/sundarananda; 67 © iStock/robas; 72 Gail Johnson/Shutterstock.com; 72 Photodisc; 76 © Stock/Beboy_ltd; 93 Purestock/Thinkstock; 108 Thinkstock/Andrzej WÃ³jcicki; 113 Vincent van Gogh/Getty Images; 113 SuperStock/Getty Images; 117 NASA/JPL-Caltech/Las Campanas; 125 DEA/G. DAGLI ORTI/ Getty Images; 125 Leonardo da Vinci/Getty Images; 125 Collection: De Agostini Picture Library/ Getty Images; 126 Monkey Business Images/Shutterstock; 126 Lawren S. Harris *North Shore, Lake Superior,* 1926 oil on canvas 102.2 × 128.3 cm Purchased 1930 National Gallery of Canada, Ottawa Photo © National Gallery of Canada; 127 Art Resource, NY; 128 Thinkstock/iStock; 133 Thinkstock/ Photos.com; 141 Thinkstock/iStock; 143 Monkey Business Images/iStock/Thinkstock; 145 © iStock/ stevenallan; 150 © iStock/asuseeut; 156 Antonio Guillem/Shutterstock; 156 © iStock/drbimages; 156 © iStock/drbimages; 156 eurobanks/Shutterstock; 165 © iStock/asiseeit; 166 © iStock/aabejon; 172 KatarzynaBialasiewicz/iStock/Thinkstock; 179 Thinkstock/Ingram Publishers; 181 © iStock/ ShotShare; 184 Thinkstock/iStock; 187 Thinkstock/iStock; 190 © iStock/asuseeit; 192 © iStock/ Joe_Potato; 196 Jamie Carroll/Thinkstock; 199 Thinkstock/Stockbyte; 206 Wavebreakmedia Ltd./ Thinkstock; 209 Thinkstock/martiapunts; 213 © iStock/epicurean; 214 Goodshoot/Thinkstock; 215 Monkey Business Images/Shutterstock; 217 wrangler/Shutterstock; 223 LuckyBusiness/ iStock/Thinkstock; 225 © iStock/diego_cervo; 225 © Stock/monkeybusinessimages; 225 © iStock/ andresrimaging; 235 bikeriderlondon/Shutterstock; 238 Thinkstock/Purestock; 242 Eddie~S; 243 Zurijeta/iStock/Thinkstock; 246 © iStock/Kyslynskyy; 248 Thinkstock/rosieyoung27; 255 © iStock johavel; 256 Thinkstock/KatarzynaBialasiewicz; 260 © iStock/sturti; 263 © iStock/ EHStock; 268 Thinkstock/4774344sean; 272 Thinkstock/Kesu01; 276 © iStock/GA161016; 281 Thinkstock/XiXinXing; 285 Robert Kneschke/iStock/Thinkstock

VOCABULARY INDEX

Practice Test A

General Information

This practice test measures your ability to understand and use English in an academic context. There are four sections. Before each section, you will see specific directions that explain how to answer the questions in that section.

In the **Reading** section, you will read and answer questions about three passages. The passages will be similar to excerpts from introductory college-level textbooks. The passages will cover a variety of different subjects. You do not need existing knowledge because all the information needed to answer the questions will be in the passage.

In the **Listening** section, you will hear two conversations and four lectures. The conversations will be about typical topics that affect students at university in North America. After each conversation, you must answer five questions. The lectures will be about academic topics that students in their first year at college are likely to study. The lectures will cover a variety of different subjects. You do not need existing knowledge because all the information needed to answer the questions will be mentioned by the speaker or speakers. After each lecture, you must answer six questions.

In the **Speaking** section, you will see six questions. The first two questions ask you to respond based on your experience and opinions. The third and fourth questions ask you to speak about information that you have read and heard. The final two questions ask you to speak about information you have heard. For each question, you will have a specific amount of time to prepare and deliver your response.

In the **Writing** section, you will answer two questions. In the first question, you will have to write about the relationship between the information in a passage that you have read and the information in a lecture that you have heard. In the second question, you will have to write a response based on your experience and opinions.

You may now begin the test by looking at the next page. Alternatively, you can take Practice Test A online at www.oxfordenglishtesting.com.

Reading Section Directions

The Reading section measures your ability to understand academic passages in English. You will have 60 minutes to read three passages and answer 40 questions about what you have read.

Most questions are worth 1 point but the last question in each set is worth more than 1 point. The directions for these questions indicate how many points you may receive.

For most questions, you should choose one answer. For some questions, however, you may need to choose from two to five answers. These questions have special directions that explain how many answers you should choose.

You may now begin the Reading section.

Cloud Seeding

Weather modification, or weather control as it is sometimes known, is any scientific manipulation of the environment intended to change weather patterns. The goal of weather modification is typically either to produce desirable weather, generally rain or snow, or to prevent adverse weather events, such as hail or severe storms. It is distinct from well-intentioned but unscientific attempts to influence the weather used by various cultures since prehistoric times. For example, the Zuni people from the southwestern United States tried to coax water from the sky by performing ritual dances. And there are reports from a few hundred years ago of farmers in Switzerland, Austria, and Italy ringing bells and firing guns in an effort to prevent hailstorms from damaging their crops.

Cloud seeding is the most common form of weather modification. The first attempt at cloud seeding took place in 1946 when scientist Vincent Schaefer dropped six pounds of dry ice (frozen carbon dioxide) from an airplane into a cloud and produced snow. The experiment was only modestly successful, but it spawned optimism among farmers everywhere. It seemed to them that science had finally triumphed over nature. Unfortunately, that was not the case. Although there were extensive cloud-seeding operations during the late 1940s and early 1950s, there was no compelling evidence to indicate that they had any significant effect on precipitation. Clearly, cloud seeding was more complicated than had been believed. It was not until the 1970s that scientists better understood the processes involved. New experiments indicated that only certain kinds of clouds are amenable to seeding. One of the most responsive is the winter orographic cloud, formed when winter air currents encounter a mountain slope and rise. If the temperature in such a cloud is right, seeding may increase precipitation by five to 15 percent. However, to judge the success of cloud seeding accurately, scientists must determine how much precipitation would have fallen without seeding, and this is always difficult to gauge.

One form of cloud seeding, static seeding, was developed by Bernard Vonnegut, brother of the famous novelist Kurt Vonnegut. Silver iodide, which has a crystalline structure similar to that of ice, is heated on the ground in a generator fueled by propane gas. The heat and smoke carry particles of silver iodide up to the clouds where they act as nuclei for the formation of ice crystals, which then fall as rain or snow. The system first used by Schaefer, the glaciogenic method, employs airplanes – or sometimes rockets – to deliver dry ice pellets. Aircraft seeding is typically more effective than ground-based seeding because accurate delivery of the seeding agent is possible. However, it is considerably more expensive. A third method, hygroscopic seeding, has been in use only for a few years and requires more research. This method involves using planes to carry salt crystals to the lower portions of clouds.

Cloud seeding in the United States has mostly taken place in western states. The population of the West has expanded rapidly over recent decades, and this area relies more heavily on snowfall than other regions of the United States. About 75 percent of the water in western rivers comes from melted snow. Indeed, without consistent and heavy snowfall in the Rocky Mountains and the Sierra Nevada range, the West would experience droughts. The most intensive effort to produce precipitation, mainly conducted by the federal government, took place during the West's snow drought in the winter of 1976–77. Although it is difficult to judge the effectiveness of cloud seeding based on one crash program, most experts doubted that large-scale cloud seeding led to a significant increase in the amount of snow that fell during that period. Because the program was not a clear-cut success, the US federal government discontinued cloud-seeding operations in the late 1970s, but some individual states continue to seed clouds as do nongovernmental organizations, including ski resorts and agricultural cooperatives. Cloud seeding is also practiced in other countries, particularly those with regions prone to drought, such as Australia, India, and China. In fact, China probably has the most extensive weather-modification programs of any nation in the world.

1. The word "adverse" in paragraph 1 most likely means
   - Ⓐ advanced
   - Ⓑ discovered
   - Ⓒ impossible
   - Ⓓ undesirable

2. Why does the author mention farmers from Switzerland, Austria, and Italy in paragraph 1?
   - Ⓐ To compare their goals with those of the Zuni people of the US Southwest
   - Ⓑ To give an example of a nonscientific attempt to control weather patterns
   - Ⓒ To point out that they were successful at producing the weather they wanted
   - Ⓓ To emphasize how important it was for them to protect their crops from hail

3. The word "spawned" in paragraph 2 is closest in meaning to
   - Ⓐ came up with
   - Ⓑ gave rise to
   - Ⓒ grew out of
   - Ⓓ went in for

4. What can be inferred about the feelings of farmers after the cloud-seeding operations of the late 1940s and early 1950s?
   - Ⓐ They were pleased that these extensive operations were producing significant evidence.
   - Ⓑ They were optimistic that future cloud-seeding operations would be even more successful.
   - Ⓒ They were upset that scientists were trying to modify the weather without consulting with them.
   - Ⓓ They were disappointed because these operations were less successful than the first experiment.

5. According to paragraph 2, what had scientists learned about cloud seeding by the 1970s?
   - Ⓐ Not all types of clouds can be successfully seeded.
   - Ⓑ It is difficult to seed clouds in mountainous areas.
   - Ⓒ Seeding is more successful when the weather is cold.
   - Ⓓ Seeding always leads to higher levels of precipitation.

6. The word "gauge" in paragraph 2 is closest in meaning to
   - Ⓐ define
   - Ⓑ prevent
   - Ⓒ measure
   - Ⓓ observe

7. According to the author, in what way are the glaciogenic and hygroscopic methods of cloud seeding similar?
   - Ⓐ They were developed at about the same time.
   - Ⓑ They use chemicals with similar structures.
   - Ⓒ They employ the same delivery method.
   - Ⓓ They were developed by the same scientist.

8. The word "it" in paragraph 3 refers to
   - Ⓐ the seeding agent
   - Ⓑ accurate delivery
   - Ⓒ ground-based seeding
   - Ⓓ aircraft seeding

9. In paragraph 3, the author states that clouds are seeded with all of the following substances EXCEPT
   - Ⓐ silver iodide
   - Ⓑ propane gas
   - Ⓒ dry ice pellets
   - Ⓓ salt crystals

10. Which of the following best expresses the essential information in the highlighted sentence in paragraph 4? Incorrect choices change the meaning in important ways or leave out essential information.
    - Ⓐ Although a large amount of snow fell during the period, experts were unsure how to judge cloud seeding.
    - Ⓑ Most experts felt that, on balance, the program did not contribute to increased snowfall during the period.
    - Ⓒ Experts asked to judge if cloud seeding was effective felt there was insufficient time to make an assessment.
    - Ⓓ So much snow fell during the period that it was difficult to judge whether clouds had been seeded or not.

11. What point does the author make in paragraph 4?
    - Ⓐ Although the US government no longer has a weather modification program, other nations and organizations do.
    - Ⓑ Because the US government has stopped cloud-seeding operations, other countries have increased their efforts.
    - Ⓒ Few regions of the US are prone to drought, so the US government made the decision to discontinue cloud seeding.
    - Ⓓ Countries like Australia, India, and China have used data from the US government to develop extensive programs.

12. Look at the four squares (■) that indicate where the following sentence could be added to the passage.

Unlike silver iodide, dry ice works not by providing ice-forming nuclei, but by lowering the temperature near the water droplets in the clouds, causing them to freeze instantly.

Where would the sentence best fit? Choose position **A**, **B**, **C**, or **D**.

One form of cloud seeding, static seeding, was developed by Bernard Vonnegut, brother of the famous novelist Kurt Vonnegut. Silver iodide, which has a crystalline structure similar to that of ice, is heated on the ground in a generator fueled by propane gas. The heat and smoke carry particles of silver iodide up to the clouds where they act as nuclei for the formation of ice crystals, which then fall as rain or snow. **A** The system first used by Schaefer, the glaciogenic method, employs airplanes – or sometimes rockets – to deliver dry ice pellets. **B** Aircraft seeding is typically more effective than ground-based seeding because accurate delivery of the seeding agent is possible. **C** However, it is considerably more expensive. **D** A third method, hygroscopic seeding, has been in use only for a few years and requires more research. This method involves using planes to carry salt crystals to the lower portions of clouds.

13. **Directions:** An introductory sentence for a brief summary of the passage is provided below. Complete the summary by selecting the THREE answer choices that express the most important ideas in the passage. Some sentences do not belong in the summary because they express ideas that are not presented in the passage or are minor ideas in the passage. **This question is worth 2 points.**

> **Weather modification involves using scientific methods to change the weather in ways that benefit humans.**
>
> -
> -
> -

Ⓐ Hygroscopic seeding is a common method of cloud seeding, although scientists are still researching its effectiveness.

Ⓑ One scientist involved in cloud-seeding experiments is famous because of his sibling, who is a well-known writer.

Ⓒ The most common form of weather modification involves seeding clouds with chemicals to induce precipitation.

Ⓓ Scientists' knowledge of the processes involved in cloud seeding improved as they conducted more experiments.

Ⓔ A snow drought during the winter of 1976–77 led to a variety of efforts to modify the weather in mountainous areas.

Ⓕ An early experiment in cloud seeding was successful, but later experiments did not have such impressive results.

North American Colonial Furniture

Britain's North American colonies covered a vast area, far larger than most European nations, and during the Colonial Period from roughly 1620 to 1776, no single metropolis emerged as a cultural center equivalent to London or Paris. There was, therefore, no single "American" style of furniture-making during that period. A transplanted British style of furniture-making predominated throughout most of the Colonies, but artisans of British ancestry in different locations adjusted their products to suit local differences in materials, climate, and taste. Cities as close geographically as Boston, in the Massachusetts colony, and Hartford, in the colony of Connecticut, produced strikingly different styles of furniture even though both were derived from the same British sources. Although the British influence was strong, many artisans in the Colonies continued to work in the idiom of their respective mother countries. Colonists of Dutch ancestry in the Hudson Valley of the New York colony, for instance, produced wardrobes and other pieces in the style of the Netherlands. In the colonies of Pennsylvania and North Carolina, furniture-makers of German ancestry maintained furniture traditions from their homeland, as did Swedish artisans in Delaware.

In the early Colonial Period (pre-1720), few colonists could afford to furnish their homes with more than strictly essential and utilitarian pieces: stools, benches, chests, straight chairs, tables, and beds. Most furniture of this period was of a style known as Jacobean, though Colonial Jacobean furniture is far plainer than British Jacobean furniture. Few pieces had the kinds of decorative, elaborately carved features seen on European furniture at that time. Jacobean pieces were simple in design and heavy-looking, and frequently served multiple purposes. Houses of the time often consisted of only one small room with a low ceiling. The table-chair, a chair that could tilt forward to form a table, was typical of the space-saving furniture popular at the time. Only a few simple tools were required to build these pieces, and they were made of readily available native woods such as pine, maple, oak, and walnut. Many pieces were literally homemade and used construction techniques that would have been considered outmoded in Europe.

However, around 1720, the Colonies became more affluent, and wealthy merchants demanded grander furniture. For the next three and a half decades, the Queen Anne furniture style was the rage. Unlike the boxy, bulky furniture of the early Colonial Period, Queen Anne pieces were more graceful and curved. The most distinctive feature of Queen Anne pieces was the *cyma*, or S-shaped curve, and carved ornaments such as seashells were common. Simple, multi-purpose pieces such as the bench gave way to more specialized pieces like the tea table. Colonial homes, especially in cities, grew larger and contained more rooms: several bedrooms, a dining room, a central hall, and a parlor, each requiring specific items of furniture.

Although published in London in 1754, British craftsman Thomas Chippendale's book of furniture patterns, *The Gentleman and Cabinet-Maker's Director*, did not become available in the Colonies until the 1760s. When it did arrive, it had such a profound influence on furniture-makers that Chippendale furniture is the name given to Colonial furniture of this period. Chippendale furniture has a refined and graceful form, with curving lines and elaborate carvings. Some Chippendale pieces clearly show the influence of Chinese furnishings. Many were made not of native woods but of tropical woods, especially mahogany, which were imported from Caribbean islands under British rule. Sofas and chairs of this period were upholstered in expensive fabrics such as velvet. The father and son team of John and Thomas Goddard, whose workshop was in Newport, in the Rhode Island colony, produced splendid Chippendale cabinets, desks, and bookshelves. William Savery of Philadelphia, the largest city in the Colonies, also produced high-quality Chippendale furniture, and his pieces were as popular in the Colonies as Thomas Chippendale's were in England.

Around 1900, a style of furniture called Colonial Revival (or Early American), which mimicked Colonial styles, became popular in part because of the efforts of a historian and furniture-maker named Wallace Nutting. Mass-produced reproductions of Colonial pieces were common sights in suburban homes across the United States during the mid-twentieth century. Pieces of Colonial Revival furniture can still be seen in thrift shops and secondhand furniture stores.

14. Which of the following best expresses the essential information in the highlighted sentence in paragraph 1? Incorrect choices change the meaning in important ways or leave out essential information.

   Ⓐ Furniture made in Boston was different from that made in Hartford even though the two cities were in the same colony.

   Ⓑ Although Boston and Hartford are close to each other, the styles of furniture produced in those cities were dissimilar.

   Ⓒ People in Boston and Hartford produced furniture that was different from furniture made in nearby Colonial cities.

   Ⓓ Furniture-makers in Boston and Hartford wanted to produce furniture that was different from furniture made in Britain.

15. The word "idiom" in paragraph 1 is closest in meaning to

   Ⓐ language

   Ⓑ style

   Ⓒ materials

   Ⓓ effect

16. Which of the following can be inferred from paragraph 1?

   Ⓐ There was high demand for furniture made by colonists originally from the Netherlands.

   Ⓑ People in Delaware liked traditional furniture more than people in the New York colony.

   Ⓒ British furniture styles had little influence on furniture made by people from other countries.

   Ⓓ Many people of German ancestry lived in Pennsylvania or North Carolina after emigrating.

17. The word "utilitarian" in paragraph 2 is closest in meaning to

   Ⓐ practical

   Ⓑ precious

   Ⓒ primitive

   Ⓓ profitable

18. Why does the author mention the "table-chair" in paragraph 2?

   Ⓐ To suggest that not every piece of furniture could be made with simple tools

   Ⓑ To show that furniture-makers in the colonies produced some clever designs

   Ⓒ To give an example of a piece of furniture that had more than one purpose

   Ⓓ To contrast Colonial Jacobean furniture with Jacobean furniture from Britain

19. The word "outmoded" in paragraph 2 is closest in meaning to

   Ⓐ rarely seen

   Ⓑ old-fashioned

   Ⓒ overpriced

   Ⓓ little-known

20. How does the author organize the information in paragraph 3?

   Ⓐ By contrasting Queen Anne furniture with pieces made in earlier times

   Ⓑ By discussing one piece of ornamental Queen Anne furniture in detail

   Ⓒ By explaining why the design of Queen Anne furniture was so attractive

   Ⓓ By giving examples of Queen Anne furniture designed for specific rooms

21. The word "Many" in paragraph 4 refers to

   Ⓐ curving lines

   Ⓑ elaborate carvings

   Ⓒ Chippendale pieces

   Ⓓ Chinese furnishings

22. In paragraph 4, the author mentions all of the following about Chippendale furniture EXCEPT:

   Ⓐ Some pieces were influenced by Chinese designs.

   Ⓑ Chairs and sofas were the most popular pieces.

   Ⓒ Pieces were often made using costly materials.

   Ⓓ It was popular both in the Colonies and Britain.

23. What can be inferred from paragraph 4?
    - (A) During the 1760s, Britain had other colonies in addition to North America.
    - (B) Native woods were not strong enough to use in making Chippendale furniture.
    - (C) Thomas Goddard learned how to make Chippendale furniture from his father.
    - (D) At first, Thomas Chippendale's book was not successful in North America.

24. The word "mimicked" in paragraph 5 is closest in meaning to
    - (A) illustrated
    - (B) designed
    - (C) copied
    - (D) produced

25. What does the author imply about Colonial Revival furniture in paragraph 5?
    - (A) It became popular because of the success of Wallace Nutting's furniture designs.
    - (B) Like Colonial furniture, it was mostly handmade by individual furniture-makers.
    - (C) Homeowners liked to have it in their homes because their neighbors also had it.
    - (D) It was more popular during the middle of the twentieth century than it is now.

26. Look at the four squares (■) that indicate where the following sentence could be added to the passage.

Although the Colonial Period ended in 1776, furniture from that period had an influence on later styles.

Where would the sentence best fit? Choose position **A**, **B**, **C**, or **D**.

A Around 1900, a style of furniture called Colonial Revival (or Early American), which mimicked Colonial styles, became popular in part because of the efforts of a historian and furniture-maker named Wallace Nutting. **B** Mass-produced reproductions of Colonial pieces were common sights in suburban homes across the United States during the mid-twentieth century. **C** Pieces of Colonial Revival furniture can still be seen in thrift shops and secondhand furniture stores. **D**

27. **Directions:** Select the phrases that correctly describe features associated with each type of furniture. One of the answer choices will NOT be used. **This question is worth 3 points.**

Jacobean
•
•

Queen Anne
•

Chippendale
•
•

- (A) Designed to be easy to construct
- (B) Featured curves and carved marine motifs
- (C) Had relatively few decorative elements
- (D) Influenced by a book of design patterns
- (E) Made from imported types of wood
- (F) Produced by Dutch and Swedish artisans

Urban Zoning

Zoning regulations are laws that control land use in towns and cities. Their primary purpose is to segregate areas of land that are considered incompatible. They divide a municipality into geographic areas (zones) where, for example, only residences or only factories may be built. Exceptions to zoning laws, known as variances, are sometimes allowed with the permission of the government involved when the laws would cause hardships for property owners. In the United States, most zoning regulations are passed by local governments – cities, towns, and counties – but a few states, including Vermont and Hawaii, have retained considerable power to administer land use through zoning.

Until the late nineteenth century, few cities and towns had land-use regulations of any kind, and no tough laws governing urban land use were passed at all. A few cities did enact some legislation, including San Francisco, which in 1883 restricted the location of laundries, and Boston, which in 1891 became the first of several cities to limit the height of buildings. A few years later, Washington, DC, followed the "City Beautiful" movement and planned redevelopment in the center. This movement was inspired by the model communities built for the 1893 Chicago World's Fair and provided momentum for reform. The first zoning law that provided a city with sweeping powers over land use was the New York City law of 1916. This law was passed in reaction to the construction of the Equitable Building. This skyscraper towered over other buildings in its neighborhood. It blocked both sunlight and the views from the windows of nearby buildings. The law gave the New York City government control over the construction of new buildings, and served as a blueprint for zoning regulations in other large cities.

There are various types of zoning laws in use today. One system of zoning laws is called Euclidian zoning, named for Euclid, Ohio, the small city where it was first used. This is by far the most common zoning system in the United States, and it is used in both big cities and small towns. It creates zones and strictly limits the kind of development that can take place inside each zone. The most common types of zones are agricultural, one-family residential, multi-family residential, commercial, light industrial, and industrial. There may also be mixed zones, such as commercial/industrial.

Another type of zoning regulation is design-based zoning. A relatively new type of zoning, design-based laws are more flexible than Euclidian zoning and provide local zoning committees with a wide range of powers. As a result, critics say they are more difficult to understand and enforce. Design-based zoning regulations focus more on the type of building than on the use of the land and they allow some mixed use. For example, businesses might be allowed to operate in buildings that were formerly used as residences. On the other hand, a modern-looking twenty-first-century ten-story apartment building would not be permitted in a neighborhood of two-story nineteenth-century houses.

Supporters say that zoning keeps local taxes low, preserves the quality of neighborhoods, and protects the environment. However, there has been much criticism of various aspects of zoning, some of it well deserved. Critics say that zoning interferes with the building of low-cost homes and slows the growth of business and industry. They also say zoning laws, such as those that require houses to be on very large lots, keep less wealthy families out of desirable neighborhoods. More recently, zoning laws have been criticized by some urban planners and scholars, such as Jane Jacobs. They say, with some justification, that zoning laws have helped create unsightly urban sprawl or the spread of buildings into open areas around a city, and made US cities less distinctive. They also say that zoning has promoted the American "car culture," since people must drive to the places where they work and shop if residential zones are separate from commercial and industrial zones. Critics associated with the New Urbanism school of urban planning want a return to the 1920s, when residences, shops, and offices could all be found on the same block and even in the same building.

28. The word "segregate" in paragraph 1 is closest in meaning to
- Ⓐ deviate
- Ⓑ eliminate
- Ⓒ separate
- Ⓓ validate

29. Based on the information in paragraph 1, which of these people might be given a variance?
- Ⓐ A factory owner who wanted to build a new residence near her factory
- Ⓑ A store owner whose shop would have to close because of zoning laws
- Ⓒ A home owner who accidentally violated zoning regulations in the past
- Ⓓ A city resident who lived in one zone but traveled to work in another zone

30. Why does the author mention Vermont and Hawaii in paragraph 1?
- Ⓐ To contrast land-use laws in these states with those in other states
- Ⓑ To emphasize that zoning regulations give states a great deal of power
- Ⓒ To give an example of states that have an atypical approach to zoning
- Ⓓ To suggest that zoning regulations are more relaxed in these states

31. The phrase "sweeping powers" in paragraph 2 is closest in meaning to
- Ⓐ clear knowledge
- Ⓑ broad control
- Ⓒ careful analysis
- Ⓓ typical behavior

32. Which of the following best expresses the essential information in the highlighted sentence in paragraph 2? Incorrect choices change the meaning in important ways or leave out essential information.
- Ⓐ The governments of New York City and other large urban areas were able to construct new buildings in various zones.
- Ⓑ A law passed in New York City gave the city government control over zoning; it was also used as a model by other cities.
- Ⓒ The law that passed in New York City served as a blueprint for the successful construction of buildings in zoned areas.
- Ⓓ Other cities that instituted zoning regulations wanted the same degree of control that New York City government had.

33. It can be inferred from paragraph 2 that early land-use legislation
- Ⓐ did not affect rural communities
- Ⓑ was inspired by global reforms
- Ⓒ did not apply to tall buildings
- Ⓓ was intended to make cities safer

34. What point does the author NOT make about Euclidean zoning in paragraph 3?
- Ⓐ It sets strict limits on land use within each zone.
- Ⓑ It is the most widespread zoning system in the US.
- Ⓒ There are a variety of different types of single-use zones.
- Ⓓ It is predominantly used as a zoning system in small cities.

35. How does design-based zoning differ from Euclidean zoning? *Choose two answers.*
- Ⓐ It restricts buildings based on their appearance rather than their use.
- Ⓑ It provides a varied mix of zones within different neighborhoods in a city.
- Ⓒ It divides cities into zones where some types of land use are not allowed.
- Ⓓ It permits the use of a building in a particular zone to change over time.

36. The word "it" in paragraph 5 refers to
- Ⓐ zoning
- Ⓑ criticism
- Ⓒ environment
- Ⓓ quality

37. The word "lots" in paragraph 5 is closest in meaning to
  - (A) plots of land
  - (B) types of zone
  - (C) periods of time
  - (D) amounts of money

38. What does the author imply in paragraph 5?
  - (A) Zoning regulations have ensured that cities in the US remain attractive.
  - (B) More relaxed zoning laws would mean fewer people would need cars.
  - (C) New Urbanism did not work in the 1920s but might be successful today.
  - (D) Jane Jacobs and other critics of zoning laws do not make valid arguments.

39. Look at the four squares (■) that indicate where the following sentence could be added to the passage.

For instance, they give the zoning authority control over many aspects of a building, from its architectural style to its height, from the amount of space it may occupy to its location on a lot, and even how much parking it must provide.

Where would the sentence best fit? Choose position **A**, **B**, **C**, or **D**.

A Another type of zoning regulation is design-based zoning. **B** A relatively new type of zoning, design-based laws are more flexible than Euclidian zoning and provide local zoning committees with a wide range of powers. **C** As a result, critics say they are more difficult to understand and enforce. **D** Design-based zoning regulations focus more on the type of building than on the use of the land and they allow some mixed use. For example, businesses might be allowed to operate in buildings that were formerly used as residences. On the other hand, a modern-looking twenty-first-century ten-story apartment building would not be permitted in a neighborhood of two-story nineteenth-century houses.

40. **Directions:** An introductory sentence for a brief summary of the passage is provided below. Complete the summary by selecting the THREE answer choices that express the most important ideas in the passage. Some sentences do not belong in the summary because they express ideas that are not presented in the passage or are minor ideas in the passage. **This question is worth 2 points.**

> **Zoning laws divide municipal areas into zones and regulate how the land in each zone can be used.**
>
> -
> -
> -

  - (A) Some zones in large cities are mixed zones that allow for both commercial and industrial use.
  - (B) Zoning has been criticized by some people who feel that it can lead to urban problems.
  - (C) Two main systems of zoning used in the United States are Euclidian zoning and design-based zoning.
  - (D) The "City Beautiful" movement inspired by the Chicago World's Fair created interest in land use.
  - (E) According to its critics, design-based zoning is neither flexible nor easy to understand or implement.
  - (F) Some cities had early land-use regulations, but the first tough zoning law was only enacted in 1916.

Listening Section Directions

The Listening section measures your ability to understand conversations and lectures in English. The Listening section will take about 60 minutes. This includes time to listen to the two conversations and four lectures, and 30 minutes to answer 34 questions about what you have heard. You will hear each conversation and lecture just **once**.

After each conversation or lecture, you will see some questions. Each question is worth 1 point. The questions typically ask about the main idea of the talk or about details that the speakers mention. Some questions ask about a speaker's attitude or reason for saying something. You should answer the questions based on what is stated or implied by the speakers.

You should take notes while you listen to the conversations and lectures. You can use your notes to help you answer the questions. Your notes will **not** be scored.

For some questions you will hear part of the conversation or lecture again. These questions are clearly marked.

You may now begin the Listening section by looking at the next page.

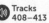

Tracks
408–413

Listen to a conversation between a student and a professor.

Now get ready to answer the questions. You may use your notes to help you answer.

1. What do the professor and student mainly discuss?
   Ⓐ The reason why the student joined the professor's class late
   Ⓑ An experiment that the student will perform next semester
   Ⓒ The grade that the student received for her final project
   Ⓓ The steps involved in undertaking a psychology experiment

2. How does the professor clarify his explanation of a "hypothesis"?
   Ⓐ He asks the student for an example she knows from her own experience.
   Ⓑ He reminds the student of an experiment he already described in class.
   Ⓒ He gives an example of an experiment conducted by his former students.
   Ⓓ He describes a common experiment that could be done in a few minutes.

3. What does the professor say about the control group and the experimental group in the experiment he describes?
   Ⓐ Those in the control group had better memories than those in the experimental group.
   Ⓑ The experimental group saw names on colored cards; the control group saw white cards.
   Ⓒ The control group did not display any meaningful difference from the experimental group.
   Ⓓ The experimental group did not understand the hypothesis, but the control group did.

4. Listen again to part of the conversation. Then answer the question. Why does the professor say this?
   Ⓐ To confirm that the student understood an earlier explanation
   Ⓑ To check that the student knows the meaning of an important term
   Ⓒ To demonstrate that the student knows more than she thinks
   Ⓓ To ask the student to summarize the information he has just said

5. Listen again to part of the conversation. Then answer the question. What can be inferred about the student when she says this?
   Ⓐ She is concerned that her lack of knowledge will be a problem.
   Ⓑ She wants the professor to spend time explaining statistics.
   Ⓒ She is surprised that statistics is so important in a psychology class.
   Ⓓ She feels that she has misunderstood some of the professor's ideas.

Track 414–420   Listen to a discussion in an anthropology class.

Now get ready to answer the questions. You may use your notes to help you answer.

6. What does the professor mainly discuss?
   - Ⓐ The ways in which Native American shelters changed over time
   - Ⓑ The various types of shelters Plains Indians used during the year
   - Ⓒ The origin and construction of a well-known kind of shelter
   - Ⓓ How teepees influenced the actions of Native American groups

 7. Listen again to part of the lecture. Then answer the question. Why does the professor say this?
   - Ⓐ To argue that scholars have good evidence for how teepees looked
   - Ⓑ To suggest that the culture of the Plains Indians changed rapidly
   - Ⓒ To point out that many aspects of life on the Plains were surprising
   - Ⓓ To correct a misconception about teepees that students might have

8. According to the professor, why were buffalo important to the Plains Indians? *Choose two answers.*
   - Ⓐ They allowed Plains Indians to follow horse herds.
   - Ⓑ They taught the Plains Indians to move quickly.
   - Ⓒ They were an important source of food.
   - Ⓓ Their skins were used for clothes and shelter.

9. The professor discusses how the daily life of Plains Indians changed over time. Put the events in the order in which they occurred.

First	
Second	
Third	
Fourth	

   - Ⓐ Their shelters became much taller than before.
   - Ⓑ They copied cone-shaped tents from Arctic Indians.
   - Ⓒ They got hold of horses and began hunting buffalo.
   - Ⓓ They used dogs to move teepees from place to place.

10. Why did the Plains Indians use lodgepole pine trees as poles for their teepees?
   - Ⓐ Their wood was durable and straight.
   - Ⓑ Their wood was light and easy to move.
   - Ⓒ They were easy to find and cut down.
   - Ⓓ They had very flexible wooden trunks.

11. Listen again to part of the lecture. Then answer the question. What does the professor imply when he says this?
   - Ⓐ Plains Indians often moved from one place to another.
   - Ⓑ The behavior of Plains Indians was affected by the weather.
   - Ⓒ Plains Indians valued wooden teepee poles highly.
   - Ⓓ The lifestyle of the Plains Indians is easy to understand.

Tracks
421–427   Listen to a lecture in a world history class.

Now get ready to answer the questions. You may use your notes to help you answer.

12. What is the main purpose of this lecture?
   - (A) To explain why people in the Middle Ages ate certain types of food
   - (B) To compare the lives of wealthy people with those of poor people
   - (C) To describe what certain aspects of daily life were like in the past
   - (D) To contrast the typical modern diet with the typical medieval one

13. What is the professor's attitude to the American history class she took when she was a student?
   - (A) She found it very influential.
   - (B) She thought it was kind of boring.
   - (C) She disliked learning about presidents.
   - (D) She enjoyed hearing her teacher's theories.

14. Indicate which foods were typically eaten by poor people in the Middle Ages. *Place a check (✓) in the correct box.*

	Yes	No
Bread made from wheat		
Vegetables, such as carrots and onions		
Meat, including deer and rabbits		
Food flavored with honey or vinegar		
Soups, stews, and porridge-like dishes		

15. What does the professor say about the diet of wealthy people in medieval times?
   - (A) They only ate food that they had hunted themselves.
   - (B) They ate a wide variety of different kinds of meat.
   - (C) They often ate bread dipped in sauce or soup.
   - (D) They typically ate vegetables preserved with salt and spices.

16. Listen again to part of the lecture. What does the professor imply when she says this?
   - (A) Trade was not the reason that Europeans originally made contact with people from other nations.
   - (B) Many people in Europe became wealthy by importing spices from countries like India and China.
   - (C) Because spice routes were very long, only the very wealthy could afford to eat spices regularly.
   - (D) Although only rich people ate spiced foods, many poor people knew about spice trade routes.

17. According to the professor, what were the main uses of spices in medieval cooking? *Choose two answers.*
   - [A] To preserve fish and meat
   - [B] To give food additional flavor
   - [C] To cover unpleasant tastes
   - [D] To make foods easier to cook

Tracks 428–433 Listen to a conversation between a student and his professor.

Now get ready to answer the questions. You may use your notes to help you answer.

18. What do the student and professor mainly discuss?
- (A) Why the student transferred from Upper State University
- (B) Why the student had not taken any statistics classes previously
- (C) Why the student lacked knowledge of some important concepts
- (D) Why the student should spend additional time in the library

19. What does the student say about the class he took at Upper State University?
- (A) He learned things that have not been discussed in his current class.
- (B) He felt that there were too many other students in the class.
- (C) He found the teaching assistant for the class to be very helpful.
- (D) He found some of the concepts difficult to understand.

20. Listen again to part of the conversation. What does the professor mean when she says this?
- (A) She feels that there are already too many students taking her class.
- (B) She will not be able to provide more help to the student during class.
- (C) She is concerned that the student has a disadvantage to overcome.
- (D) She believes it would not take long to explain concepts to the student.

21. Listen again to part of the conversation. Then answer the question. Why does the professor say this?
- (A) To suggest that the student is speaking too quickly
- (B) To imply that the student has misunderstood her idea
- (C) To emphasize that the student should talk to James Park first
- (D) To indicate that she wants to say something else to the student

22. What does the professor suggest that the student should do? *Choose two answers.*
- [A] Ask other students in the professor's class for help
- [B] Do some extra reading to increase his knowledge
- [C] Drop the professor's class and take a different one
- [D] Talk to the teaching assistant from a different class

Tracks
434–440 Listen to a discussion in a marketing class.

Now get ready to answer the questions. You may use your notes to help you answer.

23. How is the discussion mainly organized?
- Ⓐ The professor discusses each element of the marketing mix in turn.
- Ⓑ The professor asks students to give their ideas before giving his views.
- Ⓒ The professor contrasts the four Ps with other ideas about marketing.
- Ⓓ The professor explains how marketing theories have changed over time.

24. What does the professor say about Neil Borden's original concept of the marketing mix?
- Ⓐ It was a variable theory that some marketers misunderstood.
- Ⓑ It described more than 12 categories of marketing elements.
- Ⓒ It could be adjusted to help marketers understand their targets.
- Ⓓ It was widely used by managers but not by other marketers.

25. In the professor's view, which is the most important of the four Ps?
- Ⓐ Placement
- Ⓑ Pricing
- Ⓒ Product
- Ⓓ Promotion

26. Listen again to part of the lecture. What does the professor mean when he says this?
- Ⓐ Placement and distribution are different names for similar concepts.
- Ⓑ Regardless of which name is used, placement is a vital part of marketing.
- Ⓒ Consumers do not mind which name is used for distributing products.
- Ⓓ The name "placement" was chosen more for its spelling than its meaning.

27. What does the professor say about advertising? *Choose two answers.*
- Ⓐ Its purpose is to make consumers aware that a product is for sale.
- Ⓑ Some people find it confusing even though it is a simple concept.
- Ⓒ It is not the same as marketing despite what some people believe.
- Ⓓ It is a key part of the marketing mix when consumers are aware of it.

28. What is the professor's opinion of the four Ps model?
- Ⓐ He feels that it is still valid although it was developed a long time ago.
- Ⓑ He thinks that it would benefit from having one or two elements added.
- Ⓒ He finds it a useful concept even though it has a few fundamental issues.
- Ⓓ He believes it needs to be updated to account for Internet marketing.

Tracks 441–447 Listen to a lecture in a film studies class.

Now get ready to answer the questions. You may use your notes to help you answer.

29. What does the professor mainly discuss?
    (A) The rise and fall in popularity of animated movies
    (B) The history and development of animated movies
    (C) Films from the "golden age" of animated movies
    (D) Techniques used in creating animated movies

30. Indicate whether each of the following describes the work of Winsor McCay. *Place a check (✓) in the correct box.*

	Yes	No
He made the films by drawing funny faces on a blackboard.		
His characters seemed to move naturally and have personalities.		
One of his characters was the most popular one of the 1920s.		
His films were more sophisticated than earlier animations.		

31. What can be inferred about animated films before Walt Disney's *Steamboat Willie*?
    (A) They lacked star characters.
    (B) They used primitive techniques.
    (C) They were not very popular.
    (D) They did not have sound.

32. What does the professor say about the animated films of Walt Disney? *Choose two answers.*
    [A] They were based on classic children's stories.
    [B] They were longer than earlier animated films.
    [C] They were popular with people of all ages.
    [D] They were created using two kinds of animation.

33. Listen again to part of the lecture. Then answer the question. Why does the professor say this?
    (A) To emphasize the amount of work involved in making a Disney movie
    (B) To suggest that the movie *Bambi* was extremely expensive to produce
    (C) To point out that artists needed a variety of skills to make Disney movies
    (D) To illustrate a technique required to make realistic animated movies

34. What does the professor say about the "silver age" of animated movies?
    (A) The Disney studio produced a number of quality movies during this period.
    (B) The movies produced during this period were not as popular as earlier movies.
    (C) Some of the movies made during this period were produced using computers.
    (D) Each animated film released during this period took about one year to make.

Speaking Section Directions

The Speaking test measures your ability to speak about a variety of topics. You will have about 20 minutes to deliver spoken responses to six questions. This includes time for reading and listening to information that you will speak about, preparing your responses, and delivering your responses. When you respond, you should answer each of the questions as completely as possible.

In Tasks 1 and 2, you will be asked to speak about familiar topics. For each question, you will have 15 seconds to prepare and 45 seconds to speak. Your response will be scored from 0–4 based on your ability to speak clearly and coherently about the topics.

In Tasks 3 and 4, you will read a short passage and then listen to a conversation or lecture on the same topic. You will then be asked to talk about what you have read and heard. For each question, you will have 30 seconds to prepare and 60 seconds to speak. Your response will be scored from 0–4 based on your ability to speak clearly and coherently and on your ability to give an accurate summary or paraphrase of what you have read and heard.

In Tasks 5 and 6, you will listen to a conversation or a lecture. You will then be asked to talk about what you have heard. For each question, you will have 20 seconds to prepare and 60 seconds to speak. Your response will be scored from 0–4 based on your ability to speak clearly and coherently and on your ability to give an accurate summary or paraphrase of what you have read and heard.

You may now begin the Speaking section by looking at the next page.

◀)) Tracks 448–449 **Task 1**

Describe the best advice that you have ever received. Explain why you think it was good advice. Include specific details and examples to support your explanation.

Preparation time: 15 seconds

Response time: 45 seconds

◀)) Tracks 450–451 **Task 2**

Some people prefer to communicate with friends in writing using email or text messages. Others prefer to communicate with their friends using a telephone. Which method of staying in touch with friends do you prefer? Explain and support your choice.

Preparation time: 15 seconds

Response time: 45 seconds

◀)) Tracks 452–455 **Task 3**

You will now read a short passage and then listen to a conversation on the same topic. You will then be asked a question about them. After you hear the question, you will have 30 seconds to prepare your response and 60 seconds to speak.

A university official wrote a notice to all students. Read the notice. You have 45 seconds to read the letter. Begin reading now.

Food and Beverage Policy for All Campus Events

This notice serves to remind all students of the university's food and beverage policy. In order to ensure that students receive high-quality and great-value food and drink, Astoria University has an exclusive contract with NorthCo Food Services to provide food and beverage services for all events and meetings. This means that students may not bring their own food or drinks to any on-campus event. Exemptions to this policy will be made only in exceptional cases. Anybody wishing to apply for an exemption must contact Yolanda Lopez, the Director of University Dining Services, for written approval.

Now listen to two students as they discuss the notice.

The woman expresses her opinion of the policy. State her opinion and explain the reasons she gives for holding that opinion.

Preparation time: 30 seconds

Response time: 60 seconds

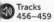 Tracks 456–459   **Task 4**

You will now read a short passage and then listen to a discussion on the same academic subject. You will then be asked a question about what you have read and heard. After you hear the question, you will have 30 seconds to prepare your response and 60 seconds to speak.

Now read the passage about metallic elements. You have 45 seconds to read the passage. Begin reading now.

Metallic Elements

There are over 80 known metallic elements. A few of these have been known for thousands of years, but most have been discovered since about 1700. The metals actually have very little in common. People think of them as being dense and heavy, and that's true of some metals, such as iron and lead, but others, like sodium, are very lightweight. People think of metals as being strong, and some are, but many pure metals are soft or brittle. Some metals, such as gold and platinum, are known as the precious metals because their rarity makes them valuable and expensive. Other metals, such as aluminum and iron, are very common.

Now listen to part of a lecture on this topic in a chemistry class.

Using details and examples from the talk, explain how titanium relates to metallic elements in general and why it is a useful element.

Preparation time: 30 seconds

Response time: 60 seconds

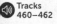 Tracks 460–462   **Task 5**

You will now listen to a conversation. You will then be asked a question about it. After you hear the question, you will have 20 seconds to prepare your response and 60 seconds to speak.

Listen to a conversation between two students.

The woman discusses two possible solutions to the man's problem. Describe the problem. Then state which of the two solutions you prefer and explain why.

Preparation time: 20 seconds

Response time: 60 seconds

Task 6

You will now listen to part of a lecture. You will then be asked a question about it. After you hear the question, you will have 20 seconds to prepare your response and 60 seconds to speak.

Listen to a lecture in an economics class.

Using examples and points from the lecture, explain the concept of opportunity cost.

Preparation time: 20 seconds

Response time: 60 seconds

Writing Section Directions

The Writing section measures your ability to use writing to communicate in an academic environment. The Writing section will take just under one hour. This includes time for reading and listening to information that you will write about, as well as for writing your responses.

In Task 1, you will read a passage and then listen to a lecture on the same topic. You may take notes while you read and listen. You will then have 20 minutes to write your response. Your response will be scored from 0–5 based on the quality of your writing, and on how accurately and completely you summarize or paraphrase the relationship between the passage and the lecture. Typically, an effective response will have between 150 and 225 words and should **not** describe your personal opinion about the topic.

In Task 2, you will be asked a question about a topic of general interest. You will have 30 minutes to write a response based on your experience and opinions. Your response will be scored from 0–5 based on the quality of your writing and on how well you have developed and organized your ideas. Typically, an effective response will have at least 300 words.

You may now begin the Writing section by looking at the next page.

Tracks 466–468 **Task 1**

Now look at the passage below. You have three minutes to read the passage.

> Biofuels are energy sources that are made from living plants, such as corn, sugar cane, palm trees, or other organic matter. Examples of biofuels include ethanol, biodiesel, green diesel, and biogas. Unlike fossil fuels, which come from plants that died millions of years ago, biofuels are renewable. Someday, our supply of coal and oil will be used up, but biofuels are a renewable resource.
>
> One major benefit of using biofuels is that countries that currently must import petroleum will become independent. They will no longer need to rely on foreign sources of energy because they can meet their energy needs by growing large quantities of biofuels.
>
> Growing biofuels provides an economic benefit for individuals, too. Using land to grow biofuels helps farmers because they can usually sell biofuels for more money than they can sell food crops. So farmers make more money, and non-farmers save money because when energy is plentiful, their fuel costs go down.
>
> We know energy based on biofuels is a workable model from the example of Brazil, where a lot of ethanol is produced by growing sugar cane. In fact, much of Brazil's energy needs are met by biofuels, and if it works in Brazil, there is no reason to think it could not work in other countries.

Now listen to a lecture on the topic you just read about.

Now answer the question. You have 20 minutes to complete your response.

Summarize the points made in the lecture, explaining how they challenge the points made in the reading passage.

Track 469 **Task 2**

Answer the question. You have 30 minutes to complete your response.

Do you agree or disagree with the following statement?

> **The most important things that people learn in their lives are not learned in school.**

Use specific reasons and examples to support your opinion.

Practice Test B

General Information

This practice test measures your ability to understand and use English in an academic context. There are four sections. Before each section, you will see specific directions that explain how to answer the questions in that section.

In the **Reading** section, you will read and answer questions about three passages. The passages will be similar to excerpts from introductory college-level textbooks. The passages will cover a variety of different subjects. You do not need existing knowledge because all the information needed to answer the questions will be in the passage.

In the **Listening** section, you will hear two conversations and four lectures. The conversations will be about typical topics that affect students at university in North America. After each conversation, you must answer five questions. The lectures will be about academic topics that students in their first year at college are likely to study. The lectures will cover a variety of different subjects. You do not need existing knowledge because all the information needed to answer the questions will be mentioned by the speaker or speakers. After each lecture, you must answer six questions.

In the **Speaking** section, you will see six questions. The first two questions ask you to respond based on your experience and opinions. The third and fourth questions ask you to speak about information that you have read and heard. The final two questions ask you to speak about information you have heard. For each question, you will have a specific amount of time to prepare and deliver your response.

In the **Writing** section, you will answer two questions. In the first question, you will have to write about the relationship between the information in a passage that you have read and the information in a lecture that you have heard. In the second question, you will have to write a response based on your experience and opinions.

You may now begin the test by looking at the next page. Alternatively, you can take Practice Test B online at www.oxfordenglishtesting.com.

Reading Section Directions

The Reading section measures your ability to understand academic passages in English. You will have 60 minutes to read three passages and answer 40 questions about what you have read.

Most questions are worth 1 point but the last question in each set is worth more than 1 point. The directions for these questions indicate how many points you may receive.

For most questions, you should choose one answer. For some questions, however, you may need to choose from two to five answers. These questions have special directions that explain how many answers you should choose.

You may now begin the Reading section by looking at the next page.

Hydrothermal Vents

Scientists have long known that creatures, such as viperfish and anglerfish, live in the ocean deeps. Even though sunlight cannot penetrate deeper than 200 meters (656 feet) and these fish live in conditions of near total darkness, they ultimately rely on sunlight for food. Small deep-ocean creatures feed on particles of organic matter that fall from the sunlit upper ocean, and predatory creatures like the viperfish in turn eat these smaller organisms. Scientists had assumed light was essential for all marine life, so it was a shock when, in 1973, researchers on the exploratory submarine DSV *Alvin* discovered colonies of creatures that, unlike other deep-ocean life forms, did not need sunlight to survive. It was almost as startling as if they had discovered living organisms not based on the element carbon.

What these marine scientists found in 1973 were entire ecosystems living around hydrothermal vents – openings in the ocean floor similar to geysers on land. They are typically found in geologically active underwater mountain ranges such as the Mid-Atlantic Ridge or the East Pacific Rise. Like geysers, vents tend to be found in groups, called vent fields, many of which have been given colorful names: Lost City, Rose Garden, and Clam Acres, for example. Vents form when water seeps deep into the oceanic crust where it is heated by subsurface magma. The superheated water dissolves minerals such as sulfides as it rises before exiting the seabed through a cylindrical structure known as a black smoker. As it exits, the water may be as much as 400 degrees Celsius (752 Fahrenheit) hotter than the near-freezing ambient water temperature, and this difference causes the dissolved minerals to precipitate out, adding to the height of the structure. One smoker off the coast of Oregon with the rather unscientific nickname of Godzilla reached 40 meters (131 feet) before it fell over, but is now growing again. There are also white smokers, which emit plumes of superheated water rich in boron, calcium, and other elements.

Although the discovery of life around the vents was a shock, the discovery of thermal vents themselves was not unanticipated. Scientists knew that there were greater amounts of certain minerals such as manganese present in seawater than could be accounted for by runoff from rivers. It is the chemical soup and the warmth provided by the black smokers that permit life to exist there. Bacteria convert hydrogen sulfide from the vents into usable nutrients, a process called chemosynthesis. To animals other than those in vent communities, these chemicals would be highly toxic, but in vent communities, hydrogen sulfide–eating bacteria form the lower link of the food chain. Small organisms can safely eat these bacteria and, in turn, act as a food source for larger organisms.

It is remarkable how concentrated life is in small areas around these vents, far more so than in other regions of the deep oceans. There are mats of bacteria several inches thick, enormous beds of clams and mussels, millions of eyeless shrimp, swarms of crabs, and clumps of giant tubeworms called tubeworm bushes. For unknown reasons, tubeworms and many other vent-community creatures display gigantism. That is, they are much larger than similar species found in shallow waters. These tubeworms are among the most extraordinary members of the vent community. Their bodies consist of a tube up to 3 meters (10 feet) long – one end anchored to the seabed, the other waving in the currents. They have no digestive system, depending instead on bacteria that line the inside of their tubes for their nutritional needs. The bacteria convert chemicals from the vent into food that they share with the tubeworms. In turn, the tubeworms supply the bacteria with hemoglobin, a chemical found in blood, which carries oxygen that the bacteria need in order to break down the minerals in the water.

Studying these phenomena deep beneath the ocean may seem of little value, but in fact hydrothermal vents may provide a source of valuable mineral resources. They may also provide insights into how life on Earth originated. Some scientists believe that early life evolved under conditions similar to those found at deep-ocean vents. Furthermore, astronomers believe phenomena similar to hydrothermal vents may exist on other worlds, such as Europa, an icy moon of Jupiter. If so, hydrothermal vents may also provide clues about possible extraterrestrial life.

1. The word "ultimately" in paragraph 1 is closest in meaning to
   - (A) to the maximum extent
   - (B) for the longest time
   - (C) at the most basic level
   - (D) for the most part

2. How does the author explain the surprise felt by scientists when they first discovered vent communities in 1973?
   - (A) By comparing it to an even more unlikely finding
   - (B) By providing comments made by the scientists
   - (C) By contrasting it with the reaction of other scholars
   - (D) By giving examples of additional exciting discoveries

3. Which of the following can be inferred from paragraph 2 about the East Pacific Rise?
   - (A) It is less geologically active than the Mid-Atlantic Range.
   - (B) Magma is found under the surface of the seabed there.
   - (C) It contains all the hydrothermal vent fields with colorful names.
   - (D) More vent fields are found there than in other parts of the ocean.

4. The word "ambient" in paragraph 2 is closest in meaning to
   - (A) average
   - (B) surface
   - (C) surrounding
   - (D) estimated

5. The author's description of Godzilla in paragraph 2 mentions which of the following?
   - (A) It has been both taller and shorter than it is at present.
   - (B) It is the name both of a black smoker and a vent field.
   - (C) It was the highest black smoker in the world before it fell over.
   - (D) Scientists have not studied it as much as other black smokers.

6. According to paragraph 2, what is one way in which black smokers differ from white smokers?
   - (A) The water emitted from black smokers is not as hot as that from white smokers.
   - (B) Black smokers build up quickly, whereas white smokers tend to grow slowly.
   - (C) Black smokers and white smokers contain different types of chemicals.
   - (D) There are vent communities around black smokers but not around white smokers.

7. Why does the author mention the mineral "manganese" in paragraph 3?
   - (A) To suggest that it alerted scientists to the possibility of finding communities of live organisms around vents
   - (B) To describe a substance that posed a possible threat to the future safety of vent-community organisms
   - (C) To point out that rivers were depositing more manganese into the ocean than had been previously thought
   - (D) To indicate that its presence in large amounts in seawater signaled the existence of undersea vents

8. The word "clumps" in paragraph 4 is closest in meaning to
   - (A) masses
   - (B) extensions
   - (C) remnants
   - (D) images

9. The word "they" in paragraph 4 refers to
   - (A) chemicals
   - (B) bacteria
   - (C) needs
   - (D) tubes

10. According to paragraph 4, which of the following best describes the relationship between giant tubeworms and the bacteria found inside their tubes?

   Ⓐ The bacteria harm the tubeworms by removing hemoglobin from their blood.

   Ⓑ The tubeworms and the bacteria both benefit from their relationship.

   Ⓒ The tubeworms receive useful nutrients, but the bacteria do not benefit.

   Ⓓ The bacteria are harmed by chemicals that the tubeworms use for digestion.

11. According to paragraph 5, which of the following is NOT a reason to study hydrothermal vents?

   Ⓐ To understand the origins of life on Earth

   Ⓑ To exploit minerals found around vent sites

   Ⓒ To develop useful techniques for astronomy

   Ⓓ To learn how life on other planets may develop

12. Look at the four squares (■) that indicate where the following sentence could be added to the passage.

At the apex of this chain are several species of predatory octopuses.

Where would the sentence best fit? Choose position **A**, **B**, **C**, or **D**.

Although the discovery of life around the vents was a shock, the discovery of thermal vents themselves was not unanticipated. Scientists knew that there were greater amounts of certain minerals such as manganese present in seawater than could be accounted for by runoff from rivers. It is the chemical soup and the warmth provided by the black smokers that permit life to exist there. **A** Bacteria convert hydrogen sulfide from the vents into usable nutrients, a process called chemosynthesis. **B** To animals other than those in vent communities, these chemicals would be highly toxic, but in vent communities, hydrogen sulfide–eating bacteria form the lower link of the food chain. **C** Small organisms can safely eat these bacteria and, in turn, act as a food source for larger organisms. **D**

13. **Directions:** An introductory sentence for a brief summary of the passage is provided below. Complete the summary by selecting the THREE answer choices that express the most important ideas in the passage. Some sentences do not belong in the summary because they express ideas that are not presented in the passage or are minor ideas in the passage. **This question is worth 2 points.**

> **The discovery of creatures living around hydrothermal vents was a surprise to scientists.**
>
> •
>
> •
>
> •

   Ⓐ Tubeworms consist of a long tube filled with bacteria plus a digestive tract and anchor.

   Ⓑ The study of hydrothermal vents may provide the answer to several scientific questions.

   Ⓒ DSV *Alvin* was the submarine that made the initial exploration of deep-sea vents.

   Ⓓ Numerous organisms cluster around hydrothermal vents to form concentrated communities.

   Ⓔ Chemicals and heat released by black and white smokers allow life to exist at vents.

   Ⓕ Vent fields often have interesting names like Rose Garden, Clam Acres, or Godzilla.

The Stages of Sleep

We all think we know what sleep is and how sleep and wakefulness differ. However, according to scientists, any definition of sleep must involve at least four components. One component is reduced movement. Most voluntary muscle functions cease during sleep. If a person is writing an email, dancing, or playing soccer, the odds are good that he or she is not asleep. Another is reduced response to stimuli. There is very little awareness of the external environment during sleep, and sleepers are unaware of low-level noises or visual cues that are easily detected when awake. The third component is a characteristic posture. In humans, this usually, though not always, involves lying down. The final component is reversibility: unlike people in a coma or animals in a state of hibernation, sleepers can be woken fairly easily.

Sleep can be divided into two broad categories: rapid eye movement (REM) sleep and non-rapid eye movement (NREM) sleep. Each category has a set of associated physical and psychological features. The discovery that different kinds of sleep exist was first made by psychologists in 1937. They used an electroencephalogram (EEG), a device that can track rhythmic brain activity, usually called brain waves, by measuring the electrical impulses of neurons inside people's brains. Originally, they divided sleep into five stages, A through E, from wakefulness through deep sleep. Then, in 1953, REM sleep was identified as a distinct stage of sleep. Fifteen years later, the older model was superseded and scientific definitions of the stages of sleep were standardized as REM sleep and NREM sleep, with the latter being divided into four stages: N1, N2, N3, and N4. In 2007, the N3 and N4 stages were combined.

Stage N1, sometimes called "drowsy sleep," is the transition from wakefulness to sleep. During N1, which typically lasts only about ten minutes, sleepers lose most awareness of the external environment and their muscles relax, though they may experience involuntary twitches. During N2, muscular activity further decreases, and awareness of the environment disappears. This stage generally represents 45 to 50 percent of a subject's sleep, the most of any stage. N3, the deepest stage of sleep, is also known as delta sleep because slow-moving delta waves appear in EEG readings. Breathing is regular during NREM sleep, and not many motor events occur; however, body repositioning and, in some people, sleepwalking can occur, especially during N3.

REM sleep, which accounts on average for about 25 percent of total sleep, is marked by the rapid movement of a sleeper's eyeballs. As a sleeper's brain is more active during this stage than NREM sleep, but his or her muscles are most relaxed, it is also known as paradoxical sleep. The EEG pattern during REM sleep is nearly the same as it is when a person is awake, and almost all dreaming occurs during this phase. Psychologists believe that the body is relaxed during this stage to prevent dreamers from acting out scenes from the vivid dreams that often occur. Psychologists also believe that the eye movement represents a visual scanning of the images seen in dreams.

Sleep is something of a roller coaster. From a study of EEG patterns, scientists know that subjects first enter N1 sleep, then N2, and then slip into deep N3 sleep. Sleepers next return to N2 sleep and then enter the REM sleep state. In a typical night, a sleeper might go through the cycle of N2-N3-N2-REM sleep from five to eight times. As the night progresses, the periods of time spent in REM sleep increase, and late-night REM episodes may last as long as an hour, with more bursts of eye movements and more dreams than during those that occur earlier in the night.

The amount of REM sleep that a person needs varies according to age. For example, infants sleep about sixteen hours per day and spend about 50 percent of that time in REM sleep. Adults typically sleep six to eight hours per day and spend 20 to 30 percent of that time in REM sleep. And assuming that people dream whenever they are in REM sleep, in an average lifetime, a person may have around 150,000 dreams. Although the amount of REM sleep may vary with age, it remains a vital part of the sleep cycle: studies have shown that a lack of REM sleep can negatively affect the brain's ability to learn and remember.

14. According to the passage, which of the following is NOT an essential part of the scientific definition of sleep?

- Ⓐ   The sleeper must be able to wake up relatively easily.
- Ⓑ   The sleeper must have reduced environmental awareness.
- Ⓒ   The sleeper must be lying down in a comfortable position.
- Ⓓ   The sleeper must make few, if any, voluntary movements.

15. In stating that "the odds are good" in paragraph 1, the author means

- Ⓐ   it is beneficial
- Ⓑ   it is relevant
- Ⓒ   it is certain
- Ⓓ   it is unusual

16. Why does the author mention "hibernation" in paragraph 1?

- Ⓐ   To compare the characteristics of being in a coma with those of hibernation
- Ⓑ   To point out a mistaken belief some people have about animals that hibernate
- Ⓒ   To explain why it is both difficult and dangerous to wake some sleepers up
- Ⓓ   To contrast one component of sleep with the same aspect of hibernation

17. Which of the following can be inferred from paragraph 2?

- Ⓐ   Electroencephalograms were not available for use in research until the 1930s.
- Ⓑ   Psychologists modified their classification of sleep as new data was identified.
- Ⓒ   REM sleep is such a distinct stage that it should have been classified sooner.
- Ⓓ   The electrical impulses of neurons cannot be measured when people are awake.

18. The word "they" in paragraph 2 refers to

- Ⓐ   sleepers' brains
- Ⓑ   electrical impulses
- Ⓒ   brain waves
- Ⓓ   psychologists

19. What does the author say about the N3 stage of sleep?

- Ⓐ   It was originally considered a less important stage than N4 sleep.
- Ⓑ   It is the stage of NREM sleep when people are most likely to move.
- Ⓒ   It accounts for about half of most people's total amount of sleep.
- Ⓓ   Scientists cannot easily take EEG readings during this stage.

20. The word "twitches" in paragraph 3 is closest in meaning to

- Ⓐ   sudden movements
- Ⓑ   environmental changes
- Ⓒ   mild sensations
- Ⓓ   dreamlike feelings

21. Why is REM sleep also known as "paradoxical sleep"?

- Ⓐ   The eyes move quickly during this stage, but the rest of the body is relaxed.
- Ⓑ   It is the longest stage of sleep but provides the least amount of rest for the body.
- Ⓒ   This stage is marked both by high levels of mental activity and physical relaxation.
- Ⓓ   It is the deepest form of sleep and the stage when the most vivid dreams occur.

22. According to paragraph 5, which stage of sleep comes immediately after REM sleep?

- Ⓐ   N1 sleep
- Ⓑ   N2 sleep
- Ⓒ   N3 sleep
- Ⓓ   Deeper REM sleep

23. Why does the author describe sleep as "something of a roller coaster" in paragraph 5?
  Ⓐ Some sleepers occasionally dream about activities that scare them.
  Ⓑ Sleepers move from deep sleep to lighter sleep and back again.
  Ⓒ The night seems to pass very quickly for many sleepers.
  Ⓓ Discoveries made by sleep scientists have been very exciting.

24. Which of the following best expresses the essential information in the highlighted sentence in paragraph 5? Incorrect choices change the meaning in important ways or leave out essential information.
  Ⓐ A person who goes to sleep early will have more REM episodes and more dreams than someone who goes to sleep late.
  Ⓑ The number of dreams that a sleeper has depends on the length of the REM episodes that he or she experiences.
  Ⓒ REM sleep episodes grow longer as the night goes on and sleepers experience more eye movements and dreams.
  Ⓓ Bursts of rapid eye movements and dreams that occur in REM sleep late at night may be an hour or more in length.

25. Look at the four squares (■) that indicate where the following sentence could be added to the passage.

Toddlers and school-age children generally spend about ten to thirteen hours asleep, one-third of which is REM sleep, while adolescents sleep nine to ten hours a day and spend about one-quarter of their total sleep time in the REM stage.

Where would the sentence best fit? Choose position Ⓐ, Ⓑ, Ⓒ, or Ⓓ.

The amount of REM sleep that a person needs varies according to age. For example, infants sleep about sixteen hours per day and spend about 50 percent of that time in REM sleep. Ⓐ Adults typically sleep six to eight hours per day and spend 20 to 30 percent of that time in REM sleep. Ⓑ And assuming that people dream whenever they are in REM sleep, in an average lifetime, a person may have around 150,000 dreams. Ⓒ Although the amount of REM sleep may vary with age, it remains a vital part of the sleep cycle: studies have shown that a lack of REM sleep can negatively affect the brain's ability to learn and remember. Ⓓ

26. **Directions:** Select the phrases that correctly describe features associated with each type of sleep. TWO of the answer choices will NOT be used. **This question is worth 3 points.**

NREM Sleep

-
-
-

REM Sleep

-
-

  Ⓐ Involves regular breathing but few motor movements
  Ⓑ Shows brain waves similar to a state of wakefulness
  Ⓒ Is divided into a number of named stages
  Ⓓ Cannot be observed through EEG readings
  Ⓔ Is not experienced by infants or children
  Ⓕ Is related to learning and memory
  Ⓖ Includes the deepest form of sleep

The Story of the Piano

The piano is such an integral part of many types of music. It was for the piano that Mozart wrote 27 concertos and Beethoven wrote his famous sonatas. Chopin, Schubert, and Liszt composed music for the piano in the nineteenth century that opened up new worlds of sound. In the twentieth century, some of the most memorable jazz was produced by bands centered on pianists such as Duke Ellington and Oscar Peterson, and popular music standards were composed on the pianos of George Gershwin, Irving Berlin, and Cole Porter. Rock music has also had its share of outstanding pianists, including Elton John, Stevie Wonder, and Billy Joel. Despite all of this, the piano is only about 300 years old.

The ultimate ancestor of the piano – and of all stringed instruments, including the lute, guitar, and violin – is the harp. The clavichord and the harpsichord, which are the piano's immediate predecessors, were influenced by the harp, too. As instruments for public performances, however, both the clavichord and the harpsichord had drawbacks. The clavichord produces sound when a metal blade, the tangent, strikes a string inside the body of the instrument. The tangent remains in contact with the string while the note is played, which dampens the vibrations and lowers the volume. The harpsichord works on a different principle. When a key is pressed, a plectrum plucks the corresponding string. Since the plectrum does not remain in contact with the string, the volume of the note is not reduced, but there is no way to change how hard or for how long the plectrum strikes the string, and thus no way to vary the volume or sustain the note.

Around the beginning of the eighteenth century, Italian instrument maker Bartolomeo Cristofori di Francesco was credited with developing an instrument with a completely novel method of striking the strings. When a key was pressed, a metal hammer struck a metal string and rebounded, allowing the string to vibrate. This vibration was carried through a bridge to a sounding board – technology that Cristofori borrowed from the harpsichord – which released the acoustic energy into the air as sound. The volume of the sound depended on the musician's touch: the harder a key was struck, the more forcefully the hammer hit the string, and the louder the note. At first, Cristofori's invention was called "gravicembalo col piano e forte," which can be loosely translated as "soft and loud keyboard instrument." This rather clumsy name was soon changed to *pianoforte* and eventually *piano*.

Despite its advantages, the piano was not an immediate success. It was not until an Italian writer, Francesco Scipione, wrote a glowing review of the new instrument that it became popular. During the eighteenth and early nineteenth centuries, the piano underwent many changes. Foot pedals were added to give more control over volume and the ability to sustain a note. Stronger, heavier piano wire was used for the strings, giving the piano greater volume. The hammers, originally covered with leather, were covered with cloth, producing a more consistent tone. And the tonal range of a standard piano increased from five octaves to seven and one-third octaves or even more.

The piano's golden age arguably lasted from the mid-nineteenth century to the mid-twentieth. Pianos appeared in the parlors and living rooms of private homes of both the working class and the wealthy, suggesting they were valued not just as a musical instrument, but also as a piece of furniture and a status symbol. The piano's popularity provided employment for piano teachers, piano tuners, and piano movers. Music publishers churned out millions of pages of sheet music for the popular songs of the day, though tastes have changed and few are played or even remembered today. Concert pianists were as popular as musical superstars of today, and their social lives were written up in newspapers and discussed at social gatherings.

Even today, the piano remains popular. Technological developments have continued, with electric pianos using an amplifier to boost the sound, and digital pianos employing computer technology in place of piano strings. These latter instruments not only are far more portable than standard pianos, but also are capable of producing sounds that no acoustic piano could make.

27. Which of the following is true of the people mentioned in paragraph 1?
   - (A) All of them are well-known composers of piano music.
   - (B) They were all well-known pianists from the 1900s.
   - (C) They were pioneers in the development of the piano.
   - (D) They are famous figures in the history of piano music.

28. The word "immediate" in paragraph 2 is closest in meaning to
   - (A) oldest
   - (B) fastest
   - (C) closest
   - (D) loudest

29. Which of the following statements is supported by paragraph 2?
   - (A) Stringed instruments like the lute and violin are ancestors of the piano.
   - (B) The action of a tangent both produces notes and reduces their volume.
   - (C) The techniques used when playing a harp have an influence on its sound.
   - (D) Harpsichords are more suited for public performances than clavichords.

30. The word "sustain" in paragraph 2 is closest in meaning to
   - (A) prolong
   - (B) increase
   - (C) repeat
   - (D) soften

31. According to the passage, what was Bartolomeo Cristofori's primary accomplishment?
   - (A) Inventing a new arrangement of the keys on a piano keyboard
   - (B) Utilizing hammers to strike the strings when keys are touched
   - (C) Inventing a bridge to carry sound from the strings to the sounding board
   - (D) Using a plectrum to construct a new style of piano with a louder sound

32. Which of the following can be inferred about the original Italian name for the piano?
   - (A) It could not easily be translated into other languages.
   - (B) It did not describe the features of the piano accurately.
   - (C) It was both too long and inconvenient for everyday use.
   - (D) It was first used by Scipione to describe Cristofori's invention.

33. The phrase "glowing review" in paragraph 4 is closest in meaning to
   - (A) positive assessment
   - (B) famous remembrance
   - (C) careful analysis
   - (D) fictional account

34. According to paragraph 4, all of the following changes occurred in the eighteenth or nineteenth century EXCEPT:
   - (A) The piano became louder because new types of strings were developed.
   - (B) The piano's hammers were covered with a different type of material.
   - (C) The piano's keyboard was expanded to include a greater number of keys.
   - (D) Foot pedals were added to give the piano a more consistent tone.

35. Which of the following best expresses the essential information in the highlighted sentence in paragraph 5? Incorrect choices change the meaning in important ways or leave out essential information.
   - (A) All kinds of people enjoyed listening to the music that pianos could produce.
   - (B) People from all social groups appreciated pianos for a number of reasons.
   - (C) Like other items of furniture, pianos were considered to be a status symbol.
   - (D) Pianos commonly appeared in private homes because they were valuable.

36. The word "few" in paragraph 5 refers to
    (A) piano teachers
    (B) music publishers
    (C) millions of pages
    (D) popular songs

37. Why does the author mention musical superstars of today in paragraph 5?
    (A) To show how they were influenced by pianists from the golden age
    (B) To explain why piano music continues to be popular in modern times
    (C) To illustrate how well known concert pianists of the golden age were
    (D) To contrast the musical ability of golden age pianists and modern ones

38. In the discussion of technological developments in paragraph 6, which of the following points does the author make?
    (A) Computers have replaced strings in electric pianos.
    (B) Digital pianos are more easily moved than other pianos.
    (C) Amplifiers allow acoustic pianos to produce more volume.
    (D) Digital and electric pianos are replacing traditional pianos.

39. Look at the four squares (■) that indicate where the following sentence could be added to the passage.

This required a larger keyboard, and the standard piano eventually settled at 36 black keys and 52 white ones.

Where would the sentence best fit? Choose position **A**, **B**, **C**, or **D**.

Despite its advantages, the piano was not an immediate success. It was not until an Italian writer, Francesco Scipione , wrote a glowing review of the new instrument that it became popular. During the eighteenth and early nineteenth centuries, the piano underwent many changes. **A** Foot pedals were added to give more control over volume and the ability to sustain a note. Stronger, heavier piano wire was used for the strings, giving the piano greater volume. **B** The hammers, originally covered with leather, were covered with cloth, producing a more consistent tone. **C** And the tonal range of a standard piano increased from five octaves to seven and one-third octaves or even more. **D**

40. **Directions:** An introductory sentence for a brief summary of the passage is provided below. Complete the summary by selecting the THREE answer choices that express the most important ideas in the passage. Some sentences do not belong in the summary because they express ideas that are not presented in the passage or are minor ideas in the passage. **This question is worth 2 points.**

> **Though only about 300 years old, the piano has played a major role in many forms of music.**
>
> •
>
> •
>
> •

    (A) The piano became famous after Francesco Scipione wrote about it and gave it a shorter name.
    (B) During the eighteenth century, many people found jobs teaching, tuning, and moving pianos.
    (C) All stringed instruments – including keyboard instruments – originally evolved from the harp.
    (D) The piano was at the height of its popularity from the mid-nineteenth to mid-twentieth centuries.
    (E) Digital pianos use computer technology to produce sounds that people have never heard before.
    (F) Cristofori's piano gave musicians more control over volume than previous keyboard instruments.

Listening Section Directions

The Listening section measures your ability to understand conversations and lectures in English. The Listening section will take about 60 minutes. This includes time to listen to the two conversations and four lectures, and 30 minutes to answer 34 questions about what you have heard. You will hear each conversation and lecture just **once**.

After each conversation or lecture, you will see some questions. Each question is worth 1 point. The questions typically ask about the main idea of the talk or about details that the speakers mention. Some questions ask about a speaker's attitude or reason for saying something. You should answer the questions based on what is stated or implied by the speakers.

You should take notes while you listen to the conversations and lectures. You can use your notes to help you answer the questions. Your notes will **not** be scored.

For some questions you will hear part of the conversation or lecture again. These questions are clearly marked.

You may now begin the Listening section by looking at the next page.

Conversation 1

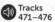 Tracks
471–476
Listen to a conversation between a professor of American literature and a student.

Now get ready to answer the questions. You may use your notes to help you answer.

1. Why does the student go to see the professor?
   - Ⓐ To ask him to change a grade
   - Ⓑ To discuss the symbolist poets
   - Ⓒ To ask for his opinion about her paper
   - Ⓓ To ask him to speak to Professor Bryant

2. What problems with the student's essay did Professor Bryant mention? *Choose two answers.*
   - Ⓐ The paper was not long enough.
   - Ⓑ She cited too few research sources.
   - Ⓒ She turned it in after the specified due date.
   - Ⓓ The essay did not include enough examples.

 3. Listen again to part of the conversation. Then answer the question. What does the student mean when she says this?
   - Ⓐ She is unsure what grade she will receive.
   - Ⓑ She believes she will receive a poor grade.
   - Ⓒ She thinks Professor Bryant is a great teacher.
   - Ⓓ She thinks it is too late to drop the class now.

4. What can be inferred about the student's friend?
   - Ⓐ He is currently a student in Professor White's poetry class.
   - Ⓑ He received a good grade when he took Professor Bryant's class.
   - Ⓒ He agrees with Professor White's opinion of Professor Bryant.
   - Ⓓ He thinks the student should drop Professor Bryant's class.

5. Indicate which suggestions the professor gives the student. *Place a check (✓) in the correct box.*

	Yes	No
Rewrite her paper so it includes more specific examples		
Transfer out of Professor Bryant's class into another class		
Discuss her academic concerns with Professor Bryant		
Talk about her paper with the dean of academic affairs		

Lecture 1

 Tracks 477–483 Listen to a lecture in an art history class.

Now get ready to answer the questions. You may use your notes to help you answer.

6. What does the professor mainly discuss?
   - Ⓐ Famous artists and performers from the 1960s
   - Ⓑ A history and comparison of Op art and Pop art
   - Ⓒ The ways in which Op art influenced Pop art
   - Ⓓ An analysis of how art trends follow fashion

7. According to the professor, what mistaken idea do many people have about Op art and Pop art?
   - Ⓐ That they both appeared about the same time
   - Ⓑ That they were both equally popular with critics
   - Ⓒ That they were similar in a number of important ways
   - Ⓓ That they were both dominated by the same artists

8. Why does the lecturer mention the bands The Beatles and The Who?
   - Ⓐ To illustrate an aspect of British culture that was popular in the 1960s
   - Ⓑ To imply that musicians were more popular in the 1960s than visual artists
   - Ⓒ To point out that musicians influenced the styles of clothing people wore
   - Ⓓ To remind students of the influence these musicians had on the visual arts

9. What difference between Bridget Riley and Victor Vasarely does the professor discuss?
   - Ⓐ The critics appreciated Vasarely's work, but did not like Riley's.
   - Ⓑ Riley's works were exhibited in New York in 1965 but Vasarely's were not.
   - Ⓒ Vasarely worked in color, but Riley worked only in black and white.
   - Ⓓ Unlike Riley, Vasarely didn't object to his designs being used in fashion.

10. Indicate whether each of the following is a characteristic of Op art, Pop art, or both Op art and Pop art. *Place a check (✓) in the correct box.*

	Op art	Pop art	Both Op art and Pop art
Mostly black and white rather than color			
Popular with critics and ordinary people			
Used in fashion designs			
Nonrepresentational			

11. What is the professor's opinion of Andy Warhol?
   - Ⓐ He could have been successful if he had worked harder.
   - Ⓑ He took too many of his ideas from other Pop artists.
   - Ⓒ He is among the best known of all American artists.
   - Ⓓ He made some unusual choices of objects to paint.

Lecture 2

 Tracks 484–490 Listen to part of a discussion in an astronomy class.

Now get ready to answer the questions. You may use your notes to help you answer.

12. What is the main purpose of this discussion?
    - Ⓐ To discuss impact damage caused by meteorites
    - Ⓑ To contrast meteoroids and micro-meteoroids
    - Ⓒ To introduce meteors, meteoroids, and meteorites
    - Ⓓ To review evidence for life on other planets

13. Listen again to part of the discussion. Then answer the question. What does the professor imply about micro-meteoroids?
    - Ⓐ Some of them are the size of small boulders.
    - Ⓑ They are smaller than a small pebble.
    - Ⓒ They are the most commonly seen meteor.
    - Ⓓ They sometimes affect the weather on Earth.

14. What does the professor say about the fireball of 1972? *Choose two answers.*
    - Ⓐ It entered the Earth's atmosphere and then returned to space.
    - Ⓑ It caused only a small amount of damage when it struck Earth.
    - Ⓒ It could be seen from Earth despite appearing in the afternoon.
    - Ⓓ It could be observed from everywhere in North America.

15. What does the professor say about asteroids and comets?
    - Ⓐ Both comets and asteroids are sources of meteoroids.
    - Ⓑ Comets are made from different materials than asteroids.
    - Ⓒ Scientists do not know exactly what they are made of.
    - Ⓓ They usually appear in the sky at the same time each year.

16. What does the professor indicate about meteors that appear during meteor showers?
    - Ⓐ They are usually much brighter than other meteors.
    - Ⓑ They are fragments of stony or stony-metal meteoroids.
    - Ⓒ They appear when Earth passes through the tails of comets.
    - Ⓓ They can have an effect on the orbits of comets or asteroids.

17. What does the professor imply about Mars?
    - Ⓐ It has always had conditions too harsh for life.
    - Ⓑ There is no evidence for any kind of life there.
    - Ⓒ Intelligent life exists there, but it is very rare.
    - Ⓓ It is possible that life exists or has existed there.

Conversation 2

 Tracks 491–496 Listen to a conversation between a student and a department administrator.

Now get ready to answer the questions. You may use your notes to help you answer.

18. Why does the student visit the department?
  - Ⓐ To make an appointment with a professor
  - Ⓑ To arrange to make a payment for a class
  - Ⓒ To get information about an unusual class
  - Ⓓ To ask when spring break will take place

19. How did the student first learn about the Ecology of Tropical Reefs course?
  - Ⓐ From the university website
  - Ⓑ From Professor Garrison
  - Ⓒ From a poster on campus
  - Ⓓ From talking to a friend

20. According to the administrator, which two components of the Ecology of Tropical Reefs class take place before the field trip? *Choose two answers.*
  - Ⓐ Getting diving certification
  - Ⓑ Giving an oral progress report
  - Ⓒ Attending evening lectures
  - Ⓓ Collecting data and observations

21. What can be inferred about the Ecology of Tropical Reefs course?
  - Ⓐ Most participants already have diving certification.
  - Ⓑ It usually involves a field trip to a tropical destination.
  - Ⓒ It is not popular among students because of its cost.
  - Ⓓ Participants will stay in luxurious accommodation.

22. Indicate whether each of the following is a step that the student will probably take before registering for Professor Garrison's class. *Place a check (✓) in the correct box.*

	Yes	No
Attend an organizational meeting		
Discuss the situation with his parents		
Have a talk with Professor Garrison		
Learn more about the course online		
Pay travel and accommodation fees		

Lecture 3

 Tracks 497–503   Listen to a lecture in a political science class.

Now get ready to answer the questions. You may use your notes to help you answer.

23. What is the main topic of this lecture?
- Ⓐ Name changes among political parties in the US.
- Ⓑ Well-known leaders of the main US political parties
- Ⓒ The development of the US political party system
- Ⓓ Factors that led to the success of some political parties

24. According to the professor, what were two policies of the Federalist party? *Choose two answers.*
- Ⓐ They supported a strong central government.
- Ⓑ They wanted Britain, not France, as their main ally.
- Ⓒ They favored agriculture over business.
- Ⓓ They opposed the creation of a central bank.

25. Listen again to part of the conversation. Then answer the question. Why does the professor say this?
- Ⓐ To emphasize that history has many hard-to-answer questions
- Ⓑ To express surprise that no one is able to answer his question
- Ⓒ To point out that there is actually no answer to his question
- Ⓓ To imply that the students should read the US Constitution

26. Which of these politicians acted as official leader of the Republican party?
- Ⓐ Alexander Hamilton
- Ⓑ George Washington
- Ⓒ James Madison
- Ⓓ Thomas Jefferson

27. What point does the professor make about the Whigs?
- Ⓐ They were led by Andrew Jackson.
- Ⓑ They were not formed until 1854.
- Ⓒ They used to be called Federalists.
- Ⓓ They favored progressive policies.

28. Indicate whether each statement is related to the First Party System, the Era of Good Feelings, or the Second Party System. *Place a check (✓) in the correct box.*

	First Party System	Era of Good Feelings	Second Party System
The nation had one rather weak political party.			
Andrew Jackson and Henry Clay were leaders.			
First one party was dominant and then another.			
Lack of competition led to parties being formed.			

Lecture 4

 Tracks 504–510 Listen a lecture in an archaeology class.

Now get ready to answer the questions. You may use your notes to help you answer.

29. What does the professor mainly discuss?
- Ⓐ How Folsom points were made
- Ⓑ Where Clovis people were from
- Ⓒ How people lived at Monte Verde
- Ⓓ Who first arrived in the Americas

30. According to the lecture, what is fluting?
- Ⓐ A way to make Folsom points easier to produce
- Ⓑ A wooden shaft attached to a Folsom point
- Ⓒ A groove carved into the face of a Folsom point
- Ⓓ A tool used in the manufacture of Folsom points

31. Listen again to part of the lecture. Then answer the question. Why does the professor say this?
- Ⓐ To argue that special tools were needed to make Folsom points
- Ⓑ To point out that making Folsom points required little training
- Ⓒ To suggest that she lacks the skill to manufacture useful objects
- Ⓓ To emphasize the skill required to make Folsom points

32. The professor discusses the discovery of Paleo-Indian artifacts. Put the events in the order in which they occurred.

First	
Second	
Third	
Fourth	

- Ⓐ An amateur scientist found the bones of an extinct giant bison.
- Ⓑ Archaeologists discovered stone tools and the remains of houses.
- Ⓒ Archaeologists found points in the bones of a type of extinct elephant.
- Ⓓ Museum scientists learned about and looked into the discovery.

33. Listen again to part of the lecture. What does the professor imply when she says this?
- Ⓐ The hunting sites in North America were temporary sites.
- Ⓑ The people who lived at Monte Verde rarely hunted.
- Ⓒ Archaeologists studied the Monte Verde site in more detail than other sites.
- Ⓓ The North American hunting sites were not as interesting as Monte Verde.

34. How does the professor organize the information about Paleo-Indians in her lecture?
- Ⓐ In chronological order from the earliest known culture to the most recent
- Ⓑ According to the relative importance of the artifacts that were discovered
- Ⓒ In the order in which archaeologists discovered and identified each culture
- Ⓓ According to the amount of information that is known about each culture

Speaking Section Directions

The Speaking test measures your ability to speak about a variety of topics. You will have about 20 minutes to deliver spoken responses to six questions. This includes time for reading and listening to information that you will speak about, preparing your responses, and delivering your responses. When you respond, you should answer each of the questions as completely as possible.

In Tasks 1 and 2, you will be asked to speak about familiar topics. For each question, you will have 15 seconds to prepare and 45 seconds to speak. Your response will be scored from 0–4 based on your ability to speak clearly and coherently about the topics.

In Tasks 3 and 4, you will read a short passage and then listen to a conversation or lecture on the same topic. You will then be asked to talk about what you have read and heard. For each question, you will have 30 seconds to prepare and 60 seconds to speak. Your response will be scored from 0–4 based on your ability to speak clearly and coherently and on your ability to give an accurate summary or paraphrase of what you have read and heard.

In Tasks 5 and 6, you will listen to a conversation or a lecture. You will then be asked to talk about what you have heard. For each question, you will have 20 seconds to prepare and 60 seconds to speak. Your response will be scored from 0–4 based on your ability to speak clearly and coherently and on your ability to give an accurate summary or paraphrase of what you have read and heard.

You may now begin the Speaking section by looking at the next page.

Tracks 511–512   **Task 1**

What is the most enjoyable vacation that you have ever taken? Explain why you liked this vacation. Include specific details and examples to support your explanation.

Preparation time: 15 seconds

Response time: 45 seconds

Tracks 513–514   **Task 2**

When they want to relax, some people enjoy reading books. Other people prefer watching television. Which of these two options do you prefer? Explain your choice. Support your opinion with specific details and examples.

Preparation time: 15 seconds

Response time: 45 seconds

Tracks 515–518   **Task 3**

You will now read a short passage and then listen to a conversation on the same topic. You will then be asked a question about them. After you hear the question, you will have 30 seconds to prepare your response and 60 seconds to speak.

A university official wrote a letter to campus tour guides. Read the letter. You have 45 seconds to read the letter. Begin reading now.

Letter to Campus Tour Guides

I'd like to begin by thanking all the students who have interrupted their summer activities to serve as guides for incoming first-year students and their families. Since it was instituted five years ago, the Summer Campus Tours have become a valuable and popular program. However, I'm sorry to inform you that the university can no longer provide guides with payment for their services. This is partially due to budget cuts, but also because the new president is trying to encourage a spirit of community service and volunteerism among students. We'll continue to provide guides from out of town with dormitory rooms and with meals at the cafeteria.

Now listen to two students as they discuss the letter.

The man expresses his opinion of the letter. State his opinion and explain the reasons he gives for having that opinion.

Preparation time: 30 seconds

Response time: 60 seconds

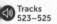

Task 4

You will now read a short passage and then listen to a discussion on the same academic subject. You will then be asked a question about what you have read and heard. After you hear the question, you will have 30 seconds to prepare your response and 60 seconds to speak.

Now read the passage about the Law of Unintended Consequences. You have 45 seconds to read the passage. Begin reading now.

The Law of Unintended Consequences

The Law of Unintended Consequences is an idea dating at least as far back as the eighteenth-century economist Adam Smith. However, American sociologist Robert Merton invented the term and popularized the concept in the 1930s. The law indicates that when a simple solution is applied to a complex problem, it often causes unexpected results. Merton lists three types of unintended consequences. One is the unexpected positive result of an action. The second is a negative result that occurs in addition to the positive result. The third is called a "perverse effect," which occurs when the result of some action is the opposite of what was intended.

Now listen to part of a lecture on this topic in an ecology class.

Using details from the talk, explain how the importation of rabbits into Australia relates to the Law of Unintended Consequences.

Preparation time: 30 seconds

Response time: 60 seconds

Task 5

You will now listen to a conversation. You will then be asked a question about it. After you hear the question, you will have 20 seconds to prepare your response and 60 seconds to speak.

Now listen to a conversation between a man and a woman.

The speakers discuss two possible solutions to a problem. Describe the problem. Then state which of the two solutions you prefer and why.

Preparation time: 20 seconds

Response time: 60 seconds

Tracks 526–528 **Task 6**

You will now listen to part of a lecture. You will then be asked a question about it. After you hear the question, you will have 20 seconds to prepare your response and 60 seconds to speak.

Now listen to part of a lecture in a finance class.

Using points and examples from the talk, say what an income statement is and what information it includes.

Preparation time: 20 seconds

Response time: 60 seconds

Writing Section Directions

The Writing section measures your ability to use writing to communicate in an academic environment. The Writing section will take just under one hour. This includes time for reading and listening to information that you will write about, as well as for writing your responses.

In Task 1, you will read a passage and then listen to a lecture on the same topic. You may take notes while you read and listen. You will then have 20 minutes to write your response. Your response will be scored from 0–5 based on the quality of your writing, and on how accurately and completely you summarize or paraphrase the relationship between the passage and the lecture. Typically, an effective response will have between 150 and 225 words and should **not** describe your personal opinion about the topic.

In Task 2, you will be asked a question about a topic of general interest. You will have 30 minutes to write a response based on your experience and opinions. Your response will be scored from 0–5 based on the quality of your writing and on how well you have developed and organized your ideas. Typically, an effective response will have at least 300 words.

You may now begin the Writing section by looking at the next page.

Tracks 529–531 **Task 1**

Now look at the passage below. You have three minutes to read the passage.

> In recent years, more and more students have been taking online courses. According to a recent report, which has tracked online learning at the university level since 2002, the rate of students in the US taking at least one online course has continued to grow at a much faster rate than regular university enrollment. In 2002, for example, 1.6 million students were taking at least one online course; but recent statistics that I've seen indicate that 5 million are studying online. That translates to a 21 percent rate of growth in online education. In contrast, total enrollment in university has grown at a rate of only 2.2 percent.
>
> What has spurred this remarkable growth? There are a number of factors, but probably the most important is financial. The cost of tuition and fees has grown drastically, at a much higher rate than general inflation. For example, face-to-face instruction at one four-year private college averages about $24,000 a year. This same university offers a mostly online degree program for about $15,000. Taking an online course also removes the cost of room and board and other assorted fees associated with attending school.
>
> Another important factor is flexibility. Students can take classes whenever they want and wherever they want. If they like, they can take classes while wearing their pajamas! And if they have a job, they can arrange their class schedule around their working hours, and get a top-quality education while continuing to earn a salary.

Now listen to a lecture on the topic you just read about.

Now answer the question. You have 20 minutes to complete your response.

Summarize the points made in the lecture, explaining how they challenge the points made in the reading passage.

Track 532 **Task 2**

Answer the question. You have 30 minutes to complete your response.

> Many people say that they would like to travel back in time to experience what life in the past was like and to witness great events. Others would like to travel into the future if they could. If it were possible to travel back or forward in time, which would you prefer to do? Why? Use specific reasons and details to explain your decision.

TACTICS FOR THE TOEFL iBT® TEST

A strategic new approach to achieving TOEFL success

Christien Lee

OXFORD

UNIVERSITY PRESS

OXFORD
UNIVERSITY PRESS

Oxford University Press is a department of the University of Oxford.
It furthers the University's objective of excellence in research, scholarship,
and education by publishing worldwide. Oxford is a registered trade mark
of Oxford University Press in the UK and in certain other countries.

Published in Canada by
Oxford University Press
8 Sampson Mews, Suite 204,
Don Mills, Ontario M3C 0H5 Canada

www.oupcanada.com

978-0-19-902019-5

Oxford University Press is committed to our environment.
This book is printed on Forest Stewardship Council® certified paper
and comes from responsible sources.

MIX
Paper from
responsible sources
FSC® C103567

Printed and bound in Canada

1 2 3 4 — 18 17 16 15

Note: All questions on the test are worth one point except questions 12 and 25. For question 12, get zero points for one correct answer, 1 point for choosing two correct answers, and 2 points if all three answers are correct. For question 25, get zero points for one or two correct answers, 1 point for choosing three correct answers, 2 points for four correct answers, and 3 points if all five answers are correct.

1. A
2. B
3. B
4. D
5. C
6. A
7. D
8. A
9. B
10. C
11. D
12. B C E (in any order)
13. D
14. B
15. B
16. A
17. C
18. D
19. C
20. B
21. C
22. A
23. A
24. C
25. Copyright or Trademarks: A D (in any order)
Patents: C E F (in any order)

UNIT 1 | READING • Factual Information Questions and Negative Factual Information Questions

Exercise B1 (p. 20)
1. organisms
2. species
3. mammal
4. reptiles
5. remains
6. fossil
7. prehistoric
8. dinosaurs

Exercise C1 (p. 21)
1. B
2. A

Exercise C2 (p. 21)
1. 2B
2. 1A 1D 2C
3. 1C 2D

Exercise D1 (p. 22)
1. B 2. C 3. D
4. E 5. F 6. A

Exercise D2 (p. 22)
1. The highlighted phrases are key phrases because:
- "paragraph 2" tells you the paragraph in which you will find the answer.
- "high prices" is a noun phrase that refers to a specific thing.
- "auction houses" is a noun phrase that refers to a specific thing.
- "rare" is an adjective with a specific meaning.
- "usually" is an adverb with a specific meaning.
- "expensive" is an adjective with a specific meaning.
- "increasingly" is an adverb with a specific meaning.
- "fashionable" is an adjective with a specific meaning.
- "works of art" is a noun phrase that refers to a specific thing.
- "more buyers" is a noun phrase that refers to a specific thing.
- "these days" is an adverb with a specific meaning.
- "100 years ago" is a time reference.
- "often" is an adverb with a specific meaning.
- "valuable" is an adjective with a specific meaning.
- "marble" is a specific term.
2. The words "dinosaur" and "fossils" are not highlighted as key phrases because they are likely to be used many times in the passage.

Exercise D3 (p. 23)
1. large size / sauropod / relatively few / natural predators / hollow bones / lakes and rivers / supported their weight / little of their energy / children

Exercise E1 (p. 23)
The two correct answers to the question are A and B. The completed table looks like this:
- Answer B
- Answer A
- Answer D
- Answer C

Exercise E2 (pp. 23–24)
1. A
   Answer A is correct because it paraphrases or simplifies an idea in the passage.
   Answer B is incorrect because it looks similar to the passage, but contradicts a point or detail.
2. B
   Answer A is incorrect because it describes a detail that is not mentioned in the passage.
   Answer B is correct because it paraphrases or simplifies an idea in the passage.
3. B
   Answer A is incorrect because it looks similar to the passage, but contradicts a point or detail.
   Answer B is correct because it paraphrases or simplifies an idea in the passage.
4. A
   Answer A is correct because it paraphrases or simplifies an idea in the passage.
   Answer B is incorrect because it looks similar to the passage, but contradicts a point or detail.

Exercise E3 (p. 24)
C

Exercise E4 (p. 24)
1. D
2. D

Exercise F1 (p. 25)
1. C
2. B

Exercise F2 (p. 25)
1. 2B
2. 1C

Exercise G1 (p. 26)
1. Contradict
2. Restate
3. Contradict
4. Not mentioned
5. Restate
6. Not mentioned

Exercise H1 (pp. 26–29)
1. D 2. C 3. A
4. D 5. B 6. B
7. C 8. A 9. D
10. B

UNIT 2 | READING • Vocabulary Questions

Exercise B1 (p. 30)
1. D 2. A 3. E
4. H 5. F 6. G
7. B 8. C

Exercise C1 (p. 31)
1. B
2. D

Exercise C2 (p. 31)
1. 1A 1D 2A
2. 2C
3. 1C 2B

Exercise D1 (p. 32)
1. A 2. B
3. B 4. A

Exercise D2 (p. 32)
- As seen in passage 4 in Exercise D1, the highlighted word may be contrasted with other words or phrases.
- As seen in passage 2, the context might include a word or phrase that is a synonym of the highlighted word.
- As seen in passage 3, an example in the context might make the meaning of the highlighted word clear.
- As seen in passage 1, the context may include other words that suggest the meaning of the highlighted word.

Exercise D3 (p. 33)
1. C. Answers will vary. Suggested answers: huge, enormous, or very large
2. A
3. C. Answers will vary. Suggested answers: living or residing
4. B

Exercise D4 (p. 33)
1. G   2. C   3. B
4. J   5. E   6. I
7. A   8. K   9. H
10. D
Answers F and L do not match any of the blanks.

Exercise D5 (p. 33)
In Exercise D3, the following words and phrases are helpful in answering the questions.
1. doubled the size / the largest territorial gain
2. Constitution / a vote by members of the House of Representatives
3. humans / founding date / settlements
4. archeological data suggest

In Exercise D4, the following words and phrases are helpful in answering the questions.
1. providing heat / cooking food
2. dangerous

3. and towns / urban cultures
4. towns / 5 million people
5. written
6. spanned the sixth to thirteenth centuries
7. War / fought / army
8. War / fought / army
9. Netherlands/ the world
10. crisis / Depression

Exercise E1 (p. 34)
1. two/twice
2. together/with
3. opposite/against
4. before
5. again/back
6. work
7. remember
8. join/bind
9. new
10. carry

Exercise E2 (p. 34)
Answers will vary.

Exercise E3 (pp. 34–35)
1. renovate
2. autonomy
3. international
4. precede
5. collaborate

Exercise E4 (p. 35)
1. Some useful number prefixes include *un(i)-*, which means "one," *tri-*, which means "three," *quadr-* or *quart-*, which means "four," *dec(a)-*, which means "ten," *cent-*, which means "hundred," and *kilo-*, which means "thousand."
2. Some common negative prefixes include *a(n)* or *ab-* as in "apolitical" or "abnormal," *anti-* as in "antibiotic," *de-* as in "destroy," *dis-* as in "disagree," *in-* (or *il-, im-,* or *ir-*) as in "incorrect," *mal-* as in "malfunction," *non-* as in "nonstop," and *un-* as in

"unscientific." Note that not every word that begins with one of these prefixes, especially *a-, de-, dis-,* and *in-,* has a negative meaning.
3. Answers will vary.

Exercise E5 (p. 35)
1. B: context clue from the passage: dictating; word clue: *mem*
2. B: context clues from the passage: across / distance
3. C: context clues from the passage: began / ended after
4. C: context clue from the passage: done by hand; word clue: *labor*
5. C: context clue from the passage: by at least 300 years; word clue: *pre*

Exercise F1 (pp. 36–37)
1. C   2. B   3. D
4. B   5. C   6. B
7. A   8. B

UNIT 3 | READING • Rhetorical Purpose Questions

Exercise B1 (p. 38)
1. currents
2. algae
3. marine
4. shore
5. seabed
6. tide
7. shallow
8. submarine

Exercise C1 (p. 39)
1. C
2. D

Exercise C2 (p. 39)
• Answer 1B is wrong because it describes a function that does not match the passage.
• Answer 1D is wrong because it describes a purpose that is contradicted by the passage.
• Answer 2A is wrong because it describes a function that does not match the passage.
• Answer 2B is wrong because it describes a purpose that is contradicted by the passage.
• Answer 2C is wrong because it describes a function that matches a different part of the passage than the question asks about.

Exercise D1 (p. 40)
1. F   2. D   3. C
4. A   5. B   6. E

Exercise D2 (p. 40)
1. describe a new concept
2. introduce an example
3. argue against an idea
4. say how two things differ

Exercise D3 (p. 41)
The following words and phrases in the passages are helpful:
1. are known as
2. such as those found on …
3. however / although it was rare / in fact still exist
4. but / differ / compared with / smaller and stouter / instead of
5. primary source / most important

Exercise D4 (p. 41)
1. C
2. A
3. B
4. E
5. F
Not used: D

Exercise D5 (p. 41)
1. A
2. B

Exercise E1 (p. 42)
• Answers that paraphrase the passage: A E G
• Answers that contradict the passage: B C H
• Answers that are not mentioned in the passage: D F

Exercise E2 (p. 43)
The answers in E1 that contradict the passage can be rewritten as follows:
• B. Scientists did not expect to find life at the bottom of the Mariana Trench.
• C. Populations of red and blue king crabs have remained low for many years.
• H. Male swordfish are not as large as females.

Exercise E3 (p. 43)
1. B
2. A
3. A
4. C Answers will vary. Suggested answer: To give an example of a condition that coral polyps need
5. C Answers will vary. Suggested answer: To describe conditions that cause coral reefs to die

Exercise E4 (p. 43)
The following words are helpful:
1. sleep in water / one hemisphere … sleeps / sleeping seals etc.
2. a chemical / acetylcholine etc.
3. calcium carbonate exoskeleton
4. warm but not too warm / 20 and 29 degrees
5. and 6.10%… already dead / 60% more at risk etc.

Exercise F1 (pp. 44–45)
1. B   2. D   3. B
4. C   5. C   6. A

UNIT 4 | READING • Inference Questions

Exercise A1 (p. 46)
1. Answers will vary.
2. Answers will vary.

Exercise B1 (p. 46)
1. H   2. A   3. E
4. F   5. B   6. G
7. C   8. D

Exercise C1 (p. 47)
1. D
2. B

Exercise C2 (p. 47)
1. 1A 2D
2. 1B 1C 2A 2C

Exercise D1 (p. 48)
• The phrase "paragraph 4" matches description B.
• The phrase "effects of wildfires" matches description C.
• The word "inferred" matches description A.

Exercise D2 (p. 48)
1. The word "inferred" matches description A from Exercise D1, the phrase "paragraph 2" matches description B, and the phrase "food webs" matches description C.
2. "Imply" matches description A, "paragraph 3" matches description B, and "keystone species model" matches description C.

3. "Concluded" matches description A, "paragraph 4" matches description B, and "recent actions of conservationists" matches description C.
4. "Suggest" matches description A, and "European oak trees" and "moderate climate change" both match description C.

Exercise D3 (p. 48)
1. The word "imply" matches description A from Exercise D1, the phrase "paragraph 1" matches description B, and the word "biodiversity" matches description C.
2. "Suggest" matches description A, and "earthworms" and "soil fertility" both match description C.
3. "Understood" matches description A, and "biotic and abiotic environments" matches description C.
4. "Inferred" matches description A, "paragraph 3" matches description B, and "honeybees" and "modern agriculture" both match description C.

Exercise D4 (p. 48)
1. Key phrases: suggest / effects of natural disturbances / wildfires. The first and second sentences in the passage give information related to the key phrases.
2. Key phrases: concluded / fire-dependent and fire-adapted organisms / differ. The third and fourth sentences in the passage give information related to the key phrases.
3. Key phrases: is implied / Our Synthetic Environment. The first sentence in the passage gives information related to the key phrases.
4. Key phrases: be inferred / loss of rainforests. The second and third sentences in the passage give information related to the key phrases.

Exercise D5 (p. 49)
1. B. Key phrases in the question: imply / start of the nineteenth century. The first sentence of the passage gives information related to the key phrases.
2. A. Key phrases in the question: concluded / feeding habits. The third and fourth sentences of the passage give information related to the key phrases.

3. B. Key phrases in the question: suggest/ hunting. The fifth and sixth sentences of the passage give information related to the key phrases.
4. A. Key phrases in the question: inferred / extinction. The tenth and eleventh sentences of the passage give information related to the key phrases.
(Note that "Passenger Pigeons" is not a useful key phrase because it occurs too often in the passage.)

Exercise E1 (p. 49)
1. B
2. A

Exercise E2 (p. 50)
1. B   2. B
3. A   4. A

Exercise E3 (p. 50)
1. Implied
2. Stated directly
3. Implied
4. Not mentioned

Exercise E4 (p. 51)
1. B D
2. A D

Exercise F1 (pp. 51–53)
1. C   2. A   3. A
4. D   5. C   6. C
7. A   8. B C

UNIT 5 | READING • Sentence Simplification Questions

Exercise B1 (p. 54)
1. F   2. C   3. G
4. A   5. H   6. E
7. B   8. D

Exercise C1 (p. 55)
1. C
2. A

Exercise C2 (p. 56)
• These answer choices change some essential information from the highlighted sentence: 1A 1B 1D 2C
• These answer choices leave out some essential information from the highlighted sentence: 2B 2D

Exercise D1 (p. 56)
1B   2A
3A   4B
5B

Exercise D2 (p. 57)
1. C   2. A   3. B
4. H   5. G   6. E

Exercise D3 (p. 57)
The correct order of the sentences is: D C A F E. (Sentence B does not belong in the restated paragraph.)

Exercise E1 (p. 58)
1. C   2. D   3. E
4. B   5. A

Exercise E2 (p. 58)
1. explains a cause, reason, or result; also describes a problem with something
2. describes all or part of a process
3. compares or contrasts two ideas
4. describes a problem with something
5. summarizes some information or an idea

Exercise E3 (p. 58)
1. B
2. A

Exercise F1 (p. 59)
• Sentence 1B changes essential information in sentence 1A.
• Sentence 2B changes the function of sentence 2A.
• Sentence 3B leaves out essential information in sentence 3A.
• Sentence 4B changes essential information in sentence 4A.

Exercise G1 (pp. 59–61)
1. C   2. B   3. A
4. D   5. D   6. C

UNIT 6 | READING • Insert Text Questions and Reference Questions

Exercise B1 (p. 62)
1. hard, outer layer
2. organisms that can cause damage
3. reproductive material
4. dead organisms, small pieces of rock, and mud
5. anchor the plant
6. substances that all organisms
7. similar form and function
8. the sun's energy into sugars

Exercise C1 (p. 63)
1. B

Exercise C2 (p. 63)
1. A / C / D

Exercise D1 (p. 64)
1. B
2. Suggested answers:
- Adding a detail or example – middle
- Comparing or contrasting ideas – middle / end
- Defining a term or concept – beginning
- Expressing a conclusion – end
- Introducing a topic – beginning

Exercise D2 (p. 64)
1. Answers will vary. Suggested answers: emphasize something / contradict some information / express an opinion / describe a problem
2. Answers will vary. Suggested answers:
- emphasize something – any position is possible, but in the middle or near the end of a paragraph are more common
- contradict some information – any position is possible, but in the middle or near the end of a paragraph are more common

- express an opinion – any position is possible, but near the start or in the middle of a paragraph are more common
- describe a problem – any position is possible, but near the start or in the middle of a paragraph are more common

Exercise D3 (p. 64)
1. D   2. A   3. B
4. E   5. C

Exercise D4 (p. 64)
The sentences should be placed in the following order to make a logically-organized paragraph:
- Various types of disease-causing pathogens affect plants, including fungi, parasites, viruses, and bacteria.
- Plant pathology is the name given to the study of diseases that are caused by such organisms.
- Rice ragged stunt virus and bacterial leaf blight, for instance, are both pathogens that can affect rice crops.
- Infections like these can affect the economy, so it can be seen that plant pathology is an important field of study.
- Many insects and other pests also affect the health of plants, but plant pathologists do not study these factors.

Exercise E1 (p. 65)
- The highlighted phrase "the former" refers to "angiosperms" in the passage.
- The highlighted phrase "the latter" refers to "gymnosperms" in the passage.

- The highlighted phrase "many of which" refers to "250,000 species (of angiosperms)" in the passage.
- The highlighted phrase "These" refers to "species (that do not bear seeds)" in the passage.
- The highlighted phrase "They" refers to "spores, (which are capsules of genetic information with a protective coating)" in the passage.
- The highlighted phrase "one" refers to "a different location" in the passage.

Exercise E2 (p. 65)
1. "Them" and "their"
2. "thin, needle-like leaves"
3. "They"
4. "Broader" and "flatter"
5. No. The word "They" that begins sentence 6 refers to "Broadleaf trees" in sentence 5.

Exercise E3 (p. 65)
A environment
B light
C forest
D soil
E temperature
F species
G oxygen
H atmosphere

Exercise F1 (p. 66)
1. C   2. B
3. B   4. A

Exercise F2 (p. 66)
- Adds details about a topic *before* the topic has been introduced or defined: 1A 2A 3A
- Introduces or defines a topic *after* details about that topic have been mentioned: 2C 3C 4B 4C

- Separates two sentences that are coherent and logically related: 1B 4B

Exercise G1 (p. 67)
1. C
2. B

Exercise G2 (p. 67)
1. Not helpful
2. Not helpful
3. Helpful
4. Helpful
5. Not helpful
6. Not helpful
7. Not helpful
8. Helpful

Exercise H1 (p. 68)
1. These words refer to or give an example of "fungi": mushrooms / yeasts / molds / they / their
2. These words refer to or give an example of "foods": fruits / they / these items / avocados / eggplants / cucumbers / tomatoes / olives
3. These words refer to or give an example of "plant": bamboo / the largest member / it / many species / its / a construction material / a food or medicine / a raw material
4. These words refer to or give an example of "story": title / fictional / tale / describes

Exercise H2 (pp. 68–69)
1. C
2. D acacias
3. D seed ferns
4. B

Exercise I1 (pp. 69–71)
1. D   2. D   3. D
4. A   5. A   6. C
7. C   8. C   9. F
10. B

UNIT 7 | READING • Fill in a Table and Prose Summary Questions

Exercise B1 (p. 72)
1. F   2. D   3. A
4. G   5. H   6. B
7. E   8. C

Exercise C1 (p. 73)
Moment Magnitude Scale:
A B (in any order)
Volcanic Explosivity Index: F
Both Moment Magnitude Scale and Volcanic Explosivity Index:
D E (in any order)
(Answer C is not used.)

Exercise D1 (p. 74)
1. A C
2. The order of the strategies is: B D E A C

Exercise D2 (p. 74)
1. Mentioned
2. Mentioned
3. Not mentioned
4. Not mentioned

Exercise D3 (p. 75)
1. Restates
2. Contradicts – Drizzle is the most common form of precipitation.
3. Contradicts – Precipitation in the form of rain constitutes a significant part of the water cycle.
4. Restates

Exercise D4 (p. 75)
1. D
2. A

Exercise D5 (p. 76)
Mafic and ultramafic lavas:
A F (in any order)
Felsic or intermediate lavas:
D E G (in any order)

Exercise E1 (p. 77)
C E F (in any order)

Exercise E2 (p. 77)
1. A
2. D
3. B

Exercise F1 (p. 78)
Step 1 – C
Step 2 – B
Step 3 – A

Exercise F2 (p. 78)
- Answers that restate information in the passage: A E (in any order)

- Answers that contradict information in the passage: B C (in any order)

Exercise F3 (p. 79)
1. Major
2. Minor
3. Major
4. Major
5. Minor

6. Major
7. Minor
8. Minor

Exercise G1 (pp. 79–83)
1. Fjords: D F (in any order)
   Fjards: C
   Fjords and Fjards: A E (in any order)
2. A C F (in any order)

3. Evidence that Wegener Initially Presented: C D G (in any order)
   Evidence that Persuaded Other Scientists: B F (in any order)
4. A B F (in any order)

READING REVIEW TEST (pp. 84–90)

Note: All questions on the test are worth one point except questions 12 and 25. For question 12, get zero points for one or two correct answers, 1 point for choosing three correct answers, 2 points for four correct answers, and 3 points if all five answers are correct. For question 25, get zero points for one correct answer, 1 point for choosing two correct answers, and 2 points if all three answers are correct.

1. C
2. D
3. A
4. B
5. A
6. D
7. A
8. D

9. B
10. C
11. D
12. Macroparasites: C E (in any order)
    Microparasites: B F (in any order)
    Parasitoids: D

13. C
14. A
15. B
16. C
17. A C
18. C
19. B
20. D

21. D
22. A
23. D
24. C
25. C D F (in any order)

LISTENING DIAGNOSTIC TEST (pp. 100–103)

1. C
2. A
3. D
4. B C
5. B
6. B
7.
- Feelings of happiness – Yes
- Improved brain activity – No
- Increased levels of doubt – No

- Reduced sensitivity to pain – Yes
8. A
9. C
10. A D
11. A
12. C
13. B
14. D
15. B D

16. C
17. D
18.
- First – Local people heard the sounds of subterranean earthquakes.
- Second – The eruption caused a fissure to form in a farmer's field.
- Third – Volcanic material

formed a cone approximately 50 meters tall.
- Fourth – Very high clouds of ash and smoke formed in the sky.
19. B
20. A
21. C
22. A

UNIT 8 | LISTENING • Gist-Content and Gist-Purpose Questions

Exercise A1 (p. 104)
Answers will vary.

Exercise B1 (p. 104)
1. assignment / term paper
2. due date
3. extension / incomplete
4. grade point average
5. office hours
6. research

Exercise C1 (p. 105)
1. B
2. The following words in the script are helpful for answering Q1:
- "Could I check a couple of things about the assignment you set for Biology 208?"
- "The paper should be 1,000 words and you want it handed in next Friday, right?"

Exercise C2 (p. 105)
1. C
2. D
3. A

Exercise D1 (p. 106)
A. 4   B. 1   C. 5
D. 6   E. 2   F. 3

Exercise D2 (p. 106)
1. A   2. A   3. B
4. A   5. B   6. A

Exercise E1 (pp. 106–107)
1. C
2. A

Exercise E2 (p. 107)
1. The speakers discuss
- an assignment that the professor gave – multiple times
- the due date of the assignment – multiple times
- a recommended article – twice
- an extension of the assignment's deadline – multiple times
- a failing grade for the assignment – once

- a visit to the Study Skills Center – once
2. C

Exercise F1 (p. 107)
1A unlikely
1B likely
1C likely
1D unlikely
2A likely
2B unlikely
2C unlikely
2D likely

Exercise F2 (p. 108)
- Answer A from Q1 in Exercise F1 matches reason 2.
- Answer D from Q1 matches reason 1.
- Answer B from Q2 matches reason 3.
- Answer C from Q2 matches reason 4.

Exercise G1 (p. 108)
1. D
2. B

Exercise G2 (p. 109)
1. F   2. B   3. E
4. A   5. C   6. D

Exercise G3 (p. 109)
1. B
2. A

Exercise H1 (p. 109)
1. molecule
2. organs
3. cells
4. element
5. nucleus
6. genetic
7. reproduction
8. offspring

Exercise I1 (pp. 110–111)
1. B   2. C   3. D
4. C   5. A   6. D

UNIT 9 | LISTENING • Detail Questions

Exercise B1 (p. 112)
1. E   2. G   3. D
4. A   5. B   6. C
7. F   8. H

Exercise C1 (p. 113)
1. B C E

Exercise C2 (p. 113)
- The phrase "letters from his brother" in answer A is a clue that this answer is wrong. The reason is that the lecture says Van Gogh sent letters to his brother, not received letters from him.
- The word "famous" in answer D is a clue because the lecture talks about "famous works" by Van Gogh, but does not say that Van Gogh believed he would become famous.
- The phrase "rarely visible" in answer F is a clue because the passage says a particular constellation is only visible to the north, not that the night sky to the north is rarely visible.

Exercise D1 (p. 114)
- A matches "$400 million wrong = actually $10 billion+"
- B matches "produces amazing images of planets + stars"
- C matches "will play in final of softball tournament" and "team traveling 2 days before deadline"
- D matches "delayed," "shuttle disaster," and "mirror had wrong shape"
- E matches "space telescope → orbiting Earth"
- F matches "Assignment set 2 weeks ago"

Exercise D2 (p. 114)
1. D   2. B C
3. A D   4. B

Exercise E1 (p. 115)
1. The following expressions match each category:

- Cause or Effect: E as a result of … / F due to …
- Contrast: A However, … / H Instead of …
- Similarity: C In the same way, … / G A related point …
- Time: B Until finally … / D To begin, …
2. Answers will vary.
3. Answers will vary.

Exercise E2 (p. 115)
1. Similarity
2. Cause/effect
3. Time
4. Contrast

Exercise F1 (p. 115)
1. A D
2. A B

Exercise G1 (p. 116)
1. Point A is a major point, B is a minor point.
2. Point A is a major point, B is a minor point.
3. Both points are major points.
4. Both points are minor points.

Exercise H1 (pp. 116–117)
1. C   2. C
3. A D   4. B

Exercise H2 (p. 117)
1. Paraphrase. The woman actually says "looks redder."
2. Repeat.
3. Repeat.
4. Paraphrase. The man actually says "As the cooling continues, the remnant star will shrink."
5. Repeat.

Exercise I1 (p. 117)
1. D   2. G   3. C
4. A   5. E   6. F
7. H   8. B

Exercise J1 (pp. 118–119)
1. C   2. B C   3. B D
4. C   5. A E   6. D
7. C   8. B C

UNIT 10 | LISTENING • Understanding the Function of What Is Said Questions

Exercise B1 (p. 120)
1. bursar
2. fees
3. financial aid
4. living expenses
5. student loan
6. scholarship
7. tuition
8. work-study program

Exercise C1 (p. 121)
1. D
2. B

Exercise D1 (p. 122)
1. E   2. D   3. A
4. B   5. C   6. F

Exercise D2 (p. 122)
1. give an example – such as
2. give a reason – the reason is that
3. clarify information – in other words
4. compare or contrast – on the other hand
5. define something – this is called
6. give some advice – you should consider

Exercise D3 (p. 122)
- Excerpt 1. give an example – for instance

- Excerpt 2. give a reason – since
- Excerpt 3. clarify information – my point here is that
- Excerpt 4. compare or contrast – unlike
- Excerpt 5. define something – we call these
- Excerpt 6. give some advice – I think you would (find it useful)

Exercise D4 (p. 122)
Answers will vary. Suggested answers:
- give an example – including
- give a reason – this is because
- clarify information – let me put that another way
- compare or contrast – in contrast
- define something – this can be defined as
- give some advice – if I were you, I would

Exercise E1 (p. 122)
1. clarify information / give a reason / give some advice
2. compare or contrast / give an example / clarify information

3. give an example / clarify information / give a reason
4. compare or contrast / give an example / give a reason

Exercise E2 (p. 123)
1A unlikely
1B likely
1C likely
2A unlikely
2B likely
2C unlikely
3A likely
3B likely
3C unlikely
4A unlikely
4B unlikely
4C likely

Exercise E3 (p. 123)
The correct answers to questions 1–4 in exercise E2 are:
1. B   2. B
3. A   4. C

Exercise F1 (p. 123)
1. B   2. A
3. B   4. A

Exercises F2 and F3 (p. 124)
1. to clarify information
2. to give an example
3. to compare two things
4. to define something

Exercise G1 (p. 124)
1A incorrect
1B correct
1C incorrect
2A correct
2B incorrect
2C incorrect
3A correct
3B incorrect
3C incorrect
4A incorrect
4B correct
4C incorrect

Exercise G2 (pp. 124–125)
1. C
2. A
3. A

Exercise H1 (p. 125)
1. pigments
2. charcoal
3. Renaissance
4. portrait
5. canvas
6. landscape
7. foreground
8. movement

Exercise I1 (pp. 125–127)
1. C   2. B   3. C
4. A   5. D   6. B

UNIT 11 | LISTENING • Understanding the Speaker's Attitude Questions

Exercise A1 (p. 128)
Answers will vary.

Exercise A2 (p. 128)
Answers will vary.

Exercise B1 (pp. 128–129)
1. major
2. minor
3. core classes
4. elective
5. prerequisite
6. Seminars
7. credits
8. audit

Exercise C1 (p. 129)
1. A
2. C

Exercise D1 (p. 130)
- Modern poetry seminar sounds good – positive
- Not taken prerequisite class – negative
- Researched modern poetry in high school – positive
- Not possible to take seminar without prerequisite – negative

- But woman can audit class if she wants – positive
- But good idea → thanks – positive

Exercise D2 (p. 130)
1. Negative
2. Positive
3. Negative
4. Negative

Exercise D3 (p. 130)
1. A   2. B
3. A   4. B

Exercise E1 (p. 131)
1. It seems to me that … – Speaker 4
2. For me, … – Speaker 6
3. My view is that … – Speaker 2
4. From my point of view, … – Speaker 5
5. My preference is for … – Speaker 1
6. In my experience, … – Speaker 4
7. I'd say that … – Speaker 3
8. I'm convinced that … – Speaker 6

Exercise E2 (p. 131)
Answers will vary. Suggested answers: I believe that … / In my opinion, … / To my way of thinking, … / I prefer … / I would rather …

Exercise E3 (p. 131)
1. A   2. C   3. A
4. A   5. B

Exercise F1 (p. 132)
1. B C

Exercise F2 (p. 132)
1. B D
The following phrases are helpful in choosing the answers: "You'll see complicated lists of additional characteristics in some of the articles on your reading list, but the five conventions are the core of what defines an epic." / "my focus is on Greek and Latin epics, so you won't be able to apply all of these ideas to epics in other languages"

Exercise F3 (p. 132)
1. A C   2. B C

Exercise G1 (p. 133)
1.
- It is emotionally powerful – Professor
- It is shocking and non-poetic – Reviewers
- It causes feelings of discomfort – Student

2.
- Jules Verne was a serious writer worthy of academic study – European academics
- The works of Jules Verne were popular, but not high quality – Contemporary critics
- Verne's writing style was new, but influenced other writers – Professor

Exercise H1 (p. 133)
1. A   2. D   3. F
4. E   5. G   6. H
7. C   8. B

Exercise I1 (pp. 134–135)
1. A   2. B   3. B
4. A   5. D   6. C D

UNIT 12 | LISTENING • Understanding Organization Questions

Exercise A1 (p. 136)
1. B   2. E   3. A
4. C   5. D

Exercise B1 (p. 136)
1. has not yet earned a degree.
2. is in his or her first year of study.
3. is in his or her second year of study.
4. is in his or her third year of study.
5. is in his or her fourth year of study.
6. a graduate-level degree.
7. enrolled at one college but is now studying at a different institution.
8. visiting from another college temporarily.

Exercise C1 (p. 137)
1. B   2. B

Exercise D1 (p. 138)
1. D   2. A   3. B
4. E   5. C

Exercise D2 (p. 138)
1. Compares two things
2. Gives an example
3. Makes a digression
4. Makes a digression
5. Gives an example

Exercise D3 (p. 138)
1. B   2. A

Exercise D4 (p. 139)
1. B   2. B   3. B
4. C   5. A   6. A C
7. B   8. A

Exercise D5 (p. 139)
1. The following words and phrases in the answers to Exercise D4 repeat what a speaker says:
- In 1, answer A, the words "make a decision" and "to specialize in" repeat what the woman says.
- In 2, answer A, the words "specialize in industrial sociology" repeat what the woman says.
- In 4, answer B, the words "Guns, Germs, and Steel" repeat what the man says.
- In 5, answers A and B, the words "participant observation" repeat what the woman says.
- In 6, answer B, the words "associated with anthropology" repeat what the woman says.
- In 7, answer B, the words "types of families" repeat what the man says.

2. In general, wrong answers more often repeat phrases that a speaker says. The reason is that answers which repeat a phrase from the conversation or lecture are good distractors. These are answer choices that are wrong but which look or sound like they might be the right answer.

Exercise E1 (p. 140)
1. D   2. B   3. E
4. A   5. C

Exercise E2 (p. 140)
1. C   2. B

Exercise E3 (p. 141)
1. Contrast
2. Cause and effect
3. Topical
4. Problem and solution
5. Chronological

Exercise E4 (p. 141)
1. Problem and solution
2. "bias and other problems" / "one solution"
3. Topical
4. "study social networks at three levels" / "we'll explore each level in more detail" / "talk about different kinds of social networks"

5. Cause and effect
6. "a number of effects on society" / "a causal link between" / "the areas most affected by"
7. Contrast
8. "Positivism is an important concept in sociology, but" / "anti-positivists argue that" / "suitable for studying the natural world but not for studying social phenomena"
9. Chronological
10. "have existed since" / "first launched in the late 1960s" / "existed in the 1970s" / "in the early 1990s" / "remains the dominant platform for such communities today"

Exercise F1 (p. 141)
1. Bias
2. individual
3. Trends
4. methods
5. interaction
6. questionnaires
7. Behavior
8. observer

Exercise G1 (pp. 142–143)
1. D   2. B   3. C
4. A   5. B   6. A

UNIT 13 | LISTENING • Connecting Content Questions

Exercise A1 (p. 144)
1. Answers will vary. Suggested answers: ambitious, charismatic, devious, diplomatic, evasive, industrious, optimistic, trustworthy.

Exercise B1 (p. 144)
1. dormitory
2. coeducational
3. Resident advisors
4. off-campus housing
5. accommodation
6. Housing Office
7. meal plan
8. roommate

Exercise C1 (p. 145)
1.
- Each member serves a six-year term and may be re-elected – Upper
- Different states have different numbers of members – Lower
- The usual name is the House of Representatives – Lower

2.
- The number of senators per state does not depend on population – Yes
- Senators meet in the south wing of the United States Capitol – No
- There are 435 members in total – No

3.
- First – The United States Congress met in locations including Philadelphia and New York.
- Second – Government officials began meeting in the Capitol building before construction was complete.
- Third – The Capitol building was used for government functions as well as church services.
- Fourth – A competition was held to encourage designs for expansions to the Capitol building.

Exercise C2 (p. 145)
- Q1 in Exercise C1 is an example of the second type of Connecting Content question.
- Q2 is an example of the first type of Connecting Content question.
- Q3 is an example of the third type of Connecting Content question.

Exercise D1 (p. 146)
1. transfer to a different dorm
2. transfer into a shared apartment
3. move out of university accommodation

Exercise D2 (pp. 146–147)
1.
- Give a presentation – No
- Produce a case study – Yes
- Write a term paper – Yes

2.
- Block plan – Yes
- Limited plan – No
- Value plan – Yes

3.
- Bilateral agreements – Yes
- Multilateral agreements – Yes
- Trilateral agreements – No
- Unilateral agreements – Yes

4.
- Authoritarianism – Yes
- Democracy – Yes
- Federalism – No
- Monarchy – Yes

Exercise E1 (p. 147)
- Less than one week – Move out of university accommodation
- From one to two weeks – Transfer to a different dormitory
- More than four weeks – Transfer into an on-campus apartment

Exercise E2 (pp. 147–148)
1.
- Should be less than 1,000 words – Term paper
- Must be submitted by week six of the course – Term paper
- Can be delivered in the form of a presentation – Case study

2.
- Students can eat in any restaurant on campus – Value plan
- Students are limited to 10 meals per week – Block plan
- Students can eat as much as they like per meal – Block plan

3.
- Only one nation benefits from the agreement – Unilateral
- All signing nations benefit from the agreement – Bilateral / Multilateral
- The agreement applies only to the export of goods – Unilateral
- The agreement applies both to imports and exports – Bilateral / Multilateral

4.
- Some groups may have fewer rights than others – Democracy
- The government holds all of the power – Authoritarianism
- Individual people have power to change government – Democracy
- The ruler has power as a result of his or her parents – Monarchy

Exercise F1 (p. 148)
1.
- He thinks some of the professor's colleagues are public law experts – No
- He really enjoyed taking the professor's class last year – Yes
- His end-of-term paper for the professor's class was very good – No
- His family might be unhappy if he chose to study political science – Yes

2.
- Citizens generally find plurality voting systems harder to understand than other systems – No
- One criticism of plurality voting is that the winning party may not have majority support – Yes
- With plurality voting, some citizens may feel that a vote for a minority party is a wasted vote – Yes
- Roughly 40 percent of countries have adopted a proportional representation voting system – No
- Countries with a proportional representation system tend to have few political parties – No

Exercise F2 (p. 149)
1. Q1, first answer / Q1, third answer
2. Q2, first answer / Q2, fifth answer
3. Q1, fifth answer / Q2, fourth answer

Exercise G1 (p. 149)
- First – Unsuccessful demonstrations for women's suffrage were held.
- Second – Women were granted limited voting rights in some regions.
- Third – A campaign led to the first nation granting full women's suffrage.
- Fourth – Several European countries gave women full voting rights.
- Fifth – Numerous countries chose to give women the right to vote.

Exercise G2 (p. 149)
1. WS for "women's suffrage" / demo for "demonstration" / C18 for "eighteenth century" / C19 for "nineteenth century" / camp for "campaign" / + for "and"
2. Suggested answers: temp for "temporary" / NZ for "New Zealand" / Euro for "European" / > for "over"

Exercise G3 (p. 150)
1.
- First – Attend an information session
- Second – Fill out and submit the application
- Third – Wait for the application to be assessed
- Fourth – Attend a group interview
  (Attend an individual training session is not used)

2.
- First – A member of Congress sponsors a bill or measure.
- Second – A committee discusses the bill and approves or rejects it.
- Third – Members of both chambers of Congress debate the bill.
- Fourth – If the bill is enrolled, the president can accept or veto it.

Exercise H1 (p. 150)
1. agreement – A; states – E
2. coalition – C; bureaucrats – F
3. election – B
4. Legislation – D
5. Representatives – G
6. veto – H

Exercise H2 (p. 150)
- Excerpt 1 – representatives
- Excerpt 2 – agreement
- Excerpt 3 – coalition
- Excerpt 4 – legislation
- Excerpt 5 – election
- Excerpt 6 – veto

Exercise I1 (pp. 151–153)

1.
- The large number of available rooms – No
- The techniques used in its construction – Yes
- The relatively inexpensive cost of living there – No
- The convenience of its location for the man – Yes

2.
- Prices tend to be expensive – Off-campus accommodation
- Not constructed recently – On-campus accommodation

- No coed accommodations – On-campus accommodation
- Less convenient location – Off-campus accommodation

3.
- Find a way to end World War I quickly – No
- Maintain peace throughout the world – Yes
- Solve international disputes diplomatically – Yes
- Cooperate with governments to promote trade – No

4.
- First – Governments discussed and founded several international organizations
- Second – The League of Nations was founded to promote world disarmament
- Third – A group of allied countries discussed and signed the Atlantic Charter
- Fourth – The United Nations Charter was drafted and signed in San Francisco

- Fifth – Members of the UN Security Council ratified the United Nations Charter

5.
- Being humorous – Not included
- Being critical – Included
- Being ironic – Included
- Being indirect – Included

6.
- First – Aristophanes
- Second – Niccolò Machiavelli
- Third – Jonathan Swift
- Fourth – Maurice Joly

UNIT 14 | LISTENING • Making Inferences Questions

Exercise A1 (p. 154)
1. recovery
2. prosperity
3. downturn
4. depression

Exercise B1 (pp. 154–155)
1. bibliography
2. coursebook
3. reading list
4. stacks
5. journal
6. catalog
7. interlibrary loan
8. special reserve

Exercise C1 (pp. 155–156)
1. B
2. C

Exercise D1 (p. 156)
C Ahmed
A Miki
B Jorgen
D Rosa

Exercise D2 (pp. 156–157)
1. B   2. A   3. B
4. A   5. B   6. B

Exercise D3 (p. 157)
1. B C
2. A D

Exercise D4 (p. 157)
1. B D
2. A B
3. A C

Exercise E1 (p. 158)
1. A B
2. The following phrases from the script are helpful: "The financial crisis of 2007–2012 was caused when property bubbles around the world burst." / "The "Lost Decade" in Japan, when the economy grew at a very slow rate, was also caused by a burst bubble"

Exercise E2 (p. 158)
1. Yes
2. Yes
3. No
4. No
5. Yes

Exercise F1 (pp. 158–159)
1.
- The woman is enjoying an economics class that she is taking – States directly
- The woman needed some extra money this semester – Implies
- Doing the reading for her economics class requires a lot of time – Implies

2.
- Some of his students used some economics terms incorrectly in their assignments – Implies
- The word fiscal is most often used to refer to government expenses and incomes – States directly
- Economists generally use the words fiscal and financial with different meanings – States directly

Exercise F2 (p. 159)
1. Imply
2. State

3. Not mention
4. Imply
5. Imply
6. State

Exercise G1 (p. 160)
1. money or property
2. goods and services
3. one market
4. customers to purchase
5. quickly
6. general decline
7. natural or economic
8. specific time

Exercise G2 (p. 160)
1. Capitalism is an economic system that aims to maximize the production of capital.
2. consume / demand / produce / supply
3. Goods are physical products, but services are not.
4. Depression

Exercise H1 (pp. 160–162)
1. A   2. B C   3. D
4. C   5. A   6. B

LISTENING REVIEW TEST (pp. 164–167)

1. D
2. B C
3. A
4. D
5. A
6. D
7. C A D E B
8. B D
9. B C

10. A
11. A
12. C
13. A B
14. D
15. A
16. C
17. C
18. A D E

19. A
20.
- Are caused by things like work or relationships – Life stressors
- Are often unexpected and may involve violence – Traumatic stressors

- May be caused by negative or positive events – Life stressors
- Affect multiple people at the same time – Ambient stressors / Traumatic stressors

21. B
22. B

UNIT 15 | SPEAKING • Independent Speaking Task 1

Exercise B1 (p. 178)
1. B 2. D 3. E
4. A 5. F 6. C

Exercise C1 (p. 179)
1. This question matches the final type of Speaking Task 1 questions.
2. This question matches the third type.
3. This question matches the first type.
4. This question matches the second type.

Exercise C2 (p. 179)
1. Question 3
2. They repeat ideas unnecessarily.

Exercise D1 (p. 180)
• Opinion – The speaker's opinion is that a book helped her to learn English effectively.
• Reason – The speaker's reason is that the book helped her to gain confidence.

Exercise D2 (p. 180)
1. Yes, the opinion, reason, and example match all three points in the checklist.

2. Answers will vary. Suggested answers:
• Opinion – A book about how to cook
• Reason – The book taught me how to cook delicious, healthy food.
• Example – Using recipes from the book I cooked for myself for one month and had no more health problems.

Exercise E1 (p. 181)
1. D 2. B 3. E
4. A 5. C

Exercise E2 (p. 181)
1. It's hard to choose
2. However, if I had to pick one, it would be
3. The main reason is that
4. For example
5. So that's why

Exercise E4 (p. 181)
1. C 2. A
3. D 4. B

Exercise E5 (p. 182)
Answers will vary.

UNIT 16 | SPEAKING • Independent Speaking Task 2

Exercise A1 (p. 184)
Answers will vary.

Exercise B1 (p. 184)
• Expressions related to education: D G
• Expressions related to work: A H
• Expressions related to health: B F
• Expressions related to free time activities: C E

Exercise C1 (p. 185)
1. This question matches the third type of Speaking Task 2 questions.
2. This question matches the first type.

3. This question matches the second type.

Exercise C2 (p. 185)
1. free
2. This response answers question 2 from Exercise C1.

Exercise D1 (p. 186)
• Choose the opinion that is easier to talk about even if it is not your real opinion – Yes
• Use stock reasons that match many topics, such as education, time, work, or health – Yes
• Think of two contrasting examples – one that is positive and one that is negative – Yes

• Make sure one example is about a person you know well, like a family member or friend – No

Exercise D2 (p. 186)
• A matches question 2
• B matches question 2
• C matches question 1
• D matches question 1

Exercise D3 (p. 186)
1. Answers will vary.
2.
• Time is the stock reason that matches answer A in Exercise D2.
• Work matches answer B.
• Education matches answer C.

• Health matches answer D.
3. Answers will vary.

Exercise D4 (p. 186)
1. B
2. Answers will vary.

Exercise E1 (p. 187)
1. C 2. E 3. D
4. B 5. A

Exercise E2 (p. 187)
1. There are some advantages to
2. However, overall I feel that
3. The main reason is that
4. For example
5. So that's why

UNIT 17 | SPEAKING • Integrated Speaking Task 3

Exercise A1 (p. 190)
Answers will vary.

Exercise B1 (p. 190)
1. Administrative Building
2. auditorium
3. campus
4. dining hall
5. Fitness Center
6. Health Services Center
7. International Student Office
8. Student Center

Exercise C1 (p. 191)
Answers will vary. Suggested answers:
1. The college announces some free lectures.
2. The man is happy about the announcement.
3. He is interested in the subjects of the lectures.
4. He is pleased that the college is offering events.

Exercise D1 (p. 192)
The following sections should be underlined in the passage:
• new registration procedure needed for student clubs
• new clubs can only be founded by full-time students
• clubs will not be approved unless at least 50 students are interested

Exercise D2 (p. 192)
Answers will vary.

Exercise D3 (p. 192)
2. Answers will vary.

Exercise D4 (p. 193)
1. The announcement states that a new fitness center is now open on campus.
2. The first detail mentioned in the announcement is that the new fitness center is open 24

hours a day, seven days a week for staff and some students.
3. The announcement also mentions that all students can use the new fitness center if they pay $50 each semester.
4. The newspaper article explains that new bulletin boards for notices and advertisements have been put up in the Student Center.
5. The first reason mentioned in the newspaper article is that the bulletin boards will provide a central place for students to put up notices and ads.
6. The newspaper article also states that the bulletin boards will make the campus look cleaner.

Exercise E1 (p. 193)
A and – +
B before – B4
C college – cllg
D (are) equal – =
E full-time – ft
F man – M
G money – $
H number (of) – #
I part-time – pt
J student – stdnt
K with – w/
L woman – W

Exercise E2 (p. 193)
2. Several other words in the notes could be abbreviated. Here are some suggestions:
• stdnt clubs or clubs – SC
• policy – plcy
• registered – regd

Exercise E3 (p. 193)
1. The man is the main speaker.
2. He is not happy about the announcement.
3. The first reason is that regular students can't use the new fitness center without paying.
4. The second reason is that the college didn't make any improvements to the existing facilities.

Exercise E4 (p. 193)
1. The woman is the main speaker.
2. She is happy about the announcement.

3. The first reason is that she thinks the bulletin boards will be useful.
4. The second reason is that parts of campus get really messy because of all the notices.

Exercise F1 (p. 194)
MP – student wants college to change policy to start clubs
OP – agree w/ student = cllg should change policy
R1 – cllg rule = ft + pt stdnts must be eql
D1 – current club policy against cllg rules

R2 – not make sense clubs need 50 stdnts B4 registered
D2 – clubs not cost cllg $ so # members not matter

Exercise G1 (p. 194)
1. MP　　2. OP　　3. R1
4. D1　　5. R2　　6. D2

Exercise G2 (p. 195)
The two people discuss a letter by a student / about changing the policy for starting student clubs. // The man supports the student's viewpoint. // First, /he states that the college has a rule that full-time and part-time students should be treated equally. //

He then adds that the college's policy about / registering student clubs is against this rule. // Next, / the man says that he doesn't think clubs need fifty potential members / before they can be registered. // He goes on to say that student clubs don't cost the college any money, / so the number of members doesn't matter.

Exercise G3 (p. 195)
Answers will vary.

Exercise G5 (p. 195)
Answers will vary.

UNIT 18 | SPEAKING • Integrated Speaking Task 4

Exercise B1 (p. 198)
1. C　　2. E　　3. B
4. H　　5. D　　6. G
7. A　　8. F

Exercise C1 (p. 199)
1. The reading gives a general description of peer pressure.
2. The professor talks about a positive example of peer pressure.
3. The people changed their behavior by recycling more than they did previously because of peer pressure from their neighbors.
4. They would probably recycle about the same amount as other people in the country if they did not experience peer pressure.

Exercise D1 (p. 200)
1.
- Summary A is too detailed.
- Summary B is good.
- Summary C is too general.
2.
- A – Not useful (because it is too general)
- B – Useful (summarizes a key point)
- C – Useful (summarizes a key point)
- D – Useful (summarizes a key point)
- E – Not useful (too general)

Exercise E1 (p. 201)
3. Yes, the note-taking suggestions are also useful for Speaking Task 3 and Writing Task 1. Many of the suggestions are also useful for TOEFL Listening.

Exercise E2 (p. 201)
1. The following abbreviations are used:
- prof – "professor"
- + – "and"
- NYC – "New York City"
- bc – "because"
- ngtv – "negative"
- opin – "opinion"
- pstv – "positive"
- CB – "confirmation bias"
2. Answers will vary. Suggested answers:
- emotional - emtnl
- experience - exp
- brochures - broch
- recommendations - recommds

Exercise F1 (p. 202)
1. To answer this question, I would need to:
- Use information from the lecture in my response.
- Explain how confirmation bias influences people's decisions.
- Explain how people can overcome confirmation bias.

2. To answer this question, I would need to:
- Use information from the lecture in my response.
- Explain how intrinsic and extrinsic motivation are different.
3. To answer this question, I would need to:
- Use information from the lecture in my response.
- Explain what peer pressure is.
- Explain how peer pressure affects what people do.

Exercise F2 (pp. 202–203)
- KP1 – "confirmation bias"
- KP2 – "people easily accept opinions they believe but reject ones they don't"
- KP3 – "people with CB can make poor decisions because of CB"
- KP4 – "prof + wife discuss vacation plans"
- KP5 – "wife suggest go NYC but prof not want NYC bc ngtv opin → emotional experience as child"
- KP6 – "prof rejects pstv points + focus on ngtv points"
- KP7 – "couple go Miami not NYC → bad experience"
- KP8 – "CB" (next to "prof rejects pstv points + focus on ngtv points")

Exercise G1 (p. 203)
1. D　　2. A　　3. C
4. B　　5. B　　6. B
7. E

Exercise G3 (p. 204)
1.
- The reading introduces the concept of
- In summary, this is
- The professor gives a personal example of this concept.
- First, she says that
- Next, she mentions that
- Finally, she states that
- This example shows how
2. The reading defines the concept of
3. The professor gives an example of this concept.
4. The professor gives two personal examples of this concept. / These examples show how
5. Cut the fifth or sixth template phrase if the speaker mentioned two points. Add a template phrase like "After that, he/she says that" before the sixth template phrase if the speaker mentioned four points.

Exercise G4 (p. 204)
Answers will vary.

UNIT 19 | SPEAKING • Integrated Speaking Task 5

Exercise B1 (p. 208)
1. G   2. D   3. A
4. H   5. B   6. E
7. F   8. C

Exercise C1 (p. 209)
Answers will vary. Suggested responses:
1. The man has a problem because a study session is at the same time as a field trip.
2. In my view, he should go on the next field trip.
3. The main reason is that there are other field trips later in the year that he can attend without changing his plans.
4. In contrast, I don't think he should see if his friends want to hold a study session on Wednesday.
5. This is because his friends would have to take time off from work.

Exercise D1 (p. 210)
- Conversation 1 – Woman – She wants to go away with friends but has to do some schoolwork.
- Conversation 2 – Both – They want to attend a concert at the same time as a student orientation.
- Conversation 3 – Man – He may have to start an internship late because of his sister's graduation.

- Conversation 4 – Woman – Her plan to stay in a friend's house over the summer is no longer possible.

Exercise D2 (p. 210)
1.
- Have you thought about – conversation 3
- Maybe we could – 2
- What I would do is – 4
- Why don't you – 1
2.
- Do her assignments and then take a break – 1
- Find out dates and times for other orientations – 2
- Try to start the internship later – 3
- Visit the Housing Office – 4

Exercise D3 (p. 210)
1. $100
2. student
3. drop out
4. budget

Exercise D4 (p. 211)
1. The man has a problem because he volunteered at an orientation so he cannot work at a conference.
2. She suggests that the man drop out as a volunteer.
3. He does not want to drop out.
4. She suggests that the man speak to the organizer of the student orientation and try to get paid for his time.

5. He thinks it is unlikely he will get paid because there is only a small budget for the event.
6. The following words are abbreviated in the notes:
- professor – prof
- conference – conf
- Monday – Mon
- Tuesday – Tue
- volunteer – volun
- and – +

Exercise E1 (p. 211)
The five circled key points in the notes should be labeled in this order:
prob – two people help at conf …
S1 – volun just one day …
R1 – other people drop out …
S2 – ask orientation organizer …
R2 – small event budget

Exercise E2 (p. 211)
1. Man
2. Woman
3. Man
4. Woman

Exercise F1 (p. 212)
1. C   2. F   3. D
4. A   5. B

Exercise F2 (p. 213)
The man has a problem because / he volunteered at an orientation / so he cannot work at a conference. // The speakers discuss a couple of possible solutions to this problem. // In

my view, / the man should speak to the organizer of the student orientation / and try to get paid for his time. // The main reason is that / even though the event budget is <u>small</u>, / he might get <u>some</u> money. // In contrast, / I <u>don't</u> think he should drop out as a volunteer. // This is because / <u>other</u> people have dropped out and / the man does <u>not</u> want to do the same thing.

Exercise F3 (p. 213)
1. The man has a problem because he volunteered at an orientation so he cannot work at a conference. The speakers discuss a couple of possible solutions to this problem. In my view, the man should drop out as a volunteer. The main reason is that he can work at the conference and get paid well. In contrast, I don't think he should speak to the organizer of the student orientation and try to get paid for his time. This is because the organizer has complained that the budget for the event is small, so he is unlikely to get any money.

Exercise F4 (p. 213)
Answers will vary.

Exercise F5 (p. 214)
Answers will vary.

UNIT 20 | SPEAKING • Integrated Speaking Task 6

Exercise A1 (p. 216)
Answers will vary. Suggested answers:
1. Macroeconomics is concerned with the performance of the whole economy.
2. Microeconomics, on the other hand, focuses on individual companies and families.
3. Loss leaders are products sold for no profit in order to drive sales of more profitable items.
4. Direct marketing involves communicating directly with customers such as by sending emails.
5. A sole proprietorship is a business owned and operated by a single individual.

Exercise B1 (p. 216)
- F consumers
- A brands
- E profit
- C marketing
- H competition
- B services
- G stockholders
- D executives

Exercise C1 (p. 217)
Answers will vary. Suggested answers:
1. He defines inflation as when the price of goods and services continues to increase over a period of time.
2. A low level of inflation is viewed positively. The main reason is that it is a sign of a growing economy.

3. A high level of inflation is viewed negatively. The main reason is that the amount of money people earn does not rise at the same level as inflation.
4. Inflation might lead to a recession because people cannot buy as many goods and services, so demand goes down, which makes a recession likely.

Exercise D1 (p. 218)
- First – C
- Second – D
- Third – B
- Fourth – A

Exercise D2 (p. 218)
1. had an impact on
2. on the other hand
3. this means
4. to give an example

Exercise D3 (p. 218)
Answers will vary. Suggested answers:
- expressions that explain how one thing has had an effect on another thing – led to / caused by / due to
- expressions that show how two things are different or one thing has changed – in contrast / eventually / in the end
- expressions that indicate definitions or explanations of important ideas – this is called / this is known as

- expressions that signal the speaker is giving an example or supporting details – for example / for instance / in one case

Exercise D4 (pp. 218–219)
1. vertical
2. factory
3. costs
4. horizontal
5. televisions
6. market

Exercise D5 (p. 219)
1. integration
2. two or more / several
3. company
4. manufacturing

Exercise D6 (p. 219)
Answers will vary. Suggested answers:
1. production – produc
2. global – glob
3. transportation – transp
4. advantages – advans or ++
5. reduced – reduc or ↓
6. increased – incr or ↑

Exercise D7 (p. 219)
Answers will vary. Suggested answers:
1. bad for econ
2. recession in many countries
3. work against stag
4. take money + time
5. lasted over 10 years

Exercise E1 (p. 220)
1. Summarize details and/or examples about the second type of integration.
2.
- Summarize details and/or examples about sole proprietorships.
- Define what a partnership is.
3.
- Introduce the first benefit of direct marketing that the speaker mentions.
- Summarize details and/or examples about the first benefit of direct marketing.
- Summarize details and/or examples about the second benefit of direct marketing.

Exercise E2 (pp. 220–221)
1. KP1
2. KP2 / KP3
3. KP4 / KP5
4. KP6 / KP7
5. KP8 / KP9

Exercise E3 (p. 221)
1. The information you need to include in the response:
- a definition of stagflation
- an explanation of why stagflation is bad for the economy
- a summary of the first example about stagflation's negative effects
- a summary of the second example about stagflation's negative effects
2. The following information in the notes is a key point:
- stagflation = combine stagnation + inflation
- high inflat + low econ growth = bad for econ

- global stag in 70s / led to recession in many countries
- hard for governments to break out / few policies ... work / take money + time

Exercise F1 (p. 221)
- KP1
- KP2 / KP3
- KP4
- KP5
- KP6 / KP7
- KP8
- KP9

Exercise F3 (p. 222)
Answers will vary.

UNIT 21 | WRITING • Integrated Writing Task 1 – Challenge Questions

Exercise B1 (p. 236)
1. C   2. B   3. D
4. E   5. A   6. G
7. F   8. H

Exercise C1 (p. 237)
1. challenge
2. oppose
3. cast doubt on
4. differ from
5. contradict

Exercise D1 (p. 238)
1. B
2. Paragraph 4
3. Paragraph 3
4. Paragraph 2

Exercise D2 (p. 238)
1.
- main view – MV
- three main points – P1 / P2 / P3
2.
- education – educ
- performance – perf
- achievement – achievem
3.
- The abbreviations S, PBP, and T are used in parentheses

after the full words:
- S – students
- PBP – performance-based pay
- T– teachers

Exercise E1 (p. 239)
1. True
2. False – The speaker's overall opinion about the topic is given at the beginning of the lecture.
3. True
4. False – In the lecture, the speaker does mention the reading passage directly.
5. True
6. False – The speaker disagrees with all the points from the reading.

Exercise E2 (p. 240)
- Use abbreviations to take notes more quickly and use the time more effectively – second
- Copy the speaker's words directly or paraphrase them, whichever is easier for you – third

- Take as many notes as you can about ideas that are related to points in the reading – first

Exercise E3 (p. 240)
1. The notes mainly copy the speaker's words directly (but with abbreviations)
2. MV / P1 / PBP / educ / T
3. money – $ / motivate – motiv

Exercise F1 (pp. 240–241)
1. The last one
2. The last one
3. The first one
4. The last one
5. The first one
6. The second one
7. The third one
8. Yes

Exercise F2 (p. 241)
Answers will vary.

Exercise G1 (pp. 241–242)
Answers will vary. Suggested answers:
1. The writer first claims that people who bully can be made to leave school because of

zero-tolerance policies.
2. The writer next says that educators can easily stop or prevent bullying from happening because of better training.
3. The writer then asserts that fewer people bully others these days because of changes in social attitudes.
4. The writer first claims that studies have shown that zero-tolerance policies have a very small impact on bullying.
5. The writer next says that educators cannot easily prevent bullying because a lot of bullying does not happen at school.
6. The writer then asserts that social attitudes have not changed and that the amount of bullying is actually increasing.

UNIT 22 | WRITING • Integrated Writing Task 1 – Problem-Solution Questions

Exercise B1 (p. 244)
1. A H   2. B E
3. D C   4. F G

Exercise C1 (p. 245)
1. Problem-Solution
2. Challenge
3. Challenge
4. Problem-Solution
5. Problem-Solution

Exercise D1 (p. 246)
1. The following information is unnecessary: "UHIE caused by city construction materials trapping heat"
2. The following abbreviations are used in the notes:
- UHIE – "urban heat island effect"
- environm – "environment"
- elec – "electricity"
- $ – "cost"
- pollut – "pollution"
- etc. – "and so on"

- temp – "temperature"
- + – "and"

Exercise E1 (p. 247)
Strategy 1 – Speaker B
Strategy 2 – Speaker C
Strategy 3 – Speaker A

Exercise E2 (p. 247)
1. B
2. D
3. A

Exercise F1 (p. 248)
Answers will vary. Suggested answers:
- *challenges the reading* → addresses issues in the reading
- *casts doubt on the reading* → answers questions in the reading
- *contradicts the reading* → takes up points in the reading

Exercise F2 (p. 248)
Answers will vary. Suggested answers:
1. the urban heat island effect results in people using more electricity, which costs money and causes pollution.
2. painting roofs a lighter color can also reduce the effect.
3. the urban heat island effect raises the temperature of nearby rivers and streams, which can harm local wildlife.
4. green roofs are beneficial because they soak up water before it gets into rivers and streams.
5. the urban heat island effect means heat waves have a more dangerous impact because they are hotter and last longer.
6. reducing temperatures in urban areas reduces

the danger of heat waves for humans.

Exercise F3 (p. 249)
Answers will vary.

Exercise G1 (p. 250)
1. The words "small system" should be replaced by "large system."
2. The words "after they are released" should be replaced by "before they are released."
3. The words "costs more than" should be replaced by "costs the same as." The words "buy organic food from grocery stores" should be replaced by "buy organic food from farmer's markets." And the words "cheaper than at farmer's markets" should be replaced by "cheaper than at grocery stores."

UNIT 23 | WRITING • Integrated Writing Task 1 – Support Questions

Exercise A1 (p. 252)
Answers will vary.

Exercise B1 (p. 252)
1. B   2. G   3. C
4. D   5. F   6. E
7. A   8. H

Exercise C1 (p. 253)
1. B   2. A   3. C

Exercise D1 (p. 254)
- Main view – the Internet has negative effects
- Point 1 – The Internet is eroding people's ability to communicate well in writing
- Point 2 – The Internet has also had an impact on people's physical health

- Point 3 – The Internet affects ... people's willingness to read lengthy texts ...and their ability to do so

Exercise D2 (p. 254)
The B set of notes are better because they accurately summarize the main view and the three main points. The A set of notes miss some of the main points, incorrectly summarize some other points, and summarize some unnecessary details.

Exercise E1 (p. 255)
Answers will vary. Suggested responses:
1. The speaker mentions that several species of animals use tools to find food and for other basic needs.

2. The speaker says that the Luddites were a group of workers who used violence to protest against machines. The Luddites were worried that they would lose their jobs because of the machines.
3. The speaker points out that ENIAC was the first electronic computer. She also mentions that it was as large as five average hotel rooms and weighed as much as several adult elephants.

Exercise F1 (p. 256)
1. I   2. D   3. B
4. H   5. A   6. E
7. J   8. F   9. G
10. C

Exercise F2 (p. 257)
Answers will vary.

Exercise F3 (p. 257)
Answers will vary.

Exercise G1 (p. 258)
- helped → helps
- due to → because / as / since
- less → fewer
- the money → money
- access to → access
- convenience → convenient
- problem → problems
- employee → employees
- easy → easily
- copied → copied
- hear often → often hear
- stored → stored in

UNIT 24 | WRITING • Independent Writing Task 2 – Single Opinion Questions

Exercise A1 (p. 260)
Answers will vary.

Exercise B1 (p. 260)
1. supervisors
2. colleagues
3. salary

4. position
5. overtime
6. promotion
7. employees
8. workplace

Exercise C1 (p. 261)
1.
- Option 1 – get a job in another country
- Option 2 – get a job in my country

2.
- Option 1 – work part time
- Option 2 – not work part time
3.
- Option 1 – need good computer skills

- Option 2 – not need good computer skills
4.
- Option 1 – doing overtime to make extra money is good
- Option 2 – avoiding overtime to enjoy free time is good

Exercise D1 (p. 262)
1. No
2. Yes
3. No
4. Yes
5. Yes

Exercise D2 (p. 262)
1. The teacher says "recognize" instead of "notice". The teacher also says "options" instead of "choices."
2. The teacher says "supporting" instead of "detailed". The teacher also says "select" instead of "choose."
3. The teacher says "Review" instead of "Look at". The teacher also says "simpler" instead of "easier."

Exercise D3 (p. 262)
1.
- first option – 1 get job overseas
- second option – 2 get job in my country
2.
- first reason – more money
- first supporting example – salaries in my country low
3.
- second reason – easy to get job
- second supporting example – lots of jobs in my country now

Exercise E1 (p. 263)
- Sentence 1 – C
- Sentence 2 – A
- Sentence 3 – D

Exercise E2 (p. 263)
- I can see why some might feel that university students should not work part time. On the whole, however, it is my opinion that students benefit when they work part

time. This piece of writing will explain my views on this topic in more detail.
- I can see why some might feel that good computer skills are useful but not necessary to find work. On the whole, however, it is my opinion that without such skills, finding a job is very hard. This piece of writing will explain my views on this topic in more detail.

Exercise E3 (p. 263)
Answers will vary.

Exercise F1 (p. 264)
- Step 1 – B
- Step 2 – A
- Step 3 – C

Exercise F2 (p. 264)
Answers will vary.

Exercise G1 (p. 265)
- First sentence – C
- Second sentence – B

Exercise G2 (p. 265)
1. C A E F
2. C D E B

Exercise H1 (p. 266)
1. Not likely
2. Likely
3. Likely
4. Not likely

Exercise H2 (p. 266)
Answers will vary.

Exercise I1 (p. 266)
- enjoy → enjoyable
- advantage → advantages
- earned → earn
- the college → college
- years → year
- than → as
- on → in
- Because of → Because
- travel → travel to
- many → much
- be definitely → definitely be
- majer → major

UNIT 25 | WRITING • Independent Writing Task 2 – Double Opinion Questions

Exercise A1 (p. 268)
Answers will vary.

Exercise B1 (p. 268)
1. patients
2. physicians
3. treatments
4. conditions / diseases
5. medicines
6. emergency
7. surgeries

Exercise C1 (p. 269)
1. factors that have led to people living longer lives than in the past.
2. qualities of a good physician.
3. ways that technology has affected people's health.
4. common health problems in my country.

Exercise D1 (p. 270)
- Step 1 – B
- Step 2 – A
- Step 3 – C

Exercise D2 (pp. 270–271)
Answers will vary. Suggested answers:
1. A good idea that matches a Writing Task 2 question should be a familiar idea.
2. A familiar idea is one that you have previously written about

or discussed in English.
3. Two advantages are that you can write about familiar ideas more quickly and accurately.
4. Second, good ideas should be simple and not complex. The reason is that simple ideas are quicker to write and may get a better score.
5. You can ask yourself if a child would understand the idea easily.
6. Finally, good ideas should be directly related to the topic because such ideas are easier to understand.

Exercise D3 (p. 271)
1.
- exercise regularly
- get different job
- visit doctor often
- eat more vegetables

Exercise D4 (p. 271)
1. Answers will vary. Suggested answer:
- good at communicating – e.g., patients feel more comfortable when nurses speak clearly and in friendly way
- careful – e.g., mistakes can happen that hurt patients if nurses are not careful

2. Answers will vary. Suggested answer:
Nurses should have lots of energy. For example, energetic nurses can use their energy to care for their patients more effectively.

Exercise D5 (p. 271)
Answers will vary.

Exercise E1 (pp. 272–273)
Introduction:
- Part 1 – C
- Part 2 – F
- Part 3 – I
Body 1:
- Part 1 – A
- Part 2 – G
- Part 3 – K
Body 2:
- Part 1 – E
- Part 2 – D
- Part 3 – B
Conclusion:
- Part 1 – J
- Part 2 – H

Exercise E2 (p. 273)
Statement C

Exercise E3 (p. 273)
Answers will vary.

Exercise F1 (p. 274)
1. From my point of view,
2. I am of the opinion that
3. It is my belief that
4. It seems to me that
5. To my way of thinking,

Exercise F2 (p. 274)
Answers will vary.

Exercise G1 (p. 274)
1. Obesity, which can have several serious effects on people's health, is definitely a problem in my country.
2. Stress, which can lead to problems like heart disease, is another health problem that many people in my country have.
3. Medical research, which includes finding better treatments for dangerous diseases, is one factor that has helped people live longer lives.
4. Another factor that has helped people live longer in my country is improved medical training for physicians, who must now study for more than six years before they get a medical license.

UNIT 26 | WRITING • Independent Writing Task 2 – Contrast Opinion Questions

Exercise A1 (p. 276)
Answers will vary.

Exercise B1 (p. 276)
1. C   2. D   3. H
4. E   5. G   6. B
7. F   8. A

Exercise C1 (p. 277)
1. Double Opinion
2. Single Opinion
3. Contrast Opinion
4. Contrast Opinion

Exercise C2 (p. 277)
Answers will vary. Suggested answers:
1. Compare taking a train with taking a bus. Which way of traveling do you prefer? Why?
2. What are the advantages and disadvantages of traveling with friends? Support your opinion with details and examples.
3. What do you like and dislike about taking a trip? Why? Give reasons in support of your view.
4. Some people feel traveling cheaply is the best way to travel. Other people think it is better to travel in luxury. Compare these views. Then explain your view.

Exercise D1 (p. 278)
• A – Step 3
• B – Step 1
• C – Step 2

Exercise D2 (p. 278)
1. B
2. A

Exercise D3 (pp. 278–279)
1.
• "very slow" – stock reason: time
• "hard to study" – stock reason: education
• "expensive" – stock reason: money
• "stressful" – stock reason: health
2.
• "learn new things" – stock reason: education
• "make new friends" – stock reason: relationships
• "can work if needed" – stock reason: work
• "less stress" – stock reason: health

Exercise D4 (p. 279)
1. First example about airplanes in question 1
2. First example about buses in question 1
3. Second example about buses in question 1 / second example about different cities in question 2 / first example about stay home in question 2
4. Both examples about different cities in question 2
5. Second example about airplanes in question 1 / second example about stay home in question 2

Exercise E1 (p. 279)
1. B   2. C
3. A   4. D

Exercise E2 (p. 279)
Answers will vary.

Exercise F1 (p. 280)
1. A
2. Single Opinion and Double Opinion Questions:
• Body Paragraph 1: A, E, F
• Body Paragraph 2: B, D, H
   Contrast Opinion Questions:
• Body Paragraph 1: G, E, F
• Body Paragraph 2: C, D, H

Exercise F2 (pp. 280–281)
A – Thinking about the first aspect of this topic, in most cases cars are a very fast and convenient way to carry out daily activities like going to a shopping mall or visiting a friend who lives nearby.
D – Recently I read an interesting article about this subject. According to what I read, on average journeys by car take less than 17 minutes, but journeys by other vehicles like bicycles or buses take much longer.
E – The article also mentioned that people prefer cars because they offer protection from the weather.
B – In contrast, bicycles are a great choice for short journeys for people who want to become healthy.
C – In my experience, riding a bicycle helps me stay fit and healthy but driving a car makes me gain weight because I am not doing any exercise.
F – To give an example, in the winter I rarely ride my bicycle because it is cold and I usually feel unhealthy and overweight, but in the summer I ride my bicycle as often as I can, so I feel healthy and strong.

Exercise F3 (p. 281)
Answers will vary.

Exercise G1 (p. 281)
1. E A
2. C D

Exercise G2 (p. 281)
Answers will vary.

Exercise H1 (p. 282)
Expressions between 0% and 33%: B C
Expressions between 34% and 66%: D E
Expressions between 67% and 100%: A F

Exercise H2 (p. 282)
Answers will vary.

Exercise I1 (p. 282)
Answers will vary. Suggested answers:
1. Traveling somewhere by train usually costs a lot of money.
2. A few days ago I went to a nearby island on a boat.
3. Around 40 out of 100 people do not enjoy flying.
4. Bicycles are a very good choice for making a short trip.
5. Over the last few years, prices for tickets have gone up by almost one quarter.
6. In general, I do not like having to wait around at an airport before I can get on my plane.
7. Taking a trip to a foreign country is often a very enjoyable experience.
8. Some vehicles, such as cars, trucks, and airplanes, cause air and noise pollution.

PRACTICE TEST A | READING

1. D
2. B
3. B
4. D
5. A
6. C
7. C
8. D
9. B
10. B
11. A
12. B
13. C D F (in any order)
14. B
15. B
16. D
17. A
18. C
19. B
20. A
21. C
22. B
23. A
24. C
25. D
26. A
27. Jacobean – A C (in any order) / Queen Anne – B / Chippendale – D E (in any order)
28. C
29. B
30. C
31. B
32. B
33. A
34. D
35. A D (in any order)
36. B
37. A
38. B
39. C
40. B C F (in any order)

PRACTICE TEST A | LISTENING

1. D
2. C
3. B
4. A
5. A
6. C
7. D
8. C D (in any order)
9. First B / Second D / Third C / Fourth A
10. A
11. C
12. C
13. A
14. No / Yes / No / Yes / Yes
15. B
16. A
17. B C (in any order)
18. C
19. A
20. B
21. D
22. B D (in any order)
23. A
24. B
25. C
26. D
27. A C (in any order)
28. A
29. B
30. No / Yes / No / Yes
31. D
32. B C (in any order)
33. A
34. A

PRACTICE TEST B | READING

1. C
2. A
3. B
4. C
5. A
6. C
7. D
8. A
9. B
10. B
11. C
12. D
13. B D E (in any order)
14. C
15. C
16. D
17. B
18. D
19. B
20. A
21. C
22. B
23. B
24. C
25. A
26. NREM Sleep – A C G (in any order) / REM Sleep – B F (in any order)
27. D
28. C
29. B
30. A
31. B
32. C
33. A
34. D
35. B
36. D
37. C
38. B
39. D
40. C D F (in any order)

PRACTICE TEST B | LISTENING

1. C
2. B D (in any order)
3. B
4. C
5. Yes / No / Yes / No
6. B
7. C
8. A
9. D
10. Op art / Pop art / Both Op art and Pop art / Op art
11. C
12. C
13. B
14. A C (in any order)
15. A
16. C
17. D
18. C
19. C
20. A C (in any order)
21. B
22. Yes / Yes / No / Yes / No
23. C
24. A B (in any order)
25. C
26. C
27. D
28. Era of Good Feelings / Second Party System / First Party System / Era of Good Feelings
29. D
30. C
31. D
32. First A / Second D / Third C / Fourth B
33. A
34. C

UNIT 4 | READING • Inference Questions

Exercise E1 (Track 1)

Male Teacher OK. Today we're going to discuss Inference questions in the reading section. As you know, Inference questions test how well you can recognize information which is implied, um, suggested, in the passage. So, can anyone tell me one way to recognize this suggested information?

Male Student I think information that is stated directly in the passage can help us to, uh, make a conclusion about the answer.

Teacher Nice. Let me give an example to clarify that point. If a passage states directly that a book called *Silent Spring* was published in 1962, we can conclude that the author of that book – Rachel Carson – was born before 1962. That's a pretty obvious example, but it demonstrates the idea, I think.

Any more ideas? Anyone? No?

OK, well let me give you one more idea. I like to imagine that an indirect idea is one where the author decided to cut some words from the passage because these words were obvious. So, if you look at the passage and think, "What words are missing?" and then add those words into the sentence, the indirect idea is often clear and easy to understand. OK?

Student Can you give an example?

Teacher Uh, well I was reading about a region of Africa recently and the book mentioned that one year there was no rain and many animals died. The author didn't say directly why the animals died, but it's easy to understand why if we add some words into the sentence. Instead of saying, "there was no rain and many animals died," we could imagine, "there was no rain and many animals died *because they had no water.*" Is that clear? I imagined adding the words "because they had no water" so that the indirect idea in the book became obvious.

UNIT 5 | READING • Sentence Simplification Questions

Exercise E1 (Track 2)

Female Teacher Hi, everyone. Today let's discuss Sentence Simplification questions. First, I'll talk about a helpful strategy for answering these questions – recognizing the function of the sentence. After that, I'll give some examples of common sentence functions that you might see in the TOEFL Test.

OK. First, recognizing the function, or purpose, of the highlighted sentence may help you to recognize which are the right and wrong answers. This is because the correct answer will have the same function as the highlighted sentence, but incorrect answers sometimes have different functions. For example, if the highlighted sentence includes the words "for instance," its function is to give an example. So you would look for an answer that also gave an example and eliminate answers with a different function. Clear?

Now, there are quite a few functions that you might see in Sentence Simplification questions, but five of them are especially common. The most common type of sentence is one that compares or contrasts two ideas. Also very common are sentences that summarize an academic theory or idea. You may also hear sentences that describe a negative idea or problem with something. Another common function, although less common than the three functions I just described, is explaining either the cause or effect of something, or the reason why something happened. And finally, some sentences have the function of describing all or part of a process.

UNIT 6 | READING • Insert Text Questions and Reference Questions

Exercise D1 (Track 3)

Female Teacher OK. Let's talk about using sentence functions as a way to answer Insert Text questions. I'll begin with three general points. First, if you cannot recognize the function of a sentence quickly, don't worry. There are other strategies you can use to answer Insert Text questions, so if the function of the sentence is not obvious, try one of those other strategies.

Next, I want to be very clear that you may see a sentence with *any* function at *any* position in a paragraph. Some positions are much more or less likely than others, of course, but any position is *possible*. This means that recognizing the function of a sentence *cannot* help you choose the exact answer. However, it *can* help you quickly decide which positions are likely or unlikely, and this might help you save time because you can focus on these positions first.

OK. Now let's talk about which types of sentences are common in certain positions. Near the beginning of a paragraph, it's common to see sentences that define a term or concept. You can also expect to see sentences that introduce a topic. In the middle of a paragraph, many types of sentences are possible, but it's especially common to see sentences that compare or contrast ideas, as well as sentences that add a detail or an example. And finally, near the end of a paragraph, it's common to have a sentence that expresses a conclusion. It's also fairly common to have a sentence that compares or contrasts ideas.

OK? Any questions?

UNIT 7 | READING • Fill in a Table and Prose Summary Questions

Exercise D1 (Track 4)

Female Teacher Hi, everyone. Today we're going to focus on the two kinds of reading to learn questions: Prose Summary questions, which are very common in the TOEFL Test, and Fill in a Table questions, which appear less often.

These questions are important because they are worth two or three points, so I strongly recommend that you leave enough time to answer them carefully.

Some students find these questions hard, but in my experience if you learn and use some strategies, you can improve your ability to answer these questions, and you will probably find them pretty easy to answer correctly; though as I suggested before, you do need some time to answer them.

OK, now let's discuss some strategies for Fill in a Table questions. The first thing you'll want to do is quickly skim and scan the whole passage to find a paragraph or sentences that looks like it matches one of the answers. If you cannot find a relevant section in the passage, probably this answer choice is wrong, so eliminate it. The next thing you need to do is decide if the section you found restates the answer choice – uh, restate is another way of saying paraphrase – or if it contradicts the answer choice. If the passage contradicts the answer, that answer is wrong so eliminate it. The final step is to scan the relevant section of the passage to match the answer choice to one of the categories in the table. Once you've done that, select the answer. Then all you need to do is repeat these steps for the remaining answer choices.

Exercise F1 (Track 5)

Female Teacher OK, let's move on and talk about Prose Summary questions. The good news is that the strategies for answering Prose Summary questions are very similar to the strategies for answering Fill in a Table questions. First, you'll want to skim and scan the passage to find a relevant section or paragraph. If you cannot find a section of the passage that seems relevant to the answer, this answer is probably wrong, so eliminate it. Next, compare the answer choice to the relevant section and decide whether the answer restates the passage or contradicts it. If it contradicts it, eliminate that answer. Finally, and this step is different from Fill in a Table questions, read the relevant section of the passage again and decide if what you're reading describes a major point or a minor point in the text. A major point means you've found one of the right answers; a minor point means you've found one of the wrong answers, so you should eliminate it.

LISTENING DIAGNOSTIC TEST

Conversation 1 (Track 6)

Narrator Listen to a conversation between a student and a university employee.

Woman Hi. Are you the right person to talk to about changing my roommate?

Man Yes, but if you live in a residence on campus, I can tell you right now that there's a very long waiting list to do that. I doubt you'd be able to move in with a new roommate before the end of the school year.

Woman That long? When I spoke to my resident advisor about the situation, she suggested it would be easy and quick to switch roommates.

Man Seriously? But the RAs know that there's a waiting list. What did your RA say exactly?

Woman Well, my roommate has a friend living in McMaster Residence who wants to move in with her, and my RA suggested that I could apply to switch rooms with that friend. So, she and my roommate would share, and I'd share with that friend's current roommate. Uh, did you follow all that?

Man Yeah, it makes sense, and it also clears up why your resident advisor said it would be easy to switch. If you've already found a person who agrees to switch rooms, then you don't have to wait. Before you get too excited, though, let me just check the computer to make sure there are no issues. Can I see your student identity card? … OK, let me just type your ID number into the computer … ah, I can see from your record that you specifically requested a single-sex dormitory, but McMaster, the dorm you're thinking of moving into, is coeducational. Each floor is segregated, but there would be male students living on the floors above and below yours.

Woman Hmm … I'd rather not live in a coed dorm, but if my floor is single-sex, I guess it'll be fine … Plus, it's closer to campus than my current dorm, so yeah, no problem about that.

Man OK, so to get this done, I'll need all of you to come in and fill out the paperwork. That's both you and your roommate, plus your roommate's friend and her roommate. If you can all come in today, we could have everything sorted out by Friday.

Woman So soon? Great! I'll round everyone up and we'll be back before the end of the day … uh, how late are you open?

Man Today we're open until five … sorry, no it's until six today.

Woman That's great. Thanks so much for your help.

Conversation 1 – questions (Tracks 7–11)

Narrator Question 1. Why does the woman go to see the man?

Narrator Question 2. What can be inferred about the man when he says this?

Man The RAs know that there's a waiting list. What did your RA say exactly?

Narrator Question 3. Listen again to part of the conversation.

Woman Well, my roommate has a friend living in McMaster Residence who wants to move in with her, and my RA suggested that I could apply to switch rooms with that friend. So, she and my roommate would share, and I'd share with that friend's current roommate. Uh, did you follow all that?

Narrator Why does the student say this?

Woman Uh, did you follow all that?

Narrator Question 4. What do the speakers say about McMaster Residence?

Narrator Question 5. How quickly could the woman move into her new residence?

Lecture 1 (Track 12)

Narrator Listen to part of a lecture in a sports science class.

Male Professor While running for sport or recreation is undoubtedly hard work, many distance runners report a beneficial side effect of running beyond just an increase in their fitness level: the so-called "runner's high." This powerful and positive sensation can occur when a person exercises strenuously for a long period, taking his or her body beyond a certain threshold. In some cases, runner's high can be so powerful that it allows a runner to push beyond his or her physical limits and keep running despite experiencing pain. There is even anecdotal evidence of people continuing to run despite developing a stress fracture or having a heart attack.

The reasons why runner's high occurs is still being researched, but studies have shown that one factor is the action of certain chemicals on the runner's brain. The body naturally produces a variety of chemicals that can cause joy and other positive emotions. These chemicals include endorphins, serotonin, and dopamine. The studies demonstrated that exercising hard for a prolonged period of time – and that means any type of vigorous exercise, not just running – causes the body to produce more of these chemicals, which leads to the feeling of runner's high. Some of these chemicals also have the effect of blocking pain, which explains why people experiencing the high can keep exercising through physical discomfort.

In addition to the physical factors, psychological effects are also thought to contribute to the feeling of runner's high. These factors are more, uh, subjective and therefore more difficult to assess or prove scientifically. Unrelated studies, however, have proven that people gain increased feelings of satisfaction from working hard or achieving a difficult goal, and there's no reason to doubt that exercise can lead to the same feelings of satisfaction.

So what are the evolutionary origins of runner's high? There is no consensus on this, but one plausible theory is that the origins lie deep in human history. The effect of runner's high brings obvious advantages and it is believed to have benefited the survival of early, pre-agricultural humans who would have had to cover long distances when hunting or foraging for food. Even now, hunter-gatherer societies in some regions are known to take part in "persistence hunting." This is a form of hunting in which animals are tracked and followed for hours over very long distances until they become so exhausted that they collapse from exhaustion and are easy to kill. In such circumstances, runner's high can enable hunters to keep running after the prey animal even though they feel pain, tiredness, or hunger. Interestingly, many species of animals that are adapted specifically for running seem to experience runner's high, too, which reinforces the theory that it developed because it provided an evolutionary advantage.

Lecture 1 – questions (Tracks 13–18)

Narrator	Question 6. What does the professor mainly discuss?
Narrator	Question 7. The professor discusses some effects of runner's high. Indicate which of these effects he mentions.
Narrator	Question 8. Listen again to part of the lecture. What does the professor imply?
Male Professor	The studies demonstrated that exercising hard for a prolonged period of time – and that means any type of vigorous exercise, not just running – causes the body to produce more of these chemicals, which leads to the feeling of runner's high. Some of these chemicals also have the effect of blocking pain, which explains why people experiencing the high can keep exercising through physical discomfort.
Narrator	Question 9. What point does the professor make about psychological factors?
Narrator	Question 10. What does the professor say about persistence hunting?
Narrator	Question 11. Listen again to part of the lecture.
Male Professor	So what are the origins of runner's high? There is no consensus on this, but one plausible theory is that the origins lie deep in human history.
Narrator	Why does the professor say this?
Male Professor	There is no consensus on this.

Conversation 2 (Track 19)

Narrator	Listen to a conversation between a student and his professor.
Male Student	Do you have a moment, Professor?
Female Professor	Sure, Bryan. Is everything OK?
Student	Well, I'm a bit confused about the ideas you discussed in class a few days ago. I thought I understood the concepts, but when I started doing the additional reading you mentioned, I realized that I'd misunderstood some of the ideas.
Professor	I see. Well, what did the teaching assistant for the class say when you spoke to her? Couldn't she help?
Student	I tried to see her, but apparently she's away for a few days. I was going to wait a couple of days and talk with her when she gets back, but I was concerned that I'd fall behind.
Professor	Well, I can try to clear up the points that confuse you this time, but I'm not sure that's the best way to help you.
Student	What do you mean?
Professor	Don't take this the wrong way, but I've been teaching this class for a few years now, and one thing I've found is that students who rely on me or the TA for help often do poorly in the final exam. But students who work things out for themselves do much better, in my experience.
Student	I agree that it would be better if I could understand it on my own, but I honestly tried to do that. I did the reading you assigned, but the more I read, the less sense everything made. So, um, I guess I'm not sure what else I could have done.
Professor	Have you thought about joining a study group with some other students from the class? I know you're not the only one who's finding some of the concepts challenging.
Student	Hmmm … I typically work alone because I like to study while listening to music, but perhaps this time it would help to work with others. I was in the library yesterday and met one other person in the class who's having trouble, though I think he's confused about different things than I am.
Professor	Then he sounds like exactly the kind of person you should be working with. If you each understand different aspects of the topic, you can help each other understand the concepts. Instead of joining an existing study group, perhaps the two of you could start your own?
Student	Yeah, I see your point.
Professor	Did you still want me to go over the concepts you don't understand?
Student	Uh, you know what, I'll try the study group idea first. If I still don't understand, I'll come speak to you or the teaching assistant. Is that OK?
Professor	I think that's a healthy attitude, Bryan. Good luck.

Conversation 2 – questions (Tracks 20–24)

Narrator	Question 12. What do the speakers mainly discuss?
Narrator	Question 13. What does the man say about the teaching assistant?
Narrator	Question 14. Listen again to part of the conversation.
Female professor	Don't take this the wrong way, but I've been teaching this class for a few years now, and one thing I've found is that students who rely on me or the TA for help often do poorly in the final exam. But students who work things out for themselves do much better, in my experience.

Narrator	Why does the professor say this?
Female Professor	Don't take this the wrong way.
Narrator	Question 15. What does the man say about his study habits?
Narrator	Question 16. What is the student likely to do next?

Lecture 2 (Track 25)

Narrator	Listen to part of a talk in an Earth sciences class.
Female Professor	Geological processes frequently take place over time spans that are too long for humans to study in detail. But the eruption of the volcano at Parícutin in Mexico occurred over a much shorter period, just nine years in fact, and presented researchers with a unique opportunity: namely, the chance to observe and analyze the complete life cycle of a cinder cone volcano, from birth to extinction, using modern scientific methods.
	Parícutin is the youngest of around 1,400 volcanoes in the Trans-Mexican Volcanic Belt. In fact, at the beginning of 1943, Parícutin did not even exist. The first sign of volcanic activity at the site occurred early in that year. Residents of two villages, San Juan and Parícutin, after which the volcano is named, heard a deep rumbling caused by underground earthquakes. Then in February 1943, two farmers were working in a field when suddenly the ground in front of them swelled and split to form a gap approximately 2 meters across. They also heard a loud hissing sound and smelled rotten eggs – both of which were caused by gas escaping from the fissure. Soon ash and small stones began erupting from the volcanic vent, and within 24 hours, this material had formed a volcanic cone estimated to be 50 meters tall.
	The eruption continued for several weeks almost continuously and grew in strength. By March 1943, huge columns of ash, smoke, and rock were erupting several kilometers into the sky. The sight was so dramatic that Parícutin became a tourist attraction for a while. Apparently flights from the United States to Mexico City were even diverted to fly near the volcano to give passengers an aerial view. Can you imagine such a thing happening these days? Anyway, um, the first year of the eruption was the most violent, with about 90% of the total volume of material being ejected during this time. The following years were a quieter phase, before the eruption became more intense again in the final six months of the volcano's active life.
	As I mentioned, scientists recorded events at Parícutin as they happened, from soon after the first eruption until it ended nine years later in 1952. They made detailed maps and measurements, took photographs, and collected numerous mineral and gas samples. This data was studied extensively, allowing scientists to build up a detailed picture of the volcano's physical and chemical evolution. Despite this happening in an era before detailed computer analysis was possible, the data greatly expanded our understanding of volcanic processes in general, and of cinder cone volcanoes in particular. As these are one of the most common types of volcano, conclusions that scientists reached about Parícutin remain relevant for the study of volcanoes across the globe.

Lecture 2 – questions (Tracks 26–31)

Narrator	Question 17. What does the professor mainly discuss?
Narrator	Question 18. The professor discusses the eruption of a volcano. Put the events in the order in which they occurred.
Narrator	Question 19. What does the professor say about the eruption of Parícutin?
Narrator	Question 20. What can be inferred about the professor when she says this?
Female Professor	The sight was so dramatic that Parícutin became a tourist attraction for a while. Apparently flights from the United States to Mexico City were even diverted to fly near the volcano to give passengers an aerial view. Can you imagine such a thing happening these days?
Narrator	Question 21. What point does the professor make about the data collected about Parícutin?
Narrator	Question 22. What does the professor imply when she says this?
Female Professor	This data was studied extensively, allowing scientists to build up a detailed picture of the volcano's physical and chemical evolution. Despite this happening in an era before detailed computer analysis was possible, the data greatly expanded our understanding of volcanic processes in general, and of cinder cone volcanoes in particular. As these are one of the most common types of volcano, conclusions that scientists reached about Parícutin remain relevant for the study of volcanoes across the globe.

UNIT 8 | LISTENING • Gist-Content and Gist-Purpose

Exercises D1 and D2 (Tracks 32–37)

Narrator	Excerpt one.
Man	Excuse me, Professor. I was hoping to get some advice about how to tackle the term paper. I've done plenty of research, but I can't seem to come up with a good approach.
Woman	Sorry, Tony, but I don't have time now. Why don't you come and see me tomorrow during my office hours, OK? They're from 11 to 1.
Narrator	Excerpt two.
Man	Good morning, everyone. Today we're going to talk about the most important molecule in biology. It's sometimes referred to as "hydrogen oxide," but you'll undoubtedly know it better by its common name – water. So, first let's...
Narrator	Excerpt three.
Woman	OK. Settle down, please. We're going to be covering the functions of the major internal organs of mammals, such as the heart, lungs, and liver, so we've got a lot to get through today. Let's begin by...
Narrator	Excerpt four.
Woman	Excuse me. I wanted to find out my current GPA. Is this the right place?
Man	Yes, it is. If you can give me your student ID number, I'll pull up your record. Once I've got that...
Narrator	Excerpt five.
Woman	OK. Let's continue our discussion of the nucleus of the cell. Last class we talked about its structure – the outer membrane, the pores, the genetic material inside it, and so on. And today we're going to talk about...
Narrator	Excerpt six.

| Man | OK, so now let's turn to methods of reproduction that animals use. There are two basic methods – giving birth to live offspring, as almost all mammals and a *few* fish do – and laying eggs, as reptiles, amphibians, birds, and *most* fish do... |

Exercise E2 (Track 38)

Narrator	Listen to a student talk with his professor.
Male Student	Hello, Professor. Can I ask you something?
Female Professor	Yes, Barry, what can I do for you?
Student	It's about the paper you assigned last week; the one that's due this Friday. I'm, uh, having some trouble with it.
Professor	I see. Well, did you read the article about cell nuclei that I suggested? It gives a different perspective on the issue that might help you see how to approach the assignment.
Student	No, er, I mean, yes, I did read the article, but understanding the assignment is not why I wanted to see you...
Professor	Oh? Then what is the issue?
Student	I don't think I'm going to be able to finish it by the due date. I didn't start looking at the assignment until yesterday and although I know what I need to do, I won't have time to finish by the end of the week ... so I was hoping for an extension.
Professor	I think you're being a bit pessimistic, Barry; after all, it's still Tuesday. Isn't three days enough time?
Student	Usually it would be, but unfortunately I've got two other papers due this week and, well, I already got an extension for those assignments, so I *have* to get them done.
Professor	I see. Hmm, give me a second, OK? ... Alright, I'm not happy about this, but I'll grant you an extension under two conditions. First, you submit the assignment before 9AM on Monday morning. If it's late, you'll get a failing grade. OK?
Student	Sure. OK. I really want to keep my grade point average up, so I'll definitely hand it in before Monday morning.
Professor	And second, you speak to a counselor at the Study Skills Center on campus. A counselor can give you advice about setting up a study plan, scheduling assignments, even overcoming procrastination ... it sounds like you need help in those areas.
Student	OK. I'll do it. Thanks, Professor. I really appreciate it. See you Monday with my assignment.

Exercise G2 (Track 39)

Male Professor	One hundred sixteen elements are known to science, 92 of which occur naturally. Roughly a quarter of these elements, say around 25, are *essential* for living organisms, with the exact number and mix of essential elements depending on the species. Plants for example, seem to need one or two different elements from animals.
	Of these two dozen vital elements, four are considered to be the most important because they comprise more than 95% of most organisms. These big four are hydrogen, carbon, nitrogen, and oxygen. Of these, carbon can be found in all living cells: it is, after all, the element that determines whether a molecule is organic, meaning related to life, or inorganic.
	In addition to these big four elements, about a half dozen other elements are considered to be of major importance for life. These are phosphorus, sulfur, calcium, potassium,

sodium, magnesium, and chlorine. Uh, I know it's hard to remember and note down all of these, but you'll see all of these element names again when you do your reading.

The other essential elements for life are needed only in trace amounts, uh, that's in tiny quantities. Although organisms don't need much of these trace elements, without them serious medical issues can arise. For example, the human body contains about 75 milligrams of the trace element copper. To put that in perspective, that amount weighs less than a single grain of rice. However, scientists have linked having too *little* copper to heart disease. And, as with many trace elements, too *much* copper in the body can be poisonous.

OK, let's look in more detail at the role of some of these essential elements...

Exercise I1 – question 1 (Tracks 40 and 41)

Narrator	Listen to a conversation between a student and a university employee.
Male Student	Excuse me? I need to apply for an incomplete grade for a biology course I'm taking. I'm not going to be able to take the final exam and my professor said I should come here.
Female Employee	You're in the right place, but in order to get official approval for an incomplete grade, you'll need to have a documented medical reason or other emergency.
Student	I was in a car accident recently and I need an operation to fix a problem with my shoulder. The operation's scheduled for the same day as my exam. I've got a letter from the hospital here.
Employee	May I see the letter and your student card, too? ... OK. Let me enter your details on the computer.
Student	Thanks. Uh, how long will it take?
Employee	Entering your information will just take a couple of minutes.
Student	Uh, no, I meant, when will I know whether I've been granted the incomplete?
Employee	Oh. Uh, the dean usually reviews applications and makes a decision within a couple of days, so you should hear by Thursday or Friday.
Narrator	Question 1. Why does the man go to see the university employee?

Exercise I1 – question 2 (Tracks 42 and 43)

Narrator	Listen to a talk in a biology class.
Female Professor	Good morning, everyone. Today we're going to be discussing something that's *definitely* going to be on your midterm exam, so pay attention, OK?
	The two most common different reproductive success strategies that species use are known as K-selection and r-selection. Let's look at these two strategies in more detail.
	In simple terms, species that are K-strategists, um, that is ones that use K-selection, have relatively few offspring throughout their lives, but try to ensure that those offspring will survive. Generally, K-strategists are large species with a long lifespan that live in stable environments. They devote a great deal of time and energy to their few offspring both before and after birth. Often the offspring do not reach maturity for a long time and require parental care during that period. From this description, you'll no doubt have recognized that humans and other large mammals follow a K-selection strategy.

The opposite of K-strategists are r-strategists. Their reproductive strategy is to have a large number of offspring but to do little or nothing to ensure the survival of those offspring. They devote little energy or time to raising or caring for their young. Often each individual can only reproduce once in its life. Compared with K-strategists, species that are r-strategists are often small and have a short life-expectancy. Many invertebrate species follow an r-selection strategy, but so do a number of mammals like rats, mice, and rabbits.

Narrator	Question 2. What main topic does the professor discuss?

Exercise I1 – question 3 (Tracks 44 and 45)

Narrator	Listen to part of a lecture in a history of science class.
Male Professor	One of the most important scientific discoveries of the twentieth century was the discovery or, uh, understanding, if you like, of the structure of DNA by Francis Crick and James Watson in 1953. Like most scientific discoveries, this one could only be made because of important and groundbreaking work by other scientists.

DNA was first isolated by scientists in the nineteenth century, but at that time neither its structure nor its role in passing on genetic information were understood. Various scholars studied DNA throughout the first decades of the twentieth century, but its vital role was not recognized.

In 1928 an experiment on two forms of a bacterium showed that DNA did, in fact, carry genetic information, but as the structure of the molecule was still not known, the precise mechanism for the transmission of this information could not be determined.

Beginning in 1937, scientists took photographs of DNA by diffracting X-rays through a crystal. These photographs were not clear enough to show the structure of DNA exactly, but they did help scientists recognize that it had a regular structure. In the early 1950s improvements in X-ray crystallography techniques led to better photos, and it was one of these, known as "photo 51," that gave Watson and Crick the information they needed to come up with their famous "double helix" model of DNA, a model that proved to be correct.

Narrator	Question 3. What is the professor mainly discussing?

Exercise I1 – question 4 (Tracks 46 and 47)

Narrator	Listen to a conversation between a student and her professor.
Female Student	You wanted to see me, Professor?
Female Professor	Adrienne, come in. Uh, as I'm sure you know, the final exam is next week, and, well, to be blunt, the grades for your assignments haven't been good. I don't want to worry you, but unless you do well on the exam, you might fail the class.
Student	Really? I know my papers haven't been great, but I didn't think the situation was that bad…
Professor	I'm not saying you've already failed, but you're obviously smart and you ask great questions in class, so, um, I guess I wanted to find out why your grades haven't been good and see if I could help.
Student	That's nice of you… It's pretty simple. I needed money so I got a part-time job, and now I don't have enough time to study.

Professor	I thought it might be something like that. Look, there are 10 days before the exam. If you work hard, I'm *sure* you can pass.
Student	I appreciate your confidence in me, and of course I want to pass, but my boss has offered me more hours and I *really* need the money.
Professor	Hmm… Look, this is unsolicited advice, I know, and ultimately it's your decision, of course, but it's almost the end of the semester, right? And during the vacation you can work as many hours as you like without affecting your grades. But if you fail the class you'll just have to take it again – and pay for it again – next semester. So passing the exam would save you money, in a way. If it were me, I'd do whatever it takes to pass the class this semester.
Student	You know, that's actually really good advice. I guess I got so focused on my money issues that I forgot studying was the most important thing. I'll speak to my boss about cutting my hours for the next 10 days and then go straight to the library. Thanks, Professor. I really appreciate your advice.
Narrator	Question 4. What do the two speakers mainly discuss?

Exercise I1 – question 5 (Tracks 48 and 49)

Narrator	Listen to part of a talk in a biotechnology class.
Female Professor	Today we're going to discuss biotechnology, which is something of a controversial field. A simple but clear definition would be that biotechnology is the use or adaptation of biological processes for a specific purpose, especially one that brings an industrial or social benefit.

As I suggested, biotechnology has become controversial, and this is for a number of reasons. I think a lot of people are, frankly, scared of the possible effects of using technology to change organisms. These days there's a lot of press coverage, much of it negative, about the possible dangers of genetically-modified food crops, for example. I encourage you to read more about this, but today's class is not the right forum for a discussion of the rights and wrongs of this issue.

What I will say, though, is that biotechnology has a much longer history than most people assume, and for most of history, the results of biotechnology have been very positive for society. Let's take farming as an example. You might not think so, but farming clearly involves the "use or adaptation of biological processes for a specific purpose" which is the definition of biotechnology I gave earlier. How so? Well, early farmers soon recognized that they could grow more food if they added certain substances to the soil – these substances acted as fertilizers. They also found that growing crops in the same field in a rotation – one crop one year, a different crop the next year – would yield better results than growing the same crop year after year. And farmers who raised animals like sheep or goats tended to use their best animals as breeding animals to ensure that the offspring would be as strong as possible, as big as possible, as good at producing milk as possible, and so on.

So, again, I'm not saying that biotechnology is good or bad, but when people consider biotechnology it's important that they think about its whole history rather than just the past 50 years or so.

Narrator	Question 5. Why does the professor talk about farming?

Exercise I1 – question 6 (Tracks 50 and 51)

Narrator	Listen to a lecture in an introduction to biological sciences class.

Female Professor	A fundamental but surprisingly basic question in biology is what is life? Or to put it another way, how can we recognize whether something is alive or not? This is not an easy question to answer, but scientists generally recognize a number of characteristics that all living organisms share, although not every list has exactly the same traits, or even the same number of them.

Here's a quick overview of some of the main characteristics of life. First, living organisms are organized. They are composed of cells, which contain structures called organelles. In multi-cellular organisms, the cells are further organized into tissues and organs.

Living organisms also respond to positive and negative stimuli in their environment. An animal might move towards food or shelter, for example, but move away from danger or cold. A plant might grow towards the light or release a chemical that makes its leaves taste bad if there are too many insects eating them.

Another characteristic is that living organisms metabolize, which is a scientific way of saying that they take in energy from food and drink and then use that energy for growth and to maintain a stable internal environment within their cells – a process known as homeostasis.

Finally, living organisms exhibit growth, of course, and they reproduce. They undertake the excretion of waste products and they respire... uh, respiration means taking gas in and releasing gas out. Animals, for example, breathe in oxygen and breathe out carbon dioxide; plant respiration, however, is the other way around – carbon dioxide in, oxygen out.

Narrator	Question 6. What is the main purpose of the lecture?

UNIT 9 | LISTENING • Detail Questions

Exercises D2 and G1 (Tracks 52–55)

Narrator	Excerpt one.
Man	Hello. I'd like to make an appointment to see the dean.
Woman	She's attending an academic conference this week, and her schedule is fully booked until the week after next.
Man	Really? I needed to see her kind of urgently.
Woman	Is it something your academic advisor could help with?
Narrator	Excerpt two.
Man	We all know that the planet Saturn is surrounded by rings composed of water ice and cosmic dust, but it may surprise you to learn that three of the other planets in our solar system – the gas giant planets Jupiter, Uranus, and Neptune – also have planetary ring systems, although they are not as well developed as those of Saturn.
Narrator	Excerpt three.
Woman	In the years between 1957 and 1975, the United States and the Soviet Union competed with each other to be the first to achieve different goals in space exploration such as launching the first satellite, sending the first person into space, and being the first to orbit and then land on the moon. This period was known as the Space Race, and although it cost the governments of both the USA and the USSR billions of dollars, that investment led to numerous advances in science and technology.
Narrator	Excerpt four.
Woman	Excuse me? I need to speak to the registrar about something. Do you know why the registrar's office is closed?
Man	Um, I think there's a training session going on, but I'm not sure.
Woman	If that's the case, they could at least have put a sign on the door.
Man	If it is a training session, try again after 11 a.m. That's usually when they finish.
Woman	Thanks, I'll do that.

Exercises E2 and H1 (Tracks 56–59)

Narrator	Excerpt one.
Man	Professor? Could I speak to you a minute? I did the reading you recommended in class, but I still don't really understand the concept of redshift.
Woman	OK, and the teaching assistant's explanation didn't make it clearer?
Man	Oh, actually I didn't speak to the TA about it. I thought I'd speak to you first.
Woman	I'll give you a quick explanation, but in the future, speak to the teaching assistant first, OK?
Man	Sure. Thanks, Professor.
Woman	OK, say you're walking down the street and you hear a police car coming towards you. When the car goes past you on the street, does the sound of the siren change or stay the same?
Man	Uh, it changes, right? The sound gets deeper after the police car goes past.
Woman	Right. It sounds deeper because it's moving away from you and the length of the sound wave is therefore extended. Redshift is similar: when light is moving away from you it looks redder because it has an extended wavelength. Got it?
Man	Yeah, I think so. Thanks, Professor.
Narrator	Excerpt two.
Woman	As you know, telescopes are one of the main tools of the astronomer. And although there are various kinds of telescopes these days, optical telescopes are still important. In simple terms, big optical telescopes have more light-gathering power than smaller instruments. The reason is that the power of an optical telescope is proportional to the area of its lens or mirror.
Narrator	Excerpt three.
Man	Stars burn hydrogen as fuel. When stars of a similar mass to our sun run out of hydrogen, gravity causes them to contract. This contraction causes heat to build up, which in turn makes the outer layers of the dying star expand. This phase is known as a red giant. After this, the helium in the star will fuse to form carbon, and when all the helium has been used up, the core of the star will cool down *and* expand again to form a planetary nebula. As the cooling continues, the remnant star will shrink to form a dwarf star. The dwarf star that forms may be a white, red, brown, or black dwarf depending on a number of factors.
Narrator	Excerpt four.
Woman	We tend to think of science as being done by professional scientists and researchers who have gone through years

of formal training. In most modern sciences this is the case, but astronomy is one discipline in which self-taught amateurs using simple tools, that is people who are *not* professional scientists, can still make a contribution, in some cases a significant one. For example, two well-known recent comets, Hale-Bopp and Shoemaker-Levy, were both jointly discovered by professional *and* amateur astronomers.

Exercise F1 (Track 60)

Narrator	Listen to part of a conversation.
Man	Hello, Yuko. Is everything OK?
Woman	To be honest, I'm having a hard time these days. I really miss my friends and family. And I try to study hard but even one assignment takes me too long.
Man	Have you spoken to anyone at the International Student Center? The counselors there are specially trained to help people who are missing their home. Plus they can give you study advice that's great for international students. And you'll probably make some new friends among the other students who go there, too.
Woman	That's a good idea. I'll try. Thank you.
Narrator	Listen to part of a lecture.
Man	We all know that outer space, which is usually just called space, is a vacuum. And a vacuum, by definition, is a space that is completely empty of matter. In fact, though, not even in outer space does a perfect vacuum exist. Experiments have shown that outer space actually contains a very low density of particles. These particles include hydrogen and helium atoms, as well as less familiar particles like neutrinos and so-called dark matter.

Exercise J1 – questions 1–2 (Tracks 61–63)

Narrator	Listen to a conversation between a student and a university employee in a Careers Office on campus.
Woman	May I help you?
Man	Yeah, uh, do you only help people find work *after* they graduate, or do you offer help finding part-time positions while they're still students?
Woman	We can help with both.
Man	Great! My finances are not in very good shape so I was thinking about getting a job now. I've got a heavy workload this semester, though, so I want something that doesn't require too many hours.
Woman	Let me see what positions we have on file right now... OK, here's one that's eight hours a week, evenings only, but the job's in Oakfield. That's a town about 40 minutes from here.
Man	The number of hours sounds good, but I'd prefer not to spend a lot of time traveling to and from work. Do you have any positions on campus? I've got a friend who works in the Housing Office and he says it pays pretty well.
Woman	There's a lot of competition for those jobs and they go pretty fast, but I'll see if there's anything on the computer... nothing in the Housing Office, I'm afraid, but here's one that's just been posted for a part-time job in the Faculty Office. The hours are flexible and the pay's pretty good, but it says candidates must have international experience.
Man	Well, I'm majoring in modern languages, and when I was a kid my mother got transferred overseas a few times, so I lived in Korea, Argentina, and Australia each for a year.

	My Spanish is pretty good, and I speak some Korean, though I'm not fluent or anything. Is that the kind of experience they would want?
Woman	I can't say for certain, of course, but it sounds impressive to me. I'll print out the details of the position for you, but my computer's kind of slow, so give me a minute or two, OK?
Man	Sure, and thanks for your help.
Narrator	Question 1. What does the man want?
Narrator	Question 2. What kind of experience does the man have?

Exercise J1 – questions 3–5 (Tracks 64–67)

Narrator	Listen to part of a talk in an astronomy class.
Male Professor	Hello, everyone. Today we're going to start by discussing how astronomers classify the planets in the solar system. Broadly speaking, solar system planets are either terrestrial or Jovian.
	The terrestrial planets are the four inner planets: Mercury, Venus, Earth, and Mars. These planets typically are composed of outer layers of solid rock and an inner core of nickel or iron. They tend to be small, and low mass – Earth is the largest of the four, though Venus is very close in size – but their metallic core means they have a high density. These terrestrial planets either have no natural satellites, in the case of Mercury or Venus, or just one or two moons, as with Earth and Mars. Except for Mercury, all of the terrestrial planets have an atmosphere.
	The Jovian planets, often known as the gas giants, are the four outer planets: Jupiter, Saturn, Uranus, and Neptune. Compared with the terrestrial planets, they are huge – even Uranus, the smallest of the Jovian planets, has a mass that is 14 times that of Earth, and Jupiter, the largest, is equivalent to 318 Earths. Because they are primarily composed of the gases hydrogen and helium, however, the Jovian planets have a low density. These planets do not have a solid, rocky surface, but they typically have numerous natural satellites. For example, scientists have so far discovered 67 satellites of Jupiter, 62 for Saturn, 27 for Uranus, and 14 for Neptune. Some of these satellites are very large and are similar to the rocky, inner planets. Ganymede, one of Jupiter's moons, for instance, is slightly larger than Mercury, has a surface composed of ice and rock, a metal-rich core, and even a thin atmosphere. All of the Jovian planets are surrounded by a planetary ring system, though only Saturn's ring system can easily be observed from Earth.
	OK. Any questions so far?
Male Student	I think I remember reading that some planets are classified as ice giants. Is that right?
Professor	Good question. Compared with Jupiter and Saturn, which are the true gas giants, Uranus and Neptune are significantly smaller, have a much lower mass, and are composed of less hydrogen and helium and more rock and ice. For this reason, they are sometimes classified as ice giant planets or, perhaps I should say, they are gas giants that can also be sub-classified as ice giants.
	Anyone else?
Female Student	Yes, Professor, where does Pluto fit in? Is it also a terrestrial planet?
Professor	Ah, another good question. Until 2006, Pluto was classed as a planet, though it has such an unusual orbit and such a low mass – about 0.2% that of Earth – that astronomers

long found it hard to classify. And the problem of how to classify it came to a head in 2005 when an object orbiting the sun was discovered that is 25% larger than Pluto. This object, known as Eris, caused astronomers to rethink the definition of a planet. At a meeting of the International Astronomical Union in 2006, scientists proposed and accepted a definition of what exactly a planet is. Under that definition, Pluto and Eris were re-classified as dwarf planets. Since then, several other dwarf planets have been discovered beyond the orbit of the gas giants, but astronomers do not consider them to be true planets.

Narrator	Question 3. What are two characteristics of the terrestrial planets?
Narrator	Question 4. What point does the professor make about Ganymede?
Narrator	Question 5. What does the professor say about dwarf planets?

Exercise J1 – questions 6–8 (Tracks 68–71)

Narrator	Now listen to part of a talk in an astronomy class.
Female Professor	One of the most famous and, in my view at least, most interesting problems in astrobiology is the Fermi paradox, which is named for Enrico Fermi, the great Italian nuclear physicist. The Fermi paradox can be summarized in a simple question – Where is everybody? – but to understand who Fermi was talking about and why he was asking that question, we need a bit of background.
	OK, the first thing we need to understand is that our galaxy, the Milky Way, is huge and contains between 100 billion and 400 billion stars – astronomers are still trying to determine exactly how many. One of those stars, of course, is our sun. And there's no reason to think that our sun is special in any way – in fact, it seems to be pretty average – so if the Sun is orbited by a planet that is home to intelligent life, it's reasonable to assume that some of the other few hundred billion stars in the galaxy are also going to have planets that can sustain intelligent life. And although distances between stars are vast, even traveling to another star using slow technology would only require hundreds or thousands of years.

Which brings us back to the Fermi paradox. Given the number of stars in the galaxy and the likelihood that our star is not special, we can assume first, that some intelligent species exist, and second, that some of them are traveling through space. And if those two points are correct, where are those intelligent species? Why have we not encountered any of them here on Earth? Why have we not found any evidence of them in space?

Now before we go on to discuss possible explanations for the Fermi paradox, I want to make it clear that I've simplified the situation. There are a couple of articles on your reading list that explain the Fermi paradox in a lot more detail, and I'll expect you to have read those before the next class. You'll also want to take a look at the Drake equation which attempts to quantify how many intelligent civilizations might exist in our galaxy.

OK, so let's see if we can explain the Fermi paradox and understand why humans have not encountered intelligent life from another planet. We believe that our star is pretty average, but we know so little about planets around other stars, that we cannot say the same about Earth. It might very well be that in fact Earth is unusual in some way and that planets on which intelligent life can develop are extremely rare. A related possibility is that Earth-like planets are common, but the conditions that led to the development of intelligent, multi-cellular life are extremely rare. Either of these options would mean the number of intelligent species is extremely small, which is why we have not met any yet.

Other possibilities are that intelligent life *does* exist but we just don't see the evidence – either we're not looking for the right things, or the evidence is being deliberately hidden. Perhaps the galaxy is just too big and the cost of traveling to other stars too great, so intelligent species cannot afford to undertake interstellar journeys. And then, of course, there's always the possibility that humans have simply not been searching for intelligent life for long enough. After all, the search only began a few decades ago.

Narrator	Question 6. What is the Fermi paradox?
Narrator	Question 7. What does the professor say about Earth?
Narrator	Question 8. What points does the professor make about the search for intelligent life?

UNIT 10 | LISTENING • Understanding the Function of What Is Said Questions

Exercise D1 (Track 72)

Female Teacher	OK, now let's talk about Understanding the Function of What is Said questions. As you know, these Function questions ask the reason why a speaker is saying something. In my experience, there are several reasons, uh, functions, that commonly appear in the TOEFL Test.
	One common reason why speakers say something is to give an example. A common expression which matches that function would be "such as."
	Another common function is to give a reason for something. A speaker might use the phrase, "The reason is that" to do this.
	Because the subjects of lectures in the TOEFL Test are academic, speakers sometimes clarify information, uh, that means to make it clearer. A common expression that has this function which you might hear is "in other words."

Discussing different things and either comparing them or contrasting them with a phrase like "on the other hand" is another function you will often hear.

When a professor discusses a new concept, explains the meaning of a word, or introduces a theory, he or she often defines something. When a speaker wants to give a definition, he or she might use a phrase like "this is called."

And finally, one speaker might give advice to the other one using a functional expression like "you should consider." This function of giving advice is especially common in conversations, but you might hear it in lectures, too.

There are other possible functions, of course, but these are the most common ones, in my experience. OK?

Exercise D3 (Tracks 73–78)

Narrator	Excerpt one. Give an example.
Man	Certain artists have had a profound impact on both the world of art and on later artists. Who? Well, Leonardo Da Vinci, for instance.
Narrator	Excerpt two. Give a reason.
Woman	I had to take out a student loan since my living expenses have been much higher than I expected.
Narrator	Excerpt three. Clarify information.
Man	My point here is that a sculptor's choice of material in which to work – stone, wood, metal, and so on – affects the types of works that he or she can create.
Narrator	Excerpt four. Contrast two things.
Woman	A corbel arch cannot bear its own weight without thick supporting walls unlike a true arch, which has a stress-bearing keystone.
Narrator	Excerpt five. Define something.
Man	The best artists' brushes are made from the fur of a kind of weasel that lives in Siberia. We call these kolinsky sable or sable-hair brushes.
Narrator	Excerpt six. Give advice.
Woman	You know, the Finance Office holds workshops on budgeting and managing your money every month or so. I think you would find it useful to attend one.

Exercise E2 (Tracks 79–82)

Narrator	Excerpt one. Listen to part of a conversation in a college library.
Female Student	I want to report a lost book. The title is *Modernism and Scandinavian Art*.
Male Librarian	You mean you lost it, or it's listed in the catalog but not on the shelves?
Student	No, I lost it. I was studying at a cafe in town and I think I left it there.
Narrator	Question 1. Which of these things is the man likely to do next?
Narrator	Excerpt two. Listen to part of a lecture in an art history class.
Female Professor	When the person who created a work of art is known with certainty, we say a work is by that artist or just give the artist's name and the name of the work – there is universal agreement, for example, that *The Night Watch* is by Rembrandt. However, in many cases, it's not possible to say a particular work is by a particular artist with 100% certainty.
Narrator	Question 2. Which of these things is the woman likely to do next?
Narrator	Excerpt three. Listen to part of a conversation in a finance office.
Male Student	Hi, my name's Dale Carpenter. I wanted to find out whether my scholarship application had been accepted.
Female Employee	Let me check that for you. Uh, I'm sorry but your application was rejected because you weren't eligible to apply for that scholarship.
Narrator	Question 3. Which of these things is the woman likely to do next?
Narrator	Excerpt four. Listen to part of a lecture in a geology class.
Male Professor	OK, this next slide is an example of a metamorphic rock known as lapis lazuli which is typically composed of

the minerals lazurite, calcite, sodalite, and pyrite. It's a semi-precious stone that is found and mined mainly in Afghanistan, although there are also deposits in Chile, Russia, and a few other countries. Its main use is, well actually, does anyone know the main use of lapis lazuli?

Female Student	Isn't it used for painting, or something?
Professor	Yeah, kind of. In earlier times, lapis lazuli was ground up and mixed with wax and oils to form a pigment known as ultramarine. This could be used to make an intensely-blue – and very expensive – paint.
Narrator	Question 4. Which of these things is the professor likely to do next?

Exercise E3 (Tracks 83–86)

Narrator	Excerpt one. Listen to a conversation in a college library.
Female Student	I want to report a lost book. The title is *Modernism and Scandinavian Art*.
Male Librarian	You mean you lost it, or it's listed in the catalog but not on the shelves?
Student	No, I lost it. I was studying at a cafe in town and I think I left it there.
Librarian	Well these things happen sometimes, but you'll need to buy a new copy of the book. Let me just check how much that's going to be... Um, that book's an expensive one, I'm afraid. It looks like it will cost almost $120.
Student	So much? That's bad news. I don't have any financial aid this semester and I'm really hard up for money just now.
Narrator	Excerpt two. Listen to part of a lecture in an art history class.
Female Professor	When the person who created a work of art is known with certainty, we say a work is by that artist or just give the artist's name and the name of the work – there is universal agreement, for example, that *The Night Watch* is by Rembrandt. However, in many cases, it's not possible to say a particular work is by a particular artist with 100% certainty. So what can we say in these cases? Well, if there is a lot of evidence to support an attribution, we can say that a work is "probably by" an artist. For example, many experts think that the painting known as *Portrait of Margaretha de Geer, Wife of Jacob Trip* is by Rembrandt but there is not 100% certainty, so this work is listed as "probably by Rembrandt," or "attributed to Rembrandt." And for works that are less certainly by an artist, we could say "possibly by." Clear?
Narrator	Excerpt three. Listen to a conversation in a finance office.
Male Student	Hi, my name's Dale Carpenter. I wanted to find out whether my scholarship application had been accepted.
Female Employee	Let me check that for you. Uh, I'm sorry but your application was rejected because you weren't eligible to apply for that scholarship. There are a couple of other options for financial aid that you *are* eligible for, though. Would you like to discuss those?
Student	Sure, that would be helpful. Thanks.
Narrator	Excerpt four. Listen to part of a lecture in a geology class.
Male Professor	OK, this next slide is an example of a metamorphic rock known as lapis lazuli which is typically composed of the minerals lazurite, calcite, sodalite, and pyrite. It's a semi-precious stone that is found and mined mainly in Afghanistan, although there are also deposits in Chile, Russia, and a few other countries. Its main use is, well actually, does anyone know the main use of lapis lazuli?

Female Student	Isn't it used for painting, or something?
Professor	Yeah, kind of. In earlier times, lapis lazuli was ground up and mixed with wax and oils to form a pigment known as ultramarine. This could be used to make an intensely-blue – and *very* expensive – paint. Once scientists learned to make artificial pigments at the end of the nineteenth century, however, the main use of lapis lazuli was – and still is – as an ornamental stone in jewelry. It can be polished to a high shine and it has an intense, deep-blue color.

Exercise F1 (Tracks 87–90)

Narrator	Excerpt one. What does the man mean?
Man	I'm sorry to have to tell you this, but the submission deadline for this scholarship was last Friday.
Narrator	Excerpt two. Why does the woman say this?
Woman	Living off-campus would be cheaper than living in a residence, but transportation costs would eat up all the savings and commuting would waste at least an hour a day.
Narrator	Excerpt three. Why does the man say this?
Man	When most people think of architecture, they imagine iconic buildings like the Taj Mahal in India, or the Chrysler Building in New York. They don't, however, tend to think of the vast majority of structures they interact with every day as examples of architecture, but in fact such buildings can be described as vernacular architecture.
Narrator	Excerpt four. Why does the woman say this?
Woman	Before we finish today, I wanted to let you know about a talk on Masaccio this evening at the Art Museum in town. You may not be that familiar with his name, but Masaccio had a big influence on famous Renaissance artists like Da Vinci, Michelangelo, and Raphael, and I think you'll find his works still have power.

Exercise F2 (Tracks 91–94)

Narrator	Excerpt one.
Man	You know not all on-campus jobs are covered by the work-study program, right? A lot of positions are open to any student.
Narrator	Question 1. Why does the man ask this?
Man	You know not all on-campus jobs are covered by the work-study program, right?
Narrator	Excerpt two.
Woman	Making a weekly or monthly budget – and sticking to it – can really help keep your living expenses under control. When I was a student I managed to cut my weekly expenses by almost $50 just by setting and following a budget.
Narrator	Question 2. Why does the woman say this?
Woman	When I was a student I managed to cut my weekly expenses by almost $50 just by setting and following a budget.
Narrator	Excerpt three.
Woman	At the end of the sixteenth century, *mezzo-fresco* painting became increasingly common and popular. Painting *mezzo-fresco* had most of the permanency of *buon fresco*, and, like *secco fresco*, the colors did not fade once dry.
Narrator	Question 3. Why does the woman say this?
Woman	Painting *mezzo-fresco* had most of the permanency of *buon fresco*, and, like *secco fresco*, the colors did not fade once dry.

Narrator	Excerpt four.
Man	Look at this painting by Claude Monet titled *Water-Lily Pond and Weeping Willow*. Notice how the yellows, greens, and blues work well together. We call groups of similar colors like these, which lie next to each other on the color wheel, analogous colors. Now look at another Monet work – *Impression, Sunrise* – with the vivid orange sun standing out strongly against the blue background. This is a good example of what we call complementary colors, which means contrasting colors like these that are opposite each other on the color wheel.
Narrator	Question 4. Why does the man say this?
Man	This is a good example of what we call complementary colors, which means contrasting colors like these that are opposite each other on the color wheel.

Exercise F3 (Tracks 95–98)

Narrator	Excerpt one.
Man	You know not all on-campus jobs are covered by the work-study program, right? A lot of positions are open to any student.
Woman	Really? I actually didn't know that – thanks for clarifying.
Narrator	Excerpt two.
Woman	Making a weekly or monthly budget – and sticking to it – can really help keep your living expenses under control. When I was a student I managed to cut my weekly expenses by almost $50 just by setting and following a budget.
Man	$50 a week? Wow! I've read that having a budget is a good idea, but hearing your example really drives the point home.
Narrator	Excerpt three.
Woman	At the end of the sixteenth century, *mezzo-fresco* painting became increasingly common and popular. Painting *mezzo-fresco* had most of the permanency of *buon fresco*, and, like *secco fresco*, the colors did not fade once dry. Those two reasons led to many artists preferring *mezzo-fresco* to *buon fresco*.
Narrator	Excerpt four.
Man	Look at this painting by Claude Monet titled *Water-Lily Pond and Weeping Willow*. Notice how the yellows, greens, and blues work well together. We call groups of similar colors like these, which lie next to each other on the color wheel, analogous colors. Now look at another Monet work – *Impression, Sunrise* – with the vivid orange sun standing out strongly against the blue background. This is a good example of what we call complementary colors, which means contrasting colors like these that are opposite each other on the color wheel. To make those definitions even clearer, let me show you the two images side by side so you can see the difference between analogous and complementary colors easily.

Exercise G1 – question 1 (Tracks 99 and 100)

Narrator	Listen to a conversation in the Finance Office.
Male Student	Excuse me? Could you give me some suggestions for financial aid that I could get?
Female Employee	I'll help if I can, but you should know that the college has only a limited number of scholarships, and competition for them is tough. Typically, only students who have a perfect or near perfect academic record will get them.

Student	That's not what I want to hear. I had to get a part-time job and now I never seem to have enough time to study to keep my grades up.
Employee	Have you considered getting a student loan? The application process is quick and most applicants are accepted.
Student	To be honest, I'd be worried about repaying a loan. I've heard that the interest rates are pretty high.
Narrator	Question 1. Listen again to part of the conversation. What does the man mean?
Student	That's not what I want to hear. I had to get a part-time job and now I never seem to have enough time to study to keep my grades up.

Exercise G1 – question 2 (Tracks 101 and 102)

Narrator	Listen to part of a discussion in an art history seminar.
Male Professor	Now, a question I get asked all the time is who was the real model for Da Vinci's *Mona Lisa*? I understand that people like a good mystery, but I don't see that there's any mystery here.
Female Student	But I'm sure I read an argument that the *Mona Lisa* is actually a self-portrait of Leonardo Da Vinci himself.
Professor	Look, there are numerous theories that the woman is actually Da Vinci, or one of his male apprentices, or his mother, or Isabella of Aragon, or even nobody at all, uh, that Da Vinci painted an ideal woman rather than an actual woman. But there is *written* evidence dating from the time when we think the painting was made that Da Vinci painted Lisa Gherardini del Giocondo, which in my view is pretty compelling evidence. And take the names by which the painting has been known for hundreds of years. In English, we call it *Mona Lisa*, meaning "My Lady Lisa." And the French and Italian names – *La Joconde* and *La Gioconda*, respectively – are feminine forms of Lisa Gherardini's married name, del Giocondo. So as far as I'm concerned, the model is Lisa Gherardini and all of the other theories are interesting but incorrect.
Narrator	Question 2. Why does the speaker talk about the meanings of the name of the painting?

Exercise G1 – questions 3 and 4 (Tracks 103–105)

Narrator	Listen to part of a lecture about Chinese art.
Female Professor	In Chinese art, the so-called Four Gentlemen, or Four Noble Ones, is the name given to four plants that are considered to symbolize both the beauty and characteristics of the four seasons and certain moral qualities. The Four Gentlemen have featured widely in Chinese ink wash art since the Song Dynasty. They also feature in the ink wash art of other East Asian cultures – Korea, Japan, and Vietnam, for instance – that have been heavily influenced by Chinese culture.
	Starting from spring, the first of the Four Gentlemen is the orchid, which has a certain fragile grace and beauty. The gentle scent of the orchid was taken to symbolize modesty, purity, and even nobility.
	Although bamboo grows prolifically throughout the year, it does so most abundantly during the summer months. It is revered for its strength and flexibility, and symbolizes inner peace, tolerance, and integrity, as well as energy and vitality.
	The chrysanthemum blooms later than other flowers and so symbolizes fall. Because it is sometimes still in flower when the first snow is on the ground, it is seen as a symbol of endurance and bravery.

The winter Gentleman is the plum blossom. It's the first flower of the new year to bloom, often when snow is still on the ground, and signals that spring will soon return. From this, it should not come as a surprise that the plum blossom symbolizes hope and faith.

Narrator	Question 3. Listen again to part of the lecture. Why does the woman say this?
Professor	Although bamboo grows prolifically throughout the year, it does so most abundantly during the summer months.
Narrator	Question 4. Listen again to part of the lecture. What does the woman mean?
Professor	It's the first flower of the new year to bloom, often when snow is still on the ground, and signals that spring will soon return. From this, it should not come as a surprise that the plum blossom symbolizes hope and faith.

Exercise G3 (Tracks 106–111)

Narrator	Question 1. Listen to part of a conversation between a student and her professor.
Female Student	Hi, Professor. Could I ask you a question about the assignment? I did the reading you recommended, but I'm still not clear on Rembrandt's influences.
Male Professor	The quick answer is the three Ls: Leiden, Lastman, and Lievens. Do some research on those names, and I think his influences will be clearer, OK?
Narrator	Listen again to part of the conversation. What reason does the student have for saying this to her professor?
Student	I did the reading you recommended, but I'm still not clear on Rembrandt's influences.
Narrator	Question 2. Listen to part of a lecture in a class about classical art.
Professor	Last class we discussed sculpture in classical and Hellenistic Greece, and today we're going to take on the Romans. The Greek influence is very strong, but despite this, Roman sculpture stands on its own in two areas. The first is portraiture, which was arguably the dominant genre of Roman sculpture. The other is relief sculptures, especially narrative reliefs commemorating a triumph. Think of a flat surface which has been carved and chiseled away so that certain areas and shapes stand out from the surface. That's a relief.
Narrator	Listen again to part of the lecture. What reason does the professor have for saying this to his students?
Professor	Think of a flat surface which has been carved and chiseled away so that certain areas and shapes stand out from the surface. That's a relief.
Narrator	Listen to part of a lecture about religious art.
Female Professor	OK, so before we move on, does anyone have any questions about triptych panel paintings?
Male Student	Yeah, I'm not clear on the period during which triptychs were common.
Professor	Your reading explains the dates more than adequately and we're almost out of time, so I'm sorry but I'm not going to get into that question more at this point, OK? Right, now let's quickly talk about Hans Memling.
Narrator	Question 3. Listen again to part of the lecture. What reason does the professor have for saying this to her student?
Professor	Your reading explains the dates more than adequately and we're almost out of time, so I'm sorry but I'm not going to get into that question more at this point, OK?

Exercise I1 – questions 1 and 2 (Tracks 112–114)

Narrator   Listen to a conversation between a student and his professor.

Male Student   Hi, Professor. Do you have a minute?

Female Professor   Sure, come in, Todd. How can I help?

Student   I'm sorry this is short notice, but I'm not going to be able to help out with the art show during spring break.

Professor   Oh, uh, well that's too bad and your help will definitely be missed. Do you... I mean, is there anything wrong?

Student   Not exactly. It's just that I realized my financial situation is really not good, so I'm going to have to try and get a part-time job.

Professor   Hmmm. You know, we have some discretionary funds for the art show and I *might* be able to use those funds to hire you rather than have you work as a volunteer.

Student   Really? Wow! That would be awesome. Thanks so much, Professor.

Professor   Hold on, Todd. Don't get too excited just yet. I'm not the only person on the organizing committee, you know. I think everyone will agree to pay you because at our last meeting we discussed the idea of hiring a couple of student assistants, but I don't want to make a promise that I might not be able to keep.

Student   Thanks. I mean, even if it doesn't work out, I appreciate that you're trying to help me.

Professor   My pleasure. When I was a student it was always a struggle to pay my tuition and fees, so I know what it feels like. Now, assuming that I can use the discretionary funds to pay you, I want to make a couple of things clear. First, I won't be able to pay you very much per hour, but you can expect to get about 8 to 10 hours of work a day for about a week. Is that OK?

Student   That sounds fine. Would I be doing the same things we discussed before?

Professor   Yes, you'd be doing the same things as the people who are just volunteering, but we'd ask you to do a lot of other things, too, some of which won't be, how can I say this?, won't be the most exciting things you've ever done.

Student   No problem! As long as I'm helping out with the show and will still get a chance to meet some of the artists, I'll be happy.

Professor   Glad to hear it. Now, the next committee meeting is on Thursday morning, so I should have an answer for you by lunchtime on that day. I'll email you with the news, OK?

Student   Thanks, Professor. Fingers crossed!

Narrator   Question 1. Listen again to part of the conversation.

Student   I'm sorry this is short notice, but I'm not going to be able to help out with the art show during spring break.

Professor   Oh, uh, well that's too bad and your help will definitely be missed.

Narrator   What does the professor mean when she says this?

Professor   Oh, uh, well that's too bad and your help will definitely be missed.

Narrator   Question 2. Listen again to part of the conversation.

Professor   Hold on, Todd. Don't get too excited just yet. I'm not the only person on the organizing committee, you know. I think everyone will agree to pay you because at our last meeting we discussed the idea of hiring a couple of student assistants, but I don't want to make a promise that I might not be able to keep.

Narrator   Why does the professor say this?

Professor   Hold on, Todd. Don't get too excited just yet. I'm not the only person on the organizing committee, you know.

Exercise I1 – questions 3 and 4 (Tracks 115–117)

Narrator   Listen to part of a lecture in an art history class.

Male Professor   The Group of Seven is the name given to a group of Canadian artists who were active from 1920 to 1933. The original members of the group, who were all from Toronto, were Arthur Lismer, A. Y. Jackson, Franklin Carmichael, Frederick Varley, J. E. H. MacDonald, Lawren Harris, and Frank Johnston, who left the group in 1926. Uh, I'm just giving you a quick overview here: all these names are listed in chapter 3 of your course book, OK? Over the next 12 years, other artists were invited to join, with A. J. Casson becoming a member in 1926, Edwin Holgate in 1930, and LeMoine Fitzgerald in 1932.

Two other Canadian artists often associated with the Group of Seven despite never being official members are Tom Thompson and Emily Carr. Thomson died before the group was officially founded, but he nevertheless had a profound influence on the style, aesthetic, philosophy, and choice of subject matter of the other members of the group.

At first, members of the group painted a variety of scenes, but after their first exhibition in 1920, they began to focus on landscape paintings, and they are best known today for their paintings inspired by the Canadian landscape. Indeed, the Group originally thought of naming themselves the Algonquin school after Algonquin Park in Ontario, the wild beauty of which inspired many of their works.

The Group of Seven were influenced by Impressionism and other modern art movements from the end of the nineteenth century, including Fauvism and Symbolism. Members of the Group favored painting outdoors, which required them to work quickly in order to finish a piece. This led to paintings that sketched or simplified the landscapes they could see, not ones that focused on accurate reproduction and imitation of natural effects. The artists used bold, bright colors – often working in *impasto* – and painted simplified, almost abstract shapes to represent the feeling of natural features like lakes, trees, and mountains.

Here's a slide of a representative painting by Lawren Harris from 1926 titled *North Shore Lake Superior*. Though I should make clear at this point that Harris's works are more simplified and stylized than other members of the Group of Seven. Still, notice how the sky, lake, rocks, clouds, even the dead tree stump in the foreground are represented by blocks and lines of strong colors.

Narrator   Question 3. Listen again to part of the lecture.

Professor   The original members of the group, who were all from Toronto, were Arthur Lismer, A. Y. Jackson, Franklin Carmichael, Frederick Varley, J. E. H. MacDonald, Lawren Harris, and Frank Johnston, who left the group in 1926. Uh, I'm just giving you a quick overview here: all these names are listed in chapter 3 of your course book, OK? Over the next 12 years, other artists were invited to join, with A. J. Casson becoming a member in 1926, Edwin Holgate in 1930, and LeMoine Fitzgerald in 1932.

Narrator	Why does the professor say this?
Professor	Uh, I'm just giving you a quick overview here: all these names are listed in chapter 3 of your course book, OK?
Narrator	Question 4. Listen again to part of the lecture.
Professor	At first, members of the group painted a variety of scenes, but after their first exhibition in 1920, they began to focus on landscape paintings, and they are best known today for their paintings inspired by the Canadian landscape. Indeed, the Group originally thought of naming themselves the Algonquin school after Algonquin Park in Ontario, the wild beauty of which inspired many of their works.
Narrator	Why does the professor say this?
Professor	Indeed, the Group originally thought of naming themselves the Algonquin school after Algonquin Park in Ontario, the wild beauty of which inspired many of their works.

Exercise I1 – questions 5 and 6 (Tracks 118–120)

Narrator	Listen to part of a talk in a paleontology class. The professor is discussing prehistoric art.
Female Professor	Today we're going to discuss the amazing prehistoric cave paintings that were found in the Chauvet Cave in southern France. The cave was discovered in, I believe, late 1994. Since then it has been studied extensively by archaeologists, but not by the public, who are not allowed into the cave. As you may know, some of the art in caves that were open to the public – such as the famous Lascaux Cave, also in France – suffered damage. As a result, very few caves with prehistoric art remain accessible to the public. The majority of paintings at Chauvet Cave have been dated to the end of the Aurignacian period, as much as 32,000 years before present, making them some of the earliest examples of cave art known. Many of the images are typical of paleolithic cave art. We see numerous prey species, including horses, mammoths, aurochs – uh, that's a kind of large wild cow. This slide shows a typical example of the art in the cave. Some of these prey animals are shown interacting – two rhinos are shown engaging in aggressive behavior towards each other, for instance.

Also typical is the absence of complete human figures. Surprisingly, however, there are also numerous images of predator species like cave lions, cave bears, and hyenas.

The art on the walls of Chauvet Cave has been praised as being of very high quality for the time. To produce these images the artists used the same mineral pigments used elsewhere, namely red and yellow ochre, charcoal for black, umber for brown, calcite for white, and so on. They also used typical techniques, including painting with fingers and primitive brushes, as well as blowing or spitting paint around their hands to produce outlined shapes. Interestingly, scientists recently analyzed 32 hand prints from caves with paleolithic paintings in France and Spain. They looked at various points of data such as overall size, length of hand, and ratio of one finger to another, and determined that a majority of the artists who created these handprints were probably female.

The artists at Chauvet – whether male or female – also used some unique techniques – or at least ones we have not seen in other cave art of the period. It appears the walls were scraped before painting to create a smooth, lighter-colored surface on which to apply the paint. Further, the artists used a tool to etch around some of the figures, thus creating a slight sense of movement and three-dimensionality. So the figures were rather lifelike, but were they accurate? Scholars have long debated how accurately cave painters depicted the animals of their natural environment. Recent DNA analysis of horse bones and teeth suggests that the types of horses shown on the walls at Chauvet did indeed exist in Europe at that time, making it likely the artists were painting real animals rather than symbolic ones.

Narrator	Question 5. Listen again to part of the lecture. What does the woman mean?
Professor	Also typical is the absence of complete human figures. Surprisingly, however, there are also numerous images of predator species like cave lions, cave bears, and hyenas.
Narrator	Question 6. Why does the professor discuss DNA analysis of horse bones and teeth?

UNIT 11 | LISTENING • Understanding the Speaker's Attitude Questions

Exercise D1 (Tracks 121 and 122)

Narrator	Listen to part of a conversation between a student and a professor.
Female Student	Excuse me, Professor? I've heard your modern poetry seminar class is really good and I'd love to take it next semester but I haven't taken the prerequisite class. I did some independent research on modern poetry in high school, though, and I'm planning to major in literature so I was hoping you'd give me permission to take the class anyway.
Male Professor	You mean take the seminar without having taken the prerequisite?
Student	Yeah. Is that possible?
Professor	No, I'm sorry. In my experience, students who haven't taken prerequisite classes always have a hard time, so I no longer give permission. I'd have no problem if you wanted to audit the class, though.
Student	I hadn't thought about auditing the class but it's actually a good idea. Thank you.
Narrator	Listen to part of a lecture in a creative writing class.

Female Professor	In storytelling, something that moves the story forward – such as a situation, event, object, or even character – is called a plot device. You'll find plot devices in pretty much every story because they're a necessary part of storytelling, but in some cases they can be too obvious and not believable to readers. One type of plot device with a particularly bad reputation is the "deus ex machina." This plot device typically involves a miraculous event, such as the arrival of a hero, that saves the lives of the main protagonists. Stories that use deus ex machina can seem unbelievable or unnatural and writers who use it may find themselves criticized for a lack of creativity. However, when authors take care to ensure that plot devices like the deus ex machina are consistent with the events of the story, these devices are often accepted by readers, in fact, readers may not even notice them. There's an example of a deus ex machina in the classic novel *Lord of the Flies* when a naval officer appears at the end of the story and rescues the children. Although this is a deus ex machina, it arises naturally from the events of the story and, as a result, seems believable and authentic rather than contrived and inept.

Exercise D2 (Tracks 123–126)

Narrator Speaker one.

Man Actually, you haven't taken the necessary prerequisite classes for this course, so you won't be able to register for it.

Narrator Speaker two.

Woman That's a very interesting and insightful question, Sophia, but one that's not easy to answer simply.

Narrator Speaker three.

Man Although it's now considered a classic, when J. D. Salinger's *The Catcher in the Rye* was first published it had mixed reviews, with some critics being especially put off by the use of strong language.

Narrator Speaker four.

Woman Your midterm assignment is due in just a couple of weeks, but so far less than half of you have come to discuss your project with me.

Exercise D3 (Tracks 127 and 128)

Narrator Excerpt one. Listen to part of a conversation between a student and his tutor.

Male Student Hi Professor. I'm having some difficulty with the assignment you set. Could you explain dramatic irony for me?

Female Professor I thought we'd covered this in class pretty thoroughly, but, uh, let's take Shakespeare's *Romeo and Juliet* as an example. Near the end of that play Romeo kills himself because he thinks Juliet's dead. But the audience knows that she's actually asleep not dead, so all Romeo has to do is wait for her to wake up.

Student So that's dramatic irony? A situation that the audience knows but the characters in the story don't know?

Professor Well, that's a little simplistic, but on the whole it's a good definition.

Narrator Excerpt two. Listen to part of a lecture in a literature class. The professor is discussing narrative fiction.

Male Professor Allegory has been used for thousands of years in art and narrative literature because it's a powerful way to express complex ideas but sometimes those ideas are not always obvious. I remember when I was a child that I had to read George Orwell's classic story *Animal Farm* for a school assignment. At first, I wasn't that interested in the story. I didn't find the concept or the actions of the characters believable. I mentioned this to my teacher one day and she told me that the story's actually an allegory about political events in the former Soviet Union. I hadn't understood that at all, but when I continued reading the story with that knowledge, I found it much more interesting; so much so, in fact, that after finishing it, I re-read the book immediately.

Exercise E1 (Tracks 129–134)

Narrator Speaker one.

Woman I haven't decided which subject to major in yet, but my preference is either for modern history or ancient history, with a minor in archaeology.

Narrator Speaker two.

Woman In the year 8 A.D., the Roman poet Ovid was banished from Rome. It's not exactly clear what he did to be exiled, but my view is that a poem he wrote caused political embarrassment to Augustus, the emperor of Rome at that time.

Narrator Speaker three.

Woman During the 1930s, 40s, and 50s cheap, poorly-produced, pulp magazines published science fiction. They often had similar names like *Astounding Stories*, *Amazing Stories*, *Wonder Stories*, and *Planet Stories*. Some of the stories in these magazines were written by acclaimed authors like Robert Heinlein, Isaac Asimov, Ray Bradbury, and Arthur C. Clarke and were excellent. I'd say that the majority of stories, though, were of very low quality.

Narrator Speaker four.

Woman I understand that you're interested in taking a couple of elective classes this semester, but it seems to me that you'd be better off taking at least one more core class. In my experience, it's usually better to take all the required classes as soon as you can.

Narrator Speaker five.

Woman Let me just define a couple of literary terms: alliteration and assonance. From my point of view, the difference between these two concepts is pretty clear, but they often seem to cause confusion. In simple terms, alliteration is a literary effect that occurs when a writer uses several words that begin with the same consonant sound, such as the D sounds in "deep and dreary" or the L sounds in "lazy languid line." Assonance, in contrast, is when a writer uses several words that have the same vowel sound, like the repeated E sound in "mellow wedding bells."

Narrator Speaker six.

Man Herman Melville is today considered one of the great American novelists of the nineteenth century, but for much of his lifetime and for decades after his death he was not seen that way at all. I'm convinced that his early travel stories, which were both popular and well-received critically, led people to assume that Melville was a writer of exciting adventure stories. When he began to write more serious novels like *Moby-Dick*, which for me is the best novel of the nineteenth century, critics and readers were confused and this led to bad reviews, poor sales, and, ultimately, a prolonged decline in his reputation.

Exercise E3 (Tracks 135 and 136)

Narrator Excerpt one. Listen to a conversation between a student and her professor.

Female student You wanted to see me, Professor?

Male Professor Yes, Sally. Thank you for coming. I wanted to ask if you'd given any thought to your choice of major.

Student Um, I'm thinking about doing sociology with a minor in business, but I haven't made up my mind yet. Why?

Professor Well, you always ask excellent questions and participate well in class. And I was impressed with some of the ideas in your most recent assignment. So I wanted to say that I think you could do really well if you chose to major in literature.

Student Wow. I really enjoy your seminar, but I'm a little shocked. I mean, I only got a B minus for my last assignment.

Professor You didn't get a higher grade because your essay wasn't long enough and, to be honest, it wasn't very well organized, but your ideas were original and interesting.

Student Well, I thought I might take a few literature electives, but I hadn't considered it as a major. Let me think about it, OK?

Professor Sure, of course. Take your time, and if you have any questions, my door's open, OK?

Narrator	Excerpt two. Listen to part of a lecture in a comparative literature class.
Female Professor	Morning, everyone. Today we're going to discuss the development of the European novel and we've got a lot to cover, so let's get started, OK? Novels can be defined as extended narratives written in prose that typically have a plot that's unified and structured, an emphasis on characters, and, despite being fictional, an illusory sense of realism.
	Some extended works of prose fiction written before the seventeenth century have been called novels. These works include the *Satyricon* and the *Golden Ass* by Roman writers Petronius and Apuleius. These are certainly interesting works, but they differ in a number of ways from what we think of as a novel today – as exemplified by the definition I just gave. There's an interesting comparison chart in the reading that explains those differences, and also covers early works from other cultures such as the *Tale of Genji* by Japanese writer Murasaki Shikibu, so I'll not be discussing them any further.
	Among the earliest works that fit into our modern definition of the novel is *Don Quixote* by Cervantes, first published in 1605. This work, which today we classify as a picaresque novel, had a major influence on the development of later writers including Fielding, Dumas, and Twain. Its influence continues to this day as evidenced by a recent survey of 100 well-known authors from around the world – people like Norman Mailer, Salman Rushdie, Nadine Gordimer – who voted it the best book ever written. I'm not sure that I would go that far, but *Don Quixote* is definitely an interesting book that's worth reading.

Exercise F3 (Tracks 137 and 138)

Narrator	Excerpt one. Listen to part of a conversation between a student and an employee in the registrar's office.
Male Student	Hi. I just got a letter telling me that I need to take three additional credits of core classes, but I'm sure I've taken all the required classes. Could you look into it for me?
Female Employee	Sure. In most cases like this, there's a simple explanation, but let me have a look at your academic record, OK? It will just take a second. Well, according to the computer, last semester you took a class called Introduction to Social Sciences but didn't complete it.
Student	Really? But I *know* I completed that class.
Employee	Uh, let me check something … just a second … Hmmm. Apparently *nobody* who took that class has completed it, which doesn't sound very likely. I don't want to blame anyone, but perhaps that professor hasn't updated the class records yet.
Student	So what should I do? Go and see my professor?
Employee	That's what I would do.
Narrator	Excerpt two. Listen to part of a lecture in a world literature class.
Male Professor	OK, let's continue our discussion of different forms of poetry from around the world with an analysis of Japanese poems. Let's start with probably the best known Japanese poetic form: haiku. Traditional Japanese haiku need three things. First, and most importantly, they need a cut – um, *juxtaposition* might be a better word – between two images or ideas. This cut is indicated by a *kireji*, or cutting word. Um, we'll look at some

examples shortly, which will make this idea clearer. OK, second, a haiku needs to have 17 *sounds* in the pattern five, seven, five. In English we often talk about haiku having 17 syllables, but "syllable" is not exactly the right translation. And third, haiku traditionally need a *kigo*, or, um, seasonal reference word that's taken from a defined list of such expressions. For example, if you were to hear or see the phrases "April showers" or "budding leaves," you'd probably think about spring. Now I'm not going to claim that those are particularly poetic phrases, but they give you a sense of what the seasonal references in haiku are like.

Exercise G1 (Tracks 139 and 140)

Narrator	Excerpt one. Listen to part of a discussion in a modern poetry class.
Male Professor	*The Love Song of J. Alfred Prufrock* is widely considered one of the seminal early works of modern poetry, but when it was first published in 1915, it came in for some fairly harsh criticism. There were a few positive reviews, but many reviewers called it obscene, vulgar, and shocking, for example, and more than a few reviewers argued that it wasn't poetry at all. As the years have passed, however, critical judgment has changed and, as I said, it's now considered a classic example of early modern poetry.
Female Student	Excuse me, Professor, but why do people think that it's a classic poem? I mean, I found it really hard and unsettling to read, and it made me feel kind of uncomfortable.
Professor	Those are interesting points, Julie, and a lot of people probably feel the same way… but that's kind of the point. Modern poetry often is deliberately unsettling and uncomfortable to read because modern poetry developed out of a desire to be very different from the Romantic ideals of earlier poetry.
Student	So do you find it unsettling, Professor?
Professor	Uh, not really, no. I actually find it very moving. For me Prufrock is a sad, lonely figure, and Eliot's powerful language and imagery serve to heighten those elements.
Narrator	Excerpt two. Listen to part of a lecture in a world literature class.
Female Professor	During the nineteenth century, French novelist Jules Verne wrote a number of best-selling adventure novels that had a major influence on both science and literature, especially the genre of science fiction. Many of his stories include surprisingly accurate descriptions of later technological advances.
	During his lifetime, Verne was at first praised by contemporary critics, but over time his broad commercial popularity with the public led critics to consider him a mere storyteller and someone who wrote low-quality works. For example, unlike many of his less-popular peers, Verne *wasn't* nominated for membership in important institutions such as the Académie Française, the, uh, French Academy. In my view this criticism of Verne was unfair – many of his ideas were at least as interesting as those of his contemporaries and his writing style was both innovative and influential.
	In his native France and in other European countries the contemporary view of Verne changed slowly but surely. I would say that these days most academics from Europe consider him a major literary figure and numerous academic studies and articles about him have been published. For various reasons, however, in English-

speaking countries, especially the UK and the USA, Verne's reputation as a mere storyteller, rather than a serious writer, has lasted much longer.

Exercise I1 – questions 1 and 2 (Tracks 141–143)

Narrator   Listen to a conversation between a student and a professor.

Female Student   Thanks for seeing me, Professor.

Male Professor   No problem, Susan. How can I help?

Student   I've completed most of my core classes, and I wanted to take a couple of electives in the film studies department next semester. I'm planning to major in comparative literature and minor in film studies and I was hoping you could give me some advice about which one of two elective classes would be most useful for me to take.

Professor   Um, I'll help if I can, but the final decision is obviously one that you'll have to make.

Student   Yeah, I've almost made up my mind already, but I just wanted to get your input before deciding. One class I'm thinking about is called Introduction to Scriptwriting, and the other one is Film Script Analysis. They both have course descriptions that sound really interesting.

Professor   Well, if you're planning to major in comparative lit, I'd say Film Script Analysis might be the better option for you. In that class you'll analyze the scripts from classic films for their plot, characterization, dialogue, and so on. In other words, you'll use many of the same kinds of thinking and critical tools that you use when you study works of literature. It's taught by Professor Nowak, too, who's a really dynamic, interesting lecturer.

Student   That *does* sound good. How about the other class, Introduction to Scriptwriting?

Professor   The focus of that class is on learning how to write your own scripts, so it's more of a creative writing class than a class on literary criticism. You know, I have a feeling that class has at least one creative writing prerequisite, too. Did you check for prerequisites?

Student   No, I didn't look at the requirements of that class. And if I'd realized the focus was on creative writing, I probably wouldn't have come to see you, to be honest, as writing's not an interest of mine. Still, it definitely sounds like the script analysis class is going to be useful and interesting for me. Thanks, Professor. I really appreciate your input.

Narrator   Question 1. What is the professor's attitude to helping the student?

Narrator   Question 2. What does the student say about creative writing?

Exercise I1 – questions 3 and 4 (Tracks 144–146)

Narrator   Listen to part of a discussion in a sociology class. The subject of the discussion is the Nobel Prize in Literature.

Male Professor   The Nobel Prize in Literature is one of five Nobel prizes awarded annually. During his lifetime, Swedish inventor and businessman Alfred Nobel made a fortune from the invention of dynamite but he wanted his legacy to be one of peace and culture rather than violence and destruction. As a result, he stated in his will that the bulk of his assets were to be used to endow some prizes named after him.

According to the terms of Nobel's will, the prize in literature was intended to be awarded to authors whose body of work best met certain ideals. In other words, and this is an important point that we'll come back to later, the award is supposed to be given not for individual novels, poems, or plays, but rather for a writer's work over his or her lifetime.

Recipients for the Nobel Prize in Literature are chosen by members of the Swedish Academy based on nominations. The first prize was awarded in 1901 to French poet and essayist Sully Prudhomme, who was well-regarded in his day but whose work is now little known. Notable winners in the first decades of the twentieth century were Irish poet William Butler Yeats in 1923, English dramatist and critic George Bernard Shaw in 1925, German writer Thomas Mann in 1929, and American playwright Eugene O'Neill in 1936. More recent winners whose names you might know include Harold Pinter, Günter Grass, Seamus Heaney, and William Golding.

Now almost since it began, the, uh, Roberta? You have a question?

Female Student   Yeah, I don't think you've mentioned any female recipients, have you? Does that mean no women have won the prize?

Professor   You picked up on that very quickly, Roberta. I was about to mention that almost since its inception, the prize has been the focus of controversy, and one of the controversies has been the number of female winners. Since 1901 about 110 people have been awarded the literature prize, but only 13 of them have been women. And I'm not alone in feeling that that figure is a pretty clear indication of gender bias.

Another issue that has caused controversy is that the members of the Swedish Academy seem very Eurocentric. Around two thirds of all prize-winners have been European.

Student   So it sounds like they're biased against writers from other continents as well as women.

Professor   A case could certainly be made for that, yes. Now I'm not going to defend the members of the Swedish Academy or argue that their decisions are impartial, but the situation has improved recently, in my view as a result of negative press coverage, especially in Sweden itself. In the last 25 years, slightly more than half the recipients have been non-European and just over a quarter have been women.

Narrator   Question 3. What does the professor think about the decisions of the Swedish Academy?

Narrator   Question 4. What does the professor think led to an improvement in the situation over the last 25 years?

Exercise I1 – questions 5 and 6 (Tracks 147–149)

Narrator   Listen to a part of a talk in an English literature class. The professor is discussing William Shakespeare.

Female Professor   Before we continue our discussion of Shakespeare's plays, I'd like to address the so-called "authorship question." Some of you might already have heard of this, but in a nutshell, there are a number of people who argue, and argue passionately, I might add, that the person who wrote the plays attributed to William Shakespeare of Stratford was not, in fact, William Shakespeare of Stratford. Different groups propose different candidates as the real author of the plays – with Sir Francis Bacon, Edward de Vere, Christopher Marlowe, and William Stanley being the main alternative candidates – but they all make the same basic arguments.

Let me give a quick overview of those arguments. First, they argue that there are no contemporary documents from the time when Shakespeare was alive that explicitly state that Shakespeare was either a dramatist or an actor, both of which we would expect if he were the author of the plays and poems. Second, the works attributed to Shakespeare are full of historical and literary references that would only have been known to somebody with a much higher level of education than William Shakespeare apparently had. And third, when Shakespeare died in 1616, it seems that nobody wrote any words praising him as a great writer, something that almost always happened in that era when a person of significance passed away. In addition, there are no references in the will of Shakespeare of Stratford to plays, poems, or indeed to books of any kind, which is a surprising omission for a person who supposedly had a career as a writer.

Those are all interesting arguments, but do they really stand up? My answer would have to be no, they don't. There's a saying that academics like to use: "absence of evidence is not evidence of absence." In other words, just

because there's no evidence for something, doesn't mean it isn't true. And for each point that the anti-Shakespeareans make, a counter-argument can be made, and evidence can be found, supporting the view that Shakespeare really *did* write the poems and plays attributed to him. Further, strong cases *against* each of the alternative candidates can easily be made. There is ample written evidence, for example, that Christopher Marlowe died in 1593, which is before most of Shakespeare's plays were written. Those who think that Marlowe was the author of the plays and poems claim that his death was faked, but, well, like most conspiracy theories, frankly that's a little hard to accept.

Narrator	Question 5. What opinion does the professor say some people hold?
Narrator	Question 6. What is the professor's opinion about the authorship question?

UNIT 12 | LISTENING • Understanding Organization Questions

Exercise D1 (Track 150)

Female Teacher	Good morning everyone. Today we're going to discuss strategies for answering Understanding Organization questions. Most Organization questions ask why the speaker discusses specific information, and there are two major strategies you can use. First, you should take notes about information that is likely to be helpful; and second, you should ask yourself questions about what you have just heard. Let's discuss these two strategies in more detail.
	In terms of taking notes, there are three things you can do that will be helpful for answering Organization questions. First, take notes when a speaker gives a long, detailed example about something. Second, take notes when a speaker compares or contrasts ideas. And third, and most importantly, take notes when a speaker seems to digress – that is when the speaker suddenly starts talking about something that seems unrelated to his or her previous point. In fact, almost all digressions in the TOEFL Test *are* related to the previous point, but the relationship may not be obvious unless you listen carefully until the end of the digression. OK? I hope that's clear.
	Now the second strategy I mentioned is asking yourself questions while you listen to the speakers. There are two helpful questions that you can ask yourself. First, as you listen you can ask "Why is the speaker saying this information?" Second, asking yourself "What is the speaker likely to talk about next?" is not only a good way to answer Organization questions, but may help you understand the whole lecture or conversation better, too. OK? Any questions?

Exercise D2 (Tracks 151–155)

Narrator	Excerpt one. Listen to a conversation between a student and a university employee.
Female Student	Excuse me. I'd like to move out of on-campus housing, and I was wondering what my options are.
Male Employee	Well, you could rent a room in a university-owned house in town or rent a privately-owned apartment. The university-owned houses are usually close to campus and you'd be sharing with other students. Privately-owned places, on the other hand, are often cheaper.

Narrator	Excerpt two. Listen to part of a lecture in a sociology class.
Female Professor	An issue with using experiments as a tool of social research is that if people are aware they are involved in an experiment, they often alter their behavior. The experiments conducted by Elton Mayo at a factory are a classic example. Mayo was trying to find the optimum set of working conditions to maximize employee output, but worker output increased regardless of whether a positive or negative change was made to working conditions. The reason? Because workers knew they were part of an experiment, they worked harder.
Narrator	Excerpt three. Listen to part of a lecture in a sociology class.
Male Professor	The Pygmalion effect can be understood in terms of expectations, with those of whom more is expected tending to perform better – in any kind of task – than people of whom less is expected. I forget his exact words, but industrialist Henry Ford made an interesting comment to the effect that "Whether you think you can do something, or whether you think you can't do it, you're right."
Narrator	Excerpt four. Listen to a conversation between a student and his academic advisor.
Female Professor	Is everything OK, Neil? You seem to have something on your mind.
Male Student	I was really looking forward to being an exchange student, but I'm finding it a lot harder than I expected. Everything's so different here.
Professor	I grew up in a tiny rural town – you'd probably call it a village – but when I was 15 my family moved to New York City. I found it really difficult because everything was so different, but my brother, who's one year younger than I am, found the experience really easy. When I asked him why, he said it was because everything was so different. I realized that he was right – I was looking at the differences as a negative thing, but he saw them as a positive.
Student	So you're suggesting that I change how I think about things? Focus on the positive not the negative?
Professor	Well, it can't hurt, right?
Narrator	Excerpt five. Listen to part of a talk about applied sociology.

Male Speaker   Today's talk is on applied sociology – also called public sociology – and, uh, I've learned from experience that before going any further, I need to define what that is. In simple terms, it's using the knowledge, tools, and methods of sociology to solve social problems. My own work provides a good illustration: over the last ten years, I've helped various state and city governments develop plans to deal with an aging population. Before that, for several years I worked with school boards to develop enhanced educational systems, especially systems designed to help students from minority backgrounds.

Exercises D4 and D5 (Tracks 156–159)

Narrator   Excerpt one. Listen to part of a conversation between a student and his academic advisor.

Female Professor   Hello, Jack. I hear you're thinking about becoming a grad student after you get your degree. Did you make a decision yet about what you're going to specialize in?

Male Student   I took a class in industrial sociology when I was a sophomore and I found it really interesting. I'd love to study it in more detail. I'm actually kind of disappointed I haven't been able to take any industrial sociology classes here as a junior or senior, in fact.

Professor   Industrial sociology? Interesting choice. Where were you thinking about applying?

Student   Well, I'd like to stay here, to be honest. I love the city, and everybody in the sociology department has been so helpful.

Professor   That's nice to hear, but you know that nobody in the department specializes in industrial sociology, right? That's why we offer so few undergraduate classes in that field.

Student   So… you're suggesting I should apply somewhere else?

Professor   If you're serious about going to grad school, I'd say yes, absolutely. Um, just off the top of my head I can think of a number of excellent schools that have faculty members who specialize in industrial sociology.

Narrator   Excerpt two. Listen to part of a lecture in a sociology class.

Male Professor   Before we finish, I'd like to give some background to two books I want you to read before next class. The first is *Guns, Germs, and Steel* by Jared Diamond. This book presents a very interesting and plausible argument about why some societies have been successful throughout history while others have not. In my view it's a particularly interesting work to study from a sociological perspective because the author is *not* a sociologist. In fact, the author was trained in physiology but is now a professor of geography. This background means that he doesn't always use the language of sociology to present his ideas, but those ideas are definitely worth studying. OK, so that's the first book I want you to read: *Guns, Germs, and Steel*, Jared Diamond. Got it?

Narrator   Excerpt three. Listen to part of a lecture in an introductory social sciences class.

Female Professor   Although participant observation as a research method is commonly associated with anthropology, it's been widely used as a tool in many other social science fields including sociology, human geography, psychology, linguistics, and behavioral economics. The basic premise is simple: a researcher joins a group – which can vary in size from a few people to a whole culture – and observes and even tries to experience what the people in that group see and feel. Although participant observation typically takes a long time – many studies last for months or longer – it often yields high quality data, and because the observer can focus on *any* aspect of behavior within the group being observed, it's one of the most flexible research methods available to scholars.

Narrator   Excerpt four. Listen to part of a discussion in a sociology seminar.

Male Professor   The family is clearly an important social structure, and therefore worthy of sociological study, but before we discuss some areas of study, can anyone give a quick overview of the main types of families? Yes, Nicola?

Female Student   Nuclear and extended families, right? With extended families being common only in developing regions, generally speaking.

Male Student   Aren't single-parent families becoming pretty common, too? I read that data from a recent census shows just over a quarter of family groups are composed of one parent and one or more children.

Professor   Good point, Tim. And that leads in to our next discussion: as a sociologist, it's not enough to know what kinds of families are common in a society, it's also important to know the answers to questions like why, where, when, and how. For example, in the case of single-parent families, we might ask *when* and *where* they first started becoming more prevalent in society. We might also ask *why* this happened and *how* the trend has affected society. Any thoughts?

Exercise E4 (Tracks 160–164)

Narrator   Excerpt one. Listen to part of a lecture in a sociology class. The professor is talking about designing experiments.

Male Professor   Sociology experiments are conducted on individuals, who often have subconscious biases, so before an experiment can be conducted, it's important to design the experiment in such a way as to minimize bias and other problems. If this is not done, the experiment may have limited internal validity and its results will be undermined. One solution to control bias is with a so-called blind experiment in which participants don't know what an experiment is designed to find out. A double-blind experiment can further reduce the problem of bias by keeping certain details of the experiment – for example, whether a participant is a member of the test group or the control group – hidden from the experimenter until after the experiment has concluded.

Narrator   Excerpt two. Listen to part of a talk in a sociology class. The professor is talking about social networks.

Female Professor   In broad terms, a social network is a social structure that is made up of interdependent individuals, groups, or organizations. In other words, each member of a network is in some way connected to and dependent upon the other members of that network. Sociologists study social networks at three levels – the micro, meso, and macro levels – and we'll explore each level in more detail today as well as talk about different kinds of social networks.

Narrator   Excerpt three. Listen to part of a discussion in a sociology class. The professor is talking about poverty.

Female Professor   Poverty has a number of effects on society, none of them good. For example, numerous studies have shown a causal link between poverty – among individuals and groups – and different types of crime, such as property crime and violent crime. One easy way to see this link is to overlay a map of crime rates in the neighborhoods of a city on a map

	showing poverty levels in the same city. By and large, the areas most affected by poverty will also be the areas with the highest crime levels.
Narrator	Excerpt four. Listen to part of a talk in a history of sociology class.
Male Professor	Positivism is the idea that society can be studied scientifically through objective observation, analysis, and classification. Taken to its logical conclusion, positivists believe that this kind of scientific analysis can reveal laws of human social behavior. Positivism is an important concept in sociology, but many scholars have questioned the validity of positivist thinking and come up with alternative ways of analyzing social data. In simple terms, these anti-positivists argue that scientific methods are suitable for studying the natural world but not for studying social phenomena.
Narrator	Excerpt five. Listen to part of a lecture in a media studies class.
Male Professor	Online communities have existed since ARPANET – the forerunner to today's Internet – was first launched in the late 1960s, but they became far more prevalent, and more important, only when personal computers hooked up to a network became widespread in the 1990s. Some early online communities existed in the 1970s. These communities were built around technologies like email and bulletin boards. As technology progressed and personal computers became more powerful, communities based around Internet chat began to develop. After the emergence of the World Wide Web in the early 1990s, websites and then web applications became the locus of many online communities. The web remains the dominant platform for such communities today, especially through social media services.

Exercise G1 – questions 1 and 2 (Tracks 165–167)

Narrator	Listen to a conversation between a student and a university official.
Female Official	Hi, can I help?
Male Student	Er, yes, I wanted some information about the exchange student program.
Official	I can help with that. What did you want to know?
Student	Well, pretty much everything, to be honest... but, uh, I guess my first question is what programs are available.
Official	We have exchange agreements with several universities in this country – those are usually for a single semester – plus universities in Germany, the UK, and New Zealand – those are all for one year.
Student	I'm really interested in going overseas, so I guess my next question is whether I would be eligible.
Official	Basically, any undergraduate who has successfully completed at least 15 credit hours is eligible. That excludes most freshman students in their first semester, but anyone else can apply. The minimum number of credits doesn't apply to grad students, but they must get permission from their department.
Student	Are spaces awarded based on academic record? My cumulative grade point average is about 3.2 right now, for what that's worth.
Official	As long as your GPA is 3.0 or better you can apply. Some programs are more competitive than others, though, like London, England, so it's a good idea to be flexible about where you apply.

Student	London would be great, but I'd be happy to study somewhere else, too. Now, what about getting credit if I get accepted into an exchange program? How does that work?
Official	You'd need to discuss that with your academic advisor if you're accepted. Every student's situation is different.
Student	I understand. Listen, thanks for your help.
Official	You're welcome. Did you want to take an application package?
Student	Yeah, that would be great. Thanks again.
Narrator	Question 1. Why does the woman talk about credit hours?
Narrator	Question 2. Why does the woman mention London?

Exercise G1 – questions 3 and 4 (Tracks 168–170)

Narrator	Listen to part of a lecture in an introductory sociology class.
Male Professor	Two important concepts in sociology that you need to understand are agency and structure. These are such central ideas that we'll come back to them again and again in class and you'll read about them often, so think of today's class as a quick overview or introduction.
	You'll obviously know the meaning of these words as they're used in everyday language, but in sociology the terms have specific meanings. Agency can be defined as the extent to which individuals have the freedom – the free will, if you like – to act as they wish and make the choices they want. Of course, individuals live in a society of patterns, norms, institutions, and traditions – what we call structure – that all influence people's behavior so that the number of actions they can take and choices they can make are, in fact, limited.
	One analogy that I think can clarify this distinction is to think of an individual employee at a company. In some matters, the employee has freedom to act as he wishes and do what he wants, but because he is an employee, he must also follow the rules, policies, and constraints of the company that employs him. Pressure from his co-workers and superiors shapes his normal actions and mode of behavior, and severely limits what he can do and still reasonably expect to keep his job. Another analogy you may come across in your reading is of a sports team – an individual member of the team has a degree of freedom, or agency, in how she acts, but must also follow the structure of her sport, that is both the written regulations and unspoken rules and codes of conduct.
	Now, a question that has been discussed – but *not* resolved – almost since the discipline of sociology was founded, is whether agency or structure has more of an impact on shaping human behavior. Early theorists tended to come down firmly on one side or the other of the debate. Some argued that individual agency is hardly limited by social structures at all and that people have a great capacity to act independently of society. Others argued, equally strongly, that social structures powerfully shape human actions, and everything that people do is a result of the society in which they live and their position within that society.
	In more modern times, various attempts have been made to argue that *both* agency and structure are important in explaining behavior and society, that *both* are valid concepts, and that one cannot exist without the other. An interesting analogy is to think of agency and structure as two sides of a sheet of paper. Just as a sheet of paper must have two sides to exist in a stable form, so agency and structure are mutually necessary.

Narrator	Question 3. How does the professor organize the lecture?
Narrator	Question 4. Why does the professor mention a sport team?

Exercise G1 – questions 5 and 6 (Tracks 171–173)

Narrator	Listen to part of a talk in a media studies class. The professor is discussing documentary films.
Female Professor	One of the most interesting trends in cinema over the past few decades has been the rise in the number of documentaries being made. Some people have even called this a golden age of documentary film-making. And many of these new documentaries are what we could call social issue documentaries.

The typical issue documentary covers a subject such as a political scandal, environmental issue, social problem, or humanitarian topic. Usually the causes and/or effects of the topic are discussed, and, in some cases, potential solutions are outlined. One of the most famous issue documentaries of recent times — and justly so, in my view – is *The Thin Blue Line* by Errol Morris. The film is not just a well-crafted, cinematically-accomplished piece, but Morris was able to tell the story in such a persuasive way that an innocent man was released from prison. Another well-known issue documentary is Al Gore's *An Inconvenient Truth* which laid out in very stark terms the effects of human activity on the environment.

How about some more examples? Anyone? |
| Male Student | What about Michael Moore's movies, like, uh, *Bowling for Columbine* and *Sicko*? I found those to be very powerful. And I really liked *Super Size Me*, though I forget the name of the director of that one. |
| Professor | Yes, Michael Moore has made a number of commercially successful issue documentaries. His film *Fahrenheit* |

9/11, for example, is the highest-grossing documentary in history. And a number of other film-makers have acknowledged Moore's influence on their documentaries. To my knowledge, Morgan Spurlock, who made *Super Size Me*, hasn't publicly stated that he was influenced by Michael Moore, but his documentaries are definitely in a very similar style to Moore's.

It's debatable, though, whether any of the documentaries by Moore or Spurlock – or indeed any of the many other excellent social issue documentaries – have had much of a social impact. And that brings me to some important questions. First, to what extent can and *do* issue documentaries change the behavior or thinking of either individuals or society? Second, and more importantly, should we expect documentaries to be able to do these things?

I've already mentioned that *The Thin Blue Line* led to the release of an innocent man, but it's hard to find other examples of documentaries that led to any concrete changes in society. And what about my second question, can we expect documentaries to be able to change people, uh, change society? At one level, I would argue that the answer should be no. Like other films, documentaries are created as a form of entertainment *not* as a means of social change. But on the other hand, these days many social issue documentaries are now backed by social action campaigns orchestrated through social media, websites, the mass media, and so on. These campaigns make it clear that the film-makers are setting out not just to make a film, but to make a social change, too.

Narrator	Question 5. How is the lecture organized?
Narrator	Question 6. Why does the professor mention *The Thin Blue Line* by Errol Morris?

UNIT 13 | LISTENING • Connecting Content Questions

Exercise C1 (Track 174)

Male Student	Professor Forster said there's going to be a quiz next class about Congress and the Capitol building. Want to do a quick review?
Female Student	Sure. Good idea... uh, let's start with Congress. There are two houses of representatives, right? The Lower and Upper.
Student	Yeah. The Lower House is usually called the House of Representatives and members serve for six years, I think.
Student	Actually, they only serve for two years. It's members of the Senate, the Upper House, who serve for six years… longer if they get re-elected.
Student	Oh, right… but I know for sure the total number of members of the Lower House is 435, and membership for each state is different according to whether the state has a small or large population.
Student	Right, but each state has two Senators and that number *doesn't* depend on a state's population. Now where does each house meet? I know it's in the Capitol building, but I forget which wing.
Student	Uh, the Lower House is in the south wing of the Capitol and the Senate meets in the north wing.
Student	OK, and the Capitol was built in the early nineteenth century, but before that Congress met in various cities like New York and Philadelphia.
Student	Right, but government wanted a permanent location so they began construction of the Capitol in Washington, D.C.
Student	Didn't they start using it before it was finished?
Student	That's right, and then after construction was finished, they used it for other purposes like church services and regular meetings as well as government functions. That's kind of strange for me.
Student	It certainly doesn't get used for other purposes these days. And if I remember correctly, the original Capitol soon became too small, so around 1850 they held a competition to get some designs for expanding the building.
Student	Right… Oh, I've got a class in a few minutes so I've got to rush. Do you want to continue reviewing later?
Student	Sure. Text me when your class is finished, OK?

Exercise D2 (Tracks 175–178)

Narrator	Excerpt one. Listen to part of a conversation between a student and his professor.
Male Student	Hi, Professor. Could you explain the assignments for your political science course? I couldn't attend yesterday's class when you discussed them, and although I tried to get the information from another student, I'm a bit confused and want to make sure I don't make a mistake.
Female Professor	Certainly. There are two assignments, a term paper and a case study. The term paper should be 750 words and is due at the end of the sixth week of the course. The case study needs to be longer – at least 1,000 words – and that must be submitted before the final week of the term.

Student	Is there a presentation, too? The student I asked mentioned something about that.
Professor	No. The case study *can* be done in the form of a presentation, if you like, but I don't want you to deliver a separate presentation as well, OK?
Narrator	Question 1. In excerpt one, which assignments does the woman say the man must do? One answer has been done for you.
Narrator	Excerpt two. Listen to part of a conversation between a student and a university housing officer.
Woman	Hi. I live in a college residence, but I didn't sign up for a meal plan yet. Could you tell me about the different plans?
Man	Sure, uh, we offer a block plan and a value plan. With the block plan, you're limited to eating in your residence dining hall and in the cafeteria in the Student Center. This plan gives you 10 meals per week, but of course you can use cash or a credit card to pay for as many additional meals as you like.
Woman	Is the block plan the one where I can eat as much as I like at each meal?
Man	Yes, that's right. Now the other plan is the value plan. With the value plan you pay in advance for a meal plan card and then every time you buy some food, the cost of the meal is deducted from your card. The big advantage of the value plan is that you can eat at any restaurant on campus, not just at your residence dining hall or the Student Center cafeteria. Another benefit is that you can use your card to eat as often as you like. You're not limited to 10 meals per week.
Narrator	Question 2. In excerpt two, which meal plans do the speakers discuss?
Narrator	Excerpt three. Listen to part of a lecture in a business class.
Female Professor	Trade agreements can be classified according to the number of countries that are involved. Unilateral agreements are ones in which one country, typically a wealthy, developed nation, offers economic incentives to one or more other nations when they export goods to the developed nation. This is a called unilateral agreement because only the exporting country gets a direct economic benefit from the agreement. A bilateral agreement, as the name suggests, is one between two nations, both of which benefit from the agreement when they import goods *from* or export goods *to* the partner country. And a multilateral agreement is one signed by several or multiple countries. Such agreements are similar to bilateral agreements in that all nations which have signed the agreement benefit from it either when importing or exporting goods.
Narrator	Question 3. In excerpt three, which types of trade agreement does the professor discuss?
Narrator	Excerpt four. Listen to part of a talk in a political science class.
Male Professor	There are many kinds of political systems, but pretty much all of them can be classified as one of three basic types. The first type is authoritarianism, in which all power is held by the government, which could be a single dictator, a ruling elite, or a coalition of bureaucrats and military leaders. Under authoritarian rule, people have no power to change the government and no input in the decisions that are made or laws that are passed by government. In a democracy, on the other hand, every person has the power to choose a different leader, repeal unpopular laws, and so on through his or her voting rights. Well, that's the

	theory. In practice, certain groups within a society may *not* have equal rights. It might surprise you to learn that Switzerland, for instance, did not pass legislation giving women the right to vote in federal elections until 1971. Under a monarchy, which is the third type of political system, power is controlled by a king or queen, a monarch, who gains and keeps power for life because of his or her birth, not through an election or even political skill.
Narrator	Question 4. In excerpt four, which types of political system does the professor describe?

Exercise E2 (Tracks 179–182)

Narrator	Excerpt one. Listen to part of a conversation between a student and his professor.
Male Student	Hi, Professor. Could you explain the assignments for your political science course? I couldn't attend yesterday's class when you discussed them, and although I tried to get the information from another student, I'm a bit confused and want to make sure I don't make a mistake.
Female Professor	Certainly. There are two assignments, a term paper and a case study. The term paper should be 750 words and is due at the end of the sixth week of the course. The case study needs to be longer – at least 1,000 words – and that must be submitted before the final week of the term.
Student	Is there a presentation, too? The student I asked mentioned something about that.
Professor	No. The case study can be done in the form of a presentation, if you like, but I don't want you to deliver a separate presentation as well, OK?
Narrator	Question 1. In excerpt one, the speakers discuss assignments for a class. Indicate which details match each assignment.
Narrator	Excerpt two. Listen to part of a conversation between a student and a university housing officer.
Woman	Hi. I live in a college residence, but I didn't sign up for a meal plan yet. Could you tell me about the different plans?
Man	Sure, uh, we offer a block plan and a value plan. With the block plan, you're limited to eating in your residence dining hall and in the cafeteria in the Student Center. This plan gives you 10 meals per week, but of course you can use cash or a credit card to pay for as many additional meals as you like.
Woman	Is the block plan the one where I can eat as much as I like at each meal?
Man	Yes, that's right … Now the other plan is the value plan. With the value plan you pay in advance for a meal plan card and then every time you buy some food, the cost of the meal is deducted from your card. The big advantage of the value plan is that you can eat at any restaurant on campus, not just at your residence dining hall or the Student Center cafeteria. Another benefit is that you can use your card to eat as often as you like. You're not limited to 10 meals per week.
Narrator	Question 2. In excerpt two, the speakers discuss meal plan options. Indicate which details match each meal plan.
Narrator	Excerpt three. Listen to part of a lecture in a business class.
Female Professor	Trade agreements can be classified according to the number of countries that are involved. Unilateral agreements are ones in which one country, typically a wealthy, developed nation, offers economic incentives to one or more other nations when they export goods to the

developed nation. This is called a unilateral agreement because only the exporting country gets a direct economic benefit from the agreement. A bilateral agreement, as the name suggests, is one between two nations, both of which benefit from the agreement when they import goods from or export goods to the partner country. And a multilateral agreement is one signed by several or multiple countries. Such agreements are similar to bilateral agreements in that all nations that have signed the agreement benefit from it either when importing or exporting goods.

Narrator   Question 3. In excerpt three, the professor discusses trade agreements. Indicate which description matches each type of agreement.

Narrator   Excerpt four. Listen to part of a talk in a political science class.

Male Professor   There are many kinds of political systems, but pretty much all of them can be classified as one of three basic types. The first type is authoritarianism, in which all power is held by the government, which could be a single dictator, a ruling elite, or a coalition of bureaucrats and military leaders. Under authoritarian rule, people have no power to change the government and no input in the decisions that are made or laws that are passed by government. In a democracy, on the other hand, every person has the power to choose a different leader, repeal unpopular laws, and so on through his or her voting rights. Well, that's the theory. In practice, certain groups within a society may not have equal rights. It might surprise you to learn that Switzerland, for instance, did not pass legislation giving women the right to vote in federal elections until 1971. Under a monarchy, which is the third type of political system, power is controlled by a king or queen, a monarch who gains and keeps power for life because of his or her birth, not through an election or even political skill.

Narrator   Question 4. In excerpt four, the professor discusses different types of political systems. Indicate which description matches each type of political system.

Exercise F1 (Tracks 183 and 184)

Narrator   Listen to part of a conversation between a student and his professor.

Male Student   Professor? Could I speak to you briefly?

Female Professor   Yes... uh, it's Jeremy, isn't it?

Student   That's right. I took your introduction to Political Science class last year.

Professor   And wrote an excellent end-of-term paper if I recall correctly. So, what can I do for you, Jeremy?

Student   Well, I loved your class – it was the most interesting class I took as a freshman, actually – and I'm thinking about majoring in political science. My family really wants me to study law, however. My parents and older sister are all lawyers and my grandfather was a judge, so it's kind of a family tradition. I think they'd be disappointed if I opted for political science.

Professor   OK, I see your problem, but not how I can help.

Student   Before I make a final decision about my major, I wanted to get a better idea of what political science is all about, and I was hoping you could suggest some books I could read.

Professor   I'd be happy to do that, Jeremy. Give me your email address and I'll send you a reading list, OK?

Student   Great! Thanks, Professor. I won't take up more of your time.

Professor   Uh, Jeremy, hold on a moment … You know, one field within political science is public law. And, well, perhaps if you took an interest in that aspect of the subject, your parents wouldn't object.

Student   Public law?

Professor   It's the study of legislation that determines how the government operates, how it interacts with individual citizens, what rights those citizens have, and so on. It's really not my field, but several of my colleagues are world-renowned experts.

Student   It sounds interesting. Could you include some texts about public law when you email me the reading list?

Professor   Sure, I'll do that.

Narrator   Listen to part of a lecture in a political science class. The professor is discussing two different voting systems.

Male Professor   Plurality voting is a common voting system in use in nations around the world. The basic principle is that during an election, citizens cast their vote for just one political party. When the votes are counted, the party with more votes is declared the winner. One obvious advantage of this voting system is that it's very easy for voters to understand, unlike some of the alternative systems. On the other hand, in countries like the USA and Canada, the winning party may receive votes from just 40% of voters meaning that the winning party does *not* have support from a majority of the population. Further, nations that operate this voting system tend to have only two or three major political parties. This reduces political choice for voters, who may feel that a vote for a minor party is a wasted vote because there is almost no chance it will change the outcome of the election.

Proportional voting systems are an alternative to plurality voting. In very simple terms, the amount of power that each political party gets after an election roughly depends on the percentage of votes that it receives in the election. A party that gets just 40% of the vote, for example, would get 40% of the seats in the government. Supporters of proportional representation argue that the system guarantees a government that more truly represents all of the citizens. Nations that operate a proportional voting system also tend to have a greater number of political parties, which may be seen as a plus. The downside of having numerous parties each with a proportion of seats in government is that no single party may have enough power to pass legislation without forming an alliance or coalition with other parties.

Exercise G3 (Tracks 185 and 186)

Narrator   Listen to a conversation between a student and an employee who works in the Housing Office.

Male Housing Officer   Hi, can I help?

Female Student   Yeah, I'm interested in becoming a resident advisor.

Housing Officer   OK, sure. Let me get you an application form. Here you go.

Student   Thanks, and could you give me some idea of the process?

Housing Officer   Sure, first you need to submit your application... uh, actually, sorry that's wrong. Starting this year, you're required to attend an information session *before* you can apply. The times and dates of the sessions are on the application form.

Student	OK.
Housing Officer	Then you'll need to submit the application form. Make sure you include a one-page essay and give the names of three people willing to act as references, one of whom *must* be a current or former RA.
Student	An essay?
Housing Officer	Yes, but not an academic paper, of course. It's more like the essay you wrote when you applied to this college to, you know, explain why you think you'd make a good RA.
Student	Ah, that makes sense.
Housing Officer	Once you've submitted your application, somebody in this office will review it and contact your references. That usually takes a week or so. After that, you might get asked to attend an interview.
Student	What kind of interview is it?
Housing Officer	It's a group interview with four other applicants. During that interview you'll be observed taking part in some team-building and problem-solving activities. And if you do well in the group interview, you'll be offered a role as an RA.
Student	I didn't realize it was so competitive. Anyway, thanks for the explanation.
Narrator	Listen to part of a lecture in a public law class. The professor is discussing the legislative process in the United States.
Female Professor	Let's quickly recap how laws are made in the United States. In the first step in the process, a proposal for a new piece of legislation – called a bill or a measure – is put forward by one or more sponsoring members of Congress. After this, the bill is referred to one or more committees in either the House of Representatives or the Senate. The committee members consider the potential effects of the bill in detail. If the committee decides to approve the bill, it is described as "reported" and a committee report is published. After this, the bill is debated by members of the House and then voted upon. If the vote is in favor of the bill, it is then referred to the other chamber of Congress where it can be approved, rejected, or amended. If a bill was approved by the Senate, for example, it must also be approved by the House of Representatives. If the bill is passed by both Houses, it is described as "enrolled" and sent to the President of the United States for approval. This is the final step in the legislative process. The bill becomes law either if the President signs it or takes no action within ten working days. The President also has the power to veto the bill, which means it does *not* pass into law unless at least two thirds of Representatives and Senators vote to override the President's veto.

Exercise H2 (Tracks 187–192)

Narrator	Excerpt one.
Female Student	Let's start with Congress. There are two houses of representatives, right? The Lower and Upper.
Narrator	Excerpt two.
Female Professor	A bilateral agreement, as the name suggests, is one between two nations, both of which benefit from the agreement when they import goods from or export goods to the partner country.
Narrator	Excerpt three.
Male Professor	The first type is authoritarianism, in which all power is held by the government, which could be a single dictator, a ruling elite, or a coalition of bureaucrats and military leaders.
Narrator	Excerpt four.
Male Professor	It might surprise you to learn that Switzerland, for instance, did not pass legislation giving women the right to vote in federal elections until 1971.
Narrator	Excerpt five.
Male Professor	The basic principle is that during an election, citizens cast their vote for just one political party.
Narrator	Excerpt six.
Female Professor	The President also has the power to veto the bill, which means it does *not* pass into law unless at least two thirds of Representatives and Senators vote to override the President's veto.

Exercise I1 – questions 1 and 2 (Tracks 193–195)

Narrator	Listen to a conversation between a student and a university employee.
Male Student	Hi. I'd like to apply to live in the new Pearson Dormitory, please. I know it's mainly for graduate students, but I read that undergraduates could also apply under special circumstances.
Female Housing Officer	Yes, that's true... um, do you think you *have* special circumstances?
Student	Yeah, I've got really bad allergies. I read that the new dorm was constructed using only environmentally-friendly techniques and materials. My doctor says that kind of building will be better for me.
Housing Officer	That's too bad. I get mild allergies sometimes, so I can sympathize.
Student	And the location will be so much better for me. Right now it can take me over an hour to get to classes if the traffic is bad.
Housing Officer	Ok, well I'll give you an application for the dorm. I obviously can't say that you'll be accepted, but it sounds like you have a pretty good case. You'll need to provide evidence for your allergies, though.
Student	That won't be a problem. The doctors and nurses at the clinic on campus know me well, and I see a specialist at a hospital in town, too.
Housing Officer	Here's the application. You know, it might be a good idea to discuss other options, in case your application for Pearson Dorm is rejected. Have you considered any of the other on-campus residences?
Student	I lived in McDonald Dorm when I was a freshman, but it's an old building and my allergies flared up really badly so I had to move out. I considered transferring into a different dorm, but they're all pretty old, so I didn't think any of them would be better for my allergies. Plus, all the dorms are single-sex and I'd rather live in a coeducational residence.
Housing Officer	So did you move into off-campus housing?
Student	Yeah. At first I found a shared room in a really nice but expensive house a couple blocks from campus. The house was constructed only a few years ago so my allergies weren't too bad at first, but then the owner got a dog and I had to move again. I've been living in a new apartment in town since last year. My allergies are OK there, but I can't really afford it and, like I mentioned, the travel time to and from campus is a big issue for me.
Housing Officer	Well, it sounds like Pearson is the best option for you. I certainly hope your application is accepted.

Student	Thanks. Me, too!
Narrator	Question 1. The speakers discuss a newly constructed dormitory. Indicate which benefits of this dormitory the speakers mention.
Narrator	Question 2. The speakers discuss two alternative housing options for the student. Indicate what the speakers say about each option.

Exercise I1 – questions 3 and 4 (Tracks 196–198)

Narrator	Listen to part of a lecture in an international relations class.
Male Professor	Today we're going to discuss the development of intergovernmental organizations like the League of Nations and the United Nations – the UN. The political thinker Immanuel Kant proposed a global organization very like the League of Nations in 1795, but it would be many years before governments, any official intergovernmental organizations, were actually created.

The first steps toward a global intergovernmental organization came in the nineteenth century when governments began discussing and creating several organizations to foster international cooperation. For example, the International Telegraph Union – now called the International Telecommunication Union – was founded in about, um, 1865. It might interest you to know that this organization actually still exists and is now a specialized agency of the United Nations.

A forerunner of the UN that resembled it in scope and purpose was the League of Nations. This intergovernmental organization was founded in 1919 after World War I with the aim of maintaining world peace through disarmament, international cooperation, and the use of diplomacy to settle disputes between states. At its peak in 1934 and 1935, 58 countries were members of the League of Nations, but over time a number of important countries, including Germany, Japan, Italy, and Spain, withdrew from the League, which weakened it. And when World War II started in 1939, it was clear that the League had failed – its primary purpose was maintaining world peace, remember – and so it was disbanded.

Around the same time that the League of Nations was dissolving, the United Nations was beginning. In 1939 the US State Department began to plan for a new world organization. Then in 1942 a group of allied governments, 26 in total I think, signed a pact called the Atlantic Charter. In addition to an agreement to continue the war effort, the Atlantic Charter included a list of ideas for what would happen after the war ended.

In the final days of World War II, the UN as we know it today began to take shape. A conference was held in San Francisco called the United Nations Conference on International Organization. At this conference, representatives from 50 governments drafted the United Nations Charter based on the Atlantic Charter. This document detailed the goals and principles of the new United Nations organization. In general terms these were similar to the aims of the old League of Nations, but they were broader in scope and with more provisions for ensuring peoples all over the world had basic rights. The San Francisco conference ended with the signing of the UN Charter in June and the UN itself officially came into existence a few months later in October, 1945 when the Charter was ratified by the five countries that were members of the so-called Security Council of the UN. These countries were the USA, the UK, the Soviet Union, France, and China.

Narrator	Question 3. The speaker mentions the aims of the League of Nations. Indicate which of these answers were League of Nation goals.
Narrator	Question 4. The speaker describes the events that led to the founding of the United Nations. Put the events in the order that they happened.

Exercise I1 – questions 5 and 6 (Tracks 199–201)

Narrator	Listen to a lecture in an introduction to world literature class.
Female Professor	Political satire has a long history, from the plays and poems of ancient Greek and Roman authors to modern satirical television shows. In today's class we're going to discuss some examples of political satire from world literature, but before continuing, I think it's important that we agree on a definition of satire. It's one of those words that people use widely, but for me the characteristics of satire are actually quite narrow.

One of the main characteristics of satire is that it should be critical. For political satire, the object of the criticism is usually a political leader or party, or a viewpoint associated with the same. In other forms of satire, the criticism may be directed at people's behavior or beliefs. To give a couple of examples, the Greek playwright Aristophanes, writing in the fifth century B.C., savagely criticized the politician Cleon in many ways, including suggesting that he gave and received bribes. And French satirist and lawyer Maurice Joly published a pamphlet towards the end of the nineteenth century A.D., so more than two thousand years after Aristophanes, in which he attacked the political ambitions of Napoleon III.

A second key characteristic of satire for me is that its message should be implicit not explicit. The satirist *doesn't* directly state that a work is satirical or even that the purpose of a work is to mock political viewpoints. Rather, the satirist suggests and hints these things. Writing in the eighteenth century A.D., the Irish writer Jonathan Swift satirized political attitudes among the ruling elite in his work *A Modest Proposal*. The satire is so indirect in this work that some people have taken Swift seriously even though the "modest proposal" in question is that eating children might bring an end to poverty.

Female Student	He suggested eating children? Isn't that a bit weird?
Professor	Well, yes, Hayley, it *is* weird, but Swift was being ironic and that's part of satire. Uh, my next point should clarify. So, the last characteristic of satire – and remember that I'm outlining *my* definition of satire here; other people will have different views – is that it uses techniques like irony, parody, caricature, and exaggeration. Of these, irony – uh, saying the opposite of what you mean – is probably the most fundamental and common. A satirist will often seem to praise a political idea which the satirical work is actually intended to attack. Or, as is the case with Swift who suggested eating children, the satirist will seem to support an idea that nobody would actually support.

You might be surprised that I haven't included humor in my list of characteristics of satire. The reason is that although a lot of satire – especially modern satire – *is* intended to be funny, humor is not actually an essential element of satire and quite a number of satirical works are not intended to be humorous in any way. For example, some scholars have argued that Niccolò Machiavelli's classic work *The Prince*, written in the sixteenth century A.D., is actually satirical, but it's certainly *not* a comedic work. And Swift's *A Modest Proposal*, which we discussed earlier, is written in a very straight manner without a hint of humor.

Narrator Question 5. The professor discusses political satire. Indicate which of these traits the professor includes in her definition of satire.

Narrator Question 6. The professor mentions some examples of political satire. Put the names of these satirical authors in order of when they were writing, from the earliest time to the most recent.

UNIT 14 | LISTENING • Making Inferences Questions

Exercise D1 (Tracks 202–205)

Man I'm Ahmed. I've found that speakers often express an idea indirectly by saying something related to their point. For example, if a professor wants to imply that an essay is too short, she might say "I asked for a minimum of 2,000 words, so please keep working on this paper."

Woman Hello. My name's Miki. In my experience, speakers often express an indirect idea by talking about the opposite of their point. For instance, a librarian might say, "That book is not due back in the library until tomorrow" to imply that the book is not available in the library today.

Man Hi, this is Jorgen. I find that speakers often make an indirect point by talking about two ideas or repeating an idea but not directly stating a conclusion. For example, if a professor says, "This journal article is interesting" and "there are many great ideas in this article," he is implying that students should read the journal article.

Woman My name is Rosa. Sometimes a speaker uses intonation to make a point indirectly. For example, if a student says, "the book is *supposed* to be on special reserve," her tone of voice makes it clear that the book is not actually on special reserve.

Exercise D2 (Tracks 206–208)

Narrator Excerpt one.

Woman I'm going to have to apply for an interlibrary loan to read one of the books on the reading list you gave us.

Man Really? I'm surprised to hear that.

Narrator Excerpt two.

Man As a general rule, fluctuations in the price of products and services are caused by changes in supply and demand. So, for example, when demand for a product or service increases, the price of that product or service usually goes up.

Narrator Excerpt three.

Woman Did you find the book you needed?

Man Yeah. I was actually able to search the library's computer catalog today. Once I knew where to look, it was easy to find the book in the stacks.

Exercise D4 (Tracks 209–211)

Narrator Excerpt one. Listen to part of a conversation in a college library.

Male Student Excuse me? I was told you might be able to tell me about any part-time jobs available in the library.

Female Librarian Let me check if we have any open postings, OK? Um, it looks like there's one position available.

Student Could you tell me what kind of work I'd be expected to do?

Librarian It would mostly be re-shelving books and journals in the stacks, but you might also be asked to help clients use the computer catalog, find audiovisual materials, apply for interlibrary loans, check books in or out, that kind of thing.

Student That sounds easy enough. And what about the pay and hours?

Librarian Er, the pay's minimum wage and it's for up to 10 hours a week. The hours are flexible, but you'd need to be able to do at least one weekend shift and two evenings a week.

Student A weekend shift? Hmmm. I'd need to adjust my schedule. When's the deadline for applying?

Librarian There's no deadline, but if you're interested, you should apply ASAP. The last position here was filled in just two days.

Student That's good to know. Thanks.

Narrator Excerpt two. Listen to part of a lecture in a business class.

Female Professor Today we're going to discuss the business cycle, which is, uh, which describes fluctuations in economic activity – things like trade, production, consumption, and so on – across the whole economy. Each business cycle, which may be called an economic cycle or a boom-bust cycle in some of the books on your reading list, typically lasts months to years before repeating.

Uh, there are various ways to describe the business cycle, but today we'll look at a simple cyclical model with four stages – the recovery stage, prosperity stage, recession stage, and depression stage.

During the recovery phase – sometimes also called the revival phase – economic activity, which of course had been at extremely low levels during the preceding stage, begins to pick up. Typically demand for goods and services increases, which leads to a rise in productivity and a corresponding rise in investment. These changes in turn lead to increased output, employment, and so on, and, importantly, economic optimism. And if the recovery phase continues for long enough, it leads into the next phase in the cycle.

Narrator Excerpt three. Listen to part of a discussion in an economics seminar.

Male Instructor OK, so I hope you all did the reading from your coursebook on risk aversion. Would anyone like to give a short and simple definition? Linda?

Female Student It's a theory, uh, a concept that when consumers are faced with uncertain situations they typically avoid risky behavior. So, for instance, a risk-averse investor would likely choose to make a safe investment with a low return rather than an investment with a higher potential return but also higher risks.

Instructor Good. Now of course from the reading we know that the reality is more complex than Linda's explanation. We know that there are levels of risk aversion – with some consumers being heavily risk-averse and others much less so. And not all consumers are averse to taking risks, of course. Some are risk-neutral, and some – the ones who look for the best ROI regardless of potential losses – are risk-seeking, uh risk-loving. We also need to take into account the concepts of absolute and relative risk aversion, which, despite how it might seem from your textbook, are actually pretty easy to understand.

Exercise E2 (Tracks 212–214)

Narrator	Excerpt one. Listen to part of a conversation.
Female Professor	Thank you for coming to see me, Bob. I had some questions about the bibliography in your last assignment.
Male Student	Oh, OK. Was there a problem?
Professor	Well, not exactly. Um, what I mean is that I was surprised your bibliography was so long. I think you cited 17 or 18 different sources, which is a lot for a 1,000-word paper. And, well, a number of the books listed in your bibliography were not cited in the body of your essay, so I'm not sure why you included them.
Student	Well, I checked out a lot of books and journals from the library to write the paper. In the end I didn't have as much time to do research as I expected, but I thought I'd include all the titles I got from the library in the bibliography.
Professor	In the future, please only include books you actually used in your research, OK?
Student	Sure. Sorry about that.
Narrator	Can you make the following conclusion from the conversation?
	Question 1. The man's bibliography for an assignment included books that he did not actually read.
Narrator	Excerpt two. Listen to part of a lecture about normative economics.
Female Professor	Normative economics is a branch of economics that, unlike positive economics, focuses on what *ought to* happen in an economy not on what *actually* happens. Two important theories based on normative economics are social choice theory and cooperative game theory. Such theories can be useful in understanding possible economic behavior, but not actual behavior, of course.
Narrator	Can you reach the following conclusions from the lecture?
	Question 2. Positive economics focuses on what actually happens in the economy not on what should happen.
	Question 3. Social choice theory is the most important theory that is based on normative economics.
Narrator	Excerpt three. Listen to part of a lecture about import quotas.
Male Professor	If the government of a country wants to benefit domestic producers of particular products, such as televisions or food items, they can choose to impose import quotas on those products. This means that foreign producers are limited as to the quantity of goods they can export to that country. This allows domestic producers to enjoy higher levels of sales – often at higher prices and so with higher profitability – than would be possible if there were unlimited foreign competition.
Narrator	Can you come to the following conclusions from the lecture?
	Question 4. Without import quotas, domestic producers of a product cannot be successful.

Question 5. Import quotas do not benefit either overseas producers or domestic consumers.

Exercise F2 (Tracks 215–217)

Narrator	Excerpt one. Listen to part of a conversation in a campus bookstore.
Man	This textbook costs $97? Wow! Is there any way to get it cheaper?
Woman	We also sell second-hand books, but used copies of this particular book are sold out. You could try one of the bookstores in town.
Man	I need to go into town anyway, so I think that's what I'll do. Thanks for the help.
Narrator	Does the man imply, state, or not mention ideas 1 and 2?
Narrator	Excerpt two. Listen to part of a lecture in a class on macroeconomics.
Woman	Gross domestic product, usually abbreviated as GDP, is the value that all of the services and finished goods produced within a country would fetch if they were sold. GDP is widely used as an economic indicator – nations having a high GDP per person, for example, are usually considered to be in good economic health and to have a high standard of living. This view is not shared by everyone, though, with some people arguing that GDP should be used solely to measure productivity, not quality of life.
Narrator	Does the woman imply, state, or not mention ideas 3 and 4?
Narrator	Excerpt three. Listen to part of a conversation in a university library.
Man	Excuse me? I'm trying to find some journals in the library catalog. Every search comes back "not found," but my professor told me these titles were in the library.
Woman	Oh, not again. We upgraded our library catalog computer database a couple days ago and, well, let's just say the upgrade hasn't gone very smoothly. Do you have anything else you need to do? It will probably take our IT people a couple of hours to resolve the issue.
Narrator	Does the woman imply, state, or not mention ideas 5 and 6?

Exercise G1 (Track 218)

Male Professor	OK, so let me define a few of the terms that you'll hear in this course.
	The word capital often means money or property that can be used to purchase or invest in something.
	A consumer, like a customer, can be defined as a person who buys or uses goods and services.
	Demand refers to the level of desire among consumers in one market for specific goods and services. Items that a company has produced in order for customers to purchase them are called goods. Productivity generally refers to how quickly and efficiently a business can produce goods.
	A recession is defined as a relatively short period of time when the economy experiences a general decline.
	Resources, such as oil, water, capital, or workers, are the natural or economic assets a country or company has.
	Supply typically refers to how much of a particular good or service is available in one market at a specific time.
	OK? Any questions about those words?

Exercise H1 – questions 1 and 2 (Tracks 219–221)

Narrator	Listen to a conversation in a university library.
Male Student	I was wondering if you could help me. I've got a reading list for a postgraduate course that I'm taking, but six of the eight titles are not in the library's catalog.
Female Librarian	Really? That's unusual. Most professors take care to assign books that are in the library.
Student	I'm actually doing a distance-learning degree, so the professor who assigned the reading list isn't on the faculty here.
Librarian	I see. And did the university you're doing the distance learning course through arrange for you to get library privileges here?
Student	No. I *could* have arranged that, but I was actually an undergraduate here, so I've already got access to the library as an alumnus.
Librarian	That makes sense. Well, let me have a look at your reading list and I'll see about those titles that are not in the library. I've just logged in to the interlibrary loan network and all six of the titles are available through interlibrary loan.
Student	That's great.
Librarian	Well, yes and no. If you were still studying here at the university there'd be no problem, but with alumni access, you can only get four books through interlibrary loan at one time.
Student	Four's better than nothing, but it would be a lot easier for me if I could borrow all six titles at once.
Librarian	Yes, I'm sure it would. You know, according to the computer, three of the titles you need are at Eastern State University across town. Do you think you'd be able to get library privileges there through your distance learning institution?
Student	Um, why would that ... Oh, I see. Having library access there plus alumni access here would give me much wider access to the books I need. I hadn't thought about doing that, but it's a pretty good idea.
Librarian	And you can still apply for up to four books through interlibrary loan, too.
Student	You're right.
Narrator	Question 1. Listen again to part of the conversation. What does the woman imply when she says this?
Female Librarian	If you were still studying here at the university there'd be no problem, but with alumni access, you can only get four books through interlibrary loan at one time.
Narrator	Question 2. What is the student likely to do next?

Exercise H1 – questions 3 and 4 (Tracks 222–224)

Narrator	Listen to part of a lecture in a European history class. The professor is talking about trade policies.
Female Professor	The fifteenth and sixteenth centuries were a time of political upheavals and social change in Europe. One effect of these changes was the rise and dominance – until at least the mid-eighteenth century – of mercantilism as an economic policy employed by several major European powers. The basic principle underlying mercantilism is the belief that a nation's strength is based on how much bullion, that's, uh, precious metals like gold and silver, it has accumulated. This belief that wealth meant power led to the adoption of economic and political policies that maximized opportunities for wealth creation, specifically by fostering a positive balance of trade –

that is by exporting more goods than are imported. A number of the policies adopted can be grouped under the umbrella term "protectionism," which in simple terms is the opposite of free trade.

Under mercantilism, powerful states would typically impose high tariffs, uh, taxes if you like, on both the import of raw materials and the export of goods. This allowed the government to collect significant amounts of taxation revenue from trading partners. Other common mercantilist policies – all designed to maximize wealth generation for a nation, remember – included the creation of overseas colonies, especially in areas rich with natural resources, restrictions on trade for those colonies, bans on the export of precious metals, offering subsidies to maximize industrial production and the export of finished goods, and even restrictions on domestic consumption of goods. Why the latter? Well, simple: exporting goods raises more revenue for governments than allowing domestic consumers to purchase those goods.

Mercantilist policies were clearly designed to greatly benefit one trading partner over the other, and they were often very effective. Major European powers of the time, like France and Great Britain, became extremely wealthy as a result of such policies. Their trading partners, however, did not, which raised political tensions. Other tensions were caused in situations where two major powers were each vying for access to potentially lucrative markets.

Mercantilism has been described as economic warfare because the trade imbalance between the powerful nation and its trading partners was so striking. It could certainly be argued that the exploitation of colonies by imperial powers as a result of mercantilism had a profound and long-lasting negative impact on those colonies. Many modern nations that were once colonies continue to struggle economically, for example, despite having an abundance of natural resources. And historians point to mercantilism as being among the causes of actual wars, too. The Anglo-Dutch Wars, for example, a series of short conflicts that took place between 1652 and 1784, were fought for control of profitable ocean trade routes.

Narrator	Question 3. Listen again to part of the lecture.
Female Professor	This belief that wealth meant power led to the adoption of economic and political policies that maximized opportunities for wealth creation, specifically by fostering a positive balance of trade – that is by exporting more goods than are imported. A number of the policies adopted can be grouped under the umbrella term "protectionism," which in simple terms is the opposite of free trade.
Narrator	What does the woman imply when she says this?
Female Professor	This belief that wealth meant power led to the adoption of economic and political policies that maximized opportunities for wealth creation, specifically by fostering a positive balance of trade.
Narrator	Question 4. What does the professor imply about mercantilism?

Exercise H1 – questions 5 and 6 (Tracks 225–227)

Narrator	Listen to part of a talk in an economics class. The professor is discussing economic goals.
Male Professor	Morning, everyone. We've got a lot to cover today, so let's begin. We're going to be discussing some socioeconomic goals that are generally considered desirable in a mixed economy. We'll begin by covering the three goals that

are macroeconomic in scope. In a later class we'll cover the two microeconomic goals of economic efficiency and economic equity. I should also say here that we're talking about goals, that is, targets to aim at, rather than targets that have actually been achieved.

OK, so in macroeconomic terms, governments tend to pursue economic policies that promote full employment, economic growth, and economic stability. When I mentioned full employment, your first natural reaction would probably be to assume I'm talking about the country having an unemployment rate of 0%, and second to think that such a thing is impossible. A low unemployment rate is certainly part of what full employment means, but not all of it. Um, perhaps a better way to describe this goal would be to talk of full employment of resources, with employment here meaning "use" rather than "having a job." To clarify, the goal of full employment is for all available resources – capital, real estate, and, yes, labor – to be fully used in the production of goods and services. Any resources that are not being used or that are being under-used are, in effect, being wasted because they are not contributing to the good of society. And yes, you'd be right in thinking that no country will ever achieve full employment as I've just defined it, but again, we're discussing *goals* here.

The second macroeconomic goal is economic growth. One common measurement of this is an increased capacity to produce goods and services, which can be achieved by increasing the quantity of resources available for production. Governments and individuals try to achieve economic growth because it leads to an improved standard of living. The reason? More jobs are generated, and economic security and economic equity – which we'll discuss later when we talk about the two microeconomic goals – are enhanced. In economies that are not growing, the only way for a group to obtain more goods and services, um, more benefit in other words, is to take away goods and services from another group. When the economy grows, however, every group can receive more goods and services even though the relative proportion that each group receives remains the same. OK?

The final macroeconomic goal is economic stability, which we can define as preventing or reducing fluctuations that affect consumers, producers, and nations. Examples include fluctuations in production, employment, prices, costs, and so on. But I should make it clear that price stability doesn't mean that prices never change; rather it means that the economy is not experiencing prolonged and hard-to-stop price changes as a result of inflation or deflation. Economic stability is usually measured by looking at economic indicators such as the rate of inflation or rate of unemployment, and achieving it allows individuals and governments to make long-term plans.

Narrator	Question 5. What does the author imply about economic goals?
Narrator	Question 6. What can be inferred about economic stability?

LISTENING REVIEW TEST

Conversation 1 (Track 228)

Narrator	Listen to a conversation between a student and one of his instructors.
Male Student	Hi, Professor. Do you have a moment?
Female Professor	Well, uh, is it something urgent Henry, or could we discuss it tomorrow?
Student	Oh, don't you have office hours today?
Professor	Usually, but this week I had to rearrange my schedule. I mentioned that in class yesterday.
Student	Actually I didn't attend class yesterday, and that's kind of why I wanted to see you, but uh, I'll come back tomorrow.
Professor	No, no, it's fine. You're here now.
Student	Well, I wanted to tell you that I've decided to drop your psychology class. That's why I didn't come yesterday.
Professor	Oh. Um, that's a surprise. You always seem engaged in class, so I got the impression you were interested in the subject.
Student	I am – really interested in fact – but I registered for many classes this semester, and dropping a class seemed like the best way to reduce my study load.
Professor	I understand your reasons for dropping *a* class, but if you're interested in psychology, I'm not sure why you want to drop *that* class.
Student	Well, it's not a core class, and I figured I'd meet my core requirements first, and then focus on more exciting classes.
Professor	I see. Um, from what you just said, it sounds like you don't find your core classes that interesting.
Student	Some are OK, I guess, but none of them inspire me.
Professor	You know, when I was an undergraduate I did something similar. I had two semesters where I *only* took classes that

weren't that interesting for me, and those were my two worst semesters at college.

Student	Really? Why?
Professor	Well, it was hard to get motivated to study because none of the classes excited me. So I changed my system to find a balance between the classes I *had* to take and the classes I *wanted* to take. After I did that, it was easier to get motivated for the less interesting classes because I also had some more interesting classes to work on. I'm not saying you would feel the same, but it's something to think about, perhaps.
Student	You know, now that you mention it, I can see I might feel the same way you did. So maybe I should drop a core class instead of the psychology class. Uh, I appreciate your advice and time, Professor.
Professor	You're welcome, Henry. And whatever you decide to do is fine, but don't take too long making a decision, OK? The deadline for dropping courses is Friday.

Conversation 1 – questions (Tracks 229–233)

Narrator	Question 1. Why does the student visit his instructor?
Narrator	Question 2. What does the man say about the woman's class?
Narrator	Question 3. Listen again to part of the conversation. What does the student imply when he says this?
Man	I registered for many classes this semester, and dropping a class seemed like the best way to reduce my study load.
Narrator	Question 4. Why does the instructor mention her time as an undergraduate?
Narrator	Question 5. What will the student most likely do next?

Lecture 1 (Track 234)

Narrator Listen to part of a lecture in a United States History class.

Male Professor OK, today we're going to continue our discussion of American political history by looking at the presidency of William Henry Harrison. Although president only for one month, Harrison's successful presidential campaign and the decisions made after his death were historically important.

Harrison began his career in the military, but moved into politics in his mid-twenties, and soon became a member of Congress and then governor of the newly-established Indiana Territory. During his tenure as governor he purchased large tracts of lands from some Native American tribes. This increased the size of Indiana Territory substantially, but led to tensions with other Native American peoples who felt the purchases were illegal. As tensions grew, Harrison was placed in command of an army and later won the Battle of Tippecanoe, a victory that made him famous. Harrison remained in the army until 1814, when disagreements with Secretary of War John Armstrong resulted in his resignation.

From 1816 Harrison held various political offices, including serving in both the Ohio State Senate and the United States Senate. In 1829 he retired from political life and settled on a farm in Ohio. In 1836 he was persuaded to re-enter politics, but narrowly lost the presidential election to Martin Van Buren. Four years later, however, this time running with John Tyler as his vice president, Harrison defeated Van Buren and was elected as the ninth president of the United States. He was not to enjoy being president for long, however. He was inaugurated on March 4, 1841, but fell ill three weeks later, and died on Apri 4, making his presidency of just 32 days the shortest in history.

Despite his short time in office, certain aspects of his presidency were influential. For one thing, Harrison's presidential campaign of 1840 laid the groundwork for many aspects of modern politics, including personal and political attacks on one's opponent. Harrison and his colleagues attempted to blame Martin Van Buren for the poor state of the US economy by giving him the nickname Van Ruin. They also criticized Van Buren as being a wealthy elitist who lived a life of luxury, in comparison with Harrison who was portrayed as a common man. His campaign was also one of the first to feature a memorable campaign slogan in "Tippecanoe and Tyler too," still among the most famous in US history. This slogan was one of many reminders to voters that Harrison, unlike Van Buren, was a war hero.

Harrison's sudden death also led to clarifications in the role of vice president. At the time, the wording of the Constitution was ambiguous as to whether the vice president would become "President" or "Acting President" after the death of a president. It was also unclear whether the vice president would remain in this role until the next scheduled election – which in the case of Harrison's death would mean almost four years – or if an emergency election were needed. In May of 1841 Congress convened to discuss these questions and passed a resolution specifying that John Tyler should (A) become president, and (B) hold that role until the end of the term that began with Harrison's inauguration. These principles of vice-presidential succession are essentially the same as the ones we have today.

Lecture 1 – questions (Tracks 235–240)

Narrator Question 6. What does the professor mainly discuss?

Narrator Question 7. The professor discusses events in the life of William Henry Harrison. Put the events in the order in which they occurred.

Narrator Question 8. What were some results of Harrison's time as governor of Indiana Territory?

Narrator Question 9. On what points was Martin Van Buren attacked during the 1840 presidential campaign?

Narrator Question 10. Listen again to part of the lecture. What does the professor imply?

Male Professor Harrison's presidential campaign of 1840 laid the groundwork for many aspects of modern politics, including personal and political attacks on one's opponent. Harrison and his colleagues attempted to blame Martin Van Buren for the poor state of the US economy by giving him the nickname Van Ruin. They also criticized Van Buren as being a wealthy elitist who lived a life of luxury, in comparison with Harrison who was portrayed as a common man. His campaign was also one of the first to feature a memorable campaign slogan in "Tippecanoe and Tyler too," still among the most famous in US history.

Narrator Question 11. What happened to Vice President John Tyler after Harrison's death?

Conversation 2 (Track 241)

Narrator Listen to a conversation between a student and a university employee.

Female Student Hi, I was told to speak to the Dining Services manager.

Male Employee That's me. How can I help?

Student I need to cancel my meal plan and get my money back, please.

Employee I'm sorry, but meal plans are non-refundable.

Student Look, when I registered for a value plus meal plan I didn't know that the cafe in the Student Center was going to be closed for renovations. I don't eat meat, fish, eggs, or dairy, and that cafe was pretty much the only place to get decent vegan food on campus. If I'd known about the renovations, I wouldn't have gotten a meal plan.

Employee I see. But the other campus dining locations offer vegetarian options, so can't you eat at one of those places until the cafe reopens in a couple of weeks?

Student I *have* been eating at other places, but I'm vegan not vegetarian, so hardly any of the options are suitable. I can't tell you how sick I am of eating salad every day. I don't want to repeat myself, but I wouldn't have paid for a meal plan if I'd known about the cafe renovations.

Employee OK, um, I don't normally do this, but under the circumstances, I'll authorize a refund of the unused portion of your meal plan, but...

Student That's great! Thanks.

Employee One second, please. As I was about to say, there's an administration fee of $175 associated with cancellations. You can pay that fee directly, or have it deducted from the refund amount.

Student What? I'm only canceling because of *your* renovations, so it's not right that I should have to pay *any* kind of fee.

Employee	I understand how you feel, but there's really nothing I can do ... unless, um, you're still going to be at the university *next* semester, aren't you?
Student	Yeah, why?
Employee	Well, instead of a refund, I could transfer the unused funds in your meal plan to next semester. That way you wouldn't have to pay an administration fee.
Student	That sounds like a better option. Great!
Employee	Those funds won't be available until next semester, though, so you'll need to be able to support yourself this semester.
Student	Oh, yeah. Um, I think my mom and dad *might* be able to help. I'll have to give them a call, though.
Employee	Of course. Come back and see me when you've decided what to do, OK?

Conversation 2 – questions (Tracks 242–246)

Narrator	Question 12. For what reason does the woman visit the man's office?
Narrator	Question 13. What do the speakers say about the cafe in the Student Center?
Narrator	Question 14. Listen again to part of the conversation. What does the student imply?
Male Employee	I see. But the other campus dining locations offer vegetarian options, so can't you eat at one of those places until the cafe reopens in a couple of weeks?
Female Student	I *have* been eating at other places, but I'm vegan not vegetarian, so hardly any of the options are suitable. I can't tell you how sick I am of eating salad every day.
Narrator	Question 15. Listen again to part of the conversation. What can be inferred about the student?
Male Employee	One second, please. As I was about to say, there's an administration fee of $175 associated with cancellations. You can pay that fee directly, or have it deducted from the refund amount.
Female Student	What? I'm only canceling because of *your* renovations, so it's not right that I should have to pay *any* kind of fee.
Narrator	Question 16. What will the student probably do next?

Lecture 2 (Track 247)

Narrator	Listen to part of a talk in a psychology class. The professor is discussing stress.
Female Professor	Good afternoon, everyone. Today we're going to discuss stress, which seems an appropriate topic given that your midterm exam is coming up in two weeks.
	A simple way to think about stress is that it's caused by change. I don't want you to think I'm saying every type of change causes stress, but in general, changes can be stressful. How stressful? Well, size is obviously a factor: big changes usually cause more stress than small ones. Other factors are time – the longer something lasts, the more stress it typically causes – level of expectation – unexpected things usually provoke greater levels of stress than ones we can predict – and whether the change is something people think they can control. Something that people perceive as being out of their control is more stressful than something that can be managed.
Female Student	Excuse me, Professor. I can see how change is stressful, but not why. I mean, what is it about change that causes stress?
Professor	Good question, Denise. Ideas, anyone?

Male Student	Uh, at a guess because change is dangerous? I mean, if nothing bad happened yesterday, and today is the same as yesterday, it's likely nothing bad will happen today, so you can feel safe and stress-free. But if something has changed since yesterday, there's a chance that the change could lead to danger, so your brain reacts by feeling stress. Does that make sense?
Professor	Interesting idea. Toby's just given us a plausible evolutionary perspective there. If we think about psychological principles, we could say that change causes stress because it forces us to react to something different in our lives. We can't go on the same way we did before, but rather must think or act in new ways, which is stressful.
	OK, let's move on and look at the types of stress. Ambient stressors are things in the environment that can cause stress, such as noise from a construction site, traffic problems, or even bad weather. Unlike life stressors, which I'll mention next, ambient stressors are global, meaning they affect many people at once.
	Another category is life stressors. These can be the routine stresses of daily life. Think about a disagreement at work with your boss, or an argument with your partner, or driving to the store *again* because you forgot to buy milk, those kinds of things. Routine stressors are typically individual – a stress trigger for one person may not affect another person. Some people don't get stressed by upcoming exams, for instance.
	Life stressors can also be caused by major life events. These are events that occur less frequently than routine stressors, but often in the same contexts. So losing your job rather than having a disagreement with your boss, getting a divorce rather than just getting into an argument, or having an accident when driving to the store for milk and having to spend time in the hospital. Positive life events can be stressors, too: marriage, for example, or a new job or new baby.
	The final category of stressor is a traumatic event, such as being involved in a natural disaster, or experiencing a violent fight or even a war. These are events that affect many at the same time, are often unexpected, completely out of a person's control, and last for a long time. And recall that I said stressors which are unexpected, which people cannot control, and which last for a long time cause higher levels of stress. Traumatic stressors clearly match all three.

Lecture 2 – questions (Tracks 248–253)

Narrator	Question 17. Listen again to part of the lecture. What does the professor imply when she says this?
Female Professor	Today we're going to discuss stress, which seems an appropriate topic given that your midterm exam is coming up in two weeks.
Narrator	Question 18. What factors make a life change more stressful?
Narrator	Question 19. What theory does the man suggest about why change causes stress?
Narrator	Question 20. The professor mentions three types of stressor. Indicate which characteristics match each type of stressor.
Narrator	Question 21. What example of a routine stressor does the professor give?
Narrator	Question 22. Listen again to part of the lecture.

Female Professor	The final category of stressor is a traumatic event, such as being involved in a natural disaster, or experiencing a violent fight or even a war. These are events that affect many at the same time, are often unexpected, completely out of a person's control, and last for a long time. And recall that I said stressors which are unexpected, which people cannot

control, and which last for a long time cause higher levels of stress. Traumatic stressors clearly match all three.

Narrator	What does the professor mean when she says this?
Female Professor	Traumatic stressors clearly match all three.

SPEAKING DIAGNOSTIC TEST

Speaking Diagnostic Test

Question 1 (Tracks 254 and 255)

Narrator	Talk about a place that was important to you when you were a child. Describe the place and say why it was important to you. Give reasons and details to support your answer.
Announcer	You may begin to prepare after the beep.
	You may begin to speak after the beep.

Question 2 (Tracks 256 and 257)

Narrator	Some college students prefer studying for assignments with other people. Other students prefer working on their own when they have an assignment. Which way of working on assignments do you prefer? Explain why.
Announcer	You may begin to prepare after the beep.
	You may begin to speak after the beep.

Question 3 (Tracks 258–261)

Narrator	In this question, you will read a short passage about a campus situation and then listen to a conversation on the same topic. You will then answer a question using information from both the reading passage and the conversation. After you hear the question, you will have 30 seconds to prepare your response and 60 seconds to speak. A student wrote a letter to the university newspaper about a problem. You have 45 seconds to read the letter. Begin reading now. Now listen to two students as they discuss the letter.
Man	You saw that letter in the university newspaper about office hours, right?
Woman	Yeah, but actually I find the instructors are all really professional about office hours. I don't think the writer of the letter made very good arguments.
Man	Why not?
Woman	Well, take his point about instructors being late for their office hours. I'm sure it happens sometimes, but most professors are pretty punctual. And if they are late, most will stay longer to make up the lost time, or even schedule another time to meet students. So, I don't think that's a serious problem.
Man	Yeah, I guess you're right. I've had professors make up missed time. But what about the idea to set a policy for a minimum number of hours?
Woman	Well, the university already has a policy like that.
Man	Really? I didn't know that.
Woman	Yeah. My roommate is a teaching assistant for a professor in the physics department, and she told me that all teaching staff must be available for a certain number of hours each

week. Apparently it's a contractual requirement, so there's no need for a new policy, I think.

Narrator	The woman expresses her opinion about the letter. State her opinion and explain the reasons she gives for holding that opinion.
Announcer	You may begin to prepare after the beep.
	You may begin to speak after the beep.

Question 4 (Tracks 262–265)

Narrator	In this question, you will read a short passage on an academic subject and then listen to a talk on the same topic. You will then answer a question using information from both the reading passage and the conversation. After you hear the question, you will have 30 seconds to prepare your response and 60 seconds to speak. Now read the passage about the conduction of heat. You have 45 seconds to read the passage. Begin reading now. Now listen to part of a lecture on this topic in an introductory science class.
Male Professor	If you're like me, scientific concepts are easier to understand when they're explained through everyday examples. With that in mind, let's see how a cup of a coffee and some cookies can explain heat conduction. Take the coffee first. Suppose you use a spoon to stir your coffee, but forget to remove the spoon. When you remember to remove it later, you'll feel that the metal of the spoon is hot, but not as hot as the coffee. This clearly demonstrates the conduction of heat. The spoon gains heat from the coffee, but doesn't become as hot as the coffee, because heat transfer from liquids to solids is not fully efficient. And the cookies? Well, cookies are usually baked on a metal baking sheet. The baking sheet gets hot and conducts that heat into the bottom of the cookie. And because both the baking sheet and cookie are solids, and because heat conducts very efficiently between two solids, the bottom of the cookie becomes crisp and brown. But hold on. Cookies may be crispy on the bottom, but they're generally soft on top. How come? Well, the top of the cookie is only touching the air inside the oven. The air is hot enough to bake the cookie, but heat does not conduct well between a gas – like the air inside the oven – and a solid – like the cookie – so the top of the cookie stays soft and pale. To sum up, heat conducts extremely efficiently between two solids, reasonably efficiently between liquids and solids, and less efficiently between gases and solids.
Narrator	Using points and examples from the lecture, explain the conduction of heat between solids, liquids, and gases.
Announcer	You may begin to prepare after the beep.
	You may begin to speak after the beep.

Question 5 (Tracks 266–269)

Narrator	In this question, you will listen to a conversation. You will then be asked to talk about the information in the conversation and to give your opinion about the ideas presented. After you hear the question, you will have 20 seconds to prepare your response and 60 seconds to speak.
	Now listen to a conversation between a man and a woman.
Woman	Hi, Bob. Is it true that you're going to lose your scholarship next semester?
Man	Yeah, I'm really frustrated. If my GPA were just one point higher, I wouldn't have this problem, but now I'm not sure I have enough money to keep studying.
Woman	What GPA do you need?
Man	I need to maintain a GPA of 3.5, but my grades have slipped a bit recently and right now I'm at 3.4.
Woman	Well, couldn't you get a part-time job next semester? That would let you keep studying and if you can raise your grades, you'll be eligible for the scholarship again, right?
Man	Yeah, but if I have to work as well as study, I think it'll be really difficult to raise my grades. I worked part-time when I was a sophomore, and I found that my grades really suffered.
Woman	Maybe there are other scholarships that you could apply for.
Man	At this stage in the year I'm sure all the scholarships have already been assigned.
Woman	Perhaps, but the people in the finance office are usually very helpful. It wouldn't hurt to ask.
Narrator	The speakers discuss two possible solutions to a problem. Describe the problem. Then state which of the two solutions you prefer and why.
Announcer	You may begin to prepare after the beep.
	You may begin to speak after the beep.

Question 6 (Tracks 270–273)

Narrator	In this question, you will listen to part of a lecture. You will then be asked to summarize important information from the lecture. After you hear the question, you will have 20 seconds to prepare your response and 60 seconds to speak.
	Now listen to part of a talk in a biology class.
Female Professor	Right, so let's continue our discussion of diseases that affect household pets. To that end, I'd like to introduce the concept of comorbidity. This word is actually used with two subtly different meanings, and you'll need to make sure you understand the difference between these two definitions.
	Most commonly, comorbidity describes situations in which an animal suffers from two unrelated medical conditions at the same time. So, for example, a dog infected with canine parvovirus that is also suffering from ear mites would be described as comorbid. The dog has two medical issues that need treatment – the virus and the parasite – but they're independent of each other.
	The second way in which the term comorbidity is used is when an animal has two medical conditions, and one of those conditions causes the other, or at least is related to it. I'll give you a personal example to clarify. A few months ago, one of my pet cats developed stomach cancer. The cancer reduced her appetite so much that she soon developed feline hepatic lipidosis, a liver disorder that can occur when cats don't eat enough. So the cancer, in effect, caused the liver problems – hence comorbidity. See?
	A positive footnote to this story is that my cat had a successful operation to remove the cancer. With the cancer gone, her appetite came back, and she's doing just fine now.
Narrator	Using points and examples from the talk, summarize the two definitions of comorbidity that the professor discusses.
Announcer	You may begin to prepare after the beep.
	You may begin to speak after the beep.

UNIT 15 | SPEAKING • Independent Speaking Task 1

Exercise E3 (Track 274)

Male Student	It's hard to choose only one book that I really liked.
	However, if I had to pick one, it would be a book about choosing a career from my parents.
	The main reason is that this book helped me decide what to do with my life.
	For example, when I was a high school student I wanted to work with cars so I was planning to get a job as a mechanic.
	However, after reading the book I decided that working with cars would be tedious, so I changed my plan.
	So that's why I really enjoyed the book about choosing a career.

Exercise F1 – question 1 (Tracks 275 and 276)

Narrator	Describe an important event from your childhood. Explain why this event is important to you. Include specific examples.
Announcer	You may begin to prepare after the beep.
	You may begin to speak after the beep.

Exercise F1 – question 2 (Tracks 277 and 278)

Narrator	Talk about a place you have visited that you did not like very much. Explain why you disliked this place.
Announcer	You may begin to prepare after the beep.
	You may begin to speak after the beep.

Exercise F1 – question 3 (Tracks 279 and 280)

Narrator	Which of the following do you use most often: a digital camera, a cell phone, or a computer? Why?
Announcer	You may begin to prepare after the beep.
	You may begin to speak after the beep.

Exercise F1 – question 4 (Tracks 281 and 282)

Narrator	Your friend has asked for advice about how to become healthier. What advice would you give your friend? Support your answer.
Announcer	You may begin to prepare after the beep.
	You may begin to speak after the beep.

UNIT 16 | SPEAKING • Independent Speaking Task 2

Exercise D1 (Track 283)

Katerina	Hi, Fabio. How are you?
Fabio	Hi, Katerina. To be honest, I'm frustrated about Speaking Task 2 in the TOEFL Test. Fifteen seconds is not enough time to prepare. Sometimes I can't even decide my opinion during that time.
Katerina	Well, I don't think about my real opinion, it's faster to choose the opinion that looks easier to talk about.
Fabio	Hmmm. I always think about my real opinion, but if I don't know about the topic that takes time. I like your suggestion – choose the easier opinion. I'll do it!
Katerina	And do you know about stock reasons?
Fabio	Stock reasons? No.
Katerina	Stock reasons match many topics and are easy to talk about. For example, "saving time" or "having a good time" are reasons that can match many questions.
Fabio	So time is a stock reason?
Katerina	Time is a good one. Education, work, and health are also good.
Fabio	So for education my reason could be, uh, "getting good grades"? And for work for my reason could be, um, "getting a good job"?
Katerina	Right. And for health your reason could be "staying healthy" or "reducing stress."
Fabio	OK! Got it! Time, education, work, and health... I'll use those stock reasons, if I can.
Katerina	And for the example, I quickly try to think about two examples, one positive, and one negative.
Fabio	What do you mean?
Katerina	Speaking Task 2 questions have two options, right? Well, I like to give a positive example about my opinion and a negative example about the other choice. For example, if the question asks is it better to study overseas or in my country and my opinion is that studying overseas is better, I would give a *positive* example about studying overseas...
Fabio	And a *negative* example about studying in your country. OK, I get it now, and I think it's a really good idea. I'll try that, too. Thanks, Katerina.
Katerina	No problem, Fabio. See you later and good luck!

Exercise E3 (Track 284)

Student	There are some advantages to children concentrating on academic subjects.

However, overall I feel that children should learn computer skills at school.

The main reason is that computer skills may help them get a good job in the future.

For example, my sister had computer lessons at school and because her computer skills are good, she easily got a great job after graduating from university.

In contrast, my cousin didn't learn about computers at school and he lacks good computer skills.

For this reason, he can't find a good job now even though he's very smart.

So that's why I think schools should teach children about computers.

Exercise F1 – question 1 (Tracks 285 and 286)

Narrator	Some college students work part-time while they are studying. Others choose not to work so they can concentrate on their studies. Which do you think is better for students? Explain why.
Announcer	You may begin to prepare after the beep.
	You may begin to speak after the beep.

Exercise F1 – question 2 (Tracks 287 and 288)

Narrator	Some people prefer doing outdoor activities in their free time. Others prefer spending their free time indoors. Which do you prefer? Include details and examples in your explanation.
Announcer	You may begin to prepare after the beep.
	You may begin to speak after the beep.

Exercise F1 – question 3 (Tracks 289 and 290)

Narrator	At some colleges, students study just one subject in order to get a deep knowledge of that subject. At other colleges, students study various subjects in order to get a broad knowledge of many subjects. Which is better for students? Why?
Announcer	You may begin to prepare after the beep.
	You may begin to speak after the beep.

Exercise F1 – question 4 (Tracks 291 and 292)

Narrator	Do you agree or disagree that it is healthier to live in a small town than in a big city? Why? Support your answer.
Announcer	You may begin to prepare after the beep.
	You may begin to speak after the beep.

UNIT 17 | SPEAKING • Independent Speaking Task 3

Exercise E2 (Track 293)

Man	Did you see that letter about student clubs?
Woman	From the student who wanted to start a chess club but couldn't? Yeah, I saw it.
Man	I think the student is right. The college really needs to change its policy.
Woman	Why do you say that?
Man	Well, for one thing, it's not fair for part-time students. I used to be a member of the student association, and the college has a rule that part-time and full-time students should be treated equally. So this policy about clubs is actually against college rules.
Woman	I didn't know about that rule.
Man	Yeah, it's true. And the whole business about needing 50 potential members before a club can be registered doesn't make sense.
Woman	Why?
Man	Clubs don't cost the college any money. If there are five members or fifty members, there's no difference to the college.

Woman	That's a good point... still, I bet you think it's good news about the improved exercise facilities, huh?

Exercise E3 (Track 294)

Woman	Still, I bet you think it's good news about the improved exercise facilities, huh?
Man	Actually, I'm disappointed, to be honest.
Woman	What? Knowing how much you love to work out, I thought you'd be really excited.
Man	Well, the improvements sound good, but you know regular students like us can't use the new fitness center without paying, right? Only students with an athletic scholarship can use it for free, and they already have special facilities for training.
Woman	Yeah, but it's only $50 a semester. That's not too bad.
Man	Maybe, but I don't think I should have to pay anything if other students get to use the facilities for free. Plus I'm angry that the college didn't make any improvements to the existing facilities.
Woman	Yeah, they are kind of old.
Man	Right. The other day my roommate went to the gym and out of all the exercise machines, he told me only about half were working and there was a long line of people waiting. I think the facilities should be improved for everyone, not just staff and some of the students.
Woman	You've got a point, that's for sure. It seems like you feel that the college can't do much right these days.

Exercise E4 (Track 295)

Woman	It seems like you feel that the college can't do much right these days.
Man	Yeah, I read about some new bulletin boards in the campus newspaper. What a waste of money.
Woman	Really? I thought they were a good idea.
Man	These days everybody posts notices and ads on the Internet. We don't need physical bulletin boards.
Woman	Well, people do post things online, of course, but there are also hundreds of notices posted all around campus, so I think the bulletin boards will be useful. Almost every student spends time in the Student Center, so it's great to have a place to post notices where everybody will see them.
Man	Yeah, OK, I can see that might be useful.
Woman	And there are some parts of campus that get really messy because of all the notices. There's paper and trash everywhere and it looks really bad. I'm looking forward to seeing a cleaner campus when notices that are posted outside the Student Center are taken down.
Man	That's true. The area near my dorm gets pretty messy with notices. It would be nice to see the campus looking a bit cleaner... so I guess the college *can* do something right after all!
Woman	Glad to hear it.

Exercise G3 (Track 296)

Student	The two people discuss a letter by a student about changing the policy for starting student clubs.
	The man supports the student's viewpoint.
	First, he states that the college has a rule that full-time and part-time students should be treated equally.
	He then adds that the college's policy about registering student clubs is against this rule.

Next, the man says that he doesn't think clubs need fifty potential members before they can be registered.

He goes on to say that student clubs don't cost the college any money, so the number of members doesn't matter.

Exercise H1 – question 1 (Tracks 297–300)

Narrator	In this question, you will read a short passage about a campus situation and then listen to a conversation on the same topic. You will then answer a question using information from both the reading passage and the conversation. After you hear the question, you will have 30 seconds to prepare your response and 60 seconds to speak.
	State University is planning to upgrade its library facilities. Read an announcement from the university about this plan.
	You will have 45 seconds to read the announcement. Begin reading now.
	Now listen to two students as they discuss the announcement.
Woman	Did you see that announcement about the library?
Man	Yeah, isn't it great?
Woman	Great? I guess you missed the part about everyone having to pay $100.
Man	No, I saw that, but I'm happy to pay it if we get a better library. Our current library is OK, but a new library with double the number of books will be awesome. No more waiting for books to be returned before borrowing them will really help with assignments and the new computer facilities sound good, too.
Woman	Yeah, I guess.
Man	And 500 individual study rooms for student use? Right now there are only 50 study rooms and those are reserved for graduate students and faculty. I can't wait to get one of those rooms and get down to some serious schoolwork.
Woman	Can't you just study in your room? That's what I do.
Man	You've met my roommate, right? He's nice, but really noisy so it's hard to study when he's around. A quiet place in the library would be perfect.
Narrator	The man expresses his opinion about the announcement. State his opinion and explain the reasons he gives for holding that opinion.
Announcer	You may begin to prepare after the beep.
	You may begin to speak after the beep.

Exercise H1 – question 2 (Tracks 301–304)

Narrator	In this question, you will read a short passage about a campus situation and then listen to a conversation on the same topic. You will then answer a question using information from both the reading passage and the conversation. After you hear the question, you will have 30 seconds to prepare your response and 60 seconds to speak.
	A student wrote a letter to City College's newspaper about a suggested improvement to the college. Read the letter.
	You will have 45 seconds to read the announcement. Begin reading now.
	Now listen as two students discuss the letter.
Man	Did you see that letter in today's newspaper?
Woman	The one about the college needing more food options?
Man	Yeah, that's the one. I think the writer has a point.

Woman	Well, not me. I think we've got plenty of good food options already. The writer mentioned something about all the restaurants and dining halls serving fast food, but that's just not true. I mean, there's a place that sells vegetarian food right next to the administrative building, and a great cafe selling Thai food near the International Student Office.
Man	Oh yeah. I'd forgotten about those places. I eat in the main dining hall pretty much every day.
Woman	I think that's what the writer does, too. The main dining hall does have a lot of fast food places, but if you go to other places on campus, there're plenty of options.
Man	I guess so.
Woman	And you don't even have to stay on campus. I mean, there're several great restaurants in town just a few minutes on foot from the campus. Their food's just as cheap as the on-campus cafeterias, too. So I really don't think we need more food places on campus.
Narrator	The woman expresses her opinion about the suggestion put forward in the letter. State her opinion and explain the reasons she gives for holding that opinion.
Announcer	You may begin to prepare after the beep. You may begin to speak after the beep.

Exercise H1 – question 3 (Tracks 305–308)

Narrator	In this question, you will read a short passage about a campus situation and then listen to a conversation on the same topic. You will then answer a question using information from both the reading passage and the conversation. After you hear the question, you will have 30 seconds to prepare your response and 60 seconds to speak. A university is changing the hours of operation at its Health Services Center. Read the notice about these changes.

	You will have 45 seconds to read the announcement. Begin reading now. Now listen to two students as they discuss the notice.
Man	Did you see that the hours are being reduced at the Health Services Center? I think the university is making a mistake.
Woman	Really? I saw the notice but didn't think it was that big of a deal. Why do you think it's a mistake?
Man	Take the reduced evening hours. I don't understand why they're only going to have evening hours on a Friday. I mean Friday and Saturday are the days when most students want to go out and relax, so it's not likely many students will make an appointment for a Friday. If they had to offer evening hours on only one day, they should have kept one of the original days.
Woman	That's a good point.
Man	And I think it's bad that the health center won't be open on the weekends any more. What happens if a student gets sick on the weekend?
Woman	Doesn't the notice say that we can go to several clinics in town?
Man	Yeah, but I got some information about those clinics, and the closest one is almost 30 minutes from campus and it's really difficult to get to unless you have a car. I think the university should keep the health center open on either Saturday or Sunday, not close it on both days.
Woman	I see your point. Let's hope neither one of us needs a doctor on the weekend.
Narrator	The man expresses his opinion about the decision stated in the notice. State his opinion and explain the reasons he gives for holding that opinion.
Announcer	You may begin to prepare after the beep. You may begin to speak after the beep.

UNIT 18 | SPEAKING • Independent Speaking Task 4

Exercise E3 (Tracks 309 and 310)

Narrator	Part one.
Male Professor	I'll tell you a personal story that illustrates the idea of confirmation bias. Recently my wife and I were planning our vacation. She wanted to go to New York City, but I had this preconceived idea that New York was a bad place to go. I had been there once when I was a child and, well, I got lost in the airport for several hours, which was a very upsetting and emotional experience for me. My wife showed me brochures about New York and shared other people's recommendations with me, but although it looked and sounded really interesting, my reaction was negative. I rejected or ignored positive things about New York and instead focused on negative aspects like crime and high prices.
Narrator	Part two.
Male Professor	In the end I persuaded my wife we should go to Miami… which turned out to be a mistake. On the first day, the weather was so hot and humid that we stayed inside our hotel which had air conditioning. And then a major storm hit the city and we couldn't leave our hotel because the winds were so strong. So you can see that my negative opinion about New York made me reject evidence that it was the better place to go and resulted in a disappointing vacation.

Exercise E4 (Track 311)

Male Professor	So, let's look at a couple of examples of people's negative reactions to development proposals. There's one I read about the other day which was very interesting. A California energy producer wanted to build a new environmentally-friendly power plant that used sunlight to produce energy during the day and then burned trash to produce energy at night. In other words, this power plant was designed to produce environmentally clean energy 24 hours a day. Now in general, Californians are well-known for their support of environmental causes, but local residents apparently did not support this plan because the power plant was to be built very close to their homes and so the energy firm had to find a different location to build it. And, well, I'm not proud of this, but a similar situation happened just recently in the neighborhood where I live. There was a proposal to build a new shopping mall just a few minutes from my home. Now I go shopping as much as the next person, but although I liked the idea of more convenient shopping, I was worried that the mall was too close to my home. I thought the mall would bring noise, pollution, and traffic problems, so like hundreds of my neighbors I opposed the plan and, to my relief, the plan was eventually canceled.

Exercise E5 (Track 312)

Female Professor OK, I'd like to tell you about a famous social psychology experiment. Back in the 1950s, a psychologist called Solomon Asch conducted a series of experiments on conformity – under what conditions people choose to act in the same way as others. In the classic experiment, a group of eight participants were shown a card with a line on it and then another card with three lines labeled A, B, and C. One of the three lines was obviously the same length as the original line, and two of them were either much longer or much shorter. The participants had to say which line – A, B, or C – was the same length as the original line.

The trick was that only one of the eight participants was a real participant. The real participant did not know that the other seven people were actors who had been told ahead of the experiment whether to give the right answer or a wrong answer.

Asch wanted to see whether the real participant would agree with – that is, conform with – the opinion of the seven actors when they gave the wrong answer even when their answer was clearly wrong. And in fact, at least 75% of real participants *did* conform to the group and give an incorrect answer at least once. This experiment shows that the real participant was affected by the answers that the other participants gave.

Exercise G2 (Track 313)

Female Student The reading introduces the concept of confirmation bias.

In summary, this is when people prefer information that matches their opinions and make bad decisions because of this preference.

The professor gives a personal example of this concept.

First, he says that his wife wanted a vacation in New York, but he did not want to go there because of a negative experience in New York when he was a child.

Next, he mentions that he rejected information about New York that did not match his negative opinion of that city.

Finally, he states that he and his wife vacationed in Miami instead of New York, but this was a bad decision.

This example shows how confirmation bias affected the professor's decision.

Exercise H1 – question 1 (Tracks 314–317)

Narrator In this question, you will read a short passage on an academic subject and then listen to a talk on the same topic. You will then answer a question using information from both the reading passage and the conversation. After you hear the question, you will have 30 seconds to prepare your response and 60 seconds to speak.

Now read the passage about sunk-cost bias. You have 45 seconds to read the passage. Begin reading now.

Now listen to part of a lecture on this topic in a business studies class.

Female Professor We've all heard the aphorism, "Don't throw good money after bad," but actually a number of companies are creating business models that encourage consumers to do precisely that. I was reading about a company that develops games for smartphones and tablets. Some of their games are not just wildly popular, but wildly profitable, too. Here's how their business model works.

First, a consumer downloads the game for free and starts playing. At first the game is fun and easy, but soon it becomes very hard. At this point, the player has a choice. He or she can either stop playing, or spend a few dollars to make the game easier. Some consumers will think, "Well, I've already spent some time on this game and I don't want to waste that time, so I'll spend some money to make the game easier." Then the game becomes even more difficult, and again the consumer has a choice – stop playing or spend more time and money on the game – and again some consumers will do the latter. They'll say to themselves, "You know, I've invested time and money on this game, so it must be fun. I guess I'll spend a few more dollars." The catch is that for many people, the game is no longer fun at this point, but they keep spending time and money trying to beat the game because they don't want to feel that the time and money they've already spent is wasted.

Narrator Using points and examples from the talk, explain how sunk-cost bias can cause people to make irrational decisions.

Announcer You may begin to prepare after the beep.

You may begin to speak after the beep.

Exercise H1 – question 2 (Tracks 319–321)

Narrator In this question, you will read a short passage on an academic subject and then listen to a talk on the same topic. You will then answer a question using information from both the reading passage and the conversation. After you hear the question, you will have 30 seconds to prepare your response and 60 seconds to speak.

Now read the passage about defense mechanisms. You have 45 seconds to read the passage. Begin reading now.

Now listen to part of a lecture on this topic in a psychology class.

Male Professor You've all done the reading about defense mechanisms, I hope, so let's talk about a couple of different strategies that many people adopt when faced with difficult situations.

I'm sure you've all heard – and maybe even used – the expression, "He's in denial" about a person who doesn't seem to be facing up to a problem or situation. Well, this expression is common precisely because denial is actually a defense mechanism that people use. In simple terms, denial is when a person either refuses to admit, or does not even recognize, a negative situation. When I was a child, my pet dog died in an accident. It was such a painful situation for me that, according to my parents, for at least a week after the dog died, I refused to accept she was dead. In short, I used denial as a strategy to reduce my emotional pain.

Rationalization is another defense mechanism that people sometimes use when things are bad. It involves avoiding the real reasons for a negative situation by finding a logical, rational explanation as a way to make the situation seem better. For example, a study conducted a few years ago showed that some students who fail an exam are likely to blame the quality of teaching they receive. When the study habits of those same students were analyzed, however, it was clear that many of the students failed because they simply didn't do enough work. Their feeling that their teachers were not good enough was just a rationalization to protect themselves from the painful reality that they were lazy.

Narrator Using details from the talk, explain why denial and rationalization are examples of defense mechanisms.

Announcer You may begin to prepare after the beep.

You may begin to speak after the beep.

Exercise H1 – question 3 (Tracks 322–325)

Narrator	In this question, you will read a short passage on an academic subject and then listen to a talk on the same topic. You will then answer a question using information from both the reading passage and the conversation. After you hear the question, you will have 30 seconds to prepare your response and 60 seconds to speak.
	Now read the passage about the halo effect. You have 45 seconds to read the passage. Begin reading now.
	Now listen to a lecture on the same topic in a marketing class.
Female Professor	Marketers can use the halo effect to boost sales in a couple of ways. One method is to use celebrity endorsement. Celebrities, such as actors or athletes, are often physically attractive, successful individuals. The bias introduced by the halo effect means that we tend to assume they're also smart, funny, kind, and so on. When a marketer pays a famous actor to promote a brand of jeans, for example, our positive image of that person rubs off on the jeans, so if we think the actor is stylish and attractive, we're likely to think the jeans are stylish and attractive as well.
	Another way that the halo effect works in marketing is when people's positive perception of one product sold by a company extends to that company's other products. Automobile manufacturers, for example, may try to develop a so-called halo vehicle that is a high-quality car which has a very positive image among consumers. The idea is that the positive perception of this high-quality vehicle will extend to other, lower-end, vehicles that the same company produces.
Narrator	Using points and examples from the talk, explain how companies try to take advantage of the halo effect.
Announcer	You may begin to prepare after the beep.
	You may begin to speak after the beep.

UNIT 19 | SPEAKING • Independent Speaking Task 5

Exercises D1 and D2 (Tracks 326–329)

Narrator	Conversation 1.
Man	Have you finalized your plans for spring break, Barbara? You're going to Florida with some friends, right?
Woman	That was the plan, but I'm not sure I can do it. I've really fallen behind on my schoolwork, and I've got several assignments due right after spring break. If I take time off, I don't think I'll have time to finish them.
Man	Well, why don't you stay at college for a few days and get your assignments done? Then you can join your friends for the last few days of spring break.
Woman	It might take more than a few days…
Narrator	Conversation 2.
Woman	Jack, hi. I was hoping I'd bump into you. I've got good news and bad news. The good news is that a Japanese *taiko* drumming group is giving a concert in the auditorium next week.
Man	Wow! That's great… so what's the bad news?
Woman	It's next Wednesday at 7, so if we go, we'd have to miss our student orientation session for med school.
Man	That's too bad. Maybe we could see if there are any other orientation sessions coming up.
Woman	It doesn't hurt to ask, I guess…
Narrator	Conversation 3.
Woman	Why the long face, Bob?
Man	I attended a career fair last week and dropped off some resumes, and I just got an email from a company inviting me to be a summer intern.
Woman	That sounds good. So what's the problem?
Man	My sister's graduating the same day the internship begins, and my mom wants the whole family to be at her graduation and then stay on for a family party a couple of days later. If I do that, I'll miss the first three days of the internship.
Woman	Have you thought about contacting the company and asking to start the internship a week later? I'm sure they'd understand.
Man	I guess I could, but I'm worried…
Narrator	Conversation 4.
Man	Hello, Lisa.
Woman	Hi, Frank. You don't know anyone who's renting out a room for the summer, do you? I'm staying at the university over the summer to attend summer session. I arranged to rent a room in a friend's house, but I've just heard there's a problem and I won't be able to stay there.
Man	What I would do is check the bulletin board in the housing office. There are usually plenty of rooms for rent listed there.
Woman	Hey, good idea!

Exercise D3 (Track 330)

Woman	Hey, Ben, my professor just asked if I knew a couple of people who could help out at a conference next Monday and Tuesday for $100 per day. What do you think? Want to do it with me?
Man	Next Monday and Tuesday? That's a shame, but I don't think I can. I already agreed to volunteer at a student orientation session both days.
Woman	Why don't you see if you could volunteer at the student orientation on just one of the days? That would mean you could work at the conference the other day.
Man	The money would sure be useful, but I don't want to let people down. I know they've had a couple of other volunteers drop out recently and I don't want to do the same.
Woman	Well then, what about explaining the situation to the people organizing the orientation and see if they could pay you for your time? You might not get $100 per day, but even a smaller sum would be better than nothing, right?
Man	That's a good idea, but the person in charge keeps complaining about how small his budget for the event is.

Exercise D5 (Tracks 331 and 332)

Narrator	Conversation 1.
Woman	How's everything, Karim?

Man	Hi Jenny. Everything's fine, except that I can't seem to focus on studying for my midterm exams, and time's running out.
Woman	I know that feeling. Two weeks ago I had the same problem.
Man	Yeah? How did you get your focus back?
Woman	Well, following a study plan helped. My plan was simple: work for 45 minutes and then take a break for 15 minutes. I've found I can work for hours like that.
Man	I tried using a study plan last year, but it didn't really out work well for me. Perhaps I could try again, though.
Woman	Another thing I did was write down everything I knew about one of my classes.
Man	How did that help?
Woman	Well, when I wrote everything down, all sorts of questions occurred to me. Like, for instance, I wrote down what I knew about a biological process, and as I was writing, I thought of all these other questions about the process. So I wrote those down, too, which helped me because I knew what to focus on.
Man	It sounds like it would take a long time, but maybe it would help.
Narrator	Conversation 2.
Man	Hi, Charlotte. I've been looking for you. Professor Givens asked me to tell you that a spot on the field trip has opened up, if you're still interested.
Woman	Seriously? Oh my gosh, that's great... Oh, actually, no it's not. I won't be able to go.
Man	What's wrong? Did you make other plans?
Woman	Yes. When I spoke to Professor Givens last week, she made it sound like there was no chance at all I'd be able to go on the field trip this year, and then Professor Andrews asked me to be his lab assistant, so I said yes.
Man	What I would do is speak to Professor Andrews and explain the situation. He's pretty cool, so I'm sure he'd understand.
Woman	Yeah, he'd definitely understand, but he mentioned the department would pay me to do the lab work and, well, some extra money would really come in handy right now.
Man	I guess you could go on next year's field trip. That was what you were originally planning, right?
Woman	It's just that this year the field trip is in a part of Oregon that I've always wanted to visit. Every year they change the location of the field trip, so next year it'll definitely be someplace else.

Exercise E2 (Track 333)

Woman	Hello, Pedro. Are you still studying for the TOEFL Test?
Man	Yeah, but I'm having trouble with Speaking Task 5. I always feel stress because I don't know which one of the two suggestions from the conversation should be my preferred suggestion that I talk about. If a suggestion is about a familiar topic, I choose that one, but if neither suggestion is familiar, I waste time trying to choose the better one to talk about.
Woman	You could also look at your notes. If you have better notes about one suggestion than the other one, choose the suggestion that has better notes as your preferred suggestion.

Man	Good idea! Thanks! I sort of do the same thing. If I don't have a good understanding of one of the suggestions, I usually choose the other suggestion.
Woman	That makes sense. There's one more strategy I use: if one suggestion might take a long time to talk about, it's generally a good idea to choose the other suggestion as your preferred suggestion.
Man	I sometimes run out of time, so that's also good advice. Thanks for the help!
Woman	My pleasure. Good luck on the test, Pedro.

Exercise F2 (Track 334)

Female Student	The man has a problem because he volunteered at an orientation so he cannot work at a conference.
	The speakers discuss a couple of possible solutions to this problem.
	In my view, the man should speak to the organizer of the student orientation and try to get paid for his time.
	The main reason is that even though the event budget is small, he might get some money.
	In contrast, I don't think he should drop out as a volunteer.
	This is because other people have dropped out and the man does not want to do the same thing.

Exercise G1 – question 1 (Tracks 335–338)

Narrator	In this question, you will listen to a conversation. You will then be asked to talk about the information in the conversation and to give your opinion about the ideas presented. After you hear the question, you will have 20 seconds to prepare your response and 60 seconds to speak.
Man	Hi, Kate. How are things with you?
Woman	Hey, Dan. Professor Camilleri has asked if I want to help her with some research until the end of the semester. I'd love to do it, as it would be great experience for the future, but it will take a lot of time, and I'm not sure I'll be able to stay on top of my assignments if I say yes.
Man	You have a part-time job as well, right?
Woman	That's right. I work at the fitness center in the evenings.
Man	Well, could you quit that job? That would free up some time, right?
Woman	Yeah, I've considered it, but the fitness center job pays pretty well, and I can't really afford to give it up.
Man	Well, could you do only some of the research for your professor and have someone else do the rest?
Woman	You mean, see if Professor Camilleri would be willing to work with two research assistants?
Man	Yeah. That way you'd have time for your schoolwork and part-time job, and still have time to help your professor with her research.
Woman	That's an option, I guess. I'll have to think about it more, though.
Narrator	The speakers discuss two possible solutions to a problem. Describe the problem. Then state which of the two solutions you prefer and why.
Announcer	You may begin to prepare after the beep.
	You may begin to speak after the beep.

Exercise G1 – question 2 (Tracks 339–342)

Narrator	In this question, you will listen to a conversation. You will then be asked to talk about the information in the conversation and to give your opinion about the ideas presented. After you hear the question, you will have 20 seconds to prepare your response and 60 seconds to speak.
Woman	Hi, Eric. Are you ready for our study group session with Sam, Carla, and Peter?
Man	Yes, uh, actually, I don't know.
Woman	What do you mean?
Man	Well, I did the reading I was supposed to do, but the other people in the group know so much about the subject that I've lost my confidence. I'm not sure I add anything that Sam, Carla, and Peter don't already know.
Woman	Wow. I feel exactly the same way. The other three studied this subject matter last semester, too, so they know a lot more than I do. I try to do the work, but I feel like I'm holding them back.
Man	I kind of wish I had joined a different group, you know?
Woman	Could we do that? Join a different group, I mean? I'm sure there are some study groups with people like us who didn't study the subject last semester.
Man	It's kind of late in the semester to join a different group, but we could ask around. We'd also have to make sure the professor doesn't mind... you know, another option might be to split off and form our own group.
Woman	Just the two of us?
Man	Yeah. I think we work pretty well together, and we seem to have about the same level of knowledge.
Woman	Well, it would mean a lot of hard work to complete our project in time, but it might be possible. And I'm sure Sam, Carla, and Peter wouldn't mind.
Narrator	The speakers discuss two possible solutions to a problem. Describe the problem. Then state which of the two solutions you prefer and why.
Announcer	You may begin to prepare after the beep.
	You may begin to speak after the beep.

Exercise G1 – question 3 (Tracks 343–346)

Narrator	In this question, you will listen to a conversation. You will then be asked to talk about the information in the conversation and to give your opinion about the ideas presented. After you hear the question, you will have 20 seconds to prepare your response and 60 seconds to speak.
Woman	Professor Braun, do you have a minute? I want to talk to you about next month's field trip to Carlsbad Caverns National Park.
Man	Hi, Sandy. Sure, come in. Is there a problem?
Woman	Well, I know the field trip is a requirement of the class, but I grew up in Carlsbad and often went to the National Park with my family. I also went there on two study trips when I was in high school, so I know the place pretty well. I'm worried that I won't learn anything new on the field trip.
Man	I see. Hmmm. You know, we don't normally do this, but I could speak with Professor Jenkins and arrange for you to join her group's field trip to Rock Hound State Park.
Woman	That might be OK, I guess, but I wouldn't know anyone in her group.
Man	Well, a field trip is required, so you have to go on one. I guess the only other option would be for you to do an independent field trip.
Woman	You mean, go somewhere on my own and do independent field research?
Man	Yes, is that something you would feel comfortable doing?
Woman	My father's interested in geology, so he might be able to take time off work and come with me. I'd have to call him to check, though.
Man	Try and let me know your final decision within the next couple of days, OK?
Narrator	The speakers discuss two possible solutions to a problem. Describe the problem. Then state which of the two solutions you prefer and why.
Announcer	You may begin to prepare after the beep.
	You may begin to speak after the beep.

UNIT 20 | SPEAKING • Independent Speaking Task 6

Exercise A1 (Track 347)

Narrator	Speaker 1.
Woman	The two most general fields of economics are macroeconomics and microeconomics. Macroeconomics is concerned with the performance of the whole economy. Microeconomics, on the other hand, focuses on individual companies and families.
Narrator	Speaker 2.
Man	Competitive industries use a variety of methods to increase profits. Loss leaders are products sold for no profit in order to drive sales of more profitable items. Food items such as bread, milk, and sugar are sometimes sold as loss leaders in supermarkets.
Narrator	Speaker 3.
Man	Businesses use many kinds of marketing to boost sales. Direct marketing involves communicating directly with customers such as by sending emails. All types of businesses use direct marketing.
Narrator	Speaker 4.
Woman	Sole proprietorships are a very common type of small business. A sole proprietorship is a business owned and operated by a single individual. In legal terms, the person who owns the business is the business.

Exercise D1 and D2 (Track 348)

Female Teacher	Hi, everyone. Today let's discuss Integrated Speaking Task 6 in the TOEFL Test. Although this task can be challenging, the key to doing well is simple: take good notes. It helps to take as many notes as you can, but specifically, there are four things to focus on.

First, make a note when the speaker gives a definition or explanation of a concept or idea. You'll often hear phrases like "this can be defined as," or "this means" when the speaker does this.

Second, listen carefully for signal words that tell you the speaker is giving supporting details or examples. The speaker will often introduce these with expressions like, "to illustrate" or "to give an example."

Third, if the speaker compares or contrasts points or says how something has changed, make a note. If the speaker does this, you might hear him or her say "on the other hand" or "at first, ... but later."

And fourth, also make a note if the speaker mentions how one thing has caused or been affected by another thing. Example expressions that you might hear include "as a result of" or "had an impact on."

OK? Any questions?

Exercise D7 (Track 349)

Male Professor OK, so we've talked about inflation. Now I'd like to discuss stagflation, which is a combination word formed by combining the word stagnation with the word inflation.

Stagflation is characterized by a high level of inflation but a low level of economic growth. Both high inflation and low economic growth have a negative effect on the economy, so it should come as no surprise that stagflation is especially bad for economies. For example, a global stagflation in the 1970s, which was in part caused by a huge increase in oil prices, led to a recession in many countries.

And not only is stagflation bad, but historically it has proven difficult for governments to break out of periods of stagflation. Few of the policies that are useful for combating inflation also work for combating stagflation, and those that do work are often expensive and take time. The global stagflation beginning in the 1970s that I mentioned lasted for more than ten years, for instance.

Exercise F3 (Track 350)

Male Student The professor discusses two types of integration, which helps businesses be efficient.

First, she talks about vertical integration, which is when a company controls several steps in producing an item.

She gives the example of a company that controls three steps in the production of clothes.

She goes on to say that vertical integration reduces costs and delays.

Next, she discusses horizontal integration, which is when a company controls companies selling the same product.

She mentions the case of a company that controls two companies that both sell computers.

She then points out that horizontal integration increases market share.

Exercise G1 – question 1 (Tracks 351–354)

Narrator In this question, you will listen to part of a lecture. You will then be asked to summarize important information from the lecture. After you hear the question, you will have 20 seconds to prepare your response and 60 seconds to speak.

Now listen to part of a lecture in a business studies class.

Male Professor One interesting trend over the past two decades has been the growing number of people offering software for free download via the Internet. Broadly speaking, there are two overlapping categories of free software: one is "freeware," and the other is "open source" software.

Freeware gets its name because it's free software. Typically, freeware is written and published by one or two programmers working on their own, or by a small independent software company. In other words, freeware is not usually published by major software companies, although that does happen from time to time. The vast majority of freeware is what I call single-function software, which is software that does one thing and does not have a huge variety of features or functions. For example, on my computer I have a freeware program that lets me easily and quickly rename multiple files.

Open source software is also often free and so technically could be called freeware, too; however, it differs from typical freeware in a couple of important ways. For one thing, open source programs are by definition available to download in the form of computer code as well as published programs. This means that you or I could download an open-source program and make changes to the code, if we wished. For freeware, though, the source code is not available. And for another thing, open source software is often worked on by hundreds or even thousands of people all over the world.

Narrator Using points and examples from the lecture, describe the two types of free software that the professor discusses.

Announcer You may begin to prepare after the beep.

You may begin to speak after the beep.

Exercise G1 – question 2 (Tracks 355–358)

Narrator In this question, you will listen to part of a lecture. You will then be asked to summarize important information from the lecture. After you hear the question, you will have 20 seconds to prepare your response and 60 seconds to speak.

Now listen to part of a talk in a marine biology course.

Male Professor As we've been reading, stocks of many wild fish are declining, mainly as a result of overfishing. Despite this, demand for fish continues to rise because consumers feel that fish is a healthy food choice. Whenever there's demand, businesses see an opportunity, and companies have turned to fish farming to meet the growing demand for fish. Initially there were just a few suppliers of farmed fish, but over the past few decades, the number of suppliers has grown significantly.

Fish farming, as its name suggests, involves breeding and raising fish or shellfish for food in the same way that a farmer on land might grow wheat or corn, or raise pigs or cows. The fish farmer must feed the fish, protect them from predators, make sure they are free of disease, and so on. When the fish are ready – that is, when they're large enough – they are harvested and sold as food.

Salmon, tilapia, carp, and catfish are all species of fish that are commonly farmed. I was reading recently about a less well-known species called cobia that is also very suitable for farming. For one thing, cobia grows very quickly – at least twice as quickly as salmon – and can reach a size of over 60 kilograms, uh, that's around 130 pounds. It handles the stresses of commercial fish farming relatively well, and it's cheaper to farm – and so likely to be more profitable to farm – than most other kinds of fish because it does not require expensive food in order to grow. Finally, its taste is considered to be particularly good. All of these factors make it ideal for fish farming.

Narrator	Using points and examples from the talk, explain what fish farming is and why cobia is a suitable species for farming.
Announcer	You may begin to prepare after the beep.
	You may begin to speak after the beep.

Exercise G1 – question 3 (Tracks 359–362)

Narrator	In this question, you will listen to part of a lecture. You will then be asked to summarize important information from the lecture. After you hear the question, you will have 20 seconds to prepare your response and 60 seconds to speak.
	Now listen to part of a discussion in a law seminar.
Female Professor	OK, let's continue our discussion of business law by talking about the corporation. We'll talk about corporations a lot in this course, but for now I just want to introduce the concept.
	It's actually quite hard to define a corporation in simple terms, but I'll do my best. A corporation is a company

created by one or more people which is considered to be legally separate from those people. The corporation also has certain legal rights and responsibilities of its own. To make that clearer, let's think about paying taxes. A person who owns a corporation has to pay taxes on any income that she receives, of course... well, the corporation also has to pay taxes on the income it makes because it's separate from its owner and has its own legal responsibilities.

Another important point to understand about corporations is the concept of limited liability. Let me give an example to make this clear. Imagine that a corporation has to pay a fine, for example, but only has enough money to pay 50% of the fine. In such a case, the executives who work for the corporation and the stockholders who own it would *not* have to pay the additional 50%. They would have no liability, er, no legal responsibility, to pay, because the corporation is a separate entity. This contrasts with other forms of business, such as a sole proprietorship, where the owner of the business would be fully liable to pay any fines that the business incurred, because the sole proprietorship is not a separate entity.

Narrator	Using points and examples from the seminar, describe the legal responsibilities of a corporation.
Announcer	You may begin to prepare after the beep.
	You may begin to speak after the beep.

SPEAKING REVIEW TEST

Question 1 (Tracks 363 and 364)

Narrator	What is one food that you do *not* enjoy eating? Why? Support your answer with specific details and examples.
Announcer	You may begin to prepare after the beep.
	You may begin to speak after the beep.

Question 2 (Tracks 365 and 366)

Narrator	Some people like going out to a theater to watch a movie. Other people prefer watching movies at home. Which way of watching movies do you prefer? Why? Support your response.
Announcer	You may begin to prepare after the beep.
	You may begin to speak after the beep.

Question 3 (Tracks 367–370)

Narrator	In this question, you will read a short passage about a campus situation and then listen to a conversation on the same topic. You will then answer a question using information from both the reading passage and the conversation. After you hear the question, you will have 30 seconds to prepare your response and 60 seconds to speak.
	State University is canceling events on campus. Read the notice about this cancellation.
	You have 45 seconds to read the notice. Begin reading now.
	Now listen as two students discuss the notice.
Man	Did you see that all on-campus events have been canceled? I think the university is totally overreacting.

Woman	Why? What do you mean?
Man	Well, there really wasn't any trouble at all at the event last week. Some students from another college tried to get into a party, but the event organizers said no. There was some shouting, but that's all.
Woman	But didn't some students go to the hospital?
Man	Those students were involved in a car accident on the other side of campus. It happened at about the same time, I think, so the university council thinks the events were connected, but there was no connection at all. So canceling all events will do nothing to improve student safety.
Woman	Oh.
Man	And I think it's unreasonable to wait until November before discussing the situation. That means it will be at least two weeks until this ban is lifted, so a lot of fun and important events will be canceled. My running club had arranged a fun run to raise money for a charity, but we'll have to cancel it now.
Woman	Even charity events are going to be canceled?
Man	Yeah, they are. The university's ban applies to all events.
Woman	Wow. Well, I really understand why you're so upset about this.
Narrator	The man expresses his opinion about the notice. State his opinion and explain the reasons he gives for holding that opinion.
Announcer	You may begin to prepare after the beep.
	You may begin to speak after the beep.

Question 4 (Tracks 371–374)

Narrator In this question, you will read a short passage on an academic subject and then listen to a talk on the same topic. You will then answer a question using information from both the reading passage and the conversation. After you hear the question, you will have 30 seconds to prepare your response and 60 seconds to speak.

Now read the passage about the conduction of heat. You have 45 seconds to read the passage. Begin reading now.

Now listen to part of a lecture on this topic in an archaeology class.

Female Professor I read an interesting article recently about the origin of some small obsidian artifacts found at an archaeological site in Germany. Obsidian is a type of glass formed by volcanoes, and it does not occur naturally in Germany. As a result, the archaeologists who discovered the obsidian artifacts were uncertain where they originally came from. So the scholars decided to use a technique from geology and chemistry called trace element analysis.

Before continuing, let me explain what that is. When rocks are formed, tiny amounts of different elements like zinc or iron may become part of the rock. These are called *trace elements*, and the trace elements in a rock from one location, or a rock formed during one period, are typically different from a rock formed in another location or during a different time, in the same way that different people have different fingerprints.

The result of the analysis showed that the trace elements in the obsidian artifacts exactly matched obsidian from two sites: one in Greece, and one in Turkey. The archaeologists had originally expected that the obsidian would turn out to be from Italy. To find obsidian coming from two different locations was a surprise, one that suggested that perhaps trade in obsidian was more widespread than expected.

Narrator Using the example of obsidian artifacts that the professor discusses, explain how trace element analysis helped answer an archaeological question.

Announcer You may begin to prepare after the beep.

You may begin to speak after the beep.

Question 5 (Tracks 375–378)

Narrator In this question, you will listen to a conversation. You will then be asked to talk about the information in the conversation and to give your opinion about the ideas presented. After you hear the question, you will have 20 seconds to prepare your response and 60 seconds to speak.

Now listen to a conversation between a man and a woman.

Man Hi, Jen. Did you hear any news about that internship you wanted?

Woman Yeah, they offered me an interview.

Man That's great... so why the long face?

Woman The interview's next Tuesday at 3pm, but I've already promised some people in my study group that I'd help them out with a survey then.

Man How about explaining the situation to the people in your study group? I'm sure they'd understand and be willing to reschedule the time for the survey.

Woman I could do that, I guess, but it was really hard to find a time when everyone could do the survey; next Tuesday was definitely the best option. Plus, I've already missed several study sessions recently because I was sick, and I don't want to miss another one.

Man Have you thought about contacting the company and trying to get a different interview time?

Woman Yeah, I thought about that, but I'm worried that the people at the company will think I'm not really interested in being an intern there if I ask for a different interview time.

Narrator The speakers discuss two possible solutions to a problem. Describe the problem. Then state which of the two solutions you prefer and why.

Announcer You may begin to prepare after the beep.

You may begin to speak after the beep.

Question 6 (Tracks 379–382)

Narrator In this question, you will listen to part of a lecture. You will then be asked to summarize important information from the lecture. After you hear the question, you will have 20 seconds to prepare your response and 60 seconds to speak.

Now listen to part of a talk in a public health class.

Male Professor Today, we're going to talk about vaccination, which is a way of protecting people from specific diseases that could make them very sick. In simple terms, doctors inject patients with either a very mild or deactivated disease. This makes the patient's body better able to fight an infection caused by this disease; in most cases, the vaccination causes the patient to become immune to this disease, meaning that he or she will not be able to catch it, and therefore will not become sick from it in the future.

There is some evidence of something similar to vaccination in places like China and India thousands of years ago, but the scientific practice of vaccination is less than 300 years old. When it was first introduced, vaccination seemed like a miracle. Doctors could inject patients with a harmless disease like cowpox, which would protect them from deadly viruses like smallpox. As soon as the benefits of vaccination were recognized, it became widely popular and a standard tool of public health, saving countless lives.

Over the last few decades, however, the public perception of vaccination has undergone something of a change, at least among some people. There is still a very widespread sense that vaccination is a good thing, but some people have begun to worry about the health effects of the practice. Some people believe that giving children vaccinations against various diseases can lead to physical and mental health issues. There is little if any definitive evidence to support these beliefs, but this has not stopped some parents from refusing to allow their children to be vaccinated.

Narrator Using points and examples from the talk, say what vaccination is. Then say how attitudes towards vaccination have changed over time.

Announcer You may begin to prepare after the beep.

You may begin to speak after the beep.

WRITING DIAGNOSTIC TEST

Writing Task 1 (Track 383)

Narrator Now listen to a lecture on the topic you just read about.

Male Professor The article suggests that Marco Polo did not really visit China and used sources written by others as the basis for his book. We're talking about events that happened more than 700 years ago, so it's obviously impossible to be absolutely certain, but the evidence that Marco Polo *did* visit China is very strong.

Take the point that Polo did not mention various aspects of Chinese culture in his work. He was a merchant, and so his book tends to focus on things that are of interest to merchants, not things like chopsticks or tea drinking that had no value. For example, he *does* mention printing, but printed money, not printed books – at that time, there was no book industry, remember. And he goes into great detail about the production of salt – a valuable commodity at that time.

The Great Wall of China as we know it today was mainly built two hundred years after Marco Polo visited China. There *was* a wall in Polo's time, but it would probably have been in a ruined condition, so it's not really surprising that Polo did not mention it. Moreover, other Europeans who traveled within China during this time did not mention the wall either.

And the point that Marco Polo and his relatives are not mentioned in contemporary Chinese documents can be explained, too. Foreigners in China at that time were usually referred to by a nickname, not a real name. We do not know Polo's Chinese nickname, so it's possible he *is* mentioned in documents, but under a different name. Also, Polo's book was widely copied by hand. It's possible the book we know today has a copying error, and Polo actually wrote that he stayed in China, not that he had political influence: the Italian words for "stay" and "political influence" are rather similar.

UNIT 21 | WRITING • Integrated Writing Task 1 Questions – Challenge Questions

Exercise E2 (Track 384)

Female Teacher Let's talk a little about Writing Task 1 in the TOEFL Test. As you know, you only get one chance to listen to the lecture for the integrated writing task, so it's really important to take good notes.

Some people say it's a good idea to understand as much as you can by listening, and take only a few notes. In my experience, though, you should take as many notes as you can about ideas that are related to the points in the reading. Most Writing Task 1 questions are Challenge questions, so usually the speaker will discuss ideas that disagree with the points in the reading passage.

I often hear students say there isn't enough time to take good notes. It's true you don't have much time, but you can use abbreviations to take notes more quickly and use the time more effectively. For example, instead of writing the word "and," you could save a little time by writing a plus symbol, or instead of writing the full word "information," you could write just "info."

And some people think that when you take notes you should paraphrase the speaker's words rather than copy them directly. In my view, paraphrasing while you listen is a difficult skill, so you can either copy the speaker's words exactly or paraphrase them, whichever is easier for you. That's a key point: taking notes can be difficult, so when you do it, focus on finding the easiest way to do it, OK?

Exercise E3 (Track 385)

Male Speaker A lot of people claim there's an education crisis these days and that offering teachers higher pay for better performance will solve the crisis. A closer look, however, suggests that performance-based pay may not be such a good idea after all.

Think back to the reading. The writer makes the point that teachers would work harder under a system of merit-based pay. It's possible this is true, but impossible to be sure because no studies have been done to prove it. However, numerous studies *have* shown that in most cases offering more money is actually a poor way to motivate people to work harder.

Exercise E4 – question 1 (Track 386)

Male Speaker The writer also argues that performance-based pay for teachers will lead to better student results. It may be true that students will perform better, but not necessarily because of better quality teaching. Why? Well, studies have shown that offering workers more money for better results leads to some people "cheating" the system, meaning they find ways to get better results without actually doing better work. There's no reason to think the teaching profession would be different.

Finally, studies have shown that many people become teachers because they want to help others and be creative, *not* because they want a large salary. So, offering performance-based pay is likely to mean that many people who care more about money than about inspiring students decide to become teachers. But teachers who are more interested in earning money than inspiring students are unlikely to solve the education crisis.

Exercise E4 – question 2 (Track 387)

Female Speaker In the reading, the author makes some arguments against a financial transaction tax and claims that such a tax might even increase poverty rather than reduce it. In my view, they're *clever* arguments, but not *good* arguments.

Take the point that retired people might see a drop in their income. There are situations in which a financial transaction tax *might* cause such a drop, but remember that the cost of the tax is only 0.05%. So a retired couple living on $5,000 per month, for example, would at worst have just $25 less per month. Such a small amount is unlikely to affect their lives in any meaningful way, and could hardly be said to put them in danger of living in poverty.

What about the argument that financial institutions would pass on increased costs to their customers? It's likely that many institutions would do this, but not all. And customers could easily switch to a different bank or brokerage firm that did not charge more. Further, the terms of the tax could specify that financial institutions would not be allowed to pass on the cost to customers, which would solve that potential problem.

Finally, the argument that a Robin Hood tax would lead to job losses also does not stand up to scrutiny. Pretty much any new tax will lead to job losses in some industries at first. This is usually a temporary phenomenon, though, and most workers will soon find work again. And in any case, the money raised through the financial transaction tax would allow governments to offer more support to those without work, such as helping them find a job.

Exercise H1 (Track 388)

Narrator	Now listen to a lecture on the topic you just read about.
Female Speaker	The article I asked you to read about electric cars makes some interesting arguments. And while I agree that auto makers should prioritize the manufacture of these vehicles, I cannot agree that they offer a range of benefits yet. The benefits will come in time, I believe, but for now, a close analysis shows there are more disadvantages than advantages to owning an electric car.

Take the argument that electric cars are cheaper to operate than gasoline-powered vehicles. Sadly that's not true if you include the cost of purchasing the vehicle. Electric cars currently cost thousands of dollars more, on average, than gasoline-powered cars, so even with lower daily operational costs, over the lifetime of their vehicle most owners of electric cars will actually spend more in total.

The point about the convenience of electric vehicles doesn't stand up, either. They're convenient if you only ever need to recharge the battery at home, but for trips away from home, locations where you can charge up an electric vehicle are few and far between. This puts drastic limits on where and how far owners can travel. For owners of traditional cars, however, gas stations are, almost literally, everywhere.

And although it's true that electric cars don't release harmful or polluting exhaust gases, sadly it's not true that they are environmentally friendly. In many countries, the owner of an electric car cannot recharge that car without using electricity mainly produced by burning fossil fuels like coal or natural gas. So, indirectly, recharging an electric car leads to the release of the same kinds of gases that gasoline-powered cars produce.

UNIT 22 | WRITING • Integrated Writing Task 1 Questions – Problem-Solution Questions

Exercise E1 (Track 389)

Female Speaker 1	Although note-taking is difficult, the more you practice it, the easier it will become. So practice taking notes often, such as when you watch TV or listen to a radio broadcast.
Male Speaker	The three points the speaker discusses in Writing Task 1 will be in the same order as the points in the reading. This knowledge helps you predict what the speaker will discuss next.
Female Speaker 2	Just after the lecture finishes, you might have a good memory of the speaker's words. If so, do not start writing immediately, but take a little time to add to your lecture notes before your memory fades. This will help you summarize the lecture more effectively.

Exercise E2 (Track 390)

Female Speaker	The article claims that the urban heat island effect has both an environmental and human impact. This is true, but there are a number of ways that people can mitigate, uh, reduce, these negative effects.

As the article notes, people's desire to stay cool is the main reason for the increased demand for electricity in the summer. A simple but proven technique for reducing city temperatures is to plant more vegetation, such as trees and grass. Painting roofs a lighter color to reflect more sunlight is also effective. Some studies have shown that these two measures can reduce the urban heat island effect by up to 50%.

Two techniques exist to prevent the urban heat island effect from heating up local bodies of water. One is to use construction materials for city streets that allow water to pass through them. This gives the water a chance to cool down before it ends up flowing into rivers and lakes. Another option is to plant green roofs – that is, roofs covered with grass and other plants – that can soak up the water before it reaches waterways.

The techniques for cooling temperatures will also help with the effect on human health, but many cities have begun to offer cooling shelters for vulnerable people when temperatures reach dangerous levels. These are places where people can go to cool off, get a drink of water, and learn about other techniques for staying cool. Taken together, these simple measures can dramatically reduce the impact of the urban heat island effect on mortality.

Exercise E3 (Track 391)

Male Speaker	The reading passage mentions that lions are a vulnerable species now and may face extinction in the future. This is a pessimistic view, as there are certain simple actions that humans can take, and *are* taking, that have the potential to remove the threats to lion populations.

A simple way to combat the hunting of lions for trophies would be to make the lion an endangered species in those countries where many of the hunters come from. Banning the import of trophies such as lion skins, skulls, and claws would also help. When this has happened in the past to other species, the number of people choosing to hunt those animals for sport has dropped significantly.

The problem of habitat loss is a harder one to solve. There are numerous national parks and game reserves in Africa, including well-known ones like Kruger National Park in South Africa, and Serengeti National Park in Tanzania. Within the borders of these parks, lions and other wildlife are protected. Habitat loss will probably continue outside of these parks, but as long as the parks remain, the effects of habitat loss will never become too severe.

Conservationists have already taken steps to address the problem of lack of genetic diversity among some surviving groups of lions. The process involves transplanting female lions, sometimes with their cubs, from one region to another. On a small scale, this has the potential to introduce new genetic stock into a small population of lions, which would reduce the effects of a population bottleneck and allow lions to survive.

Exercise G1 (Tracks 392–394)

Narrator Lecture 1.

Male Speaker Many scientists are concerned that sea levels will rise because climate change is causing ice at the North and South Pole to melt. If sea levels rise too high, millions of people who live in coastal cities might be affected. Because climate change is the main cause of sea level rise, it makes sense that reducing or reversing climate change might lessen the problem of rising sea levels. Another possible solution would be to build a huge system of earthworks to hold back the sea. This has worked in countries like Holland, though on a much smaller scale.

Narrator Lecture 2.

Female Speaker Incineration is a controversial method of waste treatment. The basic process involves heating waste at a very high temperature to destroy it. The advantage of incineration is that the process is very efficient at reducing the mass and volume of waste. The disadvantage is that incineration releases pollution into the atmosphere. The amount of pollution can be reduced to some extent by filtering the waste gases produced by incineration before they are released into the air. Another way to remove harmful pollutants from the waste gases is to force them through a liquid known as a scrubber before the gases are released into the atmosphere.

Narrator Lecture 3.

Male Speaker It is widely believed among consumers that organically-grown food is not just healthier than conventionally-grown food, but better for the environment as well. Despite this belief, sales of organic produce are still significantly below those of conventionally-farmed fruits and vegetables. In large part this is because organic produce is more expensive. One option for consumers is to limit their purchases to organic items that are in season locally, which often cost roughly the same as produce grown by the methods of conventional agriculture. Another option is to shop at farmer's markets where prices for organic food are usually lower than in grocery stores.

Exercise H1 (Track 395)

Narrator Now listen to a lecture on the topic you just read about.

Male Speaker The article I asked you to read describes some ways that industrial methods of food production lead to food wastage. The writer describes this as a growing global problem, which is true, but what the writer doesn't mention is that this is a problem with some surprisingly simple and low-cost solutions.

Take the issue of overproduction. If agricultural producers communicated among themselves more effectively, say through an Internet site, surplus crops from one farm could easily be used to make up a shortage of the same crop at another farm nearby. Any crops still not required could then be sold off as animal feed.

It's true that most supermarket chains care about the appearance of food they sell, but it's less certain whether this is something that consumers care about. Surveys of customers actually show that for many people the taste and price of food items are far more important factors than appearance. So rather than rejecting food that tastes good but does not look perfect, supermarkets could sell it, though perhaps at a lower price.

The problem of wastage during food processing is another one that could be solved relatively simply. Developing processing methods that minimize waste is not difficult and would almost certainly result in long-term cost savings for the processor, though it might be somewhat expensive initially.

UNIT 23 | WRITING • Integrated Writing Task 1 Questions – Support Questions

Exercise E1 (Tracks 396–399)

Narrator Excerpt A.

Female Speaker 1 We tend to think of technology, which can be defined as the application of science or tools to perform a particular function, as unique to humans. However, several species of birds, monkeys, apes, and even dolphins have been documented constructing and using tools to find food or fulfill other basic needs.

Narrator Excerpt B.

Male Speaker 1 Throughout history, people have often reacted to new technologies with concern about the impact on their lives. The Luddites are a famous example of this. They were a group of English textile workers who protested violently against the introduction of machinery that they felt would put them out of jobs, even going so far as to smash the machinery and get into fights.

Narrator Excerpt C.

Female Speaker 2 One important aspect of technological progress in the twentieth and twenty-first centuries has been the way that most technologies become smaller over time. Take ENIAC, the first true electronic computer. When it went into operation in 1946 it took up 1,800 square feet of space – roughly equivalent to five average-sized hotel rooms – and weighed about 60,000 pounds – or the same as four or five adult elephants. A modern computer that is more powerful than ENIAC, though, can fit easily into a pocket.

Narrator Excerpt D.

Male Speaker 2 Technological convergence can be explained as the way different technological systems often evolve or are created to perform similar tasks and functions as previous technologies. At the beginning of the twenty-first century, for instance, many people would have had a separate telephone, computer, music player, camera, and perhaps portable gaming device. These days, all these functions – and more – can easily be handled by even the most basic smartphone.

Exercise E2 (Track 400)

Female Speaker There are some interesting points in the article you read about the Internet. It's true that the Internet is an amazing invention that has had a revolutionary impact on society; but it's also true, in my opinion, that too much exposure to the Internet has led to a number of problems for people.

The passage makes the point that the Internet has had a negative impact on people's ability to communicate well in writing. It has also had a negative effect on how well people can talk to each other, uh, hold a conversation.

Because so much of online communication is written, research shows that many young people who have grown up using the Internet find it difficult, even uncomfortable, to speak to other people face-to-face.

Computer vision syndrome is another way that the Internet is affecting people's health. Sitting in front a computer screen and using the Internet for hours each day puts stress on people's vision, leading to tired eyes or vision problems. A research study published in 2009 shows that myopia, uh, the inability to focus clearly on objects that are far away has increased by more than 60% in the last 30 years.

The article gives one example of something called "intellectual laziness" caused by Internet usage. The ability to read long articles is clearly important, but equally important is the ability to read critically. In my experience, people who spend too much time on the Internet frequently accept an opinion expressed in writing without either looking for or recognizing problems with the writer's arguments.

Exercise E3 (Track 401)

Male Speaker The reading passage makes some interesting points about cloud computing. The cloud is a new technology, and as such there are definitely problems that need to get fixed, but on the whole I think the author is right: cloud computing has a lot of advantages, and it's here to stay.

As the writer mentions, one of the major benefits of cloud computing is its low cost. Let's look at a simple example. Suppose a small business with five employees wants to upgrade the software its employees use. Purchasing individual upgrade licenses for each worker would probably cost a total of around $2,000. But a cloud-computing license for those same five employees might cost just $100 a year.

The accessibility to data that cloud computing provides is also a real benefit. These days, more people are becoming concerned about quality of life, and they want to find a good balance between their work and their life outside work. As a result, the opportunity to work from home is now one of the things that job seekers look for in a position. Companies that utilize cloud computing are, therefore, in a strong position to attract good employees because their workers can access important data from home.

Surveys routinely show that the vast majority of computer users know they should back up their data regularly; the same surveys also show that the vast majority of users *never* back up their data. Because data stored in the cloud can automatically be backed up at almost no extra cost and with no administrative inconvenience, this feature of cloud computing is potentially a huge benefit to any business because it will minimize the expense and disruption caused by lost data.

Exercise F3 (Track 402)

Male Speaker The reading discusses some of the advantages of cloud computing and pretty clearly comes down in favor of it. I'm not going to say that cloud computing doesn't have a lot of benefits, because it does, and as the technology becomes more robust, the benefits will increase. But I think the points that the writer makes are, well, a little simplistic.

Take the point that cloud computing helps businesses save money. That's true, but only for some businesses and only in some situations. A huge multinational corporation with thousands of employees and offices in dozens of countries *might* save money by using the cloud. But for a small business with a handful of employees and just one office, cloud computing may not be cost efficient at all.

Cloud computing enthusiasts love to talk about the convenience of cloud computing because data is accessible 24 hours a day, seven days a week. Of course, the data is only accessible if the network is working; if the network is down, nobody can access anything. For a large company, every time there is a network issue – and every cloud computing service provider has had network problems, some of which lasted for days – literally thousands of employees are unable to work on important projects because they cannot access their data.

The reading also makes the point that data stored in the cloud is safe because it can easily be backed up or restored. What the reading doesn't discuss is the issue of security. Data that is stored in the cloud can easily be hacked, stolen, deleted, or copied. Hardly a month goes by without a news story about a major business losing private customer data like credit card details; and in most cases, these customer databases were stored in the cloud, so data safety is not a strong feature of cloud computing.

Exercise H1 (Track 403)

Narrator Now listen to a lecture on the topic you just read about.

Female Speaker Electronic voting systems are not without critics, some of whose criticisms are valid, but on the whole the advantages of electronic voting outweigh any possible disadvantages.

One advantage of electronic voting is the likelihood of higher voter turnout, especially among groups that tend to have lower levels of voter participation. Take the Arizona Democratic presidential primary election in 2000. During that election, voters were allowed to vote using the Internet. Despite a few technological problems – and this was the year 2000, right, when electronic voting technology was still very new – voter turnouts among some minority groups increased by 500 to 800 percent.

Another advantage of electronic voting is that voter mistakes caused by confusing ballot papers can be reduced or even eliminated. Take the famous example during the US presidential election, again in 2000. It is widely believed, though impossible to prove, that a significant number of voters in a specific district in Florida were confused by a paper ballot and as a consequence voted for a candidate they did not intend to choose. With an electronic voting system, such an error would be impossible.

A further advantage of electronic voting systems is accuracy. Votes in elections that use traditional paper ballots are counted by hand. A study in 2012 showed that the margin of error for hand counting was between zero point five and two percent. In some close elections, this might be enough for the wrong person to be declared the winner. Computers cannot make mistakes in the way humans can, however, so a well-designed electronic voting system should have a 0% error rate.

UNIT 24 | WRITING • Independent Writing Task 2 Questions – Single Opinion Questions

Exercise D1 (Track 404)

Female Teacher OK, today we're going to discuss how to write a great response to Independent Writing Task 2 questions in the TOEFL Test. And the first thing I want to talk about is planning your response.

As you know, you only have 30 minutes to answer Task 2 questions, and some people think that because of this limited amount of time, it's not necessary to plan what to say. Other people feel that planning can be helpful, but it's important to save time by spending just two minutes or even less on planning. In my view, however, thinking in these ways is not helpful.

In my experience of teaching for the TOEFL Test, students who plan their answers generally get better scores. The reasons are that planned answers usually repeat fewer ideas, and have a better overall organization. As a result, I would say that being able to plan effectively is truly one of the key skills for getting a good score in Task 2. Of course, time is limited so planning quickly is important, but if it takes you three or four minutes, or even longer, to plan your response, then that is still a good use of your time. And the more you practice planning, the faster and better you will be able to do it.

Before we continue, I want to make one very important point. You do *not* have to think of true ideas and examples when you are planning your response. Of course, you *can* think of true ideas and examples, but if you can't think of any true ideas quickly, it is perfectly OK to make up ideas and examples. And in fact, in my experience ideas and examples that you make up often match the topic better than true ideas and examples.

Exercise D2 (Track 405)

Female Teacher OK, now let me give you a step-by-step guide to actually planning your response to a Writing Task 2 question. There are many ways to plan, of course, but in my experience, it's a good idea to follow this simple three-step system.

First, read the question carefully and recognize the two options from the question that you could write about. Second, make a note of two reasons with supporting examples why you might select each option from the question. And third, review the reasons and examples you noted and decide which of the two options is simpler to write about.

WRITING REVIEW TEST

Writing Task 1 (Track 406)

Narrator Now listen to a lecture on the topic you just read about.

Female Professor The article lists various human activities that pose a threat to coral reefs. I'd like to say that the situation is less serious than the article suggests, but sadly the opposite is true, and human actions really *are* harming coral reefs around the world.

It has been estimated that pollution may affect up to 30% of all reef systems in the ways that the article explains. A three-year study from 2009 to 2012 by scientists based in the USA showed the effects of pollution in more detail. Coral that was exposed to pollution over this period had significantly more disease and stress than coral unaffected by pollutants. Interestingly, when the pollution was removed, the coral recovered in less than one year.

Fishing might sound like a relatively harmless activity compared to causing pollution, but a study carried out by the World Resources Institute in 2002 estimated that roughly two-thirds of reefs in southeast Asia are affected by overfishing and destructive fishing techniques. And a 2013 study by a team of scientists from Australia and Canada shows that overfishing of sharks can affect reefs. When there are fewer sharks, populations of fish that eat algae also decline. The reason is that the sharks keep the populations of smaller predator fish low. If there are fewer sharks, these smaller predator fish will feed on the algae-eating fish, which means algae levels will rise. And when this happens, reefs die, as the article explains.

Tourism may seem like another minor threat to coral, but not according to the National Oceanographic and Atmospheric Administration, the NOAA. That organization has ranked tourism and recreation as either a high priority threat or a medium priority threat to coral reefs at almost two-thirds of all reef sites around the world.

Introduction (Track 407)

Narrator Test of English as a Foreign Language. Practice Test A. Published and copyright Oxford University Press 2015.

Conversation 1 (Track 408)

Narrator Listen to a conversation between a student and a professor.

Female student Professor Maddox?

Male professor Yes? May I help you?

Student I … I'm in your Intro to Psych class, the one that meets at 10:00. I'm Beth Peterson. I just added your class yesterday so today was my first class. And this morning I heard some students talking about a final project – about doing an experiment? I wanted to find out about that.

Professor Right, it's an important part of your grade – you have to design a simple psychological experiment.

Student OK … You know, I guess I really don't understand what's involved in doing an experiment.

Professor Well, I'll have to give you a crash course, 'cause I don't have too much time now – I talked about this Monday, before you joined the class. OK, an experiment is basically a matter of testing a hypothesis … you know what I mean by *hypothesis*?

Student Umm, yeah, it's like a theory … something you try to prove?

Professor Exactly. It's usually stated in terms of cause and effect. "I think that if X happens, then Y will happen." Here's an example. Last year, some students designed an experiment to see if color had any effect on memory, to see if color cues helped people remember names. So they wrote ten common names on cards. Then they got their subjects to look at the names quickly and see how many they could remember five minutes later. Half the subjects saw the names on white cards, half saw the names on cards of various colors. So … what was the hypothesis?

Student Well, I guess it was, "If names are written on different colored cards, people will be able to remember them better."

Professor Sure, something like that. Now, every experiment has a control group and an experimental group. In this case, the students who saw the colored cards were the experimental group, and …

Student The ones that didn't were the control group.

Professor Correct. Then the students had to compare results from the control group and the experimental group to see if there was any meaningful difference, if there was any … statistically meaningful difference.

Student Wow, I don't know much about … much of anything about statistics.

Professor That's OK, next semester we'll spend a couple of weeks learning the basics of statistics. This semester, though, you won't need to do any statistical analysis.

Student OK, well, thanks for your time, Professor.

Conversation 1 – questions (Tracks 409–413)

Narrator Question 1. What do the professor and student mainly discuss?

Narrator Question 2. How does the professor clarify his explanation of a *hypothesis*?

Narrator Question 3. What does the professor say about the control group and the experimental group in the experiment he describes?

Narrator Question 4. Listen again to part of the conversation. Then answer the question.

Professor Some students designed an experiment to see if color had any effect on memory, to see if color cues helped people remember names. So they wrote ten common names on cards. Then they got their subjects to look at the names quickly and see how many they could remember five minutes later. Half the subjects saw the names on white cards, half saw the names on cards of various colors. So … what was the hypothesis?

Narrator Why does the professor say this?

Professor So … what was the hypothesis?

Narrator Question 5. Listen again to part of the conversation. Then answer the question.

Professor Correct. Then the students had to compare results from the control group and the experimental group to see if there was any meaningful difference, if there was any … statistically meaningful difference.

Student Wow, I don't know much about … much of anything about statistics.

Narrator What can be inferred about the student when she says this?

Student Wow, I don't know much about … much of anything about statistics.

Lecture 1: Anthropology (Track 414)

Narrator Listen to a discussion in an anthropology class.

Male professor Okay, we've been talking about traditional kinds of shelters from around the world. Today I'm going to talk about the shelters used by North American Indians … or Native Americans, as some people say. We'll start with the most famous type: the teepee. Now, did you know that only about 20 percent of all the different groups of Indians used teepees?

Male student Um, really? You mean, not all Indians lived in teepees?

Professor Lots of people think they did, because, you know, the teepee has kind of become a symbol for Native Americans in general. But actually only the groups who lived in the west-central United States, out on the Plains – like the Sioux, the Arapaho, the Cheyenne – they're the only ones who lived in teepees. The word *teepee* actually comes from the Sioux language. And surprisingly, the kind of teepee you see in pictures was commonly used only for a few hundred years.

Now, the first people to use tents resembling teepees were Arctic Indians, in the far north. In the summer, they lived in cone-shaped tents. The Plains Indians must have had some contact with the Arctic tribes, and learned to, um, copy this style of making shelters. At first the tents the Plains Indians used were much shorter and wider at the bottom than they later became, and they didn't move them very often. When they did, they used dogs to drag them around.

Female student Why dogs, Professor?

Professor Well, think about it. They didn't have horses. See, there weren't any horses around until the Spanish brought their horses in the sixteenth century. But once the Plains tribes got hold of horses and … and guns from the Spanish, well, that technology dramatically changed their culture. Almost overnight, they became nomads … buffalo-hunting nomads. They depended on buffalo for food, for clothing … for, you know, virtually everything. They followed these huge herds of buffalo that roamed around the Plains. A whole village could pack up their teepees and … and be ready to move in an hour or so. Teepees were transformed too; they became taller, they actually got twice as tall as they had been before.

OK, I'm no artist, but I'm going to draw a picture of a teepee, just showing the skeleton; the poles of the teepee. They'd use a dozen or more wooden poles and arrange them in a circle. They'd lean these poles together towards a central point up here, to form a cone, see, and they'd fasten them together near the top.

Male student Professor, I've driven across the Plains and … there aren't a lot of trees out there. Where would they get wooden poles?

Professor Ah, really good question, Rodney. You're right, there aren't many trees in the areas where the Plains Indians lived. So they would make special trips to the mountains to get poles for their teepees. They'd usually use a kind of pine tree called the lodgepole pine. They used that because its trunk was so straight, so it made a good pole. And it's a good strong wood – it had to be, to withstand the winds out on the Plains. So, as you can imagine, they always brought the poles with them when they moved.

OK, next I'm going to talk about the shelters used by other Native American tribes, such as the wigwams of the Algonquin Indians. Anyone have any more questions about tepees before I move on?

Lecture 1: Anthropology – questions (Tracks 415–420)

Narrator Question 6. What does the professor mainly discuss?

Narrator Question 7. Listen again to part of the lecture. Then answer the question.

Professor Lots of people think they did, because, you know, the teepee has kind of become a symbol for Native Americans in general. But actually only the groups who lived in the west-central United States, out on the Plains – like the Sioux, the Arapaho, the Cheyenne – they're the only ones who lived in teepees. The word *teepee* actually comes from the Sioux language. And surprisingly, the kind of teepee you see in pictures was commonly used only for a few hundred years.

Narrator Why does the professor say this?

Professor And surprisingly, the kind of teepee you see in pictures was commonly used only for a few hundred years.

Narrator Question 8. According to the professor, why were buffalo important to the Plains Indians?

Narrator Question 9. The professor discusses how the daily life of Plains Indians changed over time. Put the events in the order in which they occurred.

Narrator Question 10. Why did the Plains Indians use lodgepole pine trees as poles for their tepees?

Narrator Question 11. Listen again to part of the lecture. Then answer the question.

Professor You're right, there aren't many trees in the areas where the Plains Indians lived. So they would make special trips to the mountains to get poles for their teepees. They'd

usually use a kind of pine tree called the lodgepole pine. They used that because its trunk was so straight, so it made a good pole. And it's a good strong wood – it had to be, to withstand the winds out on the Plains. So, as you can imagine, they always brought the poles with them when they moved.

Narrator What does the professor imply when he says this?

Professor So, as you can imagine, they always brought the poles with them when they moved.

Lecture 2: World History (Track 421)

Narrator Listen to a lecture in a world history class.

Professor Good afternoon, everyone. You know, when I was a student, I – well, I've gotta admit, I found my history classes pretty boring. You know, we learned dates and the names of kings and presidents and so on. But, it wasn't until I took an American history course from the chairman of the history department – well, he made history come alive for me. He talked about what life was really like during, say, Colonial times, or the Great Depression. I decided, if I ever taught history, I'd do the same.

Now, imagine you live in the future, 500 years from now. You're studying a history of our time, the early twenty-first century. Suppose this book just lists a few major events – the kind of information you'd get from newspaper headlines. Would you really understand our time? No, of course not. You'd need more than that to get a feel for the way we live today. So that's why, this week, we're going to talk about how people lived during the Middle Ages in Europe. We'll start by talking about how people ate, about the food they ate during medieval times.

All right, the first thing you should know about food in the Middle Ages … there was a big difference, I mean a huge discrepancy between the foods eaten by the upper class – the aristocrats and rich merchants – and the lower class – the peasants. And, in those days, the wealthy made up just a tiny fraction of the population.

For both the wealthy and the poor, bread was the staple. However, peasants usually ate bread made from barley or rye. Bread was often used as sops – they'd dip pieces of bread in soups or sauces. Peasants would grow vegetables – cabbage, beets, onions, garlic, and carrots – to make soup or stew. Another common dish at the dinner table of peasants was frumenty, a sort of porridge, kind of like oatmeal today. They also ate dairy products, like soft cheeses, and they'd gather nuts, mushrooms, and fruit from the forest. The main way poor people flavored their food was with vinegar and honey – they couldn't afford spices. Poor people seldom ate meat, because it was too expensive. Why didn't they just go out and hunt animals, you ask? Well, nearly all the land was owned by the aristocrats – and hunting on an aristocrat's land was generally considered a crime.

So, what about rich people? Well, their food was more flavorful and varied than peasant food. As I said, bread was a staple for everyone, but the bread rich people ate was of better quality and was usually made from wheat. The rich hunted deer, rabbits, and birds, and so they ate a lot of game meat. They also ate roast beef, mutton, and so on. They ate very few vegetables, because those were considered "common."

During the late Middle Ages and Renaissance, Europe came into more contact with other lands. This contact eventually led to trade. Europeans – at least wealthy ones – developed a taste for foods seasoned with "exotic" spices. Spices were imported to Europe along the famous "spice routes," from the Middle East, India, China, all the way from Indonesia.

Why were spices so important? Not just because they gave food more flavor. Remember, there was no refrigeration, so salt was used to preserve meat and fish. The problem was, this food tasted … almost unbearably salty. Spices helped mask that strong flavor. And if the meat was close to spoiling, to going bad … well, spices would hide that taste, too.

Lecture 2: World History – questions (Tracks 422–427)

Narrator   Question 12. What is the main purpose of this lecture?

Narrator   Question 13. What is the professor's attitude to the American history class she took when she was a student?

Narrator   Question 14. Indicate which foods were typically eaten by poor people in the Middle Ages.

Narrator   Question 15. What does the professor say about the diet of wealthy people in medieval times?

Narrator   Question 16. Listen again to part of the lecture. What does the professor imply when she says this?

Professor   During the late Middle Ages and Renaissance, Europe came into more contact with other lands. This contact eventually led to trade. Europeans – at least wealthy ones – developed a taste for foods seasoned with "exotic" spices. Spices were imported to Europe along the famous "spice routes," from the Middle East, India, China, all the way from Indonesia.

Narrator   Question 17. According to the professor, what were the main uses of spices in medieval cooking?

Conversation 2 (Track 428)

Narrator   Listen to a conversation between a student and his professor.

Male student You wanted to see me, Professor?

Female professor Yes, Gordon. I graded your assignment and some of your answers were excellent, but, uh, I don't want to sound harsh, but you seem to have some pretty major gaps in your knowledge.

Student   Yeah, I think that's a fair assessment.

Professor   What surprises me – concerns me, actually – is that many of those gaps are related to things you studied in the prerequisite for this class.

Student   I'm actually a transfer student, so I didn't take the prerequisite here. I was at Upper State University before, and I spoke to, uh, Professor Harmon, and he felt that a statistics class I took there was equivalent to the prerequisite here, so he let me sign up for your class.

Professor   I see.

Student   The class I took at Upper State taught me some stuff that you haven't covered yet in your class, but there are also things I don't know about that everybody else seems to understand. I guess those are things that were covered in the prerequisite class.

Professor   Hmm. Well, that explains the gaps in your knowledge. I'm not quite sure how to handle it, though … OK, you're going to find my class increasingly difficult if you haven't

taken the prerequisite, and there are, what, 40, 50 other students in the class, and it wouldn't be fair for me to spend time explaining concepts that they already know, so I think the best thing …

Student   You think I should drop this class and take the prerequisite, right?

Professor   Actually, no, that's not what I was going to say. I think you should do the reading for that class, though. I can give you the reading list … uh … Here you go.

Student   Thank you, Professor. I'll go to the library and get started right away.

Professor   Not so fast, Gordon. I'm also going to put you in touch with James Park, the teaching assistant for that class.

Student   The TA?

Professor   James is very good at explaining things, and I think he'll be a really good resource for you. And come to think of it, he got his undergraduate degree from Upper State University, so the two of you will have something in common. I'm seeing James later, so I'll explain the situation to him then and ask him to get in touch with you.

Student   That's great, Professor. Thank you.

Conversation 2 – questions (Tracks 429–433)

Narrator   Question 18. What do the student and professor mainly discuss?

Narrator   Question 19. What does the student say about the class he took at Upper State University?

Narrator   Question 20. Listen again to part of the conversation. What does the professor mean when she says this?

Professor   OK, you're going to find my class increasingly difficult if you haven't taken the prerequisite, and there are, what, 40, 50 other students in the class, and it wouldn't be fair for me to spend time explaining concepts that they already know.

Narrator   Question 21. Listen again to part of the conversation. Then answer the question.

Professor   Actually, no, that's not what I was going to say. I think you should do the reading for that class, though. I can give you the reading list … uh … Here you go.

Student   Thank you, Professor. I'll go to the library and get started right away.

Professor   Not so fast, Gordon. I'm also going to put you in touch with James Park, the teaching assistant for that class.

Narrator   Why does the professor say this?

Professor   Not so fast, Gordon.

Narrator   Question 22. What does the professor suggest that the student should do?

Lecture 3: Marketing (Track 434)

Narrator   Listen to a discussion in a marketing class.

Male professor Good morning, everyone. OK, I asked you to look at Chapter 3 over the weekend, the chapter about *marketing mix*, right? If you recall, it was a pair of professors from Harvard Business School who came up with the concept of marketing mix. Professor Neil Borden created the original concept – he started using the term back in the 1940s. His idea was that there were these elements, "ingredients," he called them, that went into marketing, and he described a marketing manager as a "mixer of ingredients." He described lots of ingredients, over a dozen. Then in the early 1960s, another Harvard professor, E. Jerome McCarthy, came up with a simpler plan. He divided the ingredients into four categories – the famous "four Ps" that make up what we call marketing mix.

I guess the best way to define marketing mix ... well, it's a combination of variables that marketers can adjust, can manipulate in order to ... to reach their target market. Why? To make sales, of course – that's always the goal of marketing.

So, you can see I drew a diagram on the board, the same one that's in your book. What does this circle in the middle represent?

Female student   That's ... that would be the target market.

Professor   Yes. Then the other four circles represent the four "ingredients" ... the four Ps. What's the first one?

Female student   I think the first one mentioned in the book was *product*.

Professor   Yes. Who can define *product* and give me some examples?

Female student   Things that you sell, goods like ... computers, or ... I don't know ... running shoes ... soap ... cars.

Professor   All good examples. Products can also be services ... like a haircut or a piano lesson. Then there are some things that are hard to classify – like a computer operating system, which in some ways is a good, in some ways a service.

OK, so, what's another ingredient? Well, *pricing* is the only element that's relatively easy to change in a short time. And I'd say pricing is second only to product in importance. There are various strategies for pricing a product. You can use what's called the "going rate" price – you base your price on your competitors' prices. Or you can offer volume discounts if customers buy a lot of your product. You can also offer financing so customers can buy your product over time.

OK, then ... what about *placement*, the third ingredient. Really, a better name would be *distribution*, but that doesn't fit in with our other three Ps so neatly. So placement – it's how you get product to consumers. Do you sell your product to wholesalers or retailers, or directly to consumers? Do you sell your product regionally? Nationally? Internationally?

Now, the fourth P is *promotion*. People confuse *marketing* a product with *promoting* it, with *advertising* it. But marketing is more than advertising. Of course, promotion *is* important. Promotion makes people aware of your product, through advertising and other means.

Male student   Professor Ross, one question ... you said this classification system came from the '40s ...

Professor   Well ... the four Ps model comes from the early '60s ...

Male student   OK, still, that was a long time ago. Business has changed a lot since then, with uh globalization, and the Internet, so ... is this still a legitimate way to look at marketing?

Professor   I'm glad you asked that, Mike. Various people have tried to update the system, adding more Ps, like *personnel* or ... I don't know, *packaging*. I personally think the four P system is still valid, because it deals with the fundamental concepts of marketing – and those really haven't changed at all.

Lecture 3: Marketing – questions (Tracks 435–440)

Narrator   Question 23. How is the discussion mainly organized?

Narrator   Question 24. What does the professor say about Neil Borden's original concept of the marketing mix?

Narrator   Question 25. In the professor's view, which is the most important of the four Ps?

Narrator   Question 26. Listen again to part of the lecture. What does the professor mean when he says this?

Professor   What about *placement*, the third ingredient. Really, a better name would be *distribution*, but that doesn't fit in with our other three Ps so neatly. So placement – it's how you get product to consumers.

Narrator   Question 27. What does the professor say about advertising?

Narrator   Question 28. What is the professor's opinion of the four Ps model?

Lecture 4: Film Studies (Track 441)

Narrator   Listen to a lecture in a film studies class.

Professor   Hello, everyone. You know, up until today, all of the films we've talked about have had one thing in common – they've all been live-action films. Well, today, I'm going to talk a little about animated films, or cartoons as a lot of people call them. Some people just don't take animation seriously but, uh ... I consider it an important part of film history.

Okay then, the first animated film – it was called, um, *Humorous Faces* ...excuse me ... it was *Humorous Phases of Funny Faces* – was made way back in 1906. The creator was James Blackton, a newspaper illustrator – in those days, there weren't many photographs in daily newspapers, mostly just drawings ... illustrations. Anyway, all he did was draw faces on a blackboard in progressive phases. Pretty primitive, but this was, as I said, the first animated film. Just a few years later, Winsor McCay was making much more sophisticated animated films, like *Little Nemo* and *Gertie the Dinosaur*. These films ... well, the characters moved like they were actually alive. In earlier films, the figures moved in this really jerky, really stiff manner. Not only that, but um, the characters in McCay's films were really characters – they had real personalities.

Almost right away, these films caught on. By around 1915, there were several studios producing them. There was one in particular, called the uh, uh Pat Sullivan Studio that produced the series *Felix the Cat*. That cat turned out to be the most popular cartoon character of the 1920s.

Now the first cartoon with sound was *Steamboat Willie*, which was made about 1928. This film was made by Walt Disney. The "star" of the movie was – you may already have guessed – that's right, it was Mickey Mouse. Disney became the most famous producer of animated films. He began making feature films – what I mean is, full-length animated movies. Before this, cartoons were just shorts, five or ten minutes long, shown before or after full-length live-action movies. Not only that, but his movies appealed to ... to kids, sure, but also to adults.

The 1940s were really the golden age of animation. Walt Disney came out with movies like *Pinocchio*, *Fantasia*, *Dumbo*, *Bambi* – all the classics. And Disney ... he made a point to carefully train his animators. They took classes in art, anatomy, acting, motion studies, and all that to make sure that the animation … that everything was realistic. To make the movie *Bambi*, for example, Disney brought live deer into the studio to serve as models for the animated deer in the movie. And Disney's animation artists, they drew every frame – every frame – by hand. Then you have the voices, the music … well, there have never been animated movies like these – that's why they're still popular today.

So um, in the 1980s and '90s, uh full-length animated films became popular again. The Disney studios started making a series of remarkable animated feature films, starting with the movie *The Little Mermaid*. Almost like clockwork, they were turning out one great movie after another, one a year for the next few years. There was *Beauty and the Beast*, *Aladdin*, and *The Lion King*. I guess you'd call this the uh, … well the silver age of animation.

Lecture 4: Film Studies – questions (Tracks 442–447)

Narrator	Question 29. What does the professor mainly discuss?
Narrator	Question 30. Indicate whether each of the following describes the work of Winsor McCay.
Narrator	Question 31. What can be inferred about animated films before Walt Disney's *Steamboat Willie*?
Narrator	Question 32. What does the professor say about the animated films of Walt Disney?
Narrator	Question 33. Listen again to part of the lecture. Then answer the question.
Professor	To make the movie *Bambi*, for example, Disney brought live deer into the studio to serve as models for the animated deer in the movie. And Disney's animation artists, they drew every frame – every frame! – by hand.
Narrator	Why does the professor say this?
Professor	And Disney's animation artists, they drew every frame – every frame! – by hand.
Narrator	Question 34. What does the professor say about the "silver age" of animated movies?

Speaking Task 1 (Tracks 448 and 449)

Narrator	Speaking section Task 1. Describe the best advice that you have ever received. Explain why you think it was good advice. Include specific details and examples to support your explanation.
Announcer	You may begin to prepare after the beep.
Announcer	You may begin to speak after the beep.

Speaking Task 2 (Tracks 450 and 451)

Narrator	Speaking section Task 2. Some people prefer to communicate with friends in writing using e-mail or text messages. Others prefer to communicate with their friends using a telephone. Which method of staying in touch with friends do you prefer? Explain and support your choice.
Announcer	You may begin to prepare after the beep.
Announcer	You may begin to speak after the beep.

Speaking Task 3 (Tracks 452–455)

Narrator	Speaking section Task 3. A university official wrote a notice to all students. Read the notice. You have 45 seconds to read the letter. Begin reading now.
Narrator	Now listen to two students as they discuss the notice.
Woman	Did you see this memo about food at campus events? I'm really mad about it.
Man	Um, yeah, I saw it. Why has it got you so upset?
Woman	Well, you know I'm in the Cosmopolitan Club … It's an organization for international students, for anyone who wants to learn more about other countries. We meet every couple of weeks. People bring snacks from their own countries. It's fun trying different foods from around the world.
Man	Well, I've been at events where NorthCo supplied the snacks … and their food was actually pretty good.
Woman	I've been at events where NorthCo supplied the food, too, and all the food was from North America. There was nothing from other countries, and our Cosmopolitan Club meetings just wouldn't be the same if we couldn't taste foods from other countries.
Man	Well, I guess you'll have to get in touch with, uh, let's see, Yolanda Lopez.
Woman	I really hope she'll make an exception for our club. It's pretty inexpensive for us to bring our own snacks. But I looked into how much it would cost if NorthCo were to supply the food, and it's really expensive. I doubt we could afford to meet more than once or twice a semester if that.
Narrator	The woman expresses her opinion of the policy. State her opinion and explain the reasons she gives for holding that opinion.
Announcer	You may begin to prepare after the beep.
Announcer	You may begin to speak after the beep.

Speaking Task 4 (Tracks 456–459)

Narrator	Speaking section Task 4. Now read the passage about metallic elements. You have 45 seconds to read the passage. Begin reading now.
Narrator	Now listen to part of a lecture on this topic in a chemistry class.
Professor	Today we're going to talk about the metal titanium, which was first discovered in 1791 in Great Britain. In its pure state, it's a lustrous, silvery-white metal with a number of useful and important properties. For one thing, it is both very light and very strong. Some other metals like aluminum are light, and iron is strong, but titanium has both properties. It also retains its strength at relatively high temperatures. And this combination of factors makes it a very valuable metal for certain industrial processes and machinery. For example, it's commonly used in engines – jet engines for airplanes and even rocket engines. It's also used in consumer goods like racing bicycles and even jewelry. Now things made out of titanium are typically very expensive, but not because titanium is rare. In fact, it's one of the ten most common elements found in Earth's crust. So why is it so expensive? Well, for one thing, it's always found bonded to other elements, and the process required to turn titanium ore into pure titanium is costly. Moreover, in many of its applications, alloys of titanium rather than pure titanium are required, and the process of making titanium alloys is also difficult and expensive.
Narrator	Using details and examples from the talk, explain how titanium relates to metallic elements in general and why it is a useful element.

Announcer	You may begin to prepare after the beep.
Announcer	You may begin to speak after the beep.

Speaking Task 5 (Tracks 460–462)

Narrator	Speaking section Task 5. Listen to a conversation between two students.
Woman	Hi Greg.
Man	Hi Carolyn. Hey, you've taken Professor Thomas's computer science course, right?
Woman	His introductory course? Yeah, a couple years ago. Why?
Man	Well, I didn't think his course would be so hard, because I know quite a bit about computers. But now I have a midterm exam Friday and I'm really worried.
Woman	Well … you need to talk to Professor Thomas, find out what it's going to cover, what kind of questions are going to be on it.
Man	I don't know, I … tell you the truth, he kind of intimidates me. I mean, he uses so much computer jargon, so much technical language that … I don't know what he's talking about.
Woman	Yeah, he does use a lot of computer talk. Hey, maybe you should go look at his old tests in the test bank.
Man	The what?
Woman	The test bank. You know, student government keeps old tests on file in their office at the Student Union Building. There are tests from almost every professor there. I'm sure they'll have some of Professor Thomas's old exams.
Man	Hmm. That might be useful, looking at his old tests.
Narrator	The woman discusses two possible solutions to the man's problem. Describe the problem. Then state which of the two solutions you prefer and explain why.
Announcer	You may begin to prepare after the beep.
Announcer	You may begin to speak after the beep.

Speaking Task 6 (Tracks 463–465)

Narrator	Speaking section Task 6. Listen to a lecture in an economics class.
Professor	OK, today we're going to talk about an important concept: the concept of "opportunity cost." It's useful for economists, business experts, and project planners. In fact, it's helpful for almost anyone making a choice between two alternatives. An opportunity cost is the cost of something that must be given up – the value of the "next best alternative" – as a result of some decision. In other words, it's the value of the action you decide *not* to do.
	OK, this is easier to understand if I give you an example. Imagine you want to go out to eat in a restaurant. You could go out for lunch or dinner. You can only go out for one meal. If you decide to go out for lunch, your opportunity cost that day is going out for dinner, because going out for dinner is the "next best alternative."
	Here's another example. Say you decide to go to university for a year. You have to pay for tuition, books, room and board, lab fees, all that. Let's say it costs $50,000. That's your accounting cost. Now, let's say if you didn't go to a university, you could get a job and earn $75,000 a year. That's your

opportunity cost, $75,000 – the amount that you would earn if you worked instead of going to school. So, the true costs of your decision to go to school for a year would be $125,000 – accounting costs plus opportunity costs.

Narrator	Using examples and points from the lecture, explain the concept of opportunity cost.
Announcer	You may begin to prepare after the beep.
Announcer	You may begin to speak after the beep.

Writing Task 1 (Tracks 466–468)

Narrator	Writing section Task 1. Listen to a lecture on the topic you just read about.
Professor	OK, everyone read that article I gave you about biofuels, right? The author is pretty sure that biofuels will save us from dependence on fossil fuels. The author is right when he says that we need a replacement for fossil fuels. But personally, I don't think biofuels are the answer.
	The author says that if countries grow crops to make biofuels, they can become energy independent. That sounds great in theory, but in practice, it's not possible and not even a good idea. The world is too … interconnected, too interdependent. If industrialized nations suddenly stopped buying petroleum and other fossil fuels, the world economy would be seriously affected, so this so-called benefit of biofuels would actually be a problem.
	The biggest problem with biofuels is this – if you use land for growing fuel crops, you can't use that land for growing food, so food prices rise. For example, when North American corn began to be used for biofuels, the price of corn went up. Now corn is used in a lot of common foods and as animal feed, so suddenly farmers and non-farmers were not saving money or making money but spending it.
	The article says that Brazil is a success story when it comes to biofuels. It's true that making fuel from sugarcane as they do in Brazil is a fairly efficient process, more so than making fuel from corn. But sugarcane can't be grown everywhere, so what works in Brazil is unlikely to work in other countries. Besides, in Brazil, rainforests have been cut down to make room for sugarcane production, which has actually led to a rise in carbon dioxide levels, so the "success" in Brazil is not as great as people often say.
Narrator	Summarize the points made in the lecture, explaining how they challenge the points made in the reading passage.
Announcer	Begin writing now. You have 20 minutes.
	You have 10 minutes remaining.
	You have 5 minutes remaining.
	You have 2 minutes remaining.
	Stop writing now.

Writing Task 2 (Track 469)

Announcer	Begin writing now. You have 30 minutes.
	You have 15 minutes remaining.
	You have 5 minutes remaining.
	You have 2 minutes remaining.
	Stop writing now.

Practice Test B Audio Script

Introduction (Track 470)

Narrator   Test of English as a Foreign Language. Practice Test B. Published and copyright Oxford University Press 2015.

Conversation 1 (Track 471)

Narrator   Listen to a conversation between a professor of American literature and a student.

Student   Professor White? Do you have a minute?

Professor   Oh, hi, Marcia. Sure, come on in.

Student   I put a copy of a paper that I wrote in your mailbox … about symbolist poetry. … I wrote it for the class I'm taking with Professor Bryant. Did you see it?

Professor   Umm, yeah, I did. I read it over yesterday.

Student   Do you mind, uh, telling me what you thought about it?

Professor   I … well, I think it was well written, but, uh …

Student   Because the grade Professor Bryant gave me for that essay – it was pretty low, I thought. Can I ask you: What grade would you have given me?

Professor   Sorry, Marcia, but it's not really appropriate for me to comment on a grade that one of my colleagues gave you.

Student   I see. Well … I just felt like I … you know, I did well in your class last semester, but now I'm really struggling in Professor Bryant's class.

Professor   Did she write any comments on your essay?

Student   She wrote that it wasn't specific enough, that I should have provided more concrete examples. Oh, yeah, and that I should have used more research sources.

Professor   Let me see. Hmm. Well, it's true; you only cite three articles in your bibliography.

Student   I know, but I suppose I felt like those articles provided all the information I needed. The thing is I, uh, I don't think I can drop her class now – I think it's too late. And I guess I know what kind of grade I'll get if I stay in the class.

Professor   Well, you *could* ask permission from the dean of academic affairs to drop the class, but … listen, Marcia, if I were you, I would stay in Professor Bryant's class. In my opinion, she's an excellent teacher.

Student   Well, I have this friend – he took Professor Bryant's class last year, and he said … he said she was a tough grader, but he really learned a lot in her class.

Professor   Exactly. Anyway, you know what I'd do? I'd rewrite this paper. Find some other sources of information about the symbolist poets. Try to be more specific and use more examples. I don't know for sure if she'll change your grade for this assignment, but … she might.

Student   Well, yeah, I suppose I could do that.

Professor   And you know what else I'd do, Marcia? I'd make an appointment to have a talk with Professor Bryant. Talk to her about your concerns. Ask her what you can do to improve your grade in her class.

Conversation 1 – questions (Tracks 472–476)

Narrator   Question 1. Why does the student go to see the professor?

Narrator   Question 2. What problems with the student's essay did Professor Bryant mention?

Narrator   Question 3. Listen again to part of the conversation. Then answer the question.

Professor   Let me see. Hmm. Well, it's true; you only cite three articles in your bibliography.

Student   I know, but I suppose I felt like those articles provided all the information I needed. The thing is I, uh, I don't think I can drop her class now – I think it's too late. And I guess I know what kind of grade I'll get if I stay in the class.

Narrator   What does the student mean when she says this?

Student   I guess I know what kind of grade I'll get if I stay in the class.

Narrator   Question 4. What can be inferred about the student's friend?

Narrator   Question 5. Indicate which suggestions the professor gives the student.

Lecture 1: Art History (Track 477)

Narrator   Listen to a lecture in an art history class.

Professor   OK, everyone. Today we're going to talk about two styles of art that were popular in the 1960s, Op art and Pop art. A lot of people confuse these two styles and think they're closely related, but apart from both appearing around the same time and having similar names, they don't really have much in common.

So, let's look at Op art first. *Op art* is short for "optical art." It's called that because it uses optical illusions to trick your eyes. Op art is nonrepresentational. You know what I mean by that, right? You look at the painting, and you don't see a person, a landscape, or a bowl of fruit; it's completely abstract. Op art basically consists of intricate geometric patterns. Even though the images are two-dimensional, they give the impression that they're three-dimensional. Some seem to rise right out of the surface they're painted on, and some seem to sink down into it.

Op art became very popular after a 1965 exhibition in New York City called The Responsive Eye. A lot of critics didn't like it, but the public absolutely loved it. I'd say the two most important Op artists were Bridget Riley and Victor Vasarely. In the beginning, most Op art works were painted in black and white – a good example is Bridget Riley's painting *Current*. But Riley was also one of the first Op artists to paint in color.

Op art wasn't confined to painting. It was also important in the field of fashion. This was a time when just about anything British was very popular. British bands like The Beatles and The Who were dominating the worldwide music scene.

A famous clothing designer from Britain named Mary Quant came up with the notion of putting Op art patterns on clothing and the idea spread all over the fashion world. And, uh, it turns out, this was one of the differences between Victor Vasarely and Bridget Riley. Vasarely appreciated the fact that his art appeared on clothing. Riley? Well, it made her really angry. OK, now let's talk a little about Pop art. *Pop art* is short for "popular art." Remember I said Op art is nonrepresentational? Well, in contrast, Pop art featured realistic and uh, familiar images. Pop art presented colorful images taken from popular culture … from advertisements, comic books, magazines, photos, and just everyday objects. These images are often repeated over and over. One good example is a work by Andy Warhol that consists of dozens of pictures of the actress Marilyn Monroe.

Now, I mentioned Andy Warhol. It's impossible to talk about Pop art without talking about him. Warhol was … um … he was very, very original. He was the most famous Pop artist and, I think, one of the best-known American artists ever. He was also one of the most prolific, turning out thousands of prints, paintings, sculptures, and films. His most famous piece is a perfectly rendered painting of a can of tomato soup! You've probably seen it before. Some people wondered, and *you* may wonder, what's so great about a can of soup? But Pop art was wildly popular, both with art critics and the public. It was young, it was bright and colorful, it was a little crazy – a lot like the 1960s themselves. Like Op art, Pop art, especially Andy Warhol's, found its way into fashion. His soup can, bananas, and pictures of Marilyn showed up on T-shirts, dresses, and all sorts of clothes.

Lecture 1: Art History – questions (Tracks 478–483)

Narrator	Question 6. What does the professor mainly discuss?
Narrator	Question 7. According to the professor, what mistaken idea do many people have about Op art and Pop art?
Narrator	Question 8. Why does the lecturer mention the bands The Beatles and The Who?
Narrator	Question 9. What difference between Bridget Riley and Victor Vasarely does the professor discuss?
Narrator	Question 10. Indicate whether each of the following is a characteristic of Op art, Pop art, or both Op art and Pop art.
Narrator	Question 11. What is the professor's opinion of Andy Warhol?

Lecture 2: Astronomy (Track 484)

Narrator	Listen to part of a discussion in an astronomy class.
Female professor	A lot of people think a meteor is a rock from outer space, but actually, that's not quite right. In reality, a meteor is just the visible path, the trail of light you see when a rock enters Earth's atmosphere. It's sometimes called a shooting star, though it has nothing to do with stars. The rock itself is called a meteoroid. And if a meteoroid reaches the ground and survives impact, it's called a meteorite.

Scientists have only known that meteors were originally rocks from outer space for about the last 200 years. Before that, people thought they were some sort of weather phenomenon, like lightning. Most meteoroids vary from the size of a grain of sand to the size of a small boulder. The very smallest are called micro-meteoroids, but you'll never see one from Earth because meteoroids must be at least the size of a small pebble to create a visible meteor.

According to studies, about 20,000 meteoroids enter Earth's atmosphere every day. And that doesn't include micro-meteoroids, since those are too small to track. Of course, from any one location, you're only going to see a few … on average, around five an hour. Typically, astronomers track and count these objects with radar or telescopes at night, but in rare cases, it's possible to see certain especially bright meteoroids called *fireballs* during the daytime. Uh, a famous example is the Great Daylight Fireball of 1972. It appeared one afternoon over the western U.S. and Canada.

Male student	Did it do any damage when it hit?
Professor	No, luckily it entered the atmosphere somewhere over Utah and then exited over Canada and went back into space without impacting Earth.

OK, so, where do all these rocks come from? Well, a lot of them come from asteroids. There are different types of meteoroids, you see. There are stony meteoroids that come from one type of asteroid, and stony-metal meteoroids from another type of asteroid, and … and we also know that some meteoroids come from comets. Do you know how we know that?

Student	Um, because of what they're made of?
Professor	Not exactly. Remember I said you usually see around five meteors an hour? Well, there are certain times when you can see many more. These periods of intense meteor activity are called "meteor showers," and they typically occur at the same time each year. For example, the Leonid meteor shower occurs each November. Astronomers figured out that showers recur annually because Earth's orbit takes it through the tails of comets every year at about the same time, so all these meteors must come from comets.

But maybe the most interesting meteoroids are from Mars. For one thing, they're rare. I mean, thousands of meteorites have been found, but only about 35 from Mars. And one of them shows signs that it was shaped by water. And where there's water, scientists believe there's a possibility that life exists. Conditions on Mars are probably too harsh for complex, intelligent life to have developed, but some people think that one or two meteorites from Mars show signs of bacterial life, which is a very intriguing possibility.

Lecture 2: Astronomy – questions (Tracks 485–490)

Narrator	Question 12. What is the main purpose of this discussion?
Narrator	Question 13. Listen again to part of the discussion. Then answer the question.
	Scientists have only known that meteors were originally rocks from outer space for about the last 200 years. Before that, people thought they were some sort of weather phenomenon, like lightning. Most meteoroids vary from the size of a grain of sand to the size of a small boulder. The very smallest are called micro-meteoroids, but you'll never see one from Earth because meteoroids must be at least the size of a small pebble to create a visible meteor.
Narrator	What does the professor imply about micro-meteoroids?
Narrator	Question 14. What does the professor say about the fireball of 1972?
Narrator	Question 15. What does the professor say about asteroids and comets?
Narrator	Question 16. What does the professor indicate about meteors that appear during meteor showers?
Narrator	Question 17. What does the professor imply about Mars?

Conversation 2 (Track 491)

Narrator	Listen to a conversation between a student and a department administrator.
Male student	Is Professor Garrison available?
Female administrator	He's at a department lunch. Can I help?
Student	I saw a poster at the Student Union about Garrison's special class on the Ecology of Tropical Reefs, and I wanted to know a little more about the class.
Administrator	Well, for one thing, you know it partly takes place during spring break, right?
Student	Uh-huh. Actually, that appeals to me. I wanted to do something educational during spring break this year.
Administrator	You should also know it's a pretty intensive class. You'll have to attend evening lectures and diving classes to get your basic SCUBA diving certification – unless you're already certified?
Student	Umm, no, but I've got a friend who's certified, and he's always talking about how great diving is.
Administrator	OK. Then assuming you pass the diving exam, you'll fly down to Jamaica during spring break.
Student	Seriously? I knew the class involved a field trip, but Jamaica – wow!
Administrator	I know, right? This year it's Jamaica, last year it was Costa Rica, and before that it was Hawaii. Anyway, when you're in Jamaica, you'll have some seminars but you'll spend most of your time making field observations and collecting data for a research project. On the final day, you'll be expected to give an oral progress report. You'll also have to write a final paper that's due three weeks after you get back from the field trip.
Student	So, um, what about expenses?
Administrator	Well, the course isn't covered by your regular tuition. There's a registration fee, and you'll have to pay to get certified as a diver. Then there's airfare to Jamaica. We get a group rate, but it's still pretty costly.
Student	And I have to pay for a place to stay and for meals, I guess?
Administrator	Yeah, but you'll be staying at a dive camp. Don't expect five-star accommodation, but it's comfortable enough, and reasonably priced. Oh, and the cost of diving equipment's included.
Student	Well, I need to talk to my parents.
Administrator	Yes, do that, and take a look at the information on the website. Then come to the organizational meeting, which is, uh, next Tuesday.
Student	Sounds good. I'll do that. Thanks for the information. I guess I don't need to bother Professor Garrison after all.

Conversation 2 – questions (Tracks 492–496)

Narrator	Question 18. Why does the student visit the department?
Narrator	Question 19. How did the student first learn about the Ecology of Tropical Reefs course?
Narrator	Question 20. According to the administrator, which two components of the Ecology of Tropical Reefs class take place before the field trip?
Narrator	Question 21. What can be inferred about the Ecology of Tropical Reefs course?
Narrator	Question 22. Indicate whether each of the following is a step that the student will probably take before registering for Professor Garrison's class.

Lecture 3: Political Science (Track 497)

Narrator	Listen to a lecture in a political science class.
Professor	OK, everyone. You'll recall that we were talking about the Constitutional Convention of 1787, and how difficult it was to get the 13 original states to agree on anything because they jealously guarded their self-interests. One group, called the Federalists, favored a strong central government. They were opposed by the Anti-Federalists, who wanted individual states to keep most of the power. This argument had a profound effect, one that's still important today, in that it led to the birth of the political party system in the United States.

Now, does anyone know what the U.S. Constitution says about political parties? Nobody? Well, that's kind of a trick question. It's hard to imagine government without political parties, but actually there's no mention of parties in the Constitution at all. In parts that's because some people thought parties were a bad idea. George Washington, for instance, thought they'd be the source of great national disunity.

So anyway, after the Constitution was approved, a period that historians refer to as the First Party System, the Federalists continued to favor stronger power for the central government while the Anti-Federalists evolved into a party called the Democrat-Republicans. Of these two parties, the Federalists were dominant until 1800. George Washington was officially nonpartisan, but he sympathized with Federalist ideals, and the second president, John Adams, was one of the leaders of the Federalists, along with Alexander Hamilton. Basically, the Federalists fought for the merchant class, for business rather than agriculture, and they favored a national, central bank.

What about the Democrat-Republicans? They were led by Thomas Jefferson and James Madison. They were dominant after 1800 until the end of the First Party System. Most of their members were farmers, and they opposed a central bank. As far as foreign policy goes, the Democrat-Republicans favored France, whereas the Federalists wanted Britain as their main ally.

By 1816, James Madison, the leader of the Democrat-Republicans, who by now were just called the Republicans, had been elected by a huge majority, most of congress was Republican, and the Federalist party had pretty much faded away. For this one brief period in U.S. history, there was no two-party system and no partisan arguments. That's why this period, 1816 to, uh, around 1824, is called the Era of Good Feelings.

But the Republican party wasn't particularly strong. Without any competition, it broke into a variety of groups. Eventually one of those groups turned into another party, called the Whigs. So it was back to partisan politics as usual. This was the Second Party System, which lasted from about 1828 to 1854, when the Whigs opposed the Democrat-Republicans, who by now were generally just called Democrats.

Led by Andrew Jackson, the Democrats were the party of tradition, of the past. They favored farmers and opposed banks. On the other hand, the Whigs, who were led by Henry Clay and others, supported modernization and looked to the future. Like the old Federalist party, they supported business and industry. They were the reform party of the day.

Lecture 3: Political Science – questions (Tracks 498–503)

Narrator	Question 23. What is the main topic of this lecture?
Narrator	Question 24. According to the professor, what were two policies of the Federalist party?
Narrator	Question 25. Listen again to part of the lecture. Why does the professor say this?
Professor	Now, does anyone know what the U.S. Constitution says about political parties? Nobody? Well, that's kind of a trick question.
Narrator	Question 26. Which of these politicians acted as official leader of the Republican party?
Narrator	Question 27. What point does the professor make about the Whigs?
Narrator	Question 28. Indicate whether each statement is related to the First Party System, the Era of Good Feelings, or the Second Party System.

Lecture 4: Archaeology (Track 504)

Narrator	Listen to a lecture in an archaeology class.
Female professor	Today we're going to be talking about the Paleo-Indians, who were the ancestors of the Native Americans. What I want to talk about first is a remarkable archaeological find, the discovery of Folsom points. In 1908, a cowboy and amateur scientist named George McJunkin found the bones of a giant bison near a ranch in Folsom, New Mexico, where he worked. Some years later, scholars from the Denver Museum of Natural History heard about the find, and when they investigated in 1927, they discovered a man-made object embedded in the bones.
	This object was shaped like a leaf with a sharp point – hence the name Folsom points – and was made of a mineral called flint. It was thin and delicate, and a groove in the middle was hollowed out. This shallow groove is called fluting. Folsom points look simple, but the fluting makes them very hard to make. I've tried making one myself using the kinds of tools that artisans would have had available in those days, and all I got was a pile of broken flint.
Male student	So, what was the fluting for?
Professor	Well, fluting allowed the point to slide into a notch in a wooden shaft. Anyway, here's the remarkable thing about … wait, let me say this first: In the early twentieth century, archaeologists thought the earliest Paleo-Indians had crossed into the Americas only about 4,000 years before. But the giant bison in which the Folsom point was discovered had been extinct for at least 10,000 years. So this was proof that Paleo-Indians had come to the Americas much earlier than 4,000 years ago. And scientists didn't think of the Folsom people as the oldest for long. In the 1930s, archaeologists found points made by an even more ancient people. They were found in the

bones of a mammoth, which is a type of extinct elephant, near the town of Clovis, New Mexico, so these people are called Clovis people. Archaeologists used carbon dating to learn that the mammoths were about 13,000 years old. After this, many similar sites were found across the United States and Canada.

Student	So, uh, the Clovis people were the first to come to America?
Professor	Great question! There's a theory called the Clovis First theory, and until 30 years ago, pretty much every archaeologist believed that the Clovis people were the first to arrive. However, some archaeologists found hints, but nothing conclusive, of pre-Clovis cultures in Oregon, Virginia, Pennsylvania, and elsewhere. Then, in 1997, a site that seems to pre-date Clovis was found down in Monte Verde, Chile. This was a really interesting site because … well, the North American sites were hunting sites, but Monte Verde was a permanent village. Archaeologists discovered not just stone tools but also the remains of wooden houses, animal bones, even a child's footprint. Carbon dating showed these people lived over a thousand years before the Clovis people. Then in 2006, in Texas, at the Friedkin site on Buttermilk Creek, archaeologists made a huge find of more than 16,000 stone artifacts. Testing showed that these were older than Clovis points by 2,500 years.
Student	So nobody believes in the Clovis First theory anymore?
Professor	In my view, it's unlikely that the Clovis people were the first, but not every archaeologist would agree.

Lecture 4: Archaeology – questions (Tracks 505–510)

Narrator	Question 29. What does the professor mainly discuss?
Narrator	Question 30. According to the lecture, what is fluting?
Narrator	Question 31. Listen again to part of the lecture. Then answer the question.
Professor	This object was shaped like a leaf with a sharp point – hence the name Folsom points – and was made of a mineral called flint. It was thin and delicate, and a groove in the middle was hollowed out. This shallow groove is called fluting. Folsom points look simple, but the fluting makes them very hard to make. I've tried making one myself using the kinds of tools that artisans would have had available in those days, and all I got was a pile of broken flint.
Narrator	Why does the professor say this?
Professor	I've tried making one myself using the kinds of tools that artisans would have had available in those days, and all I got was a pile of broken flint.
Narrator	Question 32. The professor discusses the discovery of Paleo-Indian artifacts. Put the events in the order in which they occurred.
Narrator	Question 33. Listen again to part of the lecture. What does the professor imply when she says this?
Professor	Then, in 1997, a site that seems to pre-date Clovis was found down in Monte Verde, Chile. This was a really interesting site because … well, the North American sites were hunting sites, but Monte Verde was a permanent village. Archaeologists discovered not just stone tools but also the remains of wooden houses, animal bones, even a child's footprint.

Narrator	Question 34. How does the professor organize the information about Paleo-Indians in her lecture?

Speaking Task 1 (Tracks 511 and 512)

Narrator	Speaking section Task 1. What is the most enjoyable vacation that you have ever taken? Explain why you liked this vacation. Include specific details and examples to support your explanation.
Announcer	You may begin to prepare after the beep.
Announcer	You may begin to speak after the beep.

Speaking Task 2 (Tracks 513 and 514)

Narrator	Speaking section Task 2. When they want to relax, some people enjoy reading books. Other people prefer watching television. Which of these two options do you prefer? Explain your choice. Support your opinion with specific details and examples.
Announcer	You may begin to prepare after the beep.
Announcer	You may begin to speak after the beep.

Speaking Task 3 (Tracks 515–518)

Narrator	Speaking section Task 3.
	A university official wrote a letter to campus tour guides. Read the letter. You have 45 seconds to read the letter. Begin reading now.
Narrator	Now listen to two students as they discuss the letter.
Woman	Hi, Matt. Did you get that letter about campus tours?
Man	Yeah. I found it pretty upsetting.
Woman	Really? Why's that?
Man	The letter says the program is valuable and popular; well if that's true, the university should definitely pay us for our time. I have a job on campus in the library and I get paid for doing that, so I don't see why working as a campus tour guide is any different.
Woman	Well, the letter said the state has cut the university's budget, so I guess that's why.
Man	That's not exactly accurate, though. The budget *has* been cut, but for one thing, it's only a 2 percent cut, so it's not like the university is going to be in major financial trouble. It feels like the university is using the budget cut as an excuse, you know?
Woman	Just 2 percent, huh?
Man	And for another thing, the cut won't even take place for two years, so there's no reason for the university to stop paying campus tour guides this summer.
Woman	Oh, I didn't know that.
Man	Yeah, it's true … You know, I was looking forward to being a campus tour guide this summer, but I doubt I'll do it now.
Narrator	The man expresses his opinion of the letter. State his opinion and explain the reasons he gives for having that opinion.
Announcer	You may begin to prepare after the beep.
Announcer	You may begin to speak after the beep.

Speaking Task 4 (Tracks 519–522)

Narrator	Speaking section Task 4. Now read the passage about the Law of Unintended Consequences. You have 45 seconds to read the passage. Begin reading now.
Narrator	Now listen to part of a lecture on this topic in an ecology class.
Professor	Now we'll talk about the Law of Unintended Consequences. It's applicable in lots of fields – sociology, politics, medicine, law, and so on. It's particularly common in ecology. Unfortunately, there aren't many examples of unexpected positive results – mostly negative ones. Let's look at an actual case. Back in the eighteenth century, a small number of European rabbits were imported into Australia. At that time, there were not many sources of meat for people to eat, and it was felt that rabbits could provide a useful source of food. At first, they didn't seem to be too much of a problem, but the only natural predators of rabbits in Australia are the dog-like dingoes, and farmers often hunted the dingoes. This meant there weren't many dingoes to prey on the rabbits, and since the Australian environment suited the rabbits perfectly, the population of rabbits absolutely exploded – it's the fastest known spread of any species of mammal ever. There are probably 500 million wild rabbits in Australia today. They eat crops and destroy young fruit trees. They also cause soil erosion by eating all the plants in an area. Rabbits have cost Australia billions of dollars. Of course, none of this was intended.
Narrator	Using details from the talk, explain how the importation of rabbits into Australia relates to the Law of Unintended Consequences.
Announcer	You may begin to prepare after the beep.
Announcer	You may begin to speak after the beep.

Speaking Task 5 (Tracks 523–525)

Narrator	Speaking section Task 5.
	Now listen to a conversation between a man and a woman.
Man	Morning, Bonnie. How's it going?
Woman	Hi Josh. Oh, OK, I suppose.
Man	So is your sister still coming to town this week?
Woman	Yeah, as a matter of fact, Annie's flying in from Toronto today. Her flight gets in at 2:30.
Man	Oh, are you driving down to meet her?
Woman	Um, that's the problem. I said I would, but if I do that, I'll have to miss my biochemistry class.
Man	Well, I don't have any classes this afternoon. I could go down and pick up your sister if you like.
Woman	That's a really nice offer, but I told Annie I'd pick her up. She's expecting to see me, and it might be a little strange if I send someone she doesn't know to pick her up instead.
Man	I guess. Well, just tell your biochem teacher you have to go to the airport to get your sister and skip the class.
Woman	Yeah, I thought about that, but we have a mid-term Friday, and Professor Drake is going to review what's going to be on the test, and I don't want to miss that.
Narrator	The speakers discuss two possible solutions to a problem.

Describe the problem. Then state which of the two solutions you prefer and why.

Announcer   You may begin to prepare after the beep.

Announcer   You may begin to speak after the beep.

Speaking Task 6 (Tracks 526–528)

Narrator   Speaking section Task 6.

Now listen to part of a lecture in a finance class.

Professor   A company uses a balance sheet to show its cumulative results, that is the history of a firm's financial transactions since it started doing business. But a balance sheet does not say much about a company's *recent* financial progress. For this, companies use an income statement.

What do we mean, "income statement"? Well, it's a measurement, a snapshot, if you like, of a firm's financial gains or losses between the beginning and end of a particular period of time. This might be a month, a quarter, a year, or even longer.

In its most basic form, an income statement measures expenses against sales. The difference between the two indicates the operating results of the firm for that period. So basically, an income statement gives three pieces of information: first, sales, second, expenses, and third, net income, which is sales minus expenses. Net income can be positive – a profit – or negative – a loss. To illustrate: Let's say Company X had $1 million in sales and $900,000 in expenses, for a net income of $100,000, right?

In reality, shareholders and the board of directors want more information than that. For example, expenses might be broken into the cost of raw materials and equipment, operating expenses, salaries, interest, and so on. But the most important figure is always the final one, the net income. And because that's the final figure on an income statement, we often call net income "the bottom line."

Narrator   Using points and examples from the talk, say what an income statement is and what information it includes.

Announcer   You may begin to prepare after the beep.

Announcer   You may begin to speak after the beep.

Writing Task 1 (Tracks 529–531)

Narrator   Writing section Task 1. Now listen to a lecture on the topic you just read about.

Professor   Good afternoon. Everyone have a chance to look at the article? The author makes some pretty good points in favor of online education, doesn't he? But before you drop this class and sign up for an Internet course, there are a few things I'd like to address.

The author points out that an online degree from a four-year private university costs about $15,000 – much lower than the cost of face-to-face instruction. However, the author doesn't say that four-year private institutions are the most expensive type of school. If you attend a two-year community college or a four-year public institution in your home state, you'll spend much less on tuition for face-to-face classes. In fact, often you'll pay less than the cost of an online education at an expensive four-year private university.

And what about the author's point that taking an online course means you don't need to pay school fees like room and board? While it's true you wouldn't have to pay room and board to the university, you'd still have to live somewhere, right? And still have to buy food, right? And still have to buy books, and travel, and all the other daily expenses we have. So to suggest that online courses are going to save you money on associated expenses is, well, not really accurate.

Finally, the author emphasizes the convenience of online education. You *do* have a lot of flexibility as to when you study, where you study, and yes, you *can* attend class in pajamas. But too much flexibility and independence can be a problem for students without good self-discipline. In many online classes, about half the students who sign up fail to finish the class. They find it hard to juggle their work schedule and their study schedule, get behind, and then just quit. So, in some ways an online course is more difficult than attending classes face-to-face.

Narrator   Summarize the points made in the lecture, explaining how they challenge the points made in the reading passage.

Announcer   Begin writing now. You have 20 minutes.

You have 10 minutes remaining.

You have 5 minutes remaining.

You have 2 minutes remaining.

Stop writing now.

Writing Task 2 (Track 532)

Announcer   Begin writing now. You have 30 minutes.

You have 15 minutes remaining.

You have 5 minutes remaining.

You have 2 minutes remaining.

Stop writing now.